THE STANDARD

C

LIBRARY

P.J. Plauger

Prentice Hall
Englewood Cliffs, New Jersey 07632

Editorial/production supervision: *Brendan M. Stewart*
Manufacturing buyers: *Kelly Behr* and *Susan Brunke*

Prentice-Hall International (UK) Limited, *London*
Prentice-Hall of Australia Pty. Limited, *Sydney*
Prentice-Hall of Canada Inc., *Toronto*
Prentice-Hall Hispanoamericana, S.A., *Mexico*
Prentice-Hall of India Private Limited, *New Dehli*
Prentice-Hall of Japan, Inc., *Tokyo*
Simon & Schuster Asia Pte. Ltd., *Singapore*
Editora Prentice-Hall do Brasil, Ltda., *Rio de Janerio*

for Tana

Contents

Preface

This book shows you how to use all the library functions mandated by the ANSI and ISO Standards for the programming language C. I have chosen to focus on the library exclusively, since many other books describe the language proper. The book also shows you how to implement the library. I present about 9,000 lines of tested, working code. I believe that seeing a realistic implementation of the Standard C library can help you better understand how to use it.

As much as possible, the code for the library is written in Standard C. The primary design goal is to make the code as readable and as *exemplary* as possible. A secondary goal is to make the code highly portable across diverse computer architectures. Still another goal is to present code that makes sensible tradeoffs between accuracy, performance, and size.

Teaching you how to write C is *not* a goal of this book. I assume you know enough about C to read straightforward code. Where the code presented is not so straightforward, I explain the trickery involved.

the Standard C library The Standard C library is fairly ambitious. It provides considerable power in many different environments. It promises well-defined name spaces for both user and implementor. It imposes fairly strict requirements on the robustness and precision of its mathematical functions. And it pioneers in supporting code that adapts to varied cultures, including those with very large character sets.

To benefit from these ambitions, a user should be aware of numerous subtleties. To satisfy these ambitions, an implementor must provide for them. These subtleties are not always addressed in the C Standard proper. It is not the primary purpose of a standard to educate implementors. Nor are many of these subtleties well explained in the Rationale that accompanies the ANSI C Standard. A Rationale must serve several masters, only one of whom is the inquisitive implementor.

The pioneering features I mentioned above are not found in traditional implementations of C. An implementation can now support multiple *locales*. Each locale captures numerous conventions peculiar to a country, language, or profession. A C program can alter and query locales to adapt dynamically to a broad range of cultures. An implementation can also now support very large character sets, such as the Kanji characters used in Japan.

A C program can manipulate such character sets either as *multibyte characters* or as *wide characters*. It can also translate between these two forms. That simplifies, and standardizes, the writing of programs for this rapidly growing marketplace.

Little or no prior art exists for these new features. Hence, even the most experienced C programmers need guidance in using locales, multibyte characters, and wide characters. Particular attention is given here to these topics.

subtleties   This book explains, for users and implementors alike, how the library was *meant* to be used and how it *can* be used. By providing a working implementation of all the functions in the Standard C library, the book shows by example how to deal with their subtleties. Where no implementation is clearly the best, it also discusses alternatives and tradeoffs. An example of the subtleties involved is the function `getchar`. The header `<stdio.h>` can, in principle, mask its declaration with the macro:

```
#define getchar()    fgets(stdin)    /* NOT WISE! */
```

It must not do so, however. A valid (if useless) C program is:

```
#include <stdio.h>
#undef stdin
#undef fgets

int main(void) {
    FILE *stdin = fopen("abc");
    int i = getchar();       /* READS THE WRONG STREAM */
    int fgets = getchar();   /* PRODUCES A MYSTERIOUS ERROR */

    return (0);
    }
```

The example is admittedly perverse. Nevertheless, it illustrates practices that even a well-meaning programmer might indulge. Users have the right to expect few, if any, surprises of this ilk. Implementors have an obligation to avoid causing such surprises.

The form I settled on for the `getchar` macro is:

```
#define getchar()    (_Files[0]->_Next < _Files[0]->_Rend \
    ? *_Files[0]->_Next++ : (getchar)())
```

It is a far cry from the obvious (and more readable) form first presented above. Chapter 12: `<stdio.h>` helps explain why.

designing   Still another purpose of this book is to teach programmers how to design
libraries and implement libraries in general. By its very nature, the library provided with a programming language is a mixed bag. An implementor needs a broad spectrum of skills to deal with the varied contents of the bag. It is not enough to be a competent numerical analyst, or to be skilled in manipulating character strings efficiently, or to be knowledgable in the ways of operating system interfacing. Writing a library demands all these skills and more.

Good books have been written on how to write mathematical functions. Other books present specialized libraries for a variety of purposes. They show you how to use the library presented. Some may even justify many of the design choices for the particular library in question. Few, if any, endeavor to teach the skills required for library building in general.

reusability   A number of books present general principles for designing and implementing software. The disciplines they present have names such as structured analysis, structured design, object-oriented design, and structured programming. Most examples in these books consider only programs written for a custom application. Nevertheless, the principles and disciplines apply equally well to the writing of reusable libraries.

The goal of reusability simply raises the stakes. If a library function is not highly cohesive, in the structured-design sense, then it is less likely to find new uses. If it does not have low coupling, in the same sense, it is harder to use. Similarly, a collection of functions must hide implementation details and provide complete functionality. Otherwise, they fail at implementing reusable data abstractions, in the object-oriented sense.

So the final purpose of this book is to address the design and implementation issues peculiar to library building. The design of the Standard C library is fixed. Nevertheless, it is a good design in many ways and worthy of discussion. Implementations of the Standard C library can vary. Any number of choices are strongly dictated by general principles, such as correctness and maintainability. Other choices are dictated by priorities peculiar to a project, such as very high performance, portability, or small size. These choices and principles are also worthy of discussion.

structure of this book   The book is structured much like the Standard C library itself. Fifteen headers declare or define all the names in the library. A separate chapter covers each header. Most of the headers have reasonably cohesive contents. That makes for reasonably cohesive discussions. One or two, however, are catchalls. Their corresponding chapters are perforce wider ranging.

I include in each chapter excerpts from relevant portions of the ISO C Standard. (Aside from formatting details, the ISO and ANSI C Standards, are identical.) The excerpts supplement the narrative description of how each portion of the library is customarily used. They also help make this book a more complete reference (that is nevertheless more readable than the C Standard alone). I also show all code needed to implement that portion and to test the implementation.

Each chapter ends with references and a set of exercises. In a university course based on this book, the exercises can serve as homework problems. Many of them are simple exercises in code rewriting. They drive home a point or illustrate reasonable variations in implementation. The more ambitious exercises are labelled as such. They can serve as a basis for more extended projects. The independent reader can simply use the exercises as an impetus for further thought.

The Code

The code presented in this book has been tested with C compilers from Borland, Project GNU, and VAX ULTRIX. It has passed the widely used Plum Hall Validation Suite tests for library functions. It has also survived an assortment of public-domain programs designed to stress C implementations and illuminate their darker corners. While I have taken pains to minimize errors, I cannot guarantee that none remain. Please note the disclaimer on the copyright page.

Please note also that the code in this book is protected by copyright. It has *not* been placed in the public domain. Nor is it shareware. It is not protected by a "copyleft" agreement, like code distributed by the Free Software Foundation (Project GNU). I retain all rights.

fair use   You are welcome to transcribe the code to machine-readable form for your personal use. You can purchase the code in machine-readable from The C Users Group in Lawrence, Kansas. In either case, what you do with the code is limited by the "fair use" provisions of copyright law. Fair use does *not* permit you to distribute copies of the code, either hard copy or machine-readable, either free or for a fee.

Having said that, I do permit one important usage that goes well beyond fair use. You can compile portions of the library and link the resultant binary object modules with your own code to form an executable file. I hereby permit you to distribute unlimited copies of such an executable file. I ask no royalty on any such copies. I do, however, require that you document the presence of the library, whatever amount you use, either modified or unmodified. Please include somewhere in the executable file the following sequence of characters: `Portions of this work are derived from The Standard C Library, copyright (c) 1992 by P.J. Plauger, published by Prentice-Hall, and are used with permission`. The same message should appear prominently, and in an appropriate place, on any documentation that you distribute with the executable image. If you omit either message, you infringe the copyright.

licensing   You can also obtain permission to do more. You can distribute the entire library in the form of binary object modules. You can even distribute copies of the source files from this book, either modified or unmodified. You can, in short, incorporate the library into a product that lets people use it to make executable programs. To do so, however, requires a license. You pay a fee for the license. Contact Plum Hall Inc. in Cardiff, New Jersey for licensing terms and for on-going support of the library.

Despite the mercenary tone of these paragraphs, my primary goal is not to flog a commercial product. I believe strongly in the C Standard, having worked very hard to help bring it about. Much of my effort went into developing the specification for the Standard C library. I want to prove that we have constructed a good language standard. I wrote this implementation, and this book, to demonstrate that simple but important fact.

Acknowledgments

Compass, Inc. of Wakefield, Massachusetts believed in this project long before it was completed. They are my first customer for the library code. They helped test, debug, and improve the library extensively in the process of accepting it for use with their Intel 860 compiler. Ian Wells, in particular, bore the brunt of my delays and botches with good-natured professionalism. Don Anderson contributed many a midnight e-mail message toward making this library hang together properly. For their faith and patience, I heartily thank everyone I have worked with at Compass.

Paul Becker, my Publisher at Prentice Hall, also believed in this project. His gentle but persistent goading was instrumental in bringing this book to completion. The (anonymous) reviewers he employed helped me sharpen my focus and tone down some of the more extreme prose. Paul's professionalism reminded me why Prentice Hall has been such a major force in technical publishing for so long.

Moving to Australia for a year part way through this project presented a bouquet of impediments. My good friend and business colleague John O'Brien of Whitesmiths, Australia, was always there to help. For turning thorns into roses, he has been nonpareil. His assistance has surpassed the bounds even of friendship.

Andrew Binnie, Publishing Manager at Prentice Hall Australia kindly provided the laser printer I needed to finish this book. He was quick to help in many ways. The University of New South Wales Computer Science Department graciously gave me the time and space I needed, even though they had other plans for both.

Tom Plum has forced many of us to think deeply about fundamental aspects of C. I have enjoyed numerous fruitful discussions with him on the topics covered here. Dave Prosser has also freely shared his deep insights into the workings of C. As editor of both the ANSI and ISO C Standards, Dave provided the machine-readable text excerpted extensively in this book. Advanced Data Controls Corp. of Tokyo, Japan pioneered Kanji support in C. Takashi Kawahara and Hiroshi Fukutomi, both principals in that company, have been very helpful in educating me on the technical needs of Japanese programmers.

Much of the material presented here first appeared in monthly installments in *The C Users Journal*. Robert Ward has been a particularly easy publisher to work with. I appreciate his flexibility in letting me recycle material from his magazine. Jim Brodie has been equally generous in permitting me to use material from our book *Standard C*.

Reading technical manuscripts is never an easy task. Both John O'Brien and Tom Plum reviewed portions of this book and provided helpful feedback.

Finally, I happily acknowledge the contributions made by my family. My son, Geoffrey, helped with the layout and typographic design of this book. My wife, Tana, provided much-needed moral and logistical support over many long months. They, more than anybody, kept this project fun for me.

P.J. Plauger
Bondi, New South Wales

Chapter 0: Introduction

Background

A *library* is a collection of program components that can be reused in many programs. Most programming languages include some form of library. The programming language C is no exception. It began accreting useful *functions* right from the start. These functions help you classify characters, manipulate character strings, read input, and write output — to name just a few categories of services.

a few
definitions
You must *declare* a typical function before you use it in a program. The easiest way to do so is to incorporate into the program a *header* that declares all the library functions in a given category. A header can also define any associated *type definitions* and *macros*. A header is as much a part of the library as the functions themselves. Most often, a header is a *text file* just like the you write to make a program.

You use the `#include` directive in a C source file to make a header part of the *translation unit*. For example, the header `<stdio.h>` declares functions that perform input and output. A program that prints a simple message with the function `printf` consists of the single C source file:

```
/* a simple test program */
#include <stdio.h>

int main(void)
    {   /* say hello */
    printf("Hello\n");
    return (0);
    }
```

A *translator* converts each translation unit to an *object module*, a form suitable for use with a given *computer architecture* (or *machine*). A *linker* combines all the object modules that make up a program. It incorporates any object modules you use from the C library as well. The most popular form of translator is a *compiler*. It produces an *executable file*. Ideally at least, an executable file contains only those object modules from the library that contain functions actually used by the program. That way, the program suffers no size penalty as the C library grows more extensive. (Another form of translator is an *interpreter*. It may include the entire C library as part of the program that interprets your program.)

making a   You can construct your own libraries. A typical C compiler has a *librarian*,
library a program that assembles a library from the object modules you specify.
The linker knows to select from *any* library only the object modules used
by the program. The C library is not a special case.

You can write part or all of a library in C. The translation unit you write
to make a library object module is not that unusual:

- A library object module should contain no definition of the function `main`
  with external linkage. A programmer is unlikely to reuse code that insists
  on taking control at program startup.

- The object module should contain only functions that are easy to declare
  and use. Provide a header that declares the functions and defines any
  associated types and macros.

- Most important, a library object module should be usable in a variety of
  contexts. Writing code that is highly reusable is a skill you develop only
  with practice and by studying successful libraries.

After you have read this book, you should be comfortable designing,
writing, and constructing specialized libraries in C.

the C   The C library itself is typically written in C. That is often *not* the case
library with other programming languages. Earlier languages had libraries writ-
in C ten in *assembly language*. Different computer architectures have different
assembly languages. To move the library to another computer architecture,
you had to rewrite it completely. C lets you write powerful and efficient
code that is also highly *portable*. You can move portable code simply by
translating it with a different C translator.

Here, for example, is the library function `strlen`, declared in `<string.h>`.
The function returns the length of a null-terminated string. Its pointer
argument points to the first element of the string:

```
/* strlen function */
#include <string.h>

size_t (strlen)(const char *s)
    {   /* find length of s[] */
    const char *sc;

    for (sc = s; *sc != '\0'; ++sc)
        ;
    return (sc - s);
    }
```

`strlen` is a small function, one fairly easy to write. It is also fairly easy to
write incorrectly in many small ways. `strlen` is widely used. You might
want to provide a special version tuned to a given computer architecture.
But you don't have to. This version is correct, portable, and reasonably
efficient.

Other contemporary languages cannot be used to write significant
portions of their own libraries. You cannot, for example, write the Pascal
library function `writeln` in portable Pascal. By contrast, you *can* write the

equivalent C library function `printf` in portable C. The comparison is a bit unfair because C type checking is weaker. Nevertheless, the underlying point is significant — the C library has been expressible from its earliest beginnings almost completely in C.

nonportable code   Sometimes the code for a library function cannot be written in *portable* C. The code you write in C may work for a large class of computer architectures, but not all. In such a case, the important thing is to document clearly the nonportable portions that may have to change. You should also *isolate* nonportable code as much as possible. Even nonportable C code is easier to write, debug, and maintain than assembly language. You write assembly language only where it is unavoidable. Those places are few and far between in the C library.

This book shows you how to use the C library in its current, standardized form. Along the way, it also shows you how to write the C library in C. That can help you understand how the library works. And it illustrates many aspects of designing and writing a nontrivial library in C.

What the C Standard Says

Dennis Ritchie developed the original version of the programming language C at AT&T Bell Laboratories in the early 1970s. At first it appeared to be little more than a UNIX-specific system-implementation language for the DEC PDP-11 computer architecture. Others soon discovered, however, that it modeled a broad class of modern computers rather well. By the late 1970s, several other compiler writers had implemented C for a variety of popular targets, from microcomputers to mainframes. By the early 1980s, hundreds of implementations of C were being used by a rapidly growing community of programmers. It was time to standardize the language.

standards for C   The American National Standards Institute, or ANSI, standardizes computer programming languages in the United States. X3J11 is the name of the ANSI-authorized committee that developed the standard for C, starting in 1983. The language is now defined by ANSI Standard X3.159-1989.

The International Standards Organization, or ISO, C has a similar responsibility in the international arena. ISO formed the technical committee JTC1/SC22/WG14 to review and augment the work of X3J11. Currently, ISO has adopted a standard for C that is essentially identical to X3.159. It is called ISO 9899:1990. The C Standards differ only in format and in the numbering of sections. The wording differs in a few small places but makes no substantive change to the language definition.

I quote extensively from the ISO C Standard throughout this book. That way you can see exactly what the C Standard says about every aspect of the Standard C library. It is the final authority on what constitutes the C programming language. If you think my interpretation disagrees with the C Standard, trust the C Standard. I may very well be wrong.

You will find the C Standard hard to read from time to time. Remember that it is cast intentionally in a kind of legalese. A standard must be precise and accurate first. Readability comes a distant second. The document is not intended to be tutorial. X3J11 also produced a Rationale to accompany the C Standard. If you are curious about why X3J11 made certain decisions, go read that document. It might help. I emphasize, however, that the Rationale is also not a tutorial on the C language.

Here are two quotes from the ISO C Standard. The first quote introduces the Library section of the C Standard. It provides a few definitions and lays down several important ground rules that affect the library as a whole.

7. Library

7.1 Introduction

7.1.1 Definitions of terms

string

A *string* is a contiguous sequence of characters terminated by and including the first null character. A "pointer to" a string is a pointer to its initial (lowest addressed) character. The "length" of a string is the number of characters preceding the null character and its "value" is the sequence of the values of the contained characters, in order.

letter

A *letter* is a printing character in the execution character set corresponding to any of the 52 required lowercase and uppercase letters in the source character set, listed in 5.2.1.

decimal point

The *decimal-point character* is the character used by functions that convert floating-point numbers to or from character sequences to denote the beginning of the fractional part of such character sequences.[88] It is represented in the text and examples by a period, but may be changed by the **setlocale** function.

Forward references: character handling (7.3), the **setlocale** function (7.4.1.1).

7.1.2 Standard headers

standard headers

Each library function is declared in a *header*,[89] whose contents are made available by the **#include** preprocessing directive. The header declares a set of related functions, plus any necessary types and additional macros needed to facilitate their use.

The standard headers are

`<assert.h>`	`<locale.h>`	`<stddef.h>`
`<ctype.h>`	`<math.h>`	`<stdio.h>`
`<errno.h>`	`<setjmp.h>`	`<stdlib.h>`
`<float.h>`	`<signal.h>`	`<string.h>`
`<limits.h>`	`<stdarg.h>`	`<time.h>`

If a file with the same name as one of the above < and > delimited sequences, not provided as part of the implementation, is placed in any of the standard places for a source file to be included, the behavior is undefined.

Headers may be included in any order; each may be included more than once in a given scope, with no effect different from being included only once, except that the effect of including **<assert.h>** depends on the definition of **NDEBUG**. If used, a header shall be included outside of any external declaration or definition, and it shall first be included before the first reference to any of the functions or objects it declares, or to any of the types or macros it defines. However, if the identifier is declared or defined in more than one header, the second and subsequent associated headers may be included after the initial reference to the identifier. The program shall not have any macros with names lexically identical to keywords currently defined prior to the inclusion.

Forward references: diagnostics (7.2).

7.1.3 Reserved identifiers

reserved identifiers

Each header declares or defines all identifiers listed in its associated subclause, and optionally declares or defines identifiers listed in its associated future library directions subclause and identifiers which are always reserved either for any use or for use as file scope identifiers.

- All identifiers that begin with an underscore and either an uppercase letter or another underscore are always reserved for any use.

- All identifiers that begin with an underscore are always reserved for use as identifiers with file scope in both the ordinary identifier and tag name spaces.

- Each macro name listed in any of the following subclauses (including the future library directions) is reserved for any use if any of its associated headers is included.

- All identifiers with external linkage in any of the following subclauses (including the future library directions) are always reserved for use as identifiers with external linkage.[90]

- Each identifier with file scope listed in any of the following subclauses (including the future library directions) is reserved for use as an identifier with file scope in the same name space if any of its associated headers is included.

No other identifiers are reserved. If the program declares or defines an identifier with the same name as an identifier reserved in that context (other than as allowed by 7.1.7), the behavior is undefined.[91]

Footnotes

88. The functions that make use of the decimal-point character are **localeconv**, **fprintf**, **fscanf**, **printf**, **scanf**, **sprintf**, **sscanf**, **vfprintf**, **vprintf**, **vsprintf**, **atof**, and **strtod**.

89. A header is not necessarily a source file, nor are the **<** and **>** delimited sequences in header names necessarily valid source file names.

90. The list of reserved identifiers with external linkage includes **errno**, **setjmp**, and **va_end**.

91. Since macro names are replaced whenever found, independent of scope and name space, macro names matching any of the reserved identifier names must not be defined if an associated header, if any, is included.

The second quote describes ways to make use of the functions within the Standard C library.

7.1.7 Use of library functions

using library functions

Each of the following statements applies unless explicitly stated otherwise in the detailed descriptions that follow. If an argument to a function has an invalid value (such as a value outside the domain of the function, or a pointer outside the address space of the program, or a null pointer), the behavior is undefined. If a function argument is described as being an array, the pointer actually passed to the function shall have a value such that all address computations and accesses to objects (that would be valid if the pointer did point to the first element of such an array) are in fact valid. Any function declared in a header may be additionally implemented as a macro defined in the header, so a library function should not be declared explicitly if its header is included. Any macro definition of a function can be suppressed locally by enclosing the name of the function in parentheses, because the name is then not followed by the left parenthesis that indicates expansion of a macro function name. For the same syntactic reason, it is permitted to take the address of a library function even if it is also defined as a macro.[95] The use of **#undef** to remove any macro definition will also ensure that an actual function is referred to. Any invocation of a library function that is implemented as a macro shall expand to code that evaluates each of its arguments exactly once, fully protected by parentheses where necessary, so it is generally safe to use arbitrary expressions as arguments. Likewise, those function-like macros described in the following subclauses may be invoked in an expression anywhere a function with a compatible return type could be called.[96] All object-like macros listed as expanding to integral constant expressions shall additionally be suitable for use in **#if** preprocessing directives.

Provided that a library function can be declared without reference to any type defined in a header, it is also permissible to declare the function, either explicitly or implicitly, and use it without including its associated header. If a function that accepts a variable argument list is not declared (explicitly or by including its associated header), the behavior is undefined.

Example

The function **atoi** may be used in any of several ways

- by use of its associated header (possibly generating a macro expansion)

```
                #include <stdlib.h>
                const char *str;
                /*...*/
                i = atoi(str);
```

- by use of its associated header (assuredly generating a true function reference)

```
                #include <stdlib.h>
                #undef atoi
                const char *str;
                /*...*/
                i = atoi(str);
```
    or
```
                #include <stdlib.h>
                const char *str;
                /*...*/
                i = (atoi)(str);
```

- by explicit declaration

```
                extern int atoi(const char *);
                const char *str;
                /*...*/
                i = atoi(str);
```

- by implicit declaration

```
                const char *str;
                /*...*/
                i = atoi(str);
```

Footnotes

95.   This means that an implementation must provide an actual function for each library function, even if it also provides a macro for that function.

96.   Because external identifiers and some macro names beginning with an underscore are reserved, implementations may provide special semantics for such names. For example, the identifier **_BUILTIN_abs** could be used to indicate generation of in-line code for the **abs** function. Thus, the appropriate header could specify

```
        #define abs(x) _BUILTIN_abs(x)
```

for a compiler whose code generator will accept it.

In this manner, a user desiring to guarantee that a given library function such as **abs** will be a genuine function may write

```
        #undef abs
```

whether the implementation's header provides a macro implementation of **abs** or a built-in implementation. The prototype for the function, which precedes and is hidden by any macro definition, is thereby revealed also.

quoting the ISO Standard   Note how I have marked distinctly each quote from the ISO C Standard. The type face differs from the running text of the book and is smaller. A bold rule runs down the left side. (The notes to the left of the rule are mine.) Each quote contains at least one numbered head, to make its location within the C Standard unambiguous. I gather any footnotes and present them at the end of the quote.

I typeset the quotes from the ISO C Standard from the same machine-readable text used to produce the C Standard itself. Line and page breaks differ, of course. Be warned, however, that I edited the text extensively in altering the typesetting markup. I may have introduced errors not caught in later proofreading. The final authority on C is, as always, the printed C Standard you obtain from ISO or ANSI.

Using the Library

The C Standard has a lot to say about how the library looks to the user. Two important issues are:

- how to use library headers
- how to create names in a program

using headers   The Standard C library provides fifteen standard headers. Any predefined name not defined in the language proper is defined in one or more of these standard headers. The headers have several properties:

- They are *idempotent*. You can include the same standard header more than once. The effect is as if you included it exactly once.
- They are *mutually independent*. No standard header requires that another standard header be first included for it to work properly. Nor does any standard header include another standard header.
- They are equivalent to *file-level declarations*. You must include a standard header before you refer to anything it defines or declares. You must not include a standard header within a declaration. And you must not mask any keywords with macro definitions before you include the standard header.

The universal convention among C programmers is to include all headers near the beginning of a C source file. Only an identifying comment precedes the `#include` directives. You can write the headers in any order — I prefer to sort them alphabetically by name. Include the header for *every* library function that you use. Never mind what the C Standard says about declaring functions other ways.

Your program may require its own header files. Don't use any of the standard header names as the names of your header files. You might get away with it on one system and come to grief on another. A widespread convention, if not universal, is to choose C source file names and header file names that take the following form:

- Begin the name with a lowercase letter.
- Follow with one to seven lowercase letters and digits.
- End with .c for a C source file, .h for a header file.

Examples are `i80386.h`, `matrix.c`, and `plot.h`. Names of this form are portable to a wide variety of C translators. You can achieve even wider portability by using at most *five* additional lowercase letters and digits. That's what the C Standard suggests. I find these longer names quite portable (and cryptic) enough, however.

A header file you write may require declarations or definitions from a standard header. If so, it is a wise practice to include the standard header near the top of your header file. That eliminates the need for you to include headers in a specific order within your C source files. Don't worry if you end up including the same standard header more than once within a translation unit. That's what idempotence is all about.

It is a good practice to use a different form of the **#include** directive for your own header files. Delimit the name with double quotes instead of angle brackets. Use the angle brackets only with the standard headers. For example, you might write at the top of a C source file:

```
#include <stdio.h>
#include "plot.h"
```

My practice is to list the standard headers first. If you follow the advice I gave above, however, that practice is not mandatory. I follow it simply to minimize the arbitrary.

name   The Standard C library has fairly clean *name spaces*. The library defines **spaces** a couple hundred external names. Beyond that, it reserves certain classes of names for use by the implementors. All other names belong to the users of the language. Figure 0.1 shows the name spaces that exist in a C program. It is taken from Plauger and Brodie, *Standard C*. The figure shows that you can define an open-ended set of name spaces:

- Two new name spaces are created for each block (enclosed in braces within a function). One contains all names declared as type definitions, functions, data objects, and enumeration constants. The other contains all enumeration, structure, and union tags.

- A new name space is created for each structure or union you define. It contains the names of all the members.

- A new name space is created for each function prototype you declare. It contains the names of all the parameters.

- A new name space is created for each function you define. It contains the names of all the labels.

You can use a name only one way within a given name space. If the translator recognizes a name as belonging to a given name space, it may

Figure 0.1:
Name
Spaces

		INNERMOST BLOCK		FILE LEVEL
M A C R O S	K E Y W O R D S	type definitions functions data objects enumeration	...	type definitions functions data objects enumeration
		enumeration tag structure tag union tag	...	enumeration tag structure tag union tag
		members of a structure or union parameters within a function prototype		
		members of a structure or union parameters within a function prototype		
		...		
		goto labels		

fail to see another use of the name in a different name space. In the figure, a name space box masks any name space box to its right. Thus, a macro can mask a keyword. And either of these can mask any other use of a name. (That makes it impossible for you to define a data object whose name is **while**, for example.)

In practice, you should treat *all* keywords and library names as reserved in *all* name spaces. That minimizes confusion both for you and future readers of your code. Rely on the separate name spaces to save you only when you forget about a rarely used name in the library. If you must do something rash, like defining a macro that masks a keyword, do it carefully and document the practice clearly. You must also avoid using certain classes of names when you write programs. They are reserved for use by the implementors. Don't use:

- names of functions and data objects with external linkage that begin with an underscore, such as **_abc** or **_DEF**
- names of macros that begin with an underscore followed by a second underscore or an uppercase letter, such as **__abc** or **_DEF**.

Remember that a macro name can mask a name in any other name space. The second class of names is effectively reserved in *all* name spaces.

Implementing the Library

The code that follows in this book makes several assumptions. If you want to use any of the code with a given C implementation, you must verify that the assumptions are valid for that implementation.

assumptions
- *You can replace a standard header with a C source file of the same name, such as* **assert.h**. An implementation is permitted to treat the names of the standard headers as reserved. Including a standard header can simply turn on a set of definitions built into the translator. An implementation that does so will cause problems.
- *You can replace the standard headers piecemeal.* You may wish to experiment only with portions of the code presented here. Even if you eventually want to try it all, you don't want to have to make it all work at once.
- *You can replace a predefined function with a C source file containing a conventional definition for the function.* An implementation is permitted to treat the external names of library functions as reserved. Calling a library function can simply expand to inline code. An implementation that does so will cause problems.
- *You can replace the predefined functions piecemeal.* An implementation is permitted to combine multiple library functions into a single module. The same arguments also apply as for replacing standard headers.
- *File names for C source can have at least eight lowercase letters, followed by a dot and a single lowercase letter.* This is the form I described on page 7.

- *External names may or may not map all letters to a single case.* The code presented here works correctly either way.

  It is unlikely that your implementation violates any of these assumptions. If it does, the implementation can probably be made to cooperate by some ruse. Most C vendors write their libraries in C and use their own translators. They need this behavior too.

coding The code in this book obeys a number of style rules. Most of the rules
style make sense for any project. A few are peculiar.

- Each *visible* function in the library occupies a separate C source file. The file name is the function name, chopped to eight characters if necessary, followed by `.c`. Thus, the function `strlen` is in the file `strlen.c`. That makes for some rather small files in a few cases. It also simplifies finding functions. Appendix B: Names shows each visible name defined in the library, giving the page number where you can find the file that defines the name.

- Each *secret* name begins with an underscore followed by an uppercase letter, as in `_Getint`. Appendix B: Names also lists each secret name that has external linkage or is defined in a standard header.

- Secret functions and data objects in the library typically occupy C source files whose names begin with `x`, as in `xgetint.c`. Such a file can contain more than one function or data object. The file name typically derives from the name of one of the contained functions or data objects.

- Code layout is reasonably uniform. I usually declare data objects within functions at the innermost possible nesting level. I indent religiously to show the nesting of control structures. I also follow each left brace ({) inside a function with a one-line comment.

- The code contains no `register` declarations. They are hard to place wisely and they clutter the code. Besides, modern compilers should allocate registers much better than a programmer can.

- In the definition of a visible library function, the function name is surrounded by parentheses. (Look back at the definition of `strlen` on page 2.) Any such function can have its declaration masked by a macro definition in its corresponding header. The parentheses prevent the translator from recognizing the macro and expanding it.

- This book displays each C source file as a figure with a box around it. The figure caption gives the name of the file. Larger files appear on two facing pages — the figure caption on each page warns you that the code on that page represents only part of a C source file.

- Each figure displays C source code with horizontal tab stops set every four columns. Displayed code differs from the actual C source file in two ways — comments to the right of code are right justified on the line, and a box character (□) marks the end of the last line of code in each C source file.

The resulting code is quite dense at times. For a typical coding project, I would add white-space to make it at least twenty per cent larger. I compressed it to keep this book from getting even thicker.

The code also contains a number of files that should properly be merged. Placing all visible functions in separate files sometimes results in ridiculously small object modules, as I indicated above. I also introduced several extra C source files just to keep all files under two book pages in length. That was not my only reason for making files smaller, however. I first wrote each C source file to its natural length, however large. *Every* compiler I used failed to translate at least one of the larger files. The extra modules may sometimes be unappealing from the standpoint of good design, but they help both readability and portability in the real world.

implementing Fifteen of the source files in this implementation are the standard head-
headers ers. I listed several properties of standard headers earlier — idempotence, mutual independence, and declaration equivalence. Each of the properties has an impact on how you implement the standard headers.

Idempotence is easy to manage. You use a *macro guard* for most of the standard headers. For example, you can protect <stdio.h> by conditionally including its contents at most one time:

idempotence
```
#ifndef _STDIO_H
#define _STDIO_H
..... /* BODY OF <stdio.h> */
#endif
```

The funny macro name _STDIO_H is, of course, in the class of names reserved to the implementor.

You can't use this mechanism for the header <assert.h>. Its behavior is controlled by the macro name NDEBUG that *the programmer* can choose to define. Each time the program includes this header, the header turns the assert macro off or on, depending upon whether or not NDEBUG has a macro definition at that point in the translation unit. I discuss the matter further in Chapter 1: <assert.h>.

mutual Maintaining mutual independence among the headers takes a bit more
independence work because of a couple of issues. One is that a handful of names are defined in more than one header. A program must be able to include two different headers that define the same name without causing an error. The type definition size_t is one example. It is the type that results from applying the sizeof operator. (See Chapter 11: <stddef.h>.) You can protect against multiple definitions of this type with another macro guard:

```
#ifndef _SIZE_T
#define _SIZE_T
typedef unsigned int size_t;
#endif
```

The macro NULL is another example. You can usually write this macro wherever you want a null pointer to a data object — a pointer value that designates no data object. One way to define this macro is:

```
#define NULL (void *)0
```

It does no harm to include multiple instances of this macro definition in a translation unit. Standard C permits *benign redefinition* of a macro. Two definitions for the same macro name must have the same sequence of *tokens*. They can differ only in the *white-space* (in this case, spaces and horizontal tabs) between tokens. You need not protect against including two definitions that match in this sense.

You do have to provide the same definition in multiple places, however. That is an annoying maintenance problem. Two solutions are:

- Write the same definition in multiple places. Be prepared to hunt down all occurrences if the definition changes.
- Place the definition in a separate header file. Give the file a name that should not collide with file names created by the programmer. Include the file in each header that requires it.

I chose the second solution (most of the time) because it simplifies adapting the library to different implementations.

A similar but different issue arises with the three printing functions **vfprintf**, **vprintf**, and **vsprintf**. You call them from functions that accept a variable argument list when you want to print some or all of those arguments. Each of the three is declared in the header **<stdio.h>**. Each has an argument of type **va_list**. But that type is not defined in that particular header. It is defined only in the header **<stdarg.h>**. How can this be?

synonyms   The answer is simple, if a bit subtle. The header **<stdio.h>** must contain a *synonym* for the type **va_list**. The synonym has a name from the class reserved for macros. That's all that's needed within the standard header to express the function prototype for each of the three functions. (Of course, the implementor faces the same problems replicating either visible definitions or synonyms in multiple headers.)

It's rather difficult for you as a programmer to *use* any of these functions without a definition for **va_list**. (It can be done, but it's probably not good style.) That means you probably want to include the header **<stdarg.h>** any time you make use of any of these functions. Still, it's the programmer's problem. The implementation need not (and must not) drag in **<stdarg.h>** every time the program includes **<stdio.h>**.

headers at   The final property of standard headers is purely for the benefit of
file level   implementors. The programmer must include a standard header only where a file level declaration is permitted. That means the **#include** directive must not occur anywhere inside another declaration. Most standard headers must contain one or more *external declarations*. These are permissible only in certain contexts. Without the caveat, many standard headers would be impossible to write as ordinary C source files.

Testing the Library

Testing can be a never-ending proposition. Only the most trivial functions can be tested exhaustively. Even these can never be tested for all possible interactions with nontrivial programs that use them. You would have to test all possible input values, or at least exercise all possible paths through the code. If your goal is to prove conclusively that a function contains no bugs, you will often fall far short of your goal.

testing all paths A less ambitious goal is to write tests that exercise every part of the executable code. That is a far cry from testing every possible path through the code. It is good enough, however, to build a high level of confidence that the code is essentially correct. To write such tests, you must know:

- what the code is supposed to do (the specification)
- how it does it (the code itself)

You must then contrive tests that test each detail of the specification. (I intentionally leave vague what a "detail" might be.) In principle, those tests should visit every cranny of the code. Every piece of code should help implement some part of the specification. In practice, you must always add tests you don't anticipate when you first analyze the specification.

The result is a complex piece of code closely tied to the code you intend to test. The test program can be as complex as the program to be tested, or more so. That can double the quantity of code you must maintain in future. A change to either piece often necessitates a change to the other. You use each piece of code to debug the other. Only when the two play in harmony can you say that testing is complete — at least for the time being. The payoff for all this extra investment is a significant improvement in code reliability.

validating specifications Another form of testing is *validation*. Here, your goal is to demonstrate how well the code meets its specification. You pointedly ignore any implementation details. A vendor may know implementation details that are not easily visible to the customer. It is in the vendor's best interest to test the internal structure of the code as well as its external characteristics. A customer, however, should be concerned primarily with validating that a product meets its specification, particularly when comparing two or more competing products.

performance testing Still another form of testing is for *performance*. To many people performance means speed, pure and simple. But other factors can matter as much or more — such as memory and disk requirements, both temporary and permanent, or predictable worst-case timings. Good performance tests:

- measure parameters that are relevant to the way the code is likely to be used
- can be carried out by independent agents
- have reproducible results
- have reasonable criteria for "good enough"
- have believable criteria for "better than average" and "excellent"

An amazing number of so-called performance tests violate most or all of these principles. Many test what is easy to test for, not what is worth testing.

The wise code developer invests in as many of these forms of testing as possible, given the inevitable limits on time and money. You design a test plan alongside the code to be tested. You develop comprehensive tests as part of the project. Ideally, you have different programmers write the code and tests. You obtain vendor-independent validation suites from outside sources. You institutionalize retesting after any changes. You provide for maintenance of test machinery as well as the delivered code itself.

I heartily endorse such professionalism in developing code. Having paid lip service to that ideal, however, I intend to stop somewhat short of it. The code presented here has been extensively validated with several existing programs and suites. But I have not produced test programs to exercise every part of the executable code. This book is already overstuffed with code. To add a full set of proper tests would make it truly unwieldy.

simple testing   Instead, I present a number of simple test programs. Each tests part or all of the facilities provided by one of the standard headers in the Standard C library. You will find that these test programs focus primarily on external behavior. That means, essentially, that they comprise a simple validation suite. Occasionally, however, they stray into the realm of testing internal structure. Some implementation errors are so common, and so pernicious, that I can't resist testing for them. Rarely do they stray into the realm of performance testing.

Most of all, you will find these tests to be remarkably superficial and simplistic, given what I just said about proper testing. Nevertheless, even simple tests serve a useful purpose. You can verify that a function satisfies its basic design goals with just a few lines of code. That reassures you that your implementation is sane. When you make changes (as you inevitably will), repeating the tests renews that assurance. Simple tests are well worth writing, and keeping around.

I found that the best simple confidence tests have a number of common properties:

- Print a standard reassuring message and exit with successful status to report correct execution.
- Identify any other unavoidable output to minimize confusion on the part of the reader.
- Provide interesting implementation-dependent information that you may find otherwise difficult to obtain.
- Say nothing else.

I have adopted the convention of preceding each header name with a `t` to construct test file names. Thus, `tassert.c` tests the header `<assert.h>`. It verifies that the assert macro does what you expect. It shows you what the library prints when an assertion fails. And it ends by displaying the reassuring message `SUCCESS testing <assert.h>`.

A few of the larger headers require two or more test programs, as in `tstdio1.c` and `tstdio2.c`. Note that each of these files defines its own `main`. You link each with the Standard C library to produce a separate test program. Do *not* add any of these files to the Standard C library. I chose `t` as the leading character even though a few predefined names begin with that letter. It forms a simple mnemonic, and the file names do not to collide with any in the library proper.

References

ANSI Standard X3.159-1989 (New York: American National Standards Institute, 1989). This is the original C Standard, developed by the ANSI authorized committee X3J11. The Rationale that accompanies the C Standard explains many of the decisions that went into it.

ISO/IEC Standard 9899:1990 (Geneva: International Standards Organization, 1990). Aside from formatting details and section numbering, the ISO C Standard is identical to the ANSI C Standard. The quotes in this book are from the ISO C Standard.

B.W. Kernighan and Dennis M. Ritchie, *The C Programming Language, Second Edition* (Englewood Cliffs, N.J.: Prentice Hall, Inc., 1989). The first edition of *The C Programming Language* served for years at the de facto standard for the C language. It also provides a very good tutorial overview of C. The second edition, upgraded to reflect the ANSI C Standard, is also a good tutorial.

P.J. Plauger and Jim Brodie, *Standard C* (Redmond, Wa.: Microsoft Press, 1989). This book provides a complete but succinct reference to the entire C Standard. It covers both the language and the library.

Thomas Plum, *C Programming Guidelines* (Cardiff, N.J.: Plum Hall, Inc., 1989). Here is an excellent style guide for writing C programs. It also contains a good discussion of first-order correctness testing, on pp. 194-199.

Exercises

Exercise 0.1 Which of the following are *good* reasons for including a function in a library?

- The function is widely used.
- Performance of the function can be improved dramatically by generating inline code.
- The function is easy to write and can be written several different ways.
- The function is hard to write correctly.
- Writing the function poses several interesting challenges.
- The function proved very useful in a past application.
- The function performs a number of services that are loosely related.

Exercise 0.2 Write a (correct) program that contains the line:

```
x:  ((struct x *)x)->x = x(5);
```

Describe the five distinct uses of **x**. Can you make a case for using any two of these meanings at once in a sensible program?

Exercise 0.3 Consider the sequence:

```
double a[] = {1.0, 2.0};
double *p = a;
double sqr(x) {return (x*x); }
#define sqr(x) x*x
```

What is the result of each of the following expressions?

```
sqr(3.0)
sqr(3)
sqr(3+3)
!sqr(3)
sqr(*p++)
(sqr)(3+3)
```

Exercise 0.4 Which of the above expressions do not behave the same as the function call?

Exercise 0.5 Which of the above expressions can be repaired by altering the macro definition? Which cannot?

Exercise 0.6 If any standard header can include any other, what style must you adopt to avoid problems?

Exercise 0.7 [Harder] If a standard header can define arbitrary names, what must a programmer do to ensure that a large program runs correctly when moved from another implementation?

Exercise 0.8 [Very hard] Describe an implementation that tolerates keywords being masked by macros when you include standard headers.

Exercise 0.9 [Very hard] Describe an implementation that tolerates standard headers being included inside function definitions, or at any arbitrary place within a source file.

Chapter 1: `<assert.h>`

Background

The sole purpose of the header `<assert.h>` is to provide a definition of the macro `assert`. You use the macro to enforce assertions at critical places within your program. Should an assertion prove to be untrue, you want the program to write a suitably revealing message to the standard error stream and terminate execution abnormally. (Chapter 12: `<stdio.h>` describes how you write to a stream.) Thus, you might write:

```
#include <assert.h>
    .....
    assert(0 <= idx && idx < sizeof a / sizeof a[0]);
    /* a[idx] is now safe */
```

Any code you write following the assertion can be simpler. It need not check whether the index `idx` is in range. The assertion sees to that. And should this "impossible" situation arise while you are debugging the program, you get a handy diagnostic. The program does not stumble on to generate spurious problems at a later date.

Please note that this is *not* the best way to write production code. It is ill advised for a program in the field to terminate abnormally. No matter how revealing the accompanying message may be to you the programmer, it is assuredly cryptic to the user. Some form of error recovery is almost always preferred. Any diagnostics should be in terms that the user can understand.

What you want is some way to introduce assertions that are enforced only while you're debugging. That lets you document the assertions you need from the start, then helps you catch the worst logic errors early on. Later, you might add code to recover from errors that truly can occur during execution. You want to leave the assertions in as documentation, but you want them to generate no code.

macro NDEBUG `<assert.h>` gives you just this behavior. You can define the macro NDEBUG at some point in your program to alter the way `assert` expands. If NDEBUG is *not* defined at the point where you include `<assert.h>`, the header defines the active form of the macro `assert`. It expands to an expression that tests the assertion and writes an error message if the assertion is false. The program then terminates. If NDEBUG *is* defined, however, the header defines the passive form of the macro that does nothing.

What the C Standard Says

<assert.h>

7.2 Diagnostics <assert.h>

The header **<assert.h>** defines the **assert** macro and refers to another macro,

> **NDEBUG**

which is *not* defined by **<assert.h>**. If **NDEBUG** is defined as a macro name at the point in the source file where **<assert.h>** is included, the **assert** macro is defined simply as

```
#define assert(ignore) ((void)0)
```

The **assert** macro shall be implemented as a macro, not as an actual function. If the macro definition is suppressed in order to access an actual function, the behavior is undefined.

7.2.1 Program diagnostics

assert

7.2.1.1 The **assert** macro

Synopsis

```
#include <assert.h>
void assert(int expression);
```

Description

The **assert** macro puts diagnostics into programs. When it is executed, if **expression** is false (that is, compares equal to 0), the **assert** macro writes information about the particular call that failed (including the text of the argument, the name of the source file, and the source line number — the latter are respectively the values of the predefined macros ___FILE___ and ___LINE___) on the standard error file in an implementation-defined format.[97] It then calls the abort function.

Returns

The **assert** macro returns no value.

Forward references: the **abort** function (7.10.4.1).

Footnotes

97. The message written might be of the form

Assertion failed: *expression*, file *xyz*, line *nnn*

Using <assert.h>

I gave an example of using the **assert** macro at the beginning of this chapter. Whether active or passive, **assert** behaves essentially like a function that takes a single *int* argument and returns a *void* result. The argument to the macro is nominally an expression of type *int*. The macro writes a message and terminates execution if the value of the expression is zero.

predicates

In practice, the argument you write is a *predicate* — an expression that is either true (nonzero) or false (zero). You write predicates in *for, if,* and *while* statements to determine the flow of control through the program. An assertion is simply a compact way of writing:

```
if (!okay)
    abort();
```

The function **abort** is declared in the header **<stdlib.h>**. You call it to terminate execution of the program when something goes wrong.

Assertions help you document the assumptions behind the code you write. They also provide teeth to those assumptions while you are debugging the code. I emphasized earlier, however, that a production program should *not* terminate so abruptly. As convenient as assertions can be during debugging, they eventually prove to be a nuisance.

macro
NDEBUG
How you control the way the macro expands is a matter of taste. Somehow you must control the presence or absence of a definition for the macro **NDEBUG**. One style of programming is to change the source code. Once you believe that assertions should be disabled, just add a line before you include the header:

```
#define NDEBUG  /* disable assertions */
#include <assert.h>
```

That neatly documents that assertions are henceforth inoperative. The only drawback comes when you have to turn debugging back on again. (I can assure you that eventually you will.) You must edit the source file to remove the macro definition.

make
files
Many implementations support a somewhat more flexible approach. They let you define one or more macros outside any C source files. You specify these definitions in a command script or **make** file that rebuilds the program. That can be a better place to define **NDEBUG** and document that assertions are to be disabled. It can also be an easier file to replicate and alter when you must revert to more primitive debugging phases. Nothing in the C Standard requires such a capability, but `<assert.h>` is nevertheless designed with it in mind.

This header has an additional peculiarity. As I mentioned in the previous chapter, all other headers are idempotent. Including any of them two or more times has the same effect as including the header just once. In the case of `<assert.h>`, however, its behavior can vary each time you include it. The header alters the definition of **assert** to agree with the current definition status of **NDEBUG**.

The net effect is that you can control assertions in different ways throughout a source file. Performance may suffer dramatically, for example, when assertions occur inside frequently executed loops. Or an earlier assertion may terminate execution before you get to the revealing parts. In either case, you may need to turn assertions on and off at various places throughout a source file.

So to turn assertions on, you write:

```
#undef NDEBUG
#include <assert.h>
```

And to turn assertions off, you write:

```
#define NDEBUG
#include <assert.h>
```

benign
redefinition
Note that you can safely define the macro **NDEBUG** even if it is already defined. It is a benign redefinition, as I described on page 12. Benign redefinition was added to Standard C for just this purpose. It eliminates the need to protect multiple definitions of the same macro with macro guards and conditional directives.

Implementing `<assert.h>`

This header requires very little code, but it must be carefully crafted. To respond properly to NDEBUG, the header must have the general structure:

```
#undef assert     /* remove existing definition */
#ifdef NDEBUG
#define assert(test) ((void)0)        /* passive form */
#else
#define assert(test) .....            /* active form */
#endif
```

benign   The initial #undef directive is innocuous if no macro definition of assert
undefinition currently exists. You can always #undef a name, whether or not it has a current definition as a macro. (Think of this as *benign undefinition*.) The directive is very necessary, however, if the definition is to change.

A naive, way to write the active form of the macro is:

```
#define assert(test) if (!(test)) \
    fprintf(stderr, "Assertion failed: %s, file %s, line %i\n", \
        #test, __FILE__, __LINE__)  /* UNACCEPTABLE! */
```

This form is unacceptable for a variety of reasons:

- The macro must not directly call any of the library output functions, such as **fprintf**. Nor may it refer to the macro **stderr**. These names are properly declared or defined only in the header `<stdio.h>`. The program might not have included that header, and the header `<assert.h>` must not. A program can define macros that rename any of the names from another header, provided it doesn't include that header. That mandates that the macro call a function with a secret name to do the actual output.

- The macro must expand to a *void* expression. The program can contain an expression such as `(assert(0 < x), x < y)`. That rules out use of the *if* statement, for example. Any testing must make use of one of the conditional operators within an expression.

- The macro should expand to efficient and compact code. Otherwise, programmers will avoid writing assertions. This version always makes a function call that passes five arguments.

Figure 1.1:
assert.h

```
/* assert.h standard header */
#undef assert                          /* remove existing definition */

#ifdef NDEBUG
    #define assert(test)    ((void)0)
#else                                  /* NDEBUG not defined */
    void _Assert(char *);
        /* macros */
    #define _STR(x) _VAL(x)
    #define _VAL(x) #x
    #define assert(test)    ((test) ? (void)0 \
        : _Assert(__FILE__ ":" _STR(__LINE__) " " #test))
#endif
```

```
/* _Assert function */
#include <assert.h>
#include <stdio.h>
#include <stdlib.h>

void _Assert(char *mesg)
    {                              /* print assertion message and abort */
    fputs(mesg, stderr);
    fputs(" -- assertion failed\n", stderr);
    abort();
    }
```

Figure 1.1 shows the file **assert.h**. This implementation of the macro **assert** performs the test inline. That way an optimizing translator can often eliminate *all* code for an assertion that is obviously true. The macro composes the diagnostic information into a single string argument of the form **xyz:nnn expression** (to use the notation of the C Standard). The string-creation operator **#x** encodes much of the information. Then string-literal concatenation merges the pieces. It is a bit more compact than the form that the C standard suggests, with the words **file** and **line** in it.

_STR
_VAL One nuisance is that the builtin macro **__LINE__** does not expand to a string literal. It becomes a decimal constant. To convert it to proper form requires an additional layer of processing. That is performed by adding to the header the two secret macros **_STR** and **_VAL**. One macro replaces **__LINE__** with its decimal constant expansion. The second converts the decimal constant to a string literal. Omit either **_STR** or **_VAL** and you end up with the string literal "**__LINE__**" instead of what you want.

function
_Assert Figure 1.2 shows the file **xassert.c**. It defines the secret library function **_Assert** that the macro calls. A smart version of the function **_Assert** can parse the diagnostic message and supply the missing bits if it chooses. The version shown here does not, since the precise format of the message is implementation-defined.

forward
references The function **_Assert** uses two other library functions. It writes strings to the standard error stream by calling **fputs**, declared in **<stdio.h>**. It terminates execution abnormally by calling **abort**, declared in **<stdlib.h>**. The description of each of these headers occurs much later. If you have a general knowledge of C, such forward references should present few problems. But if you need to learn more about what they do at this point, you'll have to skip down quite a number of pages.

A good tutorial presentation minimizes the use of forward references. Unfortunately, the Standard C library is highly interconnected. Nearly every part is written in terms of the others and can be described only in terms of the others. When I must refer ahead, I describe the new material in general terms, as I have done for **fputs** and **abort**. That should minimize some page flipping for those new to Standard C, but probably not all.

Testing `<assert.h>`

Figure 1.3 shows the file `tassert.c`. This test program exercises the `assert` macro four different ways — in its passive and active forms, with the test condition met and not met. Only the active form with the test not met should abort. Correct execution should display something like:

```
Sample assertion failure message --
TASSERT.C:43 val == 0 -- assertion failed
SUCCESS testing <assert.h>
```

and terminate normally. Note, however, that the program writes text to both the standard error and standard output streams. Text lines can appear in a different order on some implementations. (See Chapter 12: `<stdio.h>` for a discussion of streams.)

The test fails if any of the earlier three invocations of `assert` cause execution to terminate, or if the program exits normally and reports the status `EXIT_FAILURE` (a nonzero value defined in `<stdlib.h>`).

`tassert.c` is a fairly sophisticated test program. Two of the functions it uses are brothers to ones you have already met. The program writes strings to the standard output stream by calling `puts`, declared in `<stdio.h>`. It terminates execution normally by calling `abort`, declared in `<stdlib.h>`. The program is more ambitious than that, however. It calls the function `signal`, declared in `<signal.h>`, to regain control after `_Assert` calls `abort`. It even uses the `assert` macro to verify that `signal` returns successful status. Imagine using the very machinery you are testing to implement part of the test harness! That's hardly the way to go about debugging new code.

program stubs In fact, it was not the way I debugged this code. My first version of `tassert.c` simply aborted on the fourth test of the `assert` macro. I confess that it took several tries even to get that far. Both `fputs` and `signal` sit atop a lot of machinery, not all of which was debugged when I began testing `<assert.h>`. I had to introduce *program stubs* (much simpler versions) for most of this code at one time or another. The needs of debugging can be quite different than the needs of simple confidence testing.

When one of these tests fails, you may have to alter it — or call on the services of an interactive debugger — to identify the exact failure. That is one of the design compromises I made to keep the tests succinct.

References

Two good books that preach programming by assertion are:

O.J. Dahl, E.W. Dijkstra, and C.A.R. Hoare, *Structured Programming* (New York: Academic Press, 1972).

E.W. Dijkstra, *A Discipline of Programming* (Englewood Cliffs, N.J.: Prentice-Hall, Inc., 1973).

Both are still topical, despite their age.

Figure 1.3:
tassert.c

```c
/* test assert macro */
#define NDEBUG
#include <assert.h>
#include <signal.h>
#include <stdio.h>
#include <stdlib.h>

        /* static data */
static int val = 0;

static void field_abort(int sig)
    {                                           /* handle SIGABRT */
    if (val == 1)
        {                                       /* expected result */
        puts("SUCCESS testing <assert.h>");
        exit(EXIT_SUCCESS);
        }
    else
        {                                       /* unexpected result */
        puts("FAILURE testing <assert.h>");
        exit(EXIT_FAILURE);
        }
    }

static void dummy()
    {                                   /* test dummy assert macro */
    int i = 0;

    assert(i == 0);
    assert(i == 1);
    }

#undef NDEBUG
#include <assert.h>

int main()
    {                       /* test both dummy and working forms */
    assert(signal(SIGABRT, &field_abort) != SIG_ERR);
    dummy();
    assert(val == 0);                           /* should not abort */
    ++val;
    fputs("Sample assertion failure message --\n", stderr);
    assert(val == 0);                           /* should abort */
    puts("FAILURE testing <assert.h>");
    return (EXIT_FAILURE);
    }                                                          □
```

Exercises

Exercise 1.1 Write a version of `assert.h`, using the version of `xassert.c` in Figure 1.2, that exactly matches the format shown in the C Standard.

Exercise 1.2 Write a version of `xassert.c`, using the version of `assert.h` in Figure 1.1, that exactly matches the format shown in the C Standard.

Exercise 1.3 What are the relative merits of the approaches in the previous two exercises?

Exercise 1.4 Write a version of `assert.h` and `xassert.c` that prints *all* assertions. Why would you want to use this version?

Exercise 1.5 [Harder] Write a handler for the signal `SIGABRT` that writes the prompt:

`Continue (y/n)?`

to the standard error stream and reads the response from the standard input stream. If the response is `yes` (in either uppercase or lowercase), the handler should reestablish itself and return control to the `abort` function. Chapter 9: `<signal.h>` describes signals. Chapter 13: `<stdlib.h>` describes the `abort` function.

Why would you want this capability?

Exercise 1.6 [Harder] Write a handler for the signal `SIGABRT` that executes a `longjmp` to a `setjmp` at the top of `main`. Chapter 8: `<setjmp.h>` describes the `longjmp` and `setjmp` functions.

Why would you want this capability? Describe a safe discipline for initializing static storage in a program that uses this capability.

Exercise 1.7 [**Very hard**] Some C translators provide a *source-level interactive debugger*. Such debuggers often let you set conditional breakpoints at various points within the executing program. Locate such a C translator and explore what is necessary to get `<assert.h>` to work with the debugger. Your goals are, in order of increasing difficulty:

- Have control revert to the debugger whenever an assertion fails. Execution should continue with the statement following the offending `assert` macro invocation.
- Have `assert` generate no inline code. It should pass instructions to the source-level debugger instead.
- Generate code at the same level of optimization whether or not `assert` macros appear, in either passive or active form.
- Have the modified `assert` accept test expressions of arbitrary complexity.

Why would you want each of these capabilities?

Chapter 2: <ctype.h>

Background

Character handling has been important since the earliest days of C. Many of us were attracted to the DEC PDP-11 because of its rich set of character-manipulation instructions. When Ken Thompson moved UNIX to the PDP-11/20, he gave us a great vehicle for manipulating streams of characters in a uniform style. When C came along, it was only natural that we should use it to write programs preoccupied with walloping characters.

This was truly a new style of programming. C programs tended to be small and devoted to a single function. The tradition until then was to write huge monoliths that offered a spectrum of services. C programs read and wrote streams of human-readable characters. The tradition until then was to have programs communicate with each other via highly structured binary files. They spoke to people by producing paginated reports with embedded carriage controls.

idioms   So the early toolsmiths writing in C under UNIX began developing idioms at a rapid rate. We often found ourselves sorting characters into different classes. To identify a letter, we wrote:

```
if ('A' <= c && c <= 'Z' || 'a' <= c && c <= 'z')
    .....
```

which gives a correct result when the execution character set is *ASCII*. (The letters stand for "American Standard Code for Information Interchange." It is a widely used set of character codes, but hardly universal. This idiom does *not* work correctly for other popular character sets, such as IBM's EBCDIC.)

To identify a digit, we wrote:

```
if ('0' <= c && c <= '9')
    .....
```

And to identify white-space, we wrote:

```
if (c == ' ' || c == '\t' || c == '\n')
    .....
```

Pretty soon, our programs became thick with tests like this. Worse, some became thick with tests *almost* like this. You can write the same idiom several different ways. That slows comprehension and increases the chance for errors.

character   Opinions also differed on the makeup of certain character classes. White-
classes space has always suffered notorious variability. Should you lump vertical
tabs in with horizontal tabs and spaces? If you include newlines (which are
actually ASCII line feeds), should you also include carriage returns (which
UNIX reserves for writing overstruck lines)? Then what do you do about
form feeds? The easier it is to get tools to work together, the more you want
them to agree on conventions.

The natural response was to introduce functions in place of these tests.
That made them at once more readable, more uniform, and more easily
adapted to changes in the execution character set. The idioms above
became:

```
if (isalpha(c))
    .....

if (isdigit(c))
    .....

if (isspace(c))
    .....
```

It wasn't long before a dozen-odd functions like these came into being.
They soon found their way into the growing library of C support functions.
More and more programs began to use them instead of reinventing their
own idioms. The character-classification functions were so useful, they
seemed almost too good to be true.

They were. A typical text-processing program might average three calls
on these functions for *every* character from the input stream. The overhead
of calling so many functions often dominates the execution time of the
program. That led some programmers to avoid using these standard character classification functions. It led others to develop a set of macros to take
their place.

surprises   C programmers tend to like macros. They let you write code that is as
with macros readable as calling functions but is much more efficient. You just have to
be alert to a few surprises:

- The macro may expand into much more code than a function call, even
  if it happens to execute faster than the function call. If your program
  expands the macro in many places, it can grow surprisingly larger.
- The macro may expand to a subexpression that doesn't bind as tight as
  a function call. This is unacceptable, and always has been. A liberal use
  of parentheses in the macro definition can eliminate such nonsense.
- The macro may expand one of its arguments to code that is executed
  more than once, or not at all. A macro argument with side effects will
  cause surprises. While some C programmers consider such surprises
  acceptable, modern practice avoids them. Only two Standard C library
  functions, **getc** and **putc**, both declared in **<stdio.h>**, can have macro
  versions with such *unsafe* behavior.

translation   So the challenge in those early days was to produce a set of macros to
tables replace the character-classification functions. Because they were used a lot,
they had to expand to compact code. They also had to be reasonably safe
to use. What evolved was a set of macros that used one or more *translation
tables*. Each macro took the form:

```
#define _XXXMASK      0x...
#define isxxx(c)      (_Cyptab[c] & _XXXMASK)
```

The character **c** indexes into the translation table named _Ctyptab.
Different bits in each table entry characterize the index character. If any of
the bits corresponding to the mask _**XXXMASK** are set, the character is in the
tested class. The macro expands to a compact expression that is nonzero
for all the right arguments.

One drawback to this approach is that the macro generates bad code for
some of the wrong arguments. Execute it with an argument not in the
expected range and it accesses storage outside the translation table. Depending on the implementation, the error can go undetected or it can
terminate execution with a cryptic message.

The functions assume they are testing values returned by one of the
functions **fgetc, getc, getch**, all declared in **<stdio.h>**. All return a character code type cast to *unsigned char* — a small non-negative value. Or they
return the value of the macro **EOF**, defined in **<stdio.h>** — a negative value
(usually –1).

On a computer architecture that represents type *char* the same as *signed
char*, a common error occurs when you test the more exotic character codes.
The function call **isprint(c)** looks safe enough. But say **c** has type *char* and
holds a value with the sign bit set. The argument will be a negative value
almost certainly out of range for the function.

Few programmers know to write **isprint((unsigned char)c)**, a much
safer form. Of course, you can use the type cast safely only where you are
certain that the argument value **EOF** cannot occur.

locales   Nevertheless, translation tables remain the basis for many modern
implementations of the character classification functions. They help the
implementor provide efficient macros, even in the presence of multiple
locales. Locales are a big topic. I discuss them at length in Chapter 6:
<locale.h>.

For now, I simply observe that a C program always begins execution in
the "c" locale. A call to the function **setlocale** can change the locale. When
that happens, certain properties of the functions declared in **<ctype.h>** can
change behavior.

The functions declared in **<ctype.h>** remain important to the modern C
programmer. You should use them wherever possible to sort characters into
classes. They greatly increase your chances of having code that is both
efficient and correct across varied character sets.

What the C Standard Says

7.3 Character handling <ctype.h>

The header **<ctype.h>** declares several functions useful for testing and mapping characters.[98] In all cases the argument is an **int**, the value of which shall be representable as an **unsigned char** or shall equal the value of the macro **EOF**. If the argument has any other value, the behavior is undefined.

The behavior of these functions is affected by the current locale. Those functions that have implementation-defined aspects only when not in the **"C"** locale are noted below.

The term *printing character* refers to a member of an implementation-defined set of characters, each of which occupies one printing position on a display device; the term *control character* refers to a member of an implementation-defined set of characters that are not printing characters.[99]

Forward references: EOF (7.9.1), localization (7.4).

7.3.1 Character testing functions

The functions in this subclause return nonzero (true) if and only if the value of the argument **c** conforms to that in the description of the function.

7.3.1.1 The isalnum function

Synopsis

```
#include <ctype.h>
int isalnum(int c);
```

Description

The **isalnum** function tests for any character for which **isalpha** or **isdigit** is true.

7.3.1.2 The isalpha function

Synopsis

```
#include <ctype.h>
int isalpha(int c);
```

Description

The **isalpha** function tests for any character for which **isupper** or **islower** is true, or any character that is one of an implementation-defined set of characters for which none of **iscntrl**, **isdigit**, **ispunct**, or **isspace** is true. In the **"C"** locale, **isalpha** returns true only for the characters for which **isupper** or **islower** is true.

7.3.1.3 The iscntrl function

Synopsis

```
#include <ctype.h>
int iscntrl(int c);
```

Description

The **iscntrl** function tests for any control character.

7.3.1.4 The isdigit function

Synopsis

```
#include <ctype.h>
int isdigit(int c);
```

Description

The **isdigit** function tests for any decimal-digit character (as defined in 5.2.1).

7.3.1.5 The isgraph function

Synopsis

```
#include <ctype.h>
int isgraph(int c);
```

Description

The **isgraph** function tests for any printing character except space (' ').

7.3.1.6 The `islower` function

Synopsis

```
#include <ctype.h>
int islower(int c);
```

Description

The **islower** function tests for any character that is a lowercase letter or is one of an implementation-defined set of characters for which none of **iscntrl**, **isdigit**, **ispunct**, or **isspace** is true. In the "**C**" locale, **islower** returns true only for the characters defined as lowercase letters (as defined in 5.2.1).

7.3.1.7 The `isprint` function

Synopsis

```
#include <ctype.h>
int isprint(int c);
```

Description

The **isprint** function tests for any printing character including space (' ').

7.3.1.8 The `ispunct` function

Synopsis

```
#include <ctype.h>
int ispunct(int c);
```

Description

The **ispunct** function tests for any printing character that is neither space (' ') nor a character for which **isalnum** is true.

7.3.1.9 The `isspace` function

Synopsis

```
#include <ctype.h>
int isspace(int c);
```

Description

The **isspace** function tests for any character that is a standard white-space character or is one of an implementation-defined set of characters for which **isalnum** is false. The standard white-space characters are the following: space (' '), form feed ('\f'), newline ('\n'), carriage return ('\r'), horizontal tab ('\t'), and vertical tab ('\v'). In the "**C**" locale, **isspace** returns true only for the standard white-space characters.

7.3.1.10 The `isupper` function

Synopsis

```
#include <ctype.h>
int isupper(int c);
```

Description

The **isupper** function tests for any character that is an uppercase letter or is one of an implementation-defined set of characters for which none of **iscntrl**, **isdigit**, **ispunct**, or **isspace** is true. In the "**C**" locale, **isupper** returns true only for the characters defined as uppercase letters (as defined in 5.2.1).

7.3.1.11 The `isxdigit` function

Synopsis

```
#include <ctype.h>
int isxdigit(int c);
```

Description

The **isxdigit** function tests for any hexadecimal-digit character (as defined in 6.1.3.2).

7.3.2 Character case mapping functions

7.3.2.1 The `tolower` function

Synopsis

```
#include <ctype.h>
int tolower(int c);
```

Description

The **tolower** function converts an uppercase letter to the corresponding lowercase letter.

Returns

If the argument is a character for which **isupper** is true and there is a corresponding character for which **islower** is true, the **tolower** function returns the corresponding character; otherwise, the argument is returned unchanged.

7.3.2.2 The `toupper` function

Synopsis

```
#include <ctype.h>
int toupper(int c);
```

Description

The **toupper** function converts a lowercase letter to the corresponding uppercase letter.

Returns

If the argument is a character for which **islower** is true and there is a corresponding character for which **isupper** is true, the **toupper** function returns the corresponding character; otherwise, the argument is returned unchanged.

Footnotes

98. See "future library directions" (7.13.2).

99. In an implementation that uses the seven-bit ASCII character set, the printing characters are those whose values lie from 0x20 (space) through 0x7E (tilde); the control characters are those whose values lie from 0 (NUL) through 0x1F (US), and the character 0x7F (DEL).

Using <ctype.h>

Use the functions declared in **<ctype.h>** to test or alter characters that you read in with **fgetc, fgetc, fgetc**, all declared in **<stdio.h>**. If you store such a value before you test it, declare the data object to have type *int*. If you store in any character type instead, you lose information. You may mistake an end-of-file indication for a valid character. Or you may convert a valid character code to a negative value, which is unacceptable.

If you generate an argument any other way, be careful. The functions work properly only for the value **EOF**, defined in **<stdio.h>**, and values that type *unsigned char* can represent. The characters in the basic C character set have positive values when represented as type *char*. Others may not.

Classifying characters is not as easy as it first appears. First you have to understand the classes. Then you have to understand where all the common characters lie within the class system. You have to know where the implementation has tucked the less common characters. You need some understanding of how everything changes when you move to an implementation with a different character set. Finally, you need to be aware of how the classes can change when the program changes its locale.

character classes   To begin at the beginning, the classes defined by the character-classification functions are:

- *digit* — one of the ten decimal digits ′0′ through ′9′
- *hexadecimal digit* — a digit or one of the first six letters of the alphabet in either case, ′a′ through ′f′ and ′A′ through ′F′
- *lowercase letter* — one of the letters ′a′ through ′z′, plus possibly others when outside the "c" locale
- *uppercase letter* — one of the letters ′A′ through ′Z′, plus possibly others when outside the "c" locale
- *letter* — one of the lowercase or uppercase letters, plus possibly others when outside the "c" locale
- *alphanumeric* — one of the letters or digits
- *graphic* — a character that occupies one print position and is visible when written to a display device
- *punctuation* — a graphic character that is not an alphanumeric, including at least the 29 such characters used to represent C source text
- *printable* — a graphic character or the space character ′ ′
- *space* — the space character ′ ′, one of the five standard motion control characters (form feed *FF*, newline *NL*, carriage return *CR*, horizontal tab *HT*, or vertical tab *VT*), plus possibly others when outside the "c" locale
- *control* — one of the five standard motion control characters, backspace *BS*, alert *BEL*, plus possibly others.

Two of these classes are open-ended even in the "c" locale. An implementation can define any number of additional punctuation or control characters. In ASCII, for example, punctuation also includes characters such as ′@′ and ′$′. Control characters include all the codes between decimal 1 and 31, plus the delete character, whose code is 127.

Figure 2.1 is taken from Plauger and Brodie, *Standard C*. It shows how the character classification functions relate to each other. The characters in

Figure 2.1:
Character
Classes

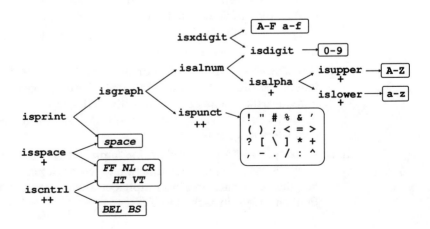

the rounded rectangles are all the members of the basic C character set. These are the characters you use to represent an arbitrary C source file. The C Standard requires that every execution character set contain all these characters. Every execution character set must also contain the null character, whose code is zero.

A single plus sign under a function name indicates that the function can represent additional characters in locales other than the "c" locale. A double plus sign indicates that the function can represent additional characters even in the "c" locale.

An execution character set can contain members that fall in none of these classes. The same character must not, however, be added at more than one place in the diagram. If it is a lowercase letter, it is also in several other classes by inheritance. But a character must not be considered both punctuation and control, for example.

As you can see from the diagram, nearly all the functions can change behavior in a program that alters its locale. Only `isdigit` and `isxdigit` remain unchanged. If your code intends to process the local language, this is good news. The locale will alter `islower`, for example, to detect any additional lowercase letters.

when locales change If your code endeavors to be locale independent, however, you must program more carefully. Supplement any tests you make with the character-classification functions to weed out any extra characters that sneak in. Or get all your locale-independent testing out of the way before the program changes out of the "c" locale.

If neither of these options is viable, you may have to revert part or all of the locale for a region of code. See page 88.

The important message is that Standard C introduces a new era. You can now write code more easily for cultures around the world, which is good. But you must now write code with more forethought. If it can end up in an international application, it may someday process characters undreamed of by early C programmers. Trust the character-classification functions to contain the problem, to help you with it, and to delineate what can change.

I conclude this section with a remark or two about each of the functions declared in `<ctype.h>`.

isalnum `isalnum` — "Alnum" is short for "alphanumeric," the fancy term for letters and digits. A common practice where a program looks for names is to require that each name begin with a letter, but permit a mixture of letters or digits to follow. You often use this function to test for the trailing characters in a name.

isalpha `isalpha` — "Alpha" is short for "alphabetic," a common term for letters of either case. You use this function to test for letters in the local alphabet. For the "c" locale, the local alphabet always consists of the familiar 26 English letters, in each of two cases.

iscntrl   **iscntrl** — Some programmers consider this function to be the exact complement of **isprint**. The two recognize disjoint sets, to be sure. But the sets do not necessarily exhaust the set of all characters. A program that uses **iscntrl** this way can fail if you present it with exotic characters.

If you use this function at all, be careful. Only seven control characters have uniform behavior across all locales — alert, backspace, carriage return, form feed, horizontal tab, newline, and vertical tab. A program that makes additional assumptions should document those assumptions in a prominent comment.

isdigit   **isdigit** — This is one of the stablest functions across locales. It matches only the ten decimal digits of the basic C character set, regardless of locale. (Some alphabets provide additional characters for various numbers.) Not only that, you can also be certain that the codes for the ten digits always have sequential values, as in the common idiom (without overflow checking):

```
for (value = 0; isdigit(*s); ++s)
    value = value * 10 + (*s - '0');
```

Knowing that you can depend on this idiom simplifies and speeds code that performs numeric conversions.

isgraph   **isgraph** — You use **isgraph** to identify characters that display when printed. This function shifts behavior when you change locale.

islower   **islower** — What constitutes a lowercase letter can vary considerably among locales. Use this function to make sure that you recognize all of them. Don't assume that every lowercase letter has a corresponding upper-case letter, or conversely. Don't even assume that every letter is either lowercase or uppercase.

isprint   **isprint** — This function recognizes all characters that occupy one print position when written to a printer.

ispunct   **ispunct** — Remember that punctuation is an open-ended set of characters, even in the "c" locale. As the description in the C Standard implies, you are better off thinking of punctuation as graphic characters other than alphanumeric.

isspace   **isspace** — This is an important function. Several library functions use **isspace** to determine which characters to treat as white-space. In the "c" locale, you use this function to identify any of the characters that alter the print position, when written to a display device, without displaying a graphic. You should assume that **isspace** is the best test for such white-space in *any* locale.

isupper   **isupper** — The same remarks apply as for **islower** above, only in reverse.

isxdigit   **isxdigit** — Like **isdigit**, this function does not change with locale. You use it for the specific purpose of identifying the digits in a hexadecimal number. Note, however, that you cannot assume letter codes are adjacent, the same way digit codes are. To convert a hexadecimal number in any locale, write:

```
#include <ctype.h>
#include <string.h>
. . . . .
    static const char xd[] =
        {"0123456789abcdefABCDEF"};
    static const char xv[] =
        {0, 1, 2, 3, 4, 5, 6, 7, 8, 9,
         10, 11, 12, 13, 14, 15,
         10, 11, 12, 13, 14, 15};

    for (value = 0; isxdigit(*s); ++s)
        value = (value << 4) + xv[strchr(xd, *s) - xd];
```

Note that this code does not check for overflow. That requires additional complexity.

tolower   **tolower** — Use this function to force any uppercase letters to lowercase. It deals with such exotica as lowercase letters that have no corresponding uppercase letter and letters that have no case. Don't assume that you can convert an uppercase letter to its corresponding lowercase letter simply by adding or subtracting a constant value. That happens to be true for ASCII and EBCDIC, two popular character sets, but it is not required by the C Standard.

toupper   **toupper** — Use this function to force any uppercase letters to lowercase. The same remarks apply as for **tolower** above, only in reverse.

Implementing `<ctype.h>`

The implementation presented here follows the traditional approach. A translation table captures the peculiarities of the execution character set. Each of the functions uses its argument as an index into the table. The function tests the selected table element against a unique mask to determine whether the character is in the class in question.

A translation table makes sense only if it is not too large. How big it gets is a product of how many elements it contains and how big each element must be. Standard C defines three "character" types — *char, signed char,* and *unsigned char.* All of these types must be able to represent all the characters in the execution character set. All are represented by at least eight bits.

range   The character classification functions each accept an argument of type
of values *int,* but with a limited range of values. Any value that type *unsigned char* can represent is valid, plus one additional value specified by the macro **EOF**, defined in **<stdio.h>**. Most sensible implementations give **EOF** the value –1. This implementation is no exception. So the number of elements in a translation table must be one more than the number of distinct values representable by a character type.

The vast majority of C implementations use exactly eight bits to represent a character type. Hence, a translation table must contain 257 elements. An implementation can, however, use more bits. C has been implemented with nine, ten, 16, and even 32 bits used to represent character types. A translation table that must represent all the values in a 16-bit character is probably too unwieldy. It would contain 65,537 elements.

Figure 2.1 shows eight distinct classes. That suggests that a translation table can be an *array of unsigned char*. But the figure also shows (with pluses) six places where an implementor can add characters to the classes. That suggests that the table must be an *array of short*. You can merge most of these additions with existing classes. Still, two sets of additions remain, outside the `"C"` locale at least:

- The function `isalpha` can recognize characters that are recognized by neither `islower` or `isupper`.
- The function `isspace` can recognize characters that are recognized by neither `iscntrl` or `isprint`.

You must either rule out locales with funny letters and spaces, or you must make each element of the translation table big enough to hold ten classification bits. If any chance exists that you may want to support locales with such alphabetic or space characters, declare the translation table to have type *array of short*. If you are willing to rule out such latitude, however, you can save space by declaring the translation table to have type *array of unsigned char*. Since this implementation aims at maximum portability, it takes the former course.

One subtle point should not get bypassed. I have consistently said that an eight-bit translation table should have elements of type *unsigned char*. Not all implementations represent integers in two's complement. In other representations, converting a negative signed representation to an unsigned one can alter low-order bits. Performing a bitwise *and* between a signed value and an unsigned mask can thus cause surprises.

So far, I have assumed that characters are represented in eight bits (or not much more). I have also assumed that a program can afford to include a translation table of 514 bytes (or not much more). To show some real code, I must make at least three more assumptions.

tolower *Assumption #1:* The case mapping functions `tolower` and `toupper` differ
toupper from the other functions in this group. They don't simply classify their argument, but return a character that may differ from the argument character. I assume that they should be implemented with mapping tables similar to the translation table shared by all the other functions.

ASCII   *Assumption #2:* The execution character set is ASCII, which is widely
and   used among modern computers. ISO 646, the international variant, has the
ISO 646   same code values and much the same *glyphs*, or visible forms of the characters. Some of the punctuation in ASCII can be replaced with alternate glyphs in ISO 646, however. That is how Europeans can introduce accented characters, such as Å and ê, without going beyond seven-bit codes.

This implementation is compatible with any variant of ISO 646 that redefines no punctuation characters as letters. It is easily changed to match other ISO 646 variants, however. You can also accommodate other character sets just as easily. IBM's EBCDIC also requires a simple change of table entries. Just be sure that your table entries agree with the character constants (such as `'a'`) produced by your C translator!

shared libraries   *Assumption #3:* The library can use writable static storage for pointers to its tables. That supports only the simple case where the translator includes code from the Standard C library C as needed. Once included in the program, library code behaves just like code supplied by the programmer. An implementation that can run multiple programs, however, often benefits from having *shared libraries.* All the code for the Standard C library occupies a single place in computer memory. A C program linked to run in this environment transfers control to functions in the shared library, rather than including its own private copy of the library code. The obvious benefits are that each program is smaller and can link faster.

writable static storage   A not-so-obvious drawback appears when one or more functions need to maintain a writable static data object that is private to the library. You can't share the same data object between different programs, or between different threads of control within the same program. You need to allocate a unique version of each writable static data object for each program or thread and initialize it to its required starting value.

Sadly, no common method exists for performing this feat. Operating systems and linkers use ad hoc machinery to make shared libraries work at all. Some simply disallow writable statics. Others require you to invoke special machinery to set up and access writable statics. You must write your code in a special way.

The character classification functions need writable static storage if they are to adapt to changing locales. One approach is to rewrite the tables when the locale changes. A better way is to alter pointers to point to different (read-only) tables. That speeds changing locales. It also minimizes the amount of writable storage that might need special handling.

This presentation largely ignores the potential problems associated with writable static storage in the library. I minimize the use of writable statics as much as possible. I also try to call attention in the code to any writable static data object that must be introduced. But I use no special notation for accessing such storage.

header <ctype.h>   Figure 2.2 shows the file `ctype.h`. The code for the functions declared in `<ctype.h>` is built around three translation tables. Three writable pointers at all times point to the tables corresponding to the current locale. Note that *every* function has a corresponding macro. I used fairly cryptic names for the macros that define the classification bits. That helps save space for the presentation. It also speeds the processing of standard headers in many implementations.

isalnum
etc.

The code for the functions looks much like the macros. Figure 2.3 (isalnum.c) through Figure 2.15 (toupper.c) shows the code for these functions.

_Tolower
_Toupper

Figure 2.16 shows the file xtolower.c. It defines the initial value of the pointer _Tolower, and the ASCII version of the translation table that accompanies tolower. Similarly, Figure 2.17 shows the file xtoupper.c. It defines

Figure 2.2:
ctype.h

```
/* ctype.h standard header */
#ifndef _CTYPE
#define _CTYPE
        /* _Ctype code bits */
#define _XA    0x200 /* extra alphabetic */
#define _XS    0x100 /* extra space */
#define _BB    0x80 /* BEL, BS, etc. */
#define _CN    0x40 /* CR, FF, HT, NL, VT */
#define _DI    0x20 /* '0'-'9' */
#define _LO    0x10 /* 'a'-'z' */
#define _PU    0x08 /* punctuation */
#define _SP    0x04 /* space */
#define _UP    0x02 /* 'A'-'Z' */
#define _XD    0x01 /* '0'-'9', 'A'-'F', 'a'-'f' */
        /* declarations */
int isalnum(int), isalpha(int), iscntrl(int), isdigit(int);
int isgraph(int), islower(int), isprint(int), ispunct(int);
int isspace(int), isupper(int), isxdigit(int);
int tolower(int), toupper(int);
extern const short *_Ctype, *_Tolower, *_Toupper;
        /* macro overrides */
#define isalnum(c)  (_Ctype[(int)(c)] & (_DI|_LO|_UP|_XA))
#define isalpha(c)  (_Ctype[(int)(c)] & (_LO|_UP|_XA))
#define iscntrl(c)  (_Ctype[(int)(c)] & (_BB|_CN))
#define isdigit(c)  (_Ctype[(int)(c)] & _DI)
#define isgraph(c)  (_Ctype[(int)(c)] & (_DI|_LO|_PU|_UP|_XA))
#define islower(c)  (_Ctype[(int)(c)] & _LO)
#define isprint(c)  \
    (_Ctype[(int)(c)] & (_DI|_LO|_PU|_SP|_UP|_XA))
#define ispunct(c)  (_Ctype[(int)(c)] & _PU)
#define isspace(c)  (_Ctype[(int)(c)] & (_CN|_SP|_XS))
#define isupper(c)  (_Ctype[(int)(c)] & _UP)
#define isxdigit(c) (_Ctype[(int)(c)] & _XD)
#define tolower(c)  _Tolower[(int)(c)]
#define toupper(c)  _Toupper[(int)(c)]
#endif                                                      □
```

Figure 2.3:
isalnum.c

```
/* isalnum function */
#include <ctype.h>

int (isalnum)(int c)
    {                           /* test for alphanumeric character */
    return (_Ctype[c] & (_DI|_LO|_UP|_XA));
    }                                                       □
```

Figure 2.4:
`isalpha.c`

```
/* isalpha function */
#include <ctype.h>

int (isalpha)(int c)
    {                                   /* test for alphabetic character */
    return (_Ctype[c] & (_LO|_UP|_XA));
    }                                                                   □
```

Figure 2.5:
`iscntrl.c`

```
/* iscntrl function */
#include <ctype.h>

int (iscntrl)(int c)
    {                                     /* test for control character */
    return (_Ctype[c] & (_BB|_CN));
    }                                                                   □
```

Figure 2.6:
`isdigit.c`

```
/* isdigit function */
#include <ctype.h>

int (isdigit)(int c)
    {                                                   /* test for digit */
    return (_Ctype[c] & _DI);
    }                                                                   □
```

Figure 2.7:
`isgraph.c`

```
/* isgraph function */
#include <ctype.h>

int (isgraph)(int c)
    {                                     /* test for graphic character */
    return (_Ctype[c] & (_DI|_LO|_PU|_UP|_XA));
    }                                                                   □
```

Figure 2.8:
`islower.c`

```
/* islower function */
#include <ctype.h>

int (islower)(int c)
    {                                   /* test for lowercase character */
    return (_Ctype[c] & _LO);
    }                                                                   □
```

Figure 2.9:
`isprint.c`

```
/* isprint function */
#include <ctype.h>

int (isprint)(int c)
    {                                   /* test for printable character */
    return (_Ctype[c] & (_DI|_LO|_PU|_SP|_UP|_XA));
    }                                                                   □
```

Figure 2.10:
`ispunct.c`

```
/* ispunct function */
#include <ctype.h>

int (ispunct)(int c)
    {                               /* test for punctuation character */
    return (_Ctype[c] & _PU);
    }                                                                    □
```

Figure 2.11:
`isspace.c`

```
/* isspace function */
#include <ctype.h>

int (isspace)(int c)
    {                               /* test for spacing character */
    return (_Ctype[c] & (_CN|_SP|_XS));
    }                                                                    □
```

Figure 2.12:
`isupper.c`

```
/* isupper function */
#include <ctype.h>

int (isupper)(int c)
    {                               /* test for uppercase character */
    return (_Ctype[c] & _UP);
    }                                                                    □
```

Figure 2.13:
`isxdigit.c`

```
/* isxdigit function */
#include <ctype.h>

int (isxdigit)(int c)
    {                               /* test for hexadecimal digit */
    return (_Ctype[c] & _XD);
    }                                                                    □
```

Figure 2.14:
`tolower.c`

```
/* tolower function */
#include <ctype.h>

int (tolower)(int c)
    {                               /* convert to lowercase character */
    return (_Tolower[c]);
    }                                                                    □
```

Figure 2.15:
`toupper.c`

```
/* toupper function */
#include <ctype.h>

int (toupper)(int c)
    {                               /* convert to uppercase character */
    return (_Toupper[c]);
    }                                                                    □
```

Figure 2.16:
xtolower.c

```
/* _Tolower conversion table -- ASCII version */
#include <ctype.h>
#include <limits.h>
#include <stdio.h>
#if EOF != -1 || UCHAR_MAX != 255
#error WRONG TOLOWER TABLE
#endif


        /* static data */
static const short tolow_tab[257] = {EOF,
 0x00, 0x01, 0x02, 0x03, 0x04, 0x05, 0x06, 0x07,
 0x08, 0x09, 0x0a, 0x0b, 0x0c, 0x0d, 0x0e, 0x0f,
 0x10, 0x11, 0x12, 0x13, 0x14, 0x15, 0x16, 0x17,
 0x18, 0x19, 0x1a, 0x1b, 0x1c, 0x1d, 0x1e, 0x1f,
 0x20, 0x21, 0x22, 0x23, 0x24, 0x25, 0x26, 0x27,
 0x28, 0x29, 0x2a, 0x2b, 0x2c, 0x2d, 0x2e, 0x2f,
 0x30, 0x31, 0x32, 0x33, 0x34, 0x35, 0x36, 0x37,
 0x38, 0x39, 0x3a, 0x3b, 0x3c, 0x3d, 0x3e, 0x3f,
 0x40, 'a',  'b',  'c',  'd',  'e',  'f',  'g',
 'h',  'i',  'j',  'k',  'l',  'm',  'n',  'o',
 'p',  'q',  'r',  's',  't',  'u',  'v',  'w',
 'x',  'y',  'z',  0x5b, 0x5c, 0x5d, 0x5e, 0x5f,
 0x60, 'a',  'b',  'c',  'd',  'e',  'f',  'g',
 'h',  'i',  'j',  'k',  'l',  'm',  'n',  'o',
 'p',  'q',  'r',  's',  't',  'u',  'v',  'w',
 'x',  'y',  'z',  0x7b, 0x7c, 0x7d, 0x7e, 0x7f,

 0x80, 0x81, 0x82, 0x83, 0x84, 0x85, 0x86, 0x87,
 0x88, 0x89, 0x8a, 0x8b, 0x8c, 0x8d, 0x8e, 0x8f,
 0x90, 0x91, 0x92, 0x93, 0x94, 0x95, 0x96, 0x97,
 0x98, 0x99, 0x9a, 0x9b, 0x9c, 0x9d, 0x9e, 0x9f,
 0xa0, 0xa1, 0xa2, 0xa3, 0xa4, 0xa5, 0xa6, 0xa7,
 0xa8, 0xa9, 0xaa, 0xab, 0xac, 0xad, 0xae, 0xaf,
 0xb0, 0xb1, 0xb2, 0xb3, 0xb4, 0xb5, 0xb6, 0xb7,
 0xb8, 0xb9, 0xba, 0xbb, 0xbc, 0xbd, 0xbe, 0xbf,
 0xc0, 0xc1, 0xc2, 0xc3, 0xc4, 0xc5, 0xc6, 0xc7,
 0xc8, 0xc9, 0xca, 0xcb, 0xcc, 0xcd, 0xce, 0xcf,
 0xd0, 0xd1, 0xd2, 0xd3, 0xd4, 0xd5, 0xd6, 0xd7,
 0xd8, 0xd9, 0xda, 0xdb, 0xdc, 0xdd, 0xde, 0xdf,
 0xe0, 0xe1, 0xe2, 0xe3, 0xe4, 0xe5, 0xe6, 0xe7,
 0xe8, 0xe9, 0xea, 0xeb, 0xec, 0xed, 0xee, 0xef,
 0xf0, 0xf1, 0xf2, 0xf3, 0xf4, 0xf5, 0xf6, 0xf7,
 0xf8, 0xf9, 0xfa, 0xfb, 0xfc, 0xfd, 0xfe, 0xff};

const short *_Tolower = &tolow_tab[1];                    □
```

the initial value of the pointer `_Toupper`, and the ASCII version of the translation table that accompanies `toupper`.

Note the use of the `#error` directive. It ensures that the code translates successfully only if its assumptions are correct. The macro `UCHAR_MAX`, defined in `<limits.h>`, gives the highest value that can be represented by type *unsigned char*.

Figure 2.17:
xtoupper.c

```c
/* _Toupper conversion table -- ASCII version */
#include <ctype.h>
#include <limits.h>
#include <stdio.h>
#if EOF != -1 || UCHAR_MAX != 255
#error WRONG TOUPPER TABLE
#endif

        /* static data */
static const short toup_tab[257] = {EOF,
 0x00, 0x01, 0x02, 0x03, 0x04, 0x05, 0x06, 0x07,
 0x08, 0x09, 0x0a, 0x0b, 0x0c, 0x0d, 0x0e, 0x0f,
 0x10, 0x11, 0x12, 0x13, 0x14, 0x15, 0x16, 0x17,
 0x18, 0x19, 0x1a, 0x1b, 0x1c, 0x1d, 0x1e, 0x1f,
 0x20, 0x21, 0x22, 0x23, 0x24, 0x25, 0x26, 0x27,
 0x28, 0x29, 0x2a, 0x2b, 0x2c, 0x2d, 0x2e, 0x2f,
 0x30, 0x31, 0x32, 0x33, 0x34, 0x35, 0x36, 0x37,
 0x38, 0x39, 0x3a, 0x3b, 0x3c, 0x3d, 0x3e, 0x3f,
 0x40, 'A', 'B', 'C', 'D', 'E', 'F', 'G',
 'H', 'I', 'J', 'K', 'L', 'M', 'N', 'O',
 'P', 'Q', 'R', 'S', 'T', 'U', 'V', 'W',
 'X', 'Y', 'Z', 0x5b, 0x5c, 0x5d, 0x5e, 0x5f,
 0x60, 'A', 'B', 'C', 'D', 'E', 'F', 'G',
 'H', 'I', 'J', 'K', 'L', 'M', 'N', 'O',
 'P', 'Q', 'R', 'S', 'T', 'U', 'V', 'W',
 'X', 'Y', 'Z', 0x7b, 0x7c, 0x7d, 0x7e, 0x7f,

 0x80, 0x81, 0x82, 0x83, 0x84, 0x85, 0x86, 0x87,
 0x88, 0x89, 0x8a, 0x8b, 0x8c, 0x8d, 0x8e, 0x8f,
 0x90, 0x91, 0x92, 0x93, 0x94, 0x95, 0x96, 0x97,
 0x98, 0x99, 0x9a, 0x9b, 0x9c, 0x9d, 0x9e, 0x9f,
 0xa0, 0xa1, 0xa2, 0xa3, 0xa4, 0xa5, 0xa6, 0xa7,
 0xa8, 0xa9, 0xaa, 0xab, 0xac, 0xad, 0xae, 0xaf,
 0xb0, 0xb1, 0xb2, 0xb3, 0xb4, 0xb5, 0xb6, 0xb7,
 0xb8, 0xb9, 0xba, 0xbb, 0xbc, 0xbd, 0xbe, 0xbf,
 0xc0, 0xc1, 0xc2, 0xc3, 0xc4, 0xc5, 0xc6, 0xc7,
 0xc8, 0xc9, 0xca, 0xcb, 0xcc, 0xcd, 0xce, 0xcf,
 0xd0, 0xd1, 0xd2, 0xd3, 0xd4, 0xd5, 0xd6, 0xd7,
 0xd8, 0xd9, 0xda, 0xdb, 0xdc, 0xdd, 0xde, 0xdf,
 0xe0, 0xe1, 0xe2, 0xe3, 0xe4, 0xe5, 0xe6, 0xe7,
 0xe8, 0xe9, 0xea, 0xeb, 0xec, 0xed, 0xee, 0xef,
 0xf0, 0xf1, 0xf2, 0xf3, 0xf4, 0xf5, 0xf6, 0xf7,
 0xf8, 0xf9, 0xfa, 0xfb, 0xfc, 0xfd, 0xfe, 0xff};

const short *_Toupper = &toup_tab[1];
```

□

data object
_Ctype

Figure 2.18 shows the file xctype.c. All the character-classification functions share a common translation table, pointed at by **_Ctype**. This file defines both the table and the pointer.

Figure 2.18:
xctype.c

```
/* _Ctype conversion table -- ASCII version */
#include <ctype.h>
#include <limits.h>
#include <stdio.h>
#if EOF != -1 || UCHAR_MAX != 255
#error WRONG CTYPE TABLE
#endif

        /* macros */
#define XDI (_DI|_XD)
#define XLO (_LO|_XD)
#define XUP (_UP|_XD)

        /* static data */
static const short ctyp_tab[257] = {0, /* EOF */
_BB,  _BB,  _BB,  _BB,  _BB,  _BB,  _BB,  _BB,
_BB,  _CN,  _CN,  _CN,  _CN,  _CN,  _BB,  _BB,
_BB,  _BB,  _BB,  _BB,  _BB,  _BB,  _BB,  _BB,
_BB,  _BB,  _BB,  _BB,  _BB,  _BB,  _BB,  _BB,
_SP,  _PU,  _PU,  _PU,  _PU,  _PU,  _PU,  _PU,
_PU,  _PU,  _PU,  _PU,  _PU,  _PU,  _PU,  _PU,
XDI,  XDI,  XDI,  XDI,  XDI,  XDI,  XDI,  XDI,
XDI,  XDI,  _PU,  _PU,  _PU,  _PU,  _PU,  _PU,
_PU,  XUP,  XUP,  XUP,  XUP,  XUP,  XUP,  _UP,
_UP,  _UP,  _UP,  _UP,  _UP,  _UP,  _UP,  _UP,
_UP,  _UP,  _UP,  _UP,  _UP,  _UP,  _UP,  _UP,
_UP,  _UP,  _UP,  _PU,  _PU,  _PU,  _PU,  _PU,
_PU,  XLO,  XLO,  XLO,  XLO,  XLO,  XLO,  _LO,
_LO,  _LO,  _LO,  _LO,  _LO,  _LO,  _LO,  _LO,
_LO,  _LO,  _LO,  _LO,  _LO,  _LO,  _LO,  _LO,
_LO,  _LO,  _LO,  _PU,  _PU,  _PU,  _PU,  _BB,
};                                      /* rest all match nothing */

const short *_Ctype = &ctyp_tab[1];
```

Testing <ctype.h>

It makes sense to test each of the functions declared in <ctype.h> for all valid argument values. It is also wise to test both the functions themselves and the macros that mask them. That goes beyond testing just the external characteristics of <ctype.h>, of course. Such double testing is looking for trouble in the inner workings of the header and its functions. Here is a case, however, where both macros and functions are important. We want some confidence that both behave as expected.

We can also profit from some additional information — a display of the characters in various printable classes, presented in order of increasing code values. That reassures us that all the expected characters match and no others. It shows any additional characters permitted in the "c" locale, such as extra punctuation. And it reveals the collating order within a class.

Figure 2.19 shows the test program tctype.c. It displays several character classes, then tests both the functions and their masking macros. Note the use of parentheses around the function names in the second set of tests. That is the same trick I use to define each of the visible functions in the library. The parentheses prevent any macro with arguments from masking the declaration of the actual function earlier in the header. If the execution character set is ASCII, the program produces the output:

```
ispunct: !"#$%&'()*+,-./:;<=>?@[\]^_'{|}~
isdigit: 0123456789
islower: abcdefghijklmnopqrstuvwxyz
isupper: ABCDEFGHIJKLMNOPQRSTUVWXYZ
isalpha: ABCDEFGHIJKLMNOPQRSTUVWXYZabcdefghijklmnopqrstuvwxyz
isalnum: 0123456789ABCDEFGHIJKLMNOPQRSTUVWXYZabcdefghijklmnopqrs
tuvwxyz
SUCCESS testing <ctype.h>
```

Note that the line showing the characters matched by `isalnum` is folded here. This book page is not wide enough to display the entire line. The line will *not* fold on a typical computer display, which has wider lines.

References

Considerable interest has arisen lately in character sets. International commerce demands better support for a richer set of characters than that traditionally used to represent English (and C) on computers. Various vendors have given meaning to all 256 codes that can be represented in the standard eight-bit byte. Nevertheless, the stalwarts are still the sets of 128 or fewer characters that can be encoded in seven bits. Two standards cover a vast number of implementations:

ANSI Standard X3.4-1968 (New York: American National Standards Institute, 1989). This defines the ASCII character set, a set of seven-bit codes widely used to represent characters in modern computers.

ISO Standard 646:1983 (Geneva: International Standards Organization, 1983). This is the international standard for seven-bit character codes.

Exercises

Exercise 2.1 List all the character classification functions that return a nonzero value for each of the characters in the string:

```
"Hello, world!\n"
```

Exercise 2.2 Modify the functions declared in `<ctype.h>` to work properly with arbitrary argument values. Treat an argument value that is out of range the same way you treat the value `EOF`. Describe at least two ways to report an error for an argument value out of range.

Exercise 2.3 A name in C begins with a letter. Any number of additional letters, digits, or underscore characters follow. Write the function `size_t idlen(const char *s)` that returns the number of characters that constitute the identifier beginning at `s`. If no identifier begins at `s`, the function returns zero.

```c
/* test ctype functions and macros */
#include <assert.h>
#include <ctype.h>
#include <limits.h>
#include <stdio.h>

static void prclass(const char *name, int (*fn)(int))
    {                           /* display a printable character class */
    int c;

    fputs(name, stdout);
    fputs(": ", stdout);
    for (c = EOF; c <= UCHAR_MAX; ++c)
        if ((*fn)(c))
            fputc(c, stdout);
    fputs("\n", stdout);
    }

int main()
    {                               /* test both macros and functions */
    char *s;
    int c;

        /* display printable classes */
    prclass("ispunct", &ispunct);
    prclass("isdigit", &isdigit);
    prclass("islower", &islower);
    prclass("isupper", &isupper);
    prclass("isalpha", &isalpha);
    prclass("isalnum", &isalnum);
        /* test macros for required characters */
    for (s = "0123456789"; *s; ++s)
        assert(isdigit(*s) && isxdigit(*s));
    for (s = "abcdefABCDEF"; *s; ++s)
        assert(isxdigit(*s));
    for (s = "abcdefghijklmnopqrstuvwxyz"; *s; ++s)
        assert(islower(*s));
    for (s = "ABCDEFGHIJKLMNOPQRSTUVWXYZ"; *s; ++s)
        assert(isupper(*s));
    for (s = "!\"#%&'();<=>?[\\]*+,-./:^_{|}~"; *s; ++s)
        assert(ispunct(*s));
    for (s = "\f\n\r\t\v"; *s; ++s)
        assert(isspace(*s) && iscntrl(*s));
    assert(isspace(' ') && isprint(' '));
    assert(iscntrl('\a') && iscntrl('\b'));
        /* test macros for all valid codes */
    for (c = EOF; c <= UCHAR_MAX; ++c)
        {                           /* test for proper class membership */
        if (isdigit(c))
            assert(isalnum(c));
        if (isupper(c))
            assert(isalpha(c));
        if (islower(c))
            assert(isalpha(c));
```

```c
            if (isalpha(c))
                assert(isalnum(c) && !isdigit(c));
            if (isalnum(c))
                assert(isgraph(c) && !ispunct(c));
            if (ispunct(c))
                assert(isgraph(c));
            if (isgraph(c))
                assert(isprint(c));
            if (isspace(c))
                assert(c == ' ' || !isprint(c));
            if (iscntrl(c))
                assert(!isalnum(c));
            }
        /* test functions for required characters */
    for (s = "0123456789"; *s; ++s)
        assert((isdigit)(*s) && (isxdigit)(*s));
    for (s = "abcdefABCDEF"; *s; ++s)
        assert((isxdigit)(*s));
    for (s = "abcdefghijklmnopqrstuvwxyz"; *s; ++s)
        assert((islower)(*s));
    for (s = "ABCDEFGHIJKLMNOPQRSTUVWXYZ"; *s; ++s)
        assert((isupper)(*s));
    for (s = "!\"#%&'();<=>?[\\]*+,-./:^_{|}~"; *s; ++s)
        assert((ispunct)(*s));
    for (s = "\f\n\r\t\v"; *s; ++s)
        assert((isspace)(*s) && (iscntrl)(*s));
    assert((isspace)(' ') && (isprint)(' '));
    assert((iscntrl)('\a') && (iscntrl)('\b'));
        /* test functions for all valid codes */
    for (c = EOF; c <= UCHAR_MAX; ++c)
        {                           /* test for proper class membership */
        if ((isdigit)(c))
            assert((isalnum)(c));
        if ((isupper)(c))
            assert((isalpha)(c));
        if ((islower)(c))
            assert((isalpha)(c));
        if ((isalpha)(c))
            assert((isalnum)(c) && !(isdigit)(c));
        if (isalnum(c))
            assert((isgraph)(c) && !(ispunct)(c));
        if ((ispunct)(c))
            assert((isgraph)(c));
        if ((isgraph)(c))
            assert((isprint)(c));
        if ((isspace)(c))
            assert(c == ' ' || !(isprint)(c));
        if ((iscntrl)(c))
            assert(!(isalnum)(c));
        }
    puts("SUCCESS testing <ctype.h>");
    return (0);
    }
```

□

Exercise 2.4 Write the function `size_t detab(char *dest, const char *src)` that copies the null-terminated string beginning at `src` to `dest`, with each horizontal tab replaced by one to four spaces. Assume tab stops every four columns. A printing character occupies one column. The only other characters that affect the print position are backspace, carriage return, and newline. Return the length of the new string at `dest`.

Exercise 2.5 Do you have to modify the function `idlen` (from Exercise 2.3) to work properly if the locale changes from `"c"`? If so, show the modified version. If not, explain why not.

Exercise 2.6 Do you have to modify the function `detab` (from Exercise 2.4) to work properly if the locale changes from `"c"`? If so, show the modified version. If not, explain why not.

Exercise 2.7 [Harder] You want to implement a library that can be shared. Describe how you would alter the code in this chapter for each of the following mechanisms:

- The translator can be instructed to place all writable static storage in the library in a section that is copied into each process that uses the library.
- You can add fields to a structure called `_Lib_stat`, declared in `<lib-stat.h>`. You can add initializers to the definition of the structure in the file `libstat.c`.
- You can add fields to a structure called `_Lib_stat`, as before. You access the structure only through a pointer to the structure called `_P`, also declared in `<libstat.h>`.
- You can add fields to a structure called `_Lib_stat`, as before. You access the structure only through a pointer to the structure returned by a call of the form `_FP()`. The function `_FP` is declared in `<libstat.h>`.

Exercise 2.8 [Harder] A *multithread* environment supports one or more threads of control;thread of that share the same static storage. Dynamic storage (with storage class `auto` or `register`) evolves separately for each thread. You want to implement a library that appears *atomic* to the threads — no function changes behavior, or misbehaves, because another thread changes the state of library static storage. You make each access to library static storage safe by surrounding it with *synchronization code,* as in:

```
_lock();
p = _Ctype;
_unlock();
```

Show how to change the code in this chapter to make it safe for multithread operation. What does that do to performance? How can you improve performance and still keep the code safe for multithread operation?

Exercise 2.9 [Very hard] Modify the macros defined in `<ctype.h>` to work properly with arbitrary argument values. Treat an argument value that is out of range the same way you treat the value `EOF`.

Chapter 3: `<errno.h>`

Background

If I had to identify one part of the C Standard that is uniformly disliked, I would not have to look far. Nobody likes `errno` or the machinery that it implies. I can't recall anybody defending this approach to error reporting, not in two dozen or more meetings of X3J11, the committee that developed the C Standard. Several alternatives were proposed over the years. At least one faction favored simply discarding `errno`. Yet it endures.

The C Standard has even added to the existing machinery. The header `<errno.h>` is an invention of the committee. We wanted to have every function and data object in the library declared in some standard header. We gave `errno` its own standard header mostly to ghettoize it. We even added some words in the hope of clarifying a notoriously murky corner of the C language.

A continuing topic among groups working to extend and improve C is how to tame `errno`. Or how to get rid of it. The fact that no clear answer has emerged to date should tell you something. There are no easy answers when it comes to reporting and handling errors.

history   C was born under UNIX. That operating system set new standards for clarity and simplicity. The interface between user program and operating system kernel is particularly clean. You specify a system call number and a handful of operands. The 40-odd system calls of early UNIX have more than doubled in number over the years. But that is still on the sparse side compared to systems of comparable power. Operands to UNIX system calls are almost always scalars — integers or pointers. They are equally spare.

Each implementation of UNIX adopts a simple method for indicating erroneous system calls. Writing in assembly language, you typically test the carry indicator in the condition code. If the carry indicator is clear, the system call was successful. Any answers you requested are returned in machine registers or in a structure within your program. (You specify the address of the structure as one of the arguments to the system call.) If the carry indicator is set, however, the system call was in error. One of the machine registers contains a small positive number to indicate the nature of the error.

handling   That scheme is great for assembly language. It is less great for programs
errors in C you write in C. You can write a library of C-callable functions, one for each
distinct system call. You'd like each function return value to be the answer
you request when making that particular system call. You can do so, but
that makes it difficult to report errors in a way that is easy to test. Alternatively, you can have each function return as its value a success or failure
indication. Do that and you have no easy way to get at the answer you want
from a successful system call.

One trick that mostly works is to do a bit of both. For a typical system
call, you can define an error return value that is distinguishable from any
valid answer. A null pointer is an obvious case in point. The value –1 can
also be set aside in many cases, with no serious conflict with valid answers.
Each UNIX system call usually has a such return value to indicate that some
form of error has occurred.

What the C-callable functions do *not* do is report exactly which error
occurred. That strains the trick a bit too much. All you can tell from the
return value is whether an error occurred. You have to look elsewhere to
get details.

The "elsewhere" that early UNIX programmers adopted was a data
object with external linkage. Any system call that fails stores the error code
from the kernel in an *int* variable called **errno**. It then returns –1, or some
other appropriately silly value, to indicate the error. Most of the time, the
program doesn't care about details. An error is an error is an error. But in
those few cases where the program does care, it knows how to get additional information. It looks in **errno** to see the last error code stored there.

Naturally, you'd better look before it's too late. Make another system call
that fails and the error code gets overwritten. You must also look at **errno**
only after a system call that fails. A successful call doesn't clear the value
stored there. It's not a great piece of machinery, but it does work.

overworked   The first problem with **errno** is that it was too handy. People started
machinery finding additional uses for it. It grew from a dirty little trick for augmenting
UNIX system calls to a C institution. And that's when it got overworked.
System calls aren't the only rich source of errors. Another well-explored
vein is the portion of the library that computes the common math functions.
(See Chapter 7: **<math.h>**.)

Some functions yield values too large to represent for certain arguments
(such as **exp(1000.0)**). Some yield values too small to represent for certain
arguments (such as **exp(-1000.0)**). Some are simply undefined for certain
argument values (such as **sqrt(-1.0)**). Some are defined, but of suspect
worth for certain argument values (such as **sin(1e30)**).

You could introduce one or more error codes for each function that can
run into trouble. Following the naming convention for UNIX error codes,
you could report **ESQRT** for the square root of a negative number. But that
is both open-ended and messy.

Fortunately, math errors fall into just a few categories:

math errors

- An *overflow* occurs when a result is too large in magnitude to represent as a floating-point value of the required type.

- An *underflow* occurs when a result is too small in magnitude to represent as a floating-point value of the required type.

- A *significance loss* occurs when a result has nowhere near the number of significant digits indicated by its type.

- A *domain error* occurs when a result is undefined for a given argument value.

Several different system calls in UNIX can yield the same error codes. Similarly, several different math functions can yield one or more of these errors. (The errors can even occur for nearly all the arithmetic operators, with floating-point operands.) In fact, you can do an adequate job of covering all the math errors with just two error codes:

- `EDOM` is reported on a domain error.

- `ERANGE` is reported on an overflow or an underflow.

Loss of significance is a chancy error to report. One programmer's notion of a serious loss may be a matter of utter indifference to another programmer. Indeed, some very stable algorithms are insensitive to serious loss of significance in portions of a calculation. Hence, it is arguable whether significance loss should even be reported by the library.

You can see what's coming. Errors can occur in the math library much as they can occur on system calls. You need some way to report math library errors. So why invent yet another mechanism when you've already got one handy? An early, and natural, evolution of the C library was to report math errors by storing `EDOM` and `ERANGE` in `errno`. That practice has been blessed by inclusion in the C Standard. The C Standard also spells out a few other places where library functions must set `errno`. The complete list is:

defined errors

- Numerous functions declared in `<math.h>` store the values of the macros `EDOM` and `ERANGE`, defined in `<errno.h>`, in `errno`.

- Several functions declared in `<stdlib.h>` convert text strings to values of assorted arithmetic types. Some or all of these can store the value of `ERANGE` in `errno`.

- Several functions declared in `<stdio.h>` alter the position in a file where the next read or write occurs. These functions can store a positive value in `errno`. That value is implementation-defined. In this implementation, I have chosen `EFPOS` as the name of the macro defined in `<errno.h>` that corresponds to that value. It is *not* a widely used name.

- The function `signal`, declared in `<signal.h>`, can store a positive value in `errno`. That value isn't even implementation-defined — an implementation can do as it chooses and not disclose what it does. Since `signal` varies so much among implementations, I chose not to specify a particular error code in this library.

What the C Standard Says

<errno.h>

7.1.4 Errors `<errno.h>`

The header `<errno.h>` defines several macros, all relating to the reporting of error conditions.

The macros are

> EDOM
> ERANGE

EDOM
ERANGE

which expand to integral constant expressions with distinct nonzero values, suitable for use in `#if` preprocessing directives; and

> errno

errno

which expands to a modifiable lvalue[92] that has type `int`, the value of which is set to a positive error number by several library functions. It is unspecified whether `errno` is a macro or an identifier declared with external linkage. If a macro definition is suppressed in order to access an actual object, or a program defines an identifier with the name `errno`, the behavior is undefined.

The value of `errno` is zero at program startup , but is never set to zero by any library function.[93] The value of `errno` may be set to nonzero by a library function call whether or not there is an error, provided the use of `errno` is not documented in the description of the function in this International Standard.

Additional macro definitions, beginning with **E** and a digit or **E** and an uppercase letter,[94] may also be specified by the implementation.

Footnotes

92.   The macro `errno` need not be the identifier of an object. It might expand to a modifiable lvalue resulting from a function call (for example, `*errno()`).

93.   Thus, a program that uses `errno` for error checking should set it to zero before a library function call, then inspect it before a subsequent library function call. Of course, a library function can save the value of `errno` on entry and then set it to zero, as long as the original value is restored if `errno`'s value is still zero just before the return.

94.   See "future library directions" (7.13.1).

Using `<errno.h>`

The C Standard leaves much unsaid about the errors that can be reported. It says even less about the values of any error codes or the macro names you use to determine those values. That's because usage varies so widely among implementations. Even different versions of UNIX define different sets of error codes.

If you are writing code for a specific system, you may have to learn its peculiar set of error codes. List the header `<errno.h>` if you can. All error codes should be defined there as macros with names beginning with **E**. Read any documentation you can find that details error codes. Then be prepared to experiment. Documentation is notoriously spotty and inaccurate in this area.

If you are writing portable code, *avoid* any assumptions about extra error codes. You can count on only the properties of `errno` specified throughout the C Standard. I listed them on page 49. Rarely do you have to know explicit error codes, however. Footnote 93 of the C Standard (shown above) tells you the safest coding style for using `errno`. Set it to zero right before a library function call, then test it *for any nonzero value* before the next library call:

```
#include <errno.h>
#include <math.h>
.....
    errno = 0;
    y = sqrt(x);
    if (errno != 0)
        printf("invalid x: %e\n", x);
```

Never assume that a library function will leave errno unaffected, no matter how simple the function. It's rather a noisy channel.

Implementing <errno.h>

On the surface, the C Standard demands little of an implementation in this area. You can write the file errno.h simply as:

```
/* errno.h standard header */
#ifndef _ERRNO
#define _ERRNO

#define EDOM    1
#define ERANGE  2

extern int errno;

#endif
```

In some library file, you must add a definition for the data object:

```
int errno = 0;
```

Your only other obligation is to store values such as EDOM and ERANGE in errno at the appropriate places within the library functions. What could be simpler?

Here is a case where the overt implementation is the easiest part of the job. errno causes trouble in two subtler ways — sometimes its specification is too vague and sometimes it is too explicit. To see why takes some explaining.

too much   The vagueness comes from the historical use of errno to register system-
and   call errors. That practice has been implicitly endorsed by the C Standard.
too little   Any library function can store nonzero values in errno. The stores can occur because the function makes one or more system calls that fail. Or they can occur because some function in the library chooses to use this reporting channel.

All you can count on is the behavior explicitly called out in the C Standard. Call sqrt(-1.0) and you can be sure that errno contains the value EDOM. Call fabs(x) and all bets are off, believe it or not. No library function will store a zero in errno. Anything else is fair game.

The overspecification mostly affects the math functions. By spelling out when errno must be set, the C Standard interferes with important optimizations. In partiular, the C Standard makes it hard for compilers to use the newest floating-point coprocessors to advantage.

Chips like the Intel 80X87 family and the Motorola MC68881 have some pretty fancy instructions. Some can compute part or all of a math function with inline code. A smart compiler can dramatically speed up calculations by using these instructions. If nothing else, the compiler can avoid the function-call and function-return overhead for a math function.

mathematical   The problem comes when a mathematical exception occurs. These math
exceptions coprocessors run autonomously, and they want to keep moving. They want to record an error by carrying along a special code, called NaN (for "Not a Number") or Inf (for "infinity"). Later operations preserve these special codes. You can test at the end of a computation whether anything went wrong along the way.

At best, these coprocessors record an error in their own condition code. The main processor has to copy the coprocessor condition code into its own to test whether an error occurred. That stops a pipelined coprocessor in full career. If a C program must set `errno` on every math exception, it can run a math coprocessor at only a fraction of its potential speed.

macro   Footnote 92 of the C Standard suggests one trick that can help. The C
errno Standard does not require that `errno` be an actual data object. It is defined as a macro that expands to a *modifiable lvalue* — an arbitrary expression that you can use on the left side of an assigning operator (such as =) to designate a data object. That gives the implementor considerable latitude. In particular, the `errno` macro can expand to an expression such as `*_Erfun()`. Every time the program wants to check for errors, it calls a function to tell the program where to look.

That has two implications. First, the implementation can be lazy about recording errors. It can wait until someone tries to peek at `errno` before it stores the latest error code. That might give the implementation sufficient latitude to leave math coprocessors alone most of the time. (The translator may be hard pressed to exploit this opportunity, however.)

The second implication is that `errno` can move about. The function can return a different address every time it is called. That can be a tremendous help in implementing shared libraries. Static storage is a real nuisance in a shared library, as I discussed on page 36. Static storage that the user program can alter at will is even worse. `errno` is the only such creature in the Standard C library.

Even as a macro, `errno` is still an annoying piece of machinery. Any program can contain the sequence:

```
y = sqrt(x);
if (errno == EDOM)
    . . . . .
```

The need to support such error tests severely constrains what an implementation can do with `sqrt` and its ilk. Since any library function can alter `errno`, programmers are also ill served. Here we have a mechanism that can be hard on both the implementor and the user.

Figure 3.1:
errno.h

```
/* errno.h standard header */
#ifndef _ERRNO
#define _ERRNO
#ifndef _YVALS
#include <yvals.h>
#endif
        /* error codes */
#define EDOM     _EDOM
#define ERANGE  _ERANGE
#define EFPOS   _EFPOS
    /* ADD YOURS HERE */
#define _NERR   _ERRMAX                     /* one more than last code */
        /* declarations */
extern int errno;
#endif                                                                         □
```

parametric   Figure 3.1 shows the code for `errno.h`. It is not as simple as I suggested
code earlier. That's because I decided to make it *parametric*. The simpler form
must be tailored for each operating system that hosts the library. Other
library functions or the operating system itself may have preconceived
notions about the values of error codes. You must change this header to
match, or endure surprising irregularities.

Most of the code that uses `<errno.h>` cares about the values of one or
two error codes. As I mentioned on page 50, these values change across
operating systems. One or two library functions need to know the valid
range of error codes. This range also varies across operating systems.

I began moving this library to an assortment of environments shortly
after I first wrote it. I found it annoying that perhaps a dozen files had to
change, each in only small ways. I was quickly overwhelmed maintaining
several versions of this double handful of files.

header   That prompted me to introduce what you might call an "internal stand-
`<yvals.h>` ard header." Several of the standard headers include the header `<yvals.h>`.
(The angle brackets tell the translator to look for this header wherever the
other standard headers are stored. That may cause problems on some
systems.) I concentrate in this file many of the changes you must make to
move this library about.

The header `<errno.h>` defines its macros in terms of other macros
defined in `<yvals.h>`. This two-step process is necessary because other
headers include `<yvals.h>`. The macro ERANGE must be defined in your
program only when you include `<errno.h>`.

Note also that the macro guard for `<yvals.h>` is in the header that
includes it, not in `<yvals.h>` itself. That is a small optimization. Since
several standard headers include this header, it is likely to be requested
several times in a translation unit. The macro guard skips the `#include`
directive once `<yvals.h>` becomes part of the translation unit. The header
is not read repeatedly.

Figure 3.2:
errno.c

```
/* errno storage */
#include <errno.h>
#undef errno

int errno = 0;                                                          □
```

The header **<yvals.h>** contains a hodgepodge of values. Appendix A:
Interfaces shows versions of the header for some popular operating sys-
tems. I list here only the macros defined in **<yvals.h>** that affect **<errno.h>**.
These values are consistent with the Standard C compiler shipped with
Borland's Turbo C++, with UNIX on Sun workstations, and with ULTRIX
on the DEC VAX:

_EDOM   `#define _EDOM   33`
_ERANGE   `#define _ERANGE 34`
_EFPOS   `#define _EFPOS  35`
_ERRMAX   `#define _ERRMAX 36`

Please note, however, that these values are by no means universal.

header   I emphasize that **<yvals.h>** doesn't do the whole job of tailoring this
"yfuns.h" library to a given operating system. Later in this book I introduce yet
another header, called **"yfuns.h"**. (See page 281.) That header serves a
similar but distinct role. Even two headers is not enough. A handful of
functions in the Standard C library differ too much among operating
systems to be parametrized. They come in different versions. You will meet
them from time to time in later chapters.

Figure 3.2 shows the file **error.c**, which defines the **errno** data object.
The **#undef** directive is just insurance against future changes to **<errno.h>**.

Figure 3.3:
terrno.c

```
/* test errno macro */
#include <assert.h>
#include <errno.h>
#include <math.h>
#include <stdio.h>

int main()
    {                              /* test basic workings of errno */
    assert(errno == 0);
    perror("No error reported as");
    errno = ERANGE;
    assert(errno == ERANGE);
    perror("Range error reported as");
    errno = 0;
    assert(errno == 0);
    sqrt(-1.0);
    assert(errno == EDOM);
    perror("Domain error reported as");
    puts("SUCCESS testing <errno.h>");
    return (0);
    }                                                                  □
```

Testing `<errno.h>`

Figure 3.3 shows the test program `terrno.c`. It doesn't do much. The C Standard says little about the properties of `<errno.h>`. Primarily, `terrno.c` ensures that a program can store values in `errno` and retrieve them.

As a courtesy, the test program also displays how the standard error codes appear when output. The function `perror`, declared in `<stdio.h>`, writes a line of text to the standard error stream. The function determines the last part of that text line from the contents of `errno`. If all goes well, running the executable version of `terrno.c` displays the output:

```
No error reported as: no error
Range error reported as: range error
Domain error reported as: domain error
SUCCESS testing <errno.h>
```

Again, I must warn that this output comes from both the standard error and the standard output streams. The possibility is remote in this case, but some implementations may rearrange the lines.

References

David Stevenson, "A Proposed Standard for Binary Floating-Point Arithmetic," *Computer*, 14:3 (1981), pp. 51-62. This and subsequent articles in the same issue (pp. 63-87) of *Computer* explain many aspects of the IEEE 754 Floating-Point Standard.

Mark J. Rochkind, *Advanced UNIX Programming* (Englewood Cliffs, N.J.: Prentice Hall, Inc., 1985). Rochkind describes the UNIX system calls, where `errno` and its error codes originated.

Exercises

Exercise 3.1 List the error codes defined for the C translator you use. Can you describe in one sentence what each error code indicates?

Exercise 3.2 For the error codes defined for the C translator you use, contrive tests that cause each of the errors to occur.

Exercise 3.3 Under what circumstances might you care exactly which error code was last reported?

Exercise 3.4 Alter the test program `terrrno.c` to call `perror` for all valid error codes. The value of the macro `_NERR`, defined in `<errno.h>`, is one greater than the largest valid error code.

Exercise 3.5 Assume you have the function `int _Getfcc(void)` that returns 0, `EDOM`, or `ERANGE` to reflect the last floating-point error (if any) since the previous call to the function. Write a version of `<errno.h>` that uses this function to collect floating-point errors only when the program uses the value stored in `errno`.

Exercise 3.6 [**Harder**] Write a version of `<errno.h>` that queues values stored in `errno` and returns them in order when the program uses the value stored in `errno`. When is it safe to remove a value from the queue?

Exercise 3.7 [**Vey hard**] Eliminate the need for `errno` in the Standard C library. Consider every function that can store values in `errno`. Ensure that each has a way to specify several different error return values.

Chapter 4: `<float.h>`

Background

Floating-point arithmetic is complicated stuff. Many small processors don't even support it with hardware instructions. Others require a separate coprocessor to handle such arithmetic. Only the most complex computers include floating-point support in the standard instruction set.

There's a pragmatic reason why chip designers often omit floating-point arithmetic. It takes about the same amount of microcode to implement floating-point compare, add, subtract, multiply, and divide as it does all the rest of the instructions combined. You can essentially halve the complexity of a microprocessor by leaving out floating-point support.

Many applications don't need floating-point arithmetic at all. Others can tolerate reasonably poor performance, and a few kilobytes of extra code, by doing the arithmetic in software. The few that need high-performance arithmetic often make other expensive demands on the hardware, so the extra cost of a coprocessor is an acceptable perturbation.

history C spent its early years on a PDP-11/45 computer. That strongly colored the treatment of floating-point arithmetic in C. For instance, the types *float* (for 32-bit format) and *double* (for 64-bit format) have been in the language from the earliest days. Those were the two formats supported by the PDP-11. That is a bit unusual for a system-implementation language, and a reasonably small one at that.

The PDP-11/45 FPP could be placed in one of two modes. It did all arithmetic either with 32-bit operands or with 64-bit operands. You had to execute an instruction to switch modes. On the other hand, you could load and convert an operand of the wrong size just as easily as you could load one of the expected size. That strongly encouraged leaving the FPP in one mode. It is no surprise that C for many years promised to produce a *double* result for any operator involving floating-point operands, even one with two *float* operands. Not even FORTRAN was so generous.

As C migrated to other computer architectures, this heritage sometimes became a nuisance. Compiler writers who felt obliged to supply the full language had to write floating-point software for some pretty tiny machines. It wasn't easy. Machines that support floating point as standard hardware present a different set of problems. Chances are, the formats are slightly different. That makes writing portable code much more challenging. You need to write math functions and conversion algorithms to retain varying ranges of values and varying amounts of precision.

Machines that provide floating point as an option combine the worst of both worlds, at least to compiler implementors. The implementors must provide software support for those machines that lack the option. They must make use of the machine instructions when the option is present. And they must deal with confused customers who inadvertently link two flavors of code, or the wrong version of the library. Rarely can the hardware and software versions of floating-point support agree on where to hold intermediate results.

From a linguistic standpoint, however, most of these issues are irrelevant. The main problem the drafters of the C Standard had to deal with was excess variety. It is a longstanding tradition in C to take what the machine gives you. A right-shift operator does whatever the underlying hardware does most rapidly. So, too, does a floating-point add operator. Neither result may please a mathematician.

overflow With floating-point arithmetic, you have the obvious issues of overflow
and and underflow. A result may be too large to represent on one machine, but
underflow not on another. The resulting overflow may cause a trap, may generate a special code value, or may produce garbage that is easily mistaken for a valid result. A result may be too small to represent on one machine but not on another. The resulting underflow may cause a trap or may be quietly replaced with an exact zero. Such a *zero fixup* is often a good idea, but not always. Novices tend to write code that is susceptible to overflow and underflow. The broad range of values supported by floating point lures the innocent into a careless disregard. Your first lesson is to estimate magnitudes and avoid silly swings in value.

significance You also have the more subtle issue of significance loss. Floating point
loss arithmetic lets you represent a tremendously broad range of values, but at a cost. A value can be represented only to a fixed precision. Multiply two values that are exact and you can keep only half the significance you might like. Subtract two values that are very close together and you can lose most or all of the significance you were carrying around.

Workaday programmers most often run afoul of unexpected significance loss. That formula that looks so elegant in a textbook is an ill-behaved pig when reduced to code. It is hard to see the danger in those alternating signs in adjacent terms of a series — until you get burned, that is, and learn to do the subtractions on paper instead of at run time.

Overflow, underflow, and significance loss are intrinsic to floating-point arithmetic. They are hard enough to deal with on a given computer architecture. Writing code that can move across computer architectures is harder. Writing a standard that tells you how to write portable code is harder still. But another problem makes the matter even worse.

variations   Two machines can use the same representation for floating-point values. Yet you can add the same two values on each machine and get different answers! The result can depend, reasonably enough, on the way the two machines round results that cannot be represented exactly. You can make a case for truncating toward zero, rounding to the nearest representable value, or doing a few other similar but subtly different operations.

Or you can just plain get the wrong answer. In some circles, getting a quick answer is considered much more virtuous than getting one that is as accurate as it could be. Seymour Cray has built several successful computer companies catering to this constituency. These machines saw off precision somewhere in the neighborhood of the least-significant bit that is retained. Sometimes that curdles a bit or two having even more significance. There have even been some computers (not designed by Cray) that scrub the four least significant bits when you multiply by one!

If the C Standard had tried to outlaw this behavior, it would never have been approved. Too many machines still use quick-and-dirty floating-point arithmetic. Too many people still use these machines. To deny them the cachet of supporting conforming C compilers would be commercially unacceptable.

describing   As a result, the C Standard is mostly descriptive in the area of floating-
floating point arithmetic. It endeavors to define enough terms to talk about the
point   parameters of floating point. But it says little that is prescriptive about getting the right answer.

Committee X3J11 added the header `<float.h>` as a companion to the existing header `<limits.h>`. We put into `<float.h>` essentially every parameter that we thought might be of use to a serious numerical programmer. From these macros, you can learn enough about the properties of the execution environment, presumably, to code your numerical algorithms wisely. (Notwithstanding my earlier slurs, the major push to help this class of programmers came from Cray Research.)

What the C Standard Says

The Library section says very little about `<float.h>`.

7.1.5 Limits `<float.h>` and `<limits.h>`

The headers `<float.h>` and `<limits.h>` define several macros that expand to various limits and parameters.

The macros, their meanings, and the constraints (or restrictions) on their values are listed in 5.2.4.2.

The detailed specification of `<float.h>` is in the Environment section

5.2.4.2.2 Characteristics of floating types `<float.h>`

`<float.h>`   The characteristics of floating types are defined in terms of a model that describes a representation of floating-point numbers and values that provide information about an implementation's floating-point arithmetic.[10] The following parameters are used to define the model for each floating-point type

s sign (± 1)

b base or radix of exponent representation (an integer > 1)

e exponent (an integer between a minimum e_{min} and a maximum e_{max})

p precision (the number of base-b digits in the significand)

f_k nonnegative integers less than b (the significand digits)

A normalized floating-point number x ($f_1 > 0$ if $x \neq 0$) is defined by the following model

$$x = s \times b^e \times \sum_{k=1}^{p} f_k \times b^{-k}, \quad e_{min} \leq e \leq e_{max}$$

Of the values in the **<float.h>** header, **FLT_RADIX** shall be a constant expression suitable for use in **#if** preprocessing directives; all other values need not be constant expressions. All except **FLT_RADIX** and **FLT_ROUNDS** have separate names for all three floating-point types. The floating-point model representation is provided for all values except **FLT_ROUNDS**.

FLT_ROUNDS

The rounding mode for floating-point addition is characterized by the value of **FLT_ROUNDS**

-1   indeterminable

0   toward zero

1   to nearest

2   toward positive infinity

3   toward negative infinity

All other values for **FLT_ROUNDS** characterize implementation-defined rounding behavior.

The values given in the following list shall be replaced by implementation-defined expressions that shall be equal or greater in magnitude (absolute value) to those shown, with the same sign

FLT_RADIX

- radix of exponent representation, b
  ```
  FLT_RADIX                              2
  ```

FLT_MANT_DIG
DBL_MANT_DIG
LDBL_MANT_DIG

- number of base-**FLT_RADIX** digits in the floating-point significand, p
  ```
  FLT_MANT_DIG
  DBL_MANT_DIG
  LDBL_MANT_DIG
  ```

FLT_DIG
DBL_DIG
LDBL_DIG

- number of decimal digits, q, such that any floating-point number with q decimal digits can be rounded into a floating-point number with p radix b digits and back again without change to the q decimal digits,
  $$\lfloor (p-1) \times \log_{10} b \rfloor + \begin{cases} 1 & \text{if } b \text{ is a power of 10} \\ 0 & \text{otherwise} \end{cases}$$
  ```
  FLT_DIG                                6
  DBL_DIG                               10
  LDBL_DIG                              10
  ```

FLT_MIN_DIG
DBL_MIN_DIG
LDBL_MIN_DIG

- minimum negative integer such that **FLT_RADIX** raised to that power minus 1 is a normalized floating-point number, e_{min}
  ```
  FLT_MIN_EXP
  DBL_MIN_EXP
  LDBL_MIN_EXP
  ```

FLT_MIN_10_EXP
DBL_MIN_10_EXP
LDBL_MIN_10_EXP

- minimum negative integer such that 10 raised to that power is in the range of normalized floating-point numbers, $\lceil \log_{10} b^{e_{min}-1} \rceil$
  ```
  FLT_MIN_10_EXP                       -37
  DBL_MIN_10_EXP                       -37
  LDBL_MIN_10_EXP                      -37
  ```

FLT_MAX_EXP
DBL_MAX_EXP
LDBL_MAX_EXP

- maximum integer such that **FLT_RADIX** raised to that power minus 1 is a representable finite floating-point number, e_{max}
  ```
  FLT_MAX_EXP
  DBL_MAX_EXP
  LDBL_MAX_EXP
  ```

FLT_MAX_10_EXP
DBL_MAX_10_EXP
LDBL_MAX_10_EXP

- maximum integer such that 10 raised to that power is in the range of representable finite floating-point numbers, $\lfloor \log_{10}((1 - b^{-p}) \times b^{e_{max}}) \rfloor$

FLT_MAX_10_EXP	+37
DBL_MAX_10_EXP	+37
LDBL_MAX_10_EXP	+37

The values given in the following list shall be replaced by implementation-defined expressions with values that shall be equal to or greater than those shown

FLT_MAX
DBL_MAX
LDBL_MAX

- maximum representable finite floating-point number, $(1 - b^{-p}) \times b^{e_{max}}$

FLT_MAX	1E+37
DBL_MAX	1E+37
LDBL_MAX	1E+37

The values given in the following list shall be replaced by implementation-defined expressions with values that shall be equal to or less than those shown

FLT_EPSILON
DBL_EPSILON
LDBL_EPSILON

- the difference between 1 and the least value greater than 1 that is representable in the given floating-point type, b^{1-p}

FLT_EPSILON	1E-5
DBL_EPSILON	1E-9
LDBL_EPSILON	1E-9

FLT_MIN
DBL_MIN
LDBL_MIN

- minimum normalized positive floating-point number, $b^{e_{min}-1}$

FLT_MIN	1E-37
DBL_MIN	1E-37
LDBL_MIN	1E-37

Examples

The following describes an artificial floating-point representation that meets the minimum requirements of this International Standard, and the appropriate values in a `<float.h>` header for type **float**

$$x = s \times 16^e \times \sum_{k=1}^{6} f_k \times 16^{-k}, \quad -31 \le e \le +32$$

FLT_RADIX	16
FLT_MANT_DIG	6
FLT_EPSILON	9.53674316E-07F
FLT_DIG	6
FLT_MIN_EXP	-31
FLT_MIN	2.93873588E-39F
FLT_MIN_10_EXP	-38
FLT_MAX_EXP	+32
FLT_MAX	3.40282347E+38F
FLT_MAX_10_EXP	+38

The following describes floating-point representations that also meet the requirements for single-precision and double-precision normalized numbers in ANSI/IEEE 754-1985,[11] and the appropriate values in a `<float.h>` header for types *float* and *double*

$$x_f = s \times 2^e \times \sum_{k=1}^{24} f_k \times 2^{-k}, \quad -125 \le e \le +128$$

$$x_d = s \times 2^e \times \sum_{k=1}^{53} f_k \times 2^{-k}, \quad -1021 \le e \le +1024$$

FLT_RADIX	2
FLT_MANT_DIG	24
FLT_EPSILON	1.19209290E-07F
FLT_DIG	6
FLT_MIN_EXP	-125
FLT_MIN	1.17549435E-38F
FLT_MIN_10_EXP	-37
FLT_MAX_EXP	+128
FLT_MAX	3.40282347E+38F
FLT_MAX_10_EXP	+38
DBL_MANT_DIG	53

```
DBL_EPSILON 2.2204460492503131E-16
DBL_DIG                              15
DBL_MIN_EXP                       -1021
DBL_MIN    2.2250738585072014E-308
DBL_MIN_10_EXP                     -307
DBL_MAX_EXP                       +1024
DBL_MAX    1.7976931348623157E+308
DBL_MAX_10_EXP                     +308
```

Forward references: conditional inclusion (6.8.1).

Footnotes

10. The floating-point model is intended to clarify the description of each floating-point characteristic and does not require the floating-point arithmetic of the implementation to be identical.

11. The floating-point model in that standard sums powers of *b* from zero, so the values of the exponent limits are one less than shown here.

Using `<float.h>`

Only the most sophisticated of numerical programs care about most of the macros defined in `<float.h>` or can adapt to changes among floating-point representations. I have found good use for these parameters on just a few occasions. You will find only a few places in this library that make good use of them. That's a bit misleading, however. In some places, I use the underlying macros from which the `<float.h>` macros derive. (See the discussion of how to implement `<float.h>` starting on page 64.) In other places, the code contains implicit assumptions about the range or maximum size of certain floating-point parameters. That limits its portability.

You *can* use these macros to detect problems before they bite. Remember that the three pitfalls of floating-point arithmetic are overflow, underflow, and significance loss. Here are ways you can use the macros defined in `<float.h>` to perform *double* arithmetic more safely. The same discussion applies, naturally, to *float* and *long double* as well.

overflow   To avoid overflow, make sure that no value ever exceeds `DBL_MAX` in magnitude. Of course, it does you no good to test the final result, as in:

```
if (DBL_MAX < fabs(y))   /* SILLY TEST */
    . . . . .
```

(The functions in this and the following examples are the common math functions declared in `<math.h>`.)

By the time you make the test, it's too late. If the value you intended to store in `y` is too large to represent, `y` may contain a special code, the value of `DBL_MAX`, or garbage — depending on the kind of floating-point arithmetic the implementation provides. Or execution may terminate during the calculation of the value. In no case will the above test likely yield a useful result. A more sensible test might be:

```
if (x < log(DBL_MAX))
    y = exp(x);
else
    . . . . .          /* HANDLE OVERFLOW */
```

You can avoid computing `log(DBL_MAX)` by using one of the related macros, as in:

```
if (x <= FLT_MAX_10_EXP)
    y = pow(10, x);
else
    .....            /* HANDLE OVERFLOW */
```

This test is more stringent than necessary if `FLT_RADIX` is not equal to 10. (Modern computers usually have `FLT_RADIX` equal to 2 or, in rare cases, 16.) If you are in the business of writing functions that accept all possible inputs, that can make a difference. Otherwise, this test is close enough.

The function `ldexp` makes it easy to scale a floating-point number by a power of 2. In the common case where `FLT_RADIX` equals 2, that can be an efficient operation. For an integer exponent n, you can make the simple test:

```
if (n < FLT_MAX_EXP)
    y = ldexp(1.0, n);
else
    .....            /* HANDLE OVERFLOW */
```

You are most likely to use this last test when writing additional functions for a math library.

underflow   To avoid underflow, make sure that no value ever goes below `DBL_MIN` in magnitude. The result is usually not quite so disastrous as overflow, but it can still cause trouble. IEEE 754 floating-point arithmetic provides *gradual underflow*. That mitigates some of the worst effects of underflow. Nearly all floating-point implementations substitute the value zero for a value too small to represent. You get in trouble only if you divide by a value that has suffered underflow. Unexpectedly, your program encounters a zero divide, with all the attendant confusion. You can make the test:

```
if (fabs(y) < DBL_MIN)
    .....       /* UNDERFLOW HAS OCCURRED */
```

That is not nearly as silly as the corresponding comparison against `DBL_MAX`. Still, you test only after any damage has been done. You can also make the corresponding tests:

```
if (log(DBL_MIN) <= x)
    y = exp(x);
else
    .....              /* HANDLE UNDERFLOW */
```

```
if (FLT_MIN10_EXP <= x)
    y = pow(10, x);
else
    .....              /* HANDLE UNDERFLOW */
```

```
if (FLT_MIN_EXP < n)
    y = ldexp(1.0, n);
else
    .....              /* HANDLE UNDERFLOW */
```

significance Significance loss occurs when you subtract two values that are nearly
loss equal. Nothing can save you from such a fate except careful analysis of the
problem before you write code. You can, however, protect against a subtler
form of significance loss — adding a small magnitude to a large one. A
floating-point representation can maintain only a finite precision. Important contributions from the smaller number can get lost in the addition.

You can get in trouble, for example, when performing a quadrature —
a sum of discrete values that approximates a continuous integration. One
form of quadrature is computing the area under a curve by summing a
sequence of rectangles that just fit under the curve. Clearly, the narrower
the rectangles, the closer the sequence approximates the area of the curve.
Unfortunately, that is true only in theory. Add a sufficiently small rectan-
gular area to a running sum and part or all of the contribution gets lost. You
can test, for example, whether adding **x** to **y** captures at least three decimal
digits of significance from **y** (assuming both are positive) by writing:

```
if (x < y * DBL_EPSILON * 1.0E+03)
    .....    /* HANDLE SIGNIFICANCE LOSS */
```

other The two macros you are least likely to use are **FLT_RADIX** and **FLT_ROUNDS**.
macros Don't be surprised, in fact, if you never have occasion to use *any* of the
macros defined in **<float.h>**, despite what I just outlined here.

You should have some awareness of the peculiarities and pitfalls of
floating-point arithmetic. You should know the safe ranges and precisions
for floating-point values in portable C code and in code you write for your
workaday machines. You might use some of the macros defined in
<float.h> to build safety checks into your code. But don't think that this
header contains some key ingredient for writing highly portable code. It
doesn't.

Implementing **<float.h>**

In principle, this header consists of nothing but a bunch of macro
definitions. For a given implementation, you merely determine the values
of the parameters and plug them in. You can even use a public-domain
program called **enquire** to generate **<float.h>** automatically.

A common implementation these days is based on the IEEE 754 Standard
for floating-point arithmetic. You will find IEEE 754 floating point arithmetic in the Intel 80X87 and the Motorola MC680X0 coprocessors, to name just
two very popular lines. It is a complex standard, but only its grosser
properties affect **<float.h>**. Type *long double* can have an 80-bit representation in the IEEE 754 Standard, but it often has the same representation
as *double*. For this common case, you might consider copying the values out
of the example in the C Standard. (See page 61.)

You may find a few problems, however. Not all translators are equally
good at converting floating-point constants. Some may curdle the least
significant bit or two. That could cause overflow or underflow in the case

of some extreme values such as `DBL_MAX` and `DBL_MIN`. Or it could ruin the critical behavior of other values such as `DBL_EPSILON`. (There is also an error in the example from the C Standard — `FLT_DIG` should have the value 7.)

using unions At the very least, you should check the bit patterns produced by the floating-point values. You can do that by stuffing the value into a union one way, then extracting it another way, as in:

```
union {
    double _D;
    unsigned short _Us[4];
    } dmax = DBL_MAX;
```

Here, I assume that *unsigned short* occupies 16 bits and *double* is the IEEE 754 64-bit representation. Some computers store the most-significant word at `dmax._Us[0]`, others at `dmax._Us[3]`. You have to check what your implementation does. Whatever the case, the most significant word should have the value 0x7FEF, and all the other words should equal 0xFFFF.

A safer approach is to do it the other way around. Initialize the union as a sequence of bit patterns, then define the macro to access the union through its floating-point member. Since you can initialize only the first member of a union, you must reverse the member declarations from the example above. With this approach, you place the following in `<float.h>`:

```
typedef union {
    unsigned short _Us[4];
    double _D;
    } _Dtype;
extern _Dtype _Dmax, _Dmin, _Deps;
#define DBL_MAX        _Dmax._D;
```

In a library source file you provide a definition for `_Dmax` and friends. For the 80X86 family, which stores the least-significant word first, you write:

```
#include <float.h>
_Dtype _Dmax = {{0xffff, 0xffff, 0xffff, 0x7fef}};
```

The code is now less readable, but it is more robust. Figure 4.1 shows the resulting version of `float.h`. Each macro refers to a field from one of three data objects of type `_Dvals` — `_Dbl`, `_Flt`, and `_Ldbl`. A separate file called `xfloat.c` defines the data objects.

In writing the corresponding data objects, I encountered another annoying problem. You need different versions of these initializers for different floating-point formats. Even if you stay within the IEEE 754 Standard you must specify the order of bytes stored in a data object and whether *long double* occupies 64 or 80 bits. Other formats with `FLT_RADIX` equal to 2 differ only in niggling ways.

parameters It was time to parametrize the code once again. On page 53, I introduced the internal header `<yvals.h>`. That's where I put any parameters that vary among translators. Error codes are one set of such parameters. The properties of floating-point representations constitue another. You can include `<yvals.h>` in any library source file that must change in small ways across implementations of C. `<yvals.h>` defines the following parameters:

Figure 4.1:
float.h

```c
/* float.h standard header -- IEEE 754 version */
#ifndef _FLOAT
#define _FLOAT
#ifndef _YVALS
#include <yvals.h>
#endif
        /* type definitions */
typedef struct {
    int _Ddig, _Dmdig, _Dmax10e, _Dmaxe, _Dmin10e, _Dmine;
    union {
        unsigned short _Us[5];
        float _F;
        double _D;
        long double _Ld;
        } _Deps, _Dmax, _Dmin;
    } _Dvals;
        /* declarations */
extern _Dvals _Dbl, _Flt, _Ldbl;
        /* double properties */
#define DBL_DIG         _Dbl._Ddig
#define DBL_EPSILON     _Dbl._Deps._D
#define DBL_MANT_DIG    _Dbl._Dmdig
#define DBL_MAX         _Dbl._Dmax._D
#define DBL_MAX_10_EXP  _Dbl._Dmax10e
#define DBL_MAX_EXP     _Dbl._Dmaxe
#define DBL_MIN         _Dbl._Dmin._D
#define DBL_MIN_10_EXP  _Dbl._Dmin10e
#define DBL_MIN_EXP     _Dbl._Dmine
        /* float properties */
#define FLT_DIG         _Flt._Ddig
#define FLT_EPSILON     _Flt._Deps._F
#define FLT_MANT_DIG    _Flt._Dmdig
#define FLT_MAX         _Flt._Dmax._F
#define FLT_MAX_10_EXP  _Flt._Dmax10e
#define FLT_MAX_EXP     _Flt._Dmaxe
#define FLT_MIN         _Flt._Dmin._F
#define FLT_MIN_10_EXP  _Flt._Dmin10e
#define FLT_MIN_EXP     _Flt._Dmine
        /* common properties */
#define FLT_RADIX       2
#define FLT_ROUNDS      _FRND
        /* long double properties */
#define LDBL_DIG        _Ldbl._Ddig
#define LDBL_EPSILON    _Ldbl._Deps._Ld
#define LDBL_MANT_DIG   _Ldbl._Dmdig
#define LDBL_MAX        _Ldbl._Dmax._Ld
#define LDBL_MAX_10_EXP _Ldbl._Dmax10e
#define LDBL_MAX_EXP    _Ldbl._Dmaxe
#define LDBL_MIN        _Ldbl._Dmin._Ld
#define LDBL_MIN_10_EXP _Ldbl._Dmin10e
#define LDBL_MIN_EXP    _Ldbl._Dmine
#endif
```

_D0 ■ _D0 is the subscript of the most significant element of the array of four *unsigned short*s that represent the *double* value. Its value is either 0 or 3. (Macros for the other three subscripts, _D1, _D2, and _D3, are defined in terms of _D0 as needed elsewhere in the library.)

_DOFF ■ _DOFF is the number of fraction bits FFF... in the most-significant
_FOFF   element. The most-significant bit of that element is the sign s of the
_LOFF   floating-point value, with value 0 or 1. The remaining bits represent the characteristic CCC..., as an unsigned bit field. See Figure 4.2 for the format of the *double* representation. _FOFF is the corresponding value for type *float*. _LOFF is the corresponding value for type *long double*.

_DBIAS ■ _DBIAS is the value subtracted from the characteristic of a *double* to
_FBIAS   determine its exponent. _FBIAS is the corresponding value for type *float*.
_LBIAS   _LBIAS is the corresponding value for type *long double*. The fraction value *F* is 1.FFF... (for *float* and *double*) or 0.FFF... (for *long double*), where FFF... are the fraction bits. The value of a *double* number is then:

$$-1^S * (1.FFF...) * 2^{(CCC...)-\_DBIAS}$$

_DLONG ■ _DLONG is nonzero if *long double* has the IEEE 754 80-bit format.

_FRND ■ _FRND is the value of the macro FLT_ROUNDS

Figure 4.2:
Double
Format

SCCCCCCCCCCCFFFF	FFFF....FFFF	FFFF....FFFF	FFFF....FFFF
x._Us[_D0]	x._Us[_D1]	x._Us[_D2]	x._Us[_D3]

xfloat.c   Figure 4.3 shows the code for xfloat.c. It is written in terms of these parameters. The code also contains a number of implicit assumptions:

■ FLT_RADIX has the value 2.

■ Type *float* has a 32-bit representation and exactly overlaps an array of 2 *unsigned short*s, while type *double* has a 64-bit representation and exactly overlaps an array of 4 *unsigned short*s.

■ Type *long double* has the IEEE 754 80-bit representation only if _DLONG is nonzero. Otherwise, it has the same representation as *double*.

■ The characteristic is never larger than 14 bits.

■ The fraction value in a *float* or *double* includes a *hidden bit*. This is the 1. prepended to the FFF... above.

As an example, here are the pertinent values for the Intel 80X87 coprocessors, assuming that *double* and *long double* have different representations:

```
#define _D0      3
#define _DBIAS   0x3fe
#define _DLONG   1 #define _DOFF  4
#define _FBIAS   0x7e
#define _FOFF    7
#define _FRND    1
#define _LBIAS   0x3ffe
#define _LOFF    15
```

```
/* values used by <float.h> macros -- IEEE 754 version */
#include <float.h>

        /* macros */
#define DFRAC   (49+_DOFF)
#define DMAXE   ((1U<<(15-_DOFF))-1)
#define FFRAC   (17+_FOFF)
#define FMAXE   ((1U<<(15-_FOFF))-1)
#define LFRAC   (49+_LOFF)
#define LMAXE   0x7fff
#define LOG2    0.30103
#if _D0 != 0                                     /* low to high words */
#define DINIT(w0, wx)   wx, wx, wx, w0
#define FINIT(w0, wx)   wx, w0
#define LINIT(w0, w1, wx)   wx, wx, wx, w1, w0
#else                                            /* high to low words */
#define DINIT(w0, wx)   w0, wx, wx, wx
#define FINIT(w0, wx)   w0, wx
#define LINIT(w0, w1, wx)   w0, w1, wx, wx, wx
#endif
        /* static data */
_Dvals _Dbl = {
    (int)(DFRAC*LOG2),                                  /* DBL_DIG */
    (int)DFRAC,                                     /* DBL_MANT_DIG */
    (int)((DMAXE-_DBIAS-1)*LOG2),               /* DBL_MAX_10_EXP */
    (int)(DMAXE-_DBIAS-1),                          /* DBL_MAX_EXP */
    (int)(-_DBIAS*LOG2),                        /* DBL_MIN_10_EXP */
    (int)(1-_DBIAS),                               /* DBL_MIN_EXP */
    {{DINIT(_DBIAS-DFRAC+2<<_DOFF, 0)}},          /* DBL_EPSILON */
    {{DINIT((DMAXE<<_DOFF)-1, ~0)}},                  /* DBL_MAX */
    {{DINIT(1<<_DOFF, 0)}},                           /* DBL_MIN */
    };
_Dvals _Flt = {
    (int)(FFRAC*LOG2),                                  /* FLT_DIG */
    (int)FFRAC,                                     /* FLT_MANT_DIG */
    (int)((FMAXE-_FBIAS-1)*LOG2),               /* FLT_MAX_10_EXP */
    (int)(FMAXE-_FBIAS-1),                          /* FLT_MAX_EXP */
    (int)(-_FBIAS*LOG2),                        /* FLT_MIN_10_EXP */
    (int)(1-_FBIAS),                               /* FLT_MIN_EXP */
    {{FINIT(_FBIAS-FFRAC+2<<_FOFF, 0)}},          /* FLT_EPSILON */
    {{FINIT((FMAXE<<_FOFF)-1, ~0)}},                  /* FLT_MAX */
    {{FINIT(1<<_FOFF, 0)}},                           /* FLT_MIN */
    };
#if _DLONG
_Dvals _Ldbl = {
    (int)(LFRAC*LOG2),                                 /* LDBL_DIG */
    (int)LFRAC,                                    /* LDBL_MANT_DIG */
    (int)((LMAXE-_LBIAS-1)*LOG2),              /* LDBL_MAX_10_EXP */
    (int)(LMAXE-_LBIAS-1),                         /* LDBL_MAX_EXP */
    (int)(-_LBIAS*LOG2),                       /* LDBL_MIN_10_EXP */
    (int)(1-_LBIAS),                              /* LDBL_MIN_EXP */
    {{LINIT(_LBIAS-LFRAC+2, 0x8000, 0)}},        /* LDBL_EPSILON */
    {{LINIT(LMAXE-1, ~0, ~0)}},                      /* LDBL_MAX */
    {{LINIT(1, 0x8000, 0)}},                         /* LDBL_MIN */
    };
```

Continuing
xfloat.c
Part 2

```
#else
_Dvals _Ldbl = {
    (int)(DFRAC*LOG2),                          /* LDBL_DIG */
    (int)DFRAC,                                 /* LDBL_MANT_DIG */
    (int)((DMAXE-_DBIAS-1)*LOG2),               /* LDBL_MAX_10_EXP */
    (int)(DMAXE-_DBIAS-1),                       /* LDBL_MAX_EXP */
    (int)(-_DBIAS*LOG2),                        /* LDBL_MIN_10_EXP */
    (int)(1-_DBIAS),                            /* LDBL_MIN_EXP */
    {{DINIT(_DBIAS-DFRAC+2<<_DOFF, 0)}},        /* LDBL_EPSILON */
    {{DINIT((DMAXE<<_DOFF)-1, ~0)}},            /* LDBL_MAX */
    {{DINIT(1<<_DOFF, 0)}},                     /* LDBL_MIN */
    };
#endif                                                                      □
```

Testing `<float.h>`

Figure 4.4 shows the test program `tfloat.c`. It begins by printing the values of the macros defined in `<float.h>` in a form that people can better understand. It then checks that the macros meet the minimum requirements spelled out in the C Standard.

Here is the output for the Intel 80X87 coprocessor, on an implementation that supports all three sizes of IEEE 754 operands:

```
FLT_RADIX = 2

DBL_DIG =               15    DBL_MANT_DIG =        53
DBL_MAX_10_EXP =       308    DBL_MAX_EXP =       1024
DBL_MIN_10_EXP =      -307    DBL_MIN_EXP =      -1021
        DBL_EPSILON =  2.220446e-16
        DBL_MAX =      1.797693e+308
        DBL_MIN =      2.225074e-308

FLT_DIG =                7    FLT_MANT_DIG =        24
FLT_MAX_10_EXP =        38    FLT_MAX_EXP =        128
FLT_MIN_10_EXP =       -37    FLT_MIN_EXP =       -125
        FLT_EPSILON =  1.192093e-07
        FLT_MAX =      3.402823e+38
        FLT_MIN =      1.175494e-38

LDBL_DIG =              19    LDBL_MANT_DIG =       64
LDBL_MAX_10_EXP =     4932    LDBL_MAX_EXP =      16384
LDBL_MIN_10_EXP =    -4931    LDBL_MIN_EXP =     -16381
        LDBL_EPSILON = 1.084202e-19
        LDBL_MAX =     1.189731e+4932
        LDBL_MIN =     3.362103e-4932
SUCCESS testing <float.h>
```

I caught any number of errors in the process of developing `<float.h>` and `xfloat.c`. Most of those errors were unearthed by running `tfloat.c`. The tests are deceptively simple.

```
/* test float macros */
#include <assert.h>
#include <float.h>
#include <math.h>
#include <stdio.h>

int main()
    {                       /* test basic properties of float.h macros */
    double radlog;
    int digs;
    static int radix = FLT_RADIX;

    printf("FLT_RADIX = %i\n\n", FLT_RADIX);
    printf("DBL_DIG =        %5i   DBL_MANT_DIG = %6i\n",
        DBL_DIG, DBL_MANT_DIG);
    printf("DBL_MAX_10_EXP = %5i   DBL_MAX_EXP =  %6i\n",
        DBL_MAX_10_EXP, DBL_MAX_EXP);
    printf("DBL_MIN_10_EXP = %5i   DBL_MIN_EXP =  %6i\n",
        DBL_MIN_10_EXP, DBL_MIN_EXP);
    printf("     DBL_EPSILON = %le\n", DBL_EPSILON);
    printf("        DBL_MAX =     %le\n", DBL_MAX);
    printf("        DBL_MIN =     %le\n\n", DBL_MIN);
    printf("FLT_DIG =        %5i   FLT_MANT_DIG = %6i\n",
        FLT_DIG, FLT_MANT_DIG);
    printf("FLT_MAX_10_EXP = %5i   FLT_MAX_EXP =  %6i\n",
        FLT_MAX_10_EXP, FLT_MAX_EXP);
    printf("FLT_MIN_10_EXP = %5i   FLT_MIN_EXP =  %6i\n",
        FLT_MIN_10_EXP, FLT_MIN_EXP);
    printf("     FLT_EPSILON = %e\n", FLT_EPSILON);
    printf("        FLT_MAX =     %e\n", FLT_MAX);
    printf("        FLT_MIN =     %e\n\n", FLT_MIN);
    printf("LDBL_DIG =        %5i  LDBL_MANT_DIG = %6i\n",
        LDBL_DIG, LDBL_MANT_DIG);
    printf("LDBL_MAX_10_EXP = %5i  LDBL_MAX_EXP =  %6i\n",
        LDBL_MAX_10_EXP, LDBL_MAX_EXP);
    printf("LDBL_MIN_10_EXP = %5i  LDBL_MIN_EXP =  %6i\n",
        LDBL_MIN_10_EXP, LDBL_MIN_EXP);
    printf("     LDBL_EPSILON = %Le\n", LDBL_EPSILON);
    printf("        LDBL_MAX =     %Le\n", LDBL_MAX);
    printf("        LDBL_MIN =     %Le\n", LDBL_MIN);
    radlog = log10(radix);
        /* test double properties */
    assert(10 <= DBL_DIG && FLT_DIG <= DBL_DIG);
    assert(DBL_EPSILON <= 1e-9);
    digs = DBL_MANT_DIG * radlog;
    assert(digs <= DBL_DIG && DBL_DIG <= digs + 1);
    assert(1e37 <= DBL_MAX);
    assert(37 <= DBL_MAX_10_EXP);
#if FLT_RADIX == 2
    assert(ldexp(1.0, DBL_MAX_EXP - 1) < DBL_MAX);
    assert(ldexp(1.0, DBL_MIN_EXP - 1) == DBL_MIN);
#endif
    assert(DBL_MIN <= 1e-37);
    assert(DBL_MIN_10_EXP <= -37);
```

```
              /* test float properties */
        assert(6 <= FLT_DIG);
        assert(FLT_EPSILON <= 1e-5);
        digs = FLT_MANT_DIG * radlog;
        assert(digs <= FLT_DIG && FLT_DIG <= digs + 1);
        assert(1e37 <= FLT_MAX);
        assert(37 <= FLT_MAX_10_EXP);
#if FLT_RADIX == 2
        assert(ldexp(1.0, FLT_MAX_EXP - 1) < FLT_MAX);
        assert(ldexp(1.0, FLT_MIN_EXP - 1) == FLT_MIN);
#endif
        assert(FLT_MIN <= 1e-37);
        assert(FLT_MIN_10_EXP <= -37);
              /* test unversal properties */
#if FLT_RADIX < 2
#error bad FLT_RADIX
#endif
        assert(-1 <= FLT_ROUNDS && FLT_ROUNDS <= 3);
              /* test long double properties */
        assert(10 <= LDBL_DIG && DBL_DIG <= LDBL_DIG);
        assert(LDBL_EPSILON <= 1e-9);
        digs = LDBL_MANT_DIG * radlog;
        assert(digs <= LDBL_DIG && LDBL_DIG <= digs + 1);
        assert(1e37 <= LDBL_MAX);
        assert(37 <= LDBL_MAX_10_EXP);
#if FLT_RADIX == 2
        assert(DBL_MAX_EXP < LDBL_MAX_EXP
            || ldexp(1.0, LDBL_MAX_EXP - 1) < LDBL_MAX);
        assert(LDBL_MIN_EXP < DBL_MIN_EXP
            || ldexp(1.0, LDBL_MIN_EXP - 1) == LDBL_MIN);
#endif
        assert(LDBL_MIN <= 1e-37);
        assert(LDBL_MIN_10_EXP <= -37);
        puts("SUCCESS testing <float.h>");
        return (0);
        }
```

References

ANSI/IEEE Standard 754-1985 (Piscataway, N.J.: Institute of Electrical and Electronics Engineers, Inc., 1985). This is the floating-point standard widely used in modern microprocessors.

Jack J. Dongarra and Eric Grosse, "Distribution of Mathematical Software via Electronic Mail," *Communications of the ACM*, 30 (1987), pp. 403-407. This article describes how you can obtain various test programs via electronic mail. Two programs you can obtain via electronic mail beat particularly hard on floating-point arithmetic:

- The program enquire tests the properties of the floating-point arithmetic that accompanies a C implementation. It prints its findings in the form of a usable float.h file. Written by Steven Pemberton of CWI, Amsterdam, enquire is available through the Internet address steve@cwi.nl.

- The program **paranoia** heavily stresses floating-point arithmetic. It was originally written by W.M. Kahan of the University of California at Berkeley. A C version is now available. Mail to the Internet address **netlib@research.att.com** the request:

  ```
  send paranoia.c from paranoia
  ```

  Pat Sterbenz, *Floating-Point Computation* (Englewood Cliffs, N.J.: Prentice-Hall, Inc., 1973). This book is old and currently out of print. Nevertheless, it is hard to find a better discussion of the basic issues.

Exercises

Exercise 4.1 Determine the parameters that characterize floating-point arithmetic for the C translator you use. Do they conform to the IEEE 754 Standard?

Exercise 4.2 Can you alter **<yvals.h>** to adapt **<float.h>** and **xfloat.c** for the C translator you use? If so, do so. If not, what else must you alter?

Exercise 4.3 Consider the following code sequence:

```
double d = 1.0;
float a[N];

for (i = 0; i < n; ++i)
    d *= a[i];
```

In IEEE 754 floating-point arithmetic, how large can **N** be before you have to worry about overflow in the computation of **d**?

Exercise 4.4 Consider the following code sequence:

```
long double ld = 1.0;
double a[N];

for (i = 0; i < n; ++i)
    ld *= a[i];
```

In IEEE 754 floating-point arithmetic, how large can **N** be before you have to worry about overflow in the computation of **ld**?

Exercise 4.5 Why is the header **<yvals.h>** included directly in **<float.h>** (as opposed to including it only in **xfloat.c**)? Alter the code in this chapter to eliminate the need.

Exercise 4.6 You are given the function **int _Getrnd(void)** that returns the current floating-point rounding status. Alter the macro **FLT_RADIX** to return the current status.

Exercise 4.7 [Harder] Write a C program that determines the values of the macros defined in **<float.h>** solely by performing arithmetic. Assume that you don't know the underlying floating-point representation.

Exercise 4.8 [Very hard] Alter the program from the previous exercise to work safely even on an implementation that aborts execution on floating-point overflow. Assume that the program cannot regain control once overflow occurs.

Chapter 5: <limits.h>

Background

One of the first attempts at standardizing any part of the C programming languages began in 1980. It was begun by an organization then called /usr/group, now called Usenix. As the first commercial organization founded to promote UNIX commercially, /usr/group had a stake in vendor-independent standards. The organization felt that technical developments couldn't simply go off in all directions, nor could they be dictated solely by AT&T. Either way, it was hard to maintain an open marketplace.

history So /usr/group began the process of defining what it means to call a system UNIX or UNIX-like. They formed a standards committee that focused, at least initially, on the C programming environment. That's where nearly all applications were written, anyway. The goal was to describe a set of C functions that you could expect to find in any UNIX-compatible system. The descriptions, of course, had to be independent of any particular architecture.

A chunk of what /usr/group described was the set of C-callable functions that let you access UNIX system services. An even larger chunk, however, was the set of functions common to *all* C environments. That larger chunk served as the basis for the library portion of the C Standard. Since Kernighan and Ritchie chose not to discuss the library except in passing, the /usr/group standard was of immense help to committee X3J11. It saved us many months, possibly even years, of additional labor.

As an aside, the /usr/group effort served another very useful purpose. IEEE committee 1003 was formed to turn this industry product into an official standard. The IEEE group turned over responsibility for the system-independent functions to X3J11 and focused on the UNIX-specific portion. You know the resultant Standard today as IEEE 1003.1, a.k.a. POSIX.

naming what changes Part of building an architecture-independent description is to recognize what changes across computer architectures. You want to avoid any unnecessary differences, to be sure. The rest you want to identify and to circumscribe. Some critical value might change when you move an application program to another flavor of UNIX. So you give it a name. You lay down rules for testing the named value in a program. And you define the limits that the value can range between.

A long-standing tradition in C is that scalar data types are represented in ways natural to each computer architecture. The fundamental type *int* is particularly elastic. It wants to be a size that supports efficient computation, at least within broad limits. That may be great for efficiency, but it's a real nuisance for portability.

/usr/group invented the standard header **<limits.h>** to capture many important properties that can change across architectures. It so happens that this header deals exclusively with the ranges of values of integer types. When X3J11 decided to add similar data on the floating-point types, we elected not to overwhelm the existing contents of **<limits.h>**. Instead, we added the standard header **<float.h>**. Perhaps we should have also renamed the existing standard header **<integer.h>**, but we didn't. Tidiness yielded to historical continuity.

What the C Standard Says

5.2.4.2 Numerical limits

A conforming implementation shall document all the limits specified in this subclause, which shall be specified in the headers **<limits.h>** and **<float.h>**.

5.2.4.2.1 Sizes of integral types **<limits.h>**

<limits.h>

The values given below shall be replaced by constant expressions suitable for use in **#if** preprocessing directives. Moreover, except for **CHAR_BIT** and **MB_LEN_MAX**, the following shall be replaced by expressions that have the same type as would an expression that is an object of the corresponding type converted according to the integral promotions. Their implementation-defined values shall be equal or greater in magnitude (absolute value) to those shown, with the same sign.

CHAR_BIT

- number of bits for smallest object that is not a bit-field (byte)
  CHAR_BIT   **8**

SCHAR_MIN

- minimum value for an object of type **signed char**
  SCHAR_MIN   **-127**

SCHAR_MAX

- maximum value for an object of type **signed char**
  SCHAR_MAX   **+127**

UCHAR_MAX

- maximum value for an object of type **unsigned char**
  UCHAR_MAX   **255**

CHAR_MIN

- minimum value for an object of type **char**
  CHAR_MIN   " see below"

CHAR_MAX

- maximum value for an object of type **char**
  CHAR_MAX   " see below"

MB_LEN_MAX

- maximum number of bytes in a multibyte character, for any supported locale
  MB_LEN_MAX   **1**

SHRT_MIN

- minimum value for an object of type **short int**
  SHRT_MIN   **-32767**

SHRT_MAX

- maximum value for an object of type **short int**
  SHRT_MAX   **+32767**

USHRT_MAX

- maximum value for an object of type **unsigned short int**
  USHRT_MAX   **65535**

INT_MIN

- minimum value for an object of type **int**
  INT_MIN   **-32767**

INT_MAX

- maximum value for an object of type **int**
  INT_MAX   **+32767**

UINT_MAX	• maximum value for an object of type **unsigned int**
	UINT_MAX 65535
LONG_MIN	• minimum value for an object of type **long int**
	LONG_MIN -2147483647
LONG_MAX	• maximum value for an object of type **long int**
	LONG_MAX +2147483647
ULONG_MAX	• maximum value for an object of type **unsigned long int**
	ULONG_MAX 4294967295

If the value of an object of type **char** is treated as a signed integer when used in an expression, the value of **CHAR_MIN** shall be the same as that of **SCHAR_MIN** and the value of **CHAR_MAX** shall be the same as that of **SCHAR_MAX**. Otherwise, the value of **CHAR_MIN** shall be 0 and the value of **CHAR_MAX** shall be the same as that of **UCHAR_MAX**.[9]

Using `<limits.h>`

You can use `<limits.h>` one of two ways. The simpler way assures that you do not produce a silly program. Let's say, for example, that you want to represent some signed data that ranges in value between **VAL_MIN** and **VAL_MAX**. You can keep the program from translating incorrectly by writing:

```
#include <assert.h>
#include <limits.h>
#if VAL_MIN < INT_MIN || INT_MAX < VAL_MAX
#error values out of range
#endif
```

You can then safely store the data in data objects declared with type *int*.

adapting types   A more elaborate way to use `<limits.h>` is to control the choice of types in a program. You can alter the example above to read:

```
#include <assert.h>
#include <limits.h>
#if VAL_MIN < LONG_MIN || LONG_MAX < VAL_MAX
    typedef double Val_t;
#elif VAL_MIN < INT_MIN || INT_MAX < VAL_MAX
    typedef long Val_t;
#else
    typedef int Val_t;
#endif
```

You then declare all data objects that must hold this range of values as having type **Val_t**. The program automatically chooses the most efficient type.

The presence of `<limits.h>` is also designed to discourage an old programming trick that is extremely nonportable. Some programs attempted to test the properties of the execution environment by writing `#if` directives:

```
#if (-1 + 0x0) >> 1 > 0x7fff
/* must have ints greater than 16 bits */
.....
#endif
```

This code assumes that whatever arithmetic the preprocessor performs is the same as what occurs in the execution environment. Those who deal

Figure 5.1:
`limits.h`

```
/* limits.h standard header -- 8-bit version */
#ifndef _LIMITS
#define _LIMITS
#ifndef _YVALS
#include <yvals.h>
#endif
        /* char properties */
#define CHAR_BIT    8
#if _CSIGN
#define CHAR_MAX    127
#define CHAR_MIN    (-127-_C2)
#else
#define CHAR_MAX    255
#define CHAR_MIN    0
#endif
        /* int properties */
#if _ILONG
#define INT_MAX     2147483647
#define INT_MIN     (-2147483647-_C2)
#define UINT_MAX    4294967295
#else
#define INT_MAX     32767
#define INT_MIN     (-32767-_C2)
#define UINT_MAX    65535
#endif
        /* long properties */
#define LONG_MAX    2147483647
#define LONG_MIN    (-2147483647-_C2)
        /* multibyte properties */
#define MB_LEN_MAX  _MBMAX
        /* signed char properties */
#define SCHAR_MAX   127
#define SCHAR_MIN   (-127-_C2)
        /* short properties */
#define SHRT_MAX    32767
#define SHRT_MIN    (-32767-_C2)
        /* unsigned properties */
#define UCHAR_MAX   255
#define ULONG_MAX   4294967295
#define USHRT_MAX   65535
#endif                                                          □
```

heavily with cross compilers know well that the translation environment can differ markedly from the execution environment. For tricks like this one to work, the C Standard would have to require that the translator mimic the execution environment very closely. And translator families with a common front end would have to adapt translation-time arithmetic to suit each environment.

X3J11 discussed such requirements at length. In the end, we decided that the preprocessor was not the creature to burden with such stringent requirements. The translator must closely model the execution environment in many ways, to be sure. It must compute constant expressions — to initialize static storage, for example — to at least as wide a range and precision as the execution environment. But it can largely define its own environment for the arithmetic within `#if` directives.

So to test the execution environment you can't do experiments on the preprocessor. You must include `<limits.h>` and test the values of the macros it provides.

One addition made by X3J11 to `<limits.h>` is the macro MB_LEN_MAX. You use it to allocate space for multibyte characters. I discuss MB_LEN_MAX in conjunction with the multibyte functions in Chapter 13: `<stdlib.h>`.

Implementing `<limits.h>`

The only code you have to provide for this header is the header itself. All the macros defined in `<limits.h>` are testable within `#if` directives and are unlikely to change during execution. (The same is *not* true of most of the macros defined in `<float.h>`.)

common choices Most modern computers have 8-bit *char*s, 2-byte *short*s, and 4-byte *long*s. There are several common variations on this principal theme:

- An *int* is either 2 or 4 bytes.
- A *char* has the same range of values as either *signed char* or *unsigned char*.
- Signed values are encoded most frequently in *two's complement*, which has only one form of zero but one negative value that has no corresponding positive value. Less common are *one's complement* and *signed magnitude*. Both have two forms of zero but no extra negative value.
- The number of bytes for a single multibyte character can be any value greater than zero.

I found it convenient, therefore, to write a version of `<limits.h>` that expands to any of these common choices. Figure 5.1 shows the file `limits.h`. It includes the configuration file `<yvals.h>`, which I introduced on page 53. That file also provides parameters for the header `<float.h>`, described on page 65. Among other things, `<yvals.h>` defines the macros:

_ILONG   ■ _ILONG — nonzero if a *long* has 4 bytes

_CSIGN   ■ _CSIGN — nonzero if a *char* is signed

_C2   ■ _C2 — 1 if the encoding is two's complement, else 0

_MBMAX   ■ _MBMAX — the worst-case length of a single multibyte character.

The use of the macro _C2 obscures an important subtlety. On a two's-complement machine, you cannot simply write the obvious value for INT_MIN. On a 16-bit machine, for example, the sequence of characters -32768 parses as two tokens, a minus sign and the integer constant with value 32,768. The latter has type *long* because it is too large to represent as type *int*. Negating this value doesn't change its type. The C Standard requires, however, that INT_MIN have type *int*. Otherwise, you can be astonished by the behavior of a statement as innocent looking as:

```
/* test limits macros */
#include <limits.h>
#include <stdio.h>

int main()
    {                   /* test basic properties of limits.h macros */
    printf("CHAR_BIT = %2i   MB_LEN_MAX = %2i\n\n",
        CHAR_BIT, MB_LEN_MAX);
    printf(" CHAR_MAX = %10i   CHAR_MIN = %10i\n",
        CHAR_MAX, CHAR_MIN);
    printf("SCHAR_MAX = %10i  SCHAR_MIN = %10i\n",
        SCHAR_MAX, SCHAR_MIN);
    printf("UCHAR_MAX = %10u\n\n", UCHAR_MAX);
    printf(" SHRT_MAX = %10i   SHRT_MIN = %10i\n",
        SHRT_MAX, SHRT_MIN);
    printf("USHRT_MAX = %10u\n\n", USHRT_MAX);
    printf("  INT_MAX = %10i    INT_MIN = %10i\n",
        INT_MAX, INT_MIN);
    printf(" UINT_MAX = %10u\n\n", UINT_MAX);
    printf(" LONG_MAX = %10li   LONG_MIN = %10li\n",
        LONG_MAX, LONG_MIN);
    printf("ULONG_MAX = %10lu\n\n", ULONG_MAX);
#if CHAR_BIT < 8 || CHAR_MAX < 127 || 0 < CHAR_MIN \
    || CHAR_MAX != SCHAR_MAX && CHAR_MAX != UCHAR_MAX
#error bad char properties
#endif
#if INT_MAX < 32767 || -32767 < INT_MIN || INT_MAX < SHRT_MAX
#error bad int properties
#endif
#if LONG_MAX < 2147483647 || -2147483647 < LONG_MIN \
    || LONG_MAX < INT_MAX
#error bad long properties
#endif
#if MB_LEN_MAX < 1
#error bad MB_LEN_MAX
#endif
#if SCHAR_MAX < 127 || -127 < SCHAR_MIN
#error bad signed char properties
#endif
```

```
printf("range is from %d to %d\n", INT_MIN, INT_MAX);
```

The only safe thing is to sneak up on the value by writing an expression such as `(-32767-1)`. Given the way I chose to parametrize `<limits.h>`, you get this trickery for free.

One other subtlety should not be overlooked. I made the point earlier that preprocessor arithmetic need not model that of the execution environment. You can, in principle, compile on a host with a 32-bit *long* for a execution environment with a 36-bit *long*. Nevertheless, the host is obliged to get the values in `<limits.h>` right. That means that it must do preprocessor arithmetic to at least 36 bits. The latitude spelled out for implementors by X3J11 isn't so broad after all.

Continuing
tlimits.c
Part 2

```
#if SHRT_MAX < 32767 || -32767 < SHRT_MIN \
    || SHRT_MAX < SCHAR_MAX
#error bad short properties
#endif
#if UCHAR_MAX < 255 || UCHAR_MAX / 2 < SCHAR_MAX
#error bad unsigned char properties
#endif
#if UINT_MAX < 65535 || UINT_MAX / 2 < INT_MAX \
    || UINT_MAX < USHRT_MAX
#error bad unsigned int properties
#endif
#if ULONG_MAX < 4294967295 || ULONG_MAX / 2 < LONG_MAX \
    || ULONG_MAX < UINT_MAX
#endif
#if USHRT_MAX < 65535 || USHRT_MAX / 2 < SHRT_MAX \
    || USHRT_MAX < UCHAR_MAX
#error bad unsigned short properties
#endif
    puts("SUCCESS testing <limits.h>");
    return (0);
    }
```

Testing `<limits.h>`

Figure 5.2 shows the test program `tlimits.c`. It provides a brief sanity check you can run on `<limits.h>`. It is by no means exhaustive, but it does tell you whether the header is basically sane. It also provides a readable summary of the values of the macros defined in `<limits.h>`.

Note that all the action occurs at translation time. That's because all the macros must be usable within `#if` directives. If this test compiles, it will surely run, print its summary and success message, then exit with successful status.

Here is the output for a PC-compatible implementation that represents *char* the same as *signed char:*

```
CHAR_BIT =  8   MB_LEN_MAX =  8

  CHAR_MAX =        127   CHAR_MIN =          -128
  SCHAR_MAX =       127   SCHAR_MIN =         -128
 UCHAR_MAX =        255

  SHRT_MAX =      32767   SHRT_MIN =        -32768
 USHRT_MAX =      65535

   INT_MAX =      32767   INT_MIN =         -32768
  UINT_MAX =      65535

  LONG_MAX = 2147483647   LONG_MIN = -2147483648
 ULONG_MAX = 4294967295
 SUCCESS testing <limits.h>
```

References

The program **enquire**, described on page 71, also produces the file **limits.h**.

IEEE Standard 1003-1987 (Piscataway, N.J.: Institute of Electrical and Electronics Engineers, Inc., 1985). This is the POSIX Standard for writing applications in C that run under UNIX and UNIX-compatible operating systems. The header **<limits.h>** arose out of this standardization effort.

Exercises

Exercise 5.1 Determine the parameters that characterize integer arithmetic for the C translator you use.

Exercise 5.2 Adapt **<limits.h>** for the C translator you use.

Exercise 5.3 Consider the following code sequence:

```
int in = 1.0;
short a[N];

for (i = 0; i < n; ++i)
    in *= a[i];
```

For the C translator you use, how large can **N** be before you have to worry about overflow in the computation of **in**? How large can **N** be in a program intended to run with an arbitrary C translator?

Exercise 5.4 Consider the following code sequence:

```
long lo = 1.0;
int a[N];

for (i = 0; i < n; ++i)
    lo *= a[i];
```

For the C translator you use, how large can **N** be before you have to worry about overflow in the computation of **lo**? How large can **N** be in a program intended to run with an arbitrary C translator?

Exercise 5.5 Can an implementation of Standard C have **sizeof (long)** equal to one byte? What are some of the peculiar properties of such an implementation?

Exercise 5.6 [Harder] Write a program that determines the values of the macros defined in **<limits.h>** solely by performing arithmetic. Assume that you don't know the underlying integer representations.

Exercise 5.7 [Very hard] Alter the program from the previous exercise to work safely even on an implementation that aborts execution on integer overflow. Assume that the program cannot regain control once overflow occurs.

Chapter 6: `<locale.h>`

Background

The header `<locale.h>` is an invention of X3J11, the committee that developed the C Standard. You will find little that resembles locales in earlier implementations of C. That stands at odds with the committee's stated purpose, to "codify existing practice." Nevertheless, those of us active within X3J11 at that time felt we were acting out of the best of motives — self defense.

history   This particular header popped up about five years after work began on the C Standard. At that time, many of us felt that the Standard was essentially complete. We were simply putting a few finishing touches on a product in which we had invested five years of our lives. Resistance was mounting to change of any sort.

About then, we learned that a number of Europeans were unhappy with certain parts of the C Standard being developed by X3J11. It was simply too American in several critical ways. They despaired of trying to educate insular Yankees about the needs of the world marketplace. Rather, they were content to wait and fight their battles on a more congenial field. The Europeans took it for granted that an ISO standard for C must differ from the ANSI C Standard.

Many of us disagreed with that position. We felt it imperative that whatever standard ANSI developed had to be acceptable to the international community. We had seen the effects in the past of computer language standards that differed around the world. Our five years of effort would be in vain, we felt, if the final word on C came from a separate committee second guessing all our decisions.

So we asked the Europeans to show us their shopping list of changes. Most of the items on the list dealt with ways to adapt C programs to different cultures. That is a much more obvious problem in a land of many languages and nations such as Europe. Americans enjoy the luxury of a single (widely used if not official) language and a fairly simple alphabet.

AT&T Bell Laboratories went so far as to host a special meeting to deal with various issues of internationalization. (This is a big word that people are uttering more and more often. It seems to have no acceptable synonym that is any shorter. The informal solution is to introduce the barbarism *I18N*, pronounced "EYE eighteen EN." The 18 stands for the number of letters omitted.) Out of that meeting came the proposal for adding locale support to Standard C. The machinery eventually adopted is remarkably close to the original proposal.

Adding locales to C had the desired effect. Many of the objections to ANSI C as an international standard were derailed. It cost X3J11 an extra year, by my estimation, to hammer out locales. And we probably spent yet another year dealing with residual issues from the international community. (WG14, the ISO C standard committee, is still working on additions to the existing C Standard.) Nevertheless, we succeeded in producing a standard for C that is currently identical at both ANSI and ISO levels.

environments   Writing adaptive code is not entirely new. An early form sprung up about fifteen years ago in the UNIX operating system. Folks got the idea of adding *environment variables* to the system call that launches new processes. (That service is called **exec**, or some variant thereof, in UNIX land.) Environment variables are an open-ended set of names, each of which identifies a null-terminated string that represents its value. You can add, alter, or delete environment variables in a process. Should that process launch another process, the environment variables are automatically copied into the image of the new process.

The new process can simply ignore environment variables. It loses a few dozen, or a few hundred, bytes of storage that it might otherwise enjoy. Or it can look for certain environment variables and study their current values. A common variable is **"TZ"**, which provides information to the library date functions about the current time zone. If the value of **"TZ"** is, say, **EST05EDT**, the time functions know to label local standard time as **EST** and local Daylight Savings Time as **EDT**. The local (standard) time zone is 5 hours later than UTC, known in the past as Greenwich Mean Time.

Environment variables have many uses. They are a great way to smuggle file names into an application program. It is almost always a bad idea to wire file names directly into a program. Prompting the user for file names is mostly a good idea, except for "secret" files about which the user should not have to be informed. Asking for such a file name on the command line that starts the program is somewhat better, but it can be a nuisance. It is a particular nuisance if several programs in a suite need access to the same file name. That's why it is often much nicer to set an environment variable to the file name once and for all in a script that starts a session. The file name is captured in one place, but is made available to a whole suite of programs.

Microsoft's MS-DOS supports environment variables too — one of many good ideas borrowed from UNIX. Several commercial software packages use environment variables to advantage. A common use is to locate special directories that contain support files or that are well suited for hosting temporary files. But they have many other uses as well.

function   The Standard C library includes the function **getenv**, declared in **<st-**
getenv **dlib.h>**. Call **getenv** with the name of an environment variable and it will

return a pointer to its value string, if there is one. It is not considered an error to reference a variable that is not defined.

function Note, however, that the C Standard does *not* include `putenv`, the usual

putenv companion to `getenv`. That is the common name for the function that lets you alter the values associated with environment variables. Simply put, committee X3J11 couldn't decide how to describe the semantics of `putenv`. They differ too much among various single-user and multiprocessing systems. So you can write portable code that reads environment variables, but you can't alter them in a standard way.

why What do locales provide that environment variables do not? In a word,

locales structure. This is the era of object-oriented hoopla. So you can look on locales, if you wish, as object-oriented environment variables. A single locale provides information on many related parameters. The values are consistent for a given culture. You would have to pump dozens of reserved names into the name space for environment variables to transmit the same amount of information. And you run a greater risk that subsets of the information get altered inconsistently.

When I talk about a culture, by the way, I don't mean just a group that speaks a common language. People in the USA write dates as 7/4/1776 (Independence Day). The same day in the UK is written as 4/7/1776 (Thanksgiving Day). Even within the USA, practices can vary. Where we civilians might write a debit as $–123.45, an accountant may well prefer ($123.45).

categories For this reason, and others, locales have substructure. You can set an entire locale, or you can alter one or more *categories*. The header `<locale.h>` defines several macros with names such as `LC_COLLATE` and `LC_TIME`. Each expands to an integer value that you can use as the category argument to `setlocale`, the function that alters locales. Separate categories exist for:

- controlling collation sequences `LC_COLLATE`)
- classification of characters (`LC_CTYPE`)
- monetary formatting (`LC_MONETARY`)
- other numeric formatting (`LC_NUMERIC`)
- times (`LC_TIME`)

An implementation can choose to provide additional categories as well. A program that uses such added categories will, of course, be less portable than one that does not.

The idea behind categories is that an application may wish to tailor its locale. It may want to print dates in the local language and by the formatting rules of that language. But it may still opt to use the dot for a decimal point even though speakers of that language customarily write a comma. Or the application may adapt completely to a given locale, then change the category `LC_MONETARY` to match a worldwide corporate standard for expressing accounting information.

What the C Standard Says

<locale.h>

7.4 Localization <locale.h>

The header **<locale.h>** declares two functions, one type, and defines several macros.

The type is

struct lconv

```
struct lconv
```

which contains members related to the formatting of numeric values. The structure shall contain at least the following members, in any order. The semantics of the members and their normal ranges is explained in 7.4.2.1. In the "**C**" locale, the members shall have the values specified in the comments.

```
char *decimal_point;        /* "." */
char *thousands_sep;        /* "" */
char *grouping;             /* "" */
char *int_curr_symbol;      /* "" */
char *currency_symbol;      /* "" */
char *mon_decimal_point;    /* "" */
char *mon_thousands_sep;    /* "" */
char *mon_grouping;         /* "" */
char *positive_sign;        /* "" */
char *negative_sign;        /* "" */
char int_frac_digits;       /* CHAR_MAX */
char frac_digits;           /* CHAR_MAX */
char p_cs_precedes;         /* CHAR_MAX */
char p_sep_by_space;        /* CHAR_MAX */
char n_cs_precedes;         /* CHAR_MAX */
char n_sep_by_space;        /* CHAR_MAX */
char p_sign_posn;           /* CHAR_MAX */
char n_sign_posn;           /* CHAR_MAX */
```

NULL

The macros defined are **NULL** (described in 7.1.6); and

LC_ALL
LC_COLLATE
LC_CTYPE
LC_MONETARY
LC_NUMERIC

```
LC_ALL
LC_COLLATE
LC_CTYPE
LC_MONETARY
LC_NUMERIC
LC_TIME
```

which expand to integral constant expressions with distinct values, suitable for use as the first argument to the **setlocale** function. Additional macro definitions, beginning with the characters **LC_** and an uppercase letter,[100] may also be specified by the implementation.

7.4.1 Locale control

7.4.1.1 The **setlocale** function

setlocale

Synopsis

```
#include <locale.h>
char *setlocale(int category, const char *locale);
```

Description

The **setlocale** function selects the appropriate portion of the program's locale as specified by the **category** and **locale** arguments. The **setlocale** function may be used to change or query the program's entire current locale or portions thereof. The value **LC_ALL** for **category** names the program's entire locale; the other values for **category** name only a portion of the program's locale. Category **LC_COLLATE** affects the behavior of the **strcoll** and **strxfrm** functions. Category **LC_CTYPE** affects the behavior of the character handling functions[101] and the multibyte functions. Category **LC_MONETARY** affects the monetary formatting information returned by the **localeconv** function. Category **LC_NUMERIC** affects the decimal-point character for the formatted input/output functions and the string conversion functions, as well as the nonmonetary formatting information returned by the **localeconv** function. Category **LC_TIME** affects the behavior of the **strftime** function.

A value of "**C**" for **locale** specifies the minimal environment for C translation; a value of "" for **locale** specifies the implementation-defined native environment. Other implementation-defined strings may be passed as the second argument to **setlocale**.

At program startup, the equivalent of

```
        setlocale(LC_ALL, "C");
```
is executed.

The implementation shall behave as if no library function calls the **setlocale** function.

Returns

If a pointer to a string is given for **locale** and the selection can be honored, the **setlocale** function returns a pointer to the string associated with the specified **category** for the new locale. If the selection cannot be honored, the **setlocale** function returns a null pointer and the program's locale is not changed.

A null pointer for **locale** causes the **setlocale** function to return a pointer to the string associated with the **category** for the program's current locale; the program's locale is not changed.[102]

The pointer to string returned by the **setlocale** function is such that a subsequent call with that string value and its associated category will restore that part of the program's locale. The string pointed to shall not be modified by the program, but may be overwritten by a subsequent call to the **setlocale** function.

Forward references: formatted input/output functions (7.9.6), the multibyte character functions (7.10.7), the multibyte string functions (7.10.8), string conversion functions (7.10.1), the **strcoll** function (7.11.4.3), the **strftime** function (7.12.3.5), the **strxfrm** function (7.11.4.5).

7.4.2 Numeric formatting convention inquiry

localeconv

7.4.2.1 The **localeconv** function

Synopsis

```
        #include <locale.h>
        struct lconv *localeconv(void);
```

Description

The **localeconv** function sets the components of an object with type **struct lconv** with values appropriate for the formatting of numeric quantities (monetary and otherwise) according to the rules of the current locale.

The members of the structure with type **char *** are pointers to strings, any of which (except **decimal_point**) can point to " ", to indicate that the value is not available in the current locale or is of zero length. The members with type **char** are nonnegative numbers, any of which can be **CHAR_MAX** to indicate that the value is not available in the current locale. The members include the following:

char *decimal_point
The decimal-point character used to format nonmonetary quantities.

char *thousands_sep
The character used to separate groups of digits before the decimal-point character in formatted nonmonetary quantities.

char *grouping
A string whose elements indicate the size of each group of digits in formatted nonmonetary quantities.

char *int_curr_symbol
The international currency symbol applicable to the current locale. The first three characters contain the alphabetic international currency symbol in accordance with those specified in ISO 4217:1987. The fourth character (immediately preceding the null character) is the character used to separate the international currency symbol from the monetary quantity.

char *currency_symbol
The local currency symbol applicable to the current locale.

char *mon_decimal_point
The decimal-point used to format monetary quantities.

char *mon_thousands_sep
The separator for groups of digits before the decimal-point in formatted monetary quantities.

char *mon_grouping
A string whose elements indicate the size of each group of digits in formatted monetary quantities.

char *positive_sign
The string used to indicate a nonnegative-valued formatted monetary quantity.

`char *negative_sign`
> The string used to indicate a negative-valued formatted monetary quantity.

`char int_frac_digits`
> The number of fractional digits (those after the decimal-point) to be displayed in a internationally formatted monetary quantity.

`char frac_digits`
> The number of fractional digits (those after the decimal-point) to be displayed in a formatted monetary quantity.

`char p_cs_precedes`
> Set to 1 or 0 if the **currency_symbol** respectively precedes or succeeds the value for a nonnegative formatted monetary quantity.

`char p_sep_by_space`
> Set to 1 or 0 if the **currency_symbol** respectively is or is not separated by a space from the value for a nonnegative formatted monetary quantity.

`char n_cs_precedes`
> Set to 1 or 0 if the **currency_symbol** respectively precedes or succeeds the value for a negative formatted monetary quantity.

`char n_sep_by_space`
> Set to 1 or 0 if the **currency_symbol** respectively is or is not separated by a space from the value for a negative formatted monetary quantity.

`char p_sign_posn`
> Set to a value indicating the positioning of the **positive_sign** for a nonnegative formatted monetary quantity.

`char n_sign_posn`
> Set to a value indicating the positioning of the **negative_sign** for a negative formatted monetary quantity.

The elements of **grouping** and **mon_grouping** are interpreted according to the following:

CHAR_MAX No further grouping is to be performed.

0 The previous element is to be repeatedly used for the remainder of the digits.

other The integer value is the number of digits that comprise the current group. The next element is examined to determine the size of the next group of digits before the current group.

The value of **p_sign_posn** and **n_sign_posn** is interpreted according to the following:

0 Parentheses surround the quantity and **currency_symbol**.

1 The sign string precedes the quantity and **currency_symbol**.

2 The sign string succeeds the quantity and **currency_symbol**.

3 The sign string immediately precedes the **currency_symbol**.

4 The sign string immediately succeeds the **currency_symbol**.

The implementation shall behave as if no library function calls the **localeconv** function.

Returns

The **localeconv** function returns a pointer to the filled-in object. The structure pointed to by the return value shall not be modified by the program, but may be overwritten by a subsequent call to the **localeconv** function. In addition, calls to the **setlocale** function with categories **LC_ALL**, **LC_MONETARY**, or **LC_NUMERIC** may overwrite the contents of the structure.

Example

The following table illustrates the rules which may well be used by four countries to format monetary quantities.

Country	Positive format	Negative format	International format
Italy	`L.1.234`	`-L.1.234`	`ITL.1.234`
Netherlands	`F 1.234,56`	`F -1.234,56`	`NLG 1.234,56`
Norway	`kr1.234,56`	`kr1.234,56-`	`NOK 1.234,56`
Switzerland	`SFrs.1,234.56`	`SFrs.1,234.56C`	`CHF 1,234.56`

For these four countries, the respective values for the monetary members of the structure returned by **localeconv** are:

	Italy	Netherlands	Norway	Switzerland
int_curr_symbol	`"ITL."`	`"NLG "`	`"NOK "`	`"CHF "`
currency_symbol	`"L."`	`"F"`	`"kr"`	`"SFrs."`
mon_decimal_point	`""`	`","`	`","`	`"."`
mon_thousands_sep	`"."`	`"."`	`"."`	`","`
mon_grouping	`"\3"`	`"\3"`	`"\3"`	`"\3"`
positive_sign	`""`	`""`	`""`	`""`
negative_sign	`"-"`	`"-"`	`"-"`	`"C"`
int_frac_digits	0	2	2	2
frac_digits	0	2	2	2
p_cs_precedes	1	1	1	1
p_sep_by_space	0	1	0	0
n_cs_precedes	1	1	1	1
n_sep_by_space	0	1	0	0
p_sign_posn	1	1	1	1
n_sign_posn	1	4	2	2

Footnotes

100. See "future library directions" (7.13.3).

101. The only functions in 7.3 whose behavior is not affected by the current locale are **isdigit** and **isxdigit**.

102. The implementation must arrange to encode in a string the various categories due to a heterogeneous locale when **category** has the value **LC_ALL**.

Using `<locale.h>`

Much of the information provided in a locale is purely informative. C has never treated monetary values as a special data type, so the rest of the Standard C library is unaffected by a change in the category **LC_MONETARY**. On the other hand, some changes in locale very definitely affect how certain library functions behave. If a culture uses a comma for a decimal point, then the scan functions should accept commas and the print functions should produce commas in the proper places. That is indeed what happens. Here are all the places where library behavior changes with locale:

library changes
- The functions **strcoll** and **strxfrm**, declared in `<string.h>`, can change how they collate when category **LC_COLLATE** changes.
- The functions declared in `<ctype.h>`, the print and scan functions, declared in `<stdio.h>`, and the numeric conversion functions, declared in `<stdlib.h>`, can change how they test and alter certain characters when category **LC_CTYPE** changes.
- The multibyte functions, declared in `<stdlib.h>`, and the print and scan functions, declared in `<stdio.h>`, can change how they parse and translate multibyte strings when category **LC_CTYPE** changes.
- The print and scan functions, declared in `<stdio.h>`, and **atof** and **strtod**, declared in `<stdlib.h>`, can change what they use for the decimal point character when category **LC_NUMERIC** changes.
- The **strftime** function, declared in `<time.h>`, can change how it converts times to character strings when category **LC_TIME** changes.
- The **localeconv** function, declared in `<locale.h>`, can change what it returns when categories **LC_MONETARY** or **LC_NUMERIC** change.

If you are half as nervous as I am, this litany of changes should scare you. How do you write portable code if large chunks of the Standard C library can change behavior underfoot? Can you ship code to Germany and know what `isalpha` will do when it runs there? If you mix your code with functions from another source, how much trouble can they cause? Each time your functions get control, you may be running in a different locale. How do you code under those conditions?

X3J11 anguished about such issues when we spelled out the behavior of locales. We recognized that many people don't want to be bothered with this machinery at all. Those folks should suffer little from the addition of locales. Still others have only modest goals. They want to trade in the Americanisms wired into older C for conventions more in tune with their culture. Still others are ambitious. They want to write code that can be sold unchanged, in object-module or executable form, in numerous markets. That code must be very sophisticated about changing locales.

"c" locale   The simplest way to use locales is to ignore them. Every Standard C program starts up in the `"c"` locale. In this locale, the traditional library functions behave pretty much as they always have. `islower` returns a nonzero value only for the 26 lowercase letters of the English alphabet, for example. The decimal point is a dot. If your program never calls `setlocale`, none of this behavior can change.

native locale   The next simplest way to use locales is to change once, just after program startup, and leave it at that. The C Standard requires no other locale names besides `"c"`. But it does define a *native locale* designated by the empty string `""`. If your program executes:

```
setlocale(LC_ALL, "")
```

it shifts to this native locale. Presumably, each implementation will devise a way to determine a native locale that pleases the locals. (An implementation that doesn't care a hoot about locales can make the native locale the same as the `"c"` locale, of course.)

reverting the locale   You must be more careful in using the library once the locale can change on you. Some things get easier, such as displaying pretty dates or skipping the appropriate characters for white-space. Other things get chancier, such as parsing strings with the functions declared in `<ctype.h>`. In a pinch, you can always revert part or all of the locale to the `"c"` locale. Begin by writing:

```
#include <locale.h>
#include <stdlib.h>
#include <string.h>
    .....
    char *ls = setlocale(LC_CTYPE, "C");
    char *ss = ls ? malloc(strlen(ls) + 1) : NULL;

    if (ss)
        strcpy(ss, ls);
```

Now you can use the functions declared in **<ctype.h>** with assurance that you are working in the **"c"** locale. When you're done, revert the locale by writing:

```
setlocale(LC_ALL, ss);
free(ss);
```

Note that the code stumbles bravely onward if the heap is exhausted and **malloc** fails. It simply avoids using any null pointers unwisely. You can omit the business about allocating space and copying the locale string returned by **setlocale** only if you are sure that no other calls to that function can intervene between the two shown above.

formatting   Two locale categories tell you how to format values to match local
values conventions:

- Category **LC_MONETARY** *suggests* how to format monetary amounts, both by local custom and in accordance with international standards (ISO 4217).

- Category **LC_NUMERIC** *dictates* the decimal point character used by the Standard C library and *suggests* how to format non-monetary amounts.

Here, for example, are various ways you can format the monetary amount $–3.00 by local custom, depending upon the values stored in three members of **struct lconv**:

		n_sep_by_space: 0			
n_sign_posn:	0	1	2	3	4
n_cs_precedes: 0	(3.00$)	-3.00$	3.00$-	3.00-$	3.00$-
1	($3.00)	-$3.00	$3.00-	-$3.00	$-3.00

		n_sep_by_space: 1			
n_sign_posn:	0	1	2	3	4
n_cs_precedes: 0	(3.00 $)	-3.00 $	3.00 $-	3.00- $	3.00 $-
1	($ 3.00)	-$ 3.00	$ 3.00-	-$ 3.00	$ -3.00

The example assumes that the member **currency_symbol** points at "$", **mon_decimal_point** points at ".", **negative_sign** points at "-", and **frac_digits** has the value 2. The example does not show the effect of the members **mon_grouping** and **mon_thousands_sep**, which describe how to group and separate digits to the left of the decimal point.

Three additional members describe how to format positive monetary amounts. These are **p_sep_by_space**, **p_sign_posn**, and **p_cs_precedes**. For international monetary amounts, the member **int_curr_symbol** determines the currency symbol (instead of **currency_symbol**) and **int_frac_digits** determines how many decimal places to display (instead of **frac_digits**). And if you want to format non-monetary amounts, you care about the members **decimal_point**, **grouping**, and **thousands_sep**.

That's a lot of complexity to keep track of. Conceivably, you can make use of this information throughout an application, but probably not. The individual pieces are at a low level of detail. What you really want is some way to format numeric data that applies *all* of the relevant information in one place. Unfortunately, the C Standard does not define such a function.

function
_Fmtval
I decided to define the missing function. After several false starts, I ended up with the declaration:

```
char *_Fmtval(char *buf, double val, int frac_digs);
```

You provide the character buffer **buf** to hold the formatted value. (The modern trend is to specify a maximum length for any such buffer. I found the function quite complicated enough without such checking, desirable as it may be.) As a convenience, the function returns the value of **buf**, which then holds the formatted value as a null-terminated string.

You also specify **val**, the value to be formatted, as a *double*. That provides for a fraction part and at least 16 decimal digits of precision. For a non-monetary value, **frac_digits** specifies the numer of fraction digits to include in the formatted value. The members of **struct lconv** offer no guidance on this parameter.

Here's where the design gets clever (perhaps too clever). The locale information suggests four distinct formats for a value:

- an international monetary amount
- a local monetary amount
- a non-monetary amount with no decimal point or fraction
- a non-monetary amount with decimal point and fraction

Only in the fourth case do you need to provide a (non-negative) value for the number of fraction digits. That means you can set aside distinct negative values for the argument **frac_digits** to signal these other cases.

Figure 6.1 shows the file **xfmtval.c**, which defines the function **_Fmtval**. It distinguishes the four formats by examining the value of **frac_digits**:

- A value of –2 (the macro **FN_INT_CUR**) tells the function to format an international monetary amount.
- A value of –1 (the macro **FN_LCL_CUR**) tells the function to format a local monetary amount.
- Any other value tells the function to format a non-monetary amount. The number of fraction digits, however determined, must be a non-negative value other than **CHAR_MAX**, defined in **<limits.h>**, for the function to include a decimal point and fraction. So if you call **_Fmtval** with the value **CHAR_MAX**, or with any negative value other than –1 or –2, you tell it to format a non-monetary amount with no decimal point or fraction.
- By elimination, any non-negative value other than **CHAR_MAX** tells the function to format a non-monetary amount with a decimal point and fraction. The value specifies the number of fraction digits.

The function is straightforward, but contains a lot of tedious detail. The first half simply gathers the appropriate set of parameters for the requested formatting case. It selects a format string **fmt** to drive the generation of characters into the buffer **buf**. Note that the code doesn't trust that members of **struct lconv** have sensible values, since locales can change. I use the function **sprintf**, declared in **<stdio.h>**, to convert the *double* value **d** into the buffer. (That is just one of may things this function can do.) The funny format string in **sprintf** ensures that a decimal point appears in the buffer, followed by the appropriate number of fraction digits (if any).

The remaining logic then determines how many separators to insert between characters to the left of the decimal point and proceeds to do so. It is careful to use the function **memmove**, declared in **<string.h>**, to move characters further along in the buffer. That guarantees a correct copy even if the source and destination areas overlap. Note that the function replaces the decimal point generated by **sprintf** (which itself can vary with locale) with a decimal point that depends on the format selected.

using
_Fmtval
To use **_Fmtval**, you must first declare it and define its associated macros in your program. I chose not to include this information in any of the headers, even though I could have easily contrived a way to do so. (See the discussion on page 95.) So you must write something like:

```
#define FV_INTEGER  -3
#define FV_INT_CUR  -2
#define FV_LCL_CUR  -1
char *_Fmtval(char *, double, int);
```

Put these lines at the top of your program, or in a separate header file that you include in your program. Now you are in a position to call the function in various ways. For example, the code:

```
#include <stdio.h>
.....
    char buf[100];

    printf("You ordered %s sheets,",
        _Fmtval(buf, (double)nitems, FV_INTEGER);
    printf(" each %s square cm.\n",
        _Fmtval(buf, size, 3));
    printf("Please remit %s to our New York office,\n",
        _Fmtval(buf, cost, FV_INT_CUR));
    printf("(that's %s).\n",
        _Fmtval(buf, cost, FV_LCL_CUR));
```

might produce the output:

```
You ordered 1,340,000 sheets, each 1,204.787 square cm.
Please remit USD 18,279 to our New York office,
(that's $18,278.85).
```

Imagine trying to produce this result by inspecting the contents of **struct lconv** directly. Function **_Fmtval** obviously has its uses.

macro
NULL
The header **<locale.h>** also defines the null-pointer macro **NULL**. I discuss this macro in detail in Chapter 11: **<stddef.h>**.

```c
/* _Fmtval function */
#include <limits.h>
#include <locale.h>
#include <stdio.h>
#include <string.h>

        /* macros */
#define FN_INT_CUR -2
#define FN_LCL_CUR -1

char *_Fmtval(char *buf, double d, int fdarg)
    {                   /* format number by locale-specific rules */
    char *cur_sym, dec_pt, *grps, grp_sep, *sign;
    const char *fmt;
    int fd, neg;
    struct lconv *p = localeconv();

    if (0 <= d)
        neg = 0;
    else
        d = -d, neg = 1;
    if (fdarg == FN_INT_CUR)
        {               /* get international currency parameters */
        cur_sym = p->int_curr_symbol;
        dec_pt = p->mon_decimal_point[0];
        fmt = "$-V";
        fd = p->int_frac_digits;
        grps = p->mon_grouping;
        grp_sep = p->mon_thousands_sep[0];
        sign = neg ? p->negative_sign : p->positive_sign;
        }
    else if (fdarg == FN_LCL_CUR)
        {                       /* get local currency parameters */
        static const char *ftab[5][2][2] = {
            "(V$)",   "-V$",   "V$-",   "V-$",   "V$-",
            "($V)",   "-$V",   "$V-",   "-$V",   "$-V",
            "(V $)",  "-V $",  "V $-",  "V- $",  "V $-",
            "($ V)",  "-$ V",  "$ V-",  "-$ V",  "$ -V"};

        cur_sym = p->currency_symbol;
        dec_pt = p->mon_decimal_point[0];
        if (neg)
            fmt = ftab[p->n_sign_posn < 0 || 4 < p->n_sign_posn
                ? 0 : p->n_sign_posn][p->n_cs_precedes == 1]
                [p->n_sep_by_space == 1];
        else
            fmt = ftab[p->p_sign_posn < 0 || 4 < p->p_sign_posn
                ? 0 : p->p_sign_posn][p->p_cs_precedes == 1]
                [p->p_sep_by_space == 1];
        fd = p->frac_digits;
        grps = p->mon_grouping;
        grp_sep = p->mon_thousands_sep[0];
        sign = neg ? p->negative_sign : p->positive_sign;
        }
```

```
    else
        {           /* get numeric parameters (cur_sym not used) */
        dec_pt = p->decimal_point[0];
        fmt = "-V";
        fd = fdarg;
        grps = p->grouping;
        grp_sep = p->thousands_sep[0];
        sign = neg ? "-" : "";
        }
    {                   /* build string in buf under control of fmt */
    char *end, *s;
    const char *g;
    size_t i, ns;

    for (s = buf; *fmt; ++fmt, s += strlen(s))
        switch (*fmt)
            {                               /* process a format char */
        case '$':               /* insert currency symbol string */
            strcpy(s, cur_sym);
            break;
        case '-':                           /* insert sign string */
            strcpy(s, sign);
            break;
        default:                    /* insert literal format char */
            *s++ = *fmt, *s = '\0';
            break;
        case 'V':                       /* insert formatted value */
            sprintf(s, "%#.*f",
                0 < fd && fd != CHAR_MAX ? fd : 0, d);
            end = strchr(s, p->decimal_point[0]);
            for (ns = 0, i = end - s, g = grps; 0 < i; ++ns)
                {                       /* count separators to add */
                if (g[0] <= 0 || i <= g[0] || g[0] == CHAR_MAX)
                    break;
                i -= g[0];
                if (g[1] != 0)
                    ++g;
                }
            memmove(end + ns, end, strlen(end) + 1);
            i = end - s, end += ns;
            *end = 0 <= fd && fd != CHAR_MAX ? dec_pt : '\0';
            for (g = grps; 0 < i; --ns)
                {               /* copy up and insert separators */
                if (g[0] <= 0 || i <= g[0] || g[0] == CHAR_MAX)
                    break;
                i -= g[0], end -= g[0];
                memmove(end, end - ns, g[0]);
                *--end = grp_sep;
                if (g[1] != 0)
                    ++g;
                }
            }
        }
    return (buf);
    }
```

Implementing `<locale.h>`

This chapter contains a considerable amount of code. Unlike earlier chapters, the code draws heavily on all parts of the Standard C library. You got a taste of that variety with the function `_Fmtval` in the previous section. It made use of string manipulation functions declared in `<string.h>` and an output formatting function declared in `<stdio.h>`. You will see code from those headers and others in what follows. I won't try to describe each new function, just the more exotic usages (such as the `sprintf` format `"%#.*f"`). If you see a function that you don't recognize, just look it up in a later chapter.

One assist I can provide is a road map. Figure 6.2 shows the *call tree* for functions and data objects defined in this chapter with external linkage. I enclose entries for data objects in brackets. Following each external name is the name of the C source file that defines it and the page number where you can find the file. Beneath each function name and indented one tab stop further to the right are any names that the function refers to. (I omit this subtree on any later references to the same function name.)

For example, the function `setlocale` is defined in the C source file `setlocal.c`. That function calls itself and refers to the data object `_Clocale` defined in the same C source file. It also calls the functions `_Defloc`, `_Getloc`, and `_Setloc`.

If you find yourself getting lost in the explanations that follow, refer back to this call tree from time to time. You will find it helpful to understanding the overall structure of the functions in `<locale.h>`.

Figure 6.2:
Call Tree for
`<locale.h>`

```
localeconv              localeco.c, p.  97
setlocale               setlocal.c, p. 102
    setlocale           setlocal.c, p. 102
    [_Clocale]          setlocal.c, p. 102
    _Defloc             xdefloc.c, p. 105
    _Getloc             xgetloc.c, p. 104
        _Freeloc        xfreeloc.c, p. 118
            [_Loctab]   xloctab.c, p. 117
        _Makeloc        xmakeloc.c, p. 120
            _Locvar     xlocterm.c, p. 122
            _Locterm    xlocterm.c, p. 122
                _Skip   xgetloc.c, p. 104
            _Readloc    xreadloc.c, p. 115
                [_Loctab]   xloctab.c, p. 117
                _Skip   xgetloc.c, p. 104
        _Readloc        xreadloc.c, p. 115
    _Setloc             xsetloc.c, p. 106
        [_Costate]      xstate.c, p. 107
        [_Mbcurmax]     xstate.c, p. 107
        [_Mbstate]      xstate.c, p. 107
        [_Wcstate]      xstate.c, p. 107
```

Note that I did not include the function `_Fmtval` in this call tree. That's because it is not required by the C Standard. The C Standard permits additional functions, by the way. They can certainly have funny names like `_Fmtval`. They can even have nicer names such as `fmtval`. I chose a name reserved to implementors only as a matter of style for this presentation.

What an implementation *cannot* do with such a function is:

- include a declaration for `fmtval` in a standard header, such as `<locale.h>`
- include a definition for a macro name such as `FV_INT_CUR` in a standard header
- have any of the Standard C library functions call `fmtval`

Any of these practices pollutes the name space reserved for users.

knocking out functions Consider what happens to an added library function that honors these restrictions. A program that declares and calls our hypothetical `fmtval` will cause the linker to include the function when it scans the Standard C library for unsatisfied references to external names. A program that defines its own version of `fmtval` will not cause the linker to include the function when it scans the Standard C library. Since no other library functions depend on the presence of this version of `fmtval`, no harm can occur. The user-supplied version effectively "knocks out" the added library function. Any function that can be knocked out this way can be safely added to the Standard C library.

header `<locale.h>` That's enough about `_Fmtval`, by any name. The remainder of this chapter deals with implementing the services required by the C Standard for the header `<locale.h>`.

function `localeconv` The easiest part of implementing `<locale.h>` is the function `localeconv`. All it must do is return a pointer to a structure describing (parts of) the current locale. That structure has type `struct lconv`. It is defined in `<locale.h>`. Figure 6.3 shows the file `locale.h` and Figure 6.4 shows the file `localeco.c`. (The latter name is chopped to eight letters because of file naming restrictions on various systems, as I explained on page 7.) Packed in with `localeconv` is the static data object of type `struct lconv` whose address the function returns. Note that the function `localeconv` has a masking macro defined in `<locale.h>`.

macro `_NULL` I chose once again to parametrize the header `<locale.h>` by including the internal header `<yvals.h>`. (See the original discussion of this header on page 53.) That permits an implementation to provide a definition of the macro `_NULL`, and hence of `NULL`, tailored to each implementation. (See the discussion of `NULL` in Chapter 11: `<stddef.h>`.) For now, I simply observe that a suitable definition of `_NULL`, in many cases, is:

```
#define _NULL    (void *)0
```

implementing `setlocale` The function `setlocale` has a number of tasks to perform. It must determine what locales to switch to, based on the category and name you specify when you call the function. It must find locales already in memory, or read in newly specified locales from a file. (I describe the general case,

Figure 6.3:
locale.h

```
/* locale.h standard header */
#ifndef _LOCALE
#define _LOCALE
#ifndef _YVALS
#include <yvals.h>
#endif
        /* macros */
#define NULL     _NULL
        /* locale codes */
#define LC_ALL      0
#define LC_COLLATE 1
#define LC_CTYPE    2
#define LC_MONETARY 3
#define LC_NUMERIC  4
#define LC_TIME     5
    /* ADD YOURS HERE */
#define _NCAT       6                          /* one more than last */
        /* type definitions */
struct lconv {
        /* controlled by LC_MONETARY */
    char *currency_symbol;
    char *int_curr_symbol;
    char *mon_decimal_point;
    char *mon_grouping;
    char *mon_thousands_sep;
    char *negative_sign;
    char *positive_sign;
    char frac_digits;
    char int_frac_digits;
    char n_cs_precedes;
    char n_sep_by_space;
    char n_sign_posn;
    char p_cs_precedes;
    char p_sep_by_space;
    char p_sign_posn;
        /* controlled by LC_NUMERIC */
    char *decimal_point;
    char *grouping;
    char *thousands_sep;
    };
        /* declarations */
struct lconv *localeconv(void);
char *setlocale(int, const char *);
extern struct lconv _Locale;
        /* macro overrides */
#define localeconv()    (&_Locale)
#endif                                                    □
```

of course. A minimal implementation can recognize only the "c" and ""
locales, which can be the same.) And it must return a name that it can later
use to restore the current locale.

Figure 6.4:
localeco.c

```
/* localeconv function */
#include <limits.h>
#include <locale.h>

        /* static data */
static char null[] = "";
struct lconv _Locale = {
        /* LC_MONETARY */
    null,                                    /* currency_symbol */
    null,                                    /* int_curr_symbol */
    null,                                /* mon_decimal_point */
    null,                                    /* mon_grouping */
    null,                                /* mon_thousands_sep */
    null,                                    /* negative_sign */
    null,                                    /* positive_sign */
    CHAR_MAX,                                    /* frac_digits */
    CHAR_MAX,                                /* int_frac_digits */
    CHAR_MAX,                                  /* n_cs_precedes */
    CHAR_MAX,                                 /* n_sep_by_space */
    CHAR_MAX,                                    /* n_sign_posn */
    CHAR_MAX,                                  /* p_cs_precedes */
    CHAR_MAX,                                 /* p_sep_by_space */
    CHAR_MAX,                                    /* p_sign_posn */
        /* LC_NUMERIC */
    ".",                                     /* decimal_point */
    null,                                        /* grouping */
    null};                                  /* thousands_sep */

struct lconv *(localeconv) (void)
    {                            /* get pointer to current locale */
    return (&_Locale);
    }                                                          □
```

mixed   The last task is one of the hardest. That's because you can construct a
locales *mixed locale,* one containing categories from various locales. For example,
you can write:

```
#include <locale.h>
.....
    char *s1, s2;

    setlocale(LC_ALL, "");
    s1 = setlocale(LC_CTYPE, "C");
    if ((s2 = malloc(strlen(s1) + 1)))
        strcpy(s2, s1);
```

The first call switches to the native locale — some locale preferred by the
local operating environment. The second call reverts one category to the
"C" locale. You must make a copy of the string pointed to by **s1** because
intervening calls to **setlocale** might alter it. If you later make the call:

```
    setlocale(LC_ALL, s2);
```

the locale reverts to its earlier mixed state.

locale   `setlocale` must contrive a name that it can later use to reconstruct an
names arbitrary mix of categories. The C Standard doesn't say how to do this, or
what the name looks like. It only says that an implementation must do it.

The scheme I settled on was to paste qualifiers on a locale name if it
contains mixed categories. Say, for example, that the base locale is `"USA"`,
which gives you American date formats and so on. An application adapts
the category `LC_MONETARY` to the locale `"acct"`, which has the special conventions of accounting. The name of this mixed locale is `"USA;mone-`
`tary:acct"`.

I chose semicolons to separate components of the mixed locale name.
Within a component, a colon separates a category name from its locale
name. The base locale has no category-name qualifier. When `setlocale`
constructs a name, it adds components only for categories that differ from
the base locale.

To implement `setlocale` and its descendants requires more than just the
subtree of functions shown in Figure 6.2. It requires macros, type definitions, and declarations for all the functions and data objects. That's what
header files are for. You want a central repository for all the information
shared by a collection of functions that cooperate.

That repository should *not* be `<locale.h>`, however. You need to include
in `<locale.h>` a declaration of `setlocale`, period. All the rest is under the
hood and should stay there. My practice is to include in a standard header
only those names that must be made visible. The header `<locale.h>` does
declare the data object `_Locale`. That's because the masking macro for
`localeconv` refers to `_Locale`. Nothing else need appear in that header, so
it does not.

header   I created the internal header file `"xlocale.h"` to hold everything else.
"xlocale.h" The remaining C source files in this chapter include this internal header,
plus standard headers for any other functions they use from the Standard
C library. `"xlocale.h"` in turn includes `<locale.h>`. It also includes a couple
of other internal header files. Most of the information in `"xlocale.h"`
doesn't make sense at this point. I therefore defer showing the entire file
until later in this chapter. Along the way, I show as needed the bits and
pieces that contribute to `"xlocale.h"`.

type   The first bit is the data structure that holds an entire locale. It includes,
_Linfo naturally enough, an instance of `struct lconv`. It includes pointers to the
tables used by functions declared in `<ctype.h>` — `_Ctype`, `_Tolower`, and
`_Toupper`. It also includes information from still other parts of the Standard
C library. It is, in short, a hodgepodge. `"xlocale.h"` defines a type called
`_Linfo` that looks like:

```
typedef struct _Linfo {
    const char *_Name;   /* must be first */
    struct _Linfo *_Next;
        /* controlled by LC_COLLATE */
    _Statab _Costate;
```

```
        /* controlled by LC_CTYPE */
    const short *_Ctype;
    const short *_Tolower;
    const short *_Toupper;
    unsigned char _Mbcurmax;
    _Statab _Mbstate;
    _Statab _Wcstate;
        /* controlled by LC_MONETARY and LC_NUMERIC */
    struct lconv _Lc;
        /* controlled by LC_TIME */
    _Tinfo _Times;
    } _Linfo;
```

Only one instance of this structure exists initially — the data object _Clocale defined in setlocal.c. _Clocale has a nonzero initializer only for the member _Name, which points at the string "C", the name of the locale. (That's where the name is presumed to come first in the structure.) The first call to setlocale copies all locale-specific information into this data object before the locale changes. A later call that reverts to the "C" locale can then simply copy out the pertinent information.

If _Getloc decides to read in a new locale (as described later in this chapter), the function allocates storage for a new instance of _Linfo and copies _Clocale into it. _Getloc then reads in any changes to the locale. If all changes are valid, the function adds the new locale to the linked list of alternate locales beginning with _Clocale._Next. A list member whose member _Next holds a null pointer terminates the list. (Note that _Linfo appears in this declaration both as a type name and a structure tag. Only a structure with a tag name can contain a member that points at another instance of the same structure.)

type
_Statab
The structure _Linfo contains several members of type _Statab. Several functions in this implementation of the Standard C library use *state tables* to define their behavior. That provides the maximum in flexibility with moderate performance. It also lets you specify the behavior of these functions in a locale using notation very similar to that for the <ctype.h> translation tables. Here are the affected functions:

- strcoll and strxfrm, declared in <string.h>, map a character string to another character string, to define a collating sequence.

- mbtowc and mbstowcs, declared in <stdlib.h>, map a multibyte string to a wide-character string.

- wctomb and wcstombs, declared in <stdlib.h>, map a wide-character string to a multibyte string.

header
"xstate.h"
I describe the behavior of each of these functions in later chapters. For now, I observe simply that the internal header "xstate.h" defines the type _Statab along with several useful macros. It also declares the various data objects of type _Statab. The internal header "xlocale.h" includes "xstate.h" to obtain the information needed to manipulate state tables when locales change. Figure 6.5 shows the header file xstate.h.

Figure 6.5:
xstate.h

```
/* xstate.h internal header */
            /* macros for finite state machines */
#define ST_CH        0x00ff
#define ST_STATE     0x0f00
#define ST_STOFF     8
#define ST_FOLD      0x8000
#define ST_INPUT     0x4000
#define ST_OUTPUT    0x2000
#define ST_ROTATE    0x1000
#define _NSTATE      16
            /* type definitions */
typedef struct {
    const unsigned short *_Tab[_NSTATE];
    } _Statab;
        /* declarations */
extern _Statab _Costate, _Mbstate, _Wcstate;                      □
```

type
_Tinfo   Similarly, the functions declared in <time.h> have locale-specific behavior. The structure type _Tinfo contains several members that point to null-terminated strings. These strings control how the time functions format and translate dates and times.

header
"xtinfo.h"   The internal header "xtinfo.h" defines the type _Tinfo. It also declares the data object _Times, of type _Tinfo, that holds the current information on times. The internal header "xlocale.h" also includes "xtinfo.h" to obtain the information needed to manipulate time information when locales change. Figure 6.6 shows the header file xtinfo.h.

Now you can appreciate what goes on in setlocale. Figure 6.7 shows the file setlocal.c. Much of its logic is concerned with parsing a name to determine which locale to use for each category. Another big chunk of logic builds a name that setlocale can later digest. Everything else is small potatoes by comparison.

setlocale contains the code that copies information into the "c" locale on the first attempt to change a locale. I adopted that ruse to avoid a nasty snowball effect. It's easy enough to pile all the various locale-specific tables into one structure. Do so, however, and you get the whole snowball

Figure 6.6:
xtinfo.h

```
/* xtinfo.h internal header */

            /* type definitions */
typedef struct {
    const char *_Ampm;
    const char *_Days;
    const char *_Formats;
    const char *_Isdst;
    const char *_Months;
    const char *_Tzone;
    } _Tinfo;
        /* declarations */
extern _Tinfo _Times;                                              □
```

regardless of how little of it you use. I felt it was better to have **setlocale**
do a bit more work to avoid this problem. You don't want to drag in ten
kilobytes of code when you use only the function **isspace**.

function   The function **_Getloc** determines whether a locale corresponding to a
_Getloc given category exists in memory. If it does not, **_Getloc** looks for it by
reading a *locale file*. I describe reading this file in detail below. Figure 6.8
shows the file **xgetloc.c**, which defines this function.

function   The C source file **xgetloc.c** also defines the function **_Skip**. Several
_Skip functions that read the locale file call **_Skip** to skip past a character (other
than the null character) and any white-space that follows. Here, white-
space consists of spaces and horizontal tabs. Using **_Skip** religiously en-
forces a uniform definition for white-space in locale files. It also simplifies
much of the code that follows.

function   Figure 6.9 shows the source file **xdefloc.c**. It defines the function **_De-**
_Defloc **floc** that determines the name of the native locale. To determine that name,
I chose to use the environment variable **"LOCALE"**. That's akin to using the
environment variable **"TZ"** to determine what time zone you're in. **_Defloc**
inspects the environment variable **LOCALE** at most once during program
execution.

function   Figure 6.10 shows the file **xsetloc.c**. It defines the function **_Setloc**,
_Setloc which actually copies new information out to the various bits of static data
affected by changes in the locale. (Note that it also performs a modicum of
checking for the more critical values.) A call to **setlocale** thus drags in all
this stuff. I don't know how to avoid this particular snowball. At least you
can avoid it if you leave locales alone.

state   To complete the record, I show here the initial state tables, since both
tables **setlocale** and **_Setloc** manipulate them. (The time information **_Times**
lives in the file **asctime.c**, shown on page 437.) Figure 6.11 shows the file
xstate.c. Don't try to understand it in any detail. For now, I tell you only
that the single state table shown is common to all functions that use state
tables. It is cleverly contrived to produce useful, if simple, results for all
these functions. It also makes a good starting point for state tables that you
may choose to define in a locale file.

What I have presented so far is all the basic machinery you need to
support locales. It is enough to let you build additional locales directly into
the library. Just add static declarations of type **struct lconv** and initialize
them as you see fit. Be sure to change **_Clocale._Next** to point at the list
you add.

locale   The real fun of locales, however, is the prospect of defining an open-
files ended set. To do that, you need to be able to specify a locale without altering
C code. That takes all the remaining machinery incidated in Figure 6.2 that
I have yet to describe. Before I describe that machinery, I must describe
locale files.

Figure 6.7:
setlocal.c
Part 1

```c
/* setlocale function */
#include <ctype.h>
#include <string.h>
#include "xlocale.h"

#if _NCAT != 6
#error WRONG NUMBER OF CATEGORIES
#endif
        /* static data */
_Linfo _Clocale = {"C"};
static char *curname = "C";
static char namalloc = 0;                        /* curname allocated */
static const char * const nmcats[_NCAT] = {
    NULL, "collate:", "ctype:", "monetary:",
    "numeric:", "time:"};
static _Linfo *pcats[_NCAT] = {
    &_Clocale, &_Clocale, &_Clocale, &_Clocale,
    &_Clocale, &_Clocale};

char *(setlocale)(int cat, const char *lname)
    {                                            /* set new locale */
    size_t i;

    if (cat < 0 || _NCAT <= cat)
        return (NULL);                           /* bad category */
    if (lname == NULL)
        return (curname);
    if (lname[0] == '\0')
        lname = _Defloc();
    if (_Clocale._Costate._Tab[0] == NULL)
        {                                        /* fill in "C" locale */
        _Clocale._Costate = _Costate;
        _Clocale._Ctype = _Ctype;
        _Clocale._Tolower = _Tolower;
        _Clocale._Toupper = _Toupper;
        _Clocale._Mbcurmax = _Mbcurmax;
        _Clocale._Mbstate = _Mbstate;
        _Clocale._Wcstate = _Wcstate;
        _Clocale._Lc = _Locale;
        _Clocale._Times = _Times;
        }
    {                                            /* set categories */
    _Linfo *p;
    int changed = 0;

    if (cat != LC_ALL)
        {                                        /* set a single category */
        if ((p = _Getloc(nmcats[cat], lname)) == NULL)
            return (NULL);
        if (p != pcats[cat])
            pcats[cat] = _Setloc(cat, p), changed = 1;
        }
    else
        {                                        /* set all categories */
```

```
        for (i = 0; ++i < _NCAT; )
            {                                       /* set a category */
            if ((p = _Getloc(nmcats[i], lname)) == NULL)
                {                       /* revert all on any failure */
                setlocale(LC_ALL, curname);
                return (NULL);
                }
            if (p != pcats[i])
                pcats[i] = _Setloc(i, p), changed = 1;
            }
        if ((p = _Getloc("", lname)) != NULL)
            pcats[0] = p;           /* set only if LC_ALL component */
        }
    if (changed)
        {                                           /* rebuild curname */
        char *s;
        size_t n;
        size_t len = strlen(pcats[0]->_Name);

        for (i = 0, n = 0; ++i < _NCAT; )
            if (pcats[i] != pcats[0])
                {                       /* count a changed subcategory */
                len += strlen(nmcats[i])
                    + strlen(pcats[i]->_Name) + 1;
                ++n;
                }
        if (n == 1)
            {                                       /* uniform locale */
            if (namalloc)
                free(curname);
            curname = (char *)pcats[1]->_Name, namalloc = 0;
            }
        else if ((s = malloc(len + 1)) == NULL)
            {                       /* may be rash to try to roll back */
            setlocale(LC_ALL, curname);
            return (NULL);
            }
        else
            {                                       /* build complex name */
            if (namalloc)
                free(curname);
            curname = s, namalloc = 1;
            s += strlen(strcpy(s, pcats[0]->_Name));
            for (i = 0; ++i < _NCAT; )
                if (pcats[i] != pcats[0])
                    {                               /* add a component */
                    *s = ';';
                    s += strlen(strcpy(s, nmcats[i]));
                    s += strlen(strcpy(s, pcats[i]->_Name));
                    }
            }
        }
    return (curname);
    }
```

□

```c
/* _Getloc and _Skip functions */
#include <stdio.h>
#include <stdlib.h>
#include <string.h>
#include "xlocale.h"

const char *_Skip(const char *s)
    {                               /* skip next char plus white-space */
    return (*s == '\0' ? s : s + 1 + strspn(s + 1, " \t"));
    }

_Linfo *_Getloc(const char *nmcat, const char *lname)
    {                   /* get locale pointer, given category and name */
    const char *ns, *s;
    size_t nl;
    _Linfo *p;

    {                               /* find category component of name */
    size_t n;

    for (ns = NULL, s = lname; ; s += n + 1)
        {                           /* look for exact match or LC_ALL */
        if (s[n = strcspn(s, ":;")] == '\0' || s[n] == ';')
            {                       /* memorize first LC_ALL */
            if (ns == NULL)
                ns = s, nl = n;
            if (s[n] == '\0')
                break;
            }
        else if (memcmp(nmcat, s, ++n) == 0)
            {                       /* found exact category match */
            ns = s + n, nl = strcspn(ns, ";");
            break;
            }
        else if (s[n += strcspn(s + n, ";")] == '\0')
            break;
        }
    if (ns == NULL)
        return (NULL);                          /* invalid name */
    }
    for (p = &_Clocale; p; p = p->_Next)
        if (memcmp(p->_Name, ns, nl) == 0
            && p->_Name[nl] == '\0')
            return (p);
    {                               /* look for locale in file */
    char buf[MAXLIN], *s1;
    FILE *lf;
    _Locitem *q;
    static char *locfile;                       /* locale file name */

    if (locfile)
        ;
    else if ((s = getenv("LOCFILE")) == NULL
        || ((locfile = malloc(strlen(s) + 1))) == NULL)
        return (NULL);
```

```
    else
        strcpy(locfile, s);
    if ((lf = fopen(locfile, "r")) == NULL)
        return (NULL);
    while ((q = _Readloc(lf, buf, &s)) != NULL)
        if (q->_Code == L_NAME
            && memcmp(s, ns, nl) == 0
            && *_Skip(s + nl - 1) == '\0')
            break;
    if (q == NULL)
        p = NULL;
    else if ((p = malloc(sizeof (_Linfo))) == NULL)
        ;
    else if ((s1 = malloc(nl + 1)) == NULL)
        free(p), p = NULL;
    else
        {                                             /* build locale */
        *p = _Clocale;
        p->_Name = memcpy(s1, ns, nl);
        s1[nl] = '\0';
        if (_Makeloc(lf, buf, p))
            p->_Next = _Clocale._Next, _Clocale._Next = p;
        else
            {                       /* parsing error reading locale file */
            fputs(buf, stderr);
            fputs("\n-- invalid locale file line\n", stderr);
            _Freeloc(p);
            free(p), p = NULL;
            }
        }
    fclose(lf);
    return (p);
    }
}
```                                                                   □

```
/* _Defloc function */
#include <stdlib.h>
#include <string.h>
#include "xlocale.h"

const char *_Defloc(void)
    {                                     /* find name of default locale */
    char *s;
    static char *defname = NULL;

    if (defname)
        ;
    else if ((s = getenv("LOCALE")) != NULL
        && (defname = malloc(strlen(s) + 1)) != NULL)
        strcpy(defname, s);
    else
        defname = "C";
    return (defname);
    }
```                                                                   □

Figure 6.10:
xsetloc.c

```
/* _Setloc function */
#include <ctype.h>
#include <limits.h>
#include "xlocale.h"

_Linfo *_Setloc(int cat, _Linfo *p)
    {                                       /* set category for locale */
    switch (cat)
        {                                   /* set a category */
    case LC_COLLATE:
        _Costate = p->_Costate;
        break;
    case LC_CTYPE:
        _Ctype = p->_Ctype;
        _Tolower = p->_Tolower;
        _Toupper = p->_Toupper;
        _Mbcurmax = p->_Mbcurmax <= MB_LEN_MAX
            ? p->_Mbcurmax : MB_LEN_MAX;
        _Mbstate = p->_Mbstate;
        _Wcstate = p->_Wcstate;
        break;
    case LC_MONETARY:
        _Locale.currency_symbol = p->_Lc.currency_symbol;
        _Locale.int_curr_symbol = p->_Lc.int_curr_symbol;
        _Locale.mon_decimal_point = p->_Lc.mon_decimal_point;
        _Locale.mon_grouping = p->_Lc.mon_grouping;
        _Locale.mon_thousands_sep = p->_Lc.mon_thousands_sep;
        _Locale.negative_sign = p->_Lc.negative_sign;
        _Locale.positive_sign = p->_Lc.positive_sign;
        _Locale.frac_digits = p->_Lc.frac_digits;
        _Locale.int_frac_digits = p->_Lc.int_frac_digits;
        _Locale.n_cs_precedes = p->_Lc.n_cs_precedes;
        _Locale.n_sep_by_space = p->_Lc.n_sep_by_space;
        _Locale.n_sign_posn = p->_Lc.n_sign_posn;
        _Locale.p_cs_precedes = p->_Lc.p_cs_precedes;
        _Locale.p_sep_by_space = p->_Lc.p_sep_by_space;
        _Locale.p_sign_posn = p->_Lc.p_sign_posn;
        break;
    case LC_NUMERIC:
        _Locale.decimal_point = p->_Lc.decimal_point[0] != '\0'
            ? p->_Lc.decimal_point : ".";
        _Locale.grouping = p->_Lc.grouping;
        _Locale.thousands_sep = p->_Lc.thousands_sep;
        break;
    case LC_TIME:
        _Times = p->_Times;
        break;
        }
    return (p);
    }
```
□

Figure 6.11:
xstate.c

```c
/* _Costate, _Mbstate, and _Wcstate generic tables */
#include <limits.h>
#include "xlocale.h"
#if UCHAR_MAX != 255
#error WRONG STATE TABLE
#endif

        /* macros */
#define X   (ST_FOLD|ST_OUTPUT|ST_INPUT)

        /* static data */
static const unsigned short tab0[257] = {0,      /* alloc flag */
X|0x00, X|0x01, X|0x02, X|0x03, X|0x04, X|0x05, X|0x06, X|0x07,
X|0x08, X|0x09, X|0x0a, X|0x0b, X|0x0c, X|0x0d, X|0x0e, X|0x0f,
X|0x10, X|0x11, X|0x12, X|0x13, X|0x14, X|0x15, X|0x16, X|0x17,
X|0x18, X|0x19, X|0x1a, X|0x1b, X|0x1c, X|0x1d, X|0x1e, X|0x1f,
X|0x20, X|0x21, X|0x22, X|0x23, X|0x24, X|0x25, X|0x26, X|0x27,
X|0x28, X|0x29, X|0x2a, X|0x2b, X|0x2c, X|0x2d, X|0x2e, X|0x2f,
X|0x30, X|0x31, X|0x32, X|0x33, X|0x34, X|0x35, X|0x36, X|0x37,
X|0x38, X|0x39, X|0x3a, X|0x3b, X|0x3c, X|0x3d, X|0x3e, X|0x3f,
X|0x40, X|0x41, X|0x42, X|0x43, X|0x44, X|0x45, X|0x46, X|0x47,
X|0x48, X|0x49, X|0x4a, X|0x4b, X|0x4c, X|0x4d, X|0x4e, X|0x4f,
X|0x50, X|0x51, X|0x52, X|0x53, X|0x54, X|0x55, X|0x56, X|0x57,
X|0x58, X|0x59, X|0x5a, X|0x5b, X|0x5c, X|0x5d, X|0x5e, X|0x5f,
X|0x60, X|0x61, X|0x62, X|0x63, X|0x64, X|0x65, X|0x66, X|0x67,
X|0x68, X|0x69, X|0x6a, X|0x6b, X|0x6c, X|0x6d, X|0x6e, X|0x6f,
X|0x70, X|0x71, X|0x72, X|0x73, X|0x74, X|0x75, X|0x76, X|0x77,
X|0x78, X|0x79, X|0x7a, X|0x7b, X|0x7c, X|0x7d, X|0x7e, X|0x7f,

X|0x80, X|0x81, X|0x82, X|0x83, X|0x84, X|0x85, X|0x86, X|0x87,
X|0x88, X|0x89, X|0x8a, X|0x8b, X|0x8c, X|0x8d, X|0x8e, X|0x8f,
X|0x90, X|0x91, X|0x92, X|0x93, X|0x94, X|0x95, X|0x96, X|0x97,
X|0x98, X|0x99, X|0x9a, X|0x9b, X|0x9c, X|0x9d, X|0x9e, X|0x9f,
X|0xa0, X|0xa1, X|0xa2, X|0xa3, X|0xa4, X|0xa5, X|0xa6, X|0xa7,
X|0xa8, X|0xa9, X|0xaa, X|0xab, X|0xac, X|0xad, X|0xae, X|0xaf,
X|0xb0, X|0xb1, X|0xb2, X|0xb3, X|0xb4, X|0xb5, X|0xb6, X|0xb7,
X|0xb8, X|0xb9, X|0xba, X|0xbb, X|0xbc, X|0xbd, X|0xbe, X|0xbf,
X|0xc0, X|0xc1, X|0xc2, X|0xc3, X|0xc4, X|0xc5, X|0xc6, X|0xc7,
X|0xc8, X|0xc9, X|0xca, X|0xcb, X|0xcc, X|0xcd, X|0xce, X|0xcf,
X|0xd0, X|0xd1, X|0xd2, X|0xd3, X|0xd4, X|0xd5, X|0xd6, X|0xd7,
X|0xd8, X|0xd9, X|0xda, X|0xdb, X|0xdc, X|0xdd, X|0xde, X|0xdf,
X|0xe0, X|0xe1, X|0xe2, X|0xe3, X|0xe4, X|0xe5, X|0xe6, X|0xe7,
X|0xe8, X|0xe9, X|0xea, X|0xeb, X|0xec, X|0xed, X|0xee, X|0xef,
X|0xf0, X|0xf1, X|0xf2, X|0xf3, X|0xf4, X|0xf5, X|0xf6, X|0xf7,
X|0xf8, X|0xf9, X|0xfa, X|0xfb, X|0xfc, X|0xfd, X|0xfe, X|0xff,
    };

char _Mbcurmax = 1;

_Statab _Costate = {&tab0[1]};
_Statab _Mbstate = {&tab0[1]};
_Statab _Wcstate = {&tab0[1]};
```

A locale should be easy to define. All sorts of people might have occasion to define part or all of a locale. Different groups may want to:

- print dates and times in the local language, using the local conventions
- change the decimal point character used for reading, converting, and writing floating-point values
- specify the local currency format and symbols
- specify peculiar collating sequences
- add letters, punctuation, or control characters to the character classes defined by the functions declared in `<ctype.h>`
- alter the encodings of multibyte characters and wide characters

I list these changes roughly in order of increasing sophistication. Almost anybody might want to change month and weekday names to a different language. A few might undertake to define a special collating sequence. Only the bravest would consider changing to a new multibyte-character encoding. (It might not agree with the string literals and character constants produced by the translator, for one thing.) Nevertheless, none of these operations should require a change in the Standard C library to pull off.

The goal, therefore, is to contrive a way that ordinary citizens can define a new locale and introduce it to a C program at runtime. The program must, of course, be one that calls `setlocale` under some circumstances. And the program must make use of the information altered by such a call. Given those obvious prerequisites, the Standard C library should assist program and user in agreeing on locale specifications.

The approach I take is to introduce two environment variables and a file format. The environment variables are:

"LOCALE" ■ `"LOCALE"` (described on page 101), which specifies the name of the native locale that is selected on a call such as `setlocale(LC_ALL, "")`

"LOCFILE" ■ `"LOCFILE"`, which specifies the name of the locale file to use if `setlocale` encounters a locale name that is not already represented in memory

The file format specifies how you prepare the text file so that it defines all the additional locales you want to add.

A program called **xxx** might, for example, begin by executing the call `setlocale(LC_ALL, "")` as above. Under MS-DOS, you can invoke it from a batch file that looks like:

```
set LOCFILE c:\locales\mylocs.loc
set LOCALE USA
xxx
```

That causes the program **xxx** to read the file `c:\locales\mylocs.loc` in search of a locale named `"USA"`. Assuming the program can find that locale and successfully read it in, the program **xxx** then executes with its behavior adapted to the `"USA"` locale. Change `"USA"` to `"France"` in the batch script and the program searches out a different locale in the same file. Or you can change the file name specified by `"LOCFILE"` and always ask for the generic `"native"` locale. Both are sensible ways to tailor the native locale.

A more sophisticated program might use more than just the native locale. It could determine categories and the names of locales in various ways, then oblige `setlocale` to chase them down in the locale file. Conceivably, it could even rewrite the contents of the locale file while it is running, to build new locales on the fly. In any of these case, you certainly want to defer binding locales to programs as late as possible.

locale
file
formats
A locale consists of an assortment of data types. Some are numeric values, some are strings, and some are tables of varying formats. Each entity in a locale needs a distinct name. You use these names when you write the locale file to specify which entities you wish to redefine. For the members of `struct lconv`, I use the member name as the entity name within the locale file. In other cases, I had to invent entity names.

A locale file is organized into a sequence of text lines. You begin the definition of the `"USA"` locale, for example, with the line:

```
LOCALE  USA
```

Each line that follows begins with a keyword from a predefined list. Use **NOTE** to begin a comment and **SET** to assign a value to an uppercase letter, as in:

```
NOTE    The following sets D(elta) to 'a'-'A"
SET     D    'a' - 'A'
```

You can then use **D** as a term in an expression.

If the keyword is an entity name, you specify its value on the remainder of the line. Some examples are:

```
currency_symbol    $
int_curr_symbol    "USD "
frac_digits        2
```

The quotes around a string value are optional. You need them only if you want to include a space as part of the string. You can write a fairly ornate expression wherever a numeric value is required. I describe expressions in detail on page 113.

The initial values in each new locale match those in the `"C"` locale. That typically saves a lot of typing. All you really have to specify is what you want changed from the `"C"` locale. Write more only if you want more thorough documentation of a locale.

numeric
values
You need to specify *numeric values* for some members of `struct lconv`. These include the category `LC_MONETARY` information:

```
frac_digits
int_frac_digits
n_cs_precedes
n_sep_by_spaces
n_sign_posn
p_cs_precedes
p_sep_by_spaces
p_sign_posn
```

Each of these occupies a *char* member. A value of **CHAR_MAX**, defined in `<limits.h>`, indicates that no meaningful value is provided.

The value of the macro **MB_CUR_MAX**, defined in `<locale.h>`, can change with the category **LC_CTYPE**. I adopted the entity name:

```
mb_cur_max
```

for the *char* data object that holds the value of this macro.

string You need to specify *strings* for some members of **struct lconv**. These
values include the category **LC_MONETARY** information:

```
currency_symbol
int_curr_symbol
mon_decimal_point
mon_thousands_sep
negative_sign
positive_sign
```

and the category **LC_NUMERIC** information:

```
decimal_point
thousands_sep
```

Note, by the way, that the C Standard assumes that **mon_decimal_point**, **mon_thousands_sep**, **decimal_point**, and **thousands_sep** all are strings of length one. Functions in this implementation use the first character of each of these strings, whatever it may be.

numeric You need to specify *numeric strings* for some members of **struct lconv**.
strings These include:

```
grouping          (LC_NUMERIC)
mon_grouping      (LC_MONETARY)
```

The value of each character specifies how many characters to group as you move to the left away from the decimal point. A value of zero terminates the string and causes the last grouping value to be repeated indefinitely. A value of **CHAR_MAX** terminates the string and specifies no additional grouping. To group digits by two, by five, and then by threes, for example, you want to create the string "\2\5\3". In the locale file, however, you write:

```
mon_grouping     253
```

For numeric strings, each digit is replaced by its numeric value.

I introduced a handful of additional strings to specify information for the category **LC_TIME**. (See the type **_Tinfo** defined in Figure 6.6.) Each of these strings is divided into fields. I couldn't imagine any character that would serve universally as a field delimiter. So I adopted the convention that the first character of the string delimits the start of the first field. That character also delimits the start of each subsequent field. That lets you choose a character that doesn't collide with any characters in the fields.

As an example, the **am_pm** entity specifies what the function **strftime**, declared in `<time.h>` prints for the AM/PM indicator. A common definition for this string is :AM:PM. A colon delimits the start of each field.

Here are the category LC_TIME entity names with some reasonable string values for an English-speaking country. They mostly speak for themselves:

```
  am_pm            :AM:PM
  days             :Sun:Sunday:Mon:Monday:Tue:Tuesday\
Wed:Wednesday:Thu:Thursday:Fri:Friday:Sat:Saturday
  dst_rules        :032402:102702
  time_formats     "|%b %d %H:%M:%S %Y|%b %d %Y|%H:%M:%S"
  months           :Jan:January:Feb:February:Mar:March\
Apr:April:May:May:Jun:June\
Jul:July:Aug:August:Sep:September\
Oct:October:Nov:November:Dec:December
  time_zone        :EST:EDT:+0300
```

Note that you can continue a line by ending it with a backslash. Including all continuations, a line can have up to 255 characters.

The string time_formats specifies the formats used by strftime to generate locale-specific date and time (%c), date (%x) and time(%X). I discuss these formats further in Chapter 15: `<time.h>`.

"TIMEZONE" The third field of time_zone counts *minutes* from UTC (Greenwich Mean
"TZ" Time), not hours. That allows for the various time zones around the world that are not an integral number of hours away from UTC. If this string is empty, the time functions look for a replacement string in the environment variable **"TIMEZONE"**. (You can append a similar replacement for dst_rules.) If that variable is also absent, the functions then look for the widely-used environment variable **"TZ"**. That string takes the form EST05EDT, where the number in the middle counts hours West of UTC.

The string dst_rules is even more ornate. It takes one of two general forms:

```
(YY)MMDDHH+W
(YY)MMDDHH-W
```

Daylight Here, YY in parentheses is the number of years since 1900, MM is the month
Savings number, DD is the day of the month, W is the number of days past Sunday,
Time and HH is the hour number in a 24-hour day. +W advances to the next such day of the week on or after the date MMDD in the year in question. -W backs up to the next previous such day of the week before the specified date. You can omit the fields that specify year, hour, and day of the week.

The fairly simple example above calls for Daylight Savings Time to begin on 24 March (MMDD = 0324) at 02:00 (HH = 02) and to end on 27 October at the same time. To switch on the last Sundays in March and October each year since 1990, write : (1990)040102-0:100102-0. (Years before 1990 don't correct for Daylight Savings Time, by this set of rules.)

If you live below the Equator, the year *begins* in Daylight Savings Time. You can capture that nicely by adding a third reversal field, as in :0101:030202:100202. You can also write an arbitrary number of year rules going back in time. Qualify the first rule of each set with a starting year (YY) for the rule to take effect. You could thus capture the entire history of law governing Daylight Savings Time in a given state or country, if you chose.

The functions declared in `<ctype.h>` all are organized around translation tables. (See Chapter 2: `<ctype.h>`.) Each is an array of 257 *shorts* that accepts subscripts in the interval [–1, 255]. In the locale file, you cannot alter the contents of element –1, which translates the value of the macro **EOF**, defined in `<stdio.h>`. The entity names for these tables are:

```
ctype
tolower
toupper
```

You initialize these tables an element at a time or a subrange at a time. Here, for example, is a complete specification for the `tolower` table, using ASCII characters plus the Swedish '**Å**':

```
tolower[0 : 255]          $@
tolower['A' : 'Z']        $$ + 'a' - 'A'
tolower['Å' ]             'å'
```

The special term `$@` is the value of the index for each element in the subrange. (Read the term as "where it's at.") The special term `$$` is the value of the previous contents of the table element. (Read the term as "what its value is.") Note that you can write a simple (single-character) character constant to specify its code value, and that you can add and subtract a sequence of terms. The first two lines are, of course, optional. You inherit them from the `"c"` locale.

state   Several pairs of functions in this implementation use state tables to
tables define their behavior, as I discussed on page 99. You can specify up to 16 state tables for each of the three entity names:

```
collate
mbtowc
wctomb
```

I describe these tables in greater detail in conjunction with the functions that use them. For now, I show only a simple example. Here is how you can write the specification for the simple state table in the file `xstate.c`. (See Figure 6.11.) It makes the functions `mbtowc` and `mbstowcs`, declared in `<stdlib.h>`, perform a one-to-one mapping between multibyte and wide characters:

```
mb_cur_max               1
mbtowc[0, 0:$#]          $@ $F $I $O $O
```

The first line gives the macro **MB_CUR_MAX**, defined in `<stdlib.h>`, the value 1. No multibyte sequence requires more than one character. The second line defines all elements of state table zero for `mbtowc` and `mbstowcs`. It tells the functions to:

- *fold* the translation value into the accumulated value (`$F`)
- with the input code *mapped* to itself (`$@`)
- consume the *input* (`$I`)
- write the accumulated value as the *output* (`$O`)

The successor state is state zero (`$O`). Translation ends, in this case, when a zero input code produces a zero wide character.

expressions   That's the list of entities you can specify in a locale. Now you can understand why certain funny terms can appear in expressions. An expression itself is simply a sequence of terms that get added together. The last example above shows that you can add terms simply by writing them one after the other. The plus signs are accepted in front of terms purely as a courtesy so that expressions read better.

terms   You can write lots of different terms:

- Decimal, octal, and hexadecimal numbers follow the usual rules of C constants. The sequences 10, 012, and 0xA all represent the decimal value ten.

- A plus sign before a term leaves its value unchanged. A minus sign negates the term.

- Single quotes around a character yield the value of the character, just as for a character constant in a C source file. (No escape sequences, such as '\012', are permitted, however.)

- An uppercase letter has the value last assigned by a SET. All such variables are set to zero at program startup.

$x   In addition to these terms, a dollar sign is the first character of a
terms two-character name that has a special meaning, as outlined below. Here are the special terms signalled by a leading dollar sign:

- $$ — the current contents of a table element.

- $@ — the index of a table element. $$ and $@, if present, must precede any other terms in an expression.

- $^ — the value of the macro CHAR_MAX.

- $# — the value of the macro UCHAR_MAX

- [$a $b $f $n $r $t $v] — the values of the character escape sequences, in order, ['\a' '\b' '\f' '\n' '\r' '\t' '\v'].

- [$A $C $D $H $L $M $P $S $U $W] — the character-classification bits used in the table ctype. These specify, in order: extra alphabetics, extra control characters, digits, hexadecimal digits, lowercase letters, motion-control characters, punctuation, space characters, uppercase letters, and extra white-space characters. (See the file ctype.h on page 37 for definitions of the corresponding macros.)

- [$0 $1 $2 $3 $4 $5 $6 $7] — the successor states 0 through 7 in a state-table element. (No symbols are provided for successor states 8 through 15. Write $7+$1 for state 8, and so forth.)

- [$F $I $O $R] — the command bits used in a state-table element. These specify, in order: *fold* translated value into the accumulated value, consume *input*, produce *output*, and *reverse* bytes in the accumulated value. (See the file xstate.h in Figure 6.5 for definitions of the corresponding macros.)

With these special terms, you can write expressions in locale files that don't depend on implementation-specific code values.

"USA"   I conclude with an example of a complete locale. Here is the **"USA"** locale
locale with sensible values for all the fields in **struct lconv**. It makes no changes
to the collating sequence or multibyte encoding specified in the **"C"** locale:

```
LOCALE                  USA
currency_symbol         "$"
decimal_point           "."
grouping                "3"
int_curr_symbol         "USD "
mon_decimal_point       "."
mon_grouping            "3"
mon_thousands_sep       ","
negative_sign           "-"
positive_sign           "+"
thousands_sep           ","
frac_digits             2
int_frac_digits         2
n_cs_precedes           1
n_sep_by_space          0
n_sign_posn             4
p_cs_precedes           1
p_sep_by_space          0
p_sign_posn             4
LOCALE                  end
```

The last line delimits the end of the locale. You need such a line only at the
end of the last locale in the locale file (but it is always permissible). To
improve checking, the functions that read the locale file report an error if
end-of-file occurs part way through a locale specification.

function   Now you are in a position to understand the remaining functions that
_Getloc implement **<locale.h>**. Recall that **_Getloc** (Figure 6.8) first attempts to find
revisited a locale in memory. If that fails, it then attempts to open the locale file and
scan it for the start of the desired locale. It looks only at lines in the locale
file that begin with the keyword **LOCALE**. **_Getloc** calls **_Readloc** to read each
line and identify its keyword.

Should **_Getloc** find such a line with the desired name following the
keyword, the function allocates storage for the new locale. It copies the
contents of **_Clocale**, then changes to the new name. The function **_Makeloc**
reads the remainder of the information for the locale and alters its storage
accordingly. If **_Makeloc** reports success, **_Getloc** adds the new locale to the
list beginning at **_Clocale._Next**. If **_Makeloc** reports failure, **_Getloc** writes
an error message to the standard error stream, discards any allocated
storage, and reports that it could not find the locale. Part of the error
message is the locale-file line that caused the offense.

As a rule, it is bad practice for library functions to write such error
messages. They preempt the programmer's right to decide how best to
recover from an error. I found in this case, however, that the messages are
invaluable. A malformed locale specification is hard to debug if **setlocale**
reads only part of it or quietly refuses to accept it at all. The library is already
indulging in a complex operation that involves opening and reading a file,

perhaps repeatedly — all in response to what looks to the programmer like a simple function call. Writing to the standard error stream is not such a major addition, in that light. (Still, you may choose to omit the write in certain environments.)

function Figure 6.12 shows the file `xreadloc.c`. It defines the function `_Readloc`
_Readloc that reads the locale file a line at a time. The caller provides a buffer `buf` of length `MAXLIN` to hold the line. (The header `"xlocale.h"` defines the macro `MAXLIN` as 256.) Here is where a line that ends with a backslash gets pasted onto the line that follows. Here is also where keywords are parsed, identified, and peeled off the beginning of each line.

`_Readloc` uses the expression `(n = strspn(s, kc))` to determine the extent of the keyword on an input line. The expression stores in `n` the length

Figure 6.12:
xreadloc.c

```
/* _Readloc function */
#include <stdio.h>
#include <string.h>
#include "xlocale.h"

        /* static data */
static const char kc[] =                        /* keyword chars */
    "_abcdefghijklmnopqrstuvwxyzABCDEFGHIJKLMNOPQRSTUVWXYZ";

_Locitem *_Readloc(FILE *lf, char *buf, const char **ps)
    {                               /*  get a line from locale file */
    for (; ; )
        {                           /* loop until EOF or full line */
        size_t n;

        for (buf[0] = ' ', n = 1; ; n -= 2)
            if (fgets(buf + n, MAXLIN - n, lf) == NULL
                || buf[(n += strlen(buf + n)) - 1] != '\n')
                return (NULL);          /* EOF or line too long */
            else if (n <= 1 || buf[n - 2] != '\\')
                break;                  /* continue only if ends in \ */
        buf[n - 1] = '\0';                  /* overwrite newline */
        {                               /* look for keyword on line */
        const char *s = _Skip(buf);
        _Locitem *q;

        if (0 < (n = strspn(s, kc)))
            for (q = _Loctab; q->_Name; ++q)
                if (strncmp(q->_Name, s, n) == 0
                    && strlen(q->_Name) == n)
                    {                           /* found a match */
                    *ps = _Skip(s + n - 1);
                    return (q);
                    }
        return (NULL);              /* unknown or missing keyword */
        }
        }
    }
```

of the longest sequence of characters beginning at **s** all of which are in the string **kc**. I chose not to use the character-classification functions from `<ctype.h>`, such as `isalpha`, because they can vary among locales.

type `_Readloc` stores at ***ps** a pointer to the first character on the line following
_Locitem the keyword and any white-space. The function also returns a pointer to a table entry containing information on the keyword that it recognizes. The header `"xlocale.h"` defines the type `_Locitem` as:

```
typedef struct {
    const char *_Name;
    size_t _Offset;
    enum {
        L_GSTRING, L_NAME, L_NOTE, L_SET,
        L_STATE, L_STRING, L_TABLE, L_VALUE;
        } _Code;
    } _Locitem;
```

(The scalar type `size_t` is the integer type of the result of operator `sizeof`. Several standard headers define this type. I discuss it at length in Chapter 11: `<stddef.h>`.) The member `_Name` points at the name of the keyword. `_Offset` holds the offset into the structure `_Linfo` of the member corresponding to the keyword (if any). And `_Code` holds one of the enumerated values that characterize each instance of `_Locitem`.

data object `_Readloc` scans the data object `_Loctab`, an array of `_Locitem`, to find the
_Loctab entry that matches the keyword on each line from the locale file. Figure 6.13 shows the file `xloctab.c`, which defines `_Loctab`. It uses the macro `offsetof`, defined in `<stddef.h>`, to determine the offsets into the structure `_Linfo`. I introduce the macro `OFF` here simply to shorten the lines in this C source file.

function One other function uses `_Loctab`. Figure 6.14 shows the file `xfreeloc.c`.
_Freeloc It defines the function `_Freeloc`. If `_Makeloc` encounters an invalid line while reading the locale file, it reports failure back to `_Getloc`. That function calls `_Freeloc` to free any storage allocated for the new locale (including its name), then frees the `_Linfo` data object allocated for the new locale. (It would probably be acceptable to abandon such storage — requesting a flawed locale should be a rare event — but it is tidier to reclaim heap space that is no longer needed.) `_Freeloc` scans `_Loctab` for any elements that correspond to members you can alter in `_Linfo` by writing lines in the locale file. For each such element of `_Loctab`, `_Freeloc` determines whether any storage was allocated for the new locale. To do so takes a bit of work.

Remember that each new locale begins life as a carbon copy of the "c" locale. `_Makeloc` allocates a new table or string only when a locale-file line calls for a change. Request such a change and `_Makeloc` compares the relevant pointer member of the new `_Linfo` data object against `_Clocale`. If the pointers are the same, `_Makeloc` knows to allocate a fresh version. Changes apply to the new version, leaving data for the "c" locale alone. If the pointers differ, `_Makeloc` assumes that it has already allocated a fresh version for this new locale. Changes accumulate in the new version.

_Freeloc performs similar tests. If it encounters a pointer to a string or a table that matches its brother in _Clocale, it leaves it unchanged. If it encounters a pointer that differs between the new locale and _Clocale, it frees the new storage.

Figure 6.13:
xloctab.c

```
/* _Loctab data object */
#include <stddef.h>
#include "xlocale.h"

        /* macros */
#define OFF(member)     offsetof(_Linfo, member)
        /* static data */
_Locitem _Loctab[] = {                          /* locale file info */
    "LOCALE", OFF(_Name), L_NAME,
    "NOTE", 0, L_NOTE,
    "SET", 0, L_SET,
        /* controlled by LC_COLLATE */
    "collate", OFF(_Costate._Tab), L_STATE,
        /* controlled by LC_CTYPE */
    "ctype", OFF(_Ctype), L_TABLE,
    "tolower", OFF(_Tolower), L_TABLE,
    "toupper", OFF(_Toupper), L_TABLE,
    "mb_cur_max", OFF(_Mbcurmax), L_VALUE,
    "mbtowc", OFF(_Mbstate._Tab), L_STATE,
    "wctomb", OFF(_Wcstate._Tab), L_STATE,
        /* controlled by LC_MONETARY */
    "currency_symbol", OFF(_Lc.currency_symbol), L_STRING,
    "int_curr_symbol", OFF(_Lc.int_curr_symbol), L_STRING,
    "mon_decimal_point", OFF(_Lc.mon_decimal_point), L_STRING,
    "mon_grouping", OFF(_Lc.mon_grouping), L_GSTRING,
    "mon_thousands_sep", OFF(_Lc.mon_thousands_sep), L_STRING,
    "negative_sign", OFF(_Lc.negative_sign), L_STRING,
    "positive_sign", OFF(_Lc.positive_sign), L_STRING,
    "frac_digits", OFF(_Lc.frac_digits), L_VALUE,
    "int_frac_digits", OFF(_Lc.int_frac_digits), L_VALUE,
    "n_cs_precedes", OFF(_Lc.n_cs_precedes), L_VALUE,
    "n_sep_by_space", OFF(_Lc.n_sep_by_space), L_VALUE,
    "n_sign_posn", OFF(_Lc.n_sign_posn), L_VALUE,
    "p_cs_precedes", OFF(_Lc.p_cs_precedes), L_VALUE,
    "p_sep_by_space", OFF(_Lc.p_sep_by_space), L_VALUE,
    "p_sign_posn", OFF(_Lc.p_sign_posn), L_VALUE,
        /* controlled by LC_NUMERIC */
    "decimal_point", OFF(_Lc.decimal_point), L_STRING,
    "grouping", OFF(_Lc.grouping), L_GSTRING,
    "thousands_sep", OFF(_Lc.thousands_sep), L_STRING,
        /* controlled by LC_TIME */
    "am_pm", OFF(_Times._Ampm), L_STRING,
    "days", OFF(_Times._Days), L_STRING,
    "dst_rules", OFF(_Times._Isdst), L_STRING,
    "time_formats", OFF(_Times._Formats), L_STRING,
    "months", OFF(_Times._Months), L_STRING,
    "time_zone", OFF(_Times._Tzone), L_STRING,
    NULL};
```
□

Figure 6.14:
xfreeloc.c

```
/* _Freeloc function */
#include "xlocale.h"

void _Freeloc(_Linfo *p)
    {                                                   /* free all storage */
    _Locitem *q;

    for (q = _Loctab; q->_Name; ++q)
        switch (q->_Code)
            {                                           /* free all pointers */
        case L_STATE:
            {                                           /* free all state entries */
            int i;
            unsigned short **pt
                = &ADDR(p, q, unsigned short *);

            for (i = _NSTATE; 0 <= --i; ++pt)
                if (*pt && (*pt)[-1] != 0)
                    free(*pt);
            }
            break;
        case L_TABLE:
            if (NEWADDR(p, q, short *))
                free(ADDR(p, q, short *) - 1);
            break;
        case L_GSTRING:
        case L_NAME:
        case L_STRING:
            if (NEWADDR(p, q, char *))
                free(ADDR(p, q, char *));
            }
    }
```

Both _Makeloc and _Freeloc use two rather ornate macros to do this work. The header "xlocale.h" contains the definitions:

```
#define ADDR(p, q, ty)    (*(ty *)((char *)p + q->_Offset))
#define NEWADDR(p, q, ty)  \
    (ADDR(p, q, ty) != ADDR(&_Clocale, q, ty))
```

macro   You write ADDR(p, q, char *), for example, to make an lvalue — an
ADDR expression you can use to access part or all of a data object. Here, the data object is a member of the structure of type _Linfo pointed to by p. q points to an element of _Loctab (of type _Locitem) that contains the offset of the member. The member, in this case, has type *pointer to char*.

macro   You write NEWADDR(p, q, char *), for example, to test whether a
NEWADDR member has changed since it was copied from _Clocale. The arguments are the same as for the macro ADDR.

freeing   This machinery breaks down for state tables, however. Each of these
state tables contains _NSTATE pointers to tables that you can specify in a locale file. (The header "xstate.h" defines the macro _NSTATE as 16.) The macros, as they stand, require a separate element in _Loctab for each table that you want

to conditionally free. I didn't want to pump dozens of dummy entries into _Loctab to put _Freeloc through its paces. Equally, I didn't want to make the macros ADDR and NEWADDR any more ornate.

I decided, instead, to use a different mechanism for freeing state tables. To share code, I had already chosen to make state tables look much like the character translation tables used by the functions declared in `<ctype.h>`. That meant that each has an element with subscript –1 (corresponding to the value of the macro EOF, defined in `<stdio.h>`). None of the functions that use state tables know or care about this extra element. So I commandeered it as a flag to indicate whether the state table is allocated.

The primeval state table shared by all functions in the "C" locale is defined in the file `xstate.c`. (See Figure 6.11.) Its element –1 has the value zero. If _Makeloc allocates a new state table, it stores a nonzero value in element –1. That is how _Freeloc knows whether or not to free a state table.

function _Makeloc — Figure 6.15 shows the file `xmakeloc.c`. It defines the function _Makeloc, which I have already discussed at some length. Large as it is, _Makeloc is simply a *while* loop that processes lines from the locale file. The body of the loop is a *switch* statement that processes the different kinds of lines. The code is straightforward, but tedious and *very* compact.

The one macro you haven't met is TABSIZ. The header `"xlocale.h"` contains the definition:

```
#define TABSIZ   ((UCHAR_MAX + 2) * sizeof (short))
```

This is simply a portable way of writing the size in bytes of the various tables that you can alter in a locale file.

As much as possible, _Makeloc calls the internal function getval to parse and evaluate expressions. That helps keep uniform the rules for writing expressions on a locale-file line. (Expressions for table elements are an exception — only they accept the special terms $@ and $$.) getval, in turn, calls _Locterm repeatedly to sum a sequence of terms.

function _Locterm — Figure 6.16 shows the file `xlocterm.c`, which defines the function _Locterm. Here is where the various terms get parsed and evaluated. To evaluate octal, decimal, and hexadecimal numbers, _Locterm calls strtol, declared in `<stdlib.h>`. Note how that function updates the character pointer s to point past the number it parses and converts. The code for _Locterm is *extremely* condensed.

function _Locvar — The file `xlocterm.c` also defines the function _Locvar. Only _Makeloc calls this function, when it processes a locale-file line with the SET keyword. _Locvar is also small. It could easily be replaced with inline code.

I placed _Locvar in `xlocterm.c` for a good reason, however. It shares with _Locterm the need to access the two arrays uppers and vars. These give, respectively, the names and values of the terms you can alter on a locale-file line with the SET keyword. By placing both functions in the same file, the arrays can be kept private to that file, as can details of their implementation.

```
/* _Makeloc function */
#include <stdlib.h>
#include <string.h>
#include "xlocale.h"

static const char *getval(const char *s, unsigned short *ans)
    {                                      /* accumulate terms */
    unsigned short val;

    if (!_Locterm(&s, ans))
        return (NULL);
    while (_Locterm(&s, &val))
        *ans += val;
    return (s);
    }

int _Makeloc(FILE *lf, char *buf, _Linfo *p)
    {                             /* construct locale from text file */
    const char *s;
    char *s1;
    _Locitem *q;
    unsigned short val;
    static const char gmap[] = "0123456789abcdef";

    while ((q = _Readloc(lf, buf, &s)) != NULL)
        switch (q->_Code)
            {                               /* process a line */
        case L_GSTRING:              /* alter a grouping string */
        case L_STRING:               /* alter a normal string */
            if (NEWADDR(p, q, char *))
                free(ADDR(p, q, char *));
            if (s[0] == '"'
                && (s1 = strrchr(s + 1, '"')) != NULL
                && *_Skip(s1) == '\0')
                *s1 = '\0', ++s;
            if ((s1 = malloc(strlen(s) + 1)) == NULL)
                return (0);
            ADDR(p, q, char *) = strcpy(s1, s);
            if (q->_Code == L_GSTRING)
                for (; *s1; ++s1)
                    if ((s = strchr(gmap, *s1)) != NULL)
                        *s1 = s - gmap;
            break;
        case L_TABLE:                /* alter a translation table */
        case L_STATE:                /* alter a state table */
            {                        /* process tab[#,lo:hi] $x expr */
            int inc = 0;
            unsigned short hi, lo, stno, *usp, **uspp;

            if (*s != '['
                || (s = getval(_Skip(s), &stno)) == NULL)
                return (0);
            if (*s != ',')
                lo = stno, stno = 0;
            else if (q->_Code != L_STATE || _NSTATE <= stno
```

```
                                 || (s = getval(_Skip(s), &lo)) == NULL)
                                 return (0);
                        lo = (unsigned char)lo;
                        if (*s != ':')
                                 hi = lo;
                        else if ((s = getval(_Skip(s), &hi)) == NULL)
                                 return (0);
                        else
                                 hi = (unsigned char)hi;
                        if (*s != ']')
                                 return (0);
                        for (s = _Skip(s); s[0] == '$'; s = _Skip(s + 1))
                                 if (s[1] == '@' && (inc & 1) == 0)
                                         inc |= 1;
                                 else if (s[1] == '$' && (inc & 2) == 0)
                                         inc |= 2;
                                 else
                                         break;
                        if ((s = getval(s, &val)) == NULL || *s != '\0')
                                 return (0);
                        uspp = &ADDR(p, q, unsigned short *) + stno;
                        if (q->_Code == L_TABLE)
                                 usp = NEWADDR(p, q, short *) ? *uspp : NULL;
                        else
                                 usp = (*uspp)[-1] ? *uspp : NULL;
                        if (usp == NULL)
                                 {                               /* setup a new table */
                                 if ((usp = malloc(TABSIZ)) == NULL)
                                         return (0);
                                 usp[0] = 1;                     /* allocation flag */
                                 memcpy(++usp, ADDR(p, q, short *),
                                         TABSIZ - sizeof (short));
                                 *uspp = usp;
                                 }
                        for (; lo <= hi; ++lo)
                                 usp[lo] = val + (inc & 1 ? lo : 0)
                                         + (inc & 2 ? usp[lo] : 0);
                         }
                        break;
                case L_VALUE:                    /* alter a numeric value */
                        if ((s = getval(s, &val)) == NULL || *s != '\0')
                                 return (0);
                        ADDR(p, q, char) = val;
                        break;
                case L_SET:                      /* assign to uppercase variable */
                        if (*(s1 = (char *)_Skip(s)) == '\0'
                                 || (s1 = (char *)getval(s1, &val)) == NULL
                                 || *s1 != '\0' || _Locvar(*s, val) == 0)
                                 return (0);
                        break;
                case L_NAME:                     /* end happily with next LOCALE */
                        return (1);
                }
        return (0);                      /* fail on EOF or unknown keyword */
        }                                                                    □
```

Figure 6.16:
`xlocterm.c`

```c
/* _Locterm and _Locvar functions */
#include <ctype.h>
#include <limits.h>
#include <string.h>
#include "xlocale.h"

        /* static data */
static const char dollars[] = {                    /* PLUS $@ and $$ */
    "^abfnrtv"                                      /* character codes */
    "01234567"                                      /* state values */
    "ACDHLMPSUW"                                    /* ctype codes */
    "#FIOR"};                                       /* state commands */
static const unsigned short dolvals[] = {
    CHAR_MAX, '\a', '\b', '\f', '\n', '\r', '\t', '\v',
    0x000, 0x100, 0x200, 0x300, 0x400, 0x500, 0x600, 0x700,
    _XA, _BB, _DI, _XD, _LO, _CN, _PU, _SP, _UP, _XS,
    UCHAR_MAX, ST_FOLD, ST_INPUT, ST_OUTPUT, ST_ROTATE};
static const char uppers[] = "ABCDEFGHIJKLMNOPQRSTUVWXYZ";
static short vars[sizeof (uppers) - 1] = {0};

int _Locvar(char ch, short val)
    {                                              /* set a $ variable */
    const char *s = strchr(uppers, ch);

    if (s == NULL)
        return (0);
    vars[s - uppers] = val;
    return (1);
    }

 int _Locterm(const char **ps, unsigned short *ans)
    {                     /* evaluate a term on a locale file line */
    const char *s = *ps;
    const char *s1;
    int mi;

    for (mi = 0; *s == '+' || *s == '-'; s = _Skip(s))
        mi = *s == '-' ? !mi : mi;
    if (isdigit(s[0]))
        *ans = strtol(s, (char **)&s, 0);
    else if (s[0] == '\'' && s[1] != '\0' && s[2] == '\'')
        *ans = ((unsigned char *)s)[1], s += 3;
    else if (s[0] && (s1 = strchr(uppers, s[0])) != NULL)
        *ans = vars[s1 - uppers], ++s;
    else if (s[0] == '$' && s[1]
        && (s1 = strchr(dollars, s[1])) != NULL)
        *ans = dolvals[s1 - dollars], s += 2;
    else
        return (0);
    if (mi)
        *ans = -*ans;
    *ps = _Skip(s - 1);
    return (1);
    }
```

header   I conclude this guided tour by disclosing the complete contents of the
"xlocale.h" internal header `"xlocale.h"`. Figure 6.17 shows the file `xlocale.h`. By this
point, the disclosure should be an anticlimax. You have seen all the important pieces along the way.

You have, in fact, seen approximately 800 lines of code in this chapter.
That's a lot of code to implement what appears as just two functions and a
standard header in the description of the Standard C library. I believe,
however, that the ability to define new locales offers considerable promise.
If this investment in code can deliver on that promise, it's worth it.

Testing `<locale.h>`

Figure 6.18 shows the test program `tlocale.c`. It focuses primarily on
the portable behavior you can expect from the functions in `<locale.h>`. As
a consequence, it doesn't test much of the code presented in this chapter.
To do that, you need to switch to a new locale, such as `"USA"` presented
earlier. Then you can print the results of the extra function `_Fmtval` to verify
that the behavior changes as expected.

You can use `tlocale.c` to test any implementation of Standard C. It
ensures that the `"c"` locale meets the requirements of the C Standard, both
before and after various changes of locale. It also verifies that you can
establish mixed locales, at least involving the `"c"` and native locales. It
endeavors to determine whether these two locales differ. You get one of
two messages. For this implementation, the expected output is:

```
Native locale same as "C" locale
SUCCESS testing <locale.h>
```

References

ISO Standard 4217:1987 (Geneva: International Standards Organization,
1987). This Standard specifies the three-letter codes for the currencies of
various nations.

Exercises

Exercise 6.1 Write locales that expresses the monetary conventions for Italy, the Neth-
erlands, Norway, and Switzerland. Use the information from the example
in Section 7.4.2.1 of the C Standard (See page 86).

Exercise 6.2 Write a locale that expresses the character-classification conventions for the
French language. Add the lowercase letters [á à â ç é è ê ô û] and their
corresponding uppercase letters [Á À Â Ç É È Ê Ô Û] to the translation
tables `ctype`, `tolower`, and `toupper`. How do you determine the code values
for these letters under your implementation?

Figure 6.17:
xlocale.h

```
/* xlocale.h internal header */
#include <limits.h>
#include <locale.h>
#include <stdio.h>
#include <stdlib.h>
#include "xstate.h"
#include "xtinfo.h"


        /* macros for _Getloc and friends */
#define ADDR(p, q, ty)  (*(ty *)((char *)p + q->_Offset))
#define NEWADDR(p, q, ty)  \
    (ADDR(p, q, ty) != ADDR(&_Clocale, q, ty))
#define MAXLIN 256
#define TABSIZ  ((UCHAR_MAX + 2) * sizeof (short))
        /* type definitions */
typedef const struct {
    const char *_Name;
    size_t _Offset;
    enum {
        L_GSTRING, L_NAME, L_NOTE, L_SET,
        L_STATE, L_STRING, L_TABLE, L_VALUE
        } _Code;
    } _Locitem;
typedef struct _Linfo {
    const char *_Name;                          /* must be first */
    struct _Linfo *_Next;
        /* controlled by LC_COLLATE */
    _Statab _Costate;
        /* controlled by LC_CTYPE */
    const short *_Ctype;
    const short *_Tolower;
    const short *_Toupper;
    unsigned char _Mbcurmax;
    _Statab _Mbstate;
    _Statab _Wcstate;
        /* controlled by LC_MONETARY and LC_NUMERIC */
    struct lconv _Lc;
        /* controlled by LC_TIME */
    _Tinfo _Times;
    } _Linfo;
        /* declarations */
const char *_Defloc(void);
void _Freeloc(_Linfo *);
_Linfo *_Getloc(const char *, const char *);
int _Locterm(const char **, unsigned short *);
int _Locvar(char, short);
int _Makeloc(FILE *, char *, _Linfo *);
_Locitem *_Readloc(FILE *, char *, const char **);
_Linfo *_Setloc(int, _Linfo *);
const char *_Skip(const char *);
extern _Linfo _Clocale;
extern _Locitem _Loctab[];
```

Figure 6.18:
tlocale.c

```c
/* test locales */
#include <assert.h>
#include <limits.h>
#include <locale.h>
#include <stdio.h>
#include <string.h>

static void testclocale(struct lconv *p)
    {                            /* test properties of "C" locale */
    assert(strcmp(p->currency_symbol, "") == 0);
    assert(strcmp(p->decimal_point, ".") == 0);
    assert(strcmp(p->grouping, "") == 0);
    assert(strcmp(p->int_curr_symbol, "") == 0);
    assert(strcmp(p->mon_decimal_point, "") == 0);
    assert(strcmp(p->mon_grouping, "") == 0);
    assert(strcmp(p->mon_thousands_sep, "") == 0);
    assert(strcmp(p->negative_sign, "") == 0);
    assert(strcmp(p->positive_sign, "") == 0);
    assert(strcmp(p->thousands_sep, "") == 0);
    assert(p->frac_digits == CHAR_MAX);
    assert(p->int_frac_digits == CHAR_MAX);
    assert(p->n_cs_precedes == CHAR_MAX);
    assert(p->n_sep_by_space == CHAR_MAX);
    assert(p->n_sign_posn == CHAR_MAX);
    assert(p->p_cs_precedes == CHAR_MAX);
    assert(p->p_sep_by_space == CHAR_MAX);
    assert(p->p_sign_posn == CHAR_MAX);
    }

int main()
    {                            /* test basic properties of locales */
    static int cats[] = {LC_ALL, LC_COLLATE, LC_CTYPE,
        LC_MONETARY, LC_NUMERIC, LC_TIME};
    struct lconv *p = NULL;
    char buf[32], *s;

    assert((p = localeconv()) != NULL);
    testclocale(p);
    assert((s = setlocale(LC_ALL, NULL)) != NULL);
    assert(strlen(s) < sizeof (buf));            /* OK if longer */
    strcpy(buf, s);              /* but not safe for this program */
    assert(setlocale(LC_ALL, "") != NULL);
    assert(localeconv() != NULL);
    assert((s = setlocale(LC_MONETARY, "C")) != NULL);
    puts(strcmp(s, "C") ? "Native locale differs from \"C\""
        : "Native locale same as \"C\"");
    assert(setlocale(LC_NUMERIC, "C") != NULL);
    assert((p = localeconv()) != NULL);
    testclocale(p);
    assert(setlocale(LC_ALL, buf) != NULL);
    assert((p = localeconv()) != NULL);
    testclocale(p);
    puts("SUCCESS testing <locale.h>");
    return (0);
    }                                                              □
```

Exercise 6.3 Alter the test program `tctype.c` (shown on page 44) so that it first switches to the locale in the previous exercise. Does it display what you expect when you run it?

Exercise 6.4 Write a locale that expresses the monetary and numeric conventions for the French language. At the very least, you need to alter:

`mon_decimal_point`	`decimal_point`
`mon_grouping`	`grouping`
`mon_thousands_sep`	`thousands_sep`
`negative_sign`	`positive_sign`

Test your new locale. (Hint: You may want to commandeer test programs in this and later chapters as a starting point.)

Exercise 6.5 [**Harder**] Tables of values with many fraction digits often group digits by fives going to the right from the decimal point. An example is:

```
+1.00000 00000 00
-0.16666 66666 67
+0.00833 33333 33
-0.00019 84126 98
```

Add the members `frac_grouping` and `frac_group_sep` to `struct lconv`. Define them in such a way that you can specify the format used in this example (and others, of course). Alter the code in this chapter, including `_Fmtval`, to initialize, copy, alter, and use these members properly. Is such an addition permitted by the C Standard?

Exercise 6.6 [**Harder**] You want a program to be able to construct its own locale. Rewriting the locale file is unacceptable. What function(s) would you add to `<locale.h>` to permit a program to name, construct, and add new locales on the fly? Write the user documentation that a programmer would need to add locales.

Exercise 6.7 [**Very hard**] Implement the capabilities you described in the previous exercise.

Chapter 7: `<math.h>`

Background

Writing good math function is hard. It is still commonplace to find professional implementations of programming languages that provide math functions with serious flaws. They may generate intermediate overflows for arguments with well-defined function values, or lose considerable significance, or generate results that are simply wrong in certain cases.

history What's mildly surprising about this state of affairs is that implementors have had plenty of time to learn how to do things right. The earliest use for computers was to solve problems with a distinctive engineering or mathematical slant. The first libraries, in fact, consisted almost entirely of functions that computed the common math functions. FORTRAN, a child of the 1950s, was named for its ability to simplify FORmula TRANslation. Those formulas were larded with math functions.

Over the years, implementors have become more sophisticated. The IEEE 754 Standard for floating-point is a significant milestone on the road to safer and more consistent floating-point arithmetic. (See Chapter 4: `<float.h>` for additional discussion of floating-point representations and the IEEE 754 Standard.) Yet in another sense, IEEE 754 adds to the implementor's woes. It introduces the complexity of gradual underflow, codes for infinities and not-a-numbers, and exponents of different sizes for different precisions. Small wonder that many implementors often support only parts of the IEEE 754 Standard.

I spent about as much time writing and debugging the functions declared in `<math.h>` as I did all the rest of this library combined. That surprised me, I confess. I have written math libraries at least three times beforehand over the past twenty-odd years. You'd think that I have had plenty of time to learn how to do things right, as well. I thought so too.

goals I took so long this time because I adopted several rather ambitous goals:

- The math library should be portable over a range of popular computer architectures. All functions are designed to yield 56 bits of precision. That makes them suitable for a number of machines with 64-bit *double* representation — those with IEEE 754-compatible math coprocessors (53 bits of precision), the IBM System/370 family (53 to 56 bits), and the DEC VAX family (56 bits).

- Each function should accept all argument values in its domain (the argument values for which it is mathematically defined). It should report a *domain error* for all other arguments. In this case, the function returns a special code that represents NaN for not-a-number.

- Each function should produce a finite result if its value has a finite representation. It should report a *range error* for all values too large or too small to represent. If the value is too large in magnitude, the function returns a special code +Inf that represents plus infinity, or the negative of that code –Inf that represents minus infinity, as appropriate. If the value is too small in magnitude, the function returns zero.

- Each function should produce the most sensible result for the argument values NaN, +Inf, and –Inf. On an implementation that supports multiple NaN codes, such as IEEE 754, the functions preserve particular NaN codes wherever possible. If a function has a single argument and the value of that argument is a NaN, for example, the function returns the value of the argument.

- Each function should endeavor to produce a result whose precision is within *two bits* of the best-available approximation to any representable result.

- No function should ever generate an overflow, underflow, or zero divide, regardless of its argument values and regardless of the result.

- No function requires a floating-point representation other than *double* to perform intermediate calculations.

I believe I have achieved these goals, as best as I can tell from the testing these functions have undergone to date.

non-goals   I should also point out a number of goals I chose *not* to achieve:

- The library doesn't try to distinguish +0 from –0. IEEE 754 worries quite a bit about this distinction. All the architectures I mentioned above can represent both flavors of zero. But I have trouble accepting (or even understanding) the rationale for this extra complexity. I can sympathize with recent critiques of the IEEE 754 Standard that challenge that rationale. Most of all, I found the functions quite hard enough to write without fretting about the sign of nothing.

- The library does nothing with various flavors of NaNs. IEEE 754 arithmetic, for example, distinguishes *quiet NaNs* from *signalling NaNs*. The latter should generate a signal or raise an exception. This implementation essentially treats all NaNs as quiet NaNs.

- I provide low-level primitives only for the IEEE 754 representation. They happen to work rather well with the DEC VAX floating-point representation as well, but the fit isn't perfect. The VAX hardware doesn't recognize as special the code values for things like +Inf and -Inf. Such codes can disappear in expressions that perform arithmetic with them. The primitives must be altered to support System/370 floating-point.

- I have not checked the functions on System/370. The "wobbling precision" on that architecture requires special handling. Mostly, I have tried to provide such special handling, but it may not be thorough enough.

- Many functions are probably suboptimal for machines that retain much fewer than 53 bits of precision in type *double*. The C Standard permits a *double* to retain as few as ten decimal digits of precision — about 31 bits. For such machines, you should reconsider the approximations chosen in various math functions.

- Functions that use approximations will almost certainly fail for machines that retain more than 56 bits of precision. For such machines, you *must* reconsider the approximations chosen.

- Floating-point representations with bases other than 2 or 16 are poorly supported by this implementation of the math library. An implementation with base-10 floating-point arithmetic, for example, would call for significant redesign.

Even with these constraints, you should find that this implementation of the math library is useful in a broad variety of environments.

Computing math functions safely and accurately requires a peculiar style of programming:

finite precision
- The finite precision of floating-point representation is both a blessing and a curse. It lets you choose approximations of limited accuracy. But it offers only limited accuracy for intermediate calculations that may need more.

finite range
- The finite range of floating-point representation is also both a blessing and a curse. It lets you choose safe data types to represent arbitrary exponents. But it can surprise you with overflow or underflow in intermediate calculations.

You learn to dismantle floating-point values by performing various *seminumerical operations* on them. The separate pieces are fractions with a narrow range of values, integer exponents, and sign bits. You can work on these pieces with greater speed, accuracy, and safety. Then you paste the final result together using other seminumerical operations.

Cody and Waite
An excellent book on writing math libraries is William J. Cody, Jr. and William Waite, *Software Manual for the Elementary Functions*. Many of the functions in this chapter make use of algorithms and techniques described by Cody and Waite. Quite a few use the actual approximations derived by Cody and Waite especially for their book. I confess that on a few occasions I thought I could eliminate some of the fussier steps they recommend. All too often I was proved wrong. I happily build on the work of these careful pioneers.

elefunt tests
As a final note, the acid test for many of the functions declared in `<math.h>` was the public-domain `elefunt` (for "elementary function") tests. These derive from the carefully wrought tests in Cody and Waite.

What the C Standard Says

<math.h>

7.5 Mathematics `<math.h>`

The header **`<math.h>`** declares several mathematical functions and defines one macro. The functions take **double** arguments and return **double** values.[103] Integer arithmetic functions and conversion functions are discussed later.

The macro defined is

HUGE_VAL

```
HUGE_VAL
```

which expands to a positive **double** expression, not necessarily representable as a **float**.[104]

Forward references: integer arithmetic functions (7.10.6), the **atof** function (7.10.1.1), the **strtod** function (7.10.1.4).

7.5.1 Treatment of error conditions

The behavior of each of these functions is defined for all representable values of its input arguments. Each function shall execute as if it were a single operation, without generating any externally visible exceptions.

domain error

For all functions, a *domain error* occurs if an input argument is outside the domain over which the mathematical function is defined. The description of each function lists any required domain errors; an implementation may define additional domain errors, provided that such errors are consistent with the mathematical definition of the function.[105] On a domain error, the function returns an implementation-defined value; the value of the macro **EDOM** is stored in **errno**.

range error

Similarly, a *range error* occurs if the result of the function cannot be represented as a **double** value. If the result overflows (the magnitude of the result is so large that it cannot be represented in an object of the specified type), the function returns the value of the macro **HUGE_VAL**, with the same sign (except for the **tan** function) as the correct value of the function; the value of the macro **ERANGE** is stored in **errno**. If the result underflows (the magnitude of the result is so small that it cannot be represented in an object of the specified type), the function returns zero; whether the integer expression **errno** acquires the value of the macro **ERANGE** is implementation-defined.

7.5.2 Trigonometric functions

acos

7.5.2.1 The acos function

Synopsis

```
#include <math.h>
double acos(double x);
```

Description

The **acos** function computes the principal value of the arc cosine of **x**. A domain error occurs for arguments not in the range $[-1, +1]$.

Returns

The **acos** function returns the arc cosine in the range $[0, \pi]$ radians.

asin

7.5.2.2 The asin function

Synopsis

```
#include <math.h>
double asin(double x);
```

Description

The **asin** function computes the principal value of the arc sine of **x**. A domain error occurs for arguments not in the range $[-1, +1]$.

Returns

The **asin** function returns the arc sine in the range $[-\pi/2, +\pi/2]$ radians.

atan

7.5.2.3 The atan function

Synopsis

```
#include <math.h>
double atan(double x);
```

Description

The **atan** function computes the principal value of the arc tangent of **x**.

Returns

The **atan** function returns the arc tangent in the range $[-\pi/2, +\pi/2]$ radians.

7.5.2.4 The **atan2** function

atan2

Synopsis

```
#include <math.h>
double atan2(double y, double x);
```

Description

The **atan2** function computes the principal value of the arc tangent of **y/x**, using the signs of both arguments to determine the quadrant of the return value. A domain error may occur if both arguments are zero.

Returns

The **atan2** function returns the arc tangent of **y/x**, in the range $[-\pi, +\pi]$ radians.

7.5.2.5 The **cos** function

cos

Synopsis

```
#include <math.h>
double cos(double x);
```

Description

The **cos** function computes the cosine of **x** (measured in radians).

Returns

The **cos** function returns the cosine value.

7.5.2.6 The **sin** function

sin

Synopsis

```
#include <math.h>
double sin(double x);
```

Description

The **sin** function computes the sine of **x** (measured in radians).

Returns

The **sin** function returns the sine value.

7.5.2.7 The **tan** function

tan

Synopsis

```
#include <math.h>
double tan(double x);
```

Description

The **tan** function returns the tangent of **x** (measured in radians).

Returns

The **tan** function returns the tangent value.

7.5.3 Hyperbolic functions

7.5.3.1 The **cosh** function

cosh

Synopsis

```
#include <math.h>
double cosh(double x);
```

Description

The **cosh** function computes the hyperbolic cosine of **x**. A range error occurs if the magnitude of **x** is too large.

Returns

The **cosh** function returns the hyperbolic cosine value.

7.5.3.2 The sinh function

sinh

Synopsis

```
#include <math.h>
double sinh(double x);
```

Description

The **sinh** function computes the hyperbolic sine of **x**. A range error occurs if the magnitude of **x** is too large.

Returns

The **sinh** function returns the hyperbolic sine value.

7.5.3.3 The tanh function

tanh

Synopsis

```
#include <math.h>
double tanh(double x);
```

Description

The **tanh** function computes the hyperbolic tangent of **x**.

Returns

The **tanh** function returns the hyperbolic tangent value.

7.5.4 Exponential and logarithmic functions

7.5.4.1 The exp function

exp

Synopsis

```
#include <math.h>
double exp(double x);
```

Description

The **exp** function computes the exponential function of **x**. A range error occurs if the magnitude of **x** is too large.

Returns

The **exp** function returns the exponential value.

7.5.4.2 The frexp function

frexp

Synopsis

```
#include <math.h>
double frexp(double value, int *exp);
```

Description

The **frexp** function breaks a floating-point number into a normalized fraction and an integral power of 2. It stores the integer in the **int** object pointed to by **exp**.

Returns

The **frexp** function returns the value **x**, such that **x** is a **double** with magnitude in the interval [1/2, 1) or zero, and **value** equals **x** times 2 raised to the power ***exp**. If **value** is zero, both parts of the result are zero.

7.5.4.3 The ldexp function

ldexp

Synopsis

```
#include <math.h>
double ldexp(double x, int exp);
```

Description

The **ldexp** function multiplies a floating-point number by an integral power of 2. A range error may occur.

Returns

The **ldexp** function returns the value of **x** times 2 raised to the power **exp**.

log

7.5.4.4 The log function

Synopsis

```
#include <math.h>
double log(double x);
```

Description

The **log** function computes the natural logarithm of **x**. A domain error occurs if the argument is negative. A range error may occur if the argument is zero.

Returns

The **log** function returns the natural logarithm.

log10

7.5.4.5 The log10 function

Synopsis

```
#include <math.h>
double log10(double x);
```

Description

The **log10** function computes the base-ten logarithm of **x**. A domain error occurs if the argument is negative. A range error may occur if the argument is zero.

Returns

The **log10** function returns the base-ten logarithm.

modf

7.5.4.6 The modf function

Synopsis

```
#include <math.h>
double modf(double value, double *iptr);
```

Description

The **modf** function breaks the argument **value** into integer and fraction parts, each of which has the same sign as the argument. It stores the integer part as a **double** in the object pointed to by **iptr**.

Returns

The **modf** function returns the signed fractional part of **value**.

7.5.5 Power functions

pow

7.5.5.1 The pow function

Synopsis

```
#include <math.h>
double pow(double x, double y);
```

Description

The **pow** function computes **x** raised to the power **y**. A domain error occurs if **x** is negative and **y** is not an integral value. A domain error occurs if the result cannot be represented when **x** is zero and **y** is less than or equal to zero. A range error may occur.

Returns

The **pow** function returns the value of **x** raised to the power **y**.

sqrt

7.5.5.2 The sqrt function

Synopsis

```
#include <math.h>
double sqrt(double x);
```

Description

The **sqrt** function computes the nonnegative square root of **x**. A domain error occurs if the argument is negative.

Returns

The **sqrt** function returns the value of the square root.

7.5.6 Nearest integer, absolute value, and remainder functions

7.5.6.1 The ceil function

Synopsis

```
#include <math.h>
double ceil(double x);
```

Description

The **ceil** function computes the smallest integral value not less than **x**.

Returns

The **ceil** function returns the smallest integral value not less than **x**, expressed as a double.

7.5.6.2 The fabs function

Synopsis

```
#include <math.h>
double fabs(double x);
```

Description

The **fabs** function computes the absolute value of a floating-point number **x**.

Returns

The **fabs** function returns the absolute value of **x**.

7.5.6.3 The floor function

Synopsis

```
#include <math.h>
double floor(double x);
```

Description

The **floor** function computes the largest integral value not greater than **x**.

Returns

The **floor** function returns the largest integral value not greater than **x**, expressed as a double.

7.5.6.4 The fmod function

Synopsis

```
#include <math.h>
double fmod(double x, double y);
```

Description

The **fmod** function computes the floating-point remainder of **x/y**.

Returns

The **fmod** function returns the value **x** – i * **y**, for some integer i such that, if **y** is nonzero, the result has the same sign as **x** and magnitude less than the magnitude of **y**. If **y** is zero, whether a domain error occurs or the **fmod** function returns zero is implementation-defined.

Footnotes

103. See "future library directions" (7.13.4).

104. **HUGE_VAL** can be positive infinity in an implementation that supports infinities.

105. In an implementation that supports infinities, this allows infinity as an argument to be a domain error if the mathematical domain of the function does not include infinity.

ceil

fabs

floor

fmod

Using `<math.h>`

I have to assume that you have a good notion of what you intend to do with most functions declared in `<math.h>`. Few people are struck with a sudden urge to compute a cosine. I confine my remarks, therefore, to the usual comments on individual functions:

HUGE_VAL   **HUGE_VAL** — This macro traditionally expands to a *double* constant that is supposed to be ridiculously large. Often, it equals the expansion of DBL_MAX, defined in `<float.h>`. On machines that lack a special code for infinity (Inf), returning such a large value is considered the best way to warn that a range error has occurred. Be warned, however, that HUGE_VAL may very well equal Inf. It is probably safe to compare the return value of a math function against HUGE_VAL or -HUGE_VAL. (It is probably better to test whether errno has been set to ERANGE. Both of these macros are defined in `<errno.h>`.) Don't use HUGE_VAL any other way.

acos   acos — The functions acos and asin are often computed by a common function. Each effectively computes one of the acute angles in a right triangle, given the length of one of the sides and the hypotenuse. Be wary, therefore, of arguments to acos that are ratios, particularly if one of the terms looks like sqrt (1.0 - x * x). You may very well want to call asin, atan, or even better, atan2.

asin   asin — See acos above.

atan   atan — The functions atan and atan2 are often computed by a common function. The latter is much more general, however. Use it in preference to atan, particularly if the argument is a ratio. Also see acos above.

atan2   atan2 — This function effectively computes the angle that a radius vector makes with the origin, given the coordinates of a point in the *X–Y* plane. It is by far the most general of the four functions acos, asin, atan, and atan2. Use it in preference to the others.

ceil   ceil — The functions ceil, floor, and modf let you manipulate the fraction part of a floating-point value in various ways. Using them is much safer than converting to an integer type because they can manipulate arbitrary floating-point values without causing overflow. Note that ceil rounds to the right along the *X*–axis, while floor rounds to the left. To round an arbitrary floating-point value x to the nearest integer, write:

```
x < 0.0 ? ceil(x - 0.5) : floor(x + 0.5)
```

cos   cos — The functions cos and sin are often computed by a common function. Each effectively reduces its argument to a range of π radians, centered about either the *X*– or *Y*–axis. Be wary, therefore, of arguments to cos that include the addition of some multiple of $\pi/2$. You may very well want to call sin instead. Omit adding to the argument any multiple of 2*π. The function will probably do a better job than you of eliminating multiples of 2*π. Note, however, that each multiple of 2*π in the argument reduces the useful precision of the result of cos by almost three bits. For large enough arguments, the result of the function can be meaningless even though the function reports no error.

cosh   cosh — Use this function instead of the apparent identity:

$$cosh(x) \equiv 0.5 * (exp(x) + exp(-x))$$

or any of its optimized forms. Unlike this expression, cosh should generate a more accurate result, and cover the full range of x for which the function value is representable.

exp   exp — If the argument to exp has the form y * log(x), replace the expression with pow(x, y). The latter should be more precise.

fabs   fabs — This function should be reasonably fast. It should also work properly for the arguments Inf and –Inf, if the implementation supports those special codes.

floor   floor — See ceil above.

fmod   fmod — This function determines the floating-point analog to a remainder in integer division. You can sometimes use it to advantage in reducing an argument to a subrange within a repeated interval. As such, fmod is better and safer than subtracting a multiple of the interval directly. Other techniques described later in this chapter often do a better job of argument reduction, however.

frexp   frexp — Use this function to partition a floating-point value when you can usefully work on its fraction and exponent parts separately. The companion function is often ldexp below.

ldexp   ldexp — Use this function to recombine the fraction and exponent parts of a floating-point value after you have worked on them separately. The companion function is often frexp above.

log   log — log(x) is the natural logarithm, often written $log_e(x)$ or $ln(x)$. You can, of course, obtain the logarithm of x to any base b by multiplying the value of this function by the conversion factor $log_b(e)$ (or $1/log_e(b)$).

log10   log10 — log10(x) is often computed from log(x). If you find yourself multiplying the result of log10 by a conversion factor, consider calling log instead.

modf   modf — Use this function to partition a floating-point value when you can usefully work on its integer and fraction parts separately.

pow   pow — This is often the most elaborate of all the functions declared in <math.h>. A good implementation will generate better results for pow(x, y) than the apparent equivalent exp(y * log(x)). It may take longer, however. Replace pow(e, y) with exp(y) where e is the base of natural logarithms. Replace pow(x, 0.5) with sqrt(x). And replace pow(x, 2.0) with x * x.

sin   sin — See cos above.

sinh   sinh — Use this function instead of the apparent identity:

$$sinh(x) \equiv 0.5 * (exp(x) - exp(-x))$$

or any of its optimized forms. Unlike this expression, `sinh` should generate a more accurate result, particularly for small arguments. The function also covers the full range of `x` for which the function value is representable.

sqrt   **sqrt** — This function is generally *much* faster than the apparent equivalent `pow(x, 0.5)`.

tan   **tan** — This function effectively reduces its argument to a range of π radians, centered about the X–axis. Omit adding to the argument any multiple of $2*\pi$. The function will probably do a better job than you of eliminating multiples of $2*\pi$. Note, however, that each multiple of $2*\pi$ in the argument reduces the useful precision of the result of `tan` by almost three bits. For large enough arguments, the result of the function can be meaningless even though the function reports no error.

tanh   **tanh** — Use this function instead of the apparent identity:

$$\texttt{tanh(x)} \equiv \texttt{(exp(2.0 * x) - 1.0) / (exp(2.0 * x) + 1.0)}$$

or any of its optimized forms. Unlike this expression, `tanh` should generate a more accurate result, particularly for small arguments. The function also covers the full range of `x` for which the function value is representable.

Implementing `<math.h>`

The functions in `<math.h>` vary widely. I discuss them in three groups:

- the seminumerical functions that manipulate the components of floating-point values, such as the exponent, integer, and fraction parts
- the trignometric and inverse trignometric functions
- the exponential, logarithmic, and special power functions

primitives Along the way, I also present several low-level primitives. These are used by all the functions declared in `<math.h>` to isolate dependencies on the specific representation of floating-point values. I discussed the general properties of machines covered by this particular set of primitives starting on page 127. I emphasize once again that the parametrization doesn't cover all floating-point representations used in modern computers. You may have to alter one or more of the primitives for certain computer architectures. In rarer cases, you may have to alter the higher-level functions as well.

header   Figure 7.1 shows the file `math.h`. It contains only a few surprises. One is **`<math.h>`** the masking macros. You can see that several of the math functions call other functions in turn. The masking macros eliminate one function call.

macro   Another surprise the definition of the macro `HUGE_VAL`. I define it as the **`HUGE_VAL`** IEEE 754 code for +Inf. To do so, I introduce the type `_Dconst`. It is a union that lets you initialize a data object as an array of four *unsigned shorts*, then access the data object as a *double*. (See page 65 for a similar trick.) The data object `_Hugeval` is one of a handful of floating-point values that are best constructed this way.

Figure 7.1:
math.h

```
/* math.h standard header */
#ifndef _MATH
#define _MATH
        /* macros */
#define HUGE_VAL    _Hugeval._D
        /* type definitions */
typedef const union {
    unsigned short _W[4];
    double _D;
    } _Dconst;
        /* declarations */
double acos(double);
double asin(double);
double atan(double);
double atan2(double, double);
double ceil(double);
double cos(double);
double cosh(double);
double exp(double);
double fabs(double);
double floor(double);
double fmod(double, double);
double frexp(double, int *);
double ldexp(double, int);
double log(double);
double log10(double);
double modf(double, double *);
double pow(double, double);
double sin(double);
double sinh(double);
double sqrt(double);
double tan(double);
double tanh(double);
double _Asin(double, int);
double _Log(double, int);
double _Sin(double, unsigned int);
extern _Dconst _Hugeval;
        /* macro overrides */
#define acos(x) _Asin(x, 1)
#define asin(x) _Asin(x, 0)
#define cos(x)  _Sin(x, 1)
#define log(x)  _Log(x, 0)
#define log10(x)    _Log(x, 1)
#define sin(x)  _Sin(x, 0)
#endif
```

Figure 7.2:
xvalues.c

```
/* values used by math functions -- IEEE 754 version */
#include "xmath.h"

        /* macros */
#define NBITS   (48+_DOFF)
#if _D0
#define INIT(w0)    0, 0, 0, w0
#else
#define INIT(w0)    w0, 0, 0, 0
#endif
        /* static data */
_Dconst _Hugeval = {{INIT(_DMAX<<_DOFF)}};
_Dconst _Inf = {{INIT(_DMAX<<_DOFF)}};
_Dconst _Nan = {{INIT(_DNAN)}};
_Dconst _Rteps = {{INIT((_DBIAS-NBITS/2)<<_DOFF)}};
_Dconst _Xbig = {{INIT((_DBIAS+NBITS/2)<<_DOFF)}};                    □
```

_Hugeval   Figure 7.2 shows the file **xvalues.c** that defines this handful of values.
    _Inf   It includes a definition for **_Inf** that matches **_Hugeval**. I provide both in
case you choose to alter the definition of **HUGE_VAL**. The file also defines:

_Nan ▪ **_Nan**, the code for a generated NaN that functions return when no
operand is also a NaN

_Rteps ▪ **_Rteps**, the square root of **DBL_EPSILON** (approximately), used by some
functions to choose between different approximations

_Xbig ▪ **_Xbig**, the inverse of **_Rteps._D**, used by some functions to choose
between different approximations

The need for the last two values will become clearer when you see how
functions use them.

header   The file **xvalues.c** is essentially unreadable. It is parametrized much like
<yvals.h> the file **xfloat.c**, shown on page 68. Both files make use of system-depend-
ent parameters defined in the internal header **<yvals.h>**.

header   **xvalues.c** does not directly include **<yvals.h>**. Instead, it includes the
"xmath.h" internal header **"xmath.h"** that includes **<yvals.h>** in turn. All the files that
implement **<math.h>** include **"xmath.h"**. Since that file contains an assort-
ment of distractions, I show it in pieces as the need arises. You will find a
complete listing of **"xmath.h"** in Figure 7.38. Here are the macros defined
in **"xmath.h"** that are relevant to **xvalues.c**

```
#define _DFRAC   ((1<<_DOFF)-1)
#define _DMASK   (0x7fff&~_DFRAC)
#define _DMAX    ((1<<(15-_DOFF))-1)
#define _DNAN    (0x8000|_DMAX<<_DOFF|1<<(_DOFF-1))
```

If you can sort through this nonsense, you will observe that:

▪ the code for Inf has the largest-possible characteristic (**_DMAX**) with all
fraction bits zero

▪ the code for generated NaN has the largest-possible characteristic with
the most-significant fraction bit set

Figure 7.3:
fabs.c

```
/* fabs function */
#include "xmath.h"

double (fabs)(double x)
    {                                              /* compute fabs */
    switch (_Dtest(&x))
        {                                          /* test for special codes */
    case NAN:
        errno = EDOM;
        return (x);
    case INF:
        errno = ERANGE;
        return (_Inf._D);
    case 0:
        return (0.0);
    default:                                       /* finite */
        return (x < 0.0 ? -x : x);
        }
    }                                                              □
```

In general, a NaN has at least one nonzero fraction bit. I chose this particular code for generated NaN to match the behavior of the Intel 80X87 math coprocessor.

function   The presence of all these codes makes even the simplest functions
fabs nontrivial. For example, Figure 7.3 shows the file **fabs.c**. In a simpler world, you could reduce it to the last *return* statement:

```
return (x < 0.0 ? -x : x);
```

Here, however, we want to handle NaN, –Inf, and +Inf properly along with zero and finite values of the argument **x**. That takes a lot more testing.

function   Figure 7.4 shows the file **xdtest.c**. It defines the function **_Dtest** that
_Dtest categorizes a *double* value. The internal header **"xmath.h"** defines the vari-

Figure 7.4:
xdtest.c

```
/* _Dtest function -- IEEE 754 version */
#include "xmath.h"

short _Dtest(double *px)
    {                                              /* categorize *px */
    unsigned short *ps = (unsigned short *)px;
    short xchar = (ps[_D0] & _DMASK) >> _DOFF;

    if (xchar == _DMAX)                            /* NaN or INF */
        return (ps[_D0] & _DFRAC || ps[_D1]
            || ps[_D2] || ps[_D3] ? NAN : INF);
    else if (0 < xchar || ps[_D0] & _DFRAC
        || ps[_D1] || ps[_D2] || ps[_D3])
        return (FINITE);                           /* finite */
    else
        return (0);                                /* zero */
    }                                                              □
```

ous offsets and category values that _Dtest uses. The macro definitions of interest here are:

```
            /* word offsets within double */
#if _D0==3
#define _D1    2    /* little-endian order */
#define _D2    1
#define _D3    0
#else
#define _D1    1    /* big-endian order */
#define _D2    2
#define _D3    3
#endif
            /* return values for _D functions */
#define FINITE  -1
#define INF     1
#define NAN     2
```

Note that a floating-point value with characteristic zero is not necessarily zero. IEEE 754 supports gradual underflow. The value is zero only if all bits (other than the sign) are zero.

ceil   Figure 7.5 shows the file ceil.c and Figure 7.6 shows the file floor.c.
floor   Each function defined in these files requires that any fraction part of its argument x be set to zero. Moreover, each needs to know whether the fraction part was initially nonzero. Each function then adjusts the remaining integer part in slightly different ways.

function   Figure 7.7 shows the file xdint.c that defines the function _Dint. If *px
_Dint   has a finite value, the function tests and clears all fraction bits less than a threshold value. That threshold is effectively 2 raised to the power xexp. (Other functions have occasion to call _Dint with values of xexp other than zero.) The code for clearing fraction bits is a bit tricky.

Note the use of an index within an index in the term ps[sub[xchar]]. The index sub[xchar] corrects for differences in layout of floating-point values on different computer architectures. The *switch* statement contains

Figure 7.5:
ceil.c

```
/* ceil function */
#include "xmath.h"

double (ceil)(double x)
    {                                           /* compute ceil(x) */
    return (_Dint(&x, 0) < 0 && 0.0 < x ? x + 1.0 : x);
    }                                                              □
```

Figure 7.6:
floor.c

```
/* floor function */
#include "xmath.h"

double (floor)(double x)
    {                                          /* compute floor(x) */
    return (_Dint(&x, 0) < 0 && x < 0.0 ? x - 1.0 : x);
    }                                                              □
```

Figure 7.7:
xdint.c

```c
/* _Dint function -- IEEE 754 version */
#include "xmath.h"

short _Dint(double *px, short xexp)
    {                       /* test and drop (scaled) fraction bits */
    unsigned short *ps = (unsigned short *)px;
    unsigned short frac = ps[_D0] & _DFRAC
        || ps[_D1] || ps[_D2] || ps[_D3];
    short xchar = (ps[_D0] & _DMASK) >> _DOFF;

    if (xchar == 0 && !frac)
        return (0);                                         /* zero */
    else if (xchar != _DMAX)
        ;                                                   /* finite */
    else if (!frac)
        return (INF);
    else
        {                                                   /* NaN */
        errno = EDOM;
        return (NAN);
        }
    xchar = (_DBIAS+48+_DOFF+1) - xchar - xexp;
    if (xchar <= 0)
        return (0);                          /* no frac bits to drop */
    else if ((48+_DOFF) < xchar)
        {                                       /* all frac bits */
        ps[_D0] = 0, ps[_D1] = 0;
        ps[_D2] = 0, ps[_D3] = 0;
        return (FINITE);
        }
    else
        {                                      /* strip out frac bits */
        static const unsigned short mask[] = {
            0x0000, 0x0001, 0x0003, 0x0007,
            0x000f, 0x001f, 0x003f, 0x007f,
            0x00ff, 0x01ff, 0x03ff, 0x07ff,
            0x0fff, 0x1fff, 0x3fff, 0x7fff};
        static const size_t sub[] = {_D3, _D2, _D1, _D0};

        frac = mask[xchar & 0xf];
        xchar >>= 4;
        frac &= ps[sub[xchar]];
        ps[sub[xchar]] ^= frac;
        switch (xchar)
            {                                     /* cascade through! */
        case 3:
            frac |= ps[_D1], ps[_D1] = 0;
        case 2:
            frac |= ps[_D2], ps[_D2] = 0;
        case 1:
            frac |= ps[_D3], ps[_D3] = 0;
            }
        return (frac ? FINITE : 0);
        }
    }
```

Figure 7.8: modf.c

```
/* modf function */
#include "xmath.h"

double (modf)(double x, double *pint)
    {                                      /* compute modf(x, &intpart) */
    *pint = x;
    switch (_Dint(pint, 0))
        {                                  /* test for special codes */
    case NAN:
        return (x);
    case INF:
    case 0:
        return (0.0);
    default:                               /* finite */
        return (x - *pint);
        }
    }
```
□

a cascade of *case* labels, a practice that is generally misleading and unwise. I indulge in both practices here in the interest of performance.

function modf   Figure 7.8 shows the file modf.c. It defines the function modf, which is only slightly more ornate than ceil and floor. Like those functions, modf relies on the function _Dint to do the hard part.

function frexp   Figure 7.9 shows the file frexp.c. It defines the function frexp that unpacks the exponent from a finite argument x. Once again, a reasonable simple function is complicated by the presence of the various special codes. And once again, a more flexible low-level function does most of the hard work.

Figure 7.9: frexp.c

```
/* frexp function */
#include "xmath.h"

double (frexp)(double x, int *pexp)
    {                                      /* compute frexp(x, &i) */
    short binexp;

    switch (_Dunscale(&binexp, &x))
        {                                  /* test for special codes */
    case NAN:
    case INF:
        errno = EDOM;
        *pexp = 0;
        return (x);
    case 0:
        *pexp = 0;
        return (0.0);
    default:                               /* finite */
        *pexp = binexp;
        return (x);
        }
    }
```
□

Figure 7.10:
ldexp.c

```c
/* ldexp function */
#include "xmath.h"

double (ldexp)(double x, int xexp)
    {                                           /* compute ldexp(x, xexp) */
    switch (_Dtest(&x))
        {                                       /* test for special codes */
    case NAN:
        errno = EDOM;
        break;
    case INF:
        errno = ERANGE;
        break;
    case 0:
        break;
```

Figure 7.11:
xdunscal.c

```c
/* _Dunscale function -- IEEE 754 version */
#include "xmath.h"

short _Dunscale(short *pex, double *px)
    {               /* separate *px to 1/2 <= |frac| < 1 and 2^*pex */
    unsigned short *ps = (unsigned short *)px;
    short xchar = (ps[_D0] & _DMASK) >> _DOFF;

    if (xchar == _DMAX)
        {                                               /* NaN or INF */
        *pex = 0;
        return (ps[_D0] & _DFRAC || ps[_D1]
            || ps[_D2] || ps[_D3] ? NAN : INF);
        }
    else if (0 < xchar || (xchar = _Dnorm(ps)) != 0)
        {                               /* finite, reduce to [1/2, 1) */
        ps[_D0] = ps[_D0] & ~_DMASK | _DBIAS << _DOFF;
        *pex = xchar - _DBIAS;
        return (FINITE);
        }
    else
        {                                               /* zero */
        *pex = 0;
        return (0);
        }
    }                                                            □
```

function
ldexp

Figure 7.10 shows the file `ldexp.c`. The function `ldexp` faces problems similar to `frexp`, only in reverse. Once it dispatches any special codes, it still has a nontrivial task to perform. It too calls on a low-level function. Let's look at the two low-level functions.

function
_Dunscale

Figure 7.11 shows the file `xdunscal.c`. It defines the function `_Dunscale`, which combines the actions of `_Dtest` and `frexp` in a form that is handier for several other math functions. By calling `_Dunscale`, the function `frexp` is left with little to do.

`_Dunscale` itself has a fairly easy job except when presented with a gradual underflow. A normalized value has a nonzero characteristic and an implicit fraction bit to the left of the most-significant fraction bit that is represented. Gradual underflow is signaled by a zero characteristic and a nonzero fraction with *no* implicit leading bit. Both these forms must be converted to a normalized fraction in the range [0.5, 1.0), accompanied by the appropriate binary exponent. The function `_Dnorm`, described below, handles this messy job.

function
_Dscale

Figure 7.12 shows the file `xdscale.c` that defines the function `_Dscale`. It too frets about special codes, because of the other ways that it can be called. Adding the *short* value `xexp` to the exponent of a finite `*px` can cause overflow, gradual underflow, or underflow. You even have to worry about integer overflow in forming the new exponent. That's why the function first computes the sum in a *long*.

Most of the complexity of the function `_Dscale` lies in forming a gradual underflow. The operation is essentially the reverse of `_Dnorm`.

function
_Dnorm

Figure 7.13 shows the file `xdnorm.c` that defines the function `_Dnorm`. It normalizes the fraction part of a gradual underflow and adjusts the characteristic accordingly. To improve performance, the function shifts the fraction left 16 bits at a time whenever possible. That's why it must be prepared to shift right as well as left one bit at a time. It may overshoot and be obliged to back up.

function
fmod

Figure 7.14 shows the file `fmod.c`. The function `fmod` is the last of the seminumerical functions declared in `<math.h>`. It is also the most complex. In principle, it subtracts the magnitude of `y` from the magnitude of `x` repeatedly until the remainder is smaller than the magnitude of `y`. In practice, that could take an astronomical amount of time, even if it could be done with any reasonable precision.

What `fmod` does instead is scale `y` by the largest possible power of two before each subtraction. That can still require dozens of iterations, but the result is reasonably precise. Note the way `fmod` uses `_Dscale` and `_Dunscale` to manipulate exponents. It uses `_Dunscale` to extract the exponents of `x` and `y` to perform a quick but coarse comparison of their magnitudes. If `fmod` determines that a subtraction might be possible, it uses `_Dscale` to scale `x` to approximately the right size.

Figure 7.12:
xdcsale.c
Part 1

```c
/* _Dscale function -- IEEE 754 version */
#include "xmath.h"

short _Dscale(double *px, short xexp)
    {                           /* scale *px by 2^xexp with checking */
    long lexp;
    unsigned short *ps = (unsigned short *)px;
    short xchar = (ps[_D0] & _DMASK) >> _DOFF;

    if (xchar == _DMAX)                             /* NaN or INF */
        return (ps[_D0] & _DFRAC || ps[_D1]
            || ps[_D2] || ps[_D3] ? NAN : INF);
    else if (0 < xchar)
        ;                                           /* finite */
    else if ((xchar = _Dnorm(ps)) == 0)
        return (0);                                 /* zero */
    lexp = (long)xexp + xchar;
    if (_DMAX <= lexp)
        {                           /* overflow, return +/-INF */
        *px = ps[_D0] & _DSIGN ? -_Inf._D : _Inf._D;
        return (INF);
        }
    else if (0 < lexp)
        {                           /* finite result, repack */
        ps[_D0] = ps[_D0] & ~_DMASK | (short)lexp << _DOFF;
        return (FINITE);
        }
    else
        {                           /* denormalized, scale */
        unsigned short sign = ps[_D0] & _DSIGN;

        ps[_D0] = 1 << _DOFF | ps[_D0] & _DFRAC;
        if (lexp < -(48+_DOFF+1))
            xexp = -1;                              /* certain underflow */
        else
            {                           /* might not underflow */
            for (xexp = lexp; xexp <= -16; xexp += 16)
                {                           /* scale by words */
                ps[_D3] = ps[_D2], ps[_D2] = ps[_D1];
                ps[_D1] = ps[_D0], ps[_D0] = 0;
                }
            if ((xexp = -xexp) != 0)
                {                           /* scale by bits */
                ps[_D3] = ps[_D3] >> xexp
                    | ps[_D2] << 16 - xexp;
                ps[_D2] = ps[_D2] >> xexp
                    | ps[_D1] << 16 - xexp;
                ps[_D1] = ps[_D1] >> xexp
                    | ps[_D0] << 16 - xexp;
                ps[_D0] >>= xexp;
                }
            }
```

Continuing
xdscale.c
Part 2

```
        if (0 <= xexp && (ps[_D0] || ps[_D1]
            || ps[_D2] || ps[_D3]))
            {                                   /* denormalized */
            ps[_D0] |= sign;
            return (FINITE);
            }
        else
            {                           /* underflow, return +/-0 */
            ps[_D0] = sign, ps[_D1] = 0;
            ps[_D2] = 0, ps[_D3] = 0;
            return (0);
            }
        }
```

Figure 7.13:
xdnorm.c

```
/* _Dnorm function -- IEEE 754 version */
#include "xmath.h"

short _Dnorm(unsigned short *ps)
    {                                   /* normalize double fraction */
    short xchar;
    unsigned short sign = ps[_D0] & _DSIGN;

    xchar = 0;
    if ((ps[_D0] &= _DFRAC) != 0 || ps[_D1]
        || ps[_D2] || ps[_D3])
        {                                       /* nonzero, scale */
        for (; ps[_D0] == 0; xchar -= 16)
            {                                   /* shift left by 16 */
            ps[_D0] = ps[_D1], ps[_D1] = ps[_D2];
            ps[_D2] = ps[_D3], ps[_D3] = 0;
            }
        for (; ps[_D0] < 1<<_DOFF; --xchar)
            {                                   /* shift left by 1 */
            ps[_D0] = ps[_D0] << 1 | ps[_D1] >> 15;
            ps[_D1] = ps[_D1] << 1 | ps[_D2] >> 15;
            ps[_D2] = ps[_D2] << 1 | ps[_D3] >> 15;
            ps[_D3] <<= 1;
            }
        for (; 1<<_DOFF+1 <= ps[_D0]; ++xchar)
            {                                   /* shift right by 1 */
            ps[_D3] = ps[_D3] >> 1 | ps[_D2] << 15;
            ps[_D2] = ps[_D2] >> 1 | ps[_D1] << 15;
            ps[_D1] = ps[_D1] >> 1 | ps[_D0] << 15;
            ps[_D0] >>= 1;
            }
        ps[_D0] &= _DFRAC;
        }
    ps[_D0] |= sign;
    return (xchar);
    }
```

Figure 7.14:
fmod.c

```c
/* fmod function */
#include "xmath.h"

double (fmod)(double x, double y)
    {                                           /* compute fmod(x, y) */
    const short errx = _Dtest(&x);
    const short erry = _Dtest(&y);

    if (errx == NAN || erry == NAN || errx == INF || erry == 0)
        {                                           /* fmod undefined */
        errno = EDOM;
        return (errx == NAN ? x : erry == NAN ? y : _Nan._D);
        }
    else if (errx == 0 || erry == INF)
        return (x);         /* fmod(0,nonzero) or fmod(finite,INF) */
    else
        {                                       /* fmod(finite,finite) */
        double t;
        short n, neg, ychar;

        if (y < 0.0)
            y = -y;
        if (x < 0.0)
            x = -x, neg = 1;
        else
            neg = 0;
        for (t = y, _Dunscale(&ychar, &t), n = 0; ; )
            {                           /* subtract |y| until |x|<|y| */
            short xchar;

            t = x;
            if (n < 0 || _Dunscale(&xchar, &t) == 0
                || (n = xchar - ychar) < 0)
                return (neg ? -x : x);
            for (; 0 <= n; --n)
                {                               /* try to subtract |y|*2^n */
                t = y, _Dscale(&t, n);
                if (t <= x)
                    {
                    x -= t;
                    break;
                    }
                }
            }
        }
    }
```

function
_Sin

Now let's look at the trignometric functions. Figure 7.15 shows the file `xsin.c` that defines the function `_Sin`. It computes `sin(x)` if `qoff` is zero and `cos(x)` if `qoff` is one. Using such a "quadrant offset" for cosine avoids the loss of precision that occurs in adding $\pi/2$ to the argument instead. I developed the polynomial approximations from truncated Taylor series by "economizing" them using Chebychev polynomials. (If you don't know what that means, don't worry.)

Reducing the argument to the range $[-\pi/4, \pi/4]$ must be done carefully. It is easy enough to determine how many times $\pi/2$ should be subtracted from the argument. That determines `quad`, the quadrant (centered on one of the four axes) in which the angle lies. You need the low-order two bits of `quad + qoff` to determine whether to compute the cosine or sine and whether to negate the result. Note the way the signed quadrant is converted to an unsigned value so that negative arguments get treated consistenly on all computer architectures.

What you'd like to do at this point is compute `quad`$^*\pi/2$ to arbitrary precision. You want to subtract this value from the argument and still have full *double* precision after the most-significant bits cancel. Given the wide range that floating-point values can assume, that's a tall order. It's also a bit silly. As I discussed on page 135, the circular functions become progressively grainier the larger the magnitude of the argument. Beyond some magnitude, all values are indistinguishable from exact multiples of $\pi/2$. Some people argue that this is an error condition, but the C Standard doesn't say so. The circular functions must return some sensible value, and report no error, for all finite argument values.

macro
HUGE_RAD

I chose to split the difference. Adapting the approach used by Cody and Waite in several places, I represent $\pi/2$ to "one-and-a-half" times *double* precision. The header `"xmath.h"` defines the macro **HUGE_RAD** as:

```
#define HUGE_RAD    3.14e30
```

You can divide an argument up to this magnitude by $\pi/2$ and still get an value that you can convert to a *long* with no fear of overflow. The constant `c1` represents the most-significant bits of $\pi/2$ as a *double* whose least-significant 32 fraction bits are assuredly zero. (The constant `c2` supplies a full *double*'s worth of additional precision.)

That means you can multiply `c1` by an arbitrary *long* (converted to *double*) and get an exact result. Thus, so long as the magnitude of the argument is less than **HUGE_RAD**, you can develop the reduced argument to full *double* precision. That's what happens in the expression:

```
g = (x - g * c1) - g * c2;
```

For arguments larger in magnitude than **HUGE_RAD**, the function simply slashes off a multiple of $2^*\pi$. Note the use of `_Dint` to isolate the integer part of a *double*. Put another way, once the argument goes around about a billion times, `sin` and `cos` suddenly stop trying so hard. I felt it was not worth the extra effort needed to extend smooth behavior to larger arguments.

```
/* _Sin function */
#include "xmath.h"

/* coefficients */
static const double c[8] = {
    -0.000000000011470879,
     0.0000000002087712071,
    -0.000000275573192202,
     0.000024801587292937,
    -0.001388888888888893,
     0.041666666666667325,
    -0.500000000000000000,
     1.0};
static const double s[8] = {
    -0.000000000000764723,
     0.000000000160592578,
    -0.000000025052108383,
     0.000002755731921890,
    -0.000198412698412699,
     0.008333333333333372,
    -0.166666666666666667,
     1.0};
static const double c1 = {3294198.0 / 2097152.0};
static const double c2 = {3.139164786504813217e-7};
static const double twobypi = {0.63661977236758134308};
static const double twopi = {6.28318530717958647693};

double _Sin(double x, unsigned int qoff)
    {                                       /* compute sin(x) or cos(x) */
    switch (_Dtest(&x))
        {
    case NAN:
        errno = EDOM;
        return (x);
    case 0:
        return (qoff ? 1.0 : 0.0);
    case INF:
        errno = EDOM;
        return (_Nan._D);
    default:                                            /* finite */
        {                                       /* compute sin/cos */
        double g;
        long quad;

        if (x < -HUGE_RAD || HUGE_RAD < x)
            {                           /* x huge, sauve qui peut */
            g = x / twopi;
            _Dint(&g, 0);
            x -= g * twopi;
            }
        g = x * twobypi;
        quad = (long)(0 < g ? g + 0.5 : g - 0.5);
        qoff += (unsigned long)quad & 0x3;
        g = (double)quad;
        g = (x - g * c1) - g * c2;
```

```
            if ((g < 0.0 ? -g : g) < _Rteps._D)
                {                      /* sin(tiny)==tiny, cos(tiny)==1 */
                if (qoff & 0x1)
                    g = 1.0;                           /* cos(tiny) */
                }
            else if (qoff & 0x1)
                g = _Poly(g * g, c, 7);
            else
                g *= _Poly(g * g, s, 7);
            return (qoff & 0x2 ? -g : g);
            }
        }
    }
```

Figure 7.16:
xpoly.c

```
/* _Poly function */
#include "xmath.h"

double _Poly(double x, const double *tab, int n)
    {                                    /* compute polynomial */
    double y;

    for (y = *tab; 0 <= --n; )
        y = y * x + *++tab;
    return (y);
    }
```

The rest of the function _Sin is straightforward. If the reduced angle g is sufficiently small, evaluating a polynomial approximation is a waste of time. It also runs the risk of generating an underflow when computing the squared argument g * g if the reduced angle is *really* small. Here, "sufficiently small" occurs when g * g is less than DBL_EPSILON, defined in <float.h>. Note the use of the double constant _Rteps._D to speed this test.

_Poly   Figure 7.16 shows the file xpoly.c that defines the function _Poly. The function _Sin uses _Poly to evaluate a polynomial by Horner's Rule.

cos   Figure 7.17 shows the file cos.c and Figure 7.18 shows the file sin.c.
sin These define the trivial functions cos and sin. The header <math.h> defines masking macros for both.

function   Figure 7.19 shows the file tan.c. The function tan strongly resembles the
tan other circular functions sin and cos. It too reduces its argument to the interval $[-\pi/4, \pi/4]$. The major difference is the way the function is approximated over this reduced interval. Because it has poles at multiples of $\pi/2$, the tangent is better approximated by a ratio of polynomials. Cody and Waite supplied the coefficients.

function   Now consider the inverse trignometric functions. Figure 7.20 shows the
_Asin file xasin.c that defines the function _Asin. It computes asin(x) if qoff is zero and acos(x) if qoff is one. That avoids the need to tinker twice with the result for acos.

Figure 7.17:
cos.c

```
/* cos function */
#include <math.h>

double (cos)(double x)
    {                                              /* compute cos */
    return (_Sin(x, 1));
    }                                                          □
```

Figure 7.18:
sin.c

```
/* sin function */
#include <math.h>

double (sin)(double x)
    {                                              /* compute sin */
    return (_Sin(x, 0));
    }                                                          □
```

_Asin first determines y, the magnitude of the argument. It computes the intermediate result (also in y) five different ways:

- If y < _Rteps._D, use the argument itself.
- Otherwise, if y < 0.5, use a ratio of polynomials approximation from Cody and Waite.
- Otherwise, if y < 1.0, use the same approximation to compute 2 * asin(sqrt(1 - x) / 2)) (effectively). The actual arithmetic takes pains to minimize loss of intermediate significance.
- Otherwise, if y == 1.0, use zero.
- Otherwise, y > 1.0 and the function reports a domain error.

The concern with any such piecemeal approach is introducing discontinuities at the boundaries. The most worrisome boundary in this case occurs when y equals 0.5.

_Asin determines the final result from notes taken in idx along the way:

- If idx & 1, the arccosine was requested, not the arcsine.
- If idx & 2, the argument was negated.
- If idx & 4, the magnitude of the argument was greater than 0.5.

The final fixups involve adding various multiples of $\pi/4$ and negating the works. The sums are formed in stages to prevent loss of significance.

acos   Figure 7.21 shows the file acos.c and Figure 7.22 shows the file asin.c.
asin These define the trivial functions acos and asin. The header <math.h> defines masking macros for both.

atan   The last of the inverse trignometric functions is the arctangent. It comes
atan2 in two forms, atan(x) and atan2(y, x). Both call a common function _Atan to do the actual computation. Unlike the earlier trignometric functions, however, the common function is not the best one to show first. Figure 7.23 shows the file atan.c. Figure 7.24 shows the file atan2.c. It defines the function atan2 that reveals how the three functions work together.

Figure 7.19:
tan.c

```c
/* tan function */
#include "xmath.h"

/* coefficients, after Cody & Waite, Chapter 9 */
static const double p[3] = {
    -0.17861707342254426711e-4,
     0.34248878235890589960e-2,
    -0.13338350006421960681e+0};
static const double q[4] = {
     0.49819433993786512270e-6,
    -0.31181531907010027307e-3,
     0.25663832289440112864e-1,
    -0.46671683339755294240e+0};
static const double c1 = {3294198.0 / 2097152.0};
static const double c2 = {3.139164786504813217e-7};
static const double twobypi = {0.63661977236758134308};
static const double twopi = {6.28318530717958647693};


double tan(double x)
    {                                           /* compute tan(x) */
    double g, gd;
    long quad;

    switch (_Dtest(&x))
        {
    case NAN:
        errno = EDOM;
        return (x);
    case INF:
        errno = EDOM;
        return (_Nan._D);
    case 0:
        return (0.0);
    default:                                         /* finite */
        if (x < -HUGE_RAD || HUGE_RAD < x)
            {                         /* x huge, sauve qui peut */
            g = x / twopi;
            _Dint(&g, 0);
            x -= g * twopi;
            }
        g = x * twobypi;
        quad = (long)(0 < g ? g + 0.5 : g - 0.5);
        g = (double)quad;
        g = (x - g * c1) - g * c2;
        gd = 1.0;
        if (_Rteps._D < (g < 0.0 ? -g : g))
            {                        /* g*g worth computing */
            double y = g * g;

            gd += (((q[0] * y + q[1]) * y + q[2]) * y + q[3]) * y;
            g += ((p[0] * y + p[1]) * y + p[2]) * y * g;
            }
        return ((unsigned int)quad & 0x1 ? -gd / g : g / gd);
        }
    }
```
□

```
/* _Asin function */
#include "xmath.h"

/* coefficients, after Cody & Waite, Chapter 10 */
static const double p[5] = {
    -0.69674573447350646411e+0,
     0.10152522233806463645e+2,
    -0.39688862997504877339e+2,
     0.57208227877891731407e+2,
    -0.27368494524164255994e+2};
static const double q[6] = {
     0.10000000000000000000e+1,
    -0.23823859153670238830e+2,
     0.15095270841030604719e+3,
    -0.38186303361750149284e+3,
     0.41714430248260412556e+3,
    -0.16421096714498560795e+3};
static const double piby2 = {1.57079632679489661923};
static const double piby4 = {0.78539816339744830962};

double _Asin(double x, int idx)
    {                                   /* compute asin(x) or acos(x) */
    double g, y;
    const short errx = _Dtest(&x);

    if (0 < errx)
        {                                              /* INF, NaN */
        errno = EDOM;
        return (errx == NAN ? x : _Nan._D);
        }
    if (x < 0.0)
        y = -x, idx |= 2;
    else
        y = x;
    if (y < _Rteps._D)
        ;
    else if (y < 0.5)
        {                               /* y*y worth computing */
        g = y * y;
        y += y * g * _Poly(g, p, 4) / _Poly(g, q, 5);
        }
    else if (y < 1.0)
        {                       /* find 2*asin(sqrt((1-x)/2)) */
        idx |= 4;
        g = (1.0 - y) / 2.0;                    /* NOT * 0.5! */
        y = sqrt(g);
        y += y;
        y += y * g * _Poly(g, p, 4) / _Poly(g, q, 5);
        }
    else if (y == 1.0)
        idx |= 4, y = 0.0;
    else
        {                               /* 1.0 < |x|, undefined */
        errno = EDOM;
        return (_Nan._D);
```

```
Continuing            }
  xasin.c       switch (idx)
   Part 2           {                              /* flip and fold */
                default:                         /* shouldn't happen */
                case 0:                          /* asin, [0, 1/2) */
                case 5:                          /* acos, (1/2, 1] */
                    return (y);
                case 1:                          /* acos, [0, 1/2) */
                case 4:                          /* asin, (1/2, 1] */
                    return ((piby4 - y) + piby4);
                case 2:                          /* asin, [-1/2, 0) */
                    return (-y);
                case 3:                          /* acos, [-1/2, 0) */
                    return ((piby4 + y) + piby4);
                case 6:                          /* asin, [-1, -1/2) */
                    return ((-piby4 + y) - piby4);
                case 7:                          /* acos, [-1, -1/2) */
                    return ((piby2 - y) + piby2);
                }
        }
```

Figure 7.21:
acos.c

```
/* acos function */
#include <math.h>

double (acos)(double x)
    {                                          /* compute acos(x) */
    return (_Asin(x, 1));
    }
```

Figure 7.22:
asin.c

```
/* asin function */
#include <math.h>

double (asin)(double x)
    {                                          /* compute asin(x) */
    return (_Asin(x, 0));
    }
```

macro DSIGN   As you can see, the function `atan` offers only a subset of the possibilities inherent in `atan2`. That's because `atan(y)` is equivalent to `atan2(y, 1.0)`. By the way, the header `"xmath.h"` defines the macro DSIGN as:

```
define DSIGN(x) (((unsigned short *)&(x))[D0] & _DSIGN)
```

It lets you inspect the sign bit of a special code, such as Inf, that may not test well in a normal expression. I use DSIGN to test the sign bit whenever such a special code can occur.

`atan2` first checks its arguments for a variety of special codes. It accepts any pair that define a direction for a radius vector drawn from the origin. (The treatment of `atan2(0, 0)` is controversial. I chose to return zero, based on the advice of experts.) The function then determines the two arguments

Figure 7.23:
atan.c

```
/* atan function */
#include "xmath.h"

double (atan)(double x)
    {                                              /* compute atan(x) */
    unsigned short hex;
    static const double piby2 = {1.57079632679489661923};

    switch (_Dtest(&x))
        {                                   /* test for special codes */
    case NAN:
        errno = EDOM;
        return (x);
    case INF:
        return (DSIGN(x) ? -piby2 : piby2);
    case 0:
        return (0.0);
    default:                                              /* finite */
        if (x < 0.0)
            x = -x, hex = 0x8;
        else
            hex = 0x0;
        if (1.0 < x)
            x = 1.0 / x, hex ^= 0x2;
        return (_Atan(x, hex));
        }
    }
```

to _Atan. z is the tangent argument reduced to the interval [0, 1]. hex divides the circle into sixteen equal slices:

- If hex & 0x8, negate the final result.
- If hex & 0x4, add the arctangent of z to $\pi/4$.
- If hex & 0x2, subtract the arctangent of z from $\pi/4$.
- If hex & 0x1, add $\pi/6$ to the arctangent of z

Only _Atan sets the least-significant bit, to indicate that z was initially greater than $2-3^{1/2}$ (about 0.268). It replaces z with:

```
(z*sqrt(3)-1)/sqrt(3)+z)
```

All of these machinations derive from various trignometric identities exploited to reduce the range required for approximation.

function
_Atan
Figure 7.25 shows the file xatan.c that defines the function _Atan. It assumes that it is called only by atan or atan2. Hence, it checks only whether its argument x needs to be reduced below $2-3^{1/2}$. If the magnitude of the reduced argument is less than _Rteps._D, that serves as the approximation to the arctangent. Otherwise, the function computes a ratio of polynomials taken from Cody and Waite. The function adds an element from the table a to take care of all the adding and subtracting of constants described above.

Figure 7.24:
atan2.c

```
/* atan2 function */
#include "xmath.h"

double (atan2)(double y, double x)
    {                                           /* compute atan(y/x) */
    double z;
    const short errx = _Dtest(&x);
    const short erry = _Dtest(&y);
    unsigned short hex;

    if (errx <= 0 && erry <= 0)
        {                                   /* x & y both finite or 0 */
        if (y < 0.0)
            y = -y, hex = 0x8;
        else
            hex = 0x0;
        if (x < 0.0)
            x = -x, hex ^= 0x6;
        if (x < y)
            z = x / y, hex ^= 0x2;
        else if (0.0 < x)
            z = y / x;
        else
            return (0.0);                       /* atan(0, 0) */
        }
    else if (errx == NAN || erry == NAN)
        {                                   /* return one of the NaNs */
        errno = EDOM;
        return (errx == NAN ? x : y);
        }
    else
        {                                       /* at least one INF */
        z = errx == erry ? 1.0 : 0.0;
        hex = DSIGN(y) ? 0x8 : 0x0;
        if (DSIGN(x))
            hex ^= 0x6;
        if (erry == INF)
            hex ^= 0x2;
        }
    return (_Atan(z, hex));
    }
```

□

function The final group of functions are those that compute exponentials, loga-
sqrt rithms, and special powers. Figure 7.26 shows the file sqrt.c. The function
sqrt computes the square root of its argument x, or $x^{1/2}$. It partitions a
positive, finite x, using _Dunscale, into an exponent e and a fraction f. The
argument value is $f*2^e$, where f is in the interval [0.5, 1.0). The square root
is then $f^{1/2}*2^{e/2}$.

The function first computes a quadratic keast-squares fit to $f^{1/2}$. It then
applies Newton's Method — divide and average — three times to obtain
the needed precision. Note how the function combines the last two iterations of the algorithm to improve performance slightly.

Figure 7.25:
xatan.c

```c
/* _Atan function */
#include "xmath.h"

/* coefficients, after Cody & Waite, Chapter 11 */
static const double a[8] = {
    0.0,
    0.52359877559829887308,
    1.57079632679489661923,
    1.04719755119659774615,
    1.57079632679489661923,
    2.09439510239319549231,
    3.14159265358979323846,
    2.61799387799149436538};
static const double p[4] = {
    -0.83758299368150059274e+0,
    -0.84946240351320683534e+1,
    -0.20505855195861651981e+2,
    -0.13688768894191926929e+2};
static const double q[5] = {
    0.10000000000000000000e+1,
    0.15024001160028576121e+2,
    0.59578436142597344465e+2,
    0.86157349597130242515e+2,
    0.41066306682575781263e+2};
static const double fold = {0.26794919243112270647};
static const double sqrt3 = {1.73205080756887729353};
static const double sqrt3m1 = {0.73205080756887729353};

double _Atan(double x, unsigned short idx)
    {                               /* compute atan(x), 0 <= x <= 1.0 */
    if (fold < x)
        {                                       /* 2-sqrt(3) < x */
        x = (((sqrt3m1 * x - 0.5) - 0.5) + x) / (sqrt3 + x);
        idx |= 0x1;
        }
    if (x < -_Rteps._D || _Rteps._D < x)
        {                               /* x*x worth computing */
        const double g = x * x;

        x += x * g / _Poly(g, q, 4)
            * (((p[0] * g + p[1]) * g + p[2]) * g + p[3]);
        }
    if (idx & 0x2)
        x = -x;
    x += a[idx & 07];
    return (idx & 0x8 ? -x : x);
    }
```

```
/* sqrt function */
#include <limits.h>
#include "xmath.h"

double (sqrt)(double x)
    {                                                /* compute sqrt(x) */
    short xexp;

    switch (_Dunscale(&xexp, &x))
        {                                        /* test for special codes */
    case NAN:
        errno = EDOM;
        return (x);
    case INF:
        if (DSIGN(x))
            {                                                /* -INF */
            errno = EDOM;
            return (_Nan._D);
            }
        else
            {                                                /* +INF */
            errno = ERANGE;
            return (_Inf._D);
            }
    case 0:
        return (0.0);
    default:                                                /* finite */
        if (x < 0.0)
            {                                /* sqrt undefined for reals */
            errno = EDOM;
            return (_Nan._D);
            }
        {                                /* 0 < x, compute sqrt(x) */
        double y;
        static const double sqrt2 = {1.41421356237309505};

        y = (-0.1984742 * x + 0.8804894) * x + 0.3176687;
        y = 0.5 * (y + x / y);
        y += x / y;
        x = 0.25 * y + x / y;
        if ((unsigned int)xexp & 1)
            x *= sqrt2, --xexp;
        _Dscale(&x, xexp / 2);
        return (x);
        }
        }
    }
```

Figure 7.27:
xexp.c

```c
/* _Exp function */
#include "xmath.h"

/* coefficients, after Cody & Waite, Chapter 6 */
static const double p[3] = {
    0.31555192765684646356e-4,
    0.75753180159422776666e-2,
    0.25000000000000000000e+0};
static const double q[4] = {
    0.75104028399870046114e-6,
    0.63121894374398503557e-3,
    0.56817302698551221787e-1,
    0.50000000000000000000e+0};
static const double c1 = {22713.0 / 32768.0};
static const double c2 = {1.428606820309417232e-6};
static const double hugexp = {(double)HUGE_EXP};
static const double invln2 = {1.4426950408889634074};

short _Exp(double *px, short eoff)
    {                               /* compute e^(*px)*2^eoff, x finite */
    int neg;

    if (*px < 0)
        *px = -*px, neg = 1;
    else
        neg = 0;
    if (hugexp < *px)
        {                           /* certain underflow or overflow */
        *px = neg ? 0.0 : _Inf._D;
        return (neg ? 0 : INF);
        }
    else
        {                               /* xexp won't overflow */
        double g = *px * invln2;
        short xexp = (short)(g + 0.5);

        g = (double)xexp;
        g = (*px - g * c1) - g * c2;
        if (-_Rteps._D < g && g < _Rteps._D)
            *px = 1.0;
        else
            {                           /* g*g worth computing */
            const double y = g * g;

            g *= (p[0] * y + p[1]) * y + p[2];
            *px = 0.5 + g / (((q[0] * y + q[1]) * y + q[2]) * y
                + q[3] - g);
            ++xexp;
            }
        if (neg)
            *px = 1.0 / *px, xexp = -xexp;
        return (_Dscale(px, eoff + xexp));
        }
    }
```

□

function   Figure 7.27 shows the file `xexp.c` that defines the function `_Exp`. Several
_Exp functions need to compute the exponential of a finite argument, or e^x. A
number of these actually need to compute $e^x/2$. In this case, the argument
`eoff` is -1. Overflow occurs only if $e^x/2$ overflows.

macro   The header `"xmath.h"` defines the macro `HUGE_EXP` as the carefully con-
HUGE_EXP trived value:

```
#define HUGE_EXP    (int)(_DMAX * 900L / 1000)
```

This value is large enough to cause certain overflow on all known floating-
point representations. It is also small enough not to cause integer overflow
in the computations that follow. Thus, `HUGE_EXP` offers a coarse filter for
truly silly arguments to `_Exp`.

The trick here is to divide x by $ln(2)$ and raise 2 to that power. You can
pick off the integer part and compute 2^g, for g in the interval [−0.5, 0.5]. You
add in the integer part (plus `eoff`) at the end with `_Dscale`. That function
also handles any overflow or underflow safely.

Reducing the argument this way has many of the same problems as
reducing the arguments to `_sin` and `tan`, described earlier. The one advantage here is that you can choose extended-precision constants `c1` and `c2` to
represent $1/ln(2)$ adequately for all reasonable argument values.

As usual, the reduced argument is compared against `_Rteps._D` to avoid
underflow and unnecessary computation. The ratio of polynomials is taken
from Cody and Waite. The approximation actually computes $2^g/2$, thus the
correction to `xexp`.

function   Figure 7.28 shows the file `exp.c`. The function `exp` tests its argument for
exp special codes before calling `_Exp` with a finite argument. It then tests the
return value for a zero or Inf result, to report a range error.

function   Figure 7.29 shows the file `cosh.c`. The function `cosh` also has little else to
cosh do besides test its arguments for special codes and call `_Exp`. That's because
the value of the function depends on `exp(x)/2` whichever way it's computed:

- If `x < _Xbig._D` then the value is `(exp(x) + exp(-x))/2`. The actual form
  eliminates the second function call and some arithmetic.
- Otherwise, the value is `exp(x) / 2`, obtained directly from `_Exp`.

`cosh` must also report a range error if `_Exp(x, -1)` overflows.

function   Figure 7.30 shows the file `sinh.c`. The function `sinh` is also best com-
sinh puted in terms of `_Exp` over much of its range. But it is an odd function,
unlike `cosh`. When the magnitude of its argument `x` is less than 1.0, the
conventional definition `(exp(x) - exp(-x)) / 2` loses precision. Over this
interval, it is better to approximate the function with a ratio of polynomials,
again courtesy of Cody and Waite. As usual, if the magnitude of `x` is less
than `_Rteps._D`, the argument itself is an adequate approximation to the
value of the function.

Figure 7.28:
exp.c

```
/* exp function */
#include "xmath.h"

double (exp)(double x)
    {                                              /* compute exp(x) */
    switch (_Dtest(&x))
        {                                          /* test for special codes */
    case NAN:
        errno = EDOM;
        return (x);
    case INF:
        errno = ERANGE;
        return (DSIGN(x) ? 0.0 : _Inf._D);
    case 0:
        return (1.0);
    default:                                       /* finite */
        if (0 <= _Exp(&x, 0))
            errno = ERANGE;
        return (x);
        }
    }
```

Figure 7.29:
cosh.c

```
/* cosh function */
#include "xmath.h"

double (cosh)(double x)
    {                                              /* compute cosh(x) */
    switch (_Dtest(&x))
        {                                          /* test for special codes */
    case NAN:
        errno = EDOM;
        return (x);
    case INF:
        errno = ERANGE;
        return (_Inf._D);
    case 0:
        return (1.0);
    default:                                       /* finite */
        if (x < 0.0)
            x = -x;
        if (0 <= _Exp(&x, -1))
            errno = ERANGE;                        /* x large */
        else if (x < _Xbig._D)
            x += 0.25 / x;
        return (x);
        }
    }
```

Figure 7.30:
sinh.c

```c
/* sinh function */
#include "xmath.h"

/* coefficients, after Cody & Waite, Chapter 12 */
static const double p[4] = {
    -0.78966127417357099479e+0,
    -0.16375798202630751372e+3,
    -0.11563521196851768270e+5,
    -0.35181283430177117881e+6};
static const double q[4] = {
     1.0,
    -0.27773523119650701667e+3,
     0.36162723109421836460e+5,
    -0.21108770058106271242e+7};

double (sinh)(double x)
    {                                          /* compute sinh(x) */
    switch (_Dtest(&x))
        {                                   /* test for special codes */
    case NAN:
        errno = EDOM;
        return (x);
    case INF:
        errno = ERANGE;
        return (DSIGN(x) ? -_Inf._D : _Inf._D);
    case 0:
        return (0.0);
    default:                                          /* finite */
        {                               /* compute sinh(finite) */
        short neg;

        if (x < 0.0)
            x = -x, neg = 1;
        else
            neg = 0;
        if (x < _Rteps._D)
            ;                                         /* x tiny */
        else if (x < 1.0)
            {                                         /* |x| < 1 */
            const double y = x * x;

            x += x * y
                * (((p[0] * y + p[1]) * y + p[2]) * y + p[3])
                / (((q[0] * y + q[1]) * y + q[2]) * y + q[3]);
            }
        else if (0 <= _Exp(&x, -1))
            errno = ERANGE;                          /* x large */
        else if (x < _Xbig._D)
            x -= 0.25 / x;
        return (neg ? -x : x);
        }
        }
    }
```

function   Figure 7.31 shows the file `tanh.c`. The function `tanh` is similar in many
tanh ways to `sinh`. One difference is that it cannot overflow. The function
approaches ±1.0 as the magnitude of the argument `x` increases. (The function could compare `x` to `_Xbig._D` as do `cosh` and `sinh`. The overflow code
returned `_Exp` serves as adequate notice, however.) The other difference is
where the function chooses to change to a ratio-of-polynomials approximation. The one use here, again from Cody and Waite, is accurate for
magnitudes of `x` less than $ln(3)/2$ (about 0.549).

function   Figure 7.32 shows the file `log.c`. It computes `log(x)` by calling `_Log(x,`
log `0)`. Naturally, the header `<math.h>` provides a masking macro for this
function. This may seem silly, but it is the safe way to provide a masking
macro for `log10` (described below) as well.

function   Figure 7.33 shows the file `xlog.c` that defines the function `_Log`. It
_Log computes the natural logarithm using tricks reminiscent of those used in
`_Exp`, only in reverse. The idea is to pick off the binary exponent e using
`_Dunscale`, leaving the fraction f. The argument value is $f*2^e$, where f is in
the interval [0.5, 1.0). You can compute the base-2 logarithm of these
components as $log_2(f) + e$. You get the final result by multiplying this sum
by $ln(2)$.

That approach requires a few refinements. The approximation from
Cody and Waite wants f in the interval $[0.5^{1/2}, 2.0^{1/2}]$. If f (actually `x`) is too
small, you have to double it and correct e (`xexp`). You also have to introduce
the new variable $z = (f-1)/(f+1)$. It is better to combine both operations and
eliminate some steps that can cost precision. The approximation is yet
another ratio of polynomials. Note that it actually computes the natural
logarithm, so it is only necessary to scale `xexp` before forming the sum.

You have to form the sum carefully, at least for logarithms near zero. This
is the other face of the argument reduction problem in `_Exp`. Both functions
use the same extended-precision representation of $ln(2)$. Here, the smaller
part is combined before the larger, to involve as many low-order bits of the
conversion constant as posssible in the final result.

log10   Figure 7.34 shows the file `log10.c`. It computes the base-10 logarithm by
calling `_Log` and multiplying the result by $log_{10}(e)$. The multiplication takes
place within `_Log` only for a finite result.

function   Figure 7.35 shows the file `pow.c`. The function `pow`, which raises `x` to the
pow `y` power, is easily the most complex of all the math functions. It must deal
with a broad assortment of special cases. It must also endeavor to develop
a precise result for a broad range of argument values.

By now you should be aware of the dangers in computing `exp(y *`
`log(x))`. Put simply, the logarithm displaces fraction bits to represent the
exponent of `x` as an integer part. Multiplying by `y` can make matters even
worse. The exponential turns integer bits back into exponent bits, but the
damage is already done. Unless you can perform the intermediate calculations to extended precision, you have to lose bits along the way. This

```c
/* tanh function */
#include "xmath.h"

/* coefficients, after Cody & Waite, Chapter 13 */
static const double p[3] = {
    -0.96437492777225469787e+0,
    -0.99225929672236083313e+2,
    -0.16134119023996228053e+4};
static const double q[4] = {
    0.10000000000000000000e+1,
    0.11274474380534949335e+3,
    0.22337720718962312926e+4,
    0.48402357071988688686e+4};
static const double ln3by2 = {0.54930614433405484570};

double (tanh)(double x)
    {                                           /* compute tanh(x) */
    switch (_Dtest(&x))
        {                                  /* test for special codes */
    case NAN:
        errno = EDOM;
        return (x);
    case INF:
        return (DSIGN(x) ? -1.0 : 1.0);
    case 0:
        return (0.0);
    default:                                         /* finite */
        {                                  /* compute tanh(finite) */
        short neg;

        if (x < 0.0)
            x = -x, neg = 1;
        else
            neg = 0;
        if (x < _Rteps._D)
            ;                                        /* x tiny */
        else if (x < ln3by2)
            {                                  /* |x| < ln(3)/2 */
            const double g = x * x;

            x += x * g * ((p[0] * g + p[1]) * g + p[2])
                / (((q[0] * g + q[1]) * g + q[2]) * g + q[3]);
            }
        else if (_Exp(&x, 0) < 0)
            x = 1.0 - 2.0 / (x * x + 1.0);
        else
            x = 1.0;                                 /* x large */
        return (neg ? -x : x);
        }
        }
    }
```

Figure 7.32:
log.c

```
/* log function */
#include <math.h>

double (log)(double x)
    {                                          /* compute ln(x) */
    return (_Log(x, 0));
    }                                                          □
```

Figure 7.33:
xlog.c
Part 1

```
/* _Log function */
#include "xmath.h"

/* coefficients, after Cody & Waite, Chapter 5 */
static const double p[3] = {
    -0.78956112887491257267e+0,
     0.16383943563021534222e+2,
    -0.64124943423745581147e+2};
static const double q[3] = {
    -0.35667977739034646171e+2,
     0.31203222091924532844e+3,
    -0.76949932108494879777e+3};
static const double c1 = {22713.0 / 32768.0};
static const double c2 = {1.428606820309417232e-6};
static const double loge = 0.43429448190325182765;
static const double rthalf = {0.70710678118654752440};

double _Log(double x, int decflag)
    {                                          /* compute ln(x) */
    short xexp;

    switch (_Dunscale(&xexp, &x))
        {                               /* test for special codes */
    case NAN:
        errno = EDOM;
        return (x);
    case INF:
        if (DSIGN(x))
            {                                          /* -INF */
            errno = EDOM;
            return (_Nan._D);
            }
        else
            {                                          /* INF */
            errno = ERANGE;
            return (_Inf._D);
            }
    case 0:
        errno = ERANGE;
        return (-_Inf._D);
    default:                                          /* finite */
        if (x < 0.0)
            {                              /* ln(negative) undefined */
            errno = EDOM;
            return (_Nan._D);
            }
```

```
        else
            {                                        /* 1/2 <= x < 1 */
            double z = x - 0.5;
            double w;

            if (rthalf < x)
                z = (z - 0.5) / (x * 0.5 + 0.5);
            else
                {                                    /* x <= sqrt(1/2) */
                --xexp;
                z /= (z * 0.5 + 0.5);
                }
            w = z * z;
            z += z * w * ((p[0] * w + p[1]) * w + p[2])
                / (((w + q[0]) * w + q[1]) * w + q[2]);
            if (xexp != 0)
                {                       /* form z += ln2 * xexp safely */
                const double xn = (double)xexp;

                z = (xn * c2 + z) + xn * c1;
                }
            return (decflag ? loge * z : z);
            }
        }
    }
```

Figure 7.34:
log10.c

```
/* log10 function */
#include <math.h>

double (log10)(double x)
    {                                        /* compute log10(x) */
    return (_Log(x, 1));
    }
```

implementation of **pow** effectively retains that exended precision, without benefit of a data type with more bits than *double*.

The first half of the function simply sorts out various combinations of argument values. Either **x** is zero or at least one of the arguments is Inf or NaN. I have yet to devise an illuminating way to tabulate all these cases. You'll have to trace through the code to see how it handles the various combinations. Once again, I followed the advice of people more expert than I on the treatment of the combinations with arguable results. The C Standard offers little guidance here.

You might note, by the way, how the function calls **_Dint(&y, -1)** to determine whether the integral value stored in the *double* **y** is even or odd. **_Dint** clears the least-significant bit of the integer part of **y**, in this case. It returns the negative code **FINITE** if the bit it clears was initially nonzero. You can find a similar test later in the function **pow**.

Figure 7.35:
pow.c
Part 1

```
/* pow function */
#include "xmath.h"

double (pow)(double x, double y)
    {                                                   /* compute x^y */
    double yi = y;
    double yx, z;
    short n, xexp, zexp;
    short neg = 0;
    short errx = _Dunscale(&xexp, &x);
    const short erry = _Dint(&yi, 0);
    static const short shuge = {HUGE_EXP};
    static const double dhuge = {(double)HUGE_EXP};
    static const double ln2 = {0.69314718055994530942};
    static const double rthalf = {0.70710678118654752440};

    if (0 <= errx || 0 < erry)
        {                       /* x == 0, INF, NAN; y == INF, NAN */
        z = _Nan._D;
        if (errx == NAN || erry == NAN)
            z = errx == NAN ? x : y, errx = NAN;
        else if (erry == INF)
            if (errx == INF)                            /* INF^INF */
                errx = INF;
            else                            /* 0^INF, finite^INF */
                errx = xexp <= 0 ? (DSIGN(y) ? INF : 0)
                    : xexp == 1 && (x == 0.5 || x == -0.5) ? NAN
                    : (DSIGN(y) ? 0 : INF);
        else if (y == 0.0)
            return (1.0);                       /* x^0, x not a NaN */
        else if (errx == INF)
            {       /* INF^finite (NB: erry tests y fraction) */
            errx = y < 0.0 ? 0 : INF;
            neg = DSIGN(x) && erry == 0 && _Dint(&y, -1) < 0;
            }
        else                                        /* 0^finite */
            errx = y < 0.0 ? INF : 0;
        if (errx == 0)
            return (0.0);
        else if (errx == INF)
            {                               /* return -INF or INF */
            errno = ERANGE;
            return (neg ? -_Inf._D : _Inf._D);
            }
        else
            {                                       /* return NaN */
            errno = EDOM;
            return (z);
            }
        }
    if (y == 0.0)
        return (1.0);
    if (0.0 < x)
        neg = 0;
```

```
else if (erry < 0)
    {                                   /* negative^fractional */
    errno = EDOM;
    return (_Nan._D);
    }
else
    x = -x, neg = _Dint(&yi, -1) < 0;
if (x < rthalf)
    x *= 2.0, --xexp;           /* -sqrt(.5) <= x <= sqrt(.5) */
n = 0, yx = 0.0;
if (y <= -dhuge)
    zexp = xexp < 0 ? shuge : xexp == 0 ? 0 : -shuge;
else if (dhuge <= y)
    zexp = xexp < 0 ? -shuge : xexp == 0 ? 0 : shuge;
else
    {                                   /* y*log2(x) may be reasonable */
    double dexp = (double)xexp;
    long zl = (long)(yx = y * dexp);

    if (zl != 0)
        {                       /* form yx = y*xexp-zl carefully */
        yx = y, _Dint(&yx, 16);
        yx = (yx * dexp - (double)zl) + (y - yx) * dexp;
        }
    yx *= ln2;
    zexp = zl <= -shuge ? -shuge : zl < shuge ? zl : shuge;
    if ((n = (short)y) < -SAFE_EXP || SAFE_EXP < n)
        n = 0;
    }
    {                           /* compute z = xfrac^n * 2^yx * 2^zexp */
    z = 1.0;
if (x != 1.0)
    {                                   /* z *= xfrac^n */
    if ((yi = y - (double)n) != 0.0)
        yx += log(x) * yi;
    if (n < 0)
        n = -n;
    for (yi = x; ; yi *= yi)
        {                               /* scale by x^2^n */
        if (n & 1)
            z *= yi;
        if ((n >>= 1) == 0)
            break;
        }
    if (y < 0.0)
        z = 1.0 / z;
    }
if (yx != 0.0)                                  /* z *= 2^yx */
    z = _Exp(&yx, 0) < 0 ? z * yx : yx;
if (0 <= _Dscale(&z, zexp))                     /* z *= 2^zexp */
    errno = ERANGE;                     /* underflow or overflow */
return (neg ? -z : z);
    }
}
```

macro   The second half of the function computes x^y for finite values of x and y.
SAFE_EXP   It begins by rewriting x as $f*2^e$, where f is in the interval $[0.5^{1/2}, 2.0^{1/2}]$. If
               N is the magnitude of the largest representable *double* exponent, you know
               that you can raise f to this power with no fear of overflow. The magnitude
               of the resulting exponent cannot exceed $N/2$. The header "**xmath.h**" defines
               the macro **SAFE_EXP** as:

```
#define SAFE_EXP    (_DMAX>>1)
```

pow uses this value for just such a check.

You can rewrite x^y as $f^{y}*2^{e*y}$. Then partition the product $e*y$ into an
integer plus a fraction, or $n+g$ where g is in the interval $(-1, 1)$. Now you
can rewrite the function as:

$$x^y = f^n * (f^{y-n} * 2^g) * 2^n$$

I grouped the middle two terms with malice aforethought. That reduces
the problem to forming the product of three terms:

- f^n is a loop that multiplies f by itself $|n|$ times. If n is negative, the result
  is divided into one. So long as $|n|$ is less than **SAFE_EXP**, the result cannot
  overflow or underflow, for the reasons given above.

- $(f^{y-n} * 2^g)$ can be evaluated as the exponential of $(y-n)*ln(f) + g*ln(2)$.
  Both terms in the sum are typically small, so no serious loss of precision
  should result in the addition or the exponentiation. An exception is
  when $|n|$ would exceed **SAFE_EXP**. In this case, the function sets n (also
  known as **n** in the code) to zero and throws precision to the winds. The
  sum cannot overflow, no matter how big y (**yi**) happens to be. If the
  exponential doesn't overflow, then the final result is probably domi-
  nated by this term anyway.

- 2^n is a simple call to **_Dscale**.

Much of the complexity of this computation lies in avoiding overflows
and underflows. The remainder lies in safely partitioning $e*y$ into the sum
of n and g. Note the use of **_Dint** yet another way here. It lets you preserve
an extra 16 bits of precision in **y**, using **yx** to extend its precision. That offsets
the loss of up to that much precision during the partitioning. The largest
floating-point exponents supported by this implementation are assumed
to have no more than 14 magnitude bits. The partitioning should thus be
safe over the entire range of representable values.

other   For completeness, I show two functions that are not used by the other
functions functions declared in **<math.h>**. Functions declared in the other standard
               headers need them, but these two functions need "**xmath.h**". It seemed
               wisest to park the two functions here.

function   Figure 7.37 shows the file **xdtento.c** that defines the function **_Dtento**.
_Dtento   It multiplies the *double* value **x** by ten raised to the power **n**. It is careful to
               avoid floating-point overflow or underflow in the process. Note the use of
               _Dunscale and **_Dscale** in the internal function **dmul**. Any potential over-
               flow or underflow occurs in **_Dscale**, which handles it safely. Function
               _Dtento assumes that the argument **x** is zero or finite.

function   Figure 7.36 shows the file `xldunsca.c`. It defines the function `_Ldunscale`
_Ldunscale that does the same job for *long double* arguments that `_Dunscale` does for
double arguments. In fact, if those two floating-point types have the same
representation, it does *exactly* the same job. Only if `_DLONG` is nonzero does
`_Ldunscale` handle the 10-byte IEEE 754 extended-precision format.

header   Figure 7.38 shows the file `xmath.h`. By now, you should have been
"xmath.h" introduced to all its mysteries. I show it in its entirety here also for
completeness.

Testing `<math.h>`

Testing math functions is serious business. Even the seminumerical
functions offer numerous opportunities to go astray. The rest require a
major investment in technology to validate properly. That's why I relied on
the `elefunt` tests to prove in the trignometric, exponential, logarithmic, and
special power functions.

On the Sun 3 workstation, which uses IEEE 754 floating-point arithmetic,
the worst-case errors these tests reported were a loss of less than two bits
of accuracy. The root-mean-square errors were generally much better than
two bits.

The `paranoia` tests report an occasional error of less that two bits as well.
(The offenders here are `sqrt` and some of the formatted input and output
functions for extreme values.) I described how you can obtain `paranoia` on
page 72.

I also provide a set of tests that exercise all the functions declared in
`<math.h>`. Each function has just a few test cases, enough to verify that it is
basically sane. Given all the functions declared in `<math.h>`, however, that
still amounts to a large number of tests. So I split the tests into three files,
one for each of the three general groups of functions.

program   Figure 7.39 shows the file `tmath1.c`. It tests the macro `HUGE_VAL` and all
tmath1.c the seminumerical functions. Certain tests can be expected to produce exact
results. Others may introduce small errors. For the latter, the function
`approx` checks that the result loses no more than two bits of precision. The
program also shows what the print functions display for `HUGE_VAL`.

For this library running on a computer architecture that tolerates the
special codes for Inf and NaN, the program displays the output:

```
HUGE_VAL prints as Inf
SUCCESS testing <math.h>, part 1
```

program   Figure 7.40 shows the file `tmath2.c`. It tests all the trignometric functions
tmath2.c at angles that are various multiples of $\pi/4$. These are often critical angles
for detecting loss of precision or errors in determining the sign of the result.
If all tests pass, the program displays the message:

```
SUCCESS testing <math.h>, part 2
```

```
/* _Ldunscale function -- IEEE 754 version */
#include "xmath.h"

#if _DLONG                              /* 10-byte IEEE format */
#define _LMASK  0x7fff
#define _LMAX   0x7fff
#define _LSIGN  0x8000
#if _D0==3
#define _L0     4                       /* little-endian order */
#define _L1     3
#define _L2     2
#define _L3     1
#define _L4     0
#else
#define _L0     0                       /* big-endian order */
#define _L1     1
#define _L2     2
#define _L3     3
#define _L4     4
#endif

static short dnorm(unsigned short *ps)
    {                           /* normalize long double fraction */
    short xchar;

    for (xchar = 0; ps[_L1] == 0; xchar -= 16)
        {                               /* shift left by 16 */
        ps[_L1] = ps[_L2], ps[_L2] = ps[_L3];
        ps[_L3] = ps[_L4], ps[_L4] = 0;
        }
    for (; ps[_L1] < 1U<<_LOFF; --xchar)
        {                               /* shift left by 1 */
        ps[_L1] = ps[_L1] << 1 | ps[_L2] >> 15;
        ps[_L2] = ps[_L2] << 1 | ps[_L3] >> 15;
        ps[_L3] = ps[_L3] << 1 | ps[_L4] >> 15;
        ps[_L4] <<= 1;
        }
    return (xchar);
    }

short _Ldunscale(short *pex, long double *px)
    {               /* separate *px to |frac| < 1/2 and 2^*pex */
    unsigned short *ps = (unsigned short *)px;
    short xchar = ps[_L0] & _LMASK;

    if (xchar == _LMAX)
        {                                       /* NaN or INF */
        *pex = 0;
        return (ps[_L1] & 0x7fff || ps[_L2]
            || ps[_L3] || ps[_L4] ? NAN : INF);
        }
```

```
        else if (ps[_L1] == 0 && ps[_L2] == 0
            && ps[_L3] == 0 && ps[_L4] == 0)
            {                                           /* zero */
            *pex = 0;
            return (0);
            }
        else
            {                           /* finite, reduce to [1/2, 1) */
            xchar += dnorm(ps);
            ps[_L0] = ps[_L0] & _LSIGN | _LBIAS;
            *pex = xchar - _LBIAS;
            return (FINITE);
            }
        }
#else                                   /* long double same as double */
short _Ldunscale(short *pex, long double *px)
    {                           /* separate *px to |frac| < 1/2 and 2^*pex */
    unsigned short *ps = (unsigned short *)px;
    short xchar = (ps[_D0] & _DMASK) >> _DOFF;

    if (xchar == _DMAX)
        {                                               /* NaN or INF */
        *pex = 0;
        return (ps[_D0] & _DFRAC || ps[_D1]
            || ps[_D2] || ps[_D3] ? NAN : INF);
        }
    else if (0 < xchar || (xchar = _Dnorm(ps)) != 0)
        {                           /* finite, reduce to [1/2, 1) */
        ps[_D0] = ps[_D0] & ~_DMASK | _DBIAS << _DOFF;
        *pex = xchar - _DBIAS;
        return (FINITE);
        }
    else
        {                                               /* zero */
        *pex = 0;
        return (0);
        }
    }
#endif                                                                  □
```

program   Figure 7.41 shows the file `tmath3.c`. It tests all the exponential, logarith-
tmath3.c mic, and special power functions for a few obvious properties. Note that
one or two of the tests are obliged to produce an exact result. If all tests
pass, the program displays the message:

`SUCCESS testing <math.h>, part 3`

I can report, rather sheepishly, that these simple tests caught numerous
errors. Some arose, naturally enough, while I was first writing and debugging the math functions. The more embarassing errors appeared while I
was introducing various "improvements." I learned to rerun them religiously after any changes.

Figure 7.37:
xdtento.c
Part 1

```c
/* _Dtento function -- IEEE 754 version */
#include <errno.h>
#include <float.h>
#include "xmath.h"

        /* macros */
#define NPOWS   (sizeof pows / sizeof pows[0] - 1)
        /* static data */
static const double pows[] = {
    1e1, 1e2, 1e4, 1e8, 1e16, 1e32,
#if 0x100 < _DBIAS                          /* assume IEEE 754 8-byte */
    1e64, 1e128, 1e256,
#endif
    };
static const size_t npows = {NPOWS};

static short dmul(double *px, double y)
    {                          /* multiply y by *px with checking */
    short xexp;

    _Dunscale(&xexp, px);
    *px *= y;
    return (_Dscale(px, xexp));
    }

double _Dtento(double x, short n)
    {                                       /* compute x * 10**n */
    double factor;
    short errx;
    size_t i;

    if (n == 0 || x == 0.0)
        return (x);
    factor = 1.0;
    if (n < 0)
        {                                              /* scale down */
        unsigned int nu = -(unsigned int)n;

        for (i = 0; 0 < nu && i < npows; nu >>= 1, ++i)
            if (nu & 1)
                factor *= pows[i];
        errx = dmul(&x, 1.0 / factor);
        if (errx < 0 && 0 < nu)
            for (factor = 1.0 / pows[npows]; 0 < nu; --nu)
                if (0 <= (errx = dmul(&x, factor)))
                    break;
        }
    else if (0 < n)
        {                                              /* scale up */
        for (i = 0; 0 < n && i < npows; n >>= 1, ++i)
            if (n & 1)
                factor *= pows[i];
```

Continuing
xdtento.c
Part 2

```
                errx = dmul(&x, factor);
                if (errx < 0 && 0 < n)
                    for (factor = pows[npows]; 0 < n; --n)
                        if (0 <= (errx = dmul(&x, factor)))
                            break;
            }
        if (0 <= errx)
            errno = ERANGE;
        return (x);
        }
```

□

Figure 7.38:
xmath.h

```
/* xmath.h internal header -- IEEE 754 version */
#include <errno.h>
#include <math.h>
#include <stddef.h>
#ifndef _YVALS
#include <yvals.h>
#endif
        /* IEEE 754 properties */
#define _DFRAC   ((1<<_DOFF)-1)
#define _DMASK   (0x7fff&~_DFRAC)
#define _DMAX    ((1<<(15-_DOFF))-1)
#define _DNAN    (0x8000|_DMAX<<_DOFF|1<<(_DOFF-1))
#define _DSIGN  0x8000
#define DSIGN(x)     (((unsigned short *)&(x))[_D0] & _DSIGN)
#define HUGE_EXP    (int)(_DMAX * 900L / 1000)
#define HUGE_RAD    3.14e30
#define SAFE_EXP    (_DMAX>>1)
        /* word offsets within double */
#if _D0==3
#define _D1     2                              /* little-endian order */
#define _D2     1
#define _D3     0
#else
#define _D1     1                              /* big-endian order */
#define _D2     2
#define _D3     3
#endif
        /* return values for _D functions */
#define FINITE  -1
#define INF     1
#define NAN     2
        /* declarations */
double _Atan(double, unsigned short);
short _Dint(double *, short);
short _Dnorm(unsigned short *);
short _Dscale(double *, short);
double _Dtento(double, short);
short _Dtest(double *);
short _Dunscale(short *, double *);
short _Exp(double *, short);
short _Ldunscale(short *, long double *);
double _Poly(double, const double *, int);
extern _Dconst _Inf, _Nan, _Rteps, _Xbig;
```

□

Figure 7.39:
tmath1.c
Part 1

```
/* test math functions -- part 1 */
#include <assert.h>
#include <float.h>
#include <math.h>
#include <stdio.h>

static double eps;

static int approx(double d1, double d2)
    {                               /* test for approximate equality */
    if (d2 != 0)
        return (fabs((d2 - d1) / d2) < eps);
    else
        return (fabs(d1) < eps);
    }

int main()
    {                       /* test basic workings of math functions */
    double huge_val, x;
    int xexp;

    huge_val = HUGE_VAL;
    eps = DBL_EPSILON * 4.0;
    assert(ceil(-5.1) == -5.0);
    assert(ceil(-5.0) == -5.0);
    assert(ceil(-4.9) == -4.0);
    assert(ceil(0.0) == 0.0);
    assert(ceil(4.9) == 5.0);
    assert(ceil(5.0) == 5.0);
    assert(ceil(5.1) == 6.0);
    assert(fabs(-5.0) == 5.0);
    assert(fabs(0.0) == 0.0);
    assert(fabs(5.0) == 5.0);
    assert(floor(-5.1) == -6.0);
    assert(floor(-5.0) == -5.0);
    assert(floor(-4.9) == -5.0);
    assert(floor(0.0) == 0.0);
    assert(floor(4.9) == 4.0);
    assert(floor(5.0) == 5.0);
    assert(floor(5.1) == 5.0);
    assert(fmod(-7.0, 3.0) == -1.0);
    assert(fmod(-3.0, 3.0) == 0.0);
    assert(fmod(-2.0, 3.0) == -2.0);
    assert(fmod(0.0, 3.0) == 0.0);
    assert(fmod(2.0, 3.0) == 2.0);
    assert(fmod(3.0, 3.0) == 0.0);
    assert(fmod(7.0, 3.0) == 1.0);
    assert(approx(frexp(-3.0, &xexp), -0.75) && xexp == 2);
    assert(approx(frexp(-0.5, &xexp), -0.5) && xexp == 0);
    assert(frexp(0.0, &xexp) == 0.0 && xexp == 0);
    assert(approx(frexp(0.33, &xexp), 0.66) && xexp == -1);
    assert(approx(frexp(0.66, &xexp), 0.66) && xexp == 0);
    assert(approx(frexp(96.0, &xexp), 0.75) && xexp == 7);
    assert(ldexp(-3.0, 4) == -48.0);
    assert(ldexp(-0.5, 0) == -0.5);
```

Continuing tmath1.c Part 2

```
assert(ldexp(0.0, 36) == 0.0);
assert(approx(ldexp(0.66, -1), 0.33));
assert(ldexp(96, -3) == 12.0);
assert(approx(modf(-11.7, &x), -11.7 + 11.0)
    && x == -11.0);
assert(modf(-0.5, &x) == -0.5 && x == 0.0);
assert(modf(0.0, &x) == 0.0 && x == 0.0);
assert(modf(0.6, &x) == 0.6&& x == 0.0);
assert(modf(12.0, &x) == 0.0&& x == 12.0);
printf("HUGE_VAL prints as %.16e\n", huge_val);
puts("SUCCESS testing <math.h>, part 1");
return (0);
}
```

References

William J. Cody, Jr. and William Waite, *Software Manual For the Elementary Functions* (Englewood Cliffs, N.J.: Prentice-Hall, Inc., 1980). This is an excellent reference on writing reliable and accurate math functions. It is the source of approximations for many of the functions in this chapter.

John F. Hart, E.W. Cheney, Charles L. Lawson, Hans J. Maehly, Charles K. Mesztenyi, John R. Rice, Henry G. Thacher, Jr., and Christoph Witzgall, *Computer Approximations* (Malabar, Florida: Robert E. Krieger Publishing Company, 1978). This book contains several chapters on the art and science of numerical approximation, but its great strength lies in its extensive tables of coefficients. You can probably find an approximation with just the precision you need for any of the common math functions.

`elefunt` is a collection of transportable FORTRAN programs for testing the elementary function programs provided with FORTRAN compilers. They are fanatically thorough. The programs are written in FORTRAN by William J. Cody and are described in detail in Cody and Waite. Mail to the Internet address `netlib@research.att.com` the request:

```
send index from elefunt
```

Exercises

Exercise 7.1 Determine the floating-point representation for your C translator. Can you alter the parameters in `<yvals.h>` to accommodate it? If so, do so. Otherwise, alter the primitives to suit.

Exercise 7.2 Write the function `double hypot(double, double)` that computes the square root of the sum of the squares of its arguments. (This yields the hypotenuse of a right triangle whose sides are the two arguments.) Test it with the expressions:

```
hypot(0.7 * DBL_MAX, 0.7 * DBL_MAX);
hypot(DBL_MAX, 1.0);
hypot(1.0, DBL_MAX);
hypot(3.0, 4.0);
```

Figure 7.40:
tmath2.c
Part 1

```c
/* test math functions -- part 2 */
#include <assert.h>
#include <float.h>
#include <math.h>
#include <stdio.h>

        /* static data */
static double eps;

static int approx(double d1, double d2)
    {                                   /* test for approximate equality */
    return ((d2 ? fabs((d2 - d1) / d2) : fabs(d1)) < eps);
    }

int main()
    {                           /* test basic workings of math functions */
    double x;
    int xexp;
    static double piby4 = {0.78539816339744830962};
    static double rthalf = {0.70710678118654752440};

    eps = DBL_EPSILON * 4.0;
    assert(approx(acos(-1.0), 4.0 * piby4));
    assert(approx(acos(-rthalf), 3.0 * piby4));
    assert(approx(acos(0.0), 2.0 * piby4));
    assert(approx(acos(rthalf), piby4));
    assert(approx(acos(1.0), 0.0));
    assert(approx(asin(-1.0), -2.0 * piby4));
    assert(approx(asin(-rthalf), -piby4));
    assert(approx(asin(0.0), 0.0));
    assert(approx(asin(rthalf), piby4));
    assert(approx(asin(1.0), 2.0 * piby4));
    assert(approx(atan(-DBL_MAX), -2.0 * piby4));
    assert(approx(atan(-1.0), -piby4));
    assert(approx(atan(0.0), 0.0));
    assert(approx(atan(1.0), piby4));
    assert(approx(atan(DBL_MAX), 2.0 * piby4));
    assert(approx(atan2(-1.0, -1.0), -3.0 * piby4));
    assert(approx(atan2(-1.0, 0.0), -2.0 * piby4));
    assert(approx(atan2(-1.0, 1.0), -piby4));
    assert(approx(atan2(0.0, 1.0), 0.0));
    assert(approx(atan2(1.0, 1.0), piby4));
    assert(approx(atan2(1.0, 0.0), 2.0 * piby4));
    assert(approx(atan2(1.0, -1.0), 3.0 * piby4));
    assert(approx(atan2(0.0, -1.0), 4.0 * piby4)
        || approx(atan2(0.0, -1.0), -4.0 * piby4));
    assert(approx(cos(-3.0 * piby4), -rthalf));
    assert(approx(cos(-2.0 * piby4), 0.0));
    assert(approx(cos(-piby4), rthalf));
    assert(approx(cos(0.0), 1.0));
    assert(approx(cos(piby4), rthalf));
    assert(approx(cos(2.0 * piby4), 0.0));
    assert(approx(cos(3.0 * piby4), -rthalf));
    assert(approx(cos(4.0 * piby4), -1.0));
    assert(approx(sin(-3.0 * piby4), -rthalf));
```

<table>
<tr><td>Continuing
tmath2.c
Part 2</td><td>

```
assert(approx(sin(-2.0 * piby4), -1.0));
assert(approx(sin(-piby4), -rthalf));
assert(approx(sin(0.0), 0.0));
assert(approx(sin(piby4), rthalf));
assert(approx(sin(2.0 * piby4), 1.0));
assert(approx(sin(3.0 * piby4), rthalf));
assert(approx(sin(4.0 * piby4), 0.0));
assert(approx(tan(-3.0 * piby4), 1.0));
assert(approx(tan(-piby4), -1.0));
assert(approx(tan(0.0), 0.0));
assert(approx(tan(piby4), 1.0));
assert(approx(tan(3.0 * piby4), -1.0));
puts("SUCCESS testing <math.h>, part 2");
return (0);
}
```
</td></tr>
</table>

Exercise 7.3 Devise a more comprehensive set of tests for the function **hypot** from the previous exercise.

Exercise 7.4 Write functions that perform complex arithmetic. Each complex value $x + i*y$ is represented by the pair (x, y). Provide at least the operations compare, subtract, add, divide, multiply, magnitude, and phase. Also provide functions that convert between existing floating-point types and complex. Can you use any existing functions to advantage? What other functions are desirable?

Exercise 7.5 Alter the primitives in **<math.h>** to eliminate the special codes for NaN, Inf, and –Inf. Replace primitives with macros in **"xmath.h"** wherever possible. What does this do to the sizes of functions in the Standard C library? What does it do to execution times?

Exercise 7.6 [**Harder**] Write versions of all the math functions that accept *float* arguments and produce *float* results. Append an **f** to each existing function name to obtain the new function name. How can you test these functions?

Exercise 7.7 [**Harder**] Write versions of all the math functions that accept *long double* arguments and produce *long double* results. Append an **f** to each existing function name to obtain the new function name. How can you test these functions?

Exercise 7.8 [**Harder**] Write versions of all the math functions that accept complex arguments and produce complex results. Prepend a **c** to each existing function name to obtain the new function name. How can you test these functions?

Exercise 7.9 [**Very hard**] Measure a large corpus of code to determine if any of the math functions are worth coding inline. Modify a C compiler to do so. Measure the result.

Figure 7.41:
tmath3.c

```
/* test math functions -- part 3 */
#include <assert.h>
#include <float.h>
#include <math.h>
#include <stdio.h>

static double eps;

static int approx(double d1, double d2)
    {                               /* test for approximate equality */
    return ((d2 ? fabs((d2 - d1) / d2) : fabs(d1)) < eps);
    }

int main()
    {                       /* test basic workings of math functions */
    double x;
    int xexp;
    static double e = {2.71828182845904523536};
    static double ln2 = {0.69314718055994530942};
    static double rthalf = {0.70710678118654752440};

    eps = DBL_EPSILON * 4.0;
    assert(approx(cosh(-1.0), (e + 1.0 / e) / 2.0));
    assert(approx(cosh(0.0), 1.0));
    assert(approx(cosh(1.0), (e + 1.0 / e) / 2.0));
    assert(approx(exp(-1.0), 1.0 / e));
    assert(approx(exp(0.0), 1.0));
    assert(approx(exp(ln2), 2.0));
    assert(approx(exp(1.0), e));
    assert(approx(exp(3.0), e * e * e));
    assert(log(1.0) == 0.0);
    assert(approx(log(e), 1.0));
    assert(approx(log(e * e * e), 3.0));
    assert(approx(log10(1.0), 0.0));
    assert(approx(log10(5.0), 1.0 - log10(2.0)));
    assert(approx(log10(1e5), 5.0));
    assert(approx(pow(-2.5, 2.0), 6.25));
    assert(approx(pow(-2.0, -3.0), -0.125));
    assert(pow(0.0, 6.0) == 0.0);
    assert(approx(pow(2.0, -0.5), rthalf));
    assert(approx(pow(3.0, 4.0), 81.0));
    assert(approx(sinh(-1.0), -(e - 1.0 / e) / 2.0));
    assert(approx(sinh(0.0), 0.0));
    assert(approx(sinh(1.0), (e - 1.0 / e) / 2.0));
    assert(approx(sqrt(0.0), 0.0));
    assert(approx(sqrt(0.5), rthalf));
    assert(approx(sqrt(1.0), 1.0));
    assert(approx(sqrt(2.0), 1.0 / rthalf));
    assert(approx(sqrt(144.0), 12.0));
    assert(approx(tanh(-1.0), -(e * e - 1.0) / (e * e + 1.0)));
    assert(approx(tanh(0.0), 0.0));
    assert(approx(tanh(1.0), (e * e - 1.0) / (e * e + 1.0)));
    puts("SUCCESS testing <math.h>, part 3");
    return (0);
    }
```

Chapter 8: `<setjmp.h>`

Background

The C programming language does not let you nest functions. You cannot write a function definition inside another function definition, as in:

```
int f(void)
    {    /* outer function */
    int g(void)
        {    /* NOT PERMITTED */
        .....
```

The major effect of this restriction is that you cannot hide function names inside a hierarchy. All the functions that you declare within a given translation unit are visible to each other. That is not a major drawback — you can limit visibility by grouping functions within separate C source files that belong to different translation units.

C does, however, suffer in another way because of this design decision. It provides no easy way to transfer control out of a function except by returning to the expression that called the function. For the vast majority of function calls, that is a desirable limitation. You want the discipline of nested function calls and returns to help you understand flow of control through a program. Nevertheless, on some occasions that discipline is too restrictive. The program is sometimes easier to write, and to understand, if you can jump out of one or more function invocations at a single stroke. You want to bypass the normal function returns and transfer control to somewhere in an earlier function invocation. That's often the best way to handle a serious error.

nonlocal   You can do this sort of thing in Pascal. A nested function can contain a
goto   *goto* statement that transfers control to a label outside that function. (A *void* function in C is called a procedure in Pascal. I use "function" here to refer to Pascal procedures as well.) The label can be in any of the functions containing the nested function definition, as in:

```
function x: integer; {a Pascal goto example}
    label 99;
    function y(val: integer): integer;
        begin
        if val < 0 then
            goto 99;
        .....
```

You must declare the labels in a Pascal function before you declare any nested functions so the translator can recognize a nonlocal *goto*.

A *goto* within the same function can often simply transfer control to the statement with the proper label. A nonlocal *goto* has more work to do. It must terminate execution of the active function invocation. That involves freeing any dynamically allocated storage and restoring the previous *calling environment* Pascal even closes any files associated with any `file` variables freed this way. The function that called the function containing the *goto* statement is once again the active function. If the label named in the *goto* statement is not in the now-active function, the process repeats. Eventually, the proper function is once again active and control transfers to the statement with the proper label. The expression that invoked the function containing the *goto* never completes execution.

Pascal uses the nesting of functions to impose some discipline on the nonlocal *goto* statements you can write. The language won't let you transfer control into a function that is not active. You have no way of writing a transfer of control to an unknown function. Here is one of the ways that Pascal is arguably better than C.

label   The older language PL/I has a different solution to the problem. That **variables** language lets you declare *label* variables. You can assign a label to such a variable in one context, then use that variable as the target of a *goto* statement in another context. What gets stored in the *label* variable is whatever information the program needs to perform a nonlocal *goto*. (The *goto* need not be nonlocal — it can transfer control to a label within the current invocation of the current function.)

The PL/I approach is rather less structured than the one used by Pascal. You can write a *goto* statement that names an uninitialized *label* variable. Or the label assigned to the variable may be out of date — it may designate the invocation of a function that has terminated. In either case, the effect can be disastrous. Unless the implementation can validate the contents of a label variable before it transfers control, it will make a wild jump. Such errors are hard to debug.

C implements nonlocal transfers of control by using library functions. The header `<setjmp.h>` provides the necessary machinery:

jmp_buf ■ the type `jmp_buf`, which you can think of as a label data-object type
longjmp ■ the function `longjmp`, which performs the nonlocal transfer of control
setjmp ■ the macro `setjmp` which stores information on the current calling context in a data object of type `jmp_buf` and which marks where you want control to pass on a corresponding `longjmp` call

In this regard, the C mechanism is even more primitive than the unstructured *goto* of PL/I. All you can do is memorize a place that flow of control has reached earlier in the execution of the program. You can return to that place by executing a call to `longjmp` using the proper `jmp_buf` data object. If the data object is uninitialized or out of date, you invite disaster.

longjmp and setjmp are delicate functions. They do violence to the flow of control and to the management of dynamic storage. Both of those arenas are the province of a portion of the translator that is extremely complex and hard to write. That part must generate code that is both correct and optimized for space and speed. Optimizations often involve subtle changes in flow of control or the use of dynamic storage. Yet the code generator often works in ignorance of the properties and actions of longjmp and setjmp.

subtleties   The C Standard addresses two areas where subtleties often lurk:

- the expression that contains the setjmp macro
- the dynamic storage declared in the function that executes setjmp

In both cases, you will find language in the C Standard that is puzzling. That's because the C Standard attempts to circumscribe dangerous behavior without spelling out the dangers.

One of the dangers lies in expression evaluation. A typical computer has some number of registers that it uses to hold intermediate results while evaluating an expression. Write a sufficiently complex expression, however, and you may exhaust the available registers. You then force the code generator to store intermediate results in various bits of dynamic storage.

Here is where the problem comes in. setjmp must guess how much "calling context" to store in the jmp_buf data object. It is a safe bet that certain registers must be saved. A register that can hold intermediate results across a function call is a prime candidate, since the longjmp call can be in a called function. Once the program evaluates setjmp, it needs these intermediate results to complete evaluation of the expression. If setjmp fails to save all intermediate results, a subsequent return stimulated by a longjmp call will misbehave.

executing
setjmp   The C Standard legislates the kind of expressions that can contain setjmp as a subexpression. The idea is to preclude any expressions that might store intermediate results in dynamic storage that is unknown (and unknowable) to setjmp. Thus you can write forms such as: switch (setjmp(buf)) ....., if (2 < setjmp(buf)) ....., if (!setjmp(buf)) ....., and the expression statement setjmp(buf).

You can write no forms more complex than these. Note that you *cannot* reliably assign the value of setjmp, as in n = setjmp(buf). The expression may well evaluate properly, but the C Standard doesn't require it.

reverting
storage   The second danger concerns the treatment of dynamic storage in a function that executes setjmp. Such storage comes in three flavors:

- the parameters you declare for the function
- any data objects you declare with the auto storage-class specifier, either explicitly or implicitly
- any data objects you declare with the register storage-class specifier

The problem arises because the code generator can elect to store some of these data objects in registers. This set of registers is often indistinguishable from the set that can hold temporary intermediate values in an expression evaluation. Hence, `setjmp` is obliged to save all such registers and restore them to an earlier state on a `longjmp` call. That means that certain dynamic data objects revert to an earlier state on a subsequent return from `setjmp`. Any changes in their stored values between returns from `setjmp` get lost.

Such behavior would be an annoying anomaly if it were predictable. The problem is that it is *not* predictable. You have no way of knowing which parameters and `auto` data objects end up in registers. Even data objects you declare as `register` are uncertain. A translator has no obligation to store any such data objects in registers. Hence, any number of data objects declared in a function have uncertain values if the function executes `setjmp` and a `longjmp` call transfers control back to the function. This is hardly a tidy state of affairs.

volatile X3J11 addressed the problem by adding a minor kludge to the language.
dynamic Declare a dynamic data object to have a *volatile* type and the translator
storage knows to be more cautious. Such a data object will never be stored in a place that is altered by `longmp`. This usage admittedly stretches the semantics of *volatile*, but it does provide a useful service.

What the C Standard Says

`<setjmp.h>`   ## 7.6 Nonlocal jumps `<setjmp.h>`

The header `<setjmp.h>` defines the macro `setjmp`, and declares one function and one type, for bypassing the normal function call and return discipline.[106]

The type declared is

    jmp_buf

`jmp_buf`   which is an array type suitable for holding the information needed to restore a calling environment.

It is unspecified whether `setjmp` is a macro or an identifier declared with external linkage. If a macro definition is suppressed in order to access an actual function, or a program defines an external identifier with the name `setjmp`, the behavior is undefined.

7.6.1 Save calling environment
`setjmp`   ### 7.6.1.1 The `setjmp` macro

Synopsis

    #include <setjmp.h>
    int setjmp(jmp_buf env);

Description

The `setjmp` macro saves its calling environment in its `jmp_buf` argument for later use by the `longjmp` function.

Returns

If the return is from a direct invocation, the `setjmp` macro returns the value zero. If the return is from a call to the `longjmp` function, the `setjmp` macro returns a nonzero value.

Environmental constraint

An invocation of the `setjmp` macro shall appear only in one of the following contexts:

• the entire controlling expression of a selection or iteration statement;

- one operand of a relational or equality operator with the other operand an integral constant expression, with the resulting expression being the entire controlling expression of a selection or iteration statement;

- the operand of a unary **!** operator with the resulting expression being the entire controlling expression of a selection or iteration statement; or

- the entire expression of an expression statement (possibly cast to **void**).

7.6.2 Restore calling environment

longjmp

7.6.2.1 The longjmp function

Synopsis

```
#include <setjmp.h>
void longjmp(jmp_buf env, int val);
```

Description

The **longjmp** function restores the environment saved by the most recent invocation of the **setjmp** macro in the same invocation of the program, with the corresponding **jmp_buf** argument. If there has been no such invocation, or if the function containing the invocation of the **setjmp** macro has terminated execution[107] in the interim, the behavior is undefined.

All accessible objects have values as of the time **longjmp** was called, except that the values of objects of automatic storage duration that are local to the function containing the invocation of the corresponding **setjmp** macro that do not have volatile-qualified type and have been changed between the **setjmp** invocation and **longjmp** call are indeterminate.

As it bypasses the usual function call and return mechanisms, the **longjmp** function shall execute correctly in contexts of interrupts, signals and any of their associated functions. However, if the **longjmp** function is invoked from a nested signal handler (that is, from a function invoked as a result of a signal raised during the handling of another signal), the behavior is undefined.

Returns

After **longjmp** is completed, program execution continues as if the corresponding invocation of the **setjmp** macro had just returned the value specified by **val**. The **longjmp** function cannot cause the **setjmp** macro to return the value 0; if **val** is 0, the **setjmp** macro returns the value 1.

106. These functions are useful for dealing with unusual conditions encountered in a low-level function of a program.

107. For example, by executing a **return** statement or because another **longjmp** call has caused a transfer to a **setjmp** invocation in a function earlier in the set of nested calls.

Using <setjmp.h>

You use **<setjmp.h>** whenever you need to bypass the normal function call and return discipline. The nonlocal *goto* that **<setjmp.h>** provides is a delicate mechanism. Use it only where you must and only in a few stylized ways. I recommend that you build on a standard pattern:

- Isolate each call to **setjmp** in a separate (small) function. That minimizes any issues about which dynamically declared data objects get rolled back on a **longjmp** call.

- Call **setjmp** from the controlling expression of a *switch* statement.

- Perform all the actual processing in a function (call it **process**) that you call from *case* zero of the *switch* statement.

- Report an error and restart **process** at any point by executing the call **longjmp(1)**.

- Report an error and terminate **process** at any point by executing the call **longjmp(2)**.

You can also add additional *case* labels to handle other argument values
that `longjmp` can expect.

Here is what the top-level function might look like:

```
#include <setjmp.h>

static jmp_buf jmpbuf;

void top_level(void)
    {   /* the top-level function */
    for (; ; )
        switch (setjmp(jmpbuf))
            {   /* switch on alternate returns */
        case 0: /* first time */
            process();
            return;
        case 1: /* restart */
            <report error>
            break;
        case 2: /* terminate */
            <report error>
            return;
        default:/* unknown longjmp argument */
            <report error>
            return;
            }
    }
```

I assume here that all references to `jmpbuf` are within this translation unit.
If not, you must declare `jmpbuf` with external linkage. (Drop the storage
class keyword `static`.) Alternatively, you must pass a pointer to `jmpbuf` to
those functions that must access it.

jmp_buf   Note in this regard that `jmp_buf` is an array type. If you write the
arguments argument `jmpbuf`, the translator alters it to a pointer to the first element of
the array. That's what `setjmp` and `longjmp` expect. So even though `jmpbuf`
appears to be passed by value, it is actually passed by reference. That's how
`setjmp` can store the calling environment in `jmpbuf`.

For consistency, you should declare each parameter as `jmp_buf buf` and
write the corresponding argument as `jmpbuf`. Don't declare the parameter
as `jmp_buf *pbuf` or write the argument as `&jmpbuf`. The latter form is
clearer but at odds with the long-standing conventions for calling `setjmp`
and `longjmp`.

If you choose an alternate form for using `setjmp`, execute the macro in
the smallest possible function you can write. If the translator does not treat
`setjmp` specially, it has less opportunity to surprise you. If it is aware that
`setjmp` is troublesome, it has less code to deoptimize for safety.

Additional caveats apply if you call `longjmp` from within a signal handler. Chapter 9: `<signal.h> discusses the issues in greater detail`.

Implementing `<setjmp.h>`

The only reliable way to implement **setjmp** and **longjmp** requires functions written in assembly language. You need an intimate knowledge of how the translator generates code. You also need to perform several operations that you cannot express safely in C, if at all.

Figure 8.1 shows the file **setjmp.h**. It has proved adequate for a variety of Standard C implementations. It assumes that the calling context can be stored as an *array of int*. That is usually the case even when the stored context includes data objects of diverse types. The internal header `<yvals.h>` defines the macro **_NSETJMP** that determines the number of elements in **jmp_buf**. As an example, the Borland Turbo C++ compiler for PC-compatibles requires that `<yvals.h>` contain the definition:

```
#define _NSETJMP    10
```

macro   Note that `<setjmp.h>` declares a function named **setjmp**. It then masks
setjmp   this declaration with a macro that merely calls the function. The only reason for this silly exercise is to keep programs honest. A program should assume that **setjmp** is a macro. Hence the program cannot redeclare it in a translation unit that includes `<setjmp.h>`. A program should also assume that the Standard C library defines the name **setjmp** with external linkage. Hence the program cannot also provide such a definition even if it never includes `<setjmp.h>`. This implementation of `<setjmp.h>` endeavors to generate diagnostics for programs that are not maximally portable.

Despite my initial caveat, I present here versions of the functions **setjmp** and **longjmp** written in C. I do so only to illustrate the principles involved. *Do not* use this code in a serious implementation. It barely works, and then only for implementations that have special properties:

- The calling environment for the calling function and other dynamically allocated storage are stored in a contiguous area at the top of the stack.
- The calling environment includes all information that must be preserved by **setjmp** and restored by **longjmp**. You can reliably capture this information by copying a fixed number of characters.

Figure 8.1:
setjmp.h

```
/* setjmp.h standard header */
#ifndef _SETJMP
#define _SETJMP
#ifndef _YVALS
#include <yvals.h>
#endif
        /* type definitions */
typedef int jmp_buf[_NSETJMP];
        /* declarations */
void longjmp(jmp_buf, int);
int setjmp(jmp_buf);
        /* macro overrides */
#define setjmp(env) setjmp(env)
#endif
```

- Part of the calling environment is the saved *frame pointer* from the calling function. You can locate the saved frame pointer at a fixed offset from a single declared dynamic data object.

- If the calling environment is in the right place and the frame pointer is set properly, the function can return to the caller that provided that calling environment.

Some of these assumptions are true of many implementations of C. Some, however, are only rarely true. These functions happen to (barely) work for the VAX computer architecture. To give some hint as to what is going on, I wrote them in terms of several parameters. For the VAX, the header `<yvals.h>` would contain the macro definitions:

```
#define _JBFP      1    /* int offset of frame pointer */
#define _JBMOV     60   /* number of bytes in calling context */
#define _JBOFF     4    /* byte offset of calling context */
#define _NSETJMP   17   /* number of ints in jmp_buf */
```

function   Figure 8.2 shows the file `setjmp.c`. It defines a grubby version of `setjmp`.
setjmp The function assumes that it can copy a contiguous region of the stack to the `jmp_buf` data object and save an adequate amount of the calling environment. It declares a number of **register** data objects in the hope that it will force the saving of all important registers with the calling context. It makes a sham of calling **dummy** to outsmart some optimizers who may conclude that the registers are never used.

Figure 8.2:
setjmp.c

```
/* setjmp function */
#include <setjmp.h>
#include <string.h>

static void dummy(int a, int b, int c, int d, int e,
    int f, int g, int h, int i, int j)
    {                                   /* threaten to use arguments */
    }

static int getfp(void)
    {                                   /* return frame pointer of caller */
    int arg;

    return ((int)(&arg + _JBFP));
    }

int setjmp(jmp_buf env)
    {                                   /* save environment for re-return */
    register int a = 0, b = 0, c = 0, d = 0, e = 0;
    register int f = 0, g = 0, h = 0, i = 0, j = 0;

    if (a)                              /* try to outsmart optimizer */
        dummy(a, b, c, d, e, f, g, h, i, j);
    env[1] = getfp();
    memcpy((char *)&env[2], (char *)env[1] + _JBOFF, _JBMOV);
    return (0);
    }
```

Figure 8.3:
`longjmp.c`

```
/* longjmp function */
#include <setjmp.h>
#include <string.h>

static void dummy(int a, int b, int c, int d, int e,
    int f, int g, int h, int i, int j)
    {                                   /* threaten to use arguments */
    }

static void setfp(int fp)
    {                           /* set frame pointer of caller */
    int arg;

    (&arg)[_JBFP] = fp;
    }

static int dojmp(jmp_buf env)
    {                               /* do the actual dirty business */
    memcpy((char *)env[1] + _JBOFF, (char *)&env[2], _JBMOV);
    setfp(env[1]);
    return (env[0]);
    }

void longjmp(jmp_buf env, int val)
    {                               /* re-return from setjmp */
    register int a = 0, b = 0, c = 0, d = 0, e = 0;
    register int f = 0, g = 0, h = 0, i = 0, j = 0;

    if (a)                          /* try to outsmart optimizer */
        dummy(a, b, c, d, e, f, g, h, i, j);
    env[0] = val ? val : 1;
    dojmp(env);
    }                                                              □
```

function
longjmp

Figure 8.3 shows the file `longjmp.c`. It defines an even grubbier version of `longjmp`. The function copies the saved calling context back onto the stack. It allocates registers the same as `setjmp` and calls yet another function in the hope that this wild copy won't overlap anything in active use on the stack. It then jiggers the frame pointer in the hope that it will thus return control to the function that called `setjmp` instead of its true caller.

If all goes well (and there are many reasons why it shouldn't), execution resumes where `setjmp` was first called. The value returned by `setjmp` on this occasion is the one provided as an argument to `longjmp`. Wow.

A complete implementation of these two functions must be *much* tidier. It may, for example, also have to worry about (among other things):

- the status of a floating-point coprocessor
- whether any signal handlers are active (See Chapter 9: `<signal.h>`.)

You will find that proper versions of these functions are typically just as tricky, only much more reliable.

```
/* test setjmp functions */
#include <assert.h>
#include <setjmp.h>
#include <stdio.h>

        /* static data */
static int ctr;
static jmp_buf b0;

static void jmpto(int n)
    {                                       /* jump on static buffer */
    longjmp(b0, n);
    }

static char *stackptr(void)
    {                                       /* test for stack creep */
    char ch;

    return (&ch);
    }

static int tryit(void)
    {                                       /* exercise jumps */
    jmp_buf b1;
    char *sp = stackptr();

    ctr = 0;
    switch (setjmp(b0))
        {                                   /* jump among cases */
    case 0:
        assert(sp == stackptr());
        assert(ctr == 0);
        ++ctr;
        jmpto(0);                           /* should return 1 */
        break;
    case 1:
        assert(sp == stackptr());
        assert(ctr == 1);
        ++ctr;
        jmpto(2);
        break;
    case 2:
        assert(sp == stackptr());
        assert(ctr == 2);
        ++ctr;
        switch (setjmp(b1))
            {                               /* test nesting */
        case 0:
            assert(sp == stackptr());
            assert(ctr == 3);
            ++ctr;
            longjmp(b1, -7);
            break;
```

Continuing
`tsetjmp.c`
Part 2

```
        case -7:
            assert(sp == stackptr());
            assert(ctr == 4);
            ++ctr;
            jmpto(3);
        case 5:
            return (13);
        default:
            return (0);
        }
    case 3:
        longjmp(b1, 5);
        break;
        }
    return (-1);
    }

int main()
    {                       /* test basic workings of setjmp functions */
    assert(tryit() == 13);
    printf("sizeof (jmp_buf) = %u\n", sizeof (jmp_buf));
    puts("SUCCESS testing <setjmp.h>");
    return (0);
    }                                                                    □
```

Testing `<setjmp.h>`

Figure 8.4 shows the file `tsetjmp.c`. It is much more of a stress test for `setjmp` and `longjmp` than a mere test for functionality. I assume that you might want to try your hand at writing these functions in assembly language. My experience is that it takes careful testing to shake out the bugs in code such as this. The nastier tests you can devise the better.

stack   Note, for example, that the code tests repeatedly for "stack creep." This
creep condition arises when you fail to restore the call stack exactly to an earlier state. You can often leave trash on the stack and not notice for quite some time. Only when your program starts exhausting the stack unexpectedly, or misbehaving in other strange ways, do you begin to suspect such problems. Better to catch such failings early on.

As a courtesy, the program also displays the size of a data object of type `jmp_buf`. When `tsetjmp.c` executes properly, it displays something like:

```
sizeof (jmp_buf) = 20
SUCCESS testing <setjmp.h>
```

If anything goes wrong, the program may hang or die an unnatural death. It might even display a useful error message.

References

ISO/IEC Standard 7185:1990 (Geneva: International Standards Organization, 1990). This defines the programming language Pascal, which permits a nonlocal *goto* to a containing function.

ISO/IEC Standard 6160:1979 (Geneva: International Standards Organization, 1979). This defines the programming language PL/I, *which permits a nonlocal goto using a label variable.*

Exercises

Exercise 8.1 How is the type `jmp_buf` defined for the C translator that you use? Can you represent it safely as an *array of int*? If so, how many elements must the array have?

Exercise 8.2 Write versions of `longjmp` and `setjmp` that work with the C translator that you use.

Exercise 8.3 Modify the functions you wrote in the previous exercise to check for obvious usage errors:

- Store a checksum or other signature in each `jmp_buf` data object and check it before you trust the remaining contents.
- Verify that the call stack is at least as deep as when the contents were stored in the `jmp_buf` data object.

What other checks can you envision?

Exercise 8.4 [Harder] An *exception handler* is a code sequence that gets control when an exception is reported, or *raised*. You register the handler along with the code value for an exception in a given context. Any handler already registered for the same exception code value is masked. (In other words, registrations stack.) You unregister the handler when the context terminates. That exposes any earlier handlers. A handler can register a willingness to handle any condition. It can also *reraise* an exception — pass it up the line to handlers registered earlier. If no handler is registered for a given code value, the program terminates abnormally, preferably with a nasty message.

Design functions `when` and `raise` to implement exception handling. `when` lets you register and unregister handlers. `raise` lets you report exceptions. Why would you want such a capability?

Exercise 8.5 [Harder] Implement the functions you designed for the previous exercise.

Exercise 8.6 [Very hard] Define semantics for `setjmp` and `longjmp` that eliminate the problems described earlier in this chapter. You want to be able to call `setjmp` from an arbitrary expression. You want all (surviving) data objects to remain unaffect by a `longjmp` call. Modify a Standard C translator accordingly.

Chapter 9: `<signal.h>`

Background

A *signal* is an extraordinary event that occurs during the execution of a program. *Synchronous* signals occur because of actions that your program takes. Division by zero is one example. Accessing storage improperly is another. *Asynchronous* signals occur because of actions outside your program. Someone striking an attention key is one example. A separate program (executing asynchronously) signaling yours is another.

A signal that is not ignored by your program demands immediate handling. If you do not specify handling for a signal that occurs, it is treated as a fatal error. Your program terminates execution with unsuccessful status. In some implementations, the status indicates which signal occurred. In others, the Standard C library writes an error message to the standard error stream before it terminates execution.

header
`<signal.h>` The header `<signal.h>` defines the code values for an open-ended set of signals. It also declares two functions:

raise ■ `raise`, which reports a synchronous signal

signal ■ `signal`, which lets you specify the handling of a signal

You can handle a signal one of three ways:

■ *default handling* is to terminate execution, as described above
■ *ignoring* the signal effectively discards it
■ *handling* the signal causes control to pass to a function that you designate

signal In the last case, the function that you designate is called a *signal handler*.
handlers The Standard C library calls a signal handler when its corresponding signal is reported. Normal execution of the program is suspended. If the signal handler returns to its caller, execution of the program resumes at the point where it was suspended. Aside from the delay, and any changes made by the signal handler, the behavior of the program is unaffected.

This sounds like elegant machinery, but it is not. The occurrence of a signal introduces a second thread of control within a program. That raises all sorts of issues about synchronization and reliable operation. The C Standard promises little in either regard. C programs have been handling signals since the earliest days of the language. Nevertheless, a portable program can safely take very few actions within a signal handler.

One problem is the Standard C library itself. If called with valid arguments, no library function should ever generate a synchronous signal. But an asynchronous signal can occur while the library is executing. The signal may suspend program execution part way through a print operation, for example. Should the signal handler print a message, an output stream can end up in a confused state. There is no way to determine from within a signal handler whether a library function is in an unsafe state.

volatile
data objects Another problem concerns data objects that you declare to have *volatile* types. That warns the translator that surprising agents can access the data object, so it is careful how itgenerates accesses to such a data object. In particular, it knows not to perform optimizations that move the accesses to *volatile* data objects beyond certain *sequence points*. A signal handler is, of course, a surprising agent. Thus, you should declare any data object you access within a signal handler to have a *volatile* type. That helps, provided the signal is synchronous and occurs between two sequence points where the data object is not accessed. For an asynchronous signal however, no amount of protection suffices. Signals are not confined to suspending program execution only at sequence points.

type
sig_atomic_t The C Standard offers a partial solution to the problem of writing reliable signal handlers. The header `<signal.h>` defines the type `sig_atomic_t`. It is an integer type that the program accesses atomically. A signal should never suspend program execution part way through the access of a data object declared with this type. A signal handler can share with the rest of the program only data objects declared to have type *volatile* `sig_atomic_t`.

problems As a means of communicating information, signals leave much to be desired. The semantics spelled out for signals in the C Standard is based heavily on their behavior under the early UNIX operating system. That system had serious lapses in the way it managed signals:

- Multiple signals could get lost. The system did not queue signals, but remembered only the last one reported. If a second signal occurred before a handler processed the first, a signal could go unnoticed.

- A program could terminate even when it endeavors to process all signals. When control first passes to a signal handler, handling for that signal reverts to default behavior. The signal handler must call `signal` to reestablish itself as the handler for the signal. Should that signal occur between entry to the handler and the call to `signal`, the default handler gets control and terminates the program.

- No mechanism exists for specifically terminating the handling of a signal. In other operating systems, the program enters a special state. Processing of subsequent signals blocks until the signal handler reports completion. On such systems, other functions may have to assist in processing signals properly. These can include `abort` and `exit`, declared in `<stdlib.h>`, and `longjmp`, declared in `<setjmp.h>`.

Moreover, signals arise from an odd assortment of causes on any computer. The ones named in the C Standard are a subset of those supported by UNIX. These in turn derive from the interrupts and traps defined for the PDP-11. Mapping the sources of signals for a given computer onto those defined for C is often arbitrary. Mapping the semantics of signal handling for a given operating systems can be even more creative.

The C Standard had to weaken the already weak semantics of UNIX signals to accommodate an assortment of operating systems:

- A given signal may never occur unless you report it with **raise**.
- A given signal may be ignored unless you call **signal** to turn it on.

There's not much left.

portability   Thus, no portable use for the functions declared in `<signal.h>` can be defined with complete safety. You could, in principle, specify a handler for a signal that only **raise** reports. It's hard to imagine a situation where that works better than instead using **setjmp** and **longjmp**, declared in `<setjmp.h>`. Besides, you cannot ensure that a given signal is never reported on an arbitrary implementation of C. Any time your program handles signals, accept the fact that you limit its portability.

What the C Standard Says

`<signal.h>`   ## 7.7 Signal handling `<signal.h>`

The header `<signal.h>` declares a type and two functions and defines several macros, for handling various *signals (conditions that may be reported during program execution)*.

The type defined is

sig_atomic_t   **sig_atomic_t**

which is the integral type of an object that can be accessed as an atomic entity, even in the presence of asynchronous interrupts.

The macros defined are

SIG_DFL	**SIG_DFL**
SIG_ERR	**SIG_ERR**
SIG_IGN	**SIG_IGN**

which expand to constant expressions with distinct values that have type compatible with the second argument to and the return value of the **signal** function, and whose value compares unequal to the address of any declarable function; and the following, each of which expands to a positive integral constant expression that is the signal number corresponding to the specified condition:

SIGABRT   **SIGABRT** abnormal termination, such as is initiated by the **abort** function

SIGFPE   **SIGFPE** an erroneous arithmetic operation, such as zero divide or an operation resulting in overflow

SIGILL   **SIGILL** detection of an invalid function image, such as an illegal instruction

SIGINT   **SIGINT** receipt of an interactive attention signal

SIGSEGV   **SIGSEGV** an invalid access to storage

SIGTERM   **SIGTERM** a termination request sent to the program

An implementation need not generate any of these signals, except as a result of explicit calls to the **raise** function. Additional signals and pointers to undeclarable functions, with macro definitions beginning, respectively, with the letters **SIG** and an uppercase letter or with **SIG_** and an uppercase letter,[108] may also be specified by the implementation. The complete set of signals, their semantics, and their default handling is implementation-defined; all signal numbers shall be positive.

signal

7.7.1 Specify signal handling
7.7.1.1 The `signal` function

Synopsis

```
#include <signal.h>
void (*signal(int sig, void (*func)(int)))(int);
```

Description

The **signal** function chooses one of three ways in which receipt of the signal number **sig** is to be subsequently handled. If the value of **func** is **SIG_DFL**, default handling for that signal will occur. If the value of **func** is **SIG_IGN**, the signal will be ignored. Otherwise, **func** shall point to a function to be called when that signal occurs. Such a function is called a *signal handler*.

When a signal occurs, if **func** points to a function, first the equivalent of **signal(sig, SIG_DFL);** is executed or an implementation-defined blocking of the signal is performed. (If the value of **sig** is **SIGILL**, whether the reset to **SIG_DFL** occurs is implementation-defined.) Next the equivalent of **(*func)(sig);** is executed. The function **func** may terminate by executing a **return** statement or by calling the **abort, exit,** or **longjmp** function. If **func** executes a **return** statement and the value of **sig** was **SIGFPE** or any other implementation-defined value corresponding to a computational exception, the behavior is undefined. Otherwise, the program will resume execution at the point it was interrupted.

If the signal occurs other than as the result of calling the **abort** or **raise** function, the behavior is undefined if the signal handler calls any function in the standard library other than the **signal** function itself (with a first argument of the signal number corresponding to the signal that caused the invocation of the handler) or refers to any object with static storage duration other than by assigning a value to a static storage duration variable of type **volatile sig_atomic_t**. Furthermore, if such a call to the **signal** function results in a **SIG_ERR** return, the value of **errno** is indeterminate.[109]

At program startup, the equivalent of

```
signal(sig, SIG_IGN);
```

may be executed for some signals selected in an implementation-defined manner; the equivalent of

```
signal(sig, SIG_DFL);
```

is executed for all other signals defined by the implementation.

The implementation shall behave as if no library function calls the **signal** function.

Returns

If the request can be honored, the **signal** function returns the value of **func** for the most recent call to **signal** for the specified signal **sig**. Otherwise, a value of **SIG_ERR** is returned and a positive value is stored in **errno**.

Forward references: the **abort** function (7.10.4.1), the **exit** function (7.10.4.3).

7.7.2 Send signal

raise

7.7.2.1 The `raise` function

Synopsis

```
#include <signal.h>
int raise(int sig);
```

Description

The **raise** function sends the signal **sig** to the executing program.

Returns

The **raise** function returns zero if successful, nonzero if unsuccessful.

Footnotes

108. See "future library directions" (7.13.5). The names of the signal numbers reflect the following terms (respectively): abort, floating-point exception, illegal instruction, interrupt, segmentation violation, and termination.

109. If any signal is generated by an asynchronous signal handler, the behavior is undefined.

Using `<signal.h>`

Signal handling is essentially nonportable. Use the functions declared in `<signal.h>` only when you must specify the handling of signals for a known set of operating systems. Don't try too hard to generalize the code.

handling   If default handling for a signal is acceptable, then by all means choose
signals that option. Adding your own signal handler decreases portability and raises the odds that the program will mishandle the signal. If you must provide a handler for a signal, categorize it as follows:

- a handler for a signal that must not return, such as SIGFPE reporting an arithmetic exception or SIGABRT reporting a fatal error
- a handler for a signal that must return, such as SIGINT reporting an attention interrupt that may have interrupted a library operation

As a rule, the second category contains asynchronous signals not intended to cause immediate program termination. Rarely will you find a signal that does not fit clearly in one of these categories.

A signal handler that must not return ends in a call to **abort, exit,** or **longjmp.** Do not, of course, end a handler for SIGABRT with a call to **abort.** The handler should *not* reestablish itself by calling **signal.** Leave that to some other agency, if the program does not terminate. If the signal is asynchronous, be wary of performing any input or output. You may have interrupted the library part way through such an operation.

A signal handler that must return ends in a *return* statement. If it is to reestablish itself, it should do so immediately on entry. If the signal is asynchronous, store a nonzero value in a volatile data object of type **sig_atomic_t.** *Do nothing else* that has side effects visible to the executing program, such as input or output and accessing other data objects.

A sample asynchronous signal handler might look like:

```
#include <signal.h>

static sig_atomic_t intflag = 0;

static void field_int(int sig)
    {   /* handle SIGINT */
    signal(SIGINT, &field_int);
    intflag = 1;
    return;
    }
```

The program calls **signal(SIGINT, &field_int)** to establish the handler. From time to time, it can then check for the occurrence of asynchronous interactive attention interrupts by executing code such as:

```
    if (intflag)
        {   /* act on interrupt */
        intflag = 0;
        .....
        }
```

Note that two small windows exist where these signals can go astray:

- Within `field_int` before the call to `signal`, an occurrence of `SIGINT` can terminate the program.
- Between the testing and clearing of `intflag`, an occurrence of `SIGINT` can be lost.

Those are inherent limitations of signals.

Here is a brief characterization of the signals defined for all implementations of Standard C. Note that a given implementation may well define more. Display the contents of `<signal.h>` for other defined macro names that begin with `SIG`. These should expand to (small) positive integers that represent additional signals.

SIGABRT   `SIGABRT` — This signal occurs when the program is terminating unsuccessfully, as by an explicit call to `abort`, declared in `<stdlib.h>`. *Do not* ignore this signal. If you provide a handler, do as little as possible. End the handler with a *return* statement or a call to `exit`, declared in `<stdlib.h>`.

SIGFPE   `SIGFPE` — The name originally meant "floating-point exception." The C Standard generalizes this signal to cover any arithmetic exception such as overflow, underflow, or zero divide. Implementations vary considerably on what exceptions they report, if any. Rarely does an implementation report integer overflow. Ignoring this signal may be rash. A handler must *not* return.

SIGINT   `SIGINT` — This is the conventional way of reporting an asynchronous interactive attention signal. Most systems provide some keystroke combination that you can type to generate such a signal. Examples are ctl-C, DEL, and ATTN. It offers a convenient way to terminate a tiresome loop early. But be aware that an asynchronous signal can catch the program part way through an operation that should be atomic. If the handler does not return control, the program may subsequently misbehave. You can safely ignore this signal.

SIGSEGV   `SIGSEGV` — The name originally meant "segmentation violation," because the PDP-11 managed memory as a set of segments. The C Standard generalizes this signal to cover any exception raised by an invalid storage access. The program has attempted to access storage outside any of the functions or data objects defined by C, as with an ill-formed function designator or lvalue. Or the program has attempted to store a value in a data object with a *const* type. In any event, the program cannot safely continue execution. *Do not* ignore this signal or return from its handler.

SIGTERM   `SIGTERM` — This signal is traditionally sent from the operating system or from another program executing asynchronously with yours. Treat it as a polite but firm request to terminate execution. It is an asynchronous signal, so it may occur at an inopportune point in your program. You may want to defer it, using the techniques described above. You can ignore this signal safely, although it may be bad manners to do so.

Implementing `<signal.h>`

Figure 9.1 shows the file `signal.h`. The header `<signal.h>` I present here is minimal. A UNIX system, for example, defines dozens of signals. Many systems endeavor to look as much as possible like UNIX in this regard. They too define all these signals even if they do not generate many of them. Notwithstanding this concerted group behavior, the choice of signals and their codes both vary considerably. I have endeavored here to choose codes that are most widely used.

header As usual, I make use of the internal header `<yvals.h>` to provide parame-
`<yvals.h>` ters that can vary among systems. The code for `SIGABRT` is one. The highest valid signal code is another. Some functions in this implementation use the macro `_NSIG` to determine the lowest positive number that is not a valid signal code. Thus, the header `<yvals.h>` defines two macros of interest here. For a typical UNIX system, the definitions are:

```
#define _SIGABRT    6
#define _SIGMAX    32
```

The header `<signal.h>` makes an additional concession to widespread UNIX practice. It defines the macros `SIG_ERR` and `SIG_IGN` in a moderately ugly way. The values –1 and 1 could conceivably be valid function ad-dresses in some implementation. Admittedly, that is only rarely possible. Where it is possible, the linker can be jiggered to avoid the possibility. Still, other values would be more gracious. (The addresses of `signal` and `raise`, for example, are not likely to specify useful signal handlers.) But the values chosen here are the ones used widely in UNIX implementations. They are also widely imitated under other operating systems. I chose these for compatibility with existing machinery.

UNIX That compatibility is often necessary. Almost invariably, the functions
versions `signal` and `raise` must be tailored for each operating system. UNIX is the extreme case. In that environment, the system service `signal` does the whole job. If you have access to a C-callable function of that name, just discard the code presented here. Let other functions call it directly. If the system service has a private name, such as `_Signal`, you can write `signal` as:

```
/* signal function -- UNIX version */
#include <signal.h>

_Sigfun *_Signal(int, _Sigfun *)

_Sigfun *(signal)(int sig, _Sigfun *fun)
    {   /* call the system service
    return (_Signal(sig, fun));
    }
```

This is an obvious candidate for a masking macro in `<signal.h>`.

The function `raise` is only slightly more difficult. It uses the system service `kill` to send a signal to itself. ("Kill" is a misnomer stemming from

Figure 9.1:
signal.h

```
/* signal.h standard header */
#ifndef _SIGNAL
#define _SIGNAL
#ifndef _YVALS
#include <yvals.h>
#endif
        /* type definitions */
typedef int sig_atomic_t;
typedef void _Sigfun(int);
        /* signal codes */
#define SIGABRT _SIGABRT
#define SIGINT  2
#define SIGILL  4
#define SIGFPE  8
#define SIGSEGV 11
#define SIGTERM 15
#define _NSIG   _SIGMAX              /* one more than last code */
        /* signal return values */
#define SIG_DFL (_Sigfun *)0
#define SIG_ERR (_Sigfun *)-1
#define SIG_IGN (_Sigfun *)1
        /* declarations */
int raise(int);
_Sigfun *signal(int, _Sigfun *);
#endif                                                               □
```

its earliest use for sending only the signal **SIGKILL**.) To identify itself, **raise** also needs the system service **getpid**. Assuming suitable secret names for these two system services, such a **_Kill** and **_Getpid**, you can write **raise** as:

```
/* raise function -- UNIX version */
#include <signal.h>

int _Getpid(void);
int _Raise(int, int);

int (raise)(int sig)
    {   /* raise a signal */
    return (_Kill(_Getpid(), sig));
    }
```

Here is another obvious candidate for a masking macro.

generic The formal versions of **signal** and **raise** that I choose to present are more
versions widely usable. They provide no mapping between signals in Standard C and those provided by the operating system. That is impossible to generalize. But they do provide a useful harness for adding such system-specific code. An operating system that doesn't handle signals just like UNIX usually needs just this code to split the difference.

function Figure 9.2 shows the file **raise.c**. It defines a version of **raise** that needs
raise no assist from the operating system. It contains an array of signal handler addresses **_Sigfun** that is indexed by signal code. Initially, each element of

the array is initialized to a null pointer. That happens to match `SIG_DFL`, the value that `signal` uses to indicate default handling.

`raise` first determines that the signal code is valid. If so, the function takes the action specified by the corresponding element of `_Sigtable`. Default handling is to write a one-line message to the standard error stream and terminate with unsuccessful status. It names the signals that it knows about and prints the code value for all others. You can add names for additional signals if you want more revealing error messages.

function   Figure 9.3 shows the file `signal.c`. It defines the function signal that
signal serves as a companion to `raise` above. All it does is validate its arguments and replace the appropriate entry in `_Sigtable` with a valid function pointer. (The pointer is assumed valid if it doesn't match `SIG_ERR`. That's a fairly weak check.)

declaring   Note the declaration for `_Sigtable` in this file. My usual practice is to
_Sigtable place such a declaration in a header file that is included by all C source files that need it. In this case that would be the header `<signal.h>`, but only if some masking macro referred to it. More likely, it would be some internal header with a name such as `"xsignal.h"`. I couldn't bring myself to create yet another header for a single declaration, however. Any style must have its practical exceptions.

hardware   You can add to `signal` any system-specific code needed to get control
signals when "hardware signals" occur. These are signals reported by the operating system or the computer itself. Be careful here. Many systems will transfer control to an address you specify, but not following the C function call and return discipline. You may have to provide a bit of assembly language for each signal you handle this way.

Tell the operating system (or the computer) to transfer control to the assembly-language signal handler. Have that handler save any necessary context and call the C function you specify with the proper protocol. It can determine the address from a static data object that you know how to access both from C and from assembly language. If the C function returns, the assembly-language signal handler reverses the process to return control to the interrupted program.

Some operating systems require that you report when a signal handler completes. For a signal handler that returns, this is relatively easy. The assembly-language signal handler can do what is necessary on the way out the door. But remember that a signal handler can also terminate by calling `abort` or `exit`, declared in `<stdlib.h>`, or by calling `longjmp`, declared in `<setjmp.h>`. You may have to work over all of these functions to do a proper job.

Figure 9.2:
raise.c

```
/* raise function -- simple version */
#include <signal.h>
#include <stdio.h>
#include <stdlib.h>

        /* static data */
_Sigfun *_Sigtable[_NSIG] = {0};                        /* handler table */

int (raise)(int sig)
    {                                                   /* raise a signal */
    _Sigfun *s;

    if (sig <= 0 || _NSIG <= sig)
        return (-1);                                    /* bad signal */
    if ((s = _Sigtable[sig]) != SIG_IGN && s != SIG_DFL)
        {                                       /* revert and call handler */
        _Sigtable[sig] = SIG_DFL;
        (*s)(sig);
        }
    else if (s == SIG_DFL)
        {                                               /* default handling */
        char ac[10], *p;

        switch (sig)
            {                               /* print known signals by name */
        case SIGABRT:
            p = "abort";
            break;
        case SIGFPE:
            p = "arithmetic error";
            break;
        case SIGILL:
            p = "invalid executable code";
            break;
        case SIGINT:
            p = "interruption";
            break;
        case SIGSEGV:
            p = "invalid storage access";
            break;
        case SIGTERM:
            p = "termination request";
            break;
        default:
            *(p = &ac[(sizeof ac) - 1]) = '\0';
            do *--p = sig % 10 + '0';
                while ((sig /= 10) != 0);
            fputs("signal #", stderr);
            }
        fputs(p, stderr);
        fputs(" -- terminating\n", stderr);
        exit(EXIT_FAILURE);
        }
    return (0);
    }
```

□

Figure 9.3:
signal.c

```
/* signal function -- simple version */
#include <signal.h>

        /* external declarations */
extern _Sigfun *_Sigtable[_NSIG];

_Sigfun *(signal)(int sig, _Sigfun *fun)
    {                             /* specify handling for a signal */
    _Sigfun *s;

    if (sig <= 0 || _NSIG <= sig || fun == SIG_ERR)
        return (SIG_ERR);                        /* bad signal */
    /* add machine-dependent handling here */
    s = _Sigtable[sig], _Sigtable[sig] = fun;
    return (s);
    }                                                        □
```

Testing `<signal.h>`

Figure 9.4 shows the file `tsignal.c`. It doesn't do much, because signals have so few portable properties. About all it does is test the basic workings of `signal` and `raise` using `SIGFPE`. The code assumes that no other agency will report this signal while the program executes. That's a fairly safe assumption, but not one guaranteed by the C Standard. The test program also ensures that the various macros are defined, as is the type `sig_atomic_t`. It makes no attempt to verify any associated semantics, however.

As a courtesy, the program displays the size in bytes of `sig_atomic_t`. If all goes well, the program displays something like:

```
sizeof (sig_atomic_t) = 2
SUCCESS testing <signal.h>
```

References

PDP-11/70 Processor Handbook (Maynard, Mass.: Digital Equipment Corporation, 1976). The PDP-11 traps and interrupts inspired the signals originally defined for UNIX. You can better understand the naming and semantics of UNIX signals by going back to this source.

Exercises

Exercise 9.1 List the signal codes defined for the C translator you use. Can you describe in one sentence what each signal indicates?

Exercise 9.2 For the signal codes defined for the C translator you use, contrive tests that cause each of the signals to occur?

Exercise 9.3 Under what circumstances might you care whether any signals went unreported?

Figure 9.4:
tsignal.c

```
/* test signal functions */
#include <assert.h>
#include <signal.h>
#include <stdio.h>
#include <stdlib.h>

        /* static data */
static int sigs[] = {
    SIGABRT, SIGFPE, SIGILL, SIGINT, SIGSEGV, SIGTERM};
static void (*rets[])(int) = {SIG_DFL, SIG_ERR, SIG_IGN};
static sig_atomic_t atomic;

static void field_fpe(int sig)
    {                                         /* handle SIGFPE */
    assert(sig == SIGFPE);
    puts("SUCCESS testing <signal.h>");
    exit(EXIT_SUCCESS);
    }

int main()
    {                /* test basic workings of signal functions */
    printf("sizeof (sig_atomic_t) = %u\n",
        sizeof (sig_atomic_t));
    assert(signal(SIGFPE, &field_fpe) == SIG_DFL);
    assert(signal(SIGFPE, &field_fpe) == &field_fpe);
    raise(SIGFPE);
    puts("FAILURE testing <signal.h>");
    return (EXIT_FAILURE);
    }                                                          □
```

Exercise 9.4 Alter `signal` and `raise` to work properly with the C translator you use. Handle as many hardware signals as possible.

Exercise 9.5 Write a handler for **SIGABRT** that displays a *trace back* — a list of the functions that are active, in the reverse order that they were called. Why would you want this capability?

Exercise 9.6 [**Harder**] Identify the critical regions in the Standard C library that should not be interrupted by a signal. Arrange to have signal handling deferred until the end of any such critical region if the signal is reported while the region is active. Why would you want this capability?

Exercise 9.7 [**Very hard**] Implement new semantics for signals that ensures that:

- no signals get duplicated or lost
- signals are handled in order of reporting
- a program can be sure to handle all signals reported after some point
- critical regions can be protected against interuption
- a signal handler can communicate safely with other parts of the program

Chapter 10: `<stdarg.h>`

Background

One of the great powers of the C programming language is that it lets you define functions that accept a variable argument list. Other languages have such creatures, to be sure, but the number of such functions is fixed. All are special functions built into the language. You cannot define additional ones.

To access the additional arguments in a variable argument list, you need the macros defined in `<stdarg.h>`. They let you walk along the list of extra arguments from beginning to end as often as you like. You must know the type of each argument before you encounter it. But you need not know the particulars of any given call before it occurs. You can determine the number and types of arguments from one of the fixed arguments, for example, such as a format string.

The header `<stdarg.h>` is an invention of committee X3J11. It is based heavily on the header `<varargs.h>` that was developed as part of the Berkeley enhancement to the UNIX operating system. `<varargs.h>` was one of several contemporaneous attempts at isolating implementation dependencies in walking variable argument lists. It was also one of the most widely known. The idea was to make a common operation more portable by hiding differences inside macros.

history In the early days, no such hiding was necessary. C was a language for the PDP-11, period. Everyone knew how Dennis Ritchie's compiler laid out an argument list in memory. Walking from argument to argument was a simple exercise in pointer arithmetic. It helped that pointers were the same size as *int*s and that structures were not yet permitted as arguments. That meant that an argument could be treated as either an *int*, a *long*, or a *double*. Since *double* has the same storage alignment as *int* on the PDP-11, there was no worry about holes left in the argument list to ensure proper storage alignment.

The advent of structure arguments and pointers of varied sizes made life messier. Even if you had no interest in writing portable code, you still wanted it to be readable. That increased the demand for notation that could hide the messy details of walking a variable argument list.

Then along came implementations of C designed to work with older programming languages such as FORTRAN. It was sometimes necessary for such implementations to use a calling sequence that differed dramatically from that used on the PDP-11. Argument lists sometimes grew downward in memory instead of upward. Some involved intermediate pointers to the actual argument values. Hiding the details of accessing an argument moved from being a convenience to a necessity.

header
<stdarg.h>
Committee X3J11 felt obliged to change the Berkeley macros in several small ways. That is why the C Standard specifies a standard header with a new name. **<stdarg.h>** differs just enough from **<varargs.h>** to cause confusion to programs (and programmers) that use the older header. The committee debated ways to make the capabilities of **<stdarg.h>** more a part of the language. In the end, however, the committee elected to leave as macros the mechanisms for walking a variable argument list.

What X3J11 did instead was endeavor to generalize the macros as much as possible. The idea was to define the macros in such a way that all known implementations of C could conform without major change. Some implementations had to alter their translators to provide critical information or operations. Most, however, can support **<stdarg.h>** with no help from the translator proper.

restrictions
Some of the restrictions imposed on the macros defined in **<stdarg.h>** seem unnecessarily severe. For some implementations, they are. Each was introduced, however, to meet the needs of at least one serious C implementation. For example:

macro
va_start
- A function must declare at least one fixed argument. The macro **va_start** refers to the last of the fixed arguments so that it can locate the variable argument list.

macro
va_arg
- You cannot specify argument types in **va_arg** that "widen" in the absence of a function prototype. You must write **double**, for example, instead of **float**. The macros cannot replicate the rules for altering argument types that apply to a variable argument list.

- You can write only certain argument types in **va_arg**. That's because many macro implementations need to generate a related pointer type by textually appending a ∗. The rules for writing types in C are notoriously introverted — and much too twisty for such a simple recipe to work right all the time.

macro
va_end
- A function must execute **va_end** before it returns to its caller. That's because some implementations need to tidy up control information before a return can occur.

All in all, however, the macros defined in **<stdarg.h>** work well enough. And they offer a serivce which is uniquely powerful among modern programming languages.

What the C Standard Says

7.8 Variable arguments `<stdarg.h>`

The header `<stdarg.h>` declares a type and defines three macros, for advancing through a list of arguments whose number and types are not known to the called function when it is translated.

A function may be called with a variable number of arguments of varying types. As described in 7.7.1, its parameter list contains one or more parameters. The rightmost parameter plays a special role in the access mechanism, and will be designated *parmN* in this description.

The type declared is

        va_list

which is a type suitable for holding information needed by the macros **va_start**, **va_arg**, and **va_end**. If access to the varying arguments is desired, the called function shall declare an object (referred to as **ap** in this subclause) having type **va_list**. The object **ap** may be passed as an argument to another function; if that function invokes the **va_arg** macro with parameter **ap**, the value of **ap** in the calling function is indeterminate and shall be passed to the **va_end** macro prior to any further reference to **ap**.

7.8.1 Variable argument list access macros

The **va_start** and **va_arg** macros described in this subclause shall be implemented as macros, not as actual functions. It is unspecified whether **va_end** is a macro or an identifier declared with external linkage. If a macro definition is suppressed in order to access an actual function, or a program defines an external identifier with the name **va_end**, the behavior is undefined. The **va_start** and **va_end** macros shall be invoked in the function accepting a varying number of arguments, if access to the varying arguments is desired.

7.8.1.1 The **va_start** macro

Synopsis

        #include <stdarg.h>
        void va_start(va_list ap, parmN);

Description

The **va_start** macro shall be invoked before any access to the unnamed arguments.

The **va_start** macro initializes **ap** for subsequent use by **va_arg** and **va_end**.

The parameter *parmN* is the identifier of the rightmost parameter in the variable parameter list in the function definition (the one just before the `, . . .`). If the parameter *parmN* is declared with the **register** storage class, with a function or array type, or with a type that is not compatible with the type that results after application of the default argument promotions, the behavior is undefined.

Returns

The **va_start** macro returns no value.

7.8.1.2 The **va_arg** macro

Synopsis

        #include <stdarg.h>
        type va_arg(va_list ap, type);

Description

The **va_arg** macro expands to an expression that has the type and value of the next argument in the call. The parameter **ap** shall be the same as the **va_list ap** initialized by **va_start**. Each invocation of **va_arg** modifies **ap** so that the values of successive arguments are returned in turn. The parameter *type* is a type name specified such that the type of a pointer to an object that has the specified type can be obtained simply by postfixing a ***** to *type*. If there is no actual next argument, or if *type* is not compatible with the type of the actual next argument (as promoted according to the default argument promotions), the behavior is undefined.

Returns

The first invocation of the **va_arg** macro after that of the **va_start** macro returns the value of the argument after that specified by *parmN*. Successive invocations return the values of the remaining arguments in succession.

7.8.1.3 The va_end macro

Synopsis

```
#include <stdarg.h>
void va_end(va_list ap);
```

Description

The **va_end** macro facilitates a normal return from the function whose variable argument list was referred to by the expansion of **va_start** that initialized the **va_list ap**. The **va_end** macro may modify **ap** so that it is no longer usable (without an intervening invocation of **va_start**). If there is no corresponding invocation of the **va_start** macro, or if the **va_end** macro is not invoked before the return, the behavior is undefined.

Returns

The **va_end** macro returns no value.

Example

The function **f1** gathers into an array a list of arguments that are pointers to strings (but not more than **MAXARGS** arguments), then passes the array as a single argument to function **f2**. The number of pointers is specified by the first argument to **f1**.

```
#include <stdarg.h>
#define MAXARGS   31

void f1(int n_ptrs, ...)
{
      va_list ap;
      char *array[MAXARGS];
      int ptr_no = 0;

      if (n_ptrs > MAXARGS)
            n_ptrs = MAXARGS;
      va_start(ap, n_ptrs);
      while (ptr_no < n_ptrs)
            array[ptr_no++] = va_arg(ap, char *);
      va_end(ap);
      f2(n_ptrs, array);
}
```

Each call to **f1** shall have visible the definition of the function or a declaration such as

```
void f1(int, ...);
```

Using <stdarg.h>

You use the macros defined in **<stdarg.h>** to walk a variable argument list. The macros must accommodate the needs of diverse implementations. Hence they come with a number of caveats:

- You must declare a function explicitly as having a variable argument list. (Call it **f**.) That means its argument list must end in ellipsis (, ...), both in its definition and any declarations. Moreover, all calls to the function must be in scope of a function prototype that declares the function this way.

- You must declare the function with at least one fixed argument. The last of these fixed arguments is conventionally referred to as **parmN**.

- You must declare a data object of type **va_list**, conventionally called **ap**. The data object must, of course, be visible within the function.

- You must execute **va_start(ap, parmN)** *within* **f**. You must not execute **va_list** or **va_end** until you do so.

- You can then execute `va_arg(ap, T)` in the function or in any of the functions that it calls. You must specify the proper types for each of the arguments, of course, and in the order that they appear in the function call. Note that `va_arg` is an rvalue macro. You cannot use the macro invocation as an lvalue to alter the value stored in the argument data object.

- You must not write a type *T* that widens when passed as an argument. Replace *float* with *double*. Replace *char, signed char, unsigned char, short*, and *unsigned short* with either *int* or *unsigned int*. Use *unsigned int* for an *unsigned short* that is the same size as *int*. Rarer still, use *unsigned int* for a character type that represents no negative values and is the same size as *int*.

- You must write only a type *T* that can be converted to a pointer type by appending a `*`. For example, the type designators `int` and `char *` are valid. The type designator `char (*) [5]` is not. As a general rule, be wary of type designators that contain parentheses or brackets.

- You must execute `va_end` within `f` if you earlier executed `va_start`. Once you execute `va_end` you must not again execute `va_arg` unless you first execute `va_start` to initiate a rescan. In that case, you must execute `va_end` again before the function returns.

If all that sounds too negative, consider a positive example instead. Here is a function that generalizes the function `fputs`, declared in `<stdio.h>`. That function writes a single null-terminated string to an output stream that you designate, as in:

```
fputs("this is a test", stdout);
```

This function, called `va_fputs`, writes an arbitrary number of strings to a given stream, as in:

```
va_fputs(stdout, "this is", " a test", NULL);
```

In this example, both functions should produce the same output to the stream `stdout`.

You can write `va_fputs` as:

```
#include <stdarg.h>
#include <stdout.h>

int va_fputs(FILE *str, ...)
    {   /* write zero or more strings */
    char *s;
    va_list ap;

    va_start(ap, str);
    while (s = va_arg(ap, char *))
        if (fputs(str, s) < 0)
            return (EOF);     /* write error */
    va_end(ap);
    return (0); /* all writes successful */
    }
```

You can follow this pattern to process a wide range of variable argument lists. You can even process the variable argument list in a separate function. Be sure to execute **va_start** before you call the function. Then execute **va_end** when the function returns.

rescanning   If you want to rescan a variable argument list you have to be a bit more careful. Execute **va_start** to initiate each rescan, of course. Execute **va_end** before the function returns, and *only* if you execute **va_start** at least once. I recommend an even safer discipline — execute **va_start** and **va_end** within the same loop. That way, you are more certain to execute **va_end** only when you should.

Many implementations have no need for **va_end**. The macro expands to code that does nothing. That means that any errors in using this macro become time bombs that may not go off for years. They get more expensive to find and fix with each passing year. Take pains to eliminate the bugs up front.

va_list   Another danger lurks in calling a function with the argument **ap** (the
arguments data object of type **va_list**). In some implementations, it may be an array type. That means that the function parameter actually becomes a pointer to the first element of the **va_list** array. When the called function executes **va_arg**, the data object changes in the calling function (called **f** above).

In other implementations, **va_list** is not an array type. That means that the argument **ap** passes by value as it appears to do. When the called function executes **va_arg**, the data object in the calling function **f** does *not* change.

If you process all arguments in the called function, the difference doesn't matter. If you execute **va_arg** in different function invocations with the "same" **ap**, however, it can matter. In fact, you get in trouble if your code requires that the **va_list** data object be shared or if it requires that the data object *not* be shared.

You can ensure the behavior that you need:

- If the **va_list** data object *must* be shared, write the argument as **&ap**. Declare the corresponding parameter as **va_list *pap**. Within the function, execute **va_arg(*pap, _T_)** to access each argument in the variable argument list.

- If the **va_list** data object *must not* be shared, write the argument as **ap**. Declare the corresponding parameter as **va_list xap**. Within the function, declare a data object as **va_list ap** and execute **memcpy(ap, xap, sizeof (va_list))**. (**memcpy** is declared in **<string.h>**.) Execute **va_arg(ap, _T_)** to access each argument in the variable argument list.

These two recipes will work regardless of the type defined for **va_list**.

Implementing `<stdarg.h>`

Figure 10.1 shows the file **stdarg.h**. It is the only code needed to implement **<stdarg.h>**. That's assuming that it can be made to work with a given implementation of Standard C.

assumptions   The approach assumes that:

- A variable argument list occupies a contiguous array of characters in memory.
- Successive arguments occupy successively higher elements of the character array.
- The space occupied by an argument begins on a storage boundary that is some multiple of 2^N bytes.
- The size of the space is the smallest multiple of 2^N bytes that can represent the argument.
- Any "hole" left in the space is always at the beginning or always at the end of the argument data object.

These assumptions hold for many implementations of Standard C.

header   As usual, the internal header **<yvals.h>** defines macros that describe
<yvals.h> variations among different systems. For the header **<stdarg.h>**, two parameters are relevant:

macro ▪ _AUPBND is a mask that determines the storage boundary enforced within
_AUPBND   the variable argument list. Its value is 2^N-1.

macro ▪ _ADNBND is a mask that determines whether the hole is at the beginning
_ADNBND   or at the end of an argument data object. Its value is 2^N-1 if the hole is at the end, otherwise it is zero.

A simple example is the Borland Turbo C++ compiler. For that implementation, the header **<yvals.h>** contains the definitions:

```
#define _AUPBND 1
#define _ADNBND 1
```

Figure 10.1:
stdarg.h

```
/* stdarg.h standard header */
#ifndef _STDARG
#define _STDARG
#ifndef _YVALS
#include <yvals.h>
#endif
        /* type definitions */
typedef char *va_list;
        /* macros */
#define va_arg(ap, T)   \
    (*(T *)(((ap) += _Bnd(T, _AUPBND)) - _Bnd(T, _ADNBND)))
#define va_end(ap)      (void)0
#define va_start(ap, A) \
    (void)((ap) = (char *)&(A) + _Bnd(A, _AUPBND))
#define _Bnd(X, bnd)    (sizeof (X) + (bnd) & ~(bnd))
#endif
```

I discovered the need for specifying a hole *before* an argument with the GNU C compiler for the Sun UNIX workstation. For that system, **_AUPBND** has the value 3, but **_ADNBND** is zero.

type
va_list

Perhaps now you can understand the trickery involved in **stdarg.h**. The type **va_list** is just a pointer to *char*. Such a data object holds a pointer to the start of the next argument space.

va_start
_Bnd

The macro **va_start** skips past the named argument, which should be the last of the fixed arguments. It uses the internal macro **_Bnd** to round up the size of its argument to a multiple of 2^N bytes.

macro
va_arg

The macro **va_arg** is the trickiest of the lot. It begins by incrementing the contents of the **va_list** data object to point to the start of the next argument space. Then it backs up to point to the beginning of the current argument. Then it type casts that pointer value to be a pointer to the specified type. Its last act is to dereference the pointer to access the value stored in the data object. (In this implementation, **va_arg** is an lvalue. Don't count on that being true of others.)

macro
va_end

The macro **va_end** has nothing to do in this implementation. It expands to the place-holder expression **(void)0**.

Testing <stdarg.h>

Figure 10.2 shows the file **tstdarg.c**. It stresses the macros defined in **<stdarg.h>** moderately hard. The function **tryit** accepts a variable argument list that can have a variety of argument types. A format string argument tells the function what to expect, much like the print and scan functions declared in **<stdio.h>**.

I have found more than one implementation that fails to handle a data object of type **Cstruct** correctly. It is a structure that contains a single character. Not everyone remembers that an argument can be that small.

As a courtesy, the program displays the size in bytes of a data object of type **va_list**. If all goes well, the test program displays output something like:

```
sizeof (va_list) = 4
SUCCESS testing <stdarg.h>
```

References

UNIX Programmer's Reference Manual, 4.3 Berkeley Software Distribution VirtualVAX-11 Version (Berkeley, Ca.: University of California, 1986). Here is the source of the header **<varargs.h>** that served as the model for **<stdarg.h>**.

```c
/* test stdarg macros */
#include <assert.h>
#include <stdarg.h>
#include <stdio.h>

        /* type definitions */
typedef struct {
    char c;
    } Cstruct;

static int tryit(const char *fmt, ...)
    {                                   /* test variable argument list */
    int ctr = 0;
    va_list ap;

    va_start(ap, fmt);
    for (; *fmt; ++fmt)
        switch (*fmt)
            {                                   /* switch on argument type */
        case 'i':
            assert(va_arg(ap, int) == ++ctr);
            break;
        case 'd':
            assert(va_arg(ap, double) == ++ctr);
            break;
        case 'p':
            assert(va_arg(ap, char *)[0] == ++ctr);
            break;
        case 's':
            assert(va_arg(ap, Cstruct).c == ++ctr);
            }
    va_end(ap);
    return (ctr);
    }

int main()
    {                       /* test basic workings of stdarg macros */
    Cstruct x = {3};

    assert(tryit("iisdi", '\1', 2, x, 4.0, 5) == 5);
    assert(tryit("") == 0);
    assert(tryit("pdp", "\1", 2.0, "\3") == 3);
    printf("sizeof (va_list) = %u\n", sizeof (va_list));
    puts("SUCCESS testing <stdarg.h>");
    return (0);
    }                                                               □
```

Exercises

Exercise 10.1 Determine how your C translator stores arguments in a variable argument list by reading its documentation. Does that tell you enough?

Exercise 10.2 Determine how your C translator stores arguments in a variable argument list by displaying the header `<stdarg.h>` that it provides. Does that tell you enough?

Exercise 10.3 Determine how your C translator stores arguments in a variable argument list by examining the code produced for the test program `tstdarg.c` (Figure 10.2). Does that tell you enough? If not, augment the program to provide the missing information.

Exercise 10.4 Alter the code presented in this chapter to adapt the header `<stdarg.h>` to work with the C translator you use.

Exercise 10.5 Write the function `char *scat(char *dest, const char *src, ...)` that concatenates one or more strings and writes them to `dest`. The first string starts at `src`. A null pointer terminates the list. The function returns a pointer to the terminating null character for the string starting at `dest`.

Exercise 10.6 [**Harder**] You want to test whether an argument is present in a variable argument list. If it is present, you want to determine its type. Describe a notation that lets you do this.

Exercise 10.7 [**Very hard**] Implement the notation you developed for the previous exercise.

Chapter 11: `<stddef.h>`

Background

The header `<stddef.h>` is yet another invention of committee X3J11 in forming the C Standard. The name follows the usual cryptic pattern for naming headers in the Standard C library. It is meant to suggest that here is where you find certain "standard definitions."

The only other suitable parking spot for the definitions in this header might be `<stdlib.h>`. That too is a committee invention. It earned its (equally) vague name as a place to declare various functions, old and new, that had no traditional associated standard headers. It may seem silly to create *two* such catchall repositories. Nevertheless, the committee had its reasons.

freestanding Some members of X3J11 were determined that C should be a useful
versus language even in a *freestanding environment.* That is an environment that
hosted cannot support the full Standard C library, for whatever reason. The C Standard requires of a freestanding implementation that it support all the features of the language proper. Of the Standard C library, however, such an implementation need supply the capabilities defined in only four standard headers — `<float.h>`, `<limits.h>`, `<stdarg.h>`, and `<stddef.h>`. It can supply more, but the C Standard spells out no intermediate levels.

An implementation must provide the entire Standard C library to qualify as a *hosted* environment. That is the formal term for an environment that fully implements the C Standard. This book is, of course, primarily concerned with describing a hosted environment. It assumes that any freestanding environment will want to follow the C Standard closely in any additions it supplies beyond the required four standard headers.

That requirement clarifies what should go into `<stddef.h>`. The other three standard headers apply to fairly specific areas:

- `<float.h>` describes the properties of the floating-point representations.
- `<limits.h>` describes the properties of the integer representations.
- `<stdarg.h>` provides the macros you need to walk variable argument lists.

Any other type or macro definitions of use to a freestanding program has only one place to go. That's the header `<stddef.h>`.

A later committee decision muddied the waters somewhat. Several types and macros now have definitions in more than one standard header. The header `<locale.h>`, for example, defines the macro `NULL` So too does `<stddef.h>` and four other standard headers. Similarly, the types `size_t` and `wchar_t` have definitions in other standard headers as well as in `<stddef.h>`. That weakens the case for having a standard header just for definitions if it mostly replicates information available elsewhere. Remember, however, that the other standard headers may not be available in a freestanding environment.

The types and macros defined in `<stddef.h>` have one additional thing in common. Every one has been, at one time or another, a candidate for inclusion in the language proper. That's because every one is, in the end, defined by the translator in a private way. It is not easy to write portable code that can take the place of any of these definitions. Sometimes it is essentially impossible.

On the other hand, all the types and macros defined in `<stddef.h>` *can*, as a rule, be written as conventional type and macro definitions. The implementor simply need to be privy to how a given translator defines certain types and operations.

types as synonyms Consider the three type definitions in this header — `ptrdiff_t`, `size_t`, and `wchar_t`. Each is a *synonym* for one of the standard integer types. An implementation cannot, for example, make *short* 16-bits, `wchar_t` 24-bits, and *int* 32-bits. It must make `wchar_t` the same as some type that you can specify for a type definition. The same constraints apply to the other two type definitions.

macro NULL Implementing the macro `NULL` simply requires that you choose the most suitable of several possible options — `0`, `0L`, or `(void *)0`. You pick a form that works properly as an argument of type *pointer to void* (or pointer to *char*, *signed char*, or *unsigned char*) in the absence of a function prototype. (I discuss the macro `NULL` in greater detail on page 220.)

It might be more elegant, perhaps, to include a null-pointer constant in the C language proper. The suggestion has been raised any number of times. Nevertheless, one of these forms usually suffices for the ways in which `NULL` tends to be used.

macro offsetof That leaves the macro `offsetof`. You use it to determine the offset in bytes of a structure member from the start of the structure. Standard C defines no portable way to write this macro. Each implementation, however, must have some *nonstandard* way to implement it. An implementation may, for example, reliably evaluate some expression whose behavior is undefined in the C Standard.

You can look on `offsetof` as a portable way to perform a nonportable operation. That is true of many macros and type definitions in the Standard C library. In each instance, the need to actually extend the C language proper is not quite there. That's why the header `<stddef.h>` exists.

What the C Standard Says

7.1.6 Common Definitions `<stddef.h>`

The following types and macros are defined in the standard header **`<stddef.h>`**. Some are also defined in other headers, as noted in their respective subclauses.

The types are

> **`ptrdiff_t`**

which is the signed integral type of the result of subtracting two pointers;

> **`size_t`**

which is the unsigned integral type of the result of the **`sizeof`** operator; and

> **`wchar_t`**

which is an integral type whose range of values can represent distinct codes for all members of the largest extended character set specified among the supported locales; the null character shall have the code value zero and each member of the basic character set defined in 5.2.1 shall have a code value equal to its value when used as the lone character in an integer character constant.

The macros are

> **`NULL`**

which expands to an implementation-defined null pointer constant; and

> **`offsetof`**(*type, member-designator*)

which expands to an integral constant expression that has type **`size_t`**, the value of which is the offset in bytes, to the structure member (designated by *member-designator*), from the beginning of its structure (designated by *type*). The *member-designator* shall be such that given

> **`static`** *type* **t;**

then the expression **&(t**.*member-designator*) evaluates to an address constant. (If the specified member is a bit-field, the behavior is undefined.)

Forward references: localization (7.4).

Using `<stddef.h>`

The uses for type and macro definitions in the header **`<stddef.h>`** are essentially unrelated. You include this header if you need one or more of the definitions it provides. Note, however, that only the type definition **`ptrdiff_t`** and the macro **`offsetof`** are unique to this header. You will often find that including another standard header will supply the definition you need. I discuss each of the type and macro definitions separately.

When you subtract two pointers in a C expression, the result has type **`ptrdiff_t`**. It is an integer type that can represent negative values. Almost certainly it is either *int* or *long*. It is always the signed type that has the same number of \ bits as the unsigned type chosen for **`size_t`**, described below. (I said above that the *use* of these definitions is essentially unrelated. These two definitions are themselves highly related.)

You can subtract two pointers only if they have compatible data-object types. One may have a *const* type qualifier and the other not, for example, but both must point to the same data-object type. The translator can check types and complain if they are inappropriate. It generally cannot verify the additional constraint — both pointers must point to elements within the same array data object. Write an expression that violates this constraint and you often get a nonsense result from the subtraction.

The arithmetic essentially proceeds as follows. The program represents both pointers as offsets in bytes from a common origin in a common address space. It subtracts the two offsets algebraically, producing a signed intermediate result. It then divides this intermediate result by the size in bytes of the data object pointed to by both pointers. If both pointers point to elements of a common array, the division will yield no remainder. The final result is the difference in subscripts of the two array elements, regardless of the type of the elements.

That means, for example, that the expression `&a[5] - &a[2]` always has the value 3, of type `ptrdiff_t`. Similarly `&a[2] - &a[5]` always has the value −3. I assume in both cases that `a` is an array data object with at least 5 elements. (Pointer arithmetic is still defined for the element "just off the end" of an array, in this case `&a[5]` if `a` has exactly 5 elements.)

overflow   `ptrdiff_t` can be an inadequate type, in some instances. Consider an implementation where `size_t` is the type *unsigned int*. Then `ptrdiff_t` is the type *int*. Let's say further that you can declare a data object `x` as an array of *char* whose size `N` is greater than `INT_MAX` bytes. (The header `<limits.h>` defines the macro `INT_MAX` as the largest positive value representable by type *int*.) Then you might write something like:

```
#inlcude <limits.h>
#include <stddef.h>

#define N    INT_MAX+10
. . . . .
    char x[N];
    ptrdiff_t n = &x[N] - &x[0];
```

What is the result of the expression that initializes `n`? An overflow occurs because the result is too large to represent as an integer of type `ptrdiff_t`. The result is undefined. You can't get around this problem. It is an intrinsic weakness of the Standard C language.

Having painted this bleak picture, I must now tell you that such a situation rarely arises. It can only happen with arrays whose elements occupy only one byte. Typically, these are elements of type *char, signed char,* or *unsigned char*. Rarely are they anything else. It can happen on small computer architectures where type *int* has, say, a 16-bit representation. It can also happen on architectures that let you create enormous data objects.

Even then, you get an overflow only if you subtract pointers to two character array elements more than half an adddress-space apart. And even *then* the overflow may cause no problems because two's-complement arithmetic (the commonest form today) forgives many sins. Your program may well pass through all these perils and do what you intend anyway.

I recite all this esoterica to justify a simple conclusion. You will seldom, if ever, have a need to use the type definition `ptrdiff_t`. It's only practical use that I can imagine is to store the result of a pointer subtraction or the difference between two subscripts. Usually, your program consumes such results on the fly. This type has the intrinsic limitation that it cannot reliably capture all results of pointer subtractions. That limits its usefulness in a portable program. It's nice to know that you can determine the type of the result of a pointer subtraction. But I don't know why you would care most of the time.

type
size_t   When you apply the `sizeof` operator in a C expression, the result has type `size_t`. It is an unsigned integer type that can represent the size of the largest data object you can declare. Almost certainly it is either *unsigned int* or *unsigned long*. It is always the unsigned type that has the same number of bits as the signed type chosen for `ptrdiff_t`, described above.

Unlike `ptrdiff_t`, however, `size_t` is *very* useful. It is the safest type to represent any integer data object you use as an array subscript. You don't have to worry if a small array evolves to a very large one as the program changes. Subscript arithmetic will never overflow when performed in type `size_t`. You don't have to worry if the program moves to a machine with peculiar properties, such as 32-bit bytes and 1-byte *longs*. Type `size_t` offers the greatest chance that your code won't be unduly surprised. The only sensible type to use for computing the sizes of data objects is `size_t`.

The Standard C library makes extensive use of the type `size_t`. You will find that many function arguments and return values are declared to have this type. That is a deliberate change over older practice in C that often led to program bugs. It is part of a general trend away from declaring almost all integers as type *int*.

You should make a point of using type `size_t` *anywhere* your program performs array subscripting or address arithmetic. Be warned, however, that unsigned-integer arithmetic has more pitfalls than signed. You cannot run an unsigned counter down until it goes negative — it never will. If the translator doesn't warn you of a silly test expression, the program may loop forever. You may find, in fact, that counting down to zero sometimes leads to clumsy tests. You will occasionally miss the convenience of using negative values (such as `EOF`, defined in `<stdio.h>` to signal end-of-file) and testing for them easily. Nevertheless, the improvement in robustness is well worth the learning investment.

The code in this book uses type `size_t` wherever it is appropriate. You may see an occasional place where *int* data objects hold subscripts. In all such cases, however, the size of related array data objects should be naturally limited to a safe range of sizes. I indulge in such practices only when I have an overriding need to mix negative values with proper subscript values.

type
wchar_t   You write a *wide character constant* as, for example, `L'x'`. It has type `wchar_t`. You write a *wide character string literal* as, for example, `L"hello"`. It has type *array of* `wchar_t`. `wchar_t` is an integer type that can represent all the code values for all wide-character encodings supported by the implementation.

For an implementation with only minimal support for wide characters, **wchar_t** may be as small as *char*. For a very ambitious implementation, it may be as large as *unsigned long*. More likely, **wchar_t** is a synonym for an integer type that has at least a 16-bit representation, such as *short* or *unsigned short*.

You use **wchar_t** to represent *all* data objects that must hold wide characters. Several functions declared in **<stdlib.h>** manipulate wide characters, either one at a time or as part of null-terminated strings. You will find that many function arguments and return values in this group are declared to have this type. For this reason, the header **<stdlib.h>** also defines type **wchar_t**.

macro   The macro **NULL** serves as an almost-universal null pointer constant. You
NULL   use it as the value of a data-object pointer that should point to no data object declared (or allocated) in the program. As I mentioned on page 216, the macro can have any of the definitions **0**, **0L**, or **(void *)0**.

The last definition is compatible with any data object pointer. It is *not*, however, compatible with a function pointer. That means you cannot write:

```
int (*pfun)(void) = NULL;    /* WRONG */
```

The translator may complain that the expression type is incompatible with the data object you wish to initialize.

An important traditional use for **NULL** has largely gone away. Early versions of the C language had no function prototypes. The translator could not check whether a function-call argument expression was compatible with the corresponding function parameter declaration. Hence, it could not adjust the representation of an expression that was compatible but had a different type (such as changing **tan(1)** to **tan(1.0)**. The programmer had to ensure that each argument value had the proper representation.

Modern programming style is to declare function prototypes for *all* functions that you call. Nevertheless, an important context still exists where a function argument has no corresponding parameter declaration. That is when you call a function that accepts a variable argument list (such as **printf**, declared in **<stdio.h>**). For the extra arguments, the older C rules apply. A few standard type conversionsype;converting occur, but mostly it is up to you, the programmer, to get each such argument right.

In the earliest implementations of C, all pointers had the same representation. Usually, this representation was the same size as one of the integer types *int* or *long*. Thus, one of the decimal constants **0** or **0L** masqueraded nicely as a null pointer of any type. Define **NULL** as one of these two constants and you could assign it to an arbitrary pointer. The macro was particularly useful as an argument expression. It advertized that the expression had some pointer type and was a null-pointer constant.

Then along came implementations where pointers looked quite different than any of the integer types. The only safe way to write a null pointer was with a type cast, as in **(char *)0**. If all pointers looked the same, you could still define **NULL** as, say, `(char *)0`. The macro still served as a useful way to write argument expressions.

Standard C permits different pointer types to have different representations. You are guaranteed that you can convert any data object pointer to type *pointer to char* (or *pointer to signed char* or *pointer to unsigned char*) and back again with no loss of information. The newly introduced type *pointer to void* has the same representation as *pointer to char*, but is assignment-compatible with all data-object pointers. You use *pointer to void* as a convenient generic data-object pointer type, particularly for declaring function arguments and return values.

The safest definition for **NULL** on such an implementation is `(void *)0`. There is no guarantee, however, that *pointer to void* has the same *representation* as any other pointer. It isn't even assignment-compatible with function pointers. That means that you can't write **NULL** as a universal null-pointer constant. Nor can you safely use it as an argument expression in place of an arbitrary data-object pointer. It is guaranteed to masquerade properly only as a character pointer or as a generic *pointer to void*.

One modern style of writing C is to avoid the use of **NULL** altogether. Write every null pointer constant religiously with an appropriate type cast, as in `(int *)0`. That can lead to wordy programs, but has the virtue of being most unambiguous. A modification of this style is to write a simple `0` as a null-pointer constant wherever possible. That can lead to programs clear enough to the translator but not to human readers.

The style I follow in this book is to use **NULL** as much as possible. I find it a useful signal that a null-pointer constant is present. I use type casts to generate null-pointer constants for function pointers. I also use them for arguments to functions that accept variable argument lists, particularly if the required type is other than *pointer to void*.

You will find the macro **NULL** defined in half a dozen different headers. It is easy for you to use the macro if you so choose. My only advice is that you choose a uniform style, as always, and stick with it.

macro offsetof You use the macro `offsetof` to determine the offset in bytes of a member from the start of the structure that contains it. That can be important if you wish to manipulate the individual members of a structure using a table-driven function. See, for example, the function `_Makeloc` on page 120 and the table `_Loctab` on page 117.

The result of this macro is an integer constant expression of type `size_t`. That means you can use it to initialize a static data object such as a constant table with integer elements. It is the only portable way to do so. If you write code such as:

```
struct xx {
    int a, b;
    } x;
static size_t off = (char *)&x-b - (char *)&x;
```

the behavior of the last declaration is undefined. Some implementations can choose to evaluate the initializer and obtain the obvious result. Others can choose to diagnose the expression instead.

Nor can you reliably step from member to member by performing pointer arithmetic. The macros defined in **<stdarg.h>** let you step from argument to argument in a function that accepts a variable argument list. Those macros, or others like them, are not guaranteed to work within a structure. That's because the holes between structure members can differ from the holes between function arguments. They need not follow any documented rules, in fact.

You need the macro **offsetof** to write code that is portable:

```
#include <stddef.h>

struct xx {
    int a, b;
    } x;
static size_t off = offsetof(struct xx, b);
```

Implementing <stddef.h>

Figure 11.1 shows the file **stddef.h**. It is fairly simple. Once again, I use the internal header **<yvals.h>** to supply information that can vary among implementations. In this case, that information determines all three type definitions and the form of the macro **NULL**. The header **<yvals.h>** typically contains the following definitions:

header `typedef int _Ptrdifft;`
<yvals.h> `typedef unsigned int _Sizet;`
         `typedef unsigned short _Wchart;`
         `#define _NULL    (void *)0`

These definitions work for a wide variety of implementations. Nevertheless, certain implementations may require that one or more of them change. That's why I chose to parametrize them.

macro   For the macro **offsetof** I chose to use a common trick. Many implemen-
offsetof tations let you type cast an integer zero to a data-object pointer type, then perform pointer arithmetic on the result. That is certainly undefined behavior, so you may well find an implementation that balks at this approach.

The translator must indulge you a bit further for this definition of the macro to work properly. It must let you type cast the zero-based address back to an integer type, in this case **size_t** in disguise. Moreover, it must tolerate such antics in an integer constant expression. That's what you need to initialize static data objects.

Luckily, quite a few translators grant such a triple indulgence. If you encounter one that doesn't, you will have to research how its implementors expect you to define **offsetof**. To comply with the C Standard, each implementation must provide *some* method.

Figure 11.1:
stddef.h

```
/* stddef.h standard header */
#ifndef _STDDEF
#define _STDDEF
#ifndef _YVALS
#include <yvals.h>
#endif
        /* macros */
#define NULL      _NULL
#define offsetof(T, member) ((_Sizet)&((T *)0)->member)
        /* type definitions */
#ifndef _SIZET
#define _SIZET
typedef _Sizet size_t;
#endif
#ifndef _WCHART
#define _WCHART
typedef _Wchart wchar_t;
#endif
typedef _Ptrdifft ptrdiff_t;
#endif
```

Testing `<stddef.h>`

Figure 11.2 shows the file `tstddef.c`. It verifies the basic properties of the types and macros defined in `<stddef.h>`. It is a brief program because this header offers little to test. As a courtesy, the program also displays the sizes of data objects of type `size_t` and `wchar_t`. (`ptrdiff_t` is the same size as `size_t`.) If all goes well, the program displays output something like:

```
sizeof (size_t) = 4
sizeof (wchar_t) = 2
SUCCESS testing <stddef.h>
```

References

P.J. Plauger, "Data-Object Types," *The C Users Journal,*, 6, no. 3 (March/April 1988). This article discusses a few issues related to the topics in this chapter.

Exercises

Exercise 11.1 Determine the integer types that your implementation has chosen for `ptrdiff_t`, `size_t`, and `wchar_t`.

Exercise 11.2 Write a program that determines experimentally an integer type you can use for `wchar_t`.

Exercise 11.3 Write a program that determines experimentally the integer types you can use for `ptrdiff_t` and `wchar_t`.

Figure 11.2:
tstddef.c

```
/* test stddef definitions */
#include <assert.h>
#include <limits.h>
#include <stddef.h>
#include <stdio.h>

        /* type definitions */
typedef struct {
    char f1;
    struct {
        float flt;
        } f2;
    int f3;
    } Str;

        /* static data */
static char *pc = NULL;
static double *pd = NULL;
static size_t offs[] = {
    offsetof(Str, f1),
    offsetof(Str, f2),
    offsetof(Str, f3)};

int main()
    {               /* test basic workings of stddef definitions */
    ptrdiff_t pd = &pc[INT_MAX] - &pc[0];
    wchar_t wc = L'Z';
    Str x = {1, 2, 3};
    char *ps = (char *)&x;

    assert(sizeof (ptrdiff_t) == sizeof (size_t));
    assert(sizeof (size_t) == sizeof (sizeof (char)));
    assert(pd == &pc[INT_MAX] - &pc[0]);
    assert(wc == L'Z');
    assert(offs[0] < offs[1]);
    assert(offs[1] < offs[2]);
    assert(*(char *)(ps + offs[0]) == 1);
    assert(*(float *)(ps + offs[1]) == 2);
    assert(*(int *)(ps + offs[2]) == 3);
    printf("sizeof (size_t) = %u\n", sizeof (size_t));
    printf("sizeof (wchar_t) = %u\n", sizeof (wchar_t));
    puts("SUCCESS testing <stddef.h>");
    return (0);
    }
```

Exercise 11.4 [harder] Some implementations permit you to subtract two pointers in an integer constant expression if both are based on some static data-object declaration. Write a definition for **offsetof** that uses this capability.

Exercise 11.5 [very hard] Add a null-pointer constant to the C language. The keyword **nul** is a null pointer compatible with all pointer types. How do you handle **nul** as an argument expression in the absence of a corresponding parameter declaration?

Chapter 12: `<stdio.h>`

Background

The header `<stdio.h>` declares a broad assortment of functions that perform input and output. It is a rare program that performs no output, so this header is widely used. It was, in fact, one of the earliest headers to appear in the C library. This header declares more functions than any other standard header. It also requires more explaining because of the complex machinery that underlies the functions.

I discuss several major topics in this chapter:

- the abstract input/output model implemented by the Standard C library
- the low-level functions that read and write uninterpreted data
- the higher-level functions that print and scan data under control of a format specification

I begin with some historical perspective.

input/output model   One area of computer programming has seen dramatic improvements over the years, but has received little recognition for its successes. I refer to the device-independent model of input and output that has evolved along with high-level languages over the past twenty years or so. Standard C incorporates most of the benefits that derive from this improved model.

In the early 1960s, FORTRAN II was touted as a machine-independent language. Still, it was essentially impossible to move a FORTRAN program between computer architectures without some change. The major stumbling block to portability was in the area of input/output (or I/O for short). In FORTRAN II, you named the device you were talking to right in the I/O statement in the middle of your FORTRAN code. To read an input card image, you said `READ INPUT TAPE 5` on a tape-oriented IBM 7090. But you said `READ CARD` on other machines. To print your results, you said either `WRITE OUTPUT TAPE 6`, `PRINT`, or `TYPE`.

logical unit numbers   FORTRAN IV came along and provided an escape hatch. You could now write more generic `READ` and `WRITE` statements, each specifying a *logical unit number* (or LUN) in place of the specific device name. You stacked control cards in front of your executable binary card deck to specify which devices corresponded to which LUNs during this particular run. The era of device-independent I/O had dawned.

Well, almost. Peripheral devices still had fairly strong notions about what they should be asked to do. When you wrote to a printer, for example, the first character of each line was diverted to control carriage spacing. Send the same line to a typewriter and the carriage control characters printed. And carriage control was a lightweight issue compared to blocking factors for magnetic tape and diskfiles, or binary card formats, or how to specify end-of-file on various inputs. After a while, you learned which pairs of devices you could switch between for certain flavors of input and output.

PIP utilities
A further step toward device independence came with the evolution of standard *peripheral interchange* (or PIP) utilities. These were programs that would let you specify any combination of source and destination devices, then endeavored to perform a sensible copy operation between the two. Usually, you had to specify a bizarre set of options to give PIP a reasonable chance at guessing right. And invariably, some desirable combinations just flatly failed no matter how many hints you provided.

Then along came the CRT terminal and everybody took one step backward. Do you terminate a line with a carriage return, with a carriage return followed by a line feed, with a newline character, or with some other magical incantation? Does the terminal accept horizontal tab settings and expand tabs, or are tabs anathema to it? How do you signal end-of-file from the keyboard? As you can imagine, there were about as many answers to these questions as there were vendors of CRT terminals.

enter UNIX
It was into this atmosphere that UNIX came in the early 1970s. Ken Thompson and Dennis Ritchie, the developers of that now-famous system, deservedly get credit for packing any number of bright ideas into UNIX. Their approach to device independence was one of the brightest.

UNIX adopted a standard internal form for all text streams. Each line of text is terminated by a newline character. That's what any program expects when it reads text, and that's what any program produces when it writes it. If such a convention doesn't meet the needs of a text-oriented peripheral attached to a UNIX machine, then the fixup occurs out at the edges of the system. None of the code in the middle has to change.

system call ioctl
UNIX provides two mechanisms for fixing up text streams "out at the edges." The preferred mechanism is a generic mapper that works with any text-oriented device. You can set or test the various parameters for a given device with the `ioctl` system call. Using `ioctl`, you can (among other things) choose among various conversions between the internal newline convention and the needs of numerous terminals. Over the years, `ioctl` has evolved to a fairly sophisticated little PIP for text-oriented devices.

device handlers
The second mechanism for fixing up text streams is to tailor the special software that directly controls the device. For each device that a UNIX system may need to control, someone has to add a *device handler* to the UNIX resident. (MS-DOS has adopted similar machinery.) Early on, Thompson and Ritchie established the precedent that each device should handle standard text streams wherever possible.

file descriptors When Dennis Ritchie got the first C compiler going on PDP-11 UNIX, the language naturally inherited the simple I/O model of its host operating system. Along with the uniform representation for text streams came several other contributions to elegance. Those LUNs of yore had evolved over the years into small positive integers called *file descriptors* or *handles*. The operating system assumes responsibility for handing out file descriptors. And it keeps all file control information in its own private memory, rather than burden the user with allocating and maintaining file- and record-control blocks.

To simplify matters for most programs, the UNIX shell hands out three standard file descriptors to every program that it runs. These are for the now-commonplace *standard input, standard output*, and *standard error* streams. (They are not exactly a UNIX invention, having incubated in PL/I and MULTICS, among other places.) Programmers quickly learned the wisdom of reading text from the standard input and writing text to the standard output, whenever possible. Thus was born the software tool.

binary streams Another small but important refinement was 8-bit transparency. Nothing in UNIX prevents you from writing arbitrary binary codes to any open file, or reading them back unchanged from an adequate repository. True, sending binary to a text-oriented device might have bizarre consequences, but a file or pipeline is usually ready and willing to field arbitrary stuff. Programmers eventually learned the wisdom of making their programs tolerant of arbitrary binary codes, whenever that made sense, even if the programs originated as text processing tools. Thus did UNIX obliterate the long-standing distinction between text streams (for interacting with people) and binary streams (for interacting with other programs).

file length Yet another refinement was exact-length files. Most operating systems make only a half-hearted attempt to disguise any underlying block structure in files kept on disk, tape, or other record-oriented devices. When you write data to a file and then read it back, you may be treated to anywhere between one and a thousand extra characters tacked onto the end. UNIX records the size of a file to the nearest byte, so you get back only what was put into the file. Programmers of device handlers mostly learned to provide machinery for keeping data streams to and from devices just as tidy. Thus fell one of the last needs for the once ubiquitous PIP utility. (Note, however, that UNIX still has the **dd** command, a modern-day PIP.)

Similarly, making temporary files requires no advanced preparation, and hardly any thought. Stitching together C programs from different authors via pipelines works far more often than not. Those early UNIX systems delivered to universities produced a generation of C programmers blissfully ignorant of the ugly realities involved in performing I/O on most other operating systems.

C moves out The honeymoon ended when C moved from UNIX to other operating systems. Those of us involved in those first implementations faced some tough decisions. Should we fight to preserve the simple I/O model to which C programmers had grown accustomed, or should we alter the I/O library to match local custom? That was an easy one, philosophically at least. Few C programmers want to manipulate file-control blocks or specify a gazillion parameters when opening a file — not after years of relatively painless I/O. Most of us opted to preserve the simple I/O model as much as possible. (We also learned to provide hooks to the rest of the stuff, however, for the people who actually *liked* the local operating system.)

hiding   That being the case, where do we hide the uglies? UNIX packed most of
the them into `ioctl` or the device handlers. Generally, we lacked that option.
uglies Instead, we had to make more complex libraries to deal with varied devices and differing conventions for representing text. It is important to ensure that C can read and write text files that are compatible with the local text editor. C must also, at a minimum, read text from keyboards and write it to displays and printers. The library maps as needed between newline-terminated text lines internally and local usage externally.

We could not do a perfect job of hiding the uglies on non-UNIX systems. So another tough decision we implementors had to make was how to let the uglies shine through when we couldn't make them go away. Those vendors content to implement C very well for one environment usually just added complexity to the existing I/O functions, and added great bouquets of new functions. Those of us who were striving for a uniform but powerful environment across multiple systems had to be more sparing. That meant adding minimal additional complexity to the existing I/O functions, as well as adding as few new functions as possible. It also meant weakening some of the promises of the UNIX I/O model to satisfy the least-common denominator across varied systems.

X3J11   Committee X3J11 began meeting in 1983 to draft an ANSI standard for
moves in C. Vendors of C for non-UNIX systems fought many a patient battle with the UNIX folk who could not understand why I/O had to be so messy. It was a highly educational process. An important byproduct of all this discussion was a clearer statement of the I/O model supported by C.

text   To begin with, Standard C had to reintroduce the distinction between
versus text and binary files. Almost every operating system besides UNIX forces
binary an implementation to treat these two flavors differently. MS-DOS, for example, lets you use the same system calls for both text and binary files, but it terminates each line in a text file with both a carriage return and a line feed. The C runtime must discard those terminating carriage returns when it reads a text file, but not when it reads a binary file. Hence, the distinction is there even when you think it might not have to be.

You specify whether a file is to be treated as text or binary when you open it. You write `fopen(fname, "r")` to open a file for reading, for example. In Standard C, this recipe specifies a text file by default. If you want to open a `binary` file, you write `fopen(fname, "rb")`. You can tack the `b` onto any of the other modes as well. (The `b` can either precede or follow any `+` you write as part of the mode.)

A UNIX system is free to ignore the **b** mode qualifier, as is any operating system for which the distinction has no meaning. On many systems, however, the distinction is extremely important. If you want your program to be portable, think about how each file is used and code its **fopen** mode properly. Otherwise, your program can fail in all sorts of subtle ways.

A text file is designed to support closely the UNIX model of a stream of text. This is not always easy. As I indicated on page 226, conventions for terminating text lines vary considerably. The implementation requires latitude in converting what's out there to what your C program reads, and in converting what your program writes to what makes sense to other programs once it's out there. That latitude must extend to the set of characters you write to text files, to how you construct text lines, and even to the difference between zero and nothing. Let me elaborate.

Some systems are far from 8-bit transparent when it comes to writing things in text files. A ctl-Z looks like an end-of-file in more than one popular operating system. Even characters from the basic C character set can be chancey. Form feeds and vertical tabs may not survive intact in some environments. For maximum portability, in fact, you should write to a text file only the printing characters, plus space, newline, and horizontal tab.

terminating lines Many systems balk at partial (last) lines, since they have no way to represent the concept of a line without a terminator. If the last character you write to a text file is not a newline, that partial last line may go away. Or it may be completed for you, so that you read a newline back that you did not write out. Or the program may gripe when you run it. Avoid partial last lines in text files.

line length Some systems cannot even represent an empty line. When you write one, the library may actually write a line containing a space. On input, the system then discards the space from a line containing only a single space. Some systems discard *all* trailing spaces on a text line. That gives you nicer behavior if your program reads a file consisting of fixed-length text records. All those trailing spaces conveniently disappear. But what this means is that you cannot rely on writing a text line with trailing spaces and reading those spaces back later. Don't even try, in a portable program.

At the other extreme, systems have a right to impose an upper limit on the longest text line that they can read or write. Longer lines may be truncated, so the trailing characters are lost. Or they may be folded, so you suddenly encounter newline characters that were not there originally. Or you may get a complaint when you run your program. The upper limit guaranteed by the C Standard for the length of a text line is the curious number 509. It represents an interesting committee compromise (but not interesting enough to describe in detail).

file length Some systems cannot represent an empty file. If you create a new file, write nothing to it, then close it, the system has no way to distinguish that empty file from one that is nonexistent. Hence, Standard C permits an implementation to remove empty files when you close them. Be warned.

A file that is very long, on the other hand, may also cause problems. Under UNIX, you can characterize the position of any byte in a file with a 32-bit integer. The traditional file-positioning functions of C thus assume that a *long* can represent an arbitrary file-position. That is often not true on other systems, even for files well short of 2^{32} bytes in length. The committee added an alternate set of file-positioning functions to the Standard C library to partially ameliorate this problem.

To end the discussion of text files on a more positive note, I offer one bit of encouragement. If you follow all these rules, then the sequence of characters that you write to a text file will exactly match the sequence that you later read. Just don't push your luck by bending the rules, if such symmetry is of importance to you.

binary   As for binary files, the major compromise was to reintroduce length
files uncertainty. An implementation must preserve exactly all the bytes you write at the start of a file, but it is at liberty to pad a binary file. Any number of padding characters can be added, so long as all of them have value zero (`'\0'`). Thus, you may have to be more careful in designing your binary files. Don't assume you will see end-of-file after you read the last character you earlier wrote to the file. Either have a way of knowing when the data ends or be tolerant of trailing zero bytes in the data you read.

evolution   As I indicated on page 226, UNIX I/O represents a considerable simpli-
of streams fication over earlier systems. Most systems designed before UNIX took it for granted that I/O was a complex operation whose complexity could not be hidden from the executing program. Files had all sorts of structure, reflected in various attributes such as block or record size, search keys, printer format controls, and so on seemingly *ad infinitum*. Different combinations of these attributes had to be specified on each system call that performed I/O. Still other bits of information had to be retained between system calls to keep track of the state of each stream.

So the easiest thing, it seemed, was for the system to require each user program to allocate storage space for passing and/or remembering all these attributes and other bits of state information. The storage area was called a "data control block," "file control block," "record access block," or some equally vague name. You were obliged to set aside space for a control block before you opened the file, pass a pointer to the control block on the system call that opened the file, and pass the same pointer on all subsequent system calls that performed I/O on the file. Any other arguments needed for an I/O system call get tucked into various fields of the control block.

If you were lucky, the operating system vendor provided a package of assembly-language macros for allocating these control blocks and addressing the various fields. If you were smart, you used these macros religiously, since most vendors felt quite free to change the size and layout of control blocks with each release. The macro interface tended to be reasonably stable, since the vendor's systems programmers would have been inconvenienced had *that* changed.

But even with the best macro package in the world, you still had to contend with a pretty unstructured interface. Assemblers, as a rule, can hardly enforce that you read and write data of the appropriate type from the fields of a control block. Even worse, the fields tended to be numerous and ill-documented. It was often not clear whether you could set certain fields to advantage before a system call, or whether you could rely on the fields to contain meaningful information after a system call. The one thing you could count on was that injudicious scribbling within a control block could curdle I/O, damage files, or even crash the system.

UNIX I/O model So it was a real step forward when UNIX eliminated the need for control blocks in user memory. When you open a file under UNIX, you get back just a file descriptor, a small positive integer. Any control information is retained within the system, presumably out of reach of stupid or malicious user programs. Files are sufficiently unstructured that you need specify only a few parameters on each I/O system call. It is easy to map from a few scalar arguments on a function called from C to the minimal (and transient) structure required by each UNIX system call on any given implementation.

The functions that perform UNIX-style I/O from C have names such as **open, close, read, write,** and **lseek.** They traffic in file descriptors and I/O buffers. They support a simple I/O model that has been imposed on dozens of more complex operating systems. They appear to be ideal candidates for the I/O primities in Standard C.

There is one small problem, however. While the earliest programs written for UNIX were content to call these primitives directly, later programs became more sophisticated. They imposed a layer of buffering, in user memory, to minimize the number of system calls per byte of data transferred in and out of the program. A program almost always runs substantially faster if it reads and writes hundreds of bytes per system call instead of just a few.

A standard library of functions evolved that automatically took care of allocating and freeing buffers, filling them and draining them, and tracking error conditions in a uniform style. These functions worked with data structures of type **FILE** to control streams. Each stream data object kept track of the state of I/O to the associated file. It also contained a pointer to a buffer area and additional state information to keep track of the number of useful bytes in the buffer.

choosing I/O primitives There was broad consensus among the members of X3J11 that streams were a necessary addition to the Standard C library. Many people had learned to work exclusively with streams to ensure decent I/O performance. There were even a few implementations of C that had chosen to implement stream I/O exclusively, disdaining the simpler UNIX-style primitives as too inefficient.

Some implementations based on the UNIX primitives often had to buffer data in user memory for the **read** and **write** calls, if only to pack and unpack records in structured files. Customers using the stream functions suffered from a double layer of buffering which seldom improved performance and often confused interactive programs.

So here was the dilemma: Performing I/O at the stream level is often necessary to improve program performance, even under UNIX. You can define all I/O in terms of just a few of the stream-oriented functions, such as **fopen, fclose, fgetc, fputc, fgetpos,** and **fsetpos.** If you do so, however, you ignore the widespread historical presumption that you can also do I/O with the simpler UNIX-style primitives. That eliminates the need for **FILE** data objects and allocated buffers in user space. People writing in C for very small systems would like to be able to avoid the extra space overhead, even at a potential cost in performance.

From the standpoint of a standard, however, there is something repugnant about having two separate mechanisms for achieving much the same goal. The committee debated the relative importance of cleanliness versus backward compatibility for some time before deciding to drop the UNIX-style primitives.

In the end, I think the argument that convinced most people was that an implementation could always add **open, close,** etc. as extensions. Of course, these functions must not collide with user-defined functions or data objects having the same name. That means it must be possible to knock out any such additions to the library. And that in turn means that **fopen** must not call **open,** for example. Still, it is quite possible to provide the traditional UNIX I/O primitives and conform to the C Standard.

Some implementors on the committee even argued that you could implement **read** in terms of **fgetc** just as efficiently as the other way around, or even more so. Like elementary particles in high-energy physics, you know that only a few of the functions are primitive, but you don't know for sure which ones are primitive and which ones are built on the others.

type   In a very real sense, of course, requiring streams to do I/O in Standard
FILE C represents a step backward. Each program must now contain in user memory a complex control block to remember the state of each stream. You must be careful when you allocate and deallocate the control block (**FILE** data object). You must not directly read or write the control block or the buffer it controls. You must perform I/O operations on the stream by calling functions only in certain orders.

It's not as bad as the bad old days, however. A **FILE** data object is allocated for you when you open a stream by calling **fopen** (or before program startup for the three standard streams). You don't need to know the internal structure of a **FILE** data object, because you never have to tuck parameters directly into one or fish them out. The Standard C library provides functions for reading and writing the parameters you can control on a stream. And the semantics of the I/O functions require that streams behave fairly robustly even when you try to do silly things with them.

What the C Standard Says

7.9 Input/output `<stdio.h>`

7.9.1 Introduction

The header `<stdio.h>` declares three types, several macros, and many functions for performing input and output.

`size_t`

The types declared are **`size_t`** (described in 7.1.6);

`FILE`

    `FILE`

which is an object type capable of recording all the information needed to control a stream, including its file position indicator, a pointer to its associated buffer (if any), an *error indicator* that records whether a read/write error has occurred, and an *end-of-file indicator* that records whether the end of the file has been reached; and

`fpos_t`

    `fpos_t`

which is an object type capable of recording all the information needed to specify uniquely every position within a file.

`NULL`

The macros are **NULL** (described in 7.1.6);

`_IOFBF`
`_IOLBF`
`_IONBF`

    `_IOFBF`
    `_IOLBF`
    `_IONBF`

which expand to integral constant expressions with distinct values, suitable for use as the third argument to the **`setvbuf`** function;

`BUFSIZ`

    `BUFSIZ`

which expands to an integral constant expression, which is the size of the buffer used by the **`setbuf`** function;

`EOF`

    `EOF`

which expands to a negative integral constant expression that is returned by several functions to indicate *end-of-file,* that is, no more input from a stream;

`FOPEN_MAX`

    `FOPEN_MAX`

which expands to an integral constant expression that is the minimum number of files that the implementation guarantees can be open simultaneously;

`FILENAME_MAX`

    `FILENAME_MAX`

which expands to an integral constant expression that is the size needed for an array of **char** large enough to hold the longest file name string that the implementation guarantees can be opened;[110]

`L_tmpnam`

    `L_tmpnam`

which expands to an integral constant expression that is the size needed for an array of **char** large enough to hold a temporary file name string generated by the **`tmpnam`** function;

`SEEK_CUR`
`SEEK_END`
`SEEK_SET`

    `SEEK_CUR`
    `SEEK_END`
    `SEEK_SET`

which expand to integral constant expressions with distinct values, suitable for use as the third argument to the **`fseek`** function;

`TMP_MAX`

    `TMP_MAX`

which expands to an integral constant expression that is the minimum number of unique file names that shall be generated by the **`tmpnam`** function;

`stderr`
`stdin`
`stdout`

    `stderr`
    `stdin`
    `stdout`

which are expressions of type "pointer to **FILE**" that point to the **FILE** objects associated, respectively, with the standard error, input, and output streams.

Forward references: files (7.9.3), the **`fseek`** function (7.9.9.2), streams (7.9.2), the **`tmpnam`** function (7.9.4.4).

7.9.2 Streams

streams

Input and output, whether to or from physical devices such as terminals and tape drives, or whether to or from files supported on structured storage devices, are mapped into logical data *streams,* whose properties are more uniform than their various inputs and outputs. Two forms of mapping are supported, for *text streams* and for *binary streams.*[111]

**text
streams**

A text stream is an ordered sequence of characters composed into *lines,* each line consisting of zero or more characters plus a terminating new-line character. Whether the last line requires a terminating new-line character is implementation-defined. Characters may have to be added, altered, or deleted on input and output to conform to differing conventions for representing text in the host environment. Thus, there need not be a one-to-one correspondence between the characters in a stream and those in the external representation. Data read in from a text stream will necessarily compare equal to the data that were earlier written out to that stream only if: the data consist only of printable characters and the control characters horizontal tab and new-line; no new-line character is immediately preceded by space characters; and the last character is a new-line character. Whether space characters that are written out immediately before a new-line character appear when read in is implementation-defined.

**binary
streams**

A binary stream is an ordered sequence of characters that can transparently record internal data. Data read in from a binary stream shall compare equal to the data that were earlier written out to that stream, under the same implementation. Such a stream may, however, have an implementation-defined number of null characters appended to the end of the stream.

Environmental limits

An implementation shall support text files with lines containing at least 254 characters, including the terminating new-line character. The value of the macro **BUFSIZ** shall be at least 256.

7.9.3 Files

**opening
files**

A stream is associated with an external file (which may be a physical device) by *opening* a file, which may involve *creating* a new file. Creating an existing file causes its former contents to be discarded, if necessary. If a file can support positioning requests (such as a disk file, as opposed to a terminal), then a *file position indicator*[112] associated with the stream is positioned at the start (character number zero) of the file, unless the file is opened with append mode in which case it is implementation-defined whether the file position indicator is initially positioned at the beginning or the end of the file. The file position indicator is maintained by subsequent reads, writes, and positioning requests, to facilitate an orderly progression through the file. All input takes place as if characters were read by successive calls to the **fgetc** function; all output takes place as if characters were written by successive calls to the **fputc** function.

Binary files are not truncated, except as defined in 7.9.5.3. Whether a write on a text stream causes the associated file to be truncated beyond that point is implementation-defined.

**buffering
files**

When a stream is *unbuffered,* characters are intended to appear from the source or at the destination as soon as possible. Otherwise characters may be accumulated and transmitted to or from the host environment as a block. When a stream is *fully buffered,* characters are intended to be transmitted to or from the host environment as a block when a buffer is filled. When a stream is *line buffered,* characters are intended to be transmitted to or from the host environment as a block when a new-line character is encountered. Furthermore, characters are intended to be transmitted as a block to the host environment when a buffer is filled, when input is requested on an unbuffered stream, or when input is requested on a line buffered stream that requires the transmission of characters from the host environment. Support for these characteristics is implementation-defined, and may be affected via the **setbuf** and **setvbuf** functions.

**closing
files**

A file may be disassociated from a controlling stream by *closing* the file. Output streams are flushed (any unwritten buffer contents are transmitted to the host environment) before the stream is disassociated from the file. The value of a pointer to a **FILE** object is indeterminate after the associated file is closed (including the standard text streams). Whether a file of zero length (on which no characters have been written by an output stream) actually exists is implementation-defined.

**reopening
files**

The file may be subsequently reopened, by the same or another program execution, and its contents reclaimed or modified (if it can be repositioned at its start). If the **main** function returns to its original caller, or if the **exit** function is called, all open files are closed (hence all output streams are flushed) before program termination. Other paths to program termination, such as calling the **abort** function, need not close all files properly.

The address of the **FILE** object used to control a stream may be significant; a copy of a **FILE** object may not necessarily serve in place of the original.

At program startup, three text streams are predefined and need not be opened explicitly — *standard input* (for reading conventional input), *standard output* (for writing conventional output), and *standard error* (for writing diagnostic output). When opened, the standard error stream is not fully buffered; the standard input and standard output streams are fully buffered if and only if the stream can be determined not to refer to an interactive device.

Functions that open additional (nontemporary) files require a *file name* , which is a string. The rules for composing valid file names are implementation-defined. Whether the same file can be simultaneously open multiple times is also implementation-defined.

Environmental limits

The value of **FOPEN_MAX** shall be at least eight, including the three standard text streams.

Forward references: the **exit** function (7.10.4.3), the **fgetc** function (7.9.7.1), the **fopen** function (7.9.5.3), the **fputc** function (7.9.7.3), the **setbuf** function (7.9.5.5), the **setvbuf** function (7.9.5.6).

7.9.4 Operations on files

7.9.4.1 The remove function

remove

Synopsis

```
#include <stdio.h>
int remove(const char *filename);
```

Description

The **remove** function causes the file whose name is the string pointed to by **filename** to be no longer accessible by that name. A subsequent attempt to open that file using that name will fail, unless it is created anew. If the file is open, the behavior of the **remove** function is implementation-defined.

Returns

The **remove** function returns zero if the operation succeeds, nonzero if it fails.

7.9.4.2 The rename function

rename

Synopsis

```
#include <stdio.h>
int rename(const char *old, const char *new);
```

Description

The **rename** function causes the file whose name is the string pointed to by **old** to be henceforth known by the name given by the string pointed to by **new**. The file named **old** is no longer accessible by that name. If a file named by the string pointed to by **new** exists prior to the call to the **rename** function, the behavior is implementation-defined.

Returns

The **rename** function returns zero if the operation succeeds, nonzero if it fails,[113] in which case if the file existed previously it is still known by its original name.

7.9.4.3 The tmpfile function

tmpfile

Synopsis

```
#include <stdio.h>
FILE *tmpfile(void);
```

Description

- The **tmpfile** function creates a temporary binary file that will automatically be removed when it is closed or at program termination. If the program terminates abnormally, whether an open temporary file is removed is implementation-defined. The file is opened for update with **"wb+"** mode.

Returns

The **tmpfile** function returns a pointer to the stream of the file that it created. If the file cannot be created, the **tmpfile** function returns a null pointer.

Forward references: the **fopen** function (7.9.5.3).

7.9.4.4 The **tmpnam** function

Synopsis

```
#include <stdio.h>
char *tmpnam(char *s);
```

Description

The **tmpnam** function generates a string that is a valid file name and that is not the same as the name of an existing file.[114]

The **tmpnam** function generates a different string each time it is called, up to **TMP_MAX** times. If it is called more than **TMP_MAX** times, the behavior is implementation-defined.

The implementation shall behave as if no library function calls the **tmpnam** function.

Returns

If the argument is a null pointer, the **tmpnam** function leaves its result in an internal static object and returns a pointer to that object. Subsequent calls to the **tmpnam** function may modify the same object. If the argument is not a null pointer, it is assumed to point to an array of at least **L_tmpnam char**s; the **tmpnam** function writes its result in that array and returns the argument as its value.

Environmental limits

The value of the macro **TMP_MAX** shall be at least 25.

7.9.5 File access functions

7.9.5.1 The **fclose** function

Synopsis

```
#include <stdio.h>
int fclose(FILE *stream);
```

Description

The **fclose** function causes the stream pointed to by **stream** to be flushed and the associated file to be closed. Any unwritten buffered data for the stream are delivered to the host environment to be written to the file; any unread buffered data are discarded. The stream is disassociated from the file. If the associated buffer was automatically allocated, it is deallocated.

Returns

The **fclose** function returns zero if the stream was successfully closed, or **EOF** if any errors were detected.

7.9.5.2 The **fflush** function

Synopsis

```
#include <stdio.h>
int fflush(FILE *stream);
```

Description

If **stream** points to an output stream or an update stream in which the most recent operation was not input, the **fflush** function causes any unwritten data for that stream to be delivered to the host environment to be written to the file; otherwise, the behavior is undefined.

If **stream** is a null pointer, the **fflush** function performs this flushing action on all streams for which the behavior is defined above.

Returns

The **fflush** function returns **EOF** if a write error occurs, otherwise zero.

Forward references: the **fopen** function (7.9.5.3), the **ungetc** function (7.9.7.11).

7.9.5.3 The **fopen** function

Synopsis

```
#include <stdio.h>
FILE *fopen(const char *filename, const char *mode);
```

Description

The **fopen** function opens the file whose name is the string pointed to by **filename**, and associates a stream with it.

The argument **mode** points to a string beginning with one of the following sequences:[115]

r	open text file for reading
w	truncate to zero length or create text file for writing
a	append; open or create text file for writing at end-of-file
rb	open binary file for reading
wb	truncate to zero length or create binary file for writing
ab	append; open or create binary file for writing at end-of-file
r+	open text file for update (reading and writing)
w+	truncate to zero length or create text file for update
a+	append; open or create text file for update, writing at end-of-file
r+b *or* rb+	open binary file for update (reading and writing)
w+b *or* wb+	truncate to zero length or create binary file for update
a+b *or* ab+	append; open or create binary file for update, writing at end-of-file

Opening a file with read mode (`'r'` as the first character in the **mode** argument) fails if the file does not exist or cannot be read.

Opening a file with append mode (`'a'` as the first character in the **mode** argument) causes all subsequent writes to the file to be forced to the then current end-of-file, regardless of intervening calls to the **fseek** function. In some implementations, opening a binary file with append mode (`'b'` as the second or third character in the above list of **mode** argument values) may initially position the file position indicator for the stream beyond the last data written, because of null character padding.

When a file is opened with update mode (`'+'` as the second or third character in the above list of **mode** argument values), both input and output may be performed on the associated stream. However, output may not be directly followed by input without an intervening call to the **fflush** function or to a file positioning function (**fseek**, **fsetpos**, or **rewind**), and input may not be directly followed by output without an intervening call to a file positioning function, unless the input operation encounters end-of-file. Opening (or creating) a text file with update mode may instead open (or create) a binary stream in some implementations.

When opened, a stream is fully buffered if and only if it can be determined not to refer to an interactive device. The error and end-of-file indicators for the stream are cleared.

Returns

The **fopen** function returns a pointer to the object controlling the stream. If the open operation fails, **fopen** returns a null pointer.

Forward references: file positioning functions (7.9.9).

freopen

7.9.5.4 The **freopen** function

Synopsis

```
#include <stdio.h>
FILE *freopen(const char *filename, const char *mode,
     FILE *stream);
```

Description

The **freopen** function opens the file whose name is the string pointed to by **filename** and associates the stream pointed to by **stream** with it. The mode argument is used just as in the **fopen** function.[116]

The **freopen** function first attempts to close any file that is associated with the specified stream. Failure to close the file successfully is ignored. The error and end-of-file indicators for the stream are cleared.

Returns

The **freopen** function returns a null pointer if the open operation fails. Otherwise, **freopen** returns the value of **stream**.

7.9.5.5 The **setbuf** function

Synopsis

```
#include <stdio.h>
void setbuf(FILE *stream, char *buf);
```

Description

Except that it returns no value, the **setbuf** function is equivalent to the **setvbuf** function invoked with the values _IOFBF for **mode** and BUFSIZ for **size**, or (if **buf** is a null pointer), with the value _IONBF for **mode**.

Returns

The **setbuf** function returns no value.

Forward references: the **setvbuf** function (7.9.5.6).

7.9.5.6 The **setvbuf** function

Synopsis

```
#include <stdio.h>
int setvbuf(FILE *stream, char *buf, int mode,
     size_t size);
```

Description

The **setvbuf** function may be used only after the stream pointed to by **stream** has been associated with an open file and before any other operation is performed on the stream. The argument **mode** determines how **stream** will be buffered, as follows: _IOFBF causes input/output to be fully buffered; _IOLBF causes input/output to be line buffered; _IONBF causes input/output to be unbuffered. If **buf** is not a null pointer, the array it points to may be used instead of a buffer allocated by the **setvbuf** function.[117] The argument **size** specifies the size of the array. The contents of the array at any time are indeterminate.

Returns

The **setvbuf** function returns zero on success, or nonzero if an invalid value is given for **mode** or if the request cannot be honored.

7.9.6 Formatted input/output functions

7.9.6.1 The **fprintf** function

Synopsis

```
#include <stdio.h>
int fprintf(FILE *stream, const char *format, ...);
```

Description

The **fprintf** function writes output to the stream pointed to by **stream**, under control of the string pointed to by **format** that specifies how subsequent arguments are converted for output. If there are insufficient arguments for the format, the behavior is undefined. If the format is exhausted while arguments remain, the excess arguments are evaluated (as always) but are otherwise ignored. The **fprintf** function returns when the end of the format string is encountered.

The format shall be a multibyte character sequence, beginning and ending in its initial shift state. The format is composed of zero or more directives: ordinary multibyte characters (not %), which are copied unchanged to the output stream; and conversion specifications, each of which results in fetching zero or more subsequent arguments. Each conversion specification is introduced by the character %. After the %, the following appear in sequence:

- Zero or more *flags* (in any order) that modify the meaning of the conversion specification.

- An optional minimum *field width*. If the converted value has fewer characters than the field width, it will be padded with spaces (by default) on the left (or right, if the left adjustment flag, described later, has been given) to the field width. The field width takes the form of an asterisk * (described later) or a decimal integer.[118]

- An optional *precision* that gives the minimum number of digits to appear for the **d**, **i**, **o**, **u**, **x**, and **X** conversions, the number of digits to appear after the decimal-point character for **e**, **E**, and **f** conversions, the maximum number of significant digits for the **g** and **G** conversions, or the maximum number of characters to be written from a string in **s** conversion. The precision takes the form of a period (.) followed either by an asterisk * (described later) or by an optional decimal integer; if only the period is specified, the precision is taken as zero. If a precision appears with any other conversion specifier, the behavior is undefined.

- An optional **h** specifying that a following **d**, **i**, **o**, **u**, **x**, or **X** conversion specifier applies to a **short int** or **unsigned short int** argument (the argument will have been promoted according to the integral promotions, and its value shall be converted to **short int** or **unsigned short int** before printing); an optional **h** specifying that a following **n** conversion specifier applies to a pointer to a **short int** argument; an optional **l** (ell) specifying that a following **d**, **i**, **o**, **u**, **x**, or **X** conversion specifier applies to a **long int** or **unsigned long int** argument; an optional **l** specifying that a following **n** conversion specifier applies to a pointer to a **long int** argument; or an optional **L** specifying that a following **e**, **E**, **f**, **g**, or **G** conversion specifier applies to a **long double** argument. If an **h**, **l**, or **L** appears with any other conversion specifier, the behavior is undefined.

- A character that specifies the type of conversion to be applied.

As noted above, a field width, or precision, or both, may be indicated by an asterisk. In this case, an **int** argument supplies the field width or precision. The arguments specifying field width, or precision, or both, shall appear (in that order) before the argument (if any) to be converted. A negative field width argument is taken as a − flag followed by a positive field width. A negative precision argument is taken as if the precision were omitted.

The flag characters and their meanings are

−   The result of the conversion will be left-justified within the field. (It will be right-justified if this flag is not specified.)

+   The result of a signed conversion will always begin with a plus or minus sign. (It will begin with a sign only when a negative value is converted if this flag is not specified.)

*space*If the first character of a signed conversion is not a sign, or if a signed conversion results in no characters, a space will be prefixed to the result. If the *space* and + flags both appear, the *space* flag will be ignored.

The result is to be converted to an "alternate form." For **o** conversion, it increases the precision to force the first digit of the result to be a zero. For **x** (or **X**) conversion, a nonzero result will have **0x** (or **0X**) prefixed to it. For **e**, **E**, **f**, **g**, and **G** conversions, the result will always contain a decimal-point character, even if no digits follow it. (Normally, a decimal-point character appears in the result of these conversions only if a digit follows it.) For **g** and **G** conversions, trailing zeros will *not* be removed from the result. For other conversions, the behavior is undefined.

0   For **d**, **i**, **o**, **u**, **x**, **X**, **e**, **E**, **f**, **g**, and **G** conversions, leading zeros (following any indication of sign or base) are used to pad to the field width; no space padding is performed. If the **0** and − flags both appear, the **0** flag will be ignored. For **d**, **i**, **o**, **u**, **x**, and **X** conversions, if a precision is specified, the **0** flag will be ignored. For other conversions, the behavior is undefined.

The conversion specifiers and their meanings are

d,i   The **int** argument is converted to signed decimal in the style *[−]dddd.* The precision specifies the minimum number of digits to appear; if the value being converted can be represented in fewer digits, it will be expanded with leading zeros. The default precision is 1. The result of converting a zero value with a precision of zero is no characters.

o,u,x,X   The **unsigned int** argument is converted to unsigned octal (**o**), unsigned decimal (**u**), or unsigned hexadecimal notation (**x** or **X**) in the style *dddd*; the letters **abcdef** are used for **x** conversion and the letters **ABCDEF** for **X** conversion. The precision specifies the minimum number of digits to appear; if the value being converted can be represented in fewer digits, it will be expanded with leading zeros. The default precision is 1. The result of converting a zero value with a precision of zero is no characters.

f   The **double** argument is converted to decimal notation in the style *[−]ddd.ddd,* where the number of digits after the decimal-point character is equal to the precision specification. If the precision is missing, it is taken as 6; if the precision is zero and the **#** flag is not specified, no decimal-point character appears. If a decimal-point character appears, at least one digit appears before it. The value is rounded to the appropriate number of digits.

e,E   The **double** argument is converted in the style *[−]d.ddde±dd,* where there is one digit before the decimal-point character (which is nonzero if the argument is nonzero) and the number of digits after it is equal to the precision; if the precision is missing, it is taken as 6; if the precision is zero and the **#** flag is not specified, no decimal-point character appears. The value is rounded to the appropriate number of digits. The **E** conversion specifier will produce a number with **E** instead of **e** introducing the exponent. The exponent always contains at least two digits. If the value is zero, the exponent is zero.

g,G The **double** argument is converted in style **f** or **e** (or in style **E** in the case of a **G** conversion specifier), with the precision specifying the number of significant digits. If the precision is zero, it is taken as 1. The style used depends on the value converted; style **e** (or **E**) will be used only if the exponent resulting from such a conversion is less than –4 or greater than or equal to the precision. Trailing zeros are removed from the fractional portion of the result; a decimal-point character appears only if it is followed by a digit.

c The **int** argument is converted to an **unsigned char**, and the resulting character is written.

s The argument shall be a pointer to an array of character type.[119] Characters from the array are written up to (but not including) a terminating null character; if the precision is specified, no more than that many characters are written. If the precision is not specified or is greater than the size of the array, the array shall contain a null character.

p The argument shall be a pointer to **void**. The value of the pointer is converted to a sequence of printable characters, in an implementation-defined manner.

n The argument shall be a pointer to an integer into which is *written* the number of characters written to the output stream so far by this call to **fprintf**. No argument is converted.

% A **%** is written. No argument is converted. The complete conversion specification shall be **%%**.

If a conversion specification is invalid, the behavior is undefined.[120]

If any argument is, or points to, a union or an aggregate (except for an array of character type using **%s** conversion, or a pointer using **%p** conversion), the behavior is undefined.

In no case does a nonexistent or small field width cause truncation of a field; if the result of a conversion is wider than the field width, the field is expanded to contain the conversion result.

Returns

The **fprintf** function returns the number of characters transmitted, or a negative value if an output error occurred.

Environmental limit

The minimum value for the maximum number of characters produced by any single conversion shall be 509.

Example

To print a date and time in the form "Sunday, July 3, 10:02" followed by π to five decimal places:

```
#include <math.h>
#include <stdio.h>
/*...*/
char *weekday, *month;    /* pointers to strings */
int day, hour, min;
fprintf(stdout, "%s, %s %d, %.2d:%.2d\n",
        weekday, month, day, hour, min);
fprintf(stdout, "pi = %.5f\n", 4 * atan(1.0));
```

fscanf

7.9.6.2 The **fscanf** function

Synopsis

```
#include <stdio.h>
int fscanf(FILE *stream, const char *format, ...);
```

Description

The **fscanf** function reads input from the stream pointed to by **stream**, under control of the string pointed to by **format** that specifies the admissible input sequences and how they are to be converted for assignment, using subsequent arguments as pointers to the objects to receive the converted input. If there are insufficient arguments for the format, the behavior is undefined. If the format is exhausted while arguments remain, the excess arguments are evaluated (as always) but are otherwise ignored.

The format shall be a multibyte character sequence, beginning and ending in its initial shift state. The format is composed of zero or more directives: one or more white-space characters; an ordinary multibyte character (neither **%** nor a white-space character); or a conversion specification.

Each conversion specification is introduced by the character **%**. After the **%**, the following appear in sequence:

- An optional assignment-suppressing character *****.

- An optional nonzero decimal integer that specifies the maximum field width.

- An optional **h**, **l** (ell) or **L** indicating the size of the receiving object. The conversion specifiers **d**, **i**, and **n** shall be preceded by **h** if the corresponding argument is a pointer to **short int** rather than a pointer to **int**, or by **l** if it is a pointer to **long int**. Similarly, the conversion specifiers **o**, **u**, and **x** shall be preceded by **h** if the corresponding argument is a pointer to **unsigned short int** rather than a pointer to **unsigned int**, or by **l** if it is a pointer to **unsigned long int**. Finally, the conversion specifiers **e**, **f**, and **g** shall be preceded by **l** if the corresponding argument is a pointer to **double** rather than a pointer to **float**, or by **L** if it is a pointer to **long double**. If an **h**, **l**, or **L** appears with any other conversion specifier, the behavior is undefined.

- A character that specifies the type of conversion to be applied. The valid conversion specifiers are described below.

The **fscanf** function executes each directive of the format in turn. If a directive fails, as detailed below, the **fscanf** function returns. Failures are described as input failures (due to the unavailability of input characters), or matching failures (due to inappropriate input).

A directive composed of white-space character(s) is executed by reading input up to the first non–white-space character (which remains unread), or until no more characters can be read.

A directive that is an ordinary multibyte character is executed by reading the next characters of the stream. If one of the characters differs from one comprising the directive, the directive fails, and the differing and subsequent characters remain unread.

A directive that is a conversion specification defines a set of matching input sequences, as described below for each specifier. A conversion specification is executed in the following steps:

Input white-space characters (as specified by the **isspace** function) are skipped, unless the specification includes a **[**, **c**, or **n** specifier.[121]

An input item is read from the stream, unless the specification includes an **n** specifier. An input item is defined as the longest matching sequence of input characters, unless that exceeds a specified field width, in which case it is the initial subsequence of that length in the sequence. The first character, if any, after the input item remains unread. If the length of the input item is zero, the execution of the directive fails: this condition is a matching failure, unless an error prevented input from the stream, in which case it is an input failure.

Except in the case of a **%** specifier, the input item (or, in the case of a **%n** directive, the count of input characters) is converted to a type appropriate to the conversion specifier. If the input item is not a matching sequence, the execution of the directive fails: this condition is a matching failure. Unless assignment suppression was indicated by a *****, the result of the conversion is placed in the object pointed to by the first argument following the **format** argument that has not already received a conversion result. If this object does not have an appropriate type, or if the result of the conversion cannot be represented in the space provided, the behavior is undefined.

The following conversion specifiers are valid:

d   Matches an optionally signed decimal integer, whose format is the same as expected for the subject sequence of the **strtol** function with the value 10 for the **base** argument. The corresponding argument shall be a pointer to integer.

i   Matches an optionally signed integer, whose format is the same as expected for the subject sequence of the **strtol** function with the value 0 for the **base** argument. The corresponding argument shall be a pointer to integer.

o   Matches an optionally signed octal integer, whose format is the same as expected for the subject sequence of the **strtoul** function with the value 8 for the **base** argument. The corresponding argument shall be a pointer to unsigned integer.

u   Matches an optionally signed decimal integer, whose format is the same as expected for the subject sequence of the **strtoul** function with the value 10 for the **base** argument. The corresponding argument shall be a pointer to unsigned integer.

x   Matches an optionally signed hexadecimal integer, whose format is the same as expected for the subject sequence of the **strtoul** function with the value 16 for the **base** argument. The corresponding argument shall be a pointer to unsigned integer.

e,f,g Matches an optionally signed floating-point number, whose format is the same as expected for the subject string of the **strtod** function. The corresponding argument shall be a pointer to floating.

s Matches a sequence of non–white-space characters.[122] The corresponding argument shall be a pointer to the initial character of an array large enough to accept the sequence and a terminating null character, which will be added automatically.

[Matches a nonempty sequence of characters[122] from a set of expected characters (the *scanset*). The corresponding argument shall be a pointer to the initial character of an array large enough to accept the sequence and a terminating null character, which will be added automatically. The conversion specifier includes all subsequent characters in the **format** string, up to and including the matching right bracket (**]**). The characters between the brackets (the *scanlist*) comprise the scanset, unless the character after the left bracket is a circumflex (**^**), in which case the scanset contains all characters that do not appear in the scanlist between the circumflex and the right bracket. If the conversion specifier begins with **[]** or **[^]**, the right bracket character is in the scanlist and the next right bracket character is the matching right bracket that ends the specification; otherwise the first right bracket character is the one that ends the specification. If a **–** character is in the scanlist and is not the first, nor the second where the first character is a **^**, nor the last character, the behavior is implementation-defined.

c Matches a sequence of characters[122] of the number specified by the field width (1 if no field width is present in the directive). The corresponding argument shall be a pointer to the initial character of an array large enough to accept the sequence. No null character is added.

p Matches an implementation-defined set of sequences, which should be the same as the set of sequences that may be produced by the **%p** conversion of the **fprintf** function. The corresponding argument shall be a pointer to a pointer to **void**. The interpretation of the input item is implementation-defined. If the input item is a value converted earlier during the same program execution, the pointer that results shall compare equal to that value; otherwise the behavior of the **%p** conversion is undefined.

n No input is consumed. The corresponding argument shall be a pointer to integer into which is to be written the number of characters read from the input stream so far by this call to the **fscanf** function. Execution of a **%n** directive does not increment the assignment count returned at the completion of execution of the **fscanf** function.

% Matches a single **%**; no conversion or assignment occurs. The complete conversion specification shall be **%%**.

If a conversion specification is invalid, the behavior is undefined.[123]

The conversion specifiers **E**, **G**, and **X** are also valid and behave the same as, respectively, **e**, **g**, and **x**.

If end-of-file is encountered during input, conversion is terminated. If end-of-file occurs before any characters matching the current directive have been read (other than leading white space, where permitted), execution of the current directive terminates with an input failure; otherwise, unless execution of the current directive is terminated with a matching failure, execution of the following directive (if any) is terminated with an input failure.

If conversion terminates on a conflicting input character, the offending input character is left unread in the input stream. Trailing white space (including new-line characters) is left unread unless matched by a directive. The success of literal matches and suppressed assignments*assignment suppression is not directly determinable other than via the **%n** directive.*

Returns

The **fscanf** function returns the value of the macro **EOF** if an input failure occurs before any conversion. Otherwise, the **fscanf** function returns the number of input items assigned, which can be fewer than provided for, or even zero, in the event of an early matching failure.

Examples

The call:

```
#include <stdio.h>
/*...*/
int n, i; float x; char name[50];
n = fscanf(stdin, "%d%f%s", &i, &x, name);
```

with the input line:

```
25 54.32E-1 thompson
```

will assign to *n* the value **3**, to *i* the value **25**, to *x* the value **5.432**, and *name* will contain **thompson\0**.

The call:

```
#include <stdio.h>
/*...*/
int i; float x; char name[50];
fscanf(stdin, "%2d%f%*d %[0123456789]", &i, &x, name);
```

with input:

```
56789 0123 56a72
```

will assign to *i* the value **56** and to *x* the value **789.0**, will skip **0123**, and *name* will contain **56\0**. The next character read from the input stream will be **a**.

To accept repeatedly from **stdin** a quantity, a unit of measure and an item name:

```
#include <stdio.h>
/*...*/
int count; float quant; char units[21], item[21];
while (!feof(stdin) && !ferror(stdin)) {
        count = fscanf(stdin, "%f%20s of %20s",
                &quant, units, item);
        fscanf(stdin,"%*[^\n]");
}
```

If the **stdin** stream contains the following lines:

```
2 quarts of oil
-12.8degrees Celsius
lots of luck
10.0LBS        of
dirt
100ergs of energy
```

the execution of the above example will be analogous to the following assignments:

```
quant = 2; strcpy(units, "quarts"); strcpy(item, "oil");
count = 3;
quant = -12.8; strcpy(units, "degrees");
count = 2; /* "C" fails to match "o" */
count = 0; /* "l" fails to match "%f" */
quant = 10.0; strcpy(units, "LBS"); strcpy(item, "dirt");
count = 3;
count = 0; /* "100e" fails to match "%f" */
count = EOF;
```

Forward references: the **strtod** function (7.10.1.4), the **strtol** function (7.10.1.5), the **strtoul** function (7.10.1.6).

printf

7.9.6.3 The **printf** function

Synopsis

```
#include <stdio.h>
int printf(const char *format, ...);
```

Description

The **printf** function is equivalent to **fprintf** with the argument **stdout** interposed before the arguments to **printf**.

Returns

The **printf** function returns the number of characters transmitted, or a negative value if an output error occurred.

scanfwrite

7.9.6.4 The **scanf** function

Synopsis

```
#include <stdio.h>
int scanf(const char *format, ...);
```

Description

The **scanf** function is equivalent to **fscanf** with the argument **stdin** interposed before the arguments to **scanf**.

Returns

The **scanf** function returns the value of the macro **EOF** if an input failure occurs before any conversion. Otherwise, the **scanf** function returns the number of input items assigned, which can be fewer than provided for, or even zero, in the event of an early matching failure.

7.9.6.5 The sprintf function

Synopsis

```
#include <stdio.h>
int sprintf(char *s, const char *format, ...);
```

Description

The **sprintf** function is equivalent to **fprintf**, except that the argument **s** specifies an array into which the generated output is to be written, rather than to a stream. A null character is written at the end of the characters written; it is not counted as part of the returned sum. If copying takes place between objects that overlap, the behavior is undefined.

Returns

The **sprintf** function returns the number of characters written in the array, not counting the terminating null character.

7.9.6.6 The sscanf function

Synopsis

```
#include <stdio.h>
int sscanf(const char *s, const char *format, ...);
```

Description

The **sscanf** function is equivalent to **fscanf**, except that the argument **s** specifies a string from which the input is to be obtained, rather than from a stream. Reaching the end of the string is equivalent to encountering end-of-file for the **fscanf** function. If copying takes place between objects that overlap, the behavior is undefined.

Returns

The **sscanf** function returns the value of the macro **EOF** if an input failure occurs before any conversion. Otherwise, the **sscanf** function returns the number of input items assigned, which can be fewer than provided for, or even zero, in the event of an early matching failure.

7.9.6.7 The vfprintf function

Synopsis

```
#include <stdarg.h>
#include <stdio.h>
int vfprintf(FILE *stream, const char *format, va_list arg);
```

Description

The **vfprintf** function is equivalent to **fprintf**, with the variable argument list replaced by **arg**, which shall have been initialized by the **va_start** macro (and possibly subsequent **va_arg** calls). The **vfprintf** function does not invoke the **va_end** macro.[124]

Returns

The **vfprintf** function returns the number of characters transmitted, or a negative value if an output error occurred.

Example

The following shows the use of the **vfprintf** function in a general error-reporting routine.

```
#include <stdarg.h>
#include <stdio.h>

void error(char *function_name, char *format, ...)
{
        va_list args;
```

```
                              va_start(args, format);
                              /* print out name of function causing error */

                              fprintf(stderr, "ERROR in %s: ", function_name);
                              /* print out remainder of message */
                              vfprintf(stderr, format, args);
                              va_end(args);
                      }
```

vprintf

7.9.6.8 The **vprintf** function

Synopsis

```
#include <stdarg.h>
#include <stdio.h>
int vprintf(const char *format, va_list arg);
```

Description

The **vprintf** function is equivalent to **printf**, with the variable argument list replaced by **arg**, which shall have been initialized by the **va_start** macro (and possibly subsequent **va_arg** calls). The **vprintf** function does not invoke the **va_end** macro.[124]

Returns

The **vprintf** function returns the number of characters transmitted, or a negative value if an output error occurred.

vsprintf

7.9.6.9 The **vsprintf** function

Synopsis

```
#include <stdarg.h>
#include <stdio.h>
int vsprintf(char *s, const char *format, va_list arg);
```

Description

The **vsprintf** function is equivalent to **sprintf**, with the variable argument list replaced by **arg**, which shall have been initialized by the **va_start** macro (and possibly subsequent **va_arg** calls). The **vsprintf** function does not invoke the **va_end** macro.[124] If copying takes place between objects that overlap, the behavior is undefined.

Returns

The **vsprintf** function returns the number of characters written in the array, not counting the terminating null character.

7.9.7 Character input/output functions

fgetc

7.9.7.1 The **fgetc** function

Synopsis

```
#include <stdio.h>
int fgetc(FILE *stream);
```

Description

The **fgetc** function obtains the next character (if present) as an **unsigned char** converted to an **int**, from the input stream pointed to by **stream**, and advances the associated file position indicator for the stream (if defined).

Returns

The **fgetc** function returns the next character from the input stream pointed to by **stream**. If the stream is at end-of-file, the end-of-file indicator for the stream is set and **fgetc** returns **EOF**. If a read error occurs, the error indicator for the stream is set and **fgetc** returns **EOF**.[125]

fgets

7.9.7.2 The **fgets** function

Synopsis

```
#include <stdio.h>
char *fgets(char *s, int n, FILE *stream);
```

Description

The **fgets** function reads at most one less than the number of characters specified by **n** from the stream pointed to by **stream** into the array pointed to by **s**. No additional characters are read after a new-line character (which is retained) or after end-of-file. A null character is written immediately after the last character read into the array.

Returns

The **fgets** function returns **s** if successful. If end-of-file is encountered and no characters have been read into the array, the contents of the array remain unchanged and a null pointer is returned. If a read error occurs during the operation, the array contents are indeterminate and a null pointer is returned.

7.9.7.3 The **fputc** function

fputc

Synopsis

```
#include <stdio.h>
int fputc(int c, FILE *stream);
```

Description

The **fputc** function writes the character specified by **c** (converted to an **unsigned char**) to the output stream pointed to by **stream**, at the position indicated by the associated file position indicator for the stream (if defined), and advances the indicator appropriately. If the file cannot support positioning requests, or if the stream was opened with append mode, the character is appended to the output stream.

Returns

The **fputc** function returns the character written. If a write error occurs, the error indicator for the stream is set and **fputc** returns **EOF**.

7.9.7.4 The **fputs** function

fputs

Synopsis

```
#include <stdio.h>
int fputs(const char *s, FILE *stream);
```

Description

The **fputs** function writes the string pointed to by **s** to the stream pointed to by **stream**. The terminating null character is not written.

Returns

The **fputs** function returns **EOF** if a write error occurs; otherwise it returns a nonnegative value.

7.9.7.5 The **getc** function

getc

Synopsis

```
#include <stdio.h>
int getc(FILE *stream);
```

Description

The **getc** function is equivalent to **fgetc**, except that if it is implemented as a macro, it may evaluate **stream** more than once, so the argument should never be an expression with side effects.

Returns

The **getc** function returns the next character from the input stream pointed to by **stream**. If the stream is at end-of-file, the end-of-file indicator for the stream is set and **getc** returns **EOF**. If a read error occurs, the error indicator for the stream is set and **getc** returns **EOF**.

7.9.7.6 The **getchar** function

getchar

Synopsis

```
#include <stdio.h>
int getchar(void);
```

Description

The **getchar** function is equivalent to **getc** with the argument **stdin**.

Returns

The **getchar** function returns the next character from the input stream pointed to by **stdin**. If the stream is at end-of-file, the end-of-file indicator for the stream is set and **getchar** returns **EOF**. If a read error occurs, the error indicator for the stream is set and **getchar** returns **EOF**.

7.9.7.7 The gets function

Synopsis

```
#include <stdio.h>
char *gets(char *s);
```

Description

The **gets** function reads characters from the input stream pointed to by **stdin**, into the array pointed to by **s**, until end-of-file is encountered or a new-line character is read. Any new-line character is discarded, and a null character is written immediately after the last character read into the array.

Returns

The **gets** function returns **s** if successful. If end-of-file is encountered and no characters have been read into the array, the contents of the array remain unchanged and a null pointer is returned. If a read error occurs during the operation, the array contents are indeterminate and a null pointer is returned.

7.9.7.8 The putc function

Synopsis

```
#include <stdio.h>
int putc(int c, FILE *stream);
```

Description

The **putc** function is equivalent to **fputc**, except that if it is implemented as a macro, it may evaluate **stream** more than once, so the argument should never be an expression with side effects.

Returns

The **putc** function returns the character written. If a write error occurs, the error indicator for the stream is set and **putc** returns **EOF**.

7.9.7.9 The putchar function

Synopsis

```
#include <stdio.h>
int putchar(int c);
```

Description

The **putchar** function is equivalent to with the second argument **stdout**.

Returns

The **putchar** function returns the character written. If a write error occurs, the error indicator for the stream is set and **putchar** returns **EOF**.

7.9.7.10 The puts function

Synopsis

```
#include <stdio.h>
int puts(const char *s);
```

Description

The **puts** function writes the string pointed to by **s** to the stream pointed to by **stdout**, and appends a new-line character to the output. The terminating null character is not written.

Returns

The **puts** function returns **EOF** if a write error occurs; otherwise it returns a nonnegative value.

ungetc

7.9.7.11 The ungetc function

Synopsis

```
#include <stdio.h>
int ungetc(int c, FILE *stream);
```

Description

The **ungetc** function pushes the character specified by **c** (converted to an **unsigned char**) back onto the input stream pointed to by **stream**. The pushed-back characters will be returned by subsequent reads on that stream in the reverse order of their pushing. A successful intervening call (with the stream pointed to by **stream**) to a file positioning function (**fseek**, **fsetpos**, or **rewind**) discards any pushed-back characters for the stream. The external storage corresponding to the stream is unchanged.

One character of pushback is guaranteed. If the **ungetc** function is called too many times on the same stream without an intervening read or file positioning operation on that stream, the operation may fail.

If the value of **c** equals that of the macro **EOF**, the operation fails and the input stream is unchanged.

A successful call to the **ungetc** function clears the end-of-file indicator for the stream. The value of the file position indicator for the stream after reading or discarding all pushed-back characters shall be the same as it was before the characters were pushed back. For a text stream, the value of its file position indicator after a successful call to the **ungetc** function is unspecified until all pushed-back characters are read or discarded. For a binary stream, its file position indicator is decremented by each successful call to the **ungetc** function; if its value was zero before a call, it is indeterminate after the call.

Returns

The **ungetc** function returns the character pushed back after conversion, or **EOF** if the operation fails.

Forward references: file positioning functions (7.9.9).

7.9.8 Direct input/output functions

fread

7.9.8.1 The fread function

Synopsis

```
#include <stdio.h>
size_t fread(void *ptr, size_t size, size_t nmemb, FILE *stream);
```

Description

The **fread** function reads, into the array pointed to by **ptr**, up to **nmemb** elements whose size is specified by **size**, from the stream pointed to by **stream**. The file position indicator for the stream (if defined) is advanced by the number of characters successfully read. If an error occurs, the resulting value of the file position indicator for the stream is indeterminate. If a partial element is read, its value is indeterminate.

Returns

The **fread** function returns the number of elements successfully read, which may be less than **nmemb** if a read error or end-of-file is encountered. If **size** or **nmemb** is zero, **fread** returns zero and the contents of the array and the state of the stream remain unchanged.

fwrite

7.9.8.2 The fwrite function

Synopsis

```
#include <stdio.h>
size_t fwrite(const void *ptr, size_t size, size_t nmemb,
        FILE *stream);
```

Description

The **fwrite** function writes, from the array pointed to by **ptr**, up to **nmemb** elements whose size is specified by **size**, to the stream pointed to by **stream**. The file position indicator for the stream (if defined) is advanced by the number of characters successfully written. If an error occurs, the resulting value of the file position indicator for the stream is indeterminate.

fgetpos

Returns

The **fwrite** function returns the number of elements successfully written, which will be less than **nmemb** only if a write error is encountered.

7.9.9 File positioning functions

7.9.9.1 The **fgetpos** function

Synopsis

```
#include <stdio.h>
int fgetpos(FILE *stream, fpos_t *pos);
```

Description

The **fgetpos** function stores the current value of the file position indicator for the stream pointed to by **stream** in the object pointed to by **pos**. The value stored contains unspecified information usable by the **fsetpos** function for repositioning the stream to its position at the time of the call to the **fgetpos** function.

Returns

If successful, the **fgetpos** function returns zero; on failure, the **fgetpos** function returns nonzero and stores an implementation-defined positive value in **errno**.

Forward references: the **fsetpos** function (7.9.9.3).

fseek

7.9.9.2 The **fseek** function

Synopsis

```
#include <stdio.h>
int fseek(FILE *stream, long int offset, int whence);
```

Description

The **fseek** function sets the file position indicator for the stream pointed to by **stream**.

For a binary stream, the new position, measured in characters from the beginning of the file, is obtained by adding **offset** to the position specified by **whence**. The specified position is the beginning of the file if **whence** is **SEEK_SET**, the current value of the file position indicator if **SEEK_CUR**, or end-of-file if **SEEK_END**. A binary stream need not meaningfully support **fseek** calls with a **whence** value of **SEEK_END**.

For a text stream, either **offset** shall be zero, or **offset** shall be a value returned by an earlier call to the **ftell** function on the same stream and **whence** shall be **SEEK_SET**.

A successful call to the **fseek** function clears the end-of-file indicator for the stream and undoes any effects of the **ungetc** function on the same stream. After an **fseek** call, the next operation on an update stream may be either input or output.

Returns

The **fseek** function returns nonzero only for a request that cannot be satisfied.

Forward references: the **ftell** function (7.9.9.4).

fsetpos

7.9.9.3 The **fsetpos** function

Synopsis

```
#include <stdio.h>
int fsetpos(FILE *stream, const fpos_t *pos);
```

Description

The **fsetpos** function sets the file position indicator for the stream pointed to by **stream** according to the value of the object pointed to by **pos**, which shall be a value obtained from an earlier call to the **fgetpos** function on the same stream.

A successful call to the **fsetpos** function clears the end-of-file indicator for the stream and undoes any effects of the **ungetc** function on the same stream. After an **fsetpos** call, the next operation on an update stream may be either input or output.

Returns

If successful, the **fsetpos** function returns zero; on failure, the **fsetpos** function returns nonzero and stores an implementation-defined positive value in **errno**.

ftell

7.9.9.4 The `ftell` function

Synopsis

```
#include <stdio.h>
long int ftell(FILE *stream);
```

Description

The **ftell** function obtains the current value of the file position indicator for the stream pointed to by **stream**. For a binary stream, the value is the number of characters from the beginning of the file. For a text stream, its file position indicator contains unspecified information, usable by the **fseek** function for returning the file position indicator for the stream to its position at the time of the **ftell** call; the difference between two such return values is not necessarily a meaningful measure of the number of characters written or read.

Returns

If successful, the **ftell** function returns the current value of the file position indicator for the stream. On failure, the **ftell** function returns −1L and stores an implementation-defined positive value in **errno**.

rewind

7.9.9.5 The `rewind` function

Synopsis

```
#include <stdio.h>
void rewind(FILE *stream);
```

Description

The **rewind** function sets the file position indicator for the stream pointed to by **stream** to the beginning of the file. It is equivalent to

```
(void)fseek(stream, 0L, SEEK_SET)
```

except that the error indicator for the stream is also cleared.

Returns

The **rewind** function returns no value.

7.9.10 Error-handling functions

clearerr

7.9.10.1 The `clearerr` function

Synopsis

```
#include <stdio.h>
void clearerr(FILE *stream);
```

Description

The **clearerr** function clears the end-of-file and error indicators for the stream pointed to by **stream**.

Returns

The **clearerr** function returns no value.

feof

7.9.10.2 The `feof` function

Synopsis

```
#include <stdio.h>
int feof(FILE *stream);
```

Description

The **feof** function tests the end-of-file indicator for the stream pointed to by **stream**.

Returns

The **feof** function returns nonzero if and only if the end-of-file indicator is set for **stream**.

ferror

7.9.10.3 The `ferror` function

Synopsis

```
#include <stdio.h>
int ferror(FILE *stream);
```

Description

The **ferror** function tests the error indicator for the stream pointed to by **stream**.

Returns

The **ferror** function returns nonzero if and only if the error indicator is set for **stream**.

7.9.10.4 The **perror** function

Synopsis

```
#include <stdio.h>
void perror(const char *s);
```

Description

The **perror** function maps the error number in the integer expression **errno** to an error message. It writes a sequence of characters to the standard error stream thus: first (if **s** is not a null pointer and the character pointed to by **s** is not the null character), the string pointed to by **s** followed by a colon (:) and a space; then an appropriate error message string followed by a new-line character. The contents of the error message strings are the same as those returned by the **strerror** function with argument **errno**, which are implementation-defined.

Returns

The **perror** function returns no value.

Forward references: the **strerror** function (7.11.6.2).

Footnotes

110. If the implementation imposes no practical limit on the length of file name strings, the value of **FILENAME_MAX** should instead be the recommended size of an array intended to hold a file name string. Of course, file name string contents are subject to other system-specific constraints; therefore *all* possible strings of length **FILENAME_MAX** cannot be expected to be opened successfully.

111. An implementation need not distinguish between text streams and binary streams. In such an implementation, there need be no new-line characters in a text stream nor any limit to the length of a line.

112. This is described in the Base Document as a *file pointer*. That term is not used in this International Standard to avoid confusion with a pointer to an object that has type **FILE**.

113. Among the reasons the implementation may cause the **rename** function to fail are that the file is open or that it is necessary to copy its contents to effectuate its renaming.

114. Files created using strings generated by the **tmpnam** function are temporary only in the sense that their names should not collide with those generated by conventional naming rules for the implementation. It is still necessary to use the **remove** function to remove such files when their use is ended, and before program termination.

115. Additional characters may follow these sequences.

116. The primary use of the **freopen** function is to change the file associated with a standard text stream (**stderr**, **stdin**, or **stdout**), as those identifiers need not be modifiable lvalues to which the value returned by the **fopen** function may be assigned.

117. The buffer must have a lifetime at least as great as the open stream, so the stream should be closed before a buffer that has automatic storage duration is deallocated upon block exit.

118. Note that **0** is taken as a flag, not as the beginning of a field width.

119. No special provisions are made for multibyte characters.

120. See "future library directions" (7.13.6).

121. These white-space characters are not counted against a specified field width.

122. No special provisions are made for multibyte characters.

123. See "future library directions" (7.13.6).

124. As the functions **vfprintf**, **vsprintf**, and **vprintf** invoke the **va_arg** macro, the value of **arg** after the return is indeterminate.

125. An end-of-file and a read error can be distinguished by use of the **feof** and **ferror** functions.

Using `<stdio.h>`

Most of the functions declared in `<stdio.h>` operate on a stream that is associated with an open file. At program startup, you can make immediate use of three such streams:

stdin ■ `stdin` — the standard source for text that you read

stdout ■ `stdout` — the standard destination for text that you write

stderr ■ `stderr` — the standard destination for error messages that you write

A number of the functions declared in `<stdio.h>` use one of these streams without your naming it. For those functions that require a stream argument, you can write one of these three names as the stream argument.

opening   You can also open a file by name and connect a stream to it. You associate
a file a stream with an open file by calling `fopen` or `freopen`, as in:

```
fptr = fopen(fname, fmode);
fptr = freopen(fname, fmode, fptr);
```

Either function returns a non-null value of type *pointer to* `FILE` only if it can open a file whose name is `fname` with mode `fmode` and can associate it with the stream controlled by the data object pointed to by `fptr`.

Use `fptr` only as an argument to the other stream I/O service functions in the Standard C library. Don't try to peek inside the data object it points to, not even if a particular implementation provides a declaration of `FILE` within `<stdio.h>` that reveals some of the fields. Don't try to alter any of the fields. Don't even try to copy the contents to another data object of type `FILE` and use the copy instead, since implementations are permitted to assume they know all valid addresses for the data objects that control streams. (In other words, the address returned by `fopen` may be magic, not just the values stored at that address.)

And once you close a stream, with a successful call to `fclose` (or with a partially successful call to `freopen`), *do not* use the corresponding `fptr` value again. The storage it points to may well be deallocated or recycled. (Don't even copy the pointer value. Strictly speaking, an implementation can bomb out just sniffing at a pointer that points to deallocated storage.)

type   You don't have to know what is inside a `FILE` data object. All you know
FILE is that it has some way to represent, among other things:

■ an *end-of-file indicator* that notes whether you attempt to read past the end of the file

■ an *error indicator* that notes whether a read or write resulted in an irrecoverable data transfer error

■ a *file-position indicator* that notes the next byte to read or write from the file (and that may not be defined for certain kinds of files)

■ buffer information that notes the presence and size of any buffer area for reads and writes

■ state information that determines whether a read or write may follow

As for naming files, your best bet is to avoid wiring any file names into your code. (This is a good idea for a lot of reasons.) If you have to input or construct a file name, use a buffer that can hold `FILENAME_MAX` characters. (The macro is defined in `<stdio.h>`.) Assume only that a file name is a conventional null-terminated string. Don't peek inside, and don't rule out any characters as components of a file name.

If you must make up file names, such as for the names of your header files, keep them simple. Any implementation will probably accept file names that consist of one to six alphabetic characters, followed by a dot, followed by a single alphabetic character. Some examples are `"myhdr.h"` and `"x.y"`. Don't assume that the case of these characters is significant. Don't assume that it is not. Don't expect these names to survive unscathed as names within the operating system. The Standard C library may have to map them to some other form to comply with local usage.

mode The file mode is a string that begins with one of three letters:

- `r` specifies that you want to open an existing file for reading.

- `w` specifies that you want to open an existing file for writing and discard its contents, or you want to create a new file that initially has no contents.

- `a` is the same as `w` with the added proviso that before each write to the stream the file-position indicator is positioned at the end of the file.

You can follow the mode with two optional characters, in either order:

- `+` specifies that you want also to write a file you open for reading (with `r`), or you want also to read a file you open for writing (with `w` or `a`).

- `b` specifies that you want to open a binary file rather than a text file.

You can write additional characters after these. Each implementation defines what additional parameters, if any, you can write as part of `fmode`. A system may, for example, let you write:

```
fopen(fname, "w,lrecl=132,recfm=fixed")
```

On System/370, at least one C implementation takes this as a request to create a file with fixed-length records each 132 bytes long. Be warned, however, that no standards exist for what follows the defined modes. If you move your program between implementations, an `fopen` call with extra mode information may fail or quietly misbehave.

reading and writing The Standard C library offers a number of functions for reading and writing streams. You can, for example, read a single character, read up to a given count of characters, or read characters and convert them to encoded forms under control of a format string.

function fgetc The process of reading a single character is defined in detail for the function `fgetc`. All other functions are defined *as if* they make multiple calls on `fgetc` to obtain input characters, whether they really do so or not. `fgetc` first verifies that the stream supports reading in general and that a read request can be honored at this point in time. (See page 256.) Then it determines whether a buffer needs to be allocated for the stream and, if so, endeavors to do so. Then it determines whether a physical read must be performed (to fill an empty buffer or to input the character directly) and, if so, endeavors to do so. It sets the error indicator on a physical read error, or the end-of-file indicator on a physical read at the end of the file. If, after all this, there is a character to deliver, the function delivers it and advances the file-position indicator by one character.

An implementation that performs all these operations in detail for each character would be slow indeed. Little wonder that implementors have worked hard over the years to cut corners wherever possible. The major trick is to perform physical reads of as many characters as possible as seldom as possible, then to summarize the state of the stream succintly enough for a quick test per character. The function getc in fact, traditionally is a macro that makes it a faster version of fgetc.

unsafe   Standard C requires that getc also be represented as a true function. The
macros header <stdio.h> can, and usually does, mask the function declaration with a macro. That macro can, and usually must, indulge the unsafe practice of evaluating its *pointer to* FILE argument more than once. The header can also mask the function fgetc (or any other function) with a macro definition. The only difference is that macros other than getc (and putc) must evaluate each of its arguments exactly once, so that side effects evaluate properly just as if a true function were called.

function   Writing is very similar to reading. The primitive function is fputc, which
fputc writes one character to the stream. fputc first verifies that the stream supports writing in general and that a write request can be honored at this point in time. (See page 256.) Then it determines whether a buffer needs to be allocated for the stream and, if so, endeavors to do so. Then it determines whether a physical write must be performed (to drain a full buffer or to output the character directly) and, if so endeavors to do so. It sets the error indicator on a physical write error. If, after all this, the character got delivered, the function advances the file-position indicator by one character. Again, a typical implementation will implement the related function putc with a masking macro definition that may be unsafe.

file   It is quite common to read or write a stream in one sequential pass from
positioning beginning to end. Indeed, many of the pseudo-files such as streams from terminals and pipelines can be processed only this way. Nevertheless, occasions exist when you need to reprocess data or process data in random order. Those occasions require you to alter in various ways the normal progression of the file-position indicator. They may also require you to intermix reads and writes. The Standard C library provides three (yes, three) different mechanisms for so altering the file-position indicator:

- ungetc lets you push back a character you have just read from a stream.
- fseek, ftell, and rewind let you memorize the file-position indicator and restore it to an earlier position, provided the file-position indicator can be encoded as a *long*.
- fgetpos, fsetpos, and rewind let you memorize an arbitrary file-position indicator and restore it to an earlier position.

function   The function `ungetc` will work even with a stream that does not support
ungetc file-positioning requests, such as a stream from a terminal or pipeline. It
lets you put back a different character than you just read. It even lets you
put back a character *before* the beginning of a file, if you call the function
before the first read on a stream.

Implementations can vary in the number of characters you can push
back between reads, however. You can be sure of one character of pushback even if you intersperse calls to the formatted-input functions (such as
scanf), which also require one character of push back. For a portable
program, don't assume that you can push back more than one character.

The `ungetc` function interacts poorly with the other two mechanisms for
positioning files. Committee X3J11 spent quite a bit of time sorting out the
semantics of various sequences of calls to `ungetc` and `fseek`, for instance.
The general rule is that a character you push back with `ungetc` evaporates
after any other file-positioning request. But you should read the fine print
in the function descriptions to be sure that you get just the result you expect.
My advice is to avoid mixing `ungetc` calls with anything but read requests.

fseek   The functions `fseek` and `ftell` (and `rewind`) are the traditional file-posi-
ftell tioning functions from the earliest days of C. They assume that you can
rewind encode a file-position indicator as a *long,* as I indicated on page 230. This
happens to be true under UNIX, where files never exceed 2^{32} bytes in length
and where you can position a file to an arbitrary byte. It is not necessarily
true on a system that supports larger files or that requires more elaborate
file-positioning information.

A text file, for example, may be structured into blocks and records within
blocks — packing a block number, record number, and offset within record
into a *long* may require impossible tradeoffs for an arbitrary byte. For these
reasons, the function `ftell` may fail (returning –1), rather than return a
corrupted encoding of the file-position indicator.

You use `fseek` and `ftell` to advantage in randomly accessing the bytes
of a binary file (provided, of course, that the file is not too big). In this case,
the encoded file-position indicator is the offset in bytes from the start of the
file, which is byte zero. You can perform arithmetic on such file-position
indicators, or compute them out of whole cloth, and be sure to get just the
bytes you'd expect.

The encoded file-position indicator for a text file, however, has a format
that varies among implementations. You use `ftell` to give you a magic
cookie that marks where the file is currently positioned. (It will return a
failure code if it cannot encode the current file-positon indicator.) Later in
the execution of the same program, and before you close the file, you can
pass the same value to `fseek` to restore the file-position indicator to its
earlier value. Don't assume that you can save such values from one execution of a program to the next, or even from one file opening to the next. An
implementation may play really tricky games with the encoding.

fgetpos   If you are content merely to reposition files at places you have visited
fsetpos earlier, you should use the third mechanism. The committee added the
functions **fgetpos** and **fsetpos** to support positioning within files of arbitrary size and structure. These functions work with values of type **fpos_t**,
defined in **<stdio.h>**, which can be as ornate a structure as an implementation needs to encode an arbitrary file-position indicator. Assume that
fpos_t is a structure type that you can only copy, pass as a function
argument, or receive as a function value. Even for a binary file, there is no
defined way to compare such values or perform arithmetic on them.

buffer   You can, in principle, exercise a certain amount of control over how the
control I/O functions buffer data for a stream. You must realize, however, that
buffering is an optimization based on various conjectures about patterns
of I/O. These conjectures are usually correct, and many implementations
follow your advice. But they don't have to. An implementation is free to
ignore most of your buffering requests.

setvbuf   Nevertheless, if you think a bigger buffer will improve performance or
setbuf a smaller buffer will save space, you can supply your own candidate buffer.
Call the function **setvbuf** after you open the file and before you perform
any other operations on the stream. (Avoid the older function **setbuf**, which
is less flexible.) You can specify whether I/O should be fully buffered,
buffered by text lines, or unbuffered. It just might make a difference in how
well your program performs.

function   Sometimes you want buffering most of the time, but need to exercise
fflush limited control over when output gets flushed to the outside world. The
function **fflush** ensures that one or more streams have their output flushed
when you call it. That can be useful for pushing out messages in an
interactive environment. It can also make a database more robust in the
teeth of occasional program crashes. Be warned, however, that **fflush** has
no defined effect on input streams in Standard C. You can't use this function
to reliably discard input before a prompt, as you can under UNIX.

The Standard C library disallows certain patterns of reads and writes.
The basic rule is that you cannot follow a read with a write, or a write with
a read, without an intervening file-positioning request. More specifically,
the intervening call must be to one of the functions **fflush**, **fseek**, **fsetpos**,
or **rewind**. A read that sets the end-of-file indicator can be followed immediately by a write. Curiously enough, however, a write preceded by an
implicit seek (to a file opened with an **fmode** that begins with **a**) cannot
immediately follow a read. Figure 12.1 is a state-transition diagram that
summarizes these rules.

My final piece of advice is to give the stream I/O functions all the
latitude you can. Don't try to control the buffering too closely. You may well
end up optimizing for one implementation and deoptimizing for all others.
And don't push your luck by agressively mixing reads, writes, and various
file-positioning operations. It is easy to break an implementation if you
push it in this area. It is even easier to break your own program.

Figure 12.1:
States of a
Stream

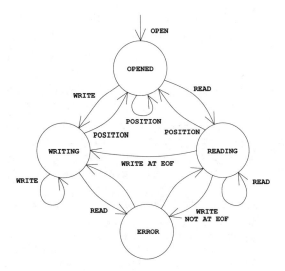

formatted   An important aspect of input/output is performing formatted output.
output That is almost invariably your first contact with I/O under C, as in the
popular first program:

```
#include <stdio.h>

int main(void)
    {   /* say hello */
    printf("hello world\n");
    }
```

Unless you write only embedded programs, formatted output is likely to
be the most important flavor of I/O that you must master.

A program can produce output that only another computer program can
love, or understand. If both programs run on the same architecture, they
share the same notion of how to encode data. One program can write out
integer and floating-point scalars, even structures and unions, and another
program can read them in and manipulate them without further ado. You
can share just about any kind of data, except pointers, between programs
just by copying the bytes to and from a binary file.

If you want to share data between programs on different computer
architectures, however, you must be far more careful. Computers frequently differ on how they encode both integer and floating-point values.
Even when two computers agree on the size of scalars and how they are
encoded, they often differ on the order in which they store in memory the
bytes of a multibyte data object.

Computers also differ widely in their requirements for storage alignment, so the holes within structures (and on the end of structures and
unions) can vary more than you might expect. Unless you are *very* careful,
you shouldn't even think of using binary files as a medium for data
interchange.

Text files have three significant advantages over binary files:

- They can be generated or altered by mere mortals such as you and me.
- They can be written to a printer or terminal with a large likelihood that human beings can understand the display.
- They can be shared between programs that share few assumptions about how data is encoded.

print functions The process of contriving a text representation of encoded data is called *output formatting*. The *print* functions (all with **print** as part of their names and all declared in **<stdio.h>**) produce formatted output. To use the print functions, you must know how to call them, how they interpret a format, and what conversions they will perform for you. The Standard C library provides six different print functions, declared as follows:

```
int fprintf(FILE *stream, const char *format, ...);
int printf(const char *format, ...);
int sprintf(char *dest, const char *format, ...);
int vfprintf(FILE *stream, const char *format, va_list ap);
int vprintf(const char *format, va_list ap);
int vsprintf(char *dest, const char *format, va_list ap);
```

All the functions accept a **format** argument, which is a pointer to a read-only null-terminated string. The format tells the function what additional arguments to expect, if any, and how to convert them. It also specifies any literal text you want to intersperse with any converted arguments. I discuss print formats in considerable detail below.

All the functions return a count of the number of text characters generated on a particular call. Two of the functions, **sprintf** and **vsprintf**, store the generated characters in a null-terminated string **dest**. You must know enough about your format and converted data to ensure that the string can fit in the storage you provide, since you cannot convey a maximum string length for these print functions to check. The remaining four functions write to a stream. (Those without a **stream** argument write to the stream **stdout**.) They return a negative value, instead of the cumulative character count, if any of the writes set the error indicator for the stream.

The functions **fprintf**, **printf**, and **sprintf** accept a variable argument list. Those extra arguments are, of course, primarily used to convey data values you want to convert to text. For maximum portability, you *must* declare these functions by including **<stdio.h>**.

vfprintf As flexible as these three functions are, they sometimes fall short of the
vprintf mark. C programmers find occasional need for print functions that behave
vsprintf slightly differently. That's where the last three functions — **vfprintf**, **vprint**, and **vsprintf** — come in. Each behaves just like the corresponding print function without the leading **v** in its name, except for the way it receives additional arguments. You use the macros defined in **<stdarg.h>** to write a wrapper function that accepts a variable argument list. These additional arguments are passed on to the print functions to do the actual conversion and text generation.

Let's say, for example, that you want to write formatted messages to stderr, each preceded by a standard prefix. You also want to log each error on a disk file. You can do all this by writing a function eprint that uses vfprintf to perform the actual output:

```
#include <stdio.h>
#include <stdarg.h>

int eprint(const char *format, ...)
    {   /* log error messages */
    extern FILE *logfile;
    int n;
    va_list ap;

    va_start(ap, format);
    fprintf(stderr, "\aERROR: ");
    vfprintf(stderr, format, ap);
    va_start(ap, format);
    n = vfprintf(logfile, format, ap);
    va_end(ap);
    return (n);
    }
```

print formats The mainspring of every print function call is the format string you specify for it. You can (and should) think of a format string as a program in a mini programming language. The print function interpretively executes this program by scanning the format string once from beginning to end. As it recognizes each component of the format string, it performs various operations. Most of these operations generate characters that the function writes to a stream or stores in memory.

Many of these operations call for argument values to be converted to character sequences. Any such arguments must appear in the variable argument list, in the order in which the format string calls for them. For example,

```
    printf("%s%c%o%i", "th", 'x', 9, 38);
```

produces the string thx1138 from four conversions (th|x|11|38). It is up to you to ensure that the type of the actual argument expression matches the type expected by the print function. Standard C has no way to check the types of additional arguments in a variable argument list.

Keep in mind that additional arguments follow the same type conversion rules as for arguments to functions called outside the scope of a prototype declaration. A *float* argument, for example, is converted to type *double*. A *char* or *short* argument is converted to *int*. The print functions type cast arguments, as needed, to restrict their range to whatever is expected for the particular conversion. The only time you are likely to see this machinery is when you specify an argument value that is out of range for the final type. For example, the conversion specifier %c expects an argument of type *int*, which it converts to *unsigned char*. So the expression printf("%c", 0x203) typically writes only 3 to the standard output stream.

printing   Not every part of a format string calls for the conversion of an additional
literal text argument. In fact, only certain *conversion specifications* gobble arguments.
Every conversion specification begins with the %per cent escape character
and matches one of the patterns shown below. The print functions treat
everything else in a format string as literal text. One character of output is
generated for each character of literal text.

Strictly speaking, a format string is a string of multibyte characters. That
lets you intersperse Kanji (or Arabic, or whatever) with your output conversions. Each sequence of literal text must begin and end in the initial shift
state, if your execution environment uses a state-dependent encoding for
multibyte characters. (See Chapter 13: `<stdlib.h>`.)

conversion   To construct a valid conversion specifications, you write four compo-
specification nents following the %. All but the last component is optional:

- Zero or more *flags* specify variations on the standard conversions.

- An optional *field width* specifies the minimum number of characters to
  generate for the conversion.

- An optional *precision* controls the number of characters generated for
  certain conversions.

- A *conversion specifier* determines the type of any argument, the type of its
  converted value, and how it is converted.

flags You write these components in the order shown above. Let's look at each
in more detail. You can specify five different flags:

- A minus (-) left-justifies a conversion. Any padding on the right is with
  spaces. An example is %-30s.

- A zero (0) pads with leading zeros (after any sign or prefix), if no other
  padding is specified. An example is %04x.

- A plus (+) generates an explicit plus sign when a positive signed-value
  is converted. An example is %+5d.

- A space generates a space in place of a sign when a positive signed-value
  is converted. An example is % 5d.

- A pound sign (#) alters the behavior of certain conversions. The o
  conversion adds a leading 0, the x conversion adds a leading 0x, the X
  conversion adds a leading 0X, and the floating-point conversions generate a decimal point even if no fraction digits follow. An example is %#x.

field   You write a field width as an unsigned decimal integer. Write an asterisk
width and the print function gobbles the next *int* argument as the field width, a
negative value contributing a minus flag. A conversion that produces fewer
than *field width* characters is padded. In the absence of minus or zero flags,
padding is on the left with spaces. Examples are %10c and %*i.

precision You write a precision as a period (.) followed by an unsigned decimal
integer. A period alone specifies a precision of zero. Write a period followed
by an asterisk and the print function takes the next *int* argument as the
precision, a negative value being taken as zero. The precision specifies:

- the minimum number of digits to generate when converting an integer
- the number of fraction digits to generate for **e**, **E**, or **f**
- the maximum number of significant digits to generate for **g** or **G**
- the maximum number of characters to generate for **s**

Examples are **%.10e** and **%.*s**.

print conversion specifiers You write a conversion specifier as a one- or two-character sequence from a predefined list of about three dozen valid sequences. The two-character sequences begin with an **h**, **l**, or **L** to indicate alternate conversion types. I list all valid sequences below. Don't write any others if you want your code to be portable.

The goal of each formatted-output conversion is to generate a text sequence that adequately represents the encoded value before conversion. Unfortunately, views differ on how you "adequately" represent even a simple integer value. That's why there are so many different ways to write conversion specifications. For many of the conversions, "adequately" means "exactly." But for floating-point conversions, any text representation is likely to be only an approximation of the original value. You can specify how many decimal digits of precision you want to retain. You can be sure that the sign and magnitude of the value will be correctly represented. You cannot, however, expect to get exactly the same value if you convert the text string back to its original encoded type.

Here are the various conversion specifiers. Remember that every conversion is subject to padding, as described above for *flags* and *field width*. If no precision **p** is specified, it assumes the stated default value:

character
- **c** — converts the *int* argument to *unsigned char* to generate a character.

decimal
- **d** — converts the *int* argument to a signed sequence of at least **p** decimal digits. Default precision is 1.

- **hd** — converts the *int* argument to *short*, then the same as **d**.

- **ld** — converts the *long* argument the same as **d**.

floating-point
- **e** — converts the *double* argument to a signed sequence of the form **d.ddde±dd**. Here, **d** stands for a decimal digit, ± is either a plus (+) or minus (-) sign, and the dot is the decimal point for the current locale. It omits the decimal point if **p** is 0 and you specify no **#** flag. It generates **p** fraction digits and at least two exponent digits. Default precision is 6.

- **Le** — converts the *long double* argument the same as **e**.

- **E** — converts the *double* argument the same as **e**, except that it replaces the **e** before the exponent with **E**.

- **LE** — converts the *long double* argument the same as **E**.

- **f** — converts the *double* argument to a signed sequence of the form **d.ddd**. Here, **d** stands for a decimal digit and the dot is the decimal point for the current locale. It generates at least one integer digit. It omits the decimal point if **p** is 0 and you specify no **#** flag. It generates **p** fraction digits. Default precision is 6.

- **Lf** — converts the *long double* argument the same as **f**.
- **g** — converts the *double* argument the same as either **e** or **f**. If **p** is unspecified or 0, it sets **p** to 1. It chooses the **f** form if the **e** form would yield an exponent in the inclusive range [–4, **p** –1]. It omits trailing zeros from any fraction. It omits the decimal point if no fraction digits remain and you specify no **#** flag.
- **Lg** — converts the *long double* argument the same as **g**.
- **G** — converts the *double* argument the same as **g**, except that it replaces the **e** before any exponent with **E**.
- **LG** — converts the *long double* argument the same as **G**.

decimal
- **i, hi, li** — are the same as **d, hd, ld**, respectively.

character count
- **n** — stores the cumulative number of generated characters in the data object pointed to by the *pointer to int* argument.
- **hn** — is the same as **n** for a *pointer to short* argument.
- **ln** — is the same as **n** for a *pointer to long* argument.

unsigne integer
- **o** — converts the *int* argument to *unsigned int* and then to an unsigned sequence of at least **p** octal digits. Default precision is 1.
- **ho** — converts the *int* argument to *unsigned short,* then the same as **o**.
- **lo** — converts the *long* argument the same as **o**.

pointer to *void*
- **p** — converts the *pointer to void* argument to an implementation-defined sequence of characters (such as the hexadecimal representation of a storage address).

string
- **s** — generates one character for each of the (non-null) characters stored in the string pointed to by the *pointer to char* argument. If you specify a precision, it generates no more than **p** characters.

unsigned decimal
- **u** — converts the *int* argument to *unsigned int* and then to an unsigned sequence of at least **p** decimal digits. Default precision is 1.
- **hu** — converts the *int* argument to *unsigned short,* then the same as **u**.
- **lu** — converts the *long* argument to *unsigned long,* then the same as **u**.

hexadecimal
- **x** — converts the *int* argument to *unsigned int,* then to an unsigned sequence of at least **p** hexadecimal digits. It represents digit values 10 through 15 by the letters **a** through **f**. Default precision is 1.
- **hx** — converts the *int* argumen to *unsigned short,* then the same as **x**.
- **lx** — converts the *long* argument to *unsigned long,* then the same as **x**
- **X** — converts the *int* argument the same as **x**, except that it represents digit values 10 through 15 by the letters **A** through **F**.
- **hX** — converts the *int* argument to *unsigned short,* then the same as **X**.
- **lX** — converts the *long* argument to *unsigned long,* then the same as **X**.

per cent
- **%** — converts *no* argument. It generates a per cent character.

Conversion specifiers handle most of your formatting needs. Where they fall short, you can get what you want in two steps. First, generate text into a buffer using **sprintf** and modify it there. Then write the text using, say, **printf**. See the function **_Fmtval** on page 92 for a practical example.

formatted input Not all programs read input. Those that do can read data directly, using an assortment of standard library functions, and interpret the data as they see fit. Converting small integers and text strings for internal consumption are both exercises that most C programmers perform easily. It is only when you must convert floating-point values, or recognize a complex mix of data fields, that standard scanning functions begin to look attractive.

Even then the choice is not always clear. The usability of a program depends heavily on how tolerant it is to variations in user input. You as a programmer may not agree with the conventions enforced by the standard formatted-input functions. You may not like the way they handle errors. In short, you are much more likely to want to roll your own input scanner.

Obtaining formatted input in not simply the inverse of producing formatted output. With output, you know what you want the program to generate next and it does it. With input, however, you are more at the mercy of the person producing the input text. Your program must *scan* the input text for recognizable patterns, then *parse* it into separate fields. Only then can it determine what to do next.

Not only that, the input text may contain no recognizable pattern. You must then decide how to respond to such an "error." Do you print a nasty message and prompt for fresh input? Do you make an educated guess and bull ahead? Or do you abort the program? Various canned input scanners have tried all these strategies. No one of them is appropriate for all cases.

It is no surprise, therefore, that the history of the formatted input functions in C is far more checkered than for the formatted output functions. Most implementations of C have long agreed on the basic properties of **printf** and its buddies. By contrast, **scanf** and its ilk have changed steadily over the years and have proliferated dialects. Committee X3J11 had to spend considerable time sorting out the proper behavior of formatted input.

scan functions The *scan* functions are so called because they all have **scan** as part of their names. These are the functions that scan input text and convert text fields to encoded data. All are declared in **<stdio.h>**. To use the scan functions, you must know how to call them, how to specify conversion formats, and what conversions they will perform for you. The Standard C library provides three different scan functions, declared as follows:

```
int fscanf(FILE *stream, const char *format, ...);
int scanf(const char *format, ...);
int sscanf(char *src, const char *format, ...);
```

The function **fscanf** obtains characters from the stream **stream**. The function **scanf** obtains characters from the stream **stdin**. Both stop scanning input early if an attempt to obtain a character sets the end-of-file or error indicator for the stream. The function **sscanf** obtains characters from the null-terminated string beginning at **src**. It stops scanning input early if it encounters the terminating null character for the string.

All the scan functions accept a variable argument list, just like the print functions. And just like the print functions, you had better declare any scan functions before you use them by including `<stdio.h>`.

All the functions accept a `format` argument, which is a pointer to a read-only null-terminated string. The format tells the function what additional arguments to expect, if any, and how to convert input fields to values to be stored. (A typical argument is a pointer to a data object that receives the converted value.) It also specifies any literal text or white-space you want to match between converted fields. If scan formats sound remarkably like print formats, the resemblance is quite intentional. But there are also important differences. I discuss scan formats in considerable detail below.

All the scan functions return a count of the number of text fields converted to values that are stored. If any of the functions stops scanning early for one of the reasons cited above, however, it returns the value of the macro `EOF`, also defined in `<stdio.h>`. Since `EOF` must have a negative value, you can easily distinguish it from any valid count, including zero. Note, however, that you can't tell how many values were stored before an early stop. If you need to locate a stopping point more precisely, break your scan call into multiple calls.

A scan function can also stop scanning early because it obtains a character that it is unprepared to deal with. In this case, the function returns the cumulative count of values converted and stored. You can determine the largest possible return value for any given call by counting all the conversions you specify in the format. The actual return value will be between zero and this maximum value, inclusive.

pushing back characters When either `fscanf` or `scanf` obtains such an unexpected character, it pushes it back to the input stream. (It also pushes back the first character beyond a valid field when it has to peek ahead to determine the end of the field.) How it does so is similar to calling the function `ungetc`. There is a very important difference, however. You cannot portably push back two characters to a stream with successive calls to `ungetc` (and no other intervening operations on the stream). You *can* portably follow an arbitrary call to a scan function with a call to `ungetc` for the same stream.

What this means effectively is that the one-character pushback limit imposed on `ungetc` is not compromised by calls to the scan functions. Either the implementation guarantees two or more characters of pushback to a stream or it provides separate machinery for the scan functions.

The scan functions push back at most one character. Say, for example, that you try to convert the invalid field `123EASY` as a floating point value. Even the subfield `123E` is invalid, since the conversion requires at least one exponent digit. The subfield `123E` is consumed and the conversion fails. No value is stored and the scan function returns. The next character to read from the stream is `A`. This behavior matters most for floating point fields, which have the most ornate syntax. Other conversions can usually digest all the characters in the longest subfield that looks valid.

scan formats   Earlier, I described the print formats as a mini programming language. The same is, of course, true of the scan formats. I also commented earlier that print and scan formats look remarkably alike. This should serve as both a comfort and a warning to you. The comfort is that the print and scan functions are designed to work together. What you write to a text file with one program should be readable as a text file by another. Any values you represent in text by calling a print function should be reclaimable by calling a scan function. (At least they should be to good accuracy, over a reasonable range of values.) You would even like the print and scan formats to resemble each other strongly. It is possible for you to write symmetric formats, ones that read back what you wrote out. Be warned, however, that that can take a bit of extra thought.

scan vs. print formats   And here lies the danger. The fact remains that the print and scan format languages are *different*. Sometimes the apparent similarity is only superficial. You can write text with a print function call that does not scan as you might expect with a scan function call using the same format. Be particularly wary when you print text using conversions with no intervening white-space. Be somewhat wary when you print adjacent white-space in two successive print calls. The scan functions tend to run together fields that you think of as separate.

The basic operation of the scan functions is, indeed the same as for the print functions. Call a scan function and it scans the format string once from beginning to end. As it recognizes each component of the format string, it performs various operations. Most of these operations consume characters sequentially from a stream (`fscanf` or `scanf`) or a string stored in memory (`sscanf`).

Many of these operations generate values that the scan function stores in various data objects that you specify with pointer arguments. Any such arguments must appear in the variable argument list, in the order in which the format string calls for them. For example:

```
sscanf("thx 1138", "%s%2o%d", &a, &b, &c);
```

stores a pointer to the string `"thx"` in the *char* array `a`, the value 11 in the *int* data object `b`, and the value 38 in the *int* data object `c`. It is up to you to ensure that the type of each actual argument pointer matches the type expected by the scan function. Standard C has no way to check the types of additional arguments in a variable argument list.

Not every part of a format string calls for the conversion of a field and the consumption of an additional argument. In fact, only certain *conversion specifications* gobble arguments. Each conversion specification begins with the escape character `%` and matches one of the patterns shown below. The scan functions treat everything else either as white-space or as literal text.

scanning white-space   White-space in a scan format is whatever the function `isspace`, declared in `<ctype.h>`, says it is. That can change if you call the function `setlocale`, declared in `<locale.h>`. In the "C" locale, white-space is what you have learned to know and love. (See Chapter 2: `<ctype.h>`.)

The scan functions treat as a single entity a sequence of one or more white-space characters in a scan format. Such a sequence causes the scan functions to consume an arbitrarily long sequence of white-space characters from the input (whatever the current locale says is white-space). The white-space in the format need not resemble that in the input. The input can contain *no* white-space. White-space in the format simply guarantees that the next input character (if any) is not a white-space character.

scanning Any character in the format that is not white-space and not part of a
literal text conversion specification calls for a literal match. The next input character must match the format character. Otherwise, the scan function returns with the current count of converted values stored. A format that ends with a literal match can produce ambiguous results. You cannot determine from the return value whether the trailing match failed. Similarly, you cannot determine whether a literal match failed or a conversion that follows it. For these reasons, literal matches have only limited use in scan formats.

A literal match can be any string of multibyte characters. Each sequence of literal text must begin and end in the initial shift state, if your execution environment uses a state-dependent encoding for multibyte characters. (See Chapter 13: `<stdlib.h>`.)

scan A scan conversion specification differs from a print conversion specifi-
conversion cation in fundamental ways. You cannot write any of the print conversion
specifications flags and you cannot write a precision (following a decimal point). Instead, scan conversions have an *assignment-suppression* flag and a conversion specification called a *scan set*. Following the % you write three components in the following order. All but the last component is optional:

assignment ▪ You write an optional asterisk (*) to specify *assignment suppression* — the
suppression   converted value is not to be stored. An example is `%*s` (which skips an arbitrary sequence of non–white-space characters).

field width ▪ You write an optional *field width* to specify the maximum number of input characters to match when determining the conversion field. The field width is an unsigned decimal integer. The amount of any leading white-space is *not* limited by the field width. An example is `%5i`.

scan ▪ You write a *conversion specifier* to determine the type of any argument,
conversion   how to determine its conversion field, and how to convert the value to
specifiers   store. You write a scan set conversion specifier between brackets (`[ ]`). All others consist of one- or two-character sequences from a predefined list of about three dozen valid sequences. The two-character sequences begin with an `h`, `l`, or `L`, to indicate alternate argument types. I describe scan sets and list all valid sequences below. Don't write anything else in a scan format if you want your code to be portable.

The goal of each formatted-input conversion is to determine the sequence of input characters that constitutes the field to convert. The scan function then converts the field, if possible, and stores the converted value in the data object designated by the next pointer argument. (If assignment is suppressed, no function argument is consumed.)

Unless otherwise specified below, each conversion first skips arbitrary white-space in the input. Skipping is just the same as for white-space in the scan format. The conversion then matches a pattern against succeeding characters in the input to determine the conversion field. You can specify a field width to limit the size of the field. Otherwise, the field extends to the last character in the input that matches the pattern.

scanning numeric fields   The scan functions convert numeric fields by calling one of the Standard C library functions `strtod`, `strtol`, or `strtoul`, all declared in F1BS<stdlib.h>. A numeric conversion field matches the longest acceptable pattern.

In the descriptions that follow, I summarize the match pattern and conversion rules for each valid conversion specifier. `w` stands for the field width you specify, or the indicated default value if you specify no field width. `ptr` stands for the next argument to consume in the variable argument list:

character
- `c` — stores `w` characters (default is 1) in the array of *char* pointed at by `ptr`. It does *not* skip leading white-space.

decimal
- `d` — converts the integer input field by calling `strtol` with a base of 10, then stores the result in the *int* pointed at by `ptr`.
- `hd` — is the same as `d`, storing in a *short*.
- `ld` — is the same as `d`, storing in a *long*.

floating-point
- `e` — converts the floating point input field by calling `strtod`, then stores the result in the *float* pointed at by `ptr`.
- `le` — is the same as `e`, storing in a *double*.
- `Le` — is the same as `e`, storing in a *long double*.
- `E, lE, LE` — are the same as `e, le, Le`, respectively.
- `f, lf, Lf` — are the same as `e, le, Le`, respectively.
- `g, lg, Lg` — are the same as `e, le, Le`, respectively.
- `G, lG, LG` — are the same as `e, le, Le`, respectively.

general integer
- `i` — converts the integer input field by calling `strtol` with a base of 0, then stores the result in the *int* pointed at by `ptr`. (That lets you write input that begins with `0, 0x`, or `0X` to specify the actual numeric base.)
- `hi` — is the same as `i`, storing in a *short*.
- `li` — is the same as `i`, storing in a *long*.

character count
- `n` — converts *no* input, but stores the cumulative number of matched input characters in the *int* pointed at by `ptr`.
- `hn` — is the same as `n`, storing in a *short*..
- `ln` — is the same as `n`, storing in a *long*..

octal
- `o` — converts the integer input field by calling `strtoul` with a base of 8, then stores the result in the *unsigned int* pointed at by `ptr`.
- `ho` — is the same as `o`, storing in an *unsigned short*..
- `lo` — is the same as `o`, storing in an *unsigned long*..

pointer   ■ **p** — converts the pointer input field, then stores the result in the *pointer*
to *void*   *to void* pointed at by **ptr**. Each implementation defines its pointer input
field to be consistent with pointers written by the print functions.

string   ■ **s** — stores up to **w** non–white-space characters (default is the rest of the
input) in the array of *char* pointed at by **ptr**. It first skips leading
white-space, and it always stores a null character after any input.

unsigned ■ **u** — converts the integer input field by calling **strtoul** with a base of 10,
decimal   then stores the result in the *unsigned int* pointed at by **ptr**.

■ **hu** — is the same as **u**, storing in an *unsigned short*.

■ **lu** — is the same as **u**, storing in an *unsigned long*.

hexadecimal ■ **x** — converts the integer input field by calling **strtoul** with a base of 16,
then stores the result in the *unsigned int* pointed at by **ptr**.

■ **hx** — is the same as **x**, storing in an *unsigned short*.

■ **lx** — is the same as **x**, storing in an *unsigned long*.

■ **X, hX, lX — are the same as x, hx, lx,** respectively.

per cent ■ **%** — converts *no* input, but matches a per cent character (**%**).

scan sets   A scan set behaves much like the **s** conversion specifier. It stores up to **w**
non–white-space characters (default is the rest of the input) in the *char* array
pointed at by **ptr**. It always stores a null character after any input. It does
not skip leading white-space. It also lets you specify what non–white-space
characters to consider as part of the field. You can specify all the characters
that match, as in **%[0123456789abcdefABCDEF]**, which matches an arbitrary
sequence of hexadecimal digits. Or you can specify all the characters that
do not match, as in **%[^0123456789]** which matches any characters other
than digits or white-space.

If you want to include the right bracket (**]**) in the set of characters you
specify, write it immediately after the opening **[** (or **[^**), as in **%[]] []** which
scans for square brackets. You cannot include the null character in the set
of characters you specify. Some implementations may let you specify a
range of characters by using a minus sign (**-**). The list of hexadecimal digits,
for example, can be written as **%[0-9abcdefABCDEF]** or even, in some cases,
as **%[0-9a-fA-F]**. Please note, however, that such usage is not universal.
Avoid it in a program that you wish to keep maximally portable.

limitations   You will find that the scan conversion specifications are not as complete
of scan as the print conversion specifications. Too often, you want to exercise more
functions control over an input scan. Or you may find it impossible to determine
where a scan failed well enough to recover properly from the failure. You
can make up for these inadequacies much the same way you augment the
print functions. First, read the data you wish to scan into a buffer. (You can
sometimes even scan with a tolerant format, such as **"%s"**.) Then use **sscanf**
to scan the buffer repeatedly until you find a successful match or determine
the nature of the input error.) Be prepared, however, to give up on the scan
functions beyond a point. Their usefulness, over the years, has proved to
be limited.

I conclude with a brief remark about each of the names in `<stdio.h>`.

BUFSIZ   **BUFSIZ** — This macro yields the preferred size of stream buffers. It typically ranges from a few hundred to a thousand-odd bytes. Favor it as the size of any buffers you declare for use with `setvbuf`.

EOF   **EOF** — This macro is used to signal end-of-file. It has a negative value, but even the functions declared in `<ctype.h>` accept it as an argument value. Some functions declared in `<stdio.h>` also use it as an error return value. Many implementations choose the value −1 for **EOF**, but don't count on it.

FILENAME_MAX   **FILENAME_MAX** — This macro defines the length of a character buffer large enough to hold an arbitrary file name. Use it to declare or allocate any such buffers. On some systems, it can be hundreds of bytes long.

FOPEN_MAX   **FOPEN_MAX** — This macro tells you how many files your program can have open simultaneously, at a minimum. The three standard I/O streams are included in the count. You use this value in a program that creates a number of temporary intermediate files, for example, so that you can plan file usage before you create any files. Every implementation must guarantee at least eight simultaneously open files. That means you can write a portable program that opens up to five additional files at once.

_IOFBF   **_IOFBF** — Use this macro as the mode (third) argument to `setvbuf` to indicate full buffering.

_IOLBF   **_IOLBF** — Use this macro as the mode (third) argument to `setvbuf` to indicate line buffering.

_IONBF   **_IONBF** — Use this macro as the mode (third) argument to `setvbuf` to indicate no buffering.

L_tmpnam   **L_tmpnam** — This macro defines the length of a character buffer large enough to hold a temporary file name. Use it to declare or allocate any such buffers. On some systems, it can be hundreds of bytes long.

NULL   **NULL** — See page 220.

SEEK_CUR   **SEEK_CUR** — Use this macro as the mode (third) argument to `fseek` to indicate a seek relative to the current file-position indicator. For a text file, this mode is valid only for a zero offset, which does nothing.

SEEK_END   **SEEK_END** — Use this macro as the mode (third) argument to `fseek` to indicate a seek relative to end-of-file. Remember that a binary file may have extra null characters appended, so this mode has uncertain results. For a text file, you can specify no offset with this mode.

SEEK_SET   **SEEK_SET** — Use this macro as the mode (third) argument to `fseek` to indicate a seek relative to beginning-of-file. For a text file, the offset must be a magic cookie returned by an earlier call to `ftell` for the same stream.

TMP_MAX   **TMP_MAX** — This macro tells you how many distinct file names, at a minimum, the function `tmpnam` will create before it starts repeating. You use this value in a program that creates a number of temporary intermediate files, for example, so that you can plan file usage before you create any files. Every implementation must guarantee at least 25 distinct file names.

stderr   stderr — Use this macro to designate the standard error stream.

stdin   stdin — Use this macro to designate the standard input stream.

stdout   stdout — Use this macro to designate the standard output stream.

FILE   FILE — You declare a *pointer to* FILE to store the value returned on a successful fopen or freopen call. You then use this value as an argument to various functions that manipulate the stream. You never have occasion to declare a data object of type FILE, however. The Standard C library provides all such creatures. Treat the contents of a FILE data object as a black box. Use the functions declared in <stdio.h> to manipulate its contents.

fpos_t   fpos_t — This is the type of the value returned by fgetpos. It can represent an arbitrary file-position indicator for any file. That means you can copy the value and pass it as an argument on a function call, but you can't perform arithmetic on it. Pass the value to fsetpos to reposition the file at the point you memorized. Note that the older functions ftell and fseek can perform much the same service, but they can also fail for certain files (particularly large ones). Use fgetpos and fsetpos wherever possible.

size_t   size_t — See page 219.

clearerr   clearerr — Use this function to clear the end-of-file and error indicators on a stream. You need it only if you also use the functions feof or ferror.

fclose   fclose — If you open a file by calling fopen, you should probably close it by a later call to fclose. A program that manipulates an arbitrary number of files may otherwise exceed the maximum number of files that may be simultaneously open. (See FOPEN_MAX above.) At program termination, the Standard C library closes any files that are still open. That is the customary way to close the three standard streams.

feof   feof — Most functions that read a stream return a special value, such as EOF, to indicate that the read encountered end-of-file. Should you miss this opportunity to check, use the function eof. It reports the state of the end-of-file indicator for a stream. A file-positioning request clears this indicator if it apparently moves the file-position indicator away from end-of-file. So too does a call to clearerr.

ferror   ferror — A read or write to a stream can fail for any number of reasons. The error indicator in a stream records all such failures. To check whether an error has occurred, call ferror. A call to clearerr or rewind clears this indicator.

fflush   fflush — You can ensure that a stream retains no buffered output by calling fflush for a stream. That may be important if you are writing prompting messages to an output stream and reading responses from an input stream. You want to ensure that the person interacting with the program knows what sort of reply the program expects next. Call fflush(NULL) to flush *all* output streams. That prepares a program for a subsequent loss of control. (The program may be about to execute unde-bugged code. Or it may have just invited the user to turn off the computer.) The Standard C library flushes all output streams at program termination.

fgetc   fgetc — You call this function to obtain the next character from an input stream. (See page 253.) All functions that read a stream behave as if they call fgetc to obtain each character. getc has the same specification as fgetc but is far more likely to have a masking macro that dramatically improves performance. As a rule, therefore, you should use getc instead of fgetc.

fgetpos   fgetpos — Use this function to memorize a position in a file to which you want to later return. It returns a value of type fpos_t, described above.

fgets   fgets — Use this function to read lines of text from a stream. It stops reading after it reads and stores a newline or when the buffer you specify is full. After any successful read, the contents of the buffer are null-terminated. *Do not* use the function gets in place of this function.

fopen   fopen — This is the function you use to open a file. I discuss it at length starting on page 252. Use freopen to redirect a standard stream.

fprintf   fprintf — This is the formatted output function that writes to the output stream you specify. See the description starting on page 257.

fputc   fputc — You call this function to write a character to an output stream. (See page 254.) All other functions that write to a stream behave as if they call fputc to deliver each character. putc has the same specification as fputc but is far more likely to have a masking macro that dramatically improves performance. As a rule, therefore, you should use putc instead of fputc.

fputs   fputs — Use this function to write characters from a null-terminated string to a stream. Unlike puts, fputs does *not* append a newline to whatever it writes. That makes it more useful for assembling lines of text or for writing binary data.

fread   fread — Use this function to read binary data into an array data object or to read up to a fixed number of characters from any stream. If the size (second) argument is greater than one, you cannot determine whether the function also read up to size - 1 additional characters beyond what it reports. As a rule, you are better off calling the function as fread(buf, 1, size * n, stream) instead of fread(buf, size, n, stream).

freopen   freopen — You use freopen only to recycle a stream that is already open. It may be convenient, for example, to redirect stdin or stdout to a different file under some circumstances. Most of the time, however, you will find that fopen is the function to use.

fscanf   fscanf — This is the formatted input function that reads from the input stream you specify.

fseek   fseek — Use this function to modify the file-position indicator for a stream. You can memorize a position in a file by executing offset = ftell(stream). Return to that position later by executing fseek(stream, offset, SEEK_CUR. fseek is more useful with a binary stream. In that case, the offset (second) argument is a *long* byte displacement within the file. The mode (third) argument must have one of the values SEEK_CUR, SEEK_END, or SEEK_SET, described above.

fsetpos   **fsetpos** — Use this function to modify the file-position indicator for a stream. Its **position** (second) argument must point to a data object of type **fpos_t** set on an earlier call to **fgetpos** for the same open stream. See the discussion of **fpos_t** above.

ftell   **ftell** — Use this function to memorize a position in a file to which you may want to later return. It returns a value of type **long**, suitable for use on a later call to **fseek**.

fwrite   **fwrite** — Use this function to write binary data from an array data object or to write a fixed number of characters to any stream. If the **size** (second) argument is greater than one, you cannot determine whether the function writes up to **size - 1** additional characters before a write error. Write errors are generally rare, so this is not a major shortcoming.

getc   **getc** — Use this function instead of **fgetc**. See **fgetc**, above.

getchar   **getchar** — This is a convenient shorthand for **getc(stdin)**. Both calls typically generate equivalent code.

gets   **gets** — Avoid using this function. You have no way to limit the number of characters it reads. Use **fgets** instead.

perror   **perror** — Use this function to write a one-line error message to the standard error stream. The message describes the current error code stored in **errno**. (See Chapter 3: **<errno.h>**.) If you want more control over how the error message appears, call **strerror**, declared in **<string.h>**, instead.

printf   **printf** — This is the formatted output function that writes to the standard output stream. It is the most widely used of the print functions. See **fprintf**, above.

putc   **putc** — Use this function instead of **fputc**. (See **fputc**.)

putchar   **putchar** — **putchar(ch)** is a convenient shorthand for **putc(ch, stdout)**. Both calls typically generate equivalent code.

puts   **puts** — Use this function to write characters from a null-terminated string to a stream. The function appends a newline to whatever it writes. Use **fputs** if you don't want the newline appended.

remove   **remove** — This function removes a file from the file system. A subsequent **fopen** call with the same file name should fail. It is good manners to remove any files you create with names generated by **tmpnam**.

rename   **rename** — This function renames a file. A subsequent **fopen** call should fail with the old file name and succeed with the new one. You can sometimes make a temporary file permanent simply by renaming it. Note, however, that **rename** is *not* obliged to copy the contents of a file to effect a renaming. Always check the function return value to see if the operation succeeds.

rewind   **rewind** — Unlike the other file-positioning functions, **rewind** clears the error indicator for a stream. It also reports no failures. You should use **fseek(stream, 0, SEEK_SET)** and **clearerr(stream)** as needed instead.

scanf   `scanf` — This is the formatted input function that reads from the standard input stream. It is the most widely used of the scan functions.

setbuf   `setbuf` — Use `setvbuf` instead of this function to get more control.

setvbuf   `setvbuf` — As a rule, it is best to let the Standard C library decide how to buffer input/output for you. If you are certain that you want no buffering or line-at-a-time buffering, then use this function to initialize the stream properly. Call `setvbuf` *immediately* after you open the stream. Almost any operation on the stream will preempt your right to choose a buffering strategy. Should you specify your own buffer with this call, don't assume that the stream will actually use it. And *never* alter the contents of the buffer while the stream is open. The `mode` (third) argument must have one of the values `_IOFBF`, `_IOLBF`, or `_IONBF`, described above. Also see the macro **BUFSIZ, described above.**

sprintf   `sprintf` — This is the formatted output function that writes a null-terminated string to the buffer you specify. It is the only way you can convert encoded values to text without writing to a stream. Note that you cannot directly specify the maximum number of characters that `sprintf` stores. Be wary of conversions that can generate enough characters to store beyond the end of the buffer. See `fprintf`, above.

sscanf   `sscanf` — This is the formatted input function that reads a null-terminated string from the buffer you specify. You can use it to scan the same sequence of characters with several different formats, until you find a scan that succeeds.

tmpfile   `tmpfile` — Use `tmpfile` instead of `tmpnam` wherever possible. The former opens the file for you and arranges to have it closed and removed on program termination. The latter requires you to assume more of these responsibilities.

tmpnam   `tmpnam` — Use this function to obtain one or more temporary file names only if `tmpfile` doesn't meet your needs. You may want to open the file in a mode other than `"wb+"`, for example. You may have to open and close the same file repeatedly. Or you may want to rename the file before program termination. See the macro `TMP_MAX`, described above.

ungetc   `ungetc` — Use this function in conjunction with the read functions only. The interaction of `ungetc` with the file-positioning functions is delicate. You can push back a different character than the last one read. You can even push back a character at beginning-of-file. But you cannot portably push back more than one character between calls to read functions.

vfprintf   `vfprintf` — Use this function to build special versions of `fprintf`, as described on page 258.

vprintf   `vprintf` — Use this function to build special versions of `printf`, as described on page 258.

vsprintf   `vsprintf` — Use this function to build special versions of `sprintf`, as described on page 258.

Implementing `<stdio.h>`

Two design decisions are critical to the implementation of `<stdio.h>`:

- the contents of the `FILE` data structure
- the low-level primitives that interact with the operating system to perform the actual input/output

I begin by discussing these two topics in detail. You can then appreciate how the low-level I/O functions work. I save the formatted input and output functions for last.

header Figure 12.2 shows the file `stdio.h`. By now you should be familiar with
`<stdio.h>` the use of the internal header `<yvals.h>` to supply implementation-dependent parameters. Here are the parameters defined in `<yvals.h>` that affect `<stdio.h>`, with some reasonable values for them:

```
#define _NULL   (void *)0   /* value for NULL */
#define _FNAMAX 64  /* value for FILENAME_MAX */
#define _FOPMAX 32  /* value for FOPEN_MAX */
#define _TNAMAX 16  /* value for TMP_MAX */
```

type The file `stdio.h` contains a few other mysteries which shall become clear
FILE in time. For now, I concentrate on the type definition `FILE`. Its members are:

- `_Mode` — a set of status bits for the stream, defined below
- `_Handle` — the handle, or file descriptor, returned by the operating system for the opened file
- `_Buf` — a pointer to the start of the stream buffer, or a null pointer if no buffer has been allocated
- `_Bend` — a pointer to the first character beyond the end of the buffer, undefined if `_Buf` is a null pointer
- `_Next` — a pointer to the next character to read or write, *never a null pointer*
- `_Rend` — a pointer to the first character beyond the end of data to be read, *never a null pointer*
- `_Rsave` — holds `_Rend` if characters have been pushed back
- `_Wend` — a pointer to the first character beyond the end of where data can be written, *never a null pointer*
- `_Back` — a stack of pushed-back characters
- `_Cbuf` — a one-character buffer to use when no other buffer is available
- `_Nback` — a count of the number of pushed-back characters
- `_Tmpnam` — a pointer to the name of a temporary file to be removed when the file is closed, or a null pointer

getc The design of the `FILE` data structure is driven by the needs of the macros
putc `getc` and `putc` (and their companions `getchar` and `putchar`). Each of these expands to a conditional expression that either accesses the stream buffer directly or calls the underlying function. The predicate (test expression) part of the conditional expression must be simple and *always safe to execute*. Thus, `str->_Next < str->_Rend` is always true if characters that can be read are in the buffer for the stream pointed at by `str`. And `str->_Next <`

`str->_Wend` is always true if space is available in the buffer to write characters to the stream. An expression such as `str->_Wend = str->_Buf`, for example, disallows writes to the buffer from these macros.

The functions that you call to read and write streams make more extensive tests. A read function, for example, distinguishes a variety of conditions such as: characters are available, buffer currently exhausted, end-of-file encountered, buffer not yet allocated, reading currently disallowed, and reading never allowed. The functions rely heavily on the various indicators in the member `_Mode` to make those distinctions.

header
"xstdio.h" Only functions within the Standard C library need be privy to the meaning of these indicators. For that reason, and others, I created the internal header `"xstdio.h"`. All the functions described in this chapter include `"xstdio.h"`. It defines macros for the stream-mode indicators. It includes `<stdio.h>` and declares all the internal functions used to implement the capabilities of `<stdio.h>`. It also defines a number of macros and types of interest only to the formatted input and output functions.

mode
indicators Unlike `<stdio.h>`, the header `"xstdio.h"` contains too many distractions to present at this point. I show you what goes into it as the need arises, then show you the whole file on page 322. Here, for example, are the macros names for the various incidators in the member `_Mode`. Each is defined as a value with a different bit set, as in `0x1, 0x2, 0x4, 0x8`, and so on. The actual values are unimportant, so I omit them here:

- `_MOPENR` — set if file is open for reading
- `_MOPENW` — set if file is open for writing
- `_MOPENA` — set if all writes append to end of file
- `_MTRUNC` — set if existing file was truncated on open (not used after open)
- `_MCREAT` — set if a new file can be created on open (not used after open)
- `_MBIN` — set if stream is binary, not set if stream is interpreted as text
- `_MALBUF` — set if the buffer must be freed on close
- `_MALFIL` — set if the `FILE` data object must be freed on close
- `_MEOF` — the end-of-file indicator
- `_MERR` — the error indicator
- `_MLBF` — set if line buffering in effect
- `_MNBF` — set if no buffering should occur
- `_MREAD` — set if a read has occurred since last file-positioning operation
- `_MWRITE` — set if a write has occurred since last file-positioning operation

These macros have private names — beginning with an underscore and an uppercase letter — even though they don't have to. As I developed the library, I found myself moving them in and out of `<stdio.h>`. Some version of the macros visible to user programs used these macro names, later versions did not. In the end, I left the names in this form as insurance. You may find occasion to introduce macros that manipulate the indicators in the member `_Mode`.

```
/* stdio.h standard header */
#ifndef _STDIO
#define _STDIO
#ifndef _YVALS
#include <yvals.h>
#endif
        /* macros */
#define NULL            _NULL
#define _IOFBF          0
#define _IOLBF          1
#define _IONBF          2
#define BUFSIZ          512
#define EOF             -1
#define FILENAME_MAX    _FNAMAX
#define FOPEN_MAX       _FOPMAX
#define L_tmpnam        _TNAMAX
#define TMP_MAX         32
#define SEEK_SET        0
#define SEEK_CUR        1
#define SEEK_END        2
#define stdin           _Files[0]
#define stdout          _Files[1]
#define stderr          _Files[2]
        /* type definitions */
#ifndef _SIZET
#define _SIZET
typedef _Sizet size_t;
#endif
typedef struct {
    unsigned long _Off;                         /* system dependent */
    } fpos_t;
typedef struct {
    unsigned short _Mode;
    short _Handle;
    unsigned char *_Buf, *_Bend, *_Next;
    unsigned char *_Rend, *_Rsave, *_Wend;
    unsigned char _Back[2], _Cbuf, _Nback;
    char *_Tmpnam;
    } FILE;
        /* declarations */
void clearerr(FILE *);
int fclose(FILE *);
int feof(FILE *);
int ferror(FILE *);
int fflush(FILE *);
int fgetc(FILE *);
int fgetpos(FILE *, fpos_t *);
char *fgets(char *, int, FILE *);
FILE *fopen(const char *, const char *);
int fprintf(FILE *, const char *, ...);
int fputc(int, FILE *);
int fputs(const char *, FILE *);
size_t fread(void *, size_t, size_t, FILE *);
FILE *freopen(const char *, const char *, FILE *);
int fscanf(FILE *, const char *, ...);
```

```
int fseek(FILE *, long, int);
int fsetpos(FILE *, const fpos_t *);
long ftell(FILE *);
size_t fwrite(const void *, size_t, size_t, FILE *);
int getc(FILE *);
int getchar(void);
char *gets(char *);
void perror(const char *);
int printf(const char *, ...);
int putc(int, FILE *);
int putchar(int);
int puts(const char *);
int remove(const char *);
int rename(const char *, const char *);
void rewind(FILE *);
int scanf(const char *, ...);
void setbuf(FILE *, char *);
int setvbuf(FILE *, char *, int, size_t);
int sprintf(char *, const char *, ...);
int sscanf(const char *, const char *, ...);
FILE *tmpfile(void);
char *tmpnam(char *);
int ungetc(int, FILE *);
int vfprintf(FILE *, const char *, char *);
int vprintf(const char *, char *);
int vsprintf(char *, const char *, char *);
long _Fgpos(FILE *, fpos_t *);
int _Fspos(FILE *, const fpos_t *, long, int);
extern FILE *_Files[FOPEN_MAX];
        /* macro overrides */
#define fgetpos(str, ptr)   (int)_Fgpos(str, ptr)
#define fseek(str, off, way)   _Fspos(str, _NULL, off, way)
#define fsetpos(str, ptr)   _Fspos(str, ptr, 0L, 0)
#define ftell(str)   _Fgpos(str, _NULL)
#define getc(str)   ((str)->_Next < (str)->_Rend \
    ? *(str)->_Next++ : (getc)(str))
#define getchar()   (_Files[0]->_Next < _Files[0]->_Rend \
    ? *_Files[0]->_Next++ : (getchar)())
#define putc(c, str)      ((str)->_Next < (str)->_Wend \
    ? (*(str)->_Next++ = c) : (putc)(c, str))
#define putchar(c)   (_Files[1]->_Next < _Files[1]->_Wend \
    ? (*_Files[1]->_Next++ = c) : (putchar)(c))
#endif
```

The indicators are actually the union of two sets. One is the set of indicators that determines how to open a file. The other is the set of indicators that helps record the state of the stream. Since the two sets partially overlap, I chose to keep them all in one "space" of bit encodings. A tidier implementation might well choose to separate the two uses. You might also want to define two sets of values if you are starved for bits in _Mode. In either case, you must add code to translate between the two representations.

function
fopen

The best way to see how the library uses a FILE data object is to track one through its lifetime. Figure 12.3 shows the file fopen.c. It defines the function fopen that you call to open a file by name. That function first looks for an idle entry in the static array of FILE pointers called _Files. It contains FOPEN_MAX elements. If all of these point to FILE data objects for open files, all subsequent open requests fail.

data object
_files

Figure 12.4 shows the file xfiles.c that defines the _Files data object. It defines static instances of FILE data objects for the three standard streams. Each is initialized to be open with appropriate parameters. I have wired in the handles 0 for standard input, 1 for standard output, and 2 for standard error. This is a widely used convention, inherited from UNIX. You may have to alter or map these values or map.

Elements beyond the first three in _Files are initialized to null pointers. Should fopen discover one of these, the function allocates a FILE data object and marks it to be freed on close. fopen discovers a closed standard stream by observing a non-null element of _Files that points at a FILE data object whose member _Mode is zero.

function
freopen

fopen calls on the internal function _Foprep to complete the process of opening a file. Figure 12.5 shows the file freopen.c. The function freopen also calls this internal function. Note how it records the state of the indicator _MALFIL until after fclose has closed the file currently associated with the stream. The one operation that freopen does *not* want fclose to perform is to free the FILE data object.

function
fclose

You may as well see fclose too, at this point. Figure 12.xx shows the file fclose.c. It undoes the work of the file-opening functions in a fairly obvious fashion. The one bit of magic is where it calls the function _Fclose to close the file associated with the stream.

function
_Foprep

Figure 12.7 shows the file xfoprep.c that defines the function _Foprep. It parses the mods (second) argument to fopen or freopen, at least as much as it can understand, and initializes members of the FILE data object accordingly. In the end, however, it must call on some outside agency to finish the job of opening the file. _Foprep passes on the file name, the encoded indicators, and whatever is left of mods to a function called _Fopen. I describe _Fopen very shortly.

primitives

_Fclose and _Fopen are the first of several low-level primitives that stand between <stdio.h> and the outside world. Each must perform a standardized function for the Standard C library. Each must also be reasonably easy to tailor for the divergent needs of different operating systems. This implementation has nine functions in <stdio.h> that must be tailored to each operating system. Three are standard functions:

- remove — Remove a named file.
- rename — Change the name of a file.
- tmpnam — Construct a reasonable name for a temporary file.

Figure 12.3:
`fopen.c`

```
/* fopen function */
#include <stdlib.h>
#include "xstdio.h"

FILE *(fopen)(const char *name, const char *mods)
    {                                           /* open a file */
    FILE *str;
    size_t i;

    for (i = 0; i < FOPEN_MAX; ++i)
        if (_Files[i] == NULL)
            {                              /* setup empty _Files[i] */
            str = malloc(sizeof (FILE));
            if (str == NULL)
                return (NULL);
            _Files[i] = str;
            str->_Mode = _MALFIL;
            break;
            }
        else if (_Files[i]->_Mode == 0)
            {                       /* setup preallocated _Files[i] */
            str = _Files[i];
            break;
            }
    if (FOPEN_MAX <= i)
        return (NULL);
    return (_Foprep(name, mods, str));
    }                                                              □
```

Figure 12.4:
`xfiles.c`

```
/* _Files data object */
#include "xstdio.h"

/* standard error buffer */
static unsigned char ebuf[80];

/* the standard streams */
static FILE sin = {                              /* standard input */
    _MOPENR, 0,
    NULL, NULL, &sin._Cbuf,
    &sin._Cbuf, NULL, &sin._Cbuf, };
static FILE sout = {                            /* standard output */
    _MOPENW, 1,
    NULL, NULL, &sout._Cbuf,
    &sout._Cbuf, NULL, &sout._Cbuf, };
static FILE serr = {                             /* standard error */
    _MOPENW|_MNBF, 2,
    ebuf, ebuf + sizeof (ebuf), ebuf,
    ebuf, NULL, ebuf, };

/* the array of stream pointers */
FILE *_Files[FOPEN_MAX] = {&sin, &sout, &serr};                      □
```

Figure 12.5:
freopen.c

```c
/* freopen function */
#include <stdlib.h>
#include "xstdio.h"

FILE *(freopen)(const char *name, const char *mods, FILE *str)
    {                                                   /* reopen a file */
    unsigned short mode = str->_Mode & _MALFIL;

    str->_Mode &= ~_MALFIL;
    fclose(str);
    str->_Mode = mode;
    return (_Foprep(name, mods, str));
    }                                                                    □
```

Figure 12.6:
fclose.c

```c
/* fclose function */
#include <stdlib.h>
#include "xstdio.h"
#include "yfuns.h"

int (fclose)(FILE *str)
    {                                                   /* close a stream */
    int stat = fflush(str);

    if (str->_Mode & _MALBUF)
        free(str->_Buf);
    str->_Buf = NULL;
    if (0 <= str->_Handle && _Fclose(str))
        stat = EOF;
    if (str->_Tmpnam)
        {                                               /* remove temp file */
        if (remove(str->_Tmpnam))
            stat = EOF;
        free(str->_Tmpnam);
        str->_Tmpnam = NULL;
        }
    str->_Mode = 0;
    str->_Next = &str->_Cbuf;
    str->_Rend = &str->_Cbuf;
    str->_Wend = &str->_Cbuf;
    str->_Nback = 0;
    if (str->_Mode & _MALFIL)
        {                                   /* find _Files[i] entry and free */
        size_t i;

        for (i = 0; i < FOPEN_MAX; ++i)
            if (_Files[i] == str)
                {                                       /* found entry */
                _Files[i] = NULL;
                break;
                }
        free(str);
        }
    return (stat);
    }                                                                    □
```

Figure 12.7:
xfoprep.c

```c
/* _Foprep function */
#include "xstdio.h"

/* open a stream */
FILE *_Foprep(const char *name, const char *mods,
    FILE *str)
    {                               /* make str safe for fclose, macros */
    str->_Handle = -1;
    str->_Tmpnam = NULL;
    str->_Buf = NULL;
    str->_Next = &str->_Cbuf;
    str->_Rend = &str->_Cbuf;
    str->_Wend = &str->_Cbuf;
    str->_Nback = 0;
    str->_Mode = (str->_Mode & _MALFIL)
        | (*mods == 'r' ? _MOPENR
        : *mods == 'w' ? _MCREAT|_MOPENW|_MTRUNC
        : *mods == 'a' ? _MCREAT|_MOPENW|_MOPENA
        : 0);
    if ((str->_Mode & (_MOPENR|_MOPENW)) == 0)
        {                                       /* bad mods */
        fclose(str);
        return (NULL);
        }
    while (*++mods== 'b' || *mods == '+')
        if (*mods == 'b')
            if (str->_Mode & _MBIN)
                break;
            else
                str->_Mode |= _MBIN;
        else
            if ((str->_Mode & (_MOPENR|_MOPENW))
                == (_MOPENR|_MOPENW))
                break;
            else
                str->_Mode |= _MOPENR|_MOPENW;
    str->_Handle = _Fopen(name, str->_Mode, mods);
    if (str->_Handle < 0)
        {                                       /* open failed */
        fclose(str);
        return (NULL);
        }
    return (str);
    }                                                          □
```

Each of these functions is small and very dependent on the peculiarities of the underlying operating system. It is not worth writing any of them in terms of lower-level primitives. You can often find versions in an existing C library that do the job nicely.

header
"yfuns.h"   Three of the primitives are macros defined in the internal header **"yfuns.h"**. I mentioned this header on page 54. It defines macros and declares functions needed only within the Standard C library to interface

to the outside world. Only certain functions written for this implementation need include `"yfuns.h"`. (The internal header `<yvals.h>`, by contrast, must be included in several standard headers.) The three macros look like internal functions with the declarations:

```
int _Fclose(FILE *str);
int _Fread(FILE *str, char *buf, int size);
int _Fwrite(FILE *str, const char *buf, int size);
```

Their semantics are:

_Fclose ■ _Fclose — Close the file associated with `str`. Return zero if successful.

_Fread ■ _Fread — Read up to `size` characters into the buffer starting at `buf` from the file associated with `str`. Return the number successfully read, or zero if at end-of-file, or a negative error code if a read error occurs.

_Fwrite ■ _Fwrite — Write `size` characters from the buffer starting at `buf` to the file associated with `str`. Return the number of characters actually written or a negative error code if a write error occurs.

Many operating systems support functions that have declarations very similar to these. You can often find existing functions that the macro expansions can call directly.

The last three primitives are internal functions. One function is declared in `"xstdio.h"`. Two are used in masking macros, and hence are declared in `<stdio.h>`. Their declarations are:

```
short _Fopen(const char *name, unsigned short mode,
      const char *mods);
long _Fgpos(FILE *str, fpos_t *fpos);
int _Fspos(FILE *str, const fpos_t *fpos, long offset, int way);
```

Their semantics are:

_Fopen ■ _Fopen — Open the file with name `name` and mode `mode` (possibly using the string `mods` as well). Return a non-negative handle if successful.

_Fgpos ■ _Fgpos — If `fpos` is not a null pointer, store the file-position indicator at `fpos` and return zero. Otherwise, encode the file-position indicator as a *long* and return its value. Return the value `EOF` if not successful.

_Fspos ■ _Fspos — If `way` has the value `SEEK_SET`, set the file-position indicator from either `fpos` or `offset`. (If `fpos` is not a null pointer, use the value stored in `fpos`. Otherwise, decode `offset` to determine the file-position indicator.) If `way` has the value `SEEK_CUR`, add `offset` to the file-position indicator. Otherwise, `way` must have the value `SEEK_END`. Set the file-position indicator to just beyond the last character in the file, plus `offset`. If successful, return zero and clear `_MEOF`, `_MREAD`, and `_MWRITE`. Otherwise, return the value `EOF`.

You are less likely to find existing functions that you can commandeer to implement part or all of these three functions. Each involves data representations that are probably peculiar to this implementation.

Appendix A: Interfaces discusses these and other interface primitives. It describes how you can use this library in conjunction with several

Figure 12.8:
remove.c

```
/* remove function -- UNIX version */
#include "xstdio.h"

        /* UNIX system call */
int _Unlink(const char *);

int (remove)(const char *fname)
    {                                          /* remove a file */
    return (_Unlink(fname));
    }                                                          □
```

Figure 12.9:
rename.c

```
/* rename function -- UNIX version */
#include "xstdio.h"

        /* UNIX system calls */
int _Link(const char *, const char *);
int _Unlink(const char *);

int (rename)(const char *old, const char *new)
    {                                          /* rename a file */
    return (_Link(old, new) ? -1 : _Unlink(old));
    }                                                          □
```

popular operating systems. For completeness, I show primitives for one environment in this chapter. Please remember, however, that these represent but one of many possibilities.

UNIX primitives   For simplicity, I *sketch* here primitives that interface to many versions of the UNIX operating system. That is often the easiest system to use as a host for the Standard C library. Even though the C language has moved to many other environments, much of the library design was shaped by the needs and capabilities of UNIX. The files I show are only sketches because they often can be augmented to advantage.

In all cases, I assume the existence of C-callable functions that perform UNIX system calls without violating the name-space restrictions of Standard C. I take the conventional UNIX name, make the first letter uppercase and prepend an underscore. Thus, `unlink` becomes `_Unlink`. You may have to write these functions in assembly language if your UNIX system supplies no adequate substitutes.

function remove   For example, Figure 12.8 shows the file `remove.c` that defines the function `remove`. This version simply invokes the UNIX system call `_Unlink`. A more careful version would verify that a program with super-user permissions is not doing something rash.

function rename   Figure 12.9 shows the file `rename.c`. It defines a simple version of `rename` that simply manipulates links to the file. That typically works only if both the new and old file names are within the same filesystem (on the same logical disk partition). A more agressive version might choose to copy a file when the `link` system service fails.

function   Figure 12.10 shows the file `tmpnam.c`. It defines a simple version of `tmpnam`
tmpnam   that concocts a temporary file name in the directory `/tmp`, the customary
place for parking temporary files. It encodes the current process-id to make
a family of names that should be unique to each thread of control.

Figure 12.10:
tmpnam.c

```
/* tmpnam function -- UNIX version */
#include <string.h>
#include "xstdio.h"


        /* UNIX system call */
int _Getpid(void);

char *(tmpnam)(char *s)
    {                                   /* create a temporary file name */
    int i;
    char *p;
    unsigned short t;
    static char buf[L_tmpnam];
    static unsigned short seed = 0;

    if (s == NULL)
        s = buf;
    seed = seed == 0 ? _Getpid() : seed + 1;
    strcpy(s, "/tmp/t");
    i = 5;
    p = s + strlen(s) + i;
    *p = '\0';
    for (t = seed; 0 <= --i; t >>= 3)
        *--p = '0' + (t & 07);
    return (s);
    }                                                                    □
```

Figure 12.11:
xfopen.c

```
/* _Fopen function -- UNIX version */
#include "xstdio.h"

        /* UNIX system call */
int _Open(const char *, int, int);

int _Fopen(const char *path, unsigned int smode,
    const char *mods)
    {                                           /* open from a file */
    unsigned int acc;

    acc = (smode & (_MOPENR|_MOPENW)) == (_MOPENR|_MOPENW) ? 2
        : smode & _MOPENW ? 1 : 0;
    if (smode & _MOPENA)
        acc |= 010;                                     /* O_APPEND */
    if (smode & _MTRUNC)
        acc |= 02000;                                   /* O_TRUNC */
    if (smode & _MCREAT)
        acc |= 01000;                                   /* O_CREAT */
    return (_Open(path, acc, 0666));
    }                                                                    □
```

Figure 12.12:
xfgpos.c

```
/* _Fgpos function -- UNIX version */
#include <errno.h>
#include "xstdio.h"

        /* UNIX system call */
long _Lseek(int, long, int);

long _Fgpos(FILE *str, fpos_t *ptr)
    {                                                   /* get file position */
    long loff = _Lseek(str->_Handle, 0L, 1);

    if (loff == -1)
        {                                               /* query failed */
        errno = EFPOS;
        return (EOF);
        }
    if (str->_Mode & _MWRITE)
        loff += str->_Next - str->_Buf;
    else if (str->_Mode & _MREAD)
        loff -= str->_Nback
            ? str->_Rsave - str->_Next + str->_Nback
            : str->_Rend - str->_Next;
    if (ptr == NULL)
        return (loff);                                  /* ftell */
    else
        {                                               /* fgetpos */
        ptr->_Off = loff;
        return (0);
        }
    }                                                                      □
```

function   Figure 12.11 shows the file **xfopen.c** that defines the function **_Fopen**. It
_Fopen maps the codes I chose for the mode indicators to the codes used by the
UNIX system service that opens a file. A proper version of this program
should not include all these magic numbers. Rather, it should include the
appropriate header that UNIX provides to define the relevant parameters.

UNIX makes no distinction between binary and text files. Other operating systems may have to worry about such distinctions at the time the
program opens a file. Similarly, UNIX has no use for any additional mode
information. (**_Fopen** could insist that the mode argument be an empty
string here. This version is not so particular.)

function   Figure 12.12 shows the file **xfgpos.c** that defines the function **_Fgpos**. It
_Fgpos asks the system to deliver the file-position indicator for the file, then
corrects for any data buffered on behalf of the stream. A file-position
indicator under UNIX can be represented in a *long*. Hence, type **fpos_t**,
defined in `<stdio.h>`, is a structure that contains only one *long* member. (I
could have defined **fpos_t** as type *long* directly, but I wanted to keep the
type as restrictive as possible.) In this case, the functions **fgetpos** and
fsetpos offer no advantage over the older file-positioning functions. The
difference can be important for other systems, however.

Figure 12.13:
xfspos.c

```
/* _Fspos function -- UNIX version */
#include <errno.h>
#include "xstdio.h"

        /* UNIX system call */
long _Lseek(int, long, int);

int _Fspos(FILE *str, const fpos_t *ptr, long loff, int way)
    {                                              /* position a file */
    if (fflush(str))
        {                                          /* write error */
        errno = EFPOS;
        return (EOF);
        }
    if (ptr)
        loff += ((fpos_t *)ptr)->_Off;             /* fsetpos */
    if (way == SEEK_CUR && str->_Mode & _MREAD)
        loff -= str->_Nback
            ? str->_Rsave - str->_Next + str->_Nback
            : str->_Rend - str->_Next;
    if (way == SEEK_CUR && loff != 0
        || way != SEEK_SET || loff != -1)
        loff = _Lseek(str->_Handle, loff, way);
    if (loff == -1)
        {                                          /* request failed */
        errno = EFPOS;
        return (EOF);
        }
    else
        {                                          /* success */
        if (str->_Mode & (_MREAD|_MWRITE))
            {                                      /* empty buffer */
            str->_Next = str->_Buf;
            str->_Rend = str->_Buf;
            str->_Wend = str->_Buf;
            str->_Nback = 0;
            }
        str->_Mode &= ~(_MEOF|_MREAD|_MWRITE);
        return (0);
        }
    }                                                            □
```

_Fgpos is simpler under UNIX in another way. No mapping occurs
between the internal and external forms of text streams. Hence, the correction for characters in internal buffers is simple. Consider, by comparison,
a system that maps text streams. Say it terminates each text line with a
carriage return plus line feed instead of just a line feed. That means that
_Fread must discard certain carriage returns and _Fwrite must insert them.
It also means that _Fgpos must correct for any alterations when it corrects
the file-position indicator. The problem is manageable, but it leads to messy
logic that I choose not to show at this point.

Figure 12.14:
tmpfile.c

```c
/* tmpfile function */
#include <stdlib.h>
#include <string.h>
#include "xstdio.h"

FILE *(tmpfile)(void)
    {                                           /* open a temporary file */
    FILE *str;
    char fname[L_tmpnam];

    tmpnam(fname);
    if ((str = fopen(fname, "wb+")) != NULL)
        {                                       /* file successfully opened */
        str->_Tmpnam = malloc(sizeof (fname) + 1);
        strcpy(str->_Tmpnam, fname);
        }
    return (str);
    }
```

Figure 12.15:
clearerr.c

```c
/* clearerr function */
#include "xstdio.h"

void (clearerr)(FILE *str)
    {                           /* clear EOF and error indicators for a stream */
    if (str->_Mode & (_MOPENR|_MOPENW))
        str->_Mode &= ~(_MEOF|_MERR);
    }
```

function
_Fspos
Figure 12.13 shows the file `xfspos.c` that defines the function `_Fspos`. It too benefits from the simple UNIX I/O model in the same ways as `_Fgpos`. Output causes no problems, since the function flushes any unwritten characters before it alters the file-position indicator.

The remaining three primitives are macros. All expand to calls on functions that perform UNIX system services directly. The UNIX version of `"yfuns.h"` contains the lines:

```c
#define _Fclose(str)        _Close((str)->_Handle)
#define _Fread(str, buf, cnt)   _Read((str)->_Handle, buf, cnt)
#define _Fwrite(str, buf, cnt)  _Write((str)->_Handle, buf, cnt)

int _Close(int);
int _Read(int, unsigned char *, int);
int _Write(int, const unsigned char *, int);
```

tmpfile
clearerr
feof
ferror
Now that you have seen the I/O primitives, most of the low-level functions declared in `<stdio.h>` should make sense. Let's begin by looking at the remaining functions that set up or administer streams without performing input or output. Figure 12.14 shows the file `tmpfile.c`. Function `tmpfile` is a simple application of the functions you have already met. Figure 12.15 (`clearerr.c`), Figure 12.16 (`feof.c`), and Figure 12.17 (`ferror.c`) are even simpler. The only reason the functions defined in these files lack masking macros in `<stdio.h>` is because they are used so seldom.

Figure 12.16:
feof.c

```
/* feof function */
#include "xstdio.h"

int (feof)(FILE *str)
    {                       /* test end-of-file indicator for a stream */
    return (str->_Mode & _MEOF);
    }                                                                    □
```

Figure 12.17:
ferror.c

```
/* ferror function */
#include "xstdio.h"

int (ferror)(FILE *str)
    {                       /* test error indicator for a stream */
    return (str->_Mode & _MERR);
    }                                                                    □
```

Figure 12.18:
setbuf.c

```
/* setbuf function */
#include "xstdio.h"

void (setbuf)(FILE *str, char *buf)
    {                       /* set up buffer for a stream */
    setvbuf(str, buf, buf ? _IOFBF : _IONBF, BUFSIZ);
    }                                                                    □
```

setbuf   Figure 12.18 shows the file `setbuf.c`. It consists simply of a call to
setvbuf `setvbuf`. Figure 12.19 shows the file `setvbuf.c`. Most of its work consists of
laundering its arguments. Note that `setvbuf` will honor requests any time
the stream is has nothing buffered. It is not obliged to succeed, however,
after any reads or writes have occurred.

file   The file-positioning functions are also trivial, given the primitive func-
positioning tions `_Fgpos` and `_Fspos`. Figure 12.20 through Figure 12.24 show the files
functions `fgetpos.c`, `fseek.c`, `fsetpos.c`, `ftell.c`, and `rewind.c`. I chose to provide
masking macros for all but `rewind` in `<stdio.h>`.

function   Now consider the functions that read characters. Figure 12.25 shows the
fgetc file `fgetc.c`, which defines the prototypical input function `fgetc`. It first
looks for characters that have been pushed back by a call to `ungetc`. If none
exist, `fgetc` tests whether any characters are in the buffer. It attempts to
refill an empty buffer by calling `_Frprep`. Should that function fail to deliver
any characters, `fgetc` returns `EOF`. Two functions are simple variations of
`fgetc`. Figure 12.26 (`getc.c`) and Figure 12.27 (`getchar.c`) both call `fgetc`.

function   One other function belongs in this group. Figure 12.28 shows the file
ungetc `ungetc.c`. You have seen the effect of the function `ungetc` on several other
functions. Here is the culprit in person. Considering all the work it causes
for other functions, **ungetc** is itself remarkably simple. Notice how it alters
the **FILE** data object for the stream to encourage the macros `getc` and
`getchar` to call the functions they normally mask. That gives the underlying
functions the opportunity to pop any characters pushed back.

Figure 12.19:
setvbuf.c

```c
/* setvbuf function */
#include <limits.h>
#include <stdlib.h>
#include "xstdio.h"

int (setvbuf)(FILE *str, char *abuf, int smode, size_t size)
    {                               /* set up buffer for a stream */
    int mode;
    unsigned char *buf = (unsigned char *)abuf;

    if (str->_Mode & (_MREAD|_MWRITE))
        return (-1);
    mode = smode == _IOFBF ? 0
        : smode == _IOLBF ? _MLBF
        : smode == _IONBF ? _MNBF : -1;
    if (mode == -1)
        return (-1);
    if (size == 0)
        buf = &str->_Cbuf, size = 1;
    else if (INT_MAX < size)
        size = INT_MAX;
    if (buf)
        ;
    else if ((buf = malloc(size)) == NULL)
        return (-1);
    else
        mode |= _MALBUF;
    if (str->_Mode & _MALBUF)
        free(str->_Buf), str->_Mode &= ~_MALBUF;
    str->_Mode |= mode;
    str->_Buf = buf;
    str->_Bend = buf + size;
    str->_Next = buf;
    str->_Rend = buf;
    str->_Wend = buf;
    return (0);
    }
```

Figure 12.20:
fgetpos.c

```c
/* fgetpos function */
#include "xstdio.h"

int (fgetpos)(FILE *str, fpos_t *p)
    {                   /* get file position indicator for stream */
    return (_Fgpos(str, p));
    }
```

Figure 12.21:
fseek.c

```c
/* fseek function */
#include "xstdio.h"

int (fseek)(FILE *str, long off, int smode)
    {                                   /* set seek offset for stream */
    return (_Fspos(str, NULL, off, smode));
    }
```

Figure 12.22:
fsetpos.c

```
/* fsetpos function */
#include "xstdio.h"

int (fsetpos)(FILE *str, const fpos_t *p)
    {                       /* set file position indicator for stream */
    return (_Fspos(str, p, 0L, SEEK_SET));
    }                                                                  □
```

Figure 12.23:
ftell.c

```
/* ftell function */
#include "xstdio.h"

long (ftell)(FILE *str)
    {                                       /* get seek offset for stream */
    return (_Fgpos(str, NULL));
    }                                                                  □
```

Figure 12.24:
rewind.c

```
/* rewind function */
#include "xstdio.h"

void (rewind)(FILE *str)
    {                                               /* rewind stream */
    _Fspos(str, NULL, 0L, SEEK_SET);
    str->_Mode &= ~_MERR;
    }                                                                  □
```

Figure 12.25:
fgetc.c

```
/* fgetc function */
#include "xstdio.h"

int (fgetc)(FILE *str)
    {                                       /* get a character from stream */
    if (0 < str->_Nback)
        {                               /* deliver pushed back char */
        if (--str->_Nback == 0)
            str->_Rend = str->_Rsave;
        return (str->_Back[str->_Nback]);
        }
    if (str->_Next < str->_Rend)
        ;
    else if (_Frprep(str) <= 0)
        return (EOF);
    return (*str->_Next++);
    }                                                                  □
```

Figure 12.26:
getc.c

```
/* getc function */
#include "xstdio.h"

int (getc)(FILE *str)
    {                                       /* get a character from stream */
    return (fgetc(str));
    }                                                                  □
```

Figure 12.27:
getchar.c

```
/* getchar function */
#include "xstdio.h"

int (getchar)(void)
    {                                        /* get a character from stdin */
    return (fgetc(stdin));
    }
```

Figure 12.28:
ungetc.c

```
/* ungetc function */
#include "xstdio.h"

int (ungetc)(int c, FILE *str)
    {                                        /* push character back on stream */
    if (c == EOF
        || sizeof (str->_Back) <= str->_Nback
        || (str->_Mode & (_MOPENR|_MWRITE)) != _MOPENR)
        return (EOF);
    str->_Mode = str->_Mode & ~_MEOF | _MREAD;
    if (str->_Nback == 0)
        {                                    /* disable buffering */
        str->_Rsave = str->_Rend;
        str->_Rend = str->_Buf;
        }
    str->_Back[str->_Nback++] = c;
    return ((unsigned char)c);
    }
```

fread
fgets
gets
Other functions have logic that parallels `fgetc` but avoids calling it in the interest of speed. One is `fread`, defined in Figure 12.29 (`fread.c`). Two others are in Figure 12.30 (`fgets.c`) and Figure 12.31 (`gets.c`). Compare these two functions carefully. They are just different enough that neither is worth writing in terms of the other.

function
_Frprep
Finally, Figure 12.32 shows the file `xfrprep.c`. It defines the function `_Frprep` which does all the serious work of reading. The function returns a negative value on a read error, zero at end-of-file, and a positive value if the stream buffer now contains characters. Here is where the stream buffer gets allocated and where `_Fread` actually gets called. All functions that read a stream rely on `_Frprep` in the end.

function
fputc
Next consider the functions that write characters. Figure 12.33 shows the file `fputc.c`, which defines the prototypical output function `fputc`. It first looks to see if the stream buffer has room to write characters. If no space is available, `fputc` attempts to set up an output buffer by calling `_Fwprep`. Should that function fail to provide space, `fputc` returns the value EOF. Once it has added a character to the buffer, `fputc` tests whether to drain the buffer before it returns. Two functions are simple variations of `fputc`. Figure 12.34 (`putc.c`) and Figure 12.35 (`putchar.c`) both call `fputc`.

function
_Fwprep
Figure 12.36 shows the file `xfwprep.c`. It defines the function `_Fwprep` which does all preparation for writing. The function returns a negative

Figure 12.29:
fread.c

```
/* fread function */
#include <string.h>
#include "xstdio.h"

size_t (fread)(void *ptr, size_t size, size_t nelem, FILE *str)
    {                                      /* read into array from stream */
    size_t ns = size * nelem;
    unsigned char *s = ptr;

    if (ns == 0)
        return (0);
    if (0 < str->_Nback)
        {                                  /* deliver pushed back chars */
        for (; 0 < ns && 0 < str->_Nback; --ns)
            *s++ = str->_Back[--str->_Nback];
        if (str->_Nback == 0)
            str->_Rend = str->_Rsave;
        }
    while (0 < ns)
        {                                        /* ensure chars in buffer */
        if (str->_Next < str->_Rend)
            ;
        else if (_Frprep(str) <= 0)
            break;
            {                              /* deliver as many as possible */
            size_t m = str->_Rend - str->_Next;

            if (ns < m)
                m = ns;
            memcpy(s, str->_Next, m);
            s += m, ns -= m;
            str->_Next += m;
            }
        }
    return ((size * nelem - ns) / size);
    }
```

value on a write error or zero if the stream buffer now contains space to write characters. Here is where the stream buffer gets allocated. All functions that write a stream rely on _Fwprep in the end.

function
fflush
Figure 12.37 shows the file fflush.c. Here is where _Fwrite actually gets called to write the contents of a stream buffer. If the argument is a null pointer, the function calls itself for each element of the array _Files that is not null. I chose to use recursion instead of looping here to keep the control flow cleaner. Performance is not likely to be an issue on such a call.

function
perror
One other function belongs in this group. Figure 12.38 shows the file perror.c. It composes an error message and writes it to the standard error stream. The function _Strerror does the work of the function strerror (both declared in <string.h>) but with a buffer supplied by the caller. It is not permissible for perror to alter the contents of the static storage in strerror. Thus, each function must call _Strerror with its own static buffer.

Figure 12.30:
fgets.c

```c
/* fgets function */
#include <string.h>
#include "xstdio.h"

char *(fgets)(char *buf, int n, FILE *str)
    {                                       /* get a line from stream */
    unsigned char *s;

    if (n <= 1)
        return (NULL);
    for (s = (unsigned char *)buf; 0 < --n && str->_Nback; )
        {                                   /* deliver pushed back chars */
        *s = str->_Back[--str->_Nback];
        if (str->_Nback == 0)
            str->_Rend = str->_Rsave;
        if (*s++ == '\n')
            {                               /* terminate full line */
            *s = '\0';
            return (buf);
            }
        }
    while (0 < n)
        {                                   /* ensure buffer has chars */
        if (str->_Next < str->_Rend)
            ;
        else if (_Frprep(str) < 0)
            return (NULL);
        else if (str->_Mode & _MEOF)
            break;
            {                               /* copy as many as possible */
        unsigned char *s1 = memchr(str->_Next,
            '\n', str->_Rend - str->_Next);
        size_t m = (s1 ? s1 + 1 : str->_Rend) - str->_Next;

        if (n < m)
            s1 = NULL, m = n;
        memcpy(s, str->_Next, m);
        s += m, n -= m;
        str->_Next += m;
        if (s1)
            {                               /* terminate full line */
            *s = '\0';
            return (buf);
            }
         }
        }
    if (s == (unsigned char *)buf)
        return (NULL);
    else
        {                                   /* terminate partial line */
        *s = '\0';
        return (buf);
        }
    }
```
□

```c
/* gets function */
#include <string.h>
#include "xstdio.h"

char *(gets)(char *buf)
    {                                      /* get a line from stdio */
    unsigned char *s;

    for (s = (unsigned char *)buf; stdin->_Nback; )
        {                                  /* deliver pushed back chars */
        *s = stdin->_Back[--stdin->_Nback];
        if (stdin->_Nback == 0)
            stdin->_Rend = stdin->_Rsave;
        if (*s++ == '\n')
            {                              /* terminate full line */
            s[-1] = '\0';
            return (buf);
            }
        }
    for (; ; )
        {                                  /* ensure chars in buffer */
        if (stdin->_Next < stdin->_Rend)
            ;
        else if (_Frprep(stdin) < 0)
            return (NULL);
        else if (stdin->_Mode & _MEOF)
            break;
        {                                  /* deliver as many as possible */
        unsigned char *s1 = memchr(stdin->_Next,
            '\n', stdin->_Rend - stdin->_Next);
        size_t m = (s1 ? s1 + 1 : stdin->_Rend)
            - stdin->_Next;

        memcpy(s, stdin->_Next, m);
        s += m; stdin->_Next += m;
        if (s1)
            {                              /* terminate full line */
            s[-1] = '\0';
            return (buf);
            }
        }
        }
    if (s == (unsigned char *)buf)
        return (NULL);
    else
        {                                  /* terminate partial line */
        *s = '\0';
        return (buf);
        }
    }
```

Figure 12.32:
xfrprep.c

```c
/* _Frprep function */
#include <stdlib.h>
#include "xstdio.h"
#include "yfuns.h"

int _Frprep(FILE *str)
    {                                       /* prepare stream for reading */
    if (str->_Next < str->_Rend)
        return (1);
    else if (str->_Mode & _MEOF)
        return (0);
    else if ((str->_Mode & (_MOPENR|_MWRITE)) != _MOPENR)
        {                                   /*can't read after write */
        str->_Mode |= _MERR;
        return (-1);
        }
    if (str->_Buf)
        ;
    else if ((str->_Buf = malloc(BUFSIZ)) == NULL)
        {                                       /* use 1-char _Cbuf */
        str->_Buf = &str->_Cbuf;
        str->_Bend = str->_Buf + 1;
        }
    else
        {                               /* set up allocated buffer */
        str->_Mode |= _MALBUF;
        str->_Bend = str->_Buf + BUFSIZ;
        }
    str->_Next = str->_Buf;
    str->_Rend = str->_Buf;
    str->_Wend = str->_Buf;
    {                               /* try to read into buffer */
    int n = _Fread(str, str->_Buf, str->_Bend - str->_Buf);

    if (n < 0)
        {                                   /* report error and fail */
        str->_Mode |= _MERR;
        return (-1);
        }
    else if (n == 0)
        {                                       /* report end of file */
        str->_Mode = (str->_Mode & ~_MREAD) | _MEOF;
        return (0);
        }
    else
        {                               /* set up data read */
        str->_Mode |= _MREAD;
        str->_Rend += n;
        return (1);
        }
    }
    }
```
□

Figure 12.33:
fputc.c

```
/* fputc function */
#include "xstdio.h"

int (fputc)(int ci, FILE *str)
    {                                        /* put a character to stream */
    unsigned char c = ci;

    if (str->_Next < str->_Wend)
        ;
    else if (_Fwprep(str) < 0)
        return (EOF);
    *str->_Next++ = c;
    if (str->_Mode & (_MLBF|_MNBF))
        {                                    /* disable macros and drain */
        str->_Wend = str->_Buf;
        if ((str->_Mode & _MNBF || c == '\n') && fflush(str))
            return (EOF);
        }
    return (c);
    }                                                                         □
```

fwrite   Other functions have logic that parallels **fputc** but avoids calling it in
fputs   the interest of speed. One variant of **fgetc** is **fwrite**, defined in Figure 12.39
puts   (**fwrite.c**). Two others are in Figure 12.40 (**fputs.c**) and Figure 12.41
(**puts.c**). The latter is a simple variant of the former.

That's the complete set of low-level input and output functions. As you
can see, none is particularly hard. Nevertheless, the whole collection adds
up to a lot of code. And that's only the beginning. The hard part of
implementing **<stdio.h>** is performing formatted input and output.

formatted   Six functions perform formatted output (the print functions). All call a
output   common function **_Printf** that has the declaration:

```
int _Printf(void *(*pfn)(void *, const char *, size_t),
    void *arg, const char *fmt, va_list ap);
```

The parameters are:

- **pfn** — a pointer to a function to call to deliver characters
- **arg** — a generic data-object pointer to pass as one of the arguments to
  the delivery function
- **fmt** — a pointer to the format string
- **ap** — a pointer to the context information that describes a variable
  argument list

The delivery function returns a new value for **arg** if successful. Otherwise,
it returns a null pointer to signal a write error.

fprintf   Figure 12.42 shows the file **fprintf.c**. It defines both **fprintf** and the
printf   delivery function **prout** that it uses. In this case, the generic pointer conveys
the **FILE** pointer from **fprintf** through **_Printf** to **prout**. **prout** uses this
pointer to write the stream you specify when you call **fprintf**. Figure 12.43
shows the file **printf.c**, which is a simple variant of **fprintf**.

Figure 12.34:
putc.c

```
/* putc function */
#include "xstdio.h"

int (putc)(int c, FILE *str)
    {                                   /* put character to stream */
    return (fputc(c, str));
    }                                                                □
```

Figure 12.35:
putchar.c

```
/* putchar function */
#include "xstdio.h"

int (putchar)(int c)
    {                                   /* put character to stdout */
    return (fputc(c, stdout));
    }                                                                □
```

Figure 12.36:
xfwprep.c

```
/* _Fwprep function */
#include <stdlib.h>
#include "xstdio.h"
#include "yfuns.h"

int _Fwprep(FILE *str)
    {                                   /* prepare stream for writing */
    if (str->_Next < str->_Wend)
        return (0);
    else if (str->_Mode & _MWRITE)
        return (fflush(str));
    else if ((str->_Mode & (_MOPENW|_MREAD)) != _MOPENW)
        {                               /* can't write after read */
        str->_Mode |= _MERR;
        return (-1);
        }
    if (str->_Buf)
        ;
    else if ((str->_Buf = malloc(BUFSIZ)) == NULL)
        {                                        /* use 1-char _Cbuf */
        str->_Buf = &str->_Cbuf;
        str->_Bend = str->_Buf + 1;
        }
    else
        {                                   /* use allocated buffer */
        str->_Mode |= _MALBUF;
        str->_Bend = str->_Buf + BUFSIZ;
        }
    str->_Next = str->_Buf;
    str->_Rend = str->_Buf;
    str->_Wend = str->_Bend;
    str->_Mode |= _MWRITE;
    return (0);
    }                                                                □
```

Figure 12.37:
fflush.c

```c
/* fflush function */
#include "xstdio.h"
#include "yfuns.h"

int (fflush)(FILE *str)
    {                                           /* flush an output stream */
    int n;
    unsigned char *s;

    if (str == NULL)
        {                                       /* recurse on all streams */
        int nf, stat;

        for (stat = 0, nf = 0; nf < FOPEN_MAX; ++nf)
            if (_Files[nf] && fflush(_Files[nf]) < 0)
                stat = EOF;
        return (stat);
        }
    if (!(str->_Mode & _MWRITE))
        return (0);
    for (s = str->_Buf; s < str->_Next; s += n)
        {                                       /* try to write buffer */
        n = _Fwrite(str, s, str->_Next - s);
        if (n <= 0)
            {                                   /* report error and fail */
            str->_Next = str->_Buf;
            str->_Wend = str->_Buf;
            str->_Mode |= _MERR;
            return (EOF);
            }
        }
    str->_Next = str->_Buf;
    str->_Wend = str->_Bend;
    return (0);
    }                                                                      □
```

Figure 12.38:
perror.c

```c
/* perror function */
#include <errno.h>
#include <string.h>
#include "xstdio.h"

void (perror)(const char *s)
    {                                           /* put error string to stderr */
    static char buf[] = {"error #xxx"};

    if (s)
        {                                       /* put user-supplied prefix */
        fputs(s, stderr);
        fputs(": ", stderr);
        }
    fputs(_Strerror(errno, buf), stderr);
    fputc('\n', stderr);
    }                                                                      □
```

```c
/* fwrite function */
#include <string.h>
#include "xstdio.h"

size_t (fwrite)(const void *ptr, size_t size,
    size_t nelem, FILE *str)
    {                                   /* write to stream from array */
    char *s = (char *)ptr;
    size_t ns = size * nelem;

    if (ns == 0)
        return (0);
    while (0 < ns)
        {                               /* ensure room in buffer */
        if (str->_Next < str->_Wend)
            ;
        else if (_Fwprep(str) < 0)
            break;
            {                           /* copy in as many as possible */
        char *s1 = str->_Mode & _MLBF
            ? memchr(s, '\n', ns) : NULL;
        size_t m = s1 ? s1 - s + 1 : ns;
        size_t n = str->_Wend - str->_Next;

        if (n < m)
            s1 = NULL, m = n;
        memcpy(str->_Next, s, m);
        s += m, ns -= m;
        str->_Next += m;
        if (s1 && fflush(str))
            {                           /* disable macros on failure */
            str->_Wend = str->_Buf;
            break;
            }
        }
        }
    if (str->_Mode & _MNBF)
        {                               /* disable and drain */
        str->_Wend = str->_Buf;
        fflush(str);
        }
    return ((size * nelem - ns) / size);
    }
```

Figure 12.40:
fputs.c

```
/* fputs function */
#include <string.h>
#include "xstdio.h"

int (fputs)(const char *s, FILE *str)
    {                                         /* put a string to stream */
    while (*s)
        {                                     /* ensure room in buffer */
        if (str->_Next < str->_Wend)
            ;
        else if (_Fwprep(str) < 0)
            return (EOF);
        {                                     /* copy in as many as possible */
        const char *s1 = str->_Mode & _MLBF
            ? strchr(s, '\n') : NULL;
        size_t m = s1 ? s1 - s + 1 : strlen(s);
        size_t n;

        n = str->_Wend - str->_Next;
        if (n < m)
            s1 = NULL, m = n;
        memcpy(str->_Next, s, m);
        s += m;
        str->_Next += m;
        if (s1 && fflush(str))
            {                                 /* fail on error */
            str->_Wend = str->_Buf;
            return (EOF);
            }
        }
        }
    if (str->_Mode & _MNBF)
        {                                     /* disable macros and drain */
        str->_Wend = str->_Buf;
        if (fflush(str))
            return (EOF);
        }
    return (0);
    }
```

Figure 12.41:
puts.c

```
/* puts function */
#include "xstdio.h"

int (puts)(const char *s)
    {                                         /* put string + newline to stdout */
    return (fputs(s, stdout) < 0
        || fputc('\n', stdout) < 0 ? EOF : 0);
    }
```

Figure 12.42:
fprintf.c

```
/* fprintf function */
#include "xstdio.h"

static void *prout(void *str, const char *buf, size_t n)
    {                                          /* write to file */
    return (fwrite(buf, 1, n, str) == n ? str : NULL);
    }

int (fprintf)(FILE *str, const char *fmt, ...)
    {                                      /* print formatted to stream */
    int ans;
    va_list ap;

    va_start(ap, fmt);
    ans = _Printf(&prout, str, fmt, ap);
    va_end(ap);
    return (ans);
    }                                                              □
```

Figure 12.43:
printf.c

```
/* printf function */
#include "xstdio.h"

static void *prout(void *str, const char *buf, size_t n)
    {                                          /* write to file */
    return (fwrite(buf, 1, n, str) == n ? str : NULL);
    }

int (printf)(const char *fmt, ...)
    {                                      /* print formatted to stdout */
    int ans;
    va_list ap;

    va_start(ap, fmt);
    ans = _Printf(&prout, stdout, fmt, ap);
    va_end(ap);
    return (ans);
    }                                                              □
```

other
print
functions

Figure 12.44 shows the file `sprintf.c`. Here, the generic pointer indicates the next place to store characters in the buffer you specify when you call `sprinf`. Note also that `sprintf` writes a terminating null character if `_Printf` succeeds. Figure 12.45 through Figure 12.47 show the files `vfprintf.c`, `vprintf.c`, and `vsprintf.c`. They are obvious variants of the three more common print functions.

function
_Printf

Figure 12.48 shows the file `xprintf.c`. It defines the function `_Printf` that does all the work. The internal function `_Mbtowc`, declared in `<stdlib.h>`, parses the format as a multibyte string using state memory of type `_Mbstate` that you provide on each call. (See Chapter 13: `<stdlib.h>`.) By calling the underlying function instead of `mbtowc`, `_Printf` avoids changing the internal state of `mbtowc`. The C Standard forbids any such change.

Figure 12.44:
sprintf.c

```
/* sprintf function */
#include <string.h>
#include "xstdio.h"

static void *prout(void *s, const char *buf, size_t n)
    {                                          /* write to string */
    return ((char *)memcpy(s, buf, n) + n);
    }

int (sprintf)(char *s, const char *fmt, ...)
    {                                          /* print formatted to string */
    int ans;
    va_list ap;

    va_start(ap, fmt);
    ans = _Printf(&prout, s, fmt, ap);
    if (0 <= ans)
        s[ans] = '\0';
    va_end(ap);
    return (ans);
    }                                                              □
```

Figure 12.45:
vfprintf.c

```
/* vfprintf function */
#include "xstdio.h"

static void *prout(void *str, const char *buf, size_t n)
    {                                          /* write to file */
    return (fwrite(buf, 1, n, str) == n ? str : NULL);
    }

int (vfprintf)(FILE *str, const char *fmt, char *ap)
    {                 /* print formatted to stream from arg list */
    return (_Printf(&prout, str, fmt, ap));
    }                                                              □
```

Figure 12.46:
vprintf.c

```
/* vprintf function */
#include "xstdio.h"

static void *prout(void *str, const char *buf, size_t n)
    {                                          /* write to file */
    return (fwrite(buf, 1, n, str) == n ? str : NULL);
    }

int (vprintf)(const char *fmt, char *ap)
    {                 /* print formatted to stdout from arg list */
    return (_Printf(&prout, stdout, fmt, ap));
    }                                                              □
```

Figure 12.47:
vsprintf.c

```
/* vsprintf function */
#include <string.h>
#include "xstdio.h"

static void *prout(void *s, const char *buf, size_t n)
    {                                        /* write to string */
    return ((char *)memcpy(s, buf, n) + n);
    }

int (vsprintf)(char *s, const char *fmt, char *ap)
    {                   /* print formatted to string from arg list */
    int ans = _Printf(&prout, s, fmt, ap);

    if (0 <= ans)
        s[ans] = '\0';
    return (ans);
    }                                                               □
```

Testing for the per cent (%) escape character is a delicate matter. The only safe way is to convert the format string to a sequence of wide characters and look for one corresponding to a per cent. You must compare the data object **wc** against the wide-character code for per cent. Unfortunately, some uncertainty surrounds what that value might be. The C Standard requires that each of the characters in the basic C character set have a wide-character code that equals the single-character code. You write the single-character code for per cent as '%'. You write the wide-character equivalent as L'%'. Some question remains, however, whether the C Standard should require such equivalence. It may thus be imprudent to write code that depends on a delicate point of law.

Still another uncertainty exists. An implementation can support multiple encodings for wide characters, at least in principle. A program can change to a locale where wide-character constants don't match the current character set. (Yes!) That may be unwise, but it is not specifically disallowed by the C Standard. Hence, a prudent program might avoid using either '%' or L'%' as the wide-character code for per cent.

The implementor has three choices for the value to compare against **wc**:

- Use '%' for maximum compatibility with older C translators. Rely on the codes being equivalent and not changing with locale.
- Use L'%' for maximum clarity. Rely on the codes not changing with locale.
- Execute the call **mbstowcs(wcs, "%", 1)** on each entry to **_Printf**, with the declaration **size_t wcs[2]**. That stores the current wide-character code for per cent in **wcs[0]**. (**mbstowcs** is declared in **<stdlib.h>**.)

I chose the first course as the wisest given the current state of C translators, the C Standard, and multibyte-character support. Be warned that this area is rapidly evolving, however. A different choice may be more prudent in the near future.

```
/* _Printf function */
#include <ctype.h>
#include <stdlib.h>
#include <string.h>
#include "xstdio.h"

#define MAX_PAD (sizeof (spaces) - 1)
#define PAD(s, n)   if (0 < (n)) {int i, j = (n); \
    for (; 0 < j; j -= i) \
        {i = MAX_PAD < j ? MAX_PAD : j; PUT(s, i); } }
#define PUT(s, n)   \
    if (0 < (n)) {if ((arg = (*pfn)(arg, s, n)) != NULL) \
        x.nchar += (n); else return (x.nchar); }

static char spaces[] = "                              ";
static char zeroes[] = "00000000000000000000000000000000";

int _Printf(void *(*pfn)(void *, const char *, size_t),
    void *arg, const char *fmt, va_list ap)
    {                                        /* print formatted */
    _Pft x;

    for (x.nchar = 0; ; )
        {                                    /* scan format string */
        const char *s = fmt;

          {                                  /* copy any literal text */
          int n;
          wchar_t wc;
          _Mbsave state = {0};

          while (0 < (n = _Mbtowc(&wc, s, MB_CUR_MAX, &state)))
              {                              /* scan for '%' or '\0' */
              s += n;
              if (wc == '%')
                  {                          /* got a conversion specifier */
                  --s;
                  break;
                  }
              }
          PUT(fmt, s - fmt);
          if (n <= 0)
              return (x.nchar);
          fmt = ++s;
          }
          {                                  /* parse a conversion specifier */
          const char *t;
          static const char fchar[] = {" +-#0"};
          static const unsigned int fbit[] = {
              _FSP, _FPL, _FMI, _FNO, _FZE, 0};
```

```
        for (x.flags = 0; (t = strchr(fchar, *s)) != NULL; ++s)
            x.flags |= fbit[t - fchar];
    if (*s == '*')
        {                                       /* get width argument */
        x.width = va_arg(ap, int);
        if (x.width < 0)
            {                                       /* same as '-' flag */
            x.width = -x.width;
            x.flags |= _FMI;
            }
        ++s;
        }
    else                            /* accumulate width digits */
        for (x.width = 0; isdigit(*s); ++s)
            if (x.width < _WMAX)
                x.width = x.width * 10 + *s - '0';
    if (*s != '.')
        x.prec = -1;
    else if (*++s == '*')
        {                                   /* get precision argument */
        x.prec = va_arg(ap, int);
        ++s;
        }
    else                            /* accumulate precision digits */
        for (x.prec = 0; isdigit(*s); ++s)
            if (x.prec < _WMAX)
                x.prec = x.prec * 10 + *s - '0';
    x.qual = strchr("hlL", *s) ? *s++ : '\0';
     }
     {                                          /* do the conversion */
    char ac[32];

    _Putfld(&x, &ap, *s, ac);
    x.width -= x.n0 + x.nz0 + x.n1 + x.nz1 + x.n2 + x.nz2;
    if (!(x.flags & _FMI))
        PAD(spaces, x.width);
    PUT(ac, x.n0);
    PAD(zeroes, x.nz0);
    PUT(x.s, x.n1);
    PAD(zeroes, x.nz1);
    PUT(x.s + x.n1, x.n2);
    PAD(zeroes, x.nz2);
    if (x.flags & _FMI)
        PAD(spaces, x.width);
     }
    fmt = s + 1;
    }
}
```
□

None of the rest of the code in `_Printf` or its subordinates need worry about multibyte characters. Conversion specifiers consist of characters from the basic C character set. Each of these has a one-character encoding. (In principle, a format string may contain redundant shift codes within a conversion specifier. I chose not to support such practices.)

PUT   `_Printf` thus frets about multibyte characters only in literal text between
PAD conversion specifiers. Once it discovers a chunk of literal text, it delivers all such characters up to but not including any per cent character it encounters. Note the use of the macro **PUT**, defined at the top of this C source file, to deliver characters. You cannot package this operation as a function. It needs to return from `_Printf` should the delivery function report an error. No good is served, on the other hand, by writing out such a messy patch of logic repeatedly. For much the same reasons, I also created the macro **PAD** to deliver padding zeros or spaces.

Once `_Printf` trips across a per cent in a format, it sets about parsing the conversion specifier that follows. It translates flags into a set of indicators used throughout `_Printf` and its subordinates. The header `"xstdio.h"` contains the macro definitions:

```
#define _FSP    0x01
#define _FPL    0x02
#define _FMI    0x04
#define _FNO    0x08
#define _FZE    0x10
```

These correspond to the presence of the flags space, +, -, #, and 0, in that order.

macro   The header `"xstdio.h"` defines the macro `_WMAX` as 999. `_Printf` uses this
_WMAX value to limit the size of field width and precision values. It must be big enough to describe the largest conversions that must be supported (at least 509 generated characters) and small enough to prevent a *short* from overflowing (no larger than 32767). I chose 999 to simplify testing in the accumulator loop.

type   `_Printf` packs information about a conversion specifier into a structure
_Pft called `x` of type `_Pft`. Subordinate functions fill in additional information. By the time they have done their work, `_Printf` knows what characters to deliver simply by examining the contents of `x`. The header `"xstdio.h"` contains the type definition:

```
typedef struct {
    union {
        long li;
        long double ld;
        } v;
    char *s;
    int n0, nz0, n1, nz1, n2, nz2, prec, width;
    size_t nchar;
    unsigned int flags;
    char qual;
    } _Pft;
```

Its members are:

- **v** — communicates an integer value (**v.li**) or a floating-point value (**v.ld**) from the function that picks up the argument (**_Putfld**) to the function that converts it to text (**_Litob** or **_Ldtob**)
- **s** — communicates the address of the text buffer to use for the conversion of **v**
- **n0** — counts the number of characters at the start of the text buffer **ac** for **_Printf** to deliver first
- **nz0** — counts the number of zeros to deliver next
- **n1** — counts the number of subsequent characters from **ac** to deliver next
- **nz1** — counts the number of zeros to deliver next
- **n2** — counts the number of subsequent characters from **ac** to deliver next
- **nz2** — counts the number of zeros to deliver next
- **prec** — holds the precision (–1 if none) from the conversion specification
- **width** — holds the field width (0 if none) from the conversion specification
- **nchar** — counts the number of characters delivered so far
- **flags** — holds the encoded flags from the conversion specification
- **qual** — holds the size qualifier (**h**, **l**, **L**) from the conversion specification

All those counters are necessary to minimize demands on the size of the text buffer **ac**. It makes sense that the buffer should be large enough to represent all the meaningful precision in a numeric conversion. You do not want to have to write long sequences of zeros in the buffer, however. Better to count them and generate them with a macro such as **PAD**.

Two examples illustrate the problem. The first is the expression **printf("%015.5f", -1e4)**. It produces the text -00010000.00000. Note the sequences of three, four, and five zeros intermixed with other text. That's not such a bad thing to assemble in a buffer. But what happens when you change the expression to **printf("%0500.200f", -1e37)**? It is a portable expression that any implementation must support. It also produces hundreds of zeros, the smallest sequence having 37 zeros. It needs a *much* bigger buffer.

Rather than wire in any additional limitations on field width or precision, I added complexity to get flexibility. You will find logic that is hard to read in the functions that convert values. The payoff is that the code handles rather perverse demands.

function
_Putfld   Figure 12.49 shows the file **xputfld.c**. It defines the function **_Putfld** that **_Printf** calls to process a conversion specification. The function consists of a large *switch* statement that processes conversion specifiers in groups. **_Putfld** gathers arguments as needed from the variable argument list. It deals directly with the signs of numeric conversions and with any conversions that involve only text. It delegates the actual numeric conversions to one of two subordinate functions.

```
/* _Putfld function */
#include <string.h>
#include "xstdio.h"

        /* macros */
#if _DLONG
#define LDSIGN(x)   \
    (((unsigned short *)&(x))[_D0 ? 4 : 0] & 0x8000)
#else
#define LDSIGN(x)    (((unsigned short *)&(x))[_D0] & 0x8000)
#endif

void _Putfld(_Pft *px, va_list *pap, char code, char *ac)
    {                                    /* convert a field for _Printf */
    px->n0 = px->nz0 = px->n1 = px->nz1 = px->n2 = px->nz2 = 0;
    switch (code)
        {                               /* switch on conversion specifier */
    case 'c':                           /* convert a single character */
        ac[px->n0++] = va_arg(*pap, int);
        break;
    case 'd': case 'i':     /* convert a signed decimal integer */
        px->v.li = px->qual == 'l' ?
            va_arg(*pap, long) : va_arg(*pap, int);
        if (px->qual == 'h')
            px->v.li = (short)px->v.li;
        if (px->v.li < 0)               /* negate safely in _Litob */
            ac[px->n0++] = '-';
        else if (px->flags & _FPL)
            ac[px->n0++] = '+';
        else if (px->flags & _FSP)
            ac[px->n0++] = ' ';
        px->s = &ac[px->n0];
        _Litob(px, code);
        break;
    case 'o': case 'u':
    case 'x': case 'X':                           /* convert unsigned */
        px->v.li = px->qual == 'l' ?
            va_arg(*pap, long) : va_arg(*pap, int);
        if (px->qual == 'h')
            px->v.li = (unsigned short)px->v.li;
        else if (px->qual == '\0')
            px->v.li = (unsigned int)px->v.li;
        if (px->flags & _FNO)
            {                           /* indicate base with prefix */
            ac[px->n0++] = '0';
            if (code == 'x' || code == 'X')
                ac[px->n0++] = code;
            }
        px->s = &ac[px->n0];
        _Litob(px, code);
        break;
    case 'e': case 'E': case 'f':                 /* convert floating */
    case 'g': case 'G':
        px->v.ld = px->qual == 'L' ?
            va_arg(*pap, long double) : va_arg(*pap, double);
```

```
        if (LDSIGN(px->v.ld))
            ac[px->n0++] = '-';
        else if (px->flags & _FPL)
            ac[px->n0++] = '+';
        else if (px->flags & _FSP)
            ac[px->n0++] = ' ';
        px->s = &ac[px->n0];
        _Ldtob(px, code);
        break;
    case 'n':                               /* return output count */
        if (px->qual == 'h')
            *va_arg(*pap, short *) = px->nchar;
        else if (px->qual != 'l')
            *va_arg(*pap, int *) = px->nchar;
        else
            *va_arg(*pap, long *) = px->nchar;
        break;
    case 'p':               /* convert a pointer, hex long version */
        px->v.li = (long)va_arg(*pap, void *);
        px->s = &ac[px->n0];
        _Litob(px, 'x');
        break;
    case 's':                               /* convert a string */
        px->s = va_arg(*pap, char *);
        px->n1 = strlen(px->s);
        if (0 <= px->prec && px->prec < px->n1)
            px->n1 = px->prec;
        break;
    case '%':                               /* put a '%' */
        ac[px->n0++] = '%';
        break;
    default:                /* undefined specifier, print it out */
        ac[px->n0++] = code;
        }
    }
```

_Putfld performs all integer conversions by calling _Litob. Figure 12.50 shows the file xlitob.c that defines the function _Litob. The value it converts, px->v.li, has type *long*. This is a bit risky. A computer architecture is at liberty to report arithmetic overflow if you store in a *long* a value of type *unsigned long* that is larger than LONG_MAX. Thus the expression printf("%x", 0x80000000L) will probably print correctly, but you can't depend on it. The C Standard says that all integer conversions have arguments of signed types. Thus, the risk stems from a genetic weakness in print functions, not from any implementation decisions.

On the positive side, _Putfld and _Litob are moderately cautious. They avoid negating a *long* because that operation can overflow on a two's-complement machine. Instead, _Putfld lets _Litob convert the value to *unsigned long* and negate the new form. That cannot overflow. So long as an arbitrary *unsigned long* can be safely converted to *long* and back again, this implementation works find. That is the case on many machines.

Figure 12.50:
xlitob.c

```c
/* _Litob function */
#include <stdlib.h>
#include <string.h>
#include "xmath.h"
#include "xstdio.h"

static char ldigs[] = "0123456789abcdef";
static char udigs[] = "0123456789ABCDEF";

void _Litob(_Pft *px, char code)
    {                               /* convert unsigned long to text */
    char ac[24];                           /* safe for 64-bit integers */
    char *digs = code == 'X' ? udigs : ldigs;
    int base = code == 'o' ? 8 :
        code != 'x' && code != 'X' ? 10 : 16;
    int i = sizeof (ac);
    unsigned long ulval = px->v.li;

    if ((code == 'd' || code == 'i') && px->v.li < 0)
        ulval = -ulval;                     /* safe against overflow */
    if (ulval || px->prec)
        ac[--i] = digs[ulval % base];
    px->v.li = ulval / base;
    while (0 < px->v.li && 0 < i)
        {                                       /* convert digits */
        ldiv_t qr = ldiv(px->v.li, base);

        px->v.li = qr.quot;
        ac[--i] = digs[qr.rem];
        }
    px->n1 = sizeof (ac) - i;
    memcpy(px->s, &ac[i], px->n1);
    if (px->n1 < px->prec)
        px->nz0 = px->prec - px->n1;
    if (px->prec < 0 && (px->flags & (_FMI|_FZE)) == _FZE
        && 0 < (i = px->width - px->n0 - px->nz0 - px->n1))
        px->nz0 += i;
    }
```

macro
LDSIGN
_Putfld is equally cautious in testing floating-point values. A special code such as NaN or Inf requires delicate handling, lest it generate an exception within _Putfld. Thus, the macro LDSIGN tests the sign bit of a _long double_ using seminumerical methods. It is modeled after the macro DSIGN on page 155.

pointer
to _void_
A more questionable implementation decision concerns the p conversion specifier. The way it prints a _void_ pointer is left implementation-defined in the C Standard. In this implementation, I chose to type cast the pointer to a _long_, then print it as a hexadecimal integer. Pointers and integers are incommensurate, however. There is no guarantee that this decision is either appropriate or safe for a given architecture. You may have to alter the code here to work usefully on some machines.

_Litob itself is reasonably straightforward. It converts one digit using *unsigned long* arithmetic for safety. It then converts any remaining digits using *long* arithmetic for greater speed on many architectures. The function develops digits from right to left in an internal buffer, then copies them into the buffer it inherits from **_Printf**. Note the careful way that the function computes the number of leading zeros. It ensures that there are at least as many as called for by the precision, but more if needed to left fill with zeros.

function   **_Putfld** performs all floating-point conversions by calling **_Ldtob**. Fig-
_Ldtob ure 12.51 shows the file **xldtob.c** that defines the function **_Ldtob**. The value it converts, **px->v.ld**, has type *long double* which is large enough to represent any floating-point value.

_Ldtob stands midway between **<stdio.h>** and **<math.h>**. It includes both **"xstdio.h"** and **"xmath.h"** to obtain all the parameters it needs. It also shares many of the assumptions that permeate this implementation of **<math.h>**. The data object **pows**, for example, contains all representable floating-point values of the form 10^{2^N}. I chose to distinguish three ranges:

- the minimum range, up to 10^{32}
- the IEEE 754 8-byte representation, up to 10^{256}
- the IEEE 754 10-byte representation, up to 10^{4096}

You may have to alter this table to suit other implementations.

_Ldtob uses the function **_Ldunscale**, declared in **"xmath.h"** to test and partition the floating-point value. For a finite value x stored in **px->v.ld**, **_Ldunscale** replaces x with the fraction f, where $|f|$ is in the half-open interval [0.5, 1.0). It stores in **xexp** the exponent e, where $x = f * 2^e$. In this case, **_Ldtob** has no use for f. It uses e only to scale x (now in **ldval**) to a reasonable range.

If **_Ldunscale** reports that x is not-a-number, **_Ldtob** generates **NaN**. If x is infinity, the function generates **Inf**. The C Standard doesn't define what happens with non-a-number or infinity, so generating these sequences is a legitimate extension.

_Ldtob picks off eight (**NDIG**) digits at a time by assigning the *long double* **ldval** to the *long* **lo**. A *long* can represent values at least up to 10^9. It is generally much faster to convert a *long* to eight decimal digits than to convert any of the floating-point types. The function also endeavors to convert only the digits required by the conversion specification.

To achieve these economies of conversion takes some careful setup. Note the bizarre assignment:

```
xexp = xexp * 30103L / 100000L - NDIG/2;
```

That provides an adequate estimate of the prescaling required for **ldval** (x). You want to multiply by the minimum number of elements of **pows**. You must end up with **ldval** strictly less than 10^8. You prefer that the first group of eight digits have at least four nonzero digits. You need to capture the actual scaling factor (in **xexp**) to generate a proper exponent later. This

```
/* _Ldtob function */
#include <float.h>
#include <stdlib.h>
#include <string.h>
#include "xmath.h"
#include "xstdio.h"

        /* macros */
#define NDIG    8

        /* static data */
static const long double pows[] = {
    1e1L, 1e2L, 1e4L, 1e8L, 1e16L, 1e32L,
#if 0x100 < _LBIAS                  /* assume IEEE 754 8- or 10-byte */
    1e64L, 1e128L, 1e256L,
#if _DLONG                             /* assume IEEE 754 10-byte */
    1e512L, 1e1024L, 1e2048L, 1e4096L,
#endif
#endif
    };

void _Ldtob(_Pft *px, char code)
    {                               /* convert long double to text */
    char ac[32];
    char *p = ac;
    long double ldval = px->v.ld;
    short errx, nsig, xexp;

    if (px->prec < 0)
        px->prec = 6;
    else if (px->prec == 0 && (code == 'g' || code == 'G'))
        px->prec = 1;
    if (0 < (errx = _Ldunscale(&xexp, &px->v.ld)))
        {                                       /* x == NaN, x == INF */
        memcpy(px->s, errx == NAN ? "NaN" : "Inf", px->n1 = 3);
        return;
        }
    else if (0 == errx)                            /* x == 0 */
        nsig = 0, xexp = 0;
    else
        {                                   /* 0 < |x|, convert it */
        {                       /* scale ldval to ~~10^(NDIG/2) */
        int i, n;

        if (ldval < 0.0)
            ldval = -ldval;
        if ((xexp = xexp * 30103L / 100000L - NDIG/2) < 0)
            {                                       /* scale up */
            n = (-xexp + (NDIG/2-1)) & ~(NDIG/2-1), xexp = -n;
            for (i = 0; 0 < n; n >>= 1, ++i)
                if (n & 1)
                    ldval *= pows[i];
            }
        else if (0 < xexp)
            {                                       /* scale down */
```

```
            long double factor = 1.0;

        xexp &= ~(NDIG/2-1);
        for (n = xexp, i = 0; 0 < n; n >>= 1, ++i)
            if (n & 1)
                factor *= pows[i];
        ldval /= factor;
        }
    }
    {                                   /* convert significant digits */
    int gen = px->prec
        + (code == 'f' ? xexp + 2+NDIG : 2+NDIG/2);

    if (LDBL_DIG+NDIG/2 < gen)
        gen = LDBL_DIG+NDIG/2;
    for (*p++ = '0'; 0 < gen && 0.0 < ldval; p += NDIG)
        {                               /* convert NDIG at a time */
        int j;
        long lo = (long)ldval;

        if (0 < (gen -= NDIG))
            ldval = (ldval - (long double)lo) * 1e8L;
        for (p += NDIG, j = NDIG; 0 < lo && 0 <= --j; )
            {                           /* convert NDIG digits */
            ldiv_t qr = ldiv(lo, 10);

            *--p = qr.rem + '0', lo = qr.quot;
            }
        while (0 <= --j)
            *--p = '0';
        }
    gen = p - &ac[1];
    for (p = &ac[1], xexp += NDIG-1; *p == '0'; ++p)
        --gen, --xexp;                  /* correct xexp */
    nsig = px->prec + (code == 'f' ? xexp + 1
        : code == 'e' || code == 'E' ? 1 : 0);
    if (gen < nsig)
        nsig = gen;
    if (0 < nsig)
        {                               /* round and strip trailing zeros */
        const char drop
            = nsig < gen && '5' <= p[nsig] ? '9' : '0';
        int n;

        for (n = nsig; p[--n] == drop; )
            --nsig;
        if (drop == '9')
            ++p[n];
        if (n < 0)
            --p, ++nsig, ++xexp;
        }
    }
    }
_Genld(px, code, p, nsig, xexp);
}
```

□

expression begins that process by effectively multiplying *e* by $log_{10}(2)$. It also allows for about four digits to the left of the decimal point. The function then scales `ldval` accordingly.

The next bizarre approximation is the initializer:

```
int gen = px-prec
        + (code == 'f' ? xexp + 2+NDIG : 2+NDIG/2);
```

That gives an adequate estimate of the number of digits to convert. It allows for at least one extra digit to round the result. By contrast, the actual conversion that follows is fairly straightforward. The conversion ends by stripping any trailing zeros and adjusting `gen` and `xexp` accordingly.

The next step is to compute the number of significant digits `nsig` required by the conversion specification. (You can't do this until you have an accurate value for the exponent `xexp`.) The remaining logic then reduces `nsig` to the actual number of significant digits present. If `nsig` is less than `gen`, the function also rounds the result. `_Ldtob` ends by calling the function `_Genld`. That offloads the tedium of altering the converted value to meet the specific needs of various conversion specifiers.

function Figure 12.52 shows the file `xgenld.c` that defines the function `_Genld`. It
_Genld generates the final representation of the various floating-point conversions in the buffer provided by `_Printf`. It does so in one left-to-right pass, copying characters as needed from the buffer in `_Ldtob`. The logic here is tedious and exacting but not tricky. One surprise to note is that `xexp` changes meaning for the `f` conversion specifier. It becomes the count of leading digits, not the exponent to display. Similarly, `px->prec` changes meaning for the `g` conversion specifier. It becomes the count of fraction digits, not the total precision.

That's the end of the code for the print functions. As you can see, converting floating-point values takes considerable effort. It also involves a lot of code. An implementation of Standard C for a very small computer may have little need to print floating-point values. In that case, you can reduce program size considerably by supplying an alternate version of `_Putfld`. Omit the code for the floating-point conversions. That eliminates the need to link in `_Ldtob` and its subordinates. It also often eliminates the need to link many other functions that provide floating-point support.

Be warned, however. Having multiple versions of the same function invariably leads to confusion sooner or later.

formatted Three functions perform formatted input (the scan functions). All call a
input common function `_Scanf` that has the declaration:

```
int _Scanf(void * (*pfn) (void **, int), void *arg,
    const char *fmt, va_list ap);
```

The parameters are:

- `pfn` — a pointer to a function to call to obtain characters
- `arg` — a generic data-object pointer to pass as one of the arguments to the obtaining function

- **fmt** — a pointer to the format string
- **ap** — a pointer to the context information that describes a variable argument list

The obtaining function obtains the next character to scan if its second argument has the value **_WANT**, defined in **"xstdio.h"** as a value distinct from any character code or **EOF**. Otherwise, it treats the second argument as a character to push back. The function returns **EOF** on failure.

fscanf Figure 12.53 shows the file **fscanf.c**. It defines both **fscanf** and the
scanf obtaining function **scin** that it uses. In this case, the generic pointer conveys
sscanf the **FILE** pointer from **fscanf** through **_Scanf** to **scin**. **scin** uses this pointer to read the stream you specify when you call **fscanf**. Figure 12.54 shows the file **scanf.c**. That function is a simple variant of **fscanf**. Figure 12.44 shows the file **sprintf.c**. Here, the generic pointer indicates the next place to obtain characters in the buffer you specify when you call **sscanf**. Unlike the other scan functions, **sscanf** rewrites the generic pointer. That's why the obtaining function needs a pointer to pointer argument.

function Figure 12.56 shows the file **xscanf.c**. It defines the function **_Scanf** that
_Scanf does all the work.

type **_Scanf** packs various bits of information into a structure called **x** of type
_Sft **_Sft**. Subordinate functions fill in additional information. By the time they have done their work for a given conversion specification, **_Scanf** knows how many characters have been scanned and whether the last conversion specifier stored a converted value by examining the contents of **x**. The header **"xstdio.h"** contains the type definition:

```
typedef struct {
    int (*pfn)(void **, int);
    void *arg;
    va_list ap;
    int nchar, nget, width;
    char noconv, qual, stored;
    } _Sft;
```

Its members are:

- **pfn** — points to the obtaining function
- **arg** — holds the generic argument for the obtaining function
- **ap** — holds the context information for the variable argument list
- **nchar** — counts the total number of characters scanned so far
- **nget** — counts the number of characters scanned so far by the macro **GETN** (described below)
- **width** — holds the width (0 if none) from the conversion specification
- **noconv** — holds a nonzero value (`'*'` to suppress storing a converted value
- **qual** — holds the size qualifier (**h, l, L**) from the conversion specification
- **stored** — set to nonzero by a function subordinate to **_Scanf** that stores a converted value

```c
/* _Genld function */
#include <locale.h>
#include <string.h>
#include "xstdio.h"

void _Genld(_Pft *px, char code, char *p, short nsig,
    short xexp)
    {                                       /* generate long double text */
    const char point = localeconv()->decimal_point[0];

    if (nsig <= 0)
        nsig = 1, p = "0";
    if (code == 'f' || (code == 'g' || code == 'G')
        && -4 <= xexp && xexp < px->prec)
        {                                       /* 'f' format */
        ++xexp;                 /* change to leading digit count */
        if (code != 'f')
            {                                   /* fixup for 'g' */
            if (!(px->flags & _FNO) && nsig < px->prec)
                px->prec = nsig;
            if ((px->prec -= xexp) < 0)
                px->prec = 0;
            }
        if (xexp <= 0)
            {                       /* digits only to right of point */
            px->s[px->n1++] = '0';
            if (0 < px->prec || px->flags & _FNO)
                px->s[px->n1++] = point;
            if (px->prec < -xexp)
                xexp = -px->prec;
            px->nz1 = -xexp;
            px->prec += xexp;
            if (px->prec < nsig)
                nsig = px->prec;
            memcpy(&px->s[px->n1], p, px->n2 = nsig);
            px->nz2 = px->prec - nsig;
            }
        else if (nsig < xexp)
            {                                   /* zeros before point */
            memcpy(&px->s[px->n1], p, nsig);
            px->n1 += nsig;
            px->nz1 = xexp - nsig;
            if (0 < px->prec || px->flags & _FNO)
                px->s[px->n1] = point, ++px->n2;
            px->nz2 = px->prec;
            }
        else
            {                       /* enough digits before point */
            memcpy(&px->s[px->n1], p, xexp);
            px->n1 += xexp;
            nsig -= xexp;
            if (0 < px->prec || px->flags & _FNO)
                px->s[px->n1++] = point;
            if (px->prec < nsig)
                nsig = px->prec;
```

```
                        memcpy(&px->s[px->n1], p + xexp, nsig);
                        px->n1 += nsig;
                        px->nz1 = px->prec - nsig;
                        }
                }
        else
                {                                       /* 'e' format */
            if (code == 'g' || code == 'G')
                {                                       /* fixup for 'g' */
                if (nsig < px->prec)
                    px->prec = nsig;
                if (--px->prec < 0)
                    px->prec = 0;
                code = code == 'g' ? 'e' : 'E';
                }
            px->s[px->n1++] = *p++;
            if (0 < px->prec || px->flags & _FNO)
                px->s[px->n1++] = point;
            if (0 < px->prec)
                {                                       /* put fraction digits */
                if (px->prec < --nsig)
                    nsig = px->prec;
                memcpy(&px->s[px->n1], p, nsig);
                px->n1 += nsig;
                px->nz1 = px->prec - nsig;
                }
            p = &px->s[px->n1];                         /* put exponent */
            *p++ = code;
            if (0 <= xexp)
                *p++ = '+';
            else
                {                                       /* negative exponent */
                *p++ = '-';
                xexp = -xexp;
                }
            if (100 <= xexp)
                {                                       /* put oversize exponent */
                if (1000 <= xexp)
                    *p++ = xexp / 1000 + '0', xexp %= 1000;
                *p++ = xexp / 100 + '0', xexp %= 100;
                }
            *p++ = xexp / 10 + '0', xexp %= 10;
            *p++ = xexp + '0';
            px->n2 = p - &px->s[px->n1];
            }
    if ((px->flags & (_FMI|_FZE)) == _FZE)
        {                                               /* pad with leading zeros */
        int n = px->n0 + px->n1 + px->nz1 + px->n2 + px->nz2;

        if (n < px->width)
            px->nz0 = px->width - n;
        }
    }
```

The internal function **_Mbtowc**, declared in **<stdlib.h>**, parses the format as a multibyte string using state memory of type **_Mbstate** that you provide on each call. The issues are the same as for **_Printf**, described on page 303. Note, however, that **_Scanf** must distinguish white-space as well as per cent characters. It assumes that any wide-character code that can be stored in an *unsigned char* can be tested properly by **isspace**. That is certainly true in the current C Standard. It would be messy to change for an environment where '\t' is not necessarily equal to L'\t'.

_Scanf, like **_Printf**, also frets about multibyte characters only in literal text between conversion specifiers. Once it discovers a chunk of literal text, it attempts to match all such characters up to but not including any per cent character it encounters. It has a funny way of matching white-space. And it matches multibyte characters only if the scanned text has exactly the same shift sequences as the literal text in the format. Both of those peculiarities can limit the utility of the scan functions, but both are also genetic. That's the way the C Standard specifies the scan functions.

GET   Note the use of the macro **GET** to obtain a character and **UNGET** to put back
UNGET the first unwanted character. Both are defined in **"xstdio.h"**, because functions subordinate to **_Scanf** must obtain characters the same way. The macros are defined as:

```
#define GET(px) (++(px)->nchar, (*px)->pfn)((px)->arg, _WANT))
#define UNGET(px, ch) \
    (--(px)->nchar, (*(px)->pfn)((px)->arg, ch))
```

You can package these operations as functions. I defined them as macros primarily to improve performance.

Figure 12.53:
fscanf.c

```
/* fscanf function */
#include "xstdio.h"

static int scin(void **str, int ch)
    {                                       /* get or put a character */
    if (ch == _WANT)
        return (fgetc((FILE *)str));
    else if (0 <= ch)
        return (ungetc(ch, (FILE *)str));
    else
        return (ch);
    }

int (fscanf)(FILE *str, const char *fmt, ...)
    {                                       /* read formatted from stream */
    int ans;
    va_list ap;

    va_start(ap, fmt);
    ans = _Scanf(&scin, str, fmt, ap);
    va_end(ap);
    return (ans);
    }
```

```
/* scanf function */
#include "xstdio.h"

static int scin(void **str, int ch)
    {                                    /* get or put a character */
    if (ch == _WANT)
        return (fgetc((FILE *)str));
    else if (0 <= ch)
        return (ungetc(ch, (FILE *)str));
    else
        return (ch);
    }

int (scanf)(const char *fmt, ...)
    {                                    /* read formatted from stdin */
    int ans;
    va_list ap;

    va_start(ap, fmt);
    ans = _Scanf(&scin, stdin, fmt, ap);
    va_end(ap);
    return (ans);
    }                                                              □
```

```
/* sscanf function */
#include "xstdio.h"

static int scin(void **str, int ch)
    {                                    /* get or put a character */
    char *s = *(char **)str;

    if (ch == _WANT)
        if (*s == '\0')
            return (EOF);
        else
            {                            /* deliver a character */
            *str = s + 1;
            return (*s);
            }
    else if (0 <= ch)
        *str = s - 1;
    return (ch);
    }

int (sscanf)(const char *buf, const char *fmt, ...)
    {                                    /* read formatted from string */
    int ans;
    va_list ap;

    va_start(ap, fmt);
    ans = _Scanf(&scin, (void **)&buf, fmt, ap);
    va_end(ap);
    return (ans);
    }                                                              □
```

Figure 12.56:
xscanf.c
Part 1

```
/* _Scanf function */
#include <ctype.h>
#include <limits.h>
#include <stdlib.h>
#include <string.h>
#include "xstdio.h"

int _Scanf(int (*pfn)(void **, int), void *arg,
    const char *fmt, va_list ap)
    {                                          /* read formatted */
    const char *s;
    int nconv = 0;
    _Sft x;

    x.pfn = pfn;
    x.arg = arg;
    x.ap = ap;
    x.nchar = 0;
    for (s = fmt; ; ++s)
        {                                      /* parse format string */
        int ch;

         {                          /* match any literal or white-space */
        int n;
        wchar_t wc;
        _Mbsave state = {0};

        while (0 < (n = _Mbtowc(&wc, s, MB_CUR_MAX, &state)))
            {                          /* check type of multibyte char */
            s += n;
            if (wc == '%')
                break;
            else if (wc <= UCHAR_MAX && isspace(wc))
                {                          /* match any white-space */
                while (isspace(*s))
                    ++s;
                while (isspace(ch = GET(&x)))
                    ;
                UNGET(&x, ch);
                }
            else                           /* match literal text */
                for (s -= n; 0 <= --n; )
                    if ((ch = GET(&x)) != *s++)
                        {                          /* bad match */
                        UNGET(&x, ch);
                        return (nconv);
                        }
            }
        if (*s == '\0')
            return (nconv);
        }
         {                          /* process a conversion specifier */
```

Continuing
xscanf.c
Part 2

```
        x.noconv = *s == '*' ? *s++ : '\0';
        for (x.width = 0; isdigit(*s); ++s)
            if (x.width < _WMAX)
                x.width = x.width * 10 + *s - '0';
        x.qual = strchr("hlL", *s) ? *s++ : '\0';
        if (!strchr("cn[", *s))
            {                           /* match leading white-space */
            while (isspace(ch = GET(&x)))
                ;
            UNGET(&x, ch);
            }
        if ((s = _Getfld(&x, s)) == NULL)
            return (0 < nconv ? nconv : EOF);
        if (x.stored)
            ++nconv;
        }
    }
}
```

GETN   The header `"xstdio.h"` defines two additional macros closely related to
UNGETN these. You can store a character count in `x.nget` to define the maximum
width of a field you wish to scan. Use the macro GETN instead of GET, and
UNGETN instead of UNGET. Once the field is exhausted, GETN yields the special
code `_WANT`. That simplifies logic in several places. The macros are defined
as:

```
#define GETN(px)       (0 <= --(px)->nget ? GET(px) : _WANT)
#define UNGET(px, ch)   {if (ch) != _WANT) UNGET(px, ch); }
```

header   That's the last major contribution to the header `"xstdio.h"`. Figure 12.57
`"xstdio.h"` shows the file `xstdio.h`. It should be reasonably devoid of surprises by this
point. I present it here simply for completeness.

      Once `_Scanf` trips across a per cent in a format, it sets about parsing the
conversion specifierconversion;specifier that follows. That is a fairly easy
task, since scan conversion specifiers have few options. For all but a few
conversion specifiers, `_Scanf` also skips leading white-space.

function   Figure 12.58 shows the file `xgetfld.c`. It defines the function `_Getfld` that
`_Getfld` `_Scanf` calls to process a conversion specification. The function consists of
a large *switch* statement that processes conversion specifiers in groups.
`_Getfld` gathers arguments as needed from the variable argument list.
(Subordinate functions also gather arguments as needed.) It deals directly
with any conversions that involve only text.

function   `_Getfld` performs all integer conversions by calling `_Getint`. Figure 12.59
`_Getint` shows the file `xgetint.c` that defines the function `_Getint`. It gathers the
characters that match the appropriate pattern for an integer, then calls
either `strtol` or `strtoul`, both declared in `<stdlib.h>`, to convert the field.
The header `"xstdio.h"` defines the macro FMAX as 512. That exceeds slightly
the requirements of the C Standard for the longest field that the scan
functions must convert.

Figure 12.57:
xstdio.h
Part 1

```
/* xstdio.h internal header */
#include <stdarg.h>
#include <stdio.h>
        /* bits for _Mode in FILE */
#define _MOPENR 0x1
#define _MOPENW 0x2
#define _MOPENA 0x4
#define _MTRUNC 0x8
#define _MCREAT 0x10
#define _MBIN   0x20
#define _MALBUF 0x40
#define _MALFIL 0x80
#define _MEOF   0x100
#define _MERR   0x200
#define _MLBF   0x400
#define _MNBF   0x800
#define _MREAD  0x1000
#define _MWRITE 0x2000
        /* codes for _Printf and _Scanf */
#define _FSP    0x01
#define _FPL    0x02
#define _FMI    0x04
#define _FNO    0x08
#define _FZE    0x10
#define _WMAX   999
#define _WANT   (EOF-1)
        /* macros for _Scanf */
#define FMAX    512                     /* widest supported field */
#define GET(px) (++(px)->nchar, (*(px)->pfn)((px)->arg, _WANT))
#define GETN(px)    (0 <= --(px)->nget ? GET(px) : _WANT)
#define UNGET(px, ch) \
    (--(px)->nchar, (*(px)->pfn)((px)->arg, ch))
#define UNGETN(px, ch) {if ((ch) != _WANT) UNGET(px, ch); }
        /* type definitions */
typedef struct {
    union {
        long li;
        long double ld;
        } v;
    char *s;
    int n0, nz0, n1, nz1, n2, nz2, prec, width;
    size_t nchar;
    unsigned int flags;
    char qual;
    } _Pft;
typedef struct {
    int (*pfn)(void **, int);
    void *arg;
    va_list ap;
    int nchar, nget, width;
    char noconv, qual, stored;
    } _Sft;
```

Continuing
xstdio.h
Part 2

```
        /* declarations */
FILE *_Foprep(const char *, const char *, FILE *);
int _Fopen(const char *, unsigned int, const char *);
int _Frprep(FILE *);
int _Ftmpnam(char *, int);
int _Fwprep(FILE *);
void _Genld(_Pft *, char, char *, short, short);
const char *_Getfld(_Sft *, const char *);
int _Getfloat(_Sft *);
int _Getint(_Sft *, char);
void _Ldtob(_Pft *, char);
void _Litob(_Pft *, char);
int _Printf(void *(*)(void *, const char *, size_t),
    void *, const char *, va_list);
void _Putfld(_Pft *, va_list *, char, char *);
int _Scanf(int (*)(void **, int),
    void *, const char *, va_list);
```

**pointer
to *void*** The p conversion specifier is the mirror image of the same conversion specifier in the print functions. The way to scan a *void* pointer is, of course, also left implementation-defined in the C Standard. In this implementation, I chose to convert the field as an *unsigned long*, then store it as a pointer to *void*. I repeat for emphasis — there is no guarantee that this decision is either appropriate or safe for a given architecture. You may have to alter the code here to work usefully on some machines.

**function
_Getfloat** _Getfld performs all floating-point conversions by calling _Getfloat. Figure 12.60 shows the file **xgetfloa.c** that defines the function _Getfloat. It gathers the characters that match the appropriate pattern for a floating-point value, then calls **strtod**, declared in **<stdlib.h>**, to convert the field. Note that even a stored value of type *long double* gets converted by **strtod**. That can limit the range of values you can convert properly if *long double* has greater precision or range than *double*. That's all the C Standard requires, however. It is arguably an acceptable extension to write a "string to long double" function (with a secret name, of course) and use it instead. I chose not to undertake the additional work here.

That's the end of the code for the scan functions. As with the print functions, converting floating-point values takes considerable effort. The scan functions also involve a lot of code. An implementation of Standard C for a very small computer probably has less need to scan floating-point values than to print them. If you need the scan functions but don't need floating-point support, you can reduce program size considerably by supplying an alternate version of _Getfld. The same considerations apply as for the print functions, discussed on page 314.

```c
/* _Getfld function */
#include <ctype.h>
#include <limits.h>
#include <string.h>
#include "xstdio.h"

const char *_Getfld(_Sft *px, const char *s)
    {                                      /* convert a field */
    int ch;
    char *p;

    px->stored = 0;
    switch (*s)
        {                          /* switch on conversion specifier */
    case 'c':                               /* convert an array of chars */
        if (px->width == 0)
            px->width = 1;
        p = va_arg(px->ap, char *);
        for (; 0 < px->width; --px->width)
            if ((ch = GET(px)) < 0)
                return (NULL);
            else if (!px->noconv)
                *p++ = ch, px->stored = 1;
        break;
    case 'p':                                    /* convert a pointer */
    case 'd': case 'i': case 'o':
    case 'u': case 'x': case 'X':
        if (_Getint(px, *s))                 /* convert an integer */
            return (NULL);
        break;
    case 'e': case 'E': case 'f':
    case 'g': case 'G':
        if (_Getfloat(px))                   /* convert a floating */
            return (NULL);
        break;
    case 'n':                                /* return output count */
        if (px->qual == 'h')
            *va_arg(px->ap, short *) = px->nchar;
        else if (px->qual != 'l')
            *va_arg(px->ap, int *) = px->nchar;
        else
            *va_arg(px->ap, long *) = px->nchar;
        break;
    case 's':                                    /* convert a string */
        px->nget = px->width <= 0 ? INT_MAX : px->width;
        p = va_arg(px->ap, char *);
        while (0 <= (ch = GETN(px)))
            if (isspace(ch))
                break;
            else if (!px->noconv)
                *p++ = ch;
        UNGETN(px, ch);
        if (!px->noconv)
            *p++ = '\0', px->stored = 1;
        break;
```

<table>
<tr><td>

</td><td>

```
      case '%':                                      /* match a '%' */
          if ((ch = GET(px)) == '%')
              break;
          UNGET(px, ch);
          return (NULL);
      case '[':
          {                                      /* convert a scan set */
          char comp = *++s == '^' ? *s++ : '\0';
          const char *t = strchr(*s == ']' ? s + 1 : s, ']');
          size_t n = t - s;

          if (t == NULL)
              return (NULL);                        /* undefined */
          px->nget = px->width <= 0 ? INT_MAX : px->width;
          p = va_arg(px->ap, char *);
          while (0 <= (ch = GETN(px)))
              if (!comp && !memchr(s, ch, n)
                  || comp && memchr(s, ch, n))
                  break;
              else if (!px->noconv)
                  *p++ = ch;
          UNGETN(px, ch);
          if (!px->noconv)
              *p++ = '\0', px->stored = 1;
          s = t;
          }
          break;
      default:                                /* undefined specifier, quit */
          return (NULL);
          }
      return (s);
      }
```

□

</td></tr>
</table>

Testing `<stdio.h>`

The header `<stdio.h>` declares too many functions to test all at once (given the limitation on C source file size in this book, at least). I chose to exercise the print and scan functions in one test program. The second program tests only the all the low-level functions.

program Figure 12.61 shows the file `tstdio1.c`. It checks that print and scan
tstdio1.c conversions are exact where that is appropriate and reasonably precise where exactness cannot be guaranteed. As a courtesy, it displays the values of several macros. And it exercises the functions `vfprintf`, `vprintf`, and `vsprintf` in the process of piecing together the final output line. For this implementation, the program displays output something like:

```
BUFSIZ = 512
L_tmpnam = 16
FILENAME_MAX = 64
FOPEN_MAX = 16
TMP_MAX = 32
SUCCESS testing <stdio.h>, part 1
```

```
/* _Getint function */
#include <stdlib.h>
#include <string.h>
#include "xstdio.h"

int _Getint(_Sft *px, char code)
    {                               /* get an integer value for _Scanf */
    char ac[FMAX+1], *p;
    char seendig = 0;
    int ch;
    static const char digits[]
        = "0123456789abcdefABCDEF";
    static const char flit[] = "diouxXp";
    static const char bases[] = {10, 0, 8, 10, 16, 16, 16};
    int base = bases[(const char *)strchr(flit, code) - flit];
    int dlen;

    px->nget = px->width <= 0
        || FMAX < px->width ? FMAX : px->width;
    p = ac, ch = GETN(px);
    if (ch == '+' || ch == '-')
        *p++ = ch, ch = GETN(px);
    if (ch == '0')
        {                               /* match possible prefix */
        seendig = 1;
        *p++ = ch, ch = GETN(px);
        if ((ch == 'x' || ch == 'X')
            && (base == 0 || base == 16))
            base = 16, *p++ = ch, ch = GETN(px);
        else
            base = 8;
        }
    dlen = base == 0 || base == 10 ? 10 : base == 8 ? 8 : 16+6;
    for (; memchr(digits, ch, dlen); seendig = 1)
        *p++ = ch, ch = GETN(px);
    UNGETN(px, ch);
    if (!seendig)
        return (-1);
    *p = '\0';
    if (px->noconv)
        ;
    else if (code == 'd' || code == 'i')
        {                               /* deliver a signed integer */
        long lval = strtol(ac, NULL, base);

        px->stored = 1;
        if (px->qual == 'h')
            *va_arg(px->ap, short *) = lval;
        else if (px->qual != 'l')
            *va_arg(px->ap, int *) = lval;
        else
            *va_arg(px->ap, long *) = lval;
        }
```

Continuing
xgetint.c
Part 2

```
else
    {                               /* deliver an unsigned integer */
    unsigned long ulval = strtoul(ac, NULL, base);

    px->stored = 1;
    if (code == 'p')
        *va_arg(px->ap, void **) = (void *)ulval;
    else if (px->qual == 'h')
        *va_arg(px->ap, unsigned short *) = ulval;
    else if (px->qual != 'l')
        *va_arg(px->ap, unsigned int *) = ulval;
    else
        *va_arg(px->ap, unsigned long *) = ulval;
    }
return (0);
}                                                                        □
```

and terminates successfully.

program   Figure 12.62 shows the file `tstdio2.h`. It checks the properties of the
tstdio2.c macros defined in this header, then exercises the various functions in
simple ways. The one informative display is from a call to **perror**. (You can't
avoid some output in testing this function — may as well make the most
of it.) If the program executes successfully, it pieces together the output:

```
Domain error reported as: domain error
SUCCESS testing <stdio.h>, part 2
```

References

Brian W. Kernighan and P.J. Plauger, *Software Tools* (Reading, Mass.:
Addison-Wesley, 1975). Also by the same authors, *Software Tools in Pascal*
(Reading, Mass.: Addison-Wesley, 1978). Both of these books illustrate how
to impose the UNIX I/O model upon a variety of operating systems by
implementing a small number of primitive interface functions.

William D. Clinger, "How to Read Floating-Point Numbers Accurately,"
*Proceedings of the ACM SIGPLAN '90 Conference on Programming Language
Design and Implementation* (New York: Association for Computing Machinery, 1990, pp. 92-101). This article discusses the difficulties of converting a
text string to floating-point representation if your goal is to maintain full
precision.

Guy L. Steele, Jr. and Jon L. White, "How to Print Floating-Point Numbers Accurately," *Proceedings of the ACM SIGPLAN '90 Conference on Programming Language Design and Implementation* (New York: Association for
Computing Machinery, 1990, pp. 112-126). This article is an interesting
companion to the one above, from the same conference proceedings.

Figure 12.60:
xgetfloa.c

```c
/* _Getfloat function */
#include <ctype.h>
#include <locale.h>
#include <stdlib.h>
#include <string.h>
#include "xstdio.h"

int _Getfloat(_Sft *px)
    {                               /* get a floating point value for _scanf */
    char *p;
    int ch;
    char ac[FMAX+1];
    char seendig = 0;

    px->nget = px->width <= 0
        || FMAX < px->width ? FMAX : px->width;
    p = ac, ch = GETN(px);
    if (ch == '+' || ch == '-')
        *p++ = ch, ch = GETN(px);
    for (; isdigit(ch); seendig = 1)
        *p++ = ch, ch = GETN(px);
    if (ch == localeconv()->decimal_point[0])
        *p++ = ch, ch = GETN(px);
    for (; isdigit(ch); seendig = 1)
        *p++ = ch, ch = GETN(px);
    if ((ch == 'e' || ch == 'E') && seendig)
        {                                           /* parse exponent */
        *p++ = ch, ch = GETN(px);
        if (ch == '+' || ch == '-')
            *p++ = ch, ch = GETN(px);
        for (seendig = 0; isdigit(ch); seendig = 1)
            *p++ = ch, ch = GETN(px);
        }
    UNGETN(px, ch);
    if (!seendig)
        return (-1);
    *p = '\0';
    if (!px->noconv)
        {                                           /* convert and store */
        double dval = strtod(ac, NULL);

        px->stored = 1;
        if (px->qual == 'l')
            *va_arg(px->ap, double *) = dval;
        else if (px->qual != 'L')
            *va_arg(px->ap, float *) = dval;
        else
            *va_arg(px->ap, long double *) = dval;
        }
    return (0);
    }
```

Exercises

Exercise 12.1 How does the operating system you use represent text files? Do you have to make any changes to match the internal represent of a text stream in Standard C?

Exercise 12.2 Write the functions `fprintf`, `printf`, and `sprintf` in terms of calls to `vfprintf` and `vsprintf`.

Exercise 12.3 Write a version of `rename` that copies a file if it cannot simply rename it. Delete the original file *only* after a successful copy.

Exercise 12.4 Write a version of `remove` that simply renames the file to be removed. Place the file in an out-of-the-way directory, or give it a name not likely to conflict with common naming conventions for files. Why would you want this version?

Exercise 12.5 Write a version of `tmpnam` that checks for conflicts with existing names. (Try to open an existing file with that file name for reading.) The function keeps generating new file names until it cannot open the corresponding file. Why would you want this version? What happens if two programs executing in parallel call this function at the same time?

The C Standard says, "The implementation shall behave as if no library function calls the tmpnam function. (See page 236.) What do you have to do to satisfy this requirement?

Exercise 12.6 Implement the primitives `_Fclose`, `_Fopen`, `_Fread`, and `_Fwrite` for the operating system you use. Do you have to write any assembly language?

Exercise 12.7 [**Harder**] Implement the functions `_Fgetpos` and `_Fsetpos` for an operating system that terminates each text line with a carriage return plus line feed.

Exercise 12.8 [**Harder**] Write a function that converts a text string to *long double* by the same rules that `strtod` uses for *double*. (See page 362.)

Exercise 12.9 [**Very hard**] Redesign the scan functions so they are more widely usable. Devise a way to communicate scan failures to the calling program so that it can:

- spot the failure more precisely
- try an alternate conversion
- recover gracefully from a read error

Figure 12.61:
tstdio1.c
Part 1

```
/* test stdio functions, part 1 */
#include <assert.h>
#include <errno.h>
#include <float.h>
#include <math.h>
#include <stdarg.h>
#include <stdio.h>
#include <string.h>

static void vfp(const char *fmt, ...)
    {                                          /* test vfprintf */
    va_list ap;

    va_start(ap, fmt);
    vfprintf(stdout, fmt, ap);
    va_end(ap);
    }

static void vp(const char *fmt, ...)
    {                                          /* test vprintf */
    va_list ap;

    va_start(ap, fmt);
    vprintf(fmt, ap);
    va_end(ap);
    }

static void vsp(char *s, const char *fmt, ...)
    {                                          /* test vsprintf */
    va_list ap;

    va_start(ap, fmt);
    vsprintf(s, fmt, ap);
    va_end(ap);
    }

int main()
    {                      /* test basic workings of stdio functions */
    char buf[32], ch;
    double db;
    float fl;
    int in;
    long lo;
    long double ld;
    short sh;
    void *pv;

    assert(sprintf(buf, "%2c|%-4d|%.4o|%#lX",
        'a', -4, 8, 12L) == 16);
    assert(strcmp(buf, " a|-4  |0010|0XC") == 0);
    assert(sscanf(buf, " %c|%hd |%i|%lx",
        &ch, &sh, &in, &lo) == 4);
    assert(ch == 'a' && sh == -4 && in == 8 && lo == 12);
    assert(sprintf(buf, "%E|%.2f|%Lg",
        1.1e20, -3.346, .02L) == 23);
```

```
assert(strcmp(buf, "1.100000E+20|-3.35|0.02") == 0);
assert(sscanf(buf, "%e|%lg|%Lf", &fl, &db, &ld) == 3);
assert(fabs(fl - 1.1e20) / 1.1e20 < 4 * FLT_EPSILON);
assert(fabs(db + 3.35) / 3.35 < 4 * DBL_EPSILON);
assert(fabs(ld - 0.02) / 0.02 < 4 * LDBL_EPSILON);
assert(4 <= sprintf(buf, "|%%%n %p",
    &in, (void *)&ch) && in == 2);
assert(sscanf(buf, "|%%%n %p", &in, &pv) == 1 && in == 2);
  {                                         /* test formatted I/O */
char buf[10];
const char *tn = tmpnam(NULL);
FILE *pf;
fpos_t fp1, fp2;
int in1, in2;
long off;

assert(tn != NULL && (pf = fopen(tn, "w+")) != NULL);
setbuf(pf, NULL);
assert(fprintf(pf, "123\n") == 4);
assert((off = ftell(pf)) != -1);
assert(fprintf(pf, "456\n") == 4);
assert(fgetpos(pf, &fp1) == 0);
assert(fprintf(pf, "789\n") == 4);
rewind(pf);
assert(fscanf(pf, "%i", &in1) == 1 && in1 == 123);
assert(fsetpos(pf, &fp1) == 0);
assert(fscanf(pf, "%i", &in1) == 1 && in1 == 789);
assert(fseek(pf, off, SEEK_SET) == 0);
assert(fscanf(pf, "%i", &in1) == 1 && in1 == 456);
assert(fclose(pf) == 0
    && freopen(tn, "r", stdin) == stdin);
assert(setvbuf(stdin, buf, _IOLBF, sizeof (buf)) == 0);
assert(scanf("%i", &in1) == 1 && in1 == 123);
assert(fclose(stdin) == 0);
assert((pf = fopen(tn, "w+b")) != NULL);
  }
printf("BUFSIZ = %u\n", BUFSIZ);
printf("L_tmpnam = %u\n", L_tmpnam);
printf("FILENAME_MAX = %u\n", FILENAME_MAX);
printf("FOPEN_MAX = %u\n", FOPEN_MAX);
printf("TMP_MAX = %u\n", TMP_MAX);
vsp(buf, "SUC%c%s", 'C', "ESS");
vfp("%s testing %s", buf, "<stdio.h>");
vp(", part 1\n");
return (0);
  }
```

Figure 12.62:
tstdio2.c

```
/* test stdio functions, part 2 */
#include <assert.h>
#include <errno.h>
#include <stdio.h>
#include <string.h>

int main()
    {                        /* test basic workings of stdio functions */
    char buf[32], tname[L_tmpnam], *tn;
    FILE *pf;
    static int macs[] = {
        _IOFBF, _IOLBF, _IONBF, BUFSIZ, EOF, FILENAME_MAX,
        FOPEN_MAX, TMP_MAX, SEEK_CUR, SEEK_END, SEEK_SET};

    assert(256 <= BUFSIZ && EOF < 0);
    assert(8 <= FOPEN_MAX && 25 <= TMP_MAX);
    assert(tmpnam(tname) == tname && strlen(tname) < L_tmpnam);
    assert((tn = tmpnam(NULL)) != NULL
        && strcmp(tn, tname) != 0);
    pf = fopen(tname, "w");
    assert(pf != NULL
        && pf != stdin && pf != stdout && pf != stderr);
    assert(feof(pf) == 0 && ferror(pf) == 0);
    assert(fgetc(pf) == EOF
        && feof(pf) == 0 && ferror(pf) != 0);
    clearerr(pf);
    assert(ferror(pf) == 0);
    assert(fputc('a', pf) == 'a' && putc('b', pf) == 'b');
    assert(0 <= fputs("cde\n", pf));
    assert(0 <= fputs("fghij\n", pf));
    assert(fflush(pf) == 0);
    assert(fwrite("klmnopq\n", 2, 4, pf) == 4);
    assert(fclose(pf) == 0);
    assert(freopen(tname, "r", stdin) == stdin);
    assert(fgetc(stdin) == 'a' && getc(stdin) == 'b');
    assert(getchar() == 'c');
    assert(fgets(buf, sizeof (buf), stdin) == buf
        && strcmp(buf, "de\n") == 0);
    assert(ungetc('x', stdin) == 'x');
    assert(gets(buf) == buf && strcmp(buf, "xfghij") == 0);
    assert(fread(buf, 2, 4, stdin) == 4
        && strncmp(buf, "klmnopq\n", 8) == 0);
    assert(getchar() == EOF && feof(stdin) != 0);
    remove(tn);
    assert(rename(tname, tn) == 0
        && fopen(tname, "r") == NULL);
    assert((pf = fopen(tn, "r")) != NULL && fclose(pf) == 0);
    assert(remove(tn) == 0 && fopen(tn, "r") == NULL);
    assert((pf = tmpfile()) != NULL && fputc('x', pf) == 'x');
    errno = EDOM;
    perror("Domain error reported as");
    putchar('S'), puts("UCCESS testing <stdio.h>, part 2");
    return (0);
    }
```

Chapter 13: `<stdlib.h>`

Background

The header `<stdlib.h>` is a hodgepodge. Committee X3J11 invented this header as a place to define macros and declare functions that had no other sensible home:

- Many existing functions, such as `abs` and `malloc`, had no traditional headers to declare them. X3J11 felt strongly that *every* functions should be declared in a standard header. If such a function seemed out of place in all other headers, it ended up declared in `<stdlib.h>`.

- New groups of macros and functions ended up in new standard headers wherever possible. `<float.h>` and `<locale.h>` are clear examples. Additions to existing groups ended up in existing headers. `strcoll`, declared in `<string.h>` and `strftime`, declared in `<time.h>` are also fairly clear. Other macros and functions are harder to categorize. These ended up defined or declared in `<stdlib.h>`.

This header is not the only hodgepodge. I discuss the evolution of the header `<stddef.h>` on page 215.

function groups
To provide some structure for this chapter, I organize the functions into six groups:

- integer math (`abs`, `div`, `labs`, and `ldiv`) — performing simple integer arithmetic
- algorithms (`bsearch`, `qsort`, `rand`, and `srand`) — capturing operations complex and widespread enough to warrant packaging as library functions
- text conversions (`atof`, `atoi`, `atol`, `strtod`, `strtol`, and `strtoul`) — determining encoded arithmetic values from text representations
- multibyte conversions (`mblen`, `mbstowcs`, `mbtowc`, `wcstombs`, and `wctomb`) — mapping between multibyte and wide-character encodings
- storage allocation (`calloc`, `free`, `malloc`, and `realloc`) — managing a heap of data objects
- environmental interactions (`abort`, `atexit`, `exit`, `getenv`, and `system`) — interfacing between the program and the execution environment

I discuss separately how to implement the functions in each of these groups.

What the C Standard Says

7.10 General utilities `<stdlib.h>`

The header **`<stdlib.h>`** declares four types and several functions of general utility, and defines several macros.[126]

The types declared are **`size_t`** and **`wchar_t`** (both described in 7.1.6),

> `div_t`

which is a structure type that is the type of the value returned by the **`div`** function, and

> `ldiv_t`

which is a structure type that is the type of the value returned by the **`ldiv`** function.

The macros defined are **`NULL`** (described in 7.1.6);

> `EXIT_FAILURE`

and

> `EXIT_SUCCESS`

which expand to integral expressions that may be used as the argument to the **`exit`** function to return unsuccessful or successful termination status, respectively, to the host environment;

> `RAND_MAX`

which expands to an integral constant expression, the value of which is the maximum value returned by the **`rand`** function; and

> `MB_CUR_MAX`

which expands to a positive integer expression whose value is the maximum number of bytes in a multibyte character for the extended character set specified by the current locale (category **`LC_CTYPE`**), and whose value is never greater than **`MB_LEN_MAX`**.

7.10.1 String conversion functions

The functions **`atof`**, **`atoi`**, and **`atol`** need not affect the value of the integer expression **`errno`** on an error. If the value of the result cannot be represented, the behavior is undefined.

7.10.1.1 The `atof` function

Synopsis

```
#include <stdlib.h>
double atof(const char *nptr);
```

Description

The **`atof`** function converts the initial portion of the string pointed to by **`nptr`** to **`double`** representation. Except for the behavior on error, it is equivalent to

```
strtod(nptr, (char **)NULL)
```

Returns

The **`atof`** function returns the converted value.

Forward references: the **`strtod`** function (7.10.1.4).

7.10.1.2 The `atoi` function

Synopsis

```
#include <stdlib.h>
int atoi(const char *nptr);
```

Description

The **`atoi`** function converts the initial portion of the string pointed to by **`nptr`** to **`int`** representation. Except for the behavior on error, it is equivalent to

```
(int)strtol(nptr, (char **)NULL, 10)
```

Returns

The **`atoi`** function returns the converted value.

Forward references: the **`strtol`** function (7.10.1.5).

7.10.1.3 The **atol** function

Synopsis

```
#include <stdlib.h>
long int atol(const char *nptr);
```

Description

The **atol** function converts the initial portion of the string pointed to by **nptr** to **long int** representation. Except for the behavior on error, it is equivalent to

```
strtol(nptr, (char **)NULL, 10)
```

Returns

The **atol** function returns the converted value.

Forward references: the **strtol** function (7.10.1.5).

7.10.1.4 The **strtod** function

Synopsis

```
#include <stdlib.h>
double strtod(const char *nptr, char **endptr);
```

Description

The **strtod** function converts the initial portion of the string pointed to by **nptr** to **double** representation. First, it decomposes the input string into three parts: an initial, possibly empty, sequence of white-space characters (as specified by the **isspace** function), a subject sequence resembling a floating-point constant; and a final string of one or more unrecognized characters, including the terminating null character of the input string. Then, it attempts to convert the subject sequence to a floating-point number, and returns the result.

The expected form of the subject sequence is an optional plus or minus sign, then a nonempty sequence of digits optionally containing a decimal-point character, then an optional exponent part as defined in 6.1.3.1, but no floating suffix. The subject sequence is defined as the longest initial subsequence of the input string, starting with the first non–white-space character, that is of the expected form. The subject sequence contains no characters if the input string is empty or consists entirely of white space, or if the first non–white-space character is other than a sign, a digit, or a decimal-point character.

If the subject sequence has the expected form, the sequence of characters starting with the first digit or the decimal-point character (whichever occurs first) is interpreted as a floating constant according to the rules of 6.1.3.1, except that the decimal-point character is used in place of a period, and that if neither an exponent part nor a decimal-point character appears, a decimal point is assumed to follow the last digit in the string. If the subject sequence begins with a minus sign, the value resulting from the conversion is negated. A pointer to the final string is stored in the object pointed to by **endptr**, provided that **endptr** is not a null pointer.

In other than the **"C"** locale, additional implementation-defined subject sequence forms may be accepted.

If the subject sequence is empty or does not have the expected form, no conversion is performed; the value of **nptr** is stored in the object pointed to by **endptr**, provided that **endptr** is not a null pointer.

Returns

The **strtod** function returns the converted value, if any. If no conversion could be performed, zero is returned. If the correct value is outside the range of representable values, plus or minus **HUGE_VAL** is returned (according to the sign of the value), and the value of the macro **ERANGE** is stored in **errno**. If the correct value would cause underflow, zero is returned and the value of the macro **ERANGE** is stored in **errno**.

7.10.1.5 The **strtol** function

Synopsis

```
#include <stdlib.h>
long int strtol(const char *nptr, char **endptr, int base);
```

Description

The **strtol** function converts the initial portion of the string pointed to by **nptr** to **long int** representation. First, it decomposes the input string into three parts: an initial, possibly empty, sequence of white-space characters (as specified by the **isspace** function), a subject sequence resembling an integer represented in some radix determined by the value of **base**, and a final string of one or more unrecognized characters, including the terminating null character of the input string. Then, it attempts to convert the subject sequence to an integer, and returns the result.

If the value of **base** is zero, the expected form of the subject sequence is that of an integer constant as described in 6.1.3.2, optionally preceded by a plus or minus sign, but not including an integer suffix. If the value of **base** is between 2 and 36, the expected form of the subject sequence is a sequence of letters and digits representing an integer with the radix specified by **base**, optionally preceded by a plus or minus sign, but not including an integer suffix. The letters from **a** (or **A**) through **z** (or **Z**) are ascribed the values 10 to 35; only letters whose ascribed values are less than that of **base** are permitted. If the value of **base** is 16, the characters **0x** or **0X** may optionally precede the sequence of letters and digits, following the sign if present.

The subject sequence is defined as the longest initial subsequence of the input string, starting with the first non–white-space character, that is of the expected form. The subject sequence contains no characters if the input string is empty or consists entirely of white space, or if the first non-white-space character is other than a sign or a permissible letter or digit.

If the subject sequence has the expected form and the value of **base** is zero, the sequence of characters starting with the first digit is interpreted as an integer constant according to the rules of 6.1.3.2. If the subject sequence has the expected form and the value of **base** is between 2 and 36, it is used as the base for conversion, ascribing to each letter its value as given above. If the subject sequence begins with a minus sign, the value resulting from the conversion is negated. A pointer to the final string is stored in the object pointed to by **endptr**, provided that **endptr** is not a null pointer.

In other than the **"C"** locale, additional implementation-defined subject sequence forms may be accepted.

If the subject sequence is empty or does not have the expected form, no conversion is performed; the value of **nptr** is stored in the object pointed to by **endptr**, provided that **endptr** is not a null pointer.

Returns

The **strtol** function returns the converted value, if any. If no conversion could be performed, zero is returned. If the correct value is outside the range of representable values, **LONG_MAX** or **LONG_MIN** is returned (according to the sign of the value), and the value of the macro **ERANGE** is stored in **errno**.

strtoul

7.10.1.6 The **strtoul** function

Synopsis

```
#include <stdlib.h>
unsigned long int strtoul(const char *nptr, char **endptr, int base);
```

Description

The **strtoul** function converts the initial portion of the string pointed to by **nptr** to **unsigned long int** representation. First, it decomposes the input string into three parts: an initial, possibly empty, sequence of white-space characters (as specified by the **isspace** function), a subject sequence resembling an unsigned integer represented in some radix determined by the value of **base**, and a final string of one or more unrecognized characters, including the terminating null character of the input string. Then, it attempts to convert the subject sequence to an unsigned integer, and returns the result.

If the value of **base** is zero, the expected form of the subject sequence is that of an integer constant as described in 6.1.3.2, optionally preceded by a plus or minus sign, but not including an integer suffix. If the value of **base** is between 2 and 36, the expected form of the subject sequence is a sequence of letters and digits representing an integer with the radix specified by **base**, optionally preceded by a plus or minus sign, but not including an integer suffix. The letters from **a** (or **A**) through **z** (or **Z**) are ascribed the values 10 to 35; only letters whose ascribed values are less than that of **base** are permitted. If the value of **base** is 16, the characters **0x** or **0X** may optionally precede the sequence of letters and digits, following the sign if present.

The subject sequence is defined as the longest initial subsequence of the input string, starting with the first non–white-space character, that is of the expected form. The subject sequence contains no characters if the input string is empty or consists entirely of white space, or if the first non–white-space character is other than a sign or a permissible letter or digit.

If the subject sequence has the expected form and the value of **base** is zero, the sequence of characters starting with the first digit is interpreted as an integer constant according to the rules of 6.1.3.2. If the subject sequence has the expected form and the value of **base** is between 2 and 36, it is used as the base for conversion, ascribing to each letter its value as given above.

If the subject sequence begins with a minus sign, the value resulting from the conversion is negated. A pointer to the final string is stored in the object pointed to by **endptr**, provided that **endptr** is not a null pointer.

In other than the **"C"** locale, additional implementation-defined subject sequence forms may be accepted.

If the subject sequence is empty or does not have the expected form, no conversion is performed; the value of **nptr** is stored in the object pointed to by **endptr**, provided that **endptr** is not a null pointer.

Returns

The **strtoul** function returns the converted value, if any. If no conversion could be performed, zero is returned. If the correct value is outside the range of representable values, **ULONG_MAX** is returned, and the value of the macro **ERANGE** is stored in **errno**.

7.10.2 Pseudo-random sequence generation functions

7.10.2.1 The rand function

Synopsis

```
#include <stdlib.h>
int rand(void);
```

Description

The **rand** function computes a sequence of pseudo-random integers in the range 0 to **RAND_MAX**.

The implementation shall behave as if no library function calls the **rand** function.

Returns

The **rand** function returns a pseudo-random integer.

Environmental limit

The value of the **RAND_MAX** macro shall be at least 32767.

7.10.2.2 The srand function

Synopsis

```
#include <stdlib.h>
void srand(unsigned int seed);
```

Description

The **srand** function uses the argument as a seed for a new sequence of pseudo-random numbers to be returned by subsequent calls to **rand**. If **srand** is then called with the same seed value, the sequence of pseudo-random numbers shall be repeated. If **rand** is called before any calls to **srand** have been made, the same sequence shall be generated as when **srand** is first called with a seed value of 1.

The implementation shall behave as if no library function calls the **srand** function.

Returns

The **srand** function returns no value.

Example

The following functions define a portable implementation of **rand** and **srand**.

```
static unsigned long int next = 1;

int rand(void)    /* RAND_MAX assumed to be 32767 */
{
        next = next * 1103515245 + 12345;
        return (unsigned int)(next/65536) % 32768;
}

void srand(unsigned int seed)
{
        next = seed;
}
```

7.10.3 Memory management functions

The order and contiguity of storage allocated by successive calls to the **calloc**, **malloc**, and **realloc** functions is unspecified. The pointer returned if the allocation succeeds is suitably aligned so that it may be assigned to a pointer to any type of object and then used to access such an object or an array of such objects in the space allocated (until the space is explicitly freed or reallocated). Each such allocation shall yield a pointer to an object disjoint from any other object. The pointer returned points to the start (lowest byte address) of the allocated space. If the space cannot be allocated, a null pointer is returned. If the size of the space requested is zero, the behavior is implementation-defined; the value returned shall be either a null pointer or a unique pointer. The value of a pointer that refers to freed space is indeterminate.

calloc

7.10.3.1 The **calloc** function

Synopsis

```
#include <stdlib.h>
void *calloc(size_t nmemb, size_t size);
```

Description

The **calloc** function allocates space for an array of **nmemb** objects, each of whose size is **size**. The space is initialized to all bits zero.[127]

Returns

The **calloc** function returns either a null pointer or a pointer to the allocated space.

free

7.10.3.2 The **free** function

Synopsis

```
#include <stdlib.h>
void free(void *ptr);
```

Description

The **free** function causes the space pointed to by **ptr** to be deallocated, that is, made available for further allocation. If **ptr** is a null pointer, no action occurs. Otherwise, if the argument does not match a pointer earlier returned by the **calloc**, **malloc**, or **realloc** function, or if the space has been deallocated by a call to **free** or **realloc**, the behavior is undefined.

Returns

The **free** function returns no value.

malloc

7.10.3.3 The **malloc** function

Synopsis

```
#include <stdlib.h>
void *malloc(size_t size);
```

Description

The **malloc** function allocates space for an object whose size is specified by **size** and whose value is indeterminate.

Returns

The **malloc** function returns either a null pointer or a pointer to the allocated space.

realloc

7.10.3.4 The **realloc** function

Synopsis

```
#include <stdlib.h>
void *realloc(void *ptr, size_t size);
```

Description

The **realloc** function changes the size of the object pointed to by **ptr** to the size specified by **size**. The contents of the object shall be unchanged up to the lesser of the new and old sizes. If the new size is larger, the value of the newly allocated portion of the object is indeterminate. If **ptr** is a null pointer, the **realloc** function behaves like the **malloc** function for the specified size. Otherwise, if **ptr** does not match a pointer earlier returned by the **calloc**, **malloc**, or **realloc** function, or if the space has been deallocated by a call to the **free** or **realloc** function, the behavior is undefined. If the space cannot be allocated, the object pointed to by **ptr** is unchanged. If **size** is zero and **ptr** is not a null pointer, the object it points to is freed.

Returns

The `realloc` function returns either a null pointer or a pointer to the possibly moved allocated space.

7.10.4 Communication with the environment

7.10.4.1 The `abort` function

Synopsis

```
#include <stdlib.h>
void abort(void);
```

Description

The **abort** function causes abnormal program termination to occur, unless the signal **SIGABRT** is being caught and the signal handler does not return. Whether open output streams are flushed or open streams closed or temporary files removed is implementation-defined. An implementation-defined form of the status *unsuccessful termination* is returned to the host environment by means of the function call **raise(SIGABRT)**.

Returns

The **abort** function cannot return to its caller.

7.10.4.2 The `atexit` function

Synopsis

```
#include <stdlib.h>
int atexit(void (*func)(void));
```

Description

The **atexit** function registers the function pointed to by **func**, to be called without arguments at normal program termination.

Implementation limits

The implementation shall support the registration of at least 32 functions.

Returns

The **atexit** function returns zero if the registration succeeds, nonzero if it fails.

Forward references: the **exit** function (7.10.4.3).

7.10.4.3 The `exit` function

Synopsis

```
#include <stdlib.h>
void exit(int status);
```

Description

The **exit** function causes normal program termination to occur. If more than one call to the **exit** function is executed by a program, the behavior is undefined.

First, all functions registered by the **atexit** function are called, in the reverse order of their registration.[128]

Next, all open streams with unwritten buffered data are flushed, all open streams are closed, and all files created by the **tmpfile** function are removed.

Finally, control is returned to the host environment. If the value of **status** is zero or **EXIT_SUCCESS**, an implementation-defined form of the status *successful termination* is returned. If the value of **status** is **EXIT_FAILURE**, an implementation-defined form of the status *unsuccessful termination* is returned. Otherwise the status returned is implementation-defined.

Returns

The **exit** function cannot return to its caller.

7.10.4.4 The `getenv` function

Synopsis

```
#include <stdlib.h>
char *getenv(const char *name);
```

Description

The **getenv** function searches an *environment list,* provided by the host environment, for a string that matches the string pointed to by **name**. The set of environment names and the method for altering the environment list are implementation-defined.

The implementation shall behave as if no library function calls the **getenv** function.

Returns

The **getenv** function returns a pointer to a string associated with the matched list member. The string pointed to shall not be modified by the program, but may be overwritten by a subsequent call to the **getenv** function. If the specified **name** cannot be found, a null pointer is returned.

system ### 7.10.4.5 The **system** function

Synopsis

```
#include <stdlib.h>
int system(const char *string);
```

Description

The **system** function passes the string pointed to by **string** to the host environment to be executed by a *command processor* in an implementation-defined manner. A null pointer may be used for **string** to inquire whether a command processor exists.

Returns

If the argument is a null pointer, the **system** function returns nonzero only if a command processor is available. If the argument is not a null pointer, the **system** function returns an implementation-defined value.

7.10.5 Searching and sorting utilities

bsearch ### 7.10.5.1 The **bsearch** function

Synopsis

```
#include <stdlib.h>
void *bsearch(const void *key, const void *base, size_t nmemb,
     size_t size, int (*compar)(const void *, const void *));
```

Description

The **bsearch** function searches an array of **nmemb** objects, the initial element of which is pointed to by **base**, for an element that matches the object pointed to by **key**. The size of each element of the array is specified by **size**.

The comparison function pointed to by **compar** is called with two arguments that point to the **key** object and to an array element, in that order. The function shall return an integer less than, equal to, or greater than zero if the **key** object is considered, respectively, to be less than, to match, or to be greater than the array element. The array shall consist of: all the elements that compare less than, all the elements that compare equal to, and all the elements that compare greater than the **key** object, in that order.[129]

Returns

The **bsearch** function returns a pointer to a matching element of the array, or a null pointer if no match is found. If two elements compare as equal, which element is matched is unspecified.

qsort ### 7.10.5.2 The **qsort** function

Synopsis

```
#include <stdlib.h>
void qsort(void *base, size_t nmemb, size_t size,
     int (*compar)(const void *, const void *));
```

Description

The **qsort** function sorts an array of **nmemb** objects, the initial element of which is pointed to by **base**. The size of each object is specified by **size**.

The contents of the array are sorted into ascending order according to a comparison function pointed to by **compar**, which is called with two arguments that point to the objects being compared. The function shall return an integer less than, equal to, or greater than zero if the first argument is considered to be respectively less than, equal to, or greater than the second.

If two elements compare as equal, their order in the sorted array is unspecified.

Returns

The **qsort** function returns no value.

7.10.6 Integer arithmetic functions

7.10.6.1 The **abs** function

abs

Synopsis

```
#include <stdlib.h>
int abs(int j);
```

Description

The **abs** function computes the absolute value of an integer **j**. If the result cannot be represented, the behavior is undefined.[130]

Returns

The **abs** function returns the absolute value.

7.10.6.2 The **div** function

div

Synopsis

```
#include <stdlib.h>
div_t div(int numer, int denom);
```

Description

The **div** function computes the quotient and remainder of the division of the numerator **numer** by the denominator **denom**. If the division is inexact, the resulting quotient is the integer of lesser magnitude that is the nearest to the algebraic quotient. If the result cannot be represented, the behavior is undefined; otherwise, **quot * denom + rem** shall equal **numer**.

Returns

The **div** function returns a structure of type **div_t**, comprising both the quotient and the remainder. The structure shall contain the following members, in either order:

```
int quot;    /* quotient */
int rem;     /* remainder */
```

7.10.6.3 The **labs** function

labs

Synopsis

```
#include <stdlib.h>
long int labs(long int j);
```

Description

The **labs** function is similar to the **abs** function, except that the argument and the returned value each have type **long int**.

7.10.6.4 The **ldiv** function

ldiv

Synopsis

```
#include <stdlib.h>
ldiv_t ldiv(long int numer, long int denom);
```

Description

The **ldiv** function is similar to the **div** function, except that the arguments and the members of the returned structure (which has type **ldiv_t**) all have type **long int**.

7.10.7 Multibyte character functions

The behavior of the multibyte character functions is affected by the **LC_CTYPE** category of the current locale. For a state-dependent encoding, each function is placed into its initial state by a call for which its character pointer argument, **s**, is a null pointer. Subsequent calls with **s** as other than a null pointer cause the internal state of the function to be altered as necessary. A call with **s** as a null pointer causes these functions to return a nonzero value if encodings have state dependency, and zero otherwise.[131] Changing the **LC_CTYPE** category causes the shift state of these functions to be indeterminate.

7.10.7.1 The `mblen` function

Synopsis

```
#include <stdlib.h>
int mblen(const char *s, size_t n);
```

Description

If **s** is not a null pointer, the **mblen** function determines the number of bytes contained in the multibyte character pointed to by **s**. Except that the shift state of the **mbtowc** function is not affected, it is equivalent to

```
mbtowc((wchar_t *)0, s, n);
```

The implementation shall behave as if no library function calls the **mblen** function.

Returns

If **s** is a null pointer, the **mblen** function returns a nonzero or zero value, if multibyte character encodings, respectively, do or do not have state-dependent encodings. If **s** is not a null pointer, the **mblen** function either returns 0 (if **s** points to the null character), or returns the number of bytes that are contained in the multibyte character (if the next **n** or fewer bytes form a valid multibyte character), or returns –1 (if they do not form a valid multibyte character).

Forward references: the **mbtowc** function (7.10.7.2).

7.10.7.2 The `mbtowc` function

Synopsis

```
#include <stdlib.h>
int mbtowc(wchar_t *pwc, const char *s, size_t n);
```

Description

If **s** is not a null pointer, the **mbtowc** function determines the number of bytes that are contained in the multibyte character pointed to by **s**. It then determines the code for the value of type **wchar_t** that corresponds to that multibyte character. (The value of the code corresponding to the null character is zero.) If the multibyte character is valid and **pwc** is not a null pointer, the **mbtowc** function stores the code in the object pointed to by **pwc**. At most **n** bytes of the array pointed to by **s** will be examined.

The implementation shall behave as if no library function calls the **mbtowc** function.

Returns

If **s** is a null pointer, the **mbtowc** function returns a nonzero or zero value, if multibyte character encodings, respectively, do or do not have state-dependent encodings. If **s** is not a null pointer, the **mbtowc** function either returns 0 (if **s** points to the null character), or returns the number of bytes that are contained in the converted multibyte character (if the next **n** or fewer bytes form a valid multibyte character), or returns –1 (if they do not form a valid multibyte character).

In no case will the value returned be greater than **n** or the value of the **MB_CUR_MAX** macro.

7.10.7.3 The `wctomb` function

Synopsis

```
#include <stdlib.h>
int wctomb(char *s, wchar_t wchar);
```

Description

The **wctomb** function determines the number of bytes needed to represent the multibyte character corresponding to the code whose value is **wchar** (including any change in shift state). It stores the multibyte character representation in the array object pointed to by **s** (if **s** is not a null pointer). At most **MB_CUR_MAX** characters are stored. If the value of **wchar** is zero, the **wctomb** function is left in the initial shift state.

The implementation shall behave as if no library function calls the **wctomb** function.

Returns

If **s** is a null pointer, the **wctomb** function returns a nonzero or zero value, if multibyte character encodings, respectively, do or do not have state-dependent encodings. If **s** is not a null pointer, the **wctomb** function returns –1 if the value of **wchar** does not correspond to a valid multibyte character, or returns the number of bytes that are contained in the multibyte character corresponding to the value of **wchar**.

In no case will the value returned be greater than the value of the **MB_CUR_MAX** macro.

7.10.8 Multibyte string functions

The behavior of the multibyte string functions is affected by the **LC_CTYPE** category of the current locale.

7.10.8.1 The **mbstowcs** function

Synopsis

```
#include <stdlib.h>
size_t mbstowcs(wchar_t *pwcs, const char *s, size_t n);
```

Description

The **mbstowcs** function converts a sequence of multibyte characters that begins in the initial shift state from the array pointed to by **s** into a sequence of corresponding codes and stores not more than **n** codes into the array pointed to by **pwcs**. No multibyte characters that follow a null character (which is converted into a code with value zero) will be examined or converted. Each multibyte character is converted as if by a call to the **mbtowc** function, except that the shift state of the **mbtowc** function is not affected.

No more than **n** elements will be modified in the array pointed to by **pwcs**. If copying takes place between objects that overlap, the behavior is undefined.

Returns

If an invalid multibyte character is encountered, the **mbstowcs** function returns **(size_t) -1**. Otherwise, the **mbstowcs** function returns the number of array elements modified, not including a terminating zero code, if any.[132]

7.10.8.2 The **wcstombs** function

Synopsis

```
#include <stdlib.h>
size_t wcstombs(char *s, const wchar_t *pwcs, size_t n);
```

Description

The **wcstombs** function converts a sequence of codes that correspond to multibyte characters from the array pointed to by **pwcs** into a sequence of multibyte characters that begins in the initial shift state and stores these multibyte characters into the array pointed to by **s**, stopping if a multibyte character would exceed the limit of **n** total bytes or if a null character is stored. Each code is converted as if by a call to the **wctomb** function, except that the shift state of the **wctomb** function is not affected.

No more than **n** bytes will be modified in the array pointed to by **s**. If copying takes place between objects that overlap, the behavior is undefined.

Returns

If a code is encountered that does not correspond to a valid multibyte character, the **wcstombs** function returns **(size_t) -1**. Otherwise, the **wcstombs** function returns the number of bytes modified, not including a terminating null character, if any.[132]

Footnotes

126. See "future library directions" (7.13.7).

127. Note that this need not be the same as the representation of floating-point zero or a null pointer constant.

128. Each function is called as many times as it was registered.

129. In practice, the entire array is sorted according to the comparison function.

130. The absolute value of the most negative number cannot be represented in two's complement.

131. If the implementation employs special bytes to change the shift state, these bytes do not produce separate wide character codes, but are grouped with an adjacent multibyte character.

132. The array will not be null- or zero-terminated if the value returned is **n**.

Using <stdlib.h>

Many of the functions declared in <stdlib.h> stand alone. You use **atexit** in conjunction with **exit**, perhaps, and **srand** in conjunction with **rand**. Still, you can use and understand most of these functions in isolation. In this crowd of individuals, two groups stand out:

- The storage allocation functions work together to manage a heap.
- The multibyte functions work together to convert among different representations for large character sets.

Each of these groups warrants some discussion.

The data objects in a Standard C program occupy three kinds of storage:

storage
allocation
functions

- The program allocates *static storage* and stores initial values in it prior to program startup. If you specify no initial value for (part or all of) a data object, the program initializes each of its scalar components to zero. Such a data object continues in existence until program termination.
- The program allocates *dynamic storage* upon each entry to a block. If you specify no initial value for a data object, its initial content is indeterminate. Such a data object continues in existence until execution of the block terminates.
- The program allocates *allocated storage* only when you call one of the functions **calloc**, **malloc**, or **realloc**. It initializes such a data object to an array of zero characters only if you call **calloc**. Otherwise, its initial content is indeterminate. Such a data object continues in existence until you call **free** with its address as the argument or else until program termination.

The functions that manipulate allocated storage are the storage allocation functions declared in <stdlib.h>.

the
heap

Static storage remains stable during program execution. Dynamic storage follows a last-in/first-out discipline. It can be implemented on a stack. Often, dynamic storage shares the call stack with function call and return information. (See the discussion beginning on page 182.) Allocated storage follows no such tidy discipline. The program can intermix the allocation and freeing of such data objects in arbitrary order. Hence, the Standard C library must maintain a separate pool of storage called a *heap* to satisfy requests for controlled storage.

In some implementations, the call stack and the heap contend for a limited amount of storage. Allocate enough storage with **malloc** and you may limit the depth to which you can call functions later in the program. Or you may simply run out of space on the heap. In any event, it is simply good hygiene to allocate only what storage you need and to free it as soon as you're done with it.

heap
overhead

Be aware that static storage involves certain overheads. Accompanying each allocated data object is enough information for **free** to determine the size of the region being freed. Allocate 1,000 one-character data objects and you can easily consume four to eight times as much storage on the heap. The heap is also subject to fragmentation. Allocating and freeing data objects on the heap in arbitrary order inevitably leaves unusable holes between some of the allocated data objects. That too lowers the usable size of the heap.

Don't overreact to this knowledge. Gather related data into a structure and allocate it all at once. That minimizes heap overhead, to be sure, but it is also good programming style. *Do not* gather unrelated data just to save heap overhead. Similarly, allocate data objects with similar lifetimes all at once, then free them at about the same time. That minimizes heap fragmentation, but it too is good style. *Do not* advance or defer unrelated heap operations just to minimize fragmentation. The storage allocation functions are an important aid to programming flexibility. Use them as they are intended to be used.

multibyte character sets The other group of related functions helps you manipulate large character sets. Standard C added this group in response to the rapidly growing use of Kanji and other large character sets in computer-based products. The functions support two representations for such character sets:

- Multibyte characters are sequences of one or more codes, where each code can be represented in a C character data type. (The character data types are *char, signed char*, and *unsigned char.* All are the same size in a given implementation. That size is at least eight bits.) A subset of any multibyte encoding is the basic C character set, each character of which is a sequence of length one.

- Wide characters are integers of type `wchar_t`, defined in both `<stddef.h>` and `<stdlib.h>`. (Assume that `wchar_t` can be any integer type from *char* to *unsigned long*.) Such an integer can represent distinct codes for each of the characters in the large character set. The codes for the basic C character set have the same values as their single-character forms.

Multibyte characters are convenient for communicating between the program and the outside world. Magnetic storage and communications links have evolved to support sequences of eight-bit characters. Wide characters are convenient for manipulating text within a program. Their fixed size simplifies handling both individual characters and arrays of characters.

The C Standard defines only the bare minimum needed to support these two encodings. `mblen`, `mbstowcs`, and `mbtowc` help you translate from multibyte characters to wide-characters. `wcstombs` and `wctomb` help you do the reverse. You can be sure that more elaborate sets of functions will soon be standardized. For now, however, this is what you have.

You may have no immediate intention to write programs that are fluent with large character sets. That should not deter you from writing programs that are *tolerant* of large character sets as much as possible. See, for example, how such characters can appear in the formats used by the print and scan functions, declared in `<stdio.h>`, and by `strftime`, declared in `<time.h>`.

I conclude with the usual description of the individual macros defined and functions declared in `<stdlib.h>`:

EXIT_FAILURE   **EXIT_FAILURE** — Use this macro as the argument to `exit` or the return value from `main` to report unsuccessful program termination. Any other nonzero value you use instead may have different meanings for different operating systems.

EXIT_SUCCESS   **EXIT_SUCCESS** — Use this macro as the argument to `exit` or the return value from `main` to report successful program termination. You can also use zero. Any other value you use may have different meanings for different operating systems.

MB_CUR_MAX   **MB_CUR_MAX** — No multibyte sequence that defines a single wide character will be longer than **MB_CUR_MAX** in the current locale. You can declare a character buffer of size **MB_LEN_MAX**, defined in `<limits.h>`, then safely store **MB_CUR_MAX** characters in the initial elements of the buffer. Calling `mbtowc` with a third argument of at least **MB_CUR_MAX** is always sufficient for the function to determine the next wide character in a valid multibyte sequence. See the example for `wctomb` on page 352

RAND_MAX   **RAND_MAX** — Use this value to scale values returned from `rand`. For example, if you want random numbers of type `float` distributed over the interval [0.0, 1.0], write the expression `(float)rand()/RAND_MAX`. The value of **RAND_MAX** is at least 32,767.

size_t   **size_t** — See page 219.

wchar_t   **wchar_t** — See page 219.

div_t   **div_t** — Declare a data object of this type to store the value returned by `div`, described below.

ldiv_t   **ldiv_t** — Declare a data object of this type to store the value returned by `ldiv`, described below.

abort   **abort** — Call this function only when things go terribly wrong. It effectively calls `raise(SIGABRT)`, as described in Chapter 13: `<signal.h>`. That gives a signal handler for **SIGABRT** the opportunity to perform any last-minute operations. On the other hand, you can't be assured that input/output streams are flushed, files closed properly, or temporary files removed. Whenever possible, call `exit(EXIT_FAILURE)` instead.

abs   **abs** — Call `abs(x)` instead of writing the idiom `x < 0 ? -x : x`. A growing number of Standard C translators generate inline code for `abs` that is smaller and faster than the idiom. In addition, you avoid the occasional surprise when you inadvertently evaluate twice an expression with side effects. Note that on a two's-complement machine, `abs` can generate an overflow. (See page 77.)

atexit   **atexit** — Use this function to register another function to be called when the program is about to terminate. You may, for example, create a set of temporary files that you wish to remove before the program terminates. Write the function `void tidy(void)` to remove the files. Call `atexit(&tidy)` once you store the name of the first file to remove. When `main` returns or a function calls **exit**, the library calls all functions registered with **atexit** in reverse order of registry. The library flushes streams, closes files, and removes temporary files only after it calls all registered functions. You can register up to 32 functions with **atexit**.

atof   **atof** — The call **atof(s)** is equivalent to **strtod(s, NULL)**, except that **atof** is not obliged to store **ERANGE** in **errno** to report a range error. (See Chapter 13: **<errno.h>**.) You also get no indication with **atof** of how many characters from the string pointed to by **s** participate in the conversion. Use **strtod** instead.

atoi   **atoi** — Replace **atoi(s)** with **(int)strtol(s, NULL, 10)**. Then consider altering the second argument so that you can determine how many characters participated in the conversion. See the discussion of **atof** above for the reasons why.

atol   **atol** — Replace **atol(s)** with **strtol(s, NULL, 10)**. See the discussions of **atof** and **atoi** above for the reasons why.

bsearch   **bsearch** — Use this function to search any array whose elements are ordered by pairwise comparisons. You define the ordering with a comparison function that you provide. For example, you can build a keyword lookup function from the basic form:

```
#include <stdlib.h>
#include <string.h>

typedef enum {FLOAT, INTEGER} Code;
typedef struct {
    char *s;
    Code code;
    } Entry;
Entry symtab[] = {
    {"float", FLOAT},
    {"integer", INTEGER}}

static int cmp(const void *ck, const void *ce)
    {   /* compare key to table element */
    return (strcmp((char *)ck, ((Entry *)ce)-s));
    }

Entry *lookup(char *key)
    {   /* lookup key in table */
    return (bsearch(key, symtab,
        sizeof symtab / sizeof symtab[0],
        sizeof symtab[0], &cmp));
    }
```

A few caveats:

- If a key compares equal to two or more elements, **bsearch** can return a pointer to any of these elements.
- Beware of changes in how elements sort when the execution character set changes — call **qsort**, described below, with a compatible comparison function to ensure that an array is properly ordered.

- Be careful using the functions `strcmp` or `strcoll`, declared in `<string.h>`, directly. Both require that strings be stored in the array to be searched. You cannot use them to search an array of pointers to strings. To use `strcmp`, for example, you must write a function pointer argument that looks like `(int (*)(const void *, const void *))&strcmp`.

`calloc`   `calloc` — Use this function to allocate an array data object and store zeros in all of the characters that constitute the data object. You can assume that the size of any character type is 1, but otherwise you should use the operator `sizeof` to determine the second argument. Do *not* specify a second argument whose value is zero.

For maximum portability, don't assume that any floating-point values thus become zero or that any pointers become null pointers. Probably they are, but you can't count on it. Nor should you assume that the product of the two arguments is all that matters. An implementation can select a storage alignment for the allocated data object based on the size specified by the second argument. Thus, you should allocate:

- an array of `N` *int* as `calloc(N, sizeof (int))`
- a data object of type `struct x` as `calloc(1, sizeof (struct x))`

`div`   `div` — You call `div` for one of two reasons:

- `div` always computes a quotient that truncates toward zero, along with the corresponding remainder, regardless of how the operators `/` and `%` behave in a given implementation. This can be important when one of the operands is negative. The expression `(-3)/2` can yield either –2 or –1, while `div(-3, 2).quot` always yields –1. Similarly, `(-3)%2` can yield either 1 or –1, while `div(-3, 2).rem` always yields –1.
- `div` computes both the quotient and remainder at the same time. That can be handy when you need both results. It might even be more efficient if the function expands to inline code that contains only a single divide.

Note that the members of the resulting structure type `div_t` can occur in either order. Don't make any assumptions about the representation of this structure.

`exit`   `exit` — Call `exit` to terminate execution from anywhere within a program. Within function `main` you can either call `exit` or write a *return* statement. The argument to `exit` (or the return value for `main`) should be zero or `EXIT_SUCCESS`, described above, to report successful termination. Otherwise it should be `EXIT_FAILURE`, also described above.

`free`   `free` — Use this function to deallocate storage you allocated earlier in the execution of the program by calling `calloc`, `malloc`, or `realloc`. You can safely call `free` with a null pointer. (The function does nothing in this case.) Otherwise, the argument to `free` *must* be the value `p` returned by one of the three functions listed above. Don't call `free((char *)p + N)` to free all but the first `N` allocated characters — call `realloc(p, N)` instead. Once you call `free(p)` don't access the value currently stored in `p` in *any* expression — some computer architectures may treat such an access as a fatal error.

You are not obliged to free storage that you allocate. A good discipline, however, is to free all allocated storage as soon as possible. Freed storage can be reallocated, making better use of a limited resource. Moreover, some implementations can report storage allocated at program termination. That helps you locate places where you unintentionally fail to free storage.

getenv   **getenv** — Use this function to obtain a pointer to the value string associated with an environment variable. (See page 82.) If you name an environment variable that has no definition, you get a null pointer as the value of the function. Don't alter the value string. A subsequent call to **getenv** can alter the string, however. To allocate a private copy, write something like:

```
#include <stdlib.h>

char *copyenv(const char *name)
    {   /* get and copy environment variable */
    char *s1 = getenv(name);
    char *s2 = s1 ? malloc(strlen(s1) + 1) : NULL;

    return (s2 ? strcpy(s2, s1) : NULL);
    }
```

labs   **labs** — See the discussion of **abs**, above.

ldiv   **ldiv** — See the discussion of **div**, above.

malloc   **malloc** — See the discussion of **calloc**, above. Use **malloc** to allocate a data object that you intend to initialize yourself. If the data object contains only integers and you want them all set to zero, call **calloc** instead. The same considerations apply for the argument to **malloc** as for the second argument to **calloc**.

mblen   **mblen** — Use this function to determine the length of the multibyte sequence that defines a single wide character. That length cannot be greater than **MB_CUR_MAX**, defined in `<stdlib.h>`. Multibyte sequences can contain locking shifts that alter the interpretation of any number of characters that follow. Hence, **mblen** stores in a private static data object the shift state for the multibyte string it is currently scanning. If the call **mblen(NULL, 0)** is nonzero, you can safely scan only one multibyte string at a time by repeated calls to **mblen**. Here, for example, is a function that checks whether a multibyte string has a valid encoding:

```
#include <stdlib.h>

int mbcheck(const char *s)
    {   /* return zero if s is valid */
    int n;

    for (mblen(NULL, 0); ; s += n)
        if ((n = mblen(s, MB_CUR_MAX)) <= 0)
            return (n);
    }
```

mbstowcs   **mbstowcs** — Use this function to convert an entire multibyte string to a wide-character string. You needn't worry about whether locking shifts occur, since the function processes the entire multibyte string. You also needn't worry that the resultant wide-character string is too long, since the third argument **n** limits the number of elements stored. If the function returns a value greater than or equal to **n**, the conversion was incomplete. If the function returns a negative value, the multibyte string has an invalid encoding.

mbtowc   **mbtowc** — Use this function much the same as you would **mblen**, described above. Two differences exist between the functions:

- If the first argument to **mbtowc** is not a null pointer, the function returns the wide character it converts. Thus, you can translate a single wide character at a time, unlike **mbstowcs** which translates the entire string at once.

- The functions **mblen** and **mbtowc** maintain separate static data objects to store shift states. Thus, you can scan different strings at the same time with the two functions even when multibyte strings have locking shifts.

qsort   **qsort** — Use this function to sort any array whose elements are ordered by pairwise comparisons. You define the ordering with a comparison function that you provide. The comparison function has a specification similar to that for the function **bsearch**, described above. Note, however, that the **bsearch** comparison function compares a key to an array element. The **sort** comparison function compares two array elements.

A few caveats:

- Don't assume that the function uses the "Quicksort" algorithm, despite the name. It may not. If two or more elements compare equal, **qsort** can leave these elements in any relative order. Hence, **qsort** is not a *stable* sort.

- Beware of changes in how elements sort when the execution character set changes.

- Be careful using the functions **strcmp** or **strcoll**, declared in **<string.h>**, directly. Both require that strings be stored in the array to be sorted. You cannot use them to sort an array of pointers to strings. To use **strcmp**, for example, you must write a function pointer argument that looks like
  (int (*)(const void *, const void *))&strcmp.

rand   **rand** — Call **rand** to obtain the next value in a pseudo-random sequence. You get exactly the same sequence following each call to **srand**, described below, with a given argument value. That is often desirable behavior, particularly when you are debugging a program. If you want less predictable behavior, call **clock** or **time**, declared in **<time.h>** to obtain an argument for **srand**. The behavior of **rand** can vary among implementations. If you want exactly the same pseudo-random sequence at all times, copy the example on page 337.

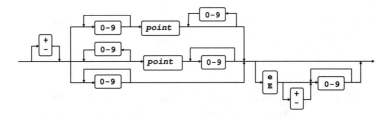

realloc   realloc — The common use for this function is to make a previously allocated data object larger or smaller. If you make it larger, the values stored in the added portion are undefined. If you make it smaller, the values stored in the retained portion remain unchanged. In either case, however, the function may alter where the data object is stored. As with **free**, described above, you shouldn't access the argument value in *any* expression once **realloc** returns. Replace the call **realloc(NULL, size)** with **malloc(size)**. The same considerations apply for the second argument to **realloc** as for the second argument to **calloc**, described above.

srand   srand — See the discussion of **rand** above. The program effectively calls **srand(1)** at program startup.

strtod   strtod — This is the function called by the scan functions, declared in Chapter 13: **<stdio.h>**, to convert a sequence of characters to an encoded value of type *double*. You can call **strtod** directly to avoid the overhead of the scan functions. That also lets you determine more precisely what part of the string argument participates in the conversion.

Note that the behavior of **strtod** can change among locales. The function effectively calls **isspace** to skip leading white-space. Figure 13.1, from Plauger and Brodie, shows the text pattern that can follow. Here, *point* matches the decimal point defined for the current locale. The figure tells you, for example, that the following are all valid ways to represent the value 12: **12**, **+12.**, and **.12e2**. An implementation can also recognize additional patterns in other than the **"c"** locale.

strtol   strtol — This is the function called by the scan functions, declared in Chapter 13: **<stdio.h>**, to convert a sequence of characters to an encoded value of type *long*. You can call **strtol** directly to avoid the overhead of the scan functions. That also lets you specify unusual bases and to determine more precisely what part of the string argument participates in the conversion.

Note that the behavior of **strtol** can change among locales. The function effectively calls **isspace** to skip leading white-space. Figure 13.2, from Plauger and Brodie, shows the text pattern that can follow. The figure tells you, for example, that the following are all valid ways to represent the value 12 (assuming the third argument to **strtol** specifies a base of zero): **12**, **+014**, and **0xC**. An implementation can also recognize additional patterns in other than the **"c"** locale.

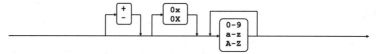

strtoul   **strtoul** — Use this function instead of **strtol**, described above, when you need a result of type *unsigned long*. The function **strtoul** reports a range error only if the converted magnitude is greater than **ULONG_MAX**, defined in **<limits.h>**. (Negating the value cannot cause overflow.) **strtol**, on the other hand, reports a range error if the converted value is less than **LONG_MIN** or greater than **LONG_MAX**, both defined in **<limits.h>**. Figure 13.2 also describes text patterns valid for **strtoul**.

system   **system** — An implementation is not obliged to have **system** do anything useful. If the call **system(NULL)** returns a nonzero value, you know that the function invokes some sort of command processor. But the C Standard imposes no requirements on what such a creature does. The only portable use for **system** is to provide uncritical access to a command processor. An editor, for example, may accept a line that begins with an exclamation point. It passes the remainder of the line as the string argument to **system**. How the local command processor interprets the line is of no concern.

wcstombs   **wcstombs** — Use this function to convert an entire wide-character string to a multibyte string. You needn't worry about whether locking shifts occur, since the function processes the entire wide-character string. You also needn't worry that the resultant multibyte string is too long, since the third argument **n** limits the number of elements stored. If the function returns a value greater than or equal to **n**, the conversion was incomplete. If the function returns a negative value, the wide-character string is invalid.

wctomb   **wctomb** — Use this function to convert a wide-character string to a multibyte string one wide character at a time. Here, for example, is a function that checks whether a wide-character string has a valid encoding:

```
#include <limits.h>
#include <stdlib.h>

int wccheck(wchar_t *wcs)
    {   /* return zero if wcs is valid */
    char buf[MB_LEN_MAX];
    int n;

    for (wctomb(NULL, 0); ; ++wcs)
        if ((n = wctomb(buf, *wcs)) <= 0)
            return (-1);
        else if (buf[n - 1] == '\0')
            return (0);
    }
```

Note that **wctomb** includes the terminating null character in the count it returns. **mbtowc** does not.

Implementing `<stdlib.h>`

header   As I indicated on page 333, the functions declared in `<stdlib.h>` fall into
`<stdlib.h>` six loosely related groups. I present those groups in the indicated order. But
first, let's look at the header itself, even though it contains a few mysteries.
Some of the mysteries are easily explained here. I explain the rest throughout the remainder of this chapter.

header   Figure 13.3 shows the file `stdlib.h`. As usual, it obtains several defini-
`<yvals.h>` tions from the internal header `<yvals.h>`. Three of these provide repeated
definitions — for the macro `NULL` and the types `size_t` and `wchar_t`. (See
Chapter 11: `<stddef.h>`.) One is unique to `<stdlib.h>` — the macro `_EXFAIL`
that determines the value of the macro `EXIT_FAILURE`.

macro   The C Standard permits each system to specify two preferred argument
`_EXFAIL` values for `exit` (or return values from `main`). The macro `EXIT_FAILURE`
reports unsuccessful termination. The macro `EXIT_SUCCESS` reports successful termination. For historical reasons, the value zero also reports successful termination. Thus, I chose to tailor only the code for unsuccessful
termination. The macro `_EXFAIL` typically has the value 1.

data object   The macro `MB_CUR_MAX` can change value when locale category `LC_CTYPE`
`_Mbcurmax` changes. It yields the value stored in the data object `_Mbcurmax`, defined in
the file `xstate.c`. (See page 107.)

type   I introduced the type `_Cmpfun` just to simplify the declaration of argu-
`_Cmpfun` ments for the functions `bsearch` and `qsort`. Don't use this declaration in
code that you write if you want it to be portable to other implementations.
(The remaining secret names I explain later.)

function   Figure 13.4 shows the file `abs.c`. The absolute value function `abs` is the
`abs` simplest of the integer math functions. You cannot provide a masking
macro, however, because you have to access the value of the argument
twice. Some computer architectures have special instructions for computing the absolute value. That makes `abs` a prime candidate for special
treatment as a builtin function generating inline code.

function   Figure 13.5 shows the file `div.c`. It provides a portable implementation
`div` of the `div` function. You can eliminate the test if you know that negative
quotients truncate toward zero. Most computer architectures have a divide
instruction that develops both quotient and remainder at the same time.
Those that develop proper negative quotients are also candidates for
builtin functions. An implementation is at liberty to reorder the members
of the structure type `div_t` to match what the hardware generates.

`labs`   Figure 13.6 shows the file `labs.c` and Figure 13.7 shows the file `ldiv.c`.
`ldiv` Both define functions that are simply *long* versions of `abs` and `div`.

function   Figure 13.8 shows the file `bsearch.c`. The function `bsearch` performs a
`bsearch` binary chop on the sorted array beginning at `base`. The logic is simple but
easy to get wrong.

Figure 13.3:
stdlib.h
Part 1

```
/* stdlib.h standard header */
#ifndef _STDLIB
#define _STDLIB
#ifndef _YVALS
#include <yvals.h>
#endif
        /* macros */
#define NULL            _NULL
#define EXIT_FAILURE    _EXFAIL
#define EXIT_SUCCESS    0
#define MB_CUR_MAX      _Mbcurmax
#define RAND_MAX        32767
        /* type definitions */
#ifndef _SIZET
#define _SIZET
typedef _Sizet size_t;
#endif
#ifndef _WCHART
#define _WCHART
typedef _Wchart wchar_t;
#endif
typedef struct {
    int quot;
    int rem;
    } div_t;
typedef struct {
    long quot;
    long rem;
    } ldiv_t;
typedef int _Cmpfun(const void *, const void *);
typedef struct {
    unsigned char _State;
    unsigned short _Wchar;
    } _Mbsave;
        /* declarations */
void abort(void);
int abs(int);
int atexit(void (*)(void));
double atof(const char *);
int atoi(const char *);
long atol(const char *);
void *bsearch(const void *, const void *,
    size_t, size_t, _Cmpfun *);
void *calloc(size_t, size_t);
div_t div(int, int);
void exit(int);
void free(void *);
char *getenv(const char *);
long labs(long);
ldiv_t ldiv(long, long);
void *malloc(size_t);
int mblen(const char *, size_t);
size_t mbstowcs(wchar_t *, const char *, size_t);
int mbtowc(wchar_t *, const char *, size_t);
void qsort(void *, size_t, size_t, _Cmpfun *);
```

```
int rand(void);
void *realloc(void *, size_t);
void srand(unsigned int);
double strtod(const char *, char **);
long strtol(const char *, char **, int);
unsigned long strtoul(const char *, char **, int);
int system(const char *);
size_t wcstombs(char *, const wchar_t *, size_t);
int wctomb(char *, wchar_t);
int _Mbtowc(wchar_t *, const char *, size_t, _Mbsave *);
double _Stod(const char *, char **);
unsigned long _Stoul(const char *, char **, int);
int _Wctomb(char *, wchar_t, char *);
extern char _Mbcurmax, _Wcxtomb;
extern _Mbsave _Mbxlen, _Mbxtowc;
extern unsigned long _Randseed;
        /* macro overrides */
#define atof(s)     _Stod(s, 0)
#define atoi(s)     (int)_Stoul(s, 0, 10)
#define atol(s)     (long)_Stoul(s, 0, 10)
#define mblen(s, n) _Mbtowc(0, s, n, &_Mbxlen)
#define mbtowc(pwc, s, n)  _Mbtowc(pwc, s, n, &_Mbxtowc)
#define srand(seed) (void)(_Randseed = (seed))
#define strtod(s, endptr)  _Stod(s, endptr)
#define strtoul(s, endptr, base)  _Stoul(s, endptr, base)
#define wctomb(s, wchar)   _Wctomb(s, wchar, &_Wcxtomb)
#endif                                                      □
```

Figure 13.4:
abs.c

```
/* abs function */
#include <stdlib.h>

int (abs)(int i)
    {                       /* compute absolute value of int argument */
    return ((i < 0) ? -i : i);
    }                                                       □
```

Figure 13.5:
div.c

```
/* div function */
#include <stdlib.h>

div_t (div)(int numer, int denom)
    {                           /* compute int quotient and remainder */
    div_t val;

    val.quot = numer / denom;
    val.rem = numer - denom * val.quot;
    if (val.quot < 0 && 0 < val.rem)
        {                           /* fix remainder with wrong sign */
        val.quot += 1;
        val.rem -= denom;
        }
    return (val);
    }                                                       □
```

Figure 13.6:
labs.c

```
/* labs function */
#include <stdlib.h>

long (labs)(long i)
    {                        /* compute absolute value of long argument */
    return ((i < 0) ? -i : i);
    }                                                                    □
```

Figure 13.7:
ldiv.c

```
/* ldiv function */
#include <stdlib.h>

ldiv_t (ldiv)(long numer, long denom)
    {                        /* compute long quotient and remainder */
    ldiv_t val;

    val.quot = numer / denom;
    val.rem = numer - denom * val.quot;
    if (val.quot < 0 && 0 < val.rem)
        {                        /* fix remainder with wrong sign */
        val.quot += 1;
        val.rem -= denom;
        }
    return (val);
    }                                                                    □
```

Figure 13.8:
bsearch.c

```
/* bsearch function */
#include <stdlib.h>

void *(bsearch)(const void *key, const void *base,
    size_t nelem, size_t size, _Cmpfun *cmp)
    {                        /* search sorted table by binary chop */
    const char *p = base;
    size_t n;

    for (p = base, n = nelem; 0 < n; )
        {                        /* check midpoint of whatever is left */
        const size_t pivot = n >> 1;
        const char *const q = p + size * pivot;
        const int val = (*cmp)(key, q);

        if (val < 0)
            n = pivot;                        /* search below pivot */
        else if (val == 0)
            return ((void *)q);                        /* found */
        else
            {                        /* search above pivot */
            p = q + size;
            n -= pivot + 1;
            }
        }
    return (NULL);                        /* no match */
    }                                                                    □
```

```c
/* qsort function */
#include <stdlib.h>
#include <string.h>

        /* macros */
#define MAX_BUF 256                          /* chunk to copy on swap */

void (qsort)(void *base, size_t n, size_t size, _Cmpfun *cmp)
    {           /* sort (char base[size])[nelem] using quicksort */
    while (1 < n)
        {                                        /* worth sorting */
        size_t i = 0;
        size_t j = n - 1;
        char *qi = base;
        char *qj = qi + size * j;
        char *qp = qj;

        while (i < j)
            {                             /* partition about pivot */
            while (i < j && (*cmp)(qi, qp) <= 0)
                ++i, qi += size;
            while (i < j && (*cmp)(qp, qj) <= 0)
                --j, qj -= size;
            if (i < j)
                {                          /* swap elements i and j */
                char buf[MAX_BUF];
                char *q1 = qi;
                char *q2 = qj;
                size_t m, ms;

                for (ms = size; 0 < ms;
                    ms -= m, q1 += m, q2 -= m)
                    {                 /* swap as many as possible */
                    m = ms < sizeof (buf) ? ms : sizeof (buf);
                    memcpy(buf, q1, m);
                    memcpy(q1, q2, m);
                    memcpy(q2, buf, m);
                    }
                ++i, qi += size;
                --j, qj -= size;
                }
            }
        if (qi != qp)
            {                            /* swap elements i and pivot */
            char buf[MAX_BUF];
            char *q1 = qi;
            char *q2 = qp;
            size_t m, ms;
```

```
                    for (ms = size; 0 < ms; ms -= m, q1 += m, q2 -= m)
                        {                        /* swap as many as possible */
                        m = ms < sizeof (buf) ? ms : sizeof (buf);
                        memcpy(buf, q1, m);
                        memcpy(q1, q2, m);
                        memcpy(q2, buf, m);
                        }
                    }
                j = n - i;
                if (j < i)
                    {                        /* recurse on smaller partition */
                    if (1 < j)
                        qsort(qi, j, size, cmp);
                    n = i;
                    }
                else
                    {                        /* lower partition is smaller */
                    if (1 < i)
                        qsort(base, i, size, cmp);
                    base = qi;
                    n = j;
                    }
                }
            }
```

function   Figure 13.9 shows the file `qsort.c`. It defines the related function `qsort`
qsort   that sorts an array beginning at **base**. This logic is much less simple and
more debatable. It is based on the Quicksort algorithm first developed by
C.A.R. Hoare. That requires you to pick a partition element, then partially
sort the array about this partition. You can then sort each of the two
partitions by recursive application of the same technique. The algorithm
can sort quite rapidly. It can also sort very slowly.

How best to choose the pivot element is the debatable issue. Pick the first
element and an array already in sort eats a lot of time. Pick the last element
and an array in reverse sort eats a lot of time. Work too hard at picking an
element and all arrays eat a lot of time. I chose simply to pick the last
element. That favors arrays that need little rearranging. You may have
reason to choose another approach.

qsort calls itself to sort the smaller of the two partitions. It loops
internally to sort the larger of the two. That minimize demands on dynamic
storage. At worst, each recursive call must sort an array half as big as the
earlier call. To sort N elements requires recursion no deeper than $log_2(N)$
calls. (You can sort 1,000,000 elements with at most ten recursive calls.)

function   Figure 13.10 shows the file **rand.c**. The function **rand** generates a pseudo-
rand   random sequence using the algorithm suggested in the C Standard. (See
page 337.) That has reasonable properties, plus the advantage of being
widely used. One virtue of a random number generator is randomness.
Another virtue, ironically, is reproducibility. You often need to check that a

Figure 13.10:
rand.c

```
/* rand function */
#include <stdlib.h>

/* the seed */
unsigned long _Randseed = 1;

int (rand)(void)
    {                                    /* compute pseudo-random value */
    _Randseed = _Randseed * 1103515245 + 12345;
    return ((unsigned int)(_Randseed >> 16) & RAND_MAX);
    }
```

Figure 13.11:
srand.c

```
/* srand function */
#include <stdlib.h>

void (srand)(unsigned int seed)
    {                                           /* alter the seed */
    _Randseed = seed;
    }
```

calculation based on pseudo-random numbers does what you expect. The arithmetic is performed using *unsigned long* integers to avoid overflows.

function
srand

Figure 13.11 shows the file **srand.c**. The function **srand** simply sets **_Randseed**, the seed for the pseudo-random sequence generated by **rand**. I provide a masking macro for **srand**. Hence, the header **<stdlib.h>** declares **_Randseed**, defined in **rand.c**.

function
_Stoul

Figure 13.12 shows the file **xstoul.c**. It defines the function **_Stoul** that performs all conversions from text string to encoded integer. The function has the same specifications as **strtoul**. I made it a separate function so that several masking macros defined in **<stdlib.h>** can call it directly. (The name **strtoul** can be redefined in some contexts.)

The first half of **_Stoul** determines the base and locates the most-significant digit. That involves stripping leading white-space, identifying any sign, and picking off any prefix such as **0x**. The function then skips any leading zeros so that it can count the number of significant digits it converts. It converts all significant digits regardless of possible overflow. For *unsigned long* arithmetic, an overflow does not cause an exception.

_Stoul makes a coarse check for overflow by first inspecting the number of significant digits. This version assumes that an *unsigned long* occupies 32 bits. (Change the array **ndigs** if such integers are larger.) For each valid base, **ndigs[base]** is the number of digits at which overflow can occur. Thus, a shorter sequence cannot overflow and a longer sequence must. A sequence of the critical length requires further checking. Take away the last digit and see whether you get back the previously accumulated value (**y**). If not, an overflow occurred.

```
/* _Stoul function */
#include <stdlib.h>
#include <ctype.h>
#include <errno.h>
#include <limits.h>
#include <stddef.h>
#include <string.h>

        /* macros */
#define BASE_MAX    36                          /* largest valid base */
        /* static data */
static const char digits[] = {                  /* valid digits */
    "0123456789abcdefghijklmnopqrstuvwxyz"};
static const char ndigs[BASE_MAX+1] = {         /* 32-bits! */
    0, 0, 33, 21, 17, 14, 13, 12, 11, 11,
    10, 10, 9, 9, 9, 9, 9, 8, 8, 8,
    8, 8, 8, 8, 7, 7, 7, 7, 7, 7,
    7, 7, 7, 7, 7, 7, 7,};

unsigned long _Stoul(const char *s, char **endptr, int base)
    {           /* convert string to unsigned long, with checking */
    const char *sc, *sd;
    const char *s1, *s2;
    char sign;
    ptrdiff_t n;
    unsigned long x, y;

    for (sc = s; isspace(*sc); ++sc)
        ;
    sign = *sc == '-' || *sc == '+' ? *sc++ : '+';
    if (base < 0 || base == 1 || BASE_MAX < base)
        {                                       /* silly base */
        if (endptr)
            *endptr = (char *)s;
        return (0);
        }
    else if (base)
        {                                       /* strip 0x or 0X */
        if (base == 16 && *sc == '0'
            && (sc[1] == 'x' || sc[1] == 'X'))
            sc += 2;
        }
    else if (*sc != '0')
        base = 10;
    else if (sc[1] == 'x' || sc[1] == 'X')
        base = 16, sc += 2;
    else
        base = 8;
    for (s1 = sc; *sc == '0'; ++sc)
        ;                                       /* skip leading zeros */
    x = 0;
```

```
    for (s2 = sc; (sd = memchr(digits,
        tolower(*sc), base)) != NULL; ++sc)
        {                                       /* accumulate digits */
        y = x;                              /* for overflow checking */
        x = x * base + (sd - digits);
        }
    if (s1 == sc)
        {                                    /* check string validity */
        if (endptr)
            *endptr = (char *)s;
        return (0);
        }
    n = sc - s2 - ndigs[base];
    if (n < 0)
        ;
    else if (0 < n || x < x - sc[-1]
        || (x - sc[-1]) / base != y)
        {                                                /* overflow */
        errno = ERANGE;
        x = ULONG_MAX;
        }
    if (sign == '-')                             /* get final value */
        x = -x;
    if (endptr)
        *endptr = (char *)sc;
    return (x);
    }                                                                □
```

Figure 13.13:
atoi.c

```
/* atoi function */
#include <stdlib.h>

int (atoi)(const char *s)
    {                                       /* convert string to int */
    return ((int)_Stoul(s, NULL, 10));
    }                                                                □
```

Figure 13.14:
atol.c

```
/* atol function */
#include <stdlib.h>

long (atol)(const char *s)
    {                                      /* convert string to long */
    return ((long)_Stoul(s, NULL, 10));
    }                                                                □
```

Figure 13.15:
strtoul.c

```
/* strtoul function */
#include <stdlib.h>

unsigned long (strtoul)(const char *s, char **endptr, int base)
    {          /* convert string to unsigned long, with checking */
    return (_Stoul(s, endptr, base));
    }                                                                □
```

Figure 13.16:
strtol.c

```c
/* strtol function */
#include <ctype.h>
#include <errno.h>
#include <limits.h>
#include <stdlib.h>

long (strtol)(const char *s, char **endptr, int base)
    {                           /* convert string to long, with checking */
    const char *sc;
    unsigned long x;

    for (sc = s; isspace(*sc); ++sc)
        ;
    x = _Stoul(s, endptr, base);                        /* not sc! */
    if (*sc == '-' && x <= LONG_MAX)
        {                               /* negative number overflowed */
        errno = ERANGE;
        return (LONG_MIN);
        }
    else if (*sc != '-' && LONG_MAX < x)
        {                               /* positive number overflowed */
        errno = ERANGE;
        return (LONG_MAX);
        }
    else
        return ((long)x);
    }                                                              □
```

Figure 13.17:
atof.c

```c
/* atof function */
#include <stdlib.h>

double (atof)(const char *s)
    {                                       /* convert string to double */
    return (_Stod(s, NULL));
    }                                                              □
```

Figure 13.18:
strtod.c

```c
/* strtod function */
#include <stdlib.h>

double (strtod)(const char *s, char **endptr)
    {                       /* convert string to double, with checking */
    return (_Stod(s, endptr));
    }                                                              □
```

Note the rare use of the type `ptrdiff_t`, defined in `<stddef.h>`. It ensures that `n` can hold the signed difference between two pointers. As I warned on page 218, `ptrdiff_t` is not a completely safe type. An argument string with over 32,767 significant digits can fail to report overflow on a computer with 16-bit pointers. That is an unlikely occurrence, but it can happen. Still, it is tedious to write the test completely safely. I chose speed in this case over absolute safety.

atoi   Figure 13.13 through Figure 13.15 show the files `atoi.c`, `atol.c`, and
atol   `strtoul.c`, respectively. These all define functions that call `_Stod` directly.
strtoul   Note that `atoi` and `atol` can overflow. The C Standard does not require that
such an overflow be reported or handled at all graciously.

function   Figure 13.16 shows the file `strtol.c`. It defines the function `strtol` that
strtol   *must* report an overflow properly. Thus, it chases down any leading minus
sign itself so that it can check the converted value as a *long*. Note that the
function must call `_Stoul` with the original pointer. Should `_Stoul` find an
invalid string, it must store that pointer at `endptr`. To point past any leading
white-space would be misleading.

atof   Floating-point conversions follow a similar pattern. Figure 13.17 shows
strtod   the file `atof.c` and Figure 13.18 shows the file `strtod.c`. Both functions
simply call the common function `_Stod` to do all the work. In this case, `atof`
enjoys the same thorough checking required of `strtod`.

function   Figure 13.19 shows the file `xstod.c`. It defines the function `_Stod` that
_Stod   performs all conversions from text string to encoded floating-point. It does
so carefully, avoiding intermediate overflow and loss of precision.

The macro `SIG_MAX`, for example, represents a careful compromise. It
limits the number of significant digits to 32. That is more than enough for
the most precise representation supported by this implementation (about
20 decimal digits for 10-byte IEEE 754 *long double*). It is also well short of
the largest integer that would cause an overflow on a conforming implementation (about 37 digits). The function pays similar care in accumulating
any exponent. As a result, any floating-point overflow or underflow is
handled safely in the function `_Dtento`, declared in `"xmath.h"`. (See the file
`xdtento.c` on page 37.)

The first half of the function checks syntax and accumulates significant
fraction digits. It then converts eight digits at a time to an array of *long*. It
converts these elements to *double*, from least-significant to most-significant,
and scales each appropriately before adding it to the running sum. This
sequence of operations is reasonably efficient and maintains precision.

mbtowc   Now let's look at the multibyte functions. Figure 13.21 shows the file
mblen   `mbtowc.c` and Figure 13.20 shows the file `mblen.c`. Both `mbtowc` and `mblen`
call the internal function `_Mbtowc` to do the actual work. Each provides
separate storage of type `_Mbsave`, defined in `<stdlib.h>`, to memorize the
shift state while walking a multibyte string. The data objects `_Mbxlen` and
`_Mbxtowc` both have names with external linkage. That permits the header
`<stdlib.h>` to define masking macros for both functions. `mblen` can, in
principle, be simpler than `mbtowc`. In this implementation, however, little
difference exists between what the two functions must do.

function   Figure 13.22 shows the file `mbstowcs.c`. The function `mbstowcs` calls
mbstowcs   `_Mbtowc` repeatedly to translate an entire multibyte string to a wide character string. It too provides storage of type `_Mbsave`, but it need not retain the
shift state between calls.

```
/* _Stod function */
#include <ctype.h>
#include <float.h>
#include <limits.h>
#include <locale.h>
#include <stdlib.h>
#include "xmath.h"

#define SIG_MAX 32

double _Stod(const char *s, char **endptr)
    {                       /* convert string to double, with checking */
    const char point = localeconv()->decimal_point[0];
    const char *sc;
    char buf[SIG_MAX], sign;
    double x;
    int ndigit, nsig, nzero, olead, opoint;

    for (sc = s; isspace(*sc); ++sc)
        ;
    sign = *sc == '-' || *sc == '+' ? *sc++ : '+';
    olead = -1, opoint = -1;
    for (ndigit = 0, nsig = 0, nzero = 0; ; ++sc)
        if (*sc == point)
            if (0 <= opoint)
                break;                      /* already seen point */
            else
                opoint = ndigit;
        else if (*sc == '0')
            ++nzero, ++ndigit;
        else if (!isdigit(*sc))
            break;
        else
            {                               /* got a nonzero digit */
            if (olead < 0)
                olead = nzero;
            else                            /* deliver zeros */
                for (; 0 < nzero && nsig < SIG_MAX; --nzero)
                    buf[nsig++] = 0;
            ++ndigit;
            if (nsig < SIG_MAX)             /* deliver digit */
                buf[nsig++] = *sc - '0';
            }
    if (ndigit == 0)
        {                                   /* set endptr */
        if (endptr)
            *endptr = (char *)s;
        return (0.0);
        }
    for (; 0 < nsig && buf[nsig - 1] == 0; --nsig)
        ;                                   /* skip trailing digits */
```

```
    {                                    /* compute significand */
    const char *pc = buf;
    int n;
    long lo[SIG_MAX/8+1];
    long *pl = &lo[nsig >> 3];
    static double fac[] = {0, 1e8, 1e16, 1e24, 1e32};

    for (*pl = 0, n = nsig; 0 < n; --n)
        if ((n & 07) == 0)                          /* start new sum */
            *--pl = *pc++;
        else
            *pl = *pl * 10 + *pc++;
    for (x = (double)lo[0], n = 0; ++n <= (nsig >> 3); )
        if (lo[n] != 0)
            x += fac[n] * (double)lo[n];
    }
    {                                /* fold in any explicit exponent */
    long lexp = 0;
    short sexp;

    if (*sc == 'e' || *sc == 'E')
        {                                           /* parse exponent */
        const char *scsav = sc;
        const char esign = *++sc == '+' || *sc == '-'
            ? *sc++ : '+';

        if (!isdigit(*sc))
            sc = scsav;                         /* ill-formed exponent */
        else
            {                                 /* exponent looks valid */
            for (; isdigit(*sc); ++sc)
                if (lexp < 100000)                  /* else overflow */
                    lexp = lexp * 10 + *sc - '0';
            if (esign == '-')
                lexp = -lexp;
            }
        }
    if (endptr)
        *endptr = (char *)sc;
    if (opoint < 0)
        lexp += ndigit - nsig;
    else
        lexp += opoint - olead - nsig;
    sexp = lexp < SHRT_MIN ? SHRT_MIN : lexp < SHRT_MAX
        ? (short)lexp : SHRT_MAX;
    x = _Dtento(x, sexp);
    return (sign == '-' ? -x : x);
    }
}
```

Figure 13.20:
mblen.c

```
/* mblen function */
#include <stdlib.h>

        /* static data */
_Mbsave _Mbxlen = {0};

int (mblen)(const char *s, size_t n)
    {                /* determine length of next multibyte code */
    return (_Mbtowc(NULL, s, n, &_Mbxlen));
    }                                                                    □
```

Figure 13.21:
mbtowc.c

```
/* mbtowc function */
#include <stdlib.h>

        /* static data */
_Mbsave _Mbxtowc = {0};

int (mbtowc)(wchar_t *pwc, const char *s, size_t n)
    {                        /* determine next multibyte code */
    return (_Mbtowc(pwc, s, n, &_Mbxtowc));
    }                                                                    □
```

Figure 13.22:
mbstowcs.c

```
/* mbstowcs function */
#include <stdlib.h>

size_t (mbstowcs)(wchar_t *wcs, const char *s, size_t n)
    {          /* translate multibyte string to wide char string */
    int i;
    wchar_t *pwc;
    _Mbsave state = {0};

    for (pwc = wcs; 0 < n; ++pwc, --n)
        {                              /* make another wide character */
        i = _Mbtowc(pwc, s, n, &state);
        if (i == -1)
            return (-1);
        else if (i == 0 || *pwc == 0)
            return (pwc - wcs);
        s += i;
        }
    return (pwc - wcs);
    }                                                                    □
```

function
_Mbtowc

Figure 13.23 shows the file **xmbtowc.c**. The function **_Mbtowc** parses a multibyte sequence far enough to develop the next wide character that it represents. It does so as a finite-state machine executing the state table stored at **_Mbstate**, defined in the file **xstate.c**. (See page 107.)

_Mbtowc must be particularly cautious because **_Mbstate** can be flawed. It can change with locale category **LC_CTYPE** in ways that the Standard C library cannot control.

Figure 13.23:
xmbtowc.c

```c
/* _Mbtowc function */
#include <limits.h>
#include <stdlib.h>
#include "xstate.h"

int _Mbtowc(wchar_t *pwc, const char *s, size_t nin,
    _Mbsave *ps)
    {                               /* translate multibyte to widechar */
    static const _Mbsave initial = {0};

    if (s == NULL)
        {                                       /* set initial state */
        *ps = initial;
        return (_Mbstate._Tab[0][0] & ST_STATE);
        }
    {                               /* run finite state machine */
    char state = ps->_State;
    int limit = 0;
    unsigned char *su = (unsigned char *)s;
    unsigned short wc = ps->_Wchar;

    if (MB_CUR_MAX < nin)
        nin = MB_CUR_MAX;
    for (; ; )
        {                           /* perform a state transformation */
        unsigned short code;
        const unsigned short *stab;

        if (_NSTATE <= state
            || (stab = _Mbstate._Tab[state]) == NULL
            || nin == 0
            || (_NSTATE*UCHAR_MAX) <= ++limit
            || (code = stab[*su]) == 0)
            break;
        state = (code & ST_STATE) >> ST_STOFF;
        if (code & ST_FOLD)
            wc = wc & ~UCHAR_MAX | code & ST_CH;
        if (code & ST_ROTATE)
            wc = wc >> CHAR_BIT & UCHAR_MAX | wc << CHAR_BIT;
        if (code & ST_INPUT && *su != '\0')
            ++su, --nin, limit = 0;
        if (code & ST_OUTPUT)
            {                                   /* produce an output wchar */
            if (pwc)
                *pwc = wc;
            ps->_State = state;
            ps->_Wchar = wc;
            return ((const char *)su - s);
            }
        }
    ps->_State = _NSTATE;                        /* error return */
    return (-1);
    }
    }
```

□

Note the various ways that the function can elect to take an error return:

- if a transfer occurs to an undefined state
- if no state table exists for a given state
- if the multibyte string ends part way through a multibyte character
- if the function makes so many state transitions since generating a wide character that it must be looping
- if the state table entry specifically signals an error

The rest of **_Mbtowc** is simple by comparison. The function retains the wide-character accumulator (**ps->_Wchar**) as part of the state memory. That simplifies generating a sequence of wide characters with a common component while in a given shift state. **_Mbtowc** returns after delivering each wide character.

function
wctomb
Figure 13.24 shows the file **wctomb.c**. The function **wctomb** calls the internal function **_Wctomb** solely to provide separate state memory. In this case, the shift state can be stored in a data object of type *char*. The data object **_Wcxtomb** has a name with external linkage so that the header **<stdlib.h>** can define a masking macro for **wctomb**.

function
wcstombs
Figure 13.25 shows the file **wcstombs.c**. The function **wcstombs** calls **_Wctomb** repeatedly to translate a wide-character string to a multibyte string. It too provides its own state memory, but it need not retain the shift state between calls.

What makes this function complex is the finite length of the *char* array it writes. If at least **MB_CUR_MAX** elements remain, **_Wctomb** can deliver characters directly. Otherwise, **wcstombs** must store the generated characters in an array of length **MB_LEN_MAX** and deliver as many as it can.

function
_Wctomb
Figure 13.26 shows the file **xwctomb.c**. The function **_Wctomb** converts a wide character to the one or more characters that comprise its multibyte representation. It does so as a finite-state machine executing the state table stored at **_Wcstate**, defined in the file **xstate.c**. (See page 107.)

_Wctomb must also be cautious because **_Wcstate** can also be flawed. It can change with locale category **LC_CTYPE** in ways that the Standard C library cannot control. Note the various ways that the function can elect to take an error return:

- if a transfer occurs to an undefined state
- if no state table exists for a given state
- if the generated multibyte string threatens to become longer than **MB_CUR_MAX** characters
- if the function makes so many state transitions since generating a character that it must be looping
- if the state table entry specifically signals an error

The rest of **_Wctomb** is likewise simple by comparison. It returns after consuming each input wide character.

Figure 13.24:
wctomb.c

```c
/* wctomb function */
#include <stdlib.h>

        /* static data */
char _Wcxtomb = {0};

int (wctomb)(char *s, wchar_t wchar)
    {           /* translate wide character to multibyte string */
    return (_Wctomb(s, wchar, &_Wcxtomb));
    }                                                           □
```

Figure 13.25:
wcstombs.c

```c
/* wcstombs function */
#include <limits.h>
#include <string.h>
#include <stdlib.h>

size_t (wcstombs)(char *s, const wchar_t *wcs, size_t n)
    {           /* translate wide char string to multibyte string */
    char *sc;
    char state = {0};
    size_t i;

    for (sc = s; 0 < n; n -= i, ++wcs)
        {                       /* translate another wide character */
        if (MB_CUR_MAX <= n)
            {                                   /* copy directly */
            if ((i = _Wctomb(sc, *wcs, &state)) <= 0)
                return (-1);
            }
        else
            {                               /* copy into local buffer */
            char buf[MB_LEN_MAX];

            if ((i = _Wctomb(buf, *wcs, &state)) <= 0)
                return (-1);
            else if (i <= n)
                memcpy(sc, buf, i);
            else
                {                                   /* won't all fit */
                memcpy(sc, buf, n);
                return (sc - s + n);
                }
            }
        sc += i;
        if (sc[-1] == '\0')
            return (sc - s - 1);
        }
    return (sc - s);
    }                                                           □
```

Figure 13.26:
xwctomb.c

```
/* _Wctomb function */
#include <limits.h>
#include <stdlib.h>
#include "xstate.h"

int _Wctomb(char *s, wchar_t wcin, char *ps)
    {                               /* translate widechar to multibyte */
    static const char initial = {0};

    if (s == NULL)
        {                                       /* set initial state */
        *ps = initial;
        return (_Mbstate._Tab[0][0] & ST_STATE);
        }
    {                                   /* run finite state machine */
    char state = *ps;
    int leave = 0;
    int limit = 0;
    int nout = 0;
    unsigned short wc = wcin;

    for (; ; )
        {                           /* perform a state transformation */
        unsigned short code;
        const unsigned short *stab;

        if (_NSTATE <= state
            || (stab = _Wcstate._Tab[state]) == NULL
            || MB_CUR_MAX <= nout
            || (_NSTATE*UCHAR_MAX) <= ++limit
            || (code = stab[wc & UCHAR_MAX]) == 0)
            break;
        state = (code & ST_STATE) >> ST_STOFF;
        if (code & ST_FOLD)
            wc = wc & ~UCHAR_MAX | code & ST_CH;
        if (code & ST_ROTATE)
            wc = wc >> CHAR_BIT & UCHAR_MAX | wc << CHAR_BIT;
        if (code & ST_OUTPUT)
            {                               /* produce an output char */
            if ((s[nout++] = code & ST_CH ? code : wc) == '\0')
                leave = 1;
            limit = 0;
            }
        if (code & ST_INPUT || leave)
            {                                       /* consume input */
            *ps = state;
            return (nout);
            }
        }
    *ps = _NSTATE;
    return (-1);
    }
    }
```

□

Figure 13.27:
xalloc.h

```
/* xalloc.h internal header */
#include <stddef.h>
#include <stdlib.h>
#ifndef _YVALS
#include <yvals.h>
#endif
        /* macros */
#define CELL_OFF    (sizeof (size_t) + _MEMBND & ~_MEMBND)
#define SIZE_BLOCK 512                    /* minimum block size */
#define SIZE_CELL  \
    ((sizeof (_Cell) + _MEMBND & ~_MEMBND) - CELL_OFF)
        /* type definitions */
typedef struct _Cell {
    size_t _Size;
    struct _Cell *_Next;
    } _Cell;
typedef struct {
    _Cell **_Plast;
    _Cell *_Head;
    } _Altab;
        /* declarations */
void *_Getmem(size_t);
extern _Altab _Aldata;                                          □
```

storage allocation   Several functions cooperate to allocate and free storage during program execution. You can implement these functions many ways. I chose to maintain a pool of available storage (the "heap") as a singly linked list. The list elements remain in sort by their addresses in storage. A static pointer points to the start of the list — the element with the lowest address.

header "xalloc.h"   Figure 13.27 shows the file `xalloc.h`. It is an internal header that is included by all of the storage allocation functions. It defines several macros and types. A list element, for example, has type `_Cell`. At least it begins with such a data object. The member `_Size` gives the useful size in bytes of the entire element, which is typically much larger than a `_Cell` data object. The member `_Next` points to the next element of the available storage list.

macro CELL_OFF   An allocated element still begins with the member `_Size`. That information may be needed later if the program elects to free the allocated element. The program does not see this size information, however. The allocation functions return a pointer to the usable area beyond the member `_Size`. The macro `CELL_OFF` gives the offset in bytes of the usable area from the start of the allocated element.

storage boundaries   Many computer architectures care about storage boundaries. Some require that certain types of data objects begin at a storage address that is some multiple of bytes. Typical multiples are two, four, or eight bytes. Other computer architectures do not require such alignment, but execute faster when manipulating data objects that are properly aligned. The macros defined in `<stdarg.h>` typically must correct for holes left by the alignment of argument data objects. (See Chapter 10: `<stdarg.h>`.)

macro
_MEMBND

The storage allocation functions also fret about storage boundaries. They assume that a worst-case storage boundary exists. Any data object aligned on such a boundary is thus suitably aligned. The internal header `<yvals.h>` defines the macro **_MEMBND** to specify this worst-case storage boundary. For a boundary of 2^N, the macro has the value 2^{N-1}. On an Intel 80X86 computer, for example, the macro can be zero (no constraints). You should probably make it at least 1 (two-byte boundaries). For such a computer with 32-bit memory, you might want to make it 3 (four-byte boundaries).

CELL_OFF
SIZE_CELL

Much of the ugly logic in the storage allocation functions results from this attempt to parametrize the worst-case storage boundary. The macro **CELL_OFF** assumes that a list element begins on a worst-case storage boundary. It determines the start of the usable area as the next such boundary beyond the space set aside for the member **_size**. Similarly, the macro **SIZE_CELL** yields the smallest permissible value of **_size** for a list element. The list element must be large enough to hold a **_Cell** data object. It must also end of a worst-case storage boundary.

function
malloc

The remainder of `"xalloc.h"` is best explained along with the function **malloc**. Figure 13.28 shows the file **malloc.c**. The function **malloc** endeavors to allocate a data object of **size** bytes. To do so, it looks for an element on the list of available storage that has a usable area at least this large. If it finds one, it splits off any excess large enough to make an additional list element. It returns a pointer to the usable area.

data object
_Aldata

The internal function **findmem**, defined in **malloc.c** scans the list of available storage. It retains two static pointers in the data object **_Aldata** of type **_Altab**, defined in `"xstdio.h"`:

- **_Head** points to the start of the list. If the list is empty, it contains a null pointer.
- **_Plast** is the *address of* the pointer to the next list element to consider. It can point to **_Aldata._Head** or to the **_Next** of an available list element. Or it can be a null pointer.

Whenever possible, **findmem** begins its scan where it left off on a previous call. That strategy reduces fragmentation at the start of a list by distributing usage over the entire list. **malloc** itself and the function **free** cooperate in maintaining these two pointers.

If **findmem** cannot find a suitable element on the available list, it endeavors to obtain more storage. (Initially the heap is empty, so the first request takes this path.) It calls the function **_Getmem**, declared in `"xalloc.h"` to do so. That primitive function must return a pointer to a storage area of at least the requested size, aligned on the worst-case storage boundary. If it cannot, it returns a null pointer.

macro
SIZE_BLOCK

The macro **SIZE_BLOCK**, defined in `"xalloc.h"`, specifies the smallest preferred list-element size. I have set it to 512, but you may want to change it. **findmem** first requests the larger of the required size and **SIZE_BLOCK**. If that fails, it halves the requested size repeatedly until the request is granted or a request of exactly the required size cannot be honored. This strategy favors larger element sizes but takes what it can get. If the request is granted, **findmem** makes the new storage look like a previously allocated element. It calls **free** to add the storage to the available list. The next iteration of the scan loop should discover this storage and use it.

function
_Getmem

The function **_Getmem** depends strongly on the execution environment. You must tailor this primitive extensively for each operating system. For completeness, I show here a version of **_Getmem** that runs under UNIX. I did the same thing for several of the primitives needed to implement the header `<stdio.h>`. (See page 283.)

Figure 13.29 shows the file **xgetmem.c**. As with the earlier UNIX primitives, it assumes the existence of a C-callable system service with its name altered to a reserved form. **_Sbrk** performs the UNIX **sbrk** system service, which allocates a block of storage. Note that **_Sbrk** expects an *int* argument. Hence **_Getmem** must ensure that a very large request is not misinterpreted.

function
calloc

Figure 13.30 shows the file **calloc.c**. It calls **malloc** to allocate storage, then sets its individual characters to zero. A more cautious version would check that the product of the two arguments is of a reasonable size.

function
free

Figure 13.31 shows the file **free.c**. It frees storage earlier allocated by **malloc** or **realloc**. Two common programming errors cause trouble for **free**:

- Invalid stores alter the value of the **_size** member.
- A program calls **free** with an invalid pointer. Either the data object was never allocated or it has already been freed.

Probably no amount of checking is enough to keep ill-formed programs from sabotaging **free**. This version makes just one or two cursory checks. If the **_size** member is not a multiple of the worst-case storage boundary, it has been altered or was never allocated. If the element to be freed overlaps an existing element on the available list, it has been freed twice. Both errors cause **free** to return without freeing the designated storage. A more helpful version might report a signal or generate a diagnostic. At the very least, is might store a nonzero value in **errno**, defined in `<errno.h>`.

Most of the work of **free** involves finding the appropriate place to insert the freed element in the list of available storage. If the freed element is adjacent to one or two existing list elements, the adjacent elements are combined. That minimizes fragmentation of the list.

Note that **free** alters the scan pointer **_Aldata._Plast**. That is necessary because the stored pointer may be to a list element now merged with another. I chose to have the scan resume just after the freed element. That's an easy address to determine here. This approach also spreads the use of storage more uniformly across the list. And it postpones as long as possible recycling freed storage (a questionable kindness to buggy programs). On the other hand, it lowers performance whenever the heap grows by calling **_Getmem**. Here is an area that can occupy a designer for a long time.

```c
/* malloc function */
#include "xalloc.h"
#include "yfuns.h"

        /* static data */
_Altab _Aldata = {0};                          /* heap initially empty */

static _Cell **findmem(size_t size)
    {                                          /* find storage */
    _Cell *q, **qb;

    for (; ; )
        {                                      /* check freed space first */
        if ((qb = _Aldata._Plast) == NULL)
            {                                  /* take it from the top */
            for (qb = &_Aldata._Head; *qb;
                qb = &(*qb)->_Next)
                if (size <= (*qb)->_Size)
                    return (qb);
            }
        else
            {                                  /* resume where we left off */
            for (; *qb; qb = &(*qb)->_Next)
                if (size <= (*qb)->_Size)
                    return (qb);
            q = *_Aldata._Plast;
            for (qb = &_Aldata._Head; *qb != q;
                qb = &(*qb)->_Next)
                if (size <= (*qb)->_Size)
                    return (qb);
            }
        {                                      /* try to buy more space */
        size_t bs;
        const size_t sz = size + CELL_OFF;

        for (bs = SIZE_BLOCK; ; bs >>= 1)
            {                                  /* try larger blocks first */
            if (bs < sz)
                bs = sz;
            if ((q = _Getmem(bs)) != NULL)
                break;
            else if (bs == sz)
                return (NULL);                 /* no storage */
            }
        /* got storage: add to heap and retry */
        q->_Size = (bs & ~_MEMBND) - CELL_OFF;
        free((char *)q + CELL_OFF);
        }
        }
    }
```

```
void *(malloc)(size_t size)
    {                               /* allocate a data object on the heap */
    _Cell *q, **qb;

    if (size < SIZE_CELL)                       /* round up size */
        size = SIZE_CELL;
    size = (size + _MEMBND) & ~_MEMBND;
    if ((qb = findmem(size)) == NULL)
        return (NULL);
    q = *qb;
    if (q->_Size < size + CELL_OFF + SIZE_CELL)
        *qb = q->_Next;                         /* use entire cell */
    else
        {                           /* peel off a residual cell */
        *qb = (_Cell *)((char *)q
            + CELL_OFF + size);
        (*qb)->_Next = q->_Next;
        (*qb)->_Size = q->_Size - CELL_OFF - size;
        q->_Size = size;
        }
    _Aldata._Plast = qb ? qb : NULL;            /* resume here */
    return ((char *)q + CELL_OFF);
    }                                                              □
```

Figure 13.29:
xgetmem.c

```
/* _Getmem function -- UNIX version */
#include "xalloc.h"

        /* UNIX system call */
void *_Sbrk(int);

void *_Getmem(size_t size)
    {                                       /* allocate raw storage */
    void *p;
    int isize = size;

    return (isize <= 0 || (p = _Sbrk(isize)) == (void *)-1
        ? NULL : p);
    }                                                              □
```

Figure 13.30:
calloc.c

```
/* calloc function */
#include <stdlib.h>
#include <string.h>

void *(calloc)(size_t nelem, size_t size)
    {           /* allocate a data object on the heap and clear it */
    const size_t n = nelem * size;
    char *p = malloc(n);

    if (p)
        memset(p, '\0', n);
    return (p);
    }                                                              □
```

Figure 13.31:
free.c

```c
/* free function */
#include "xalloc.h"

void (free)(void *ptr)
    {                                        /* free an allocated data object */
    _Cell *q;

    if (ptr == NULL)
        return;
    q = (_Cell *)((char *)ptr - CELL_OFF);
    if (q->_Size & _MEMBND)
        return;                                          /* bad pointer */
    if (_Aldata._Head == NULL
        || q < _Aldata._Head)
        {                                        /* insert at head of list */
        q->_Next = _Aldata._Head;
        _Aldata._Head = q;
        }
    else
        {                                        /* scan for insertion point */
        _Cell *qp;
        char *qpp;

        for (qp = _Aldata._Head;
            qp->_Next && q < qp->_Next; )
            qp = qp->_Next;
        qpp = (char *)qp + CELL_OFF + qp->_Size;
        if ((char *)q < qpp)
            return;                                      /* erroneous call */
        else if ((char *)q == qpp)
            {                                        /* merge qp and q */
            qp->_Size += CELL_OFF + q->_Size;
            q = qp;
            }
        else
            {                                        /* splice q after qp */
            q->_Next = qp->_Next;
            qp->_Next = q;
            }
        }
    if (q->_Next &&
        (char *)q + CELL_OFF + q->_Size == (char *)q->_Next)
        {                                        /* merge q and q->_Next */
        q->_Size += CELL_OFF + q->_Next->_Size;
        q->_Next = q->_Next->_Next;
        }
    _Aldata._Plast = &q->_Next;    /* resume scan after freed */
    }
```

Figure 13.32:
realloc.c

```
/* realloc function */
#include <string.h>
#include "xalloc.h"

void *(realloc)(void *ptr, size_t size)
    {                            /* reallocate a data object on the heap */
    _Cell *q;

    if (ptr == NULL)
        return (malloc(size));
    q = (_Cell *)((char *)ptr - CELL_OFF);
    if (q->_Size < size)
        {                                    /* try to buy a larger cell */
        char *const new_p = malloc(size);

        if (new_p == NULL)
            return (NULL);
        memcpy(new_p, ptr, q->_Size);
        free(ptr);
        return (new_p);
        }
    else if (q->_Size
        < size + CELL_OFF + SIZE_CELL)
        return (ptr);                               /* leave cell alone */
    else
        {                                           /* free excess space */
        const size_t new_n = (size + _MEMBND) & ~_MEMBND;
        _Cell *const new_q = (_Cell *)((char *)ptr + new_n);

        new_q->_Size = q->_Size - CELL_OFF - new_n;
        q->_Size = new_n;
        free((char *)new_q + CELL_OFF);
        return (ptr);
        }
    }
```

function
realloc

Figure 13.32 shows the file `realloc.c`. The function `realloc` tries to allocate a larger storage area if that is necessary. It also tries to trim the existing storage area if that proves to be worthwhile.

This version doesn't try quite as hard as it could. If a larger storage area is required, the function insists on allocating a new area before freeing the existing area. That eliminates any worries about preserving data stored in the usable area during the shuffle. But it precludes one possibility — the larger area may be available only after the existing area is freed. Here is yet another place where an ambitious implementor can make improvements.

The storage allocation functions are very important. Many programs rely on them to work rapidly and robustly. They can also provide invaluable aids to debugging. Because they are largely self-contained, they are easy to tinker with as a separate unit. For all these reasons, you can find numerous implementations of these functions. I emphasized performance and robustness here. You may well want to explore other goals.

abort   The final group of functions interfaces to the environment in various
atexit ways. Three functions deal with program termination — **abort**, **atexit**, and
exit **exit**. Figure 13.33 through Figure 13.35 show the files **abort.c**, **atexit.c**,
and **exit.c**. **abort** simply reports the signal **SIGABRT**. Should the handler
for that signal return, the function exits with unsuccessful status. **atexit** is
almost as simple. It just pushes a function pointer on the stack defined by
the data objects **_Atcount** and **_Atfuns**. A call to **exit** pops this stack and
calls the corresponding functions.

function   **exit** also closes any open files before it terminates program execution.
_Exit How a program terminates is system dependent. You can usually call some
function to do so, however. As with several other interface primitives, I
stuff that problem into the internal header **"yfuns.h"**. It either declares a
function or defines a macro called **_Exit** that accepts the exit status and
terminates execution. In a UNIX system, for example, **_Exit** can be just an
alternate name for the **exit** system service.

function   Figure 13.36 shows the file **getenv.c**. It must know how to access the
getenv environment list that defines all the environment variables. It must also
know how to walk that list to scan for an environment variable with the
requested name. The version I show here works under UNIX. It also works
under a variety of other operating systems.

     getenv assumes that **_Envp** points to the first of a sequence of null-termi-
nated strings. An empty string terminates the sequence. Each string in the
sequence has the form **name=value**. If the argument string matches all
characters before the equal sign, the function returns a pointer to the first
character past the equal sign. Once again, I leave it to the internal header
"yfuns.h" to define or declare **_Envp**.

     Some operating systems support an environment list, but not of this
form. Others support an environment list that is not directly addressable
as a C data object. Either case may require that you copy the value string
to a static buffer that is private to **getenv**. If you do so, *you must change several
functions in this implementation*. Several functions assume they can call
getenv directly. That is true only if the calls have no effect on user programs.
You must introduce a function such as **_Getenv** that lets you supply your
own static buffer to hold the value string. I chose to omit that layer of
protection against future changes.

function   Figure 13.37 shows the file **system.c**. It shows how a UNIX version of
system the function **system** might invoke a command processor from a C program.
As usual, the function assumes the existence of several UNIX system
services with suitable reserved names. And as usual, the version I show
here can be improved. Wiring in the pathname **"/bin/sh"** as the name of
the command processor is at best naive, at worst bad manners. Several
more sophisticated schemes are in common use for specifying an assortment of command processors. The function can also return more useful
status information to programs that care.

Figure 13.33:
abort.c

```
/* abort function */
#include <stdlib.h>
#include <signal.h>

void (abort)(void)
    {                                              /* terminate abruptly */
    raise(SIGABRT);
    exit(EXIT_FAILURE);
    }                                                                        □
```

Figure 13.34:
atexit.c

```
/* atexit function */
#include <stdlib.h>

        /* external declarations */
extern void (*_Atfuns[])(void);
extern size_t _Atcount;

int (atexit)(void (*func)(void))
    {                                          /* function to call at exit */
    if (_Atcount == 0)
        return (-1);                               /* list is full */
    _Atfuns[--_Atcount] = func;
    return (0);
    }                                                                        □
```

Figure 13.35:
exit.c

```
/* exit function */
#include <stdio.h>
#include <stdlib.h>
#include "yfuns.h"

        /* macros */
#define NATS    32
        /* static data */
void (*_Atfuns[NATS])(void) = {0};
size_t _Atcount = {NATS};

void (exit)(int status)
    {                                     /* tidy up and exit to system */
    while (_Atcount < NATS)
        (*_Atfuns[_Atcount++])();
    {                                              /* close all files */
    size_t i;

    for (i = 0; i < FOPEN_MAX; ++i)
        if (_Files[i])
            fclose(_Files[i]);
    }
    _Exit(status);
    }                                                                        □
```

Figure 13.36:

getenv.c

```
/* getenv function -- in-memory version */
#include <stdlib.h>
#include <string.h>
#include "yfuns.h"

char *(getenv)(const char *name)
    {                       /* search environment list for named entry */
    const char *s;
    size_t n = strlen(name);

    for (s = _Envp; *s; s += strlen(s) + 1)
        {                               /* look for name match */
        if (!strncmp(s, name, n) && s[n] == '=')
            return ((char *)&s[n + 1]);
        }
    return (NULL);
    }                                                               □
```

Figure 13.37:

system.c

```
/* system function -- UNIX version */
#include <stdlib.h>

        /* UNIX system calls */
int execl(const char *, const char *, const char *);
int fork(void);
int wait (int *);

int (system)(const char *s)
    {               /* send text to system command line processor */
    if (s)
        {                                       /* not just a test */
        int pid = fork();

        if (pid < 0)
            ;                                       /* fork failed */
        else if (pid == 0)
            execl("/bin/sh", s, NULL);
        else
            while (wait(NULL) != pid)
                ;                                   /* wait for child */
        }
    return (-1);
    }                                                               □
```

Testing <stdlib.h>

Figure 13.38 shows the file `tstdlib.c`. The test program exercises the various functions declared in `<stdlib.h>`, if sometimes only superficially. The functions `getenv` and `system`, for example, can return any value and satisfy this test. The remaining functions are obliged to do something nontrivial, at least.

As a courtesy, the program displays the values of the macros `RAND_MAX` and `MB_CUR_MAX`. It also determines whether the `"C"` locale supports multibyte strings that have shift states. For this implementation, the program displays:

```
RAND_MAX = 32767
MB_CUR_MAX = 1
Multibyte strings don't have shift states
SUCCESS testing <stdlib.h>
```

To display the final line and exit successfully, the program must do several things right. It must supply a handler for `SIGABRT` that fields the call to `abort`. That handler must call `exit` with successful status `EXIT_SUCCESS`. And `exit` must call the handler `done` registered with `atexit`. That handler must be able to write a line of text to the standard output stream. All that stuff exercises much of the logic for handling program termination.

References

Donald Knuth, *The Art of Computer Programming*, Vols. 1-3 (Reading, Mass.: Addison-Wesley, 1967 and later). Here is a rich source of algorithms, complete with analysis and tutorial introductions. Volume 1 is *Fundamental Algorithms*, volume 2 is *Seminumerical Algorithms*, and volume 3 is *Sorting and Searching*. Some are in second edition.

You will find oodles of information on:

- maintaining a heap
- computing random numbers
- searching ordered sequences
- sorting
- converting between different numeric bases

Before you tinker with the code presented in this chapter, see what Knuth has to say.

Ronald F. Brender, *Character Set Issues for Ada 9X*, SEI-89-SR-17 (Pittsburgh, Pa.: Software Engineering Institute, Carnegie Mellon University, October 1989). Here is an excellent summary of many of the issues surrounding large character sets and multiple character sets in programming languages. While the document focuses on the programming language Ada, it is largely relevant to C as well.

```
/* test stdlib functions */
#include <assert.h>
#include <limits.h>
#include <signal.h>
#include <stdio.h>
#include <stdlib.h>
#include <string.h>

static void abrt(int sig)
    {                                        /* handle SIGABRT */
    exit(EXIT_SUCCESS);
    }

static int cmp(const void *p1, const void *p2)
    {                     /* compare function for bsearch and qsort */
    unsigned char c1 = *(unsigned char *)p1;
    unsigned char c2 = *(unsigned char *)p2;

    return (*(unsigned char *)p1 - *(unsigned char *)p2);
    }

static void done(void)
    {                                        /* get control from atexit */
    puts("SUCCESS testing <stdlib.h>");
    }

int main()
    {                     /* test basic workings of stdlib functions */
    char buf[10], *s1, *s2;
    div_t iqr;
    ldiv_t lqr;
    int i1 = EXIT_FAILURE;
    int i2 = EXIT_SUCCESS;
    int i3 = MB_CUR_MAX;
    wchar_t wcs[10];
    static char abc[] = "abcdefghijklmnopqrstuvwxyz";
    static int rmax = RAND_MAX;

    assert(32767 <= rmax);
    assert(1 <= MB_CUR_MAX && MB_CUR_MAX <= MB_LEN_MAX);
    assert((s1 = malloc(sizeof (abc))) != NULL);
    strcpy(s1, abc);
    assert((s2 = calloc(sizeof (abc), 1)) != NULL
        && s2[0] == '\0');
    assert(memcmp(s2, s2 + 1, sizeof (abc) - 1) == 0);
    assert(strcmp(s1, abc) == 0);
    assert((s1 = realloc(s1, 2 * sizeof (abc) - 1)) != NULL);
    strcat(s1, abc);
    assert(strrchr(s1, 'z') == s1 + 2 * strlen(abc) - 1);
    free(s2);
    assert((s1 = realloc(s1, sizeof (abc) - 3)) != NULL);
    assert(memcmp(s1, abc, sizeof (abc) -3) == 0);
    assert(getenv("ANY") || system(NULL) || abc[0]);
    assert(abs(-4) == 4 && abs(4) == 4);
    assert(labs(-4) == 4 && labs(4) == 4);
```

```
    assert(div(7, 2).quot == 3 && div(7, 2).rem == 1);
    iqr = div(-7, 2);
    assert(iqr.quot == -3 && iqr.rem == -1);
    assert(ldiv(7, 2).quot == 3 && ldiv(7, 2).rem == 1);
    lqr = ldiv(-7, 2);
    assert(lqr.quot == -3 && lqr.rem == -1);
    assert(0 <= (i1 = rand()) && i1 <= RAND_MAX);
    assert(0 <= (i2 = rand()) && i2 <= RAND_MAX);
    srand(1);
    assert(rand() == i1 && rand() == i2);
    assert(bsearch("0", abc, sizeof (abc) - 1, 1, &cmp)
        == NULL);
    assert(bsearch("d", abc, sizeof (abc) - 1, 1, &cmp)
        == &abc[3]);
    qsort(strcpy(buf, "mishmash"), 9, 1, &cmp);
    assert(memcmp(buf, "\0ahhimmss", 9) == 0);
    assert(atof("3.0") == 3.0);
    assert(atof("-1e-17-") == -1e-17);
    assert(atoi("37") == 37 && atoi("-7192X") == -7192);
    assert(atol("+29") == 29 && atol("-077") == -77);
    assert(strtod("28G", &s1) == 28.0
        && s1 != NULL && *s1 == 'G');
    assert(strtol("-a0", &s1, 11) == -110
        && s1 != NULL && *s1 == '\0');
    assert(strtoul("54", &s1, 4) == 0
        && s1 != NULL && *s1 == '5');
    assert(strtoul("0xFfg", &s1, 16) == 255
        && s1 != NULL && *s1 == 'g');
    assert(mbstowcs(wcs, "abc", 4) == 3 && wcs[1] == 'b');
    assert(wcstombs(buf, wcs, 10) == 3
        && strcmp(buf, "abc") == 0);
    mblen(NULL, 0);
    wctomb(NULL, 0);
    assert(mblen("abc", 4) == 1);
    assert(mbtowc(&wcs[0], "abc", 4) == 1 && wcs[0] == 'a');
    assert(wctomb(buf, wcs[0]) == 1 && buf[0] == 'a');
    assert(mblen("", 1) == 0);
    assert(mbtowc(&wcs[0], "", 1) == 0 && wcs[0] == 0);
    assert(wctomb(buf, wcs[0]) == 1 && buf[0] == '\0');
    printf("RAND_MAX = %ld\n", (long)RAND_MAX);
    printf("MB_CUR_MAX = %u\n", MB_CUR_MAX);
    printf("Multibyte strings%s have shift states\n",
        mbtowc(NULL, NULL, 0) ? "" : " don't");
    atexit(&done);
    signal(SIGABRT, &abrt);
    abort();
    puts("FAILURE testing <stdlib.h>");
    return (EXIT_FAILURE);
    }
```

Exercises

Exercise 13.1 The following locale file defines the "Shift JIS" multibyte encoding for Kanji. A character code in the intervals [0x81, 0x9F] or [0xE0, 0xFC] signals the first of a two-character sequence. (Any other code is a single character.) The second character must be in the interval [0x40, 0xFC]:

```
LOCALE SHIFT_JIS
NOTE JIS codes with 0x81-0x9F or 0xE0-0xFC followed by 0x40-0xFC
SET A 0x81
SET B 0x9f
SET C 0xe0
SET D 0xfc
SET M 0x40
SET N 0xfc
SET X 0
mb_cur_max 2
mbtowc[0, 0:$#]  $@  $F      $O $I $0
mbtowc[0, A:B ]  $@  $F  $R      $I $1
mbtowc[0, C:D ]  $@  $F  $R      $I $1
mbtowc[1, 0:$#]      X
mbtowc[1, M:N ]  $@  $F      $O $I $2
mbtowc[2, 0:$#]   0  $F  $R          $0
wctomb[0, 0:$#]          $R          $1
wctomb[1, 0:$#]      X
wctomb[1, 0   ]          $R $O $I $0
wctomb[1, A:B ]  $@      $R $O      $2
wctomb[1, C:D ]  $@      $R $O      $2
wctomb[2, 0:$#]      X
wctomb[2, M:N ]              $O $I $0
LOCALE end
```

Describe the mapping between multibyte characters and wide characters defined by this locale file. Draw state-transition diagrams for both **mbtowc** and **wctomb**.

Exercise 13.2 One definition of EUC ("Extended UNIX Code") is similar to Shift JIS. A character code in the interval [0xA1, 0xFE] is the first of a two-character sequence. The second character must be in the interval [0x80, 0xFF]. Alter the locale file presented in the previous exercise to define this multibyte encoding. Describe your choice of mapping to wide characters.

Exercise 13.3 The following locale file defines the "JIS" multibyte encoding, which has locking shift states. The three-character sequence "\33(B" shifts to two-character mode The three-character sequence "\33$B" shifts back to one-character mode. In two-character mode, both character codes must be in the interval [0x21, 0x7E]:

```
LOCALE JIS
NOTE JIS codes with ESC+(+B and ESC+$+B
SET A 0x21
SET B 0x7e
SET X 0
SET Z 033
mb_cur_max 5
```

```
mbtowc[0, 0:$#] $@ $F     $O $I $0
mbtowc[0, 0   ] $@ $F     $O $I $1
mbtowc[0, Z   ]              $I $1
mbtowc[1, 0:$#]    X
mbtowc[1, '$' ]              $I $2
mbtowc[1, '(' ]              $I $3
mbtowc[2, 0:$#]    X
mbtowc[2, 'B' ]  0 $F $R     $I $0
mbtowc[3, 0:$#]    X
mbtowc[3, 'B' ]              $I $4
mbtowc[4, 0:$#]    X
mbtowc[4, Z   ]              $I $1
mbtowc[4, A:B ] $@ $F $R     $I $5
mbtowc[5, 0:$#]    X
mbtowc[5, A:B ] $@ $F     $O $I $4
wctomb[0, 0:$#]         $R      $1
wctomb[1, 0:$#]    X
wctomb[1, 0   ]         $R $O $I $0
wctomb[1, A:B ]    Z       $O    $2
wctomb[2, 0:$#] '('        $O    $3
wctomb[3, 0:$#] 'B'        $O    $4
wctomb[4, 0:$#]    X
wctomb[4, 0   ]    Z       $O    $7
wctomb[4, A:B ] $@      $R $O    $5
wctomb[5, 0:$#]    X
wctomb[5, A:B ]            $O $I $6
wctomb[6, 0:$#]         $R      $4
wctomb[7, 0:$#] '$'        $O    $7+$1
wctomb[8, 0:$#] 'B'        $O    $1
LOCALE end
```

Describe the mapping between multibyte characters and wide characters defined by this locale file. Draw state-transition diagrams for both **mbtowc** and **wctomb**.

Exercise 13.4 Alter the storage allocation functions to maintain up to eight lists of fixed-size elements. Add a freed item to an existing list of elements that have the same size. (Don't bother to sort these lists by storage address.) Otherwise, create a new list if not all eight have been established. Allocate from these lists if the request is exactly the right size. Why would you want to introduce this extra complexity?

Exercise 13.5 Alter the storage allocation functions to store a signature as well as a size in each allocated element. You might try a recipe something like:

```
p->_Signature = p->_Size ^ (int)p ^ 0x01234567;
```

(This example assumes that both **p** and **p->_Size** occupy 32 bits It is *not* portable code.) Check the signature of each element to be freed. Why would you want to introduce this extra complexity?

Exercise 13.6 Alter the storage allocation functions to require that all allocated storage be freed prior to program termination. Do you have to change **exit** as well? What discipline does that impose on the use of the storage allocation functions. Why would you want this extra constraint?

Exercise 13.7 Implement `exit`, `getenv`, and `system` for the C translator that you use. Do you have to write any assembly language?

Exercise 13.8 [**Harder**] Alter `strtod` to translate the input string `Inf` to the special code Inf. Translate the input string `NaN` to the special code NaN. Is this extension permitted by the C Standard? How can you modify the code in `<locale.h>` to turn the translation on and off? Can you devise a notation for specifying arbitrary not-a-number codes?

Exercise 13.9 [**Very hard**] Modify a C compiler to generate inline code for `abs`, `div`, `labs`, and `ldiv`.

Chapter 14: `<string.h>`

Background

The functions declared in `<string.h>` form an important addition to Standard C. They support a long tradition of using C to manipulate text as arrays of characters. Several other languages better integrate the manipulation of text strings, SNOBOL being a prime example. All that C incorporates in the language proper is the notation for null-terminated string literals such as `"abc"`. The Standard C library provides all the important functionality. These functions manipulate three forms of strings:

- Functions whose names begin with `mem` manipulate sequences of arbitrary characters. One argument (`s`) points to the start of the string — the lowest subscripted element. Another (`n`) counts the number of elements.

- Functions whose names begin with `strn` manipulate sequences of non-null characters. The arguments `s` and `n` are the same as above. The string ends just before the element `s[n]` or with the lowest value of `i` for which `s[i]` is zero (`'\0'`), whichever defines a shorter sequence.

- All other functions whose names begin with `str` manipulate null-terminated sequences of characters. These functions use only the argument `s` to determine the start of the string.

Each group has its distinct uses, as you might expect.

drawbacks   What you might not expect are several design lapses in these functions. The functions declared in `<string.h>` are not the result of a concerted design effort. Rather, they represent the accretion of contributions made by various authors over a span of years. By the time the C standardization effort began, it was too late to "fix" them. Too many programs had definite notions of how the functions should behave. Some of the problems are:

- Many of the functions that search return a null pointer when the search fails. You have to capture the return value and test it before you can safely use it further. A pointer to the end of the string is just as good a failure code and *much* more usable in expressions.

- The functions that copy return a pointer to the start of the destination area. That is sometimes useful in a larger expression, but the address of the *end* of the copy is more informative. You can perform multiple copies more effectively with the latter return value than with the former.

- The names of some functions are mysterious. **strcspn** and **strpbrk**, for example, do not loudly proclaim what they do.

- The set of functions is incomplete and inconsistent. **strnlen** and **memrchr** are two sensible additions, for example, whereas **strncat** is surprising.

Despite these aesthetic gripes, I find the functions declared in **<string.h>** to be both important and useful. Several of them are, in fact, leading contenders for generating inline code. Many C programs use these functions, and use them a lot. They are worth the effort to learn and to optimize.

What the C Standard Says

7.11 String handling **<string.h>**

7.11.1 String function conventions

The header **<string.h>** declares one type and several functions, and defines one macro useful for manipulating arrays of character type and other objects treated as arrays of character type.[133] The type is **size_t** and the macro is **NULL** (both described in 7.1.6). Various methods are used for determining the lengths of the arrays, but in all cases a **char *** or **void *** argument points to the initial (lowest addressed) character of the array. If an array is accessed beyond the end of an object, the behavior is undefined.

7.11.2 Copying functions

7.11.2.1 The **memcpy** function

Synopsis

```
#include <string.h>
void *memcpy(void *s1, const void *s2, size_t n);
```

Description

The **memcpy** function copies **n** characters from the object pointed to by **s2** into the object pointed to by **s1**. If copying takes place between objects that overlap, the behavior is undefined.

Returns

The **memcpy** function returns the value of **s1**.

7.11.2.2 The **memmove** function

Synopsis

```
#include <string.h>
void *memmove(void *s1, const void *s2, size_t n);
```

Description

The **memmove** function copies **n** characters from the object pointed to by **s2** into the object pointed to by **s1**. Copying takes place as if the **n** characters from the object pointed to by **s2** are first copied into a temporary array of **n** characters that does not overlap the objects pointed to by **s1** and **s2**, and then the **n** characters from the temporary array are copied into the object pointed to by **s1**.

Returns

The **memmove** function returns the value of **s1**.

7.11.2.3 The **strcpy** function

Synopsis

```
#include <string.h>
char *strcpy(char *s1, const char *s2);
```

Description

The **strcpy** function copies the string pointed to by **s2** (including the terminating null character) into the array pointed to by **s1**. If copying takes place between objects that overlap, the behavior is undefined.

Returns

The **strcpy** function returns the value of **s1**.

7.11.2.4 The **strncpy** function

Synopsis

```
#include <string.h>
char *strncpy(char *s1, const char *s2, size_t n);
```

Description

The **strncpy** function copies not more than **n** characters (characters that follow a null character are not copied) from the array pointed to by **s2** to the array pointed to by **s1**.[134] If copying takes place between objects that overlap, the behavior is undefined.

If the array pointed to by **s2** is a string that is shorter than **n** characters, null characters are appended to the copy in the array pointed to by **s1**, until **n** characters in all have been written.

Returns

The **strncpy** function returns the value of **s1**.

7.11.3 Concatenation functions

7.11.3.1 The **strcat** function

Synopsis

```
#include <string.h>
char *strcat(char *s1, const char *s2);
```

Description

The **strcat** function appends a copy of the string pointed to by **s2** (including the terminating null character) to the end of the string pointed to by **s1**. The initial character of **s2** overwrites the null character at the end of **s1**. If copying takes place between objects that overlap, the behavior is undefined.

Returns

The **strcat** function returns the value of **s1**.

7.11.3.2 The **strncat** function

Synopsis

```
#include <string.h>
char *strncat(char *s1, const char *s2, size_t n);
```

Description

The **strncat** function appends not more than **n** characters (a null character and characters that follow it are not appended) from the array pointed to by **s2** to the end of the string pointed to by **s1**. The initial character of **s2** overwrites the null character at the end of **s1**. A terminating null character is always appended to the result.[135] If copying takes place between objects that overlap, the behavior is undefined.

Returns

The **strncat** function returns the value of **s1**.

Forward references: the **strlen** function (7.11.6.3).

7.11.4 Comparison functions

The sign of a nonzero value returned by the comparison functions **memcmp**, **strcmp**, and **strncmp** is determined by the sign of the difference between the values of the first pair of characters (both interpreted as **unsigned char**) that differ in the objects being compared.

7.11.4.1 The **memcmp** function

Synopsis

```
#include <string.h>
int memcmp(const void *s1, const void *s2, size_t n);
```

Description

The **memcmp** function compares the first **n** characters of the object pointed to by **s1** to the first **n** characters of the object pointed to by **s2** .[136]

Returns

The **memcmp** function returns an integer greater than, equal to, or less than zero, accordingly as the object pointed to by **s1** is greater than, equal to, or less than the object pointed to by **s2**.

7.11.4.2 The `strcmp` function

Synopsis

```
#include <string.h>
int strcmp(const char *s1, const char *s2);
```

Description

The **strcmp** function compares the string pointed to by **s1** to the string pointed to by **s2**.

Returns

The **strcmp** function returns an integer greater than, equal to, or less than zero, accordingly as the string pointed to by **s1** is greater than, equal to, or less than the string pointed to by **s2**.

7.11.4.3 The `strcoll` function

Synopsis

```
#include <string.h>
int strcoll(const char *s1, const char *s2);
```

Description

The **strcoll** function compares the string pointed to by **s1** to the string pointed to by **s2**, both interpreted as appropriate to the **LC_COLLATE** category of the current locale.

Returns

The **strcoll** function returns an integer greater than, equal to, or less than zero, accordingly as the string pointed to by **s1** is greater than, equal to, or less than the string pointed to by **s2** when both are interpreted as appropriate to the current locale.

7.11.4.4 The `strncmp` function

Synopsis

```
#include <string.h>
int strncmp(const char *s1, const char *s2, size_t n);
```

Description

The **strncmp** function compares not more than **n** characters (characters that follow a null character are not compared) from the array pointed to by **s1** to the array pointed to by **s2**.

Returns

The **strncmp** function returns an integer greater than, equal to, or less than zero, accordingly as the possibly null-terminated array pointed to by **s1** is greater than, equal to, or less than the possibly null-terminated array pointed to by **s2**.

7.11.4.5 The `strxfrm` function

Synopsis

```
#include <string.h>
size_t strxfrm(char *s1, const char *s2, size_t n);
```

Description

The **strxfrm** function transforms the string pointed to by **s2** and places the resulting string into the array pointed to by **s1**. The transformation is such that if the **strcmp** function is applied to two transformed strings, it returns a value greater than, equal to, or less than zero, corresponding to the result of the **strcoll** function applied to the same two original strings. No more than **n** characters are placed into the resulting array pointed to by **s1**, including the terminating null character. If **n** is zero, **s1** is permitted to be a null pointer. If copying takes place between objects that overlap, the behavior is undefined.

Returns

The **strxfrm** function returns the length of the transformed string (not including the terminating null character). If the value returned is **n** or more, the contents of the array pointed to by **s1** are indeterminate.

Example

The value of the following expression is the size of the array needed to hold the transformation of the string pointed to by **s**.

```
1 + strxfrm(NULL, s, 0)
```

7.11.5 Search functions

7.11.5.1 The **memchr** function

Synopsis

```
#include <string.h>
void *memchr(const void *s, int c, size_t n);
```

Description

The **memchr** function locates the first occurrence of **c** (converted to an **unsigned char**) in the initial **n** characters (each interpreted as **unsigned char**) of the object pointed to by **s**.

Returns

The **memchr** function returns a pointer to the located character, or a null pointer if the character does not occur in the object.

7.11.5.2 The **strchr** function

Synopsis

```
#include <string.h>
char *strchr(const char *s, int c);
```

Description

The **strchr** function locates the first occurrence of **c** (converted to a **char**) in the string pointed to by **s**. The terminating null character is considered to be part of the string.

Returns

The **strchr** function returns a pointer to the located character, or a null pointer if the character does not occur in the string.

7.11.5.3 The **strcspn** function

Synopsis

```
#include <string.h>
size_t strcspn(const char *s1, const char *s2);
```

Description

The **strcspn** function computes the length of the maximum initial segment of the string pointed to by **s1** which consists entirely of characters *not* from the string pointed to by **s2**.

Returns

The **strcspn** function returns the length of the segment.

7.11.5.4 The **strpbrk** function

Synopsis

```
#include <string.h>
char *strpbrk(const char *s1, const char *s2);
```

Description

The **strpbrk** function locates the first occurrence in the string pointed to by **s1** of any character from the string pointed to by **s2**.

Returns

The **strpbrk** function returns a pointer to the character, or a null pointer if no character from **s2** occurs in **s1**.

7.11.5.5 The **strrchr** function

Synopsis

```
#include <string.h>
char *strrchr(const char *s, int c);
```

memchr

strchr

strcspn

strpbrk

strrchr

Description

The **strrchr** function locates the last occurrence of **c** (converted to a **char**) in the string pointed to by **s**. The terminating null character is considered to be part of the string.

Returns

The **strrchr** function returns a pointer to the character, or a null pointer if **c** does not occur in the string.

7.11.5.6 The **strspn** function

Synopsis

```
#include <string.h>
size_t strspn(const char *s1, const char *s2);
```

Description

The **strspn** function computes the length of the maximum initial segment of the string pointed to by **s1** which consists entirely of characters from the string pointed to by **s2**.

Returns

The **strspn** function returns the length of the segment.

7.11.5.7 The **strstr** function

Synopsis

```
#include <string.h>
char *strstr(const char *s1, const char *s2);
```

Description

The **strstr** function locates the first occurrence in the string pointed to by **s1** of the sequence of characters (excluding the terminating null character) in the string pointed to by **s2**

Returns

The **strstr** function returns a pointer to the located string, or a null pointer if the string is not found. If **s2** points to a string with zero length, the function returns **s1**.

7.11.5.8 The **strtok** function

Synopsis

```
#include <string.h>
char *strtok(char *s1, const char *s2);
```

Description

A sequence of calls to the **strtok** function breaks the string pointed to by **s1** into a sequence of tokens, each of which is delimited by a character from the string pointed to by **s2**. The first call in the sequence has **s1** as its first argument, and is followed by calls with a null pointer as their first argument. The separator string pointed to by **s2** may be different from call to call.

The first call in the sequence searches the string pointed to by **s1** for the first character that is *not* contained in the current separator string pointed to by **s2**. If no such character is found, then there are no tokens in the string pointed to by **s1** and the **strtok** function returns a null pointer. If such a character is found, it is the start of the first token.

The **strtok** function then searches from there for a character that *is* contained in the current separator string. If no such character is found, the current token extends to the end of the string pointed to by **s1**, and subsequent searches for a token will return a null pointer. If such a character is found, it is overwritten by a null character, which terminates the current token. The **strtok** function saves a pointer to the following character, from which the next search for a token will start.

Each subsequent call, with a null pointer as the value of the first argument, starts searching from the saved pointer and behaves as described above.

The implementation shall behave as if no library function calls the **strtok** function.

Returns

The **strtok** function returns a pointer to the first character of a token, or a null pointer if there is no token.

Example

```
#include <string.h>
 static char str[] = "?a???b,,,#c";
char *t;

t = strtok(str, "?");   /* t points to the token "a" */
t = strtok(NULL, ",");  /* t points to the token "??b" */
t = strtok(NULL, "#,"); /* t points to the token "c" */
t = strtok(NULL, "?");  /* t is a null pointer */
```

7.11.6 Miscellaneous functions

7.11.6.1 The `memset` function

Synopsis

```
#include <string.h>
void *memset(void *s, int c, size_t n);
```

Description

The **memset** function copies the value of **c** (converted to an **unsigned char**) into each of the first **n** characters of the object pointed to by **s**.

Returns

The **memset** function returns the value of **s**.

7.11.6.2 The `strerror` function

Synopsis

```
#include <string.h>
char *strerror(int errnum);
```

Description

The **strerror** function maps the error number in **errnum** to an error message string.

The implementation shall behave as if no library function calls the **strerror** function.

Returns

The **strerror** function returns a pointer to the string, the contents of which are implementation-defined. The array pointed to shall not be modified by the program, but may be overwritten by a subsequent call to the **strerror** function.

7.11.6.3 The `strlen` function

Synopsis

```
#include <string.h>
size_t strlen(const char *s);
```

Description

The **strlen** function computes the length of the string pointed to by **s**.

Returns

The **strlen** function returns the number of characters that precede the terminating null character.

Footnotes

133. See "future library directions" (7.13.8).

134. Thus, if there is no null character in the first **n** characters of the array pointed to by **s2**, the result will not be null-terminated.

135. Thus, the maximum number of characters that can end up in the array pointed to by **s1** is **strlen(s1)+n+1**.

136. The contents of "holes" used as padding for purposes of alignment within structure objects are indeterminate. Strings shorter than their allocated space and unions may also cause problems in comparison.

Using `<string.h>`

You use the functions declared in `<string.h>` to manipulate strings of characters. You characterize each string by an argument (call is **s**) which is a pointer to the start of the string.

- If a string can contain null characters, you must also specify its length (call it **n**) as an additional argument. **n** can be zero. Use the functions whose names begin with **mem**.

- If a string may or may not have a terminating null character, you must similarly specify its maximum length **n**, which can be zero. Use the functions whose names begin with **strn**.

- If a string assuredly has a terminating null character, you specify only **s**. Use the remaining functions whose names begin with **str**.

Beyond this simple categorization, the string functions are only loosely related. I describe each separately, along with the macro and the type defined in `<string.h>`:

NULL   **NULL** — See page 220.

size_t   **size_t** — See page 219.

memchr   **memchr** — Use this function to locate the first occurrence (the one having the lowest subscript) of a character in a character sequence of known length. The function type casts the first (string pointer) argument to *pointer to unsigned char*. It also type casts the second (search character) argument to *unsigned char*. That ensures that an argument expression of any character type behaves sensibly and predictably. A search failure returns a null pointer, however. Be sure to test the return value before you try to use it to access storage. Also note that the return value has type *pointer to void*. You can assign the value to a character pointer but you can't use it to access storage unless you first type cast it to some character pointer type.

memcmp   **memcmp** — This function offers the quickest way to determine whether two character sequences of the same known length match character for character. You can also use it to establish a lexical ordering between two character sequences, but that ordering can change among implementations. If a portable result is important, you must write your own comparison function.

memcpy   **memcpy** — If you can be certain that the destination **s1** and source **s2** do not overlap, **memcpy(s1, s2, n)** will perform the copy safely and rapidly. If the two might overlap, use **memmove(s1, s2, n)** instead. *Do not* assume that either function accesses storage in any particular order. In particular, if you want to store the same value throughout a contiguous sequence of elements in a character array, use **memset**.

memmove   **memmove** — See **memcpy** above.

memset   **memset** — This is the safe way to store the same value throughout a contiguous sequence of elements in a character array.

strcat   **strcat** — If you have only two strings **s1** and **s2** to concatenate, or just a few short strings, use **strcat(s1, s2)**. Otherwise, favor a form such as **strcpy(s1 += strlen(s1), s2)**. That saves repeated, and ever-lengthening, rescans of the initial part of the string. Be sure that the destination array is large enough to hold the concatenated string. Note that **strcat** returns **s1**, not a pointer to the new end of the string.

strchr   **strchr** — Use this function to locate the first occurrence (the one having the lowest subscript) of a character in a null-terminated string. The function type casts the second (search character) argument to *char*. That ensures that an argument expression of any character type behaves sensibly and predictably. A search failure returns a null pointer, however. Be sure to test the return value before you try to use it to access storage. Note that the call **strchr(s, '\0')** returns a pointer to the terminating null. See also **strcspn**, **strpbrk**, and **strrchr**, described below.

strcmp   **strcmp** — This function offers the quickest way to determine whether two null-terminated strings match character for character. You can also use it to establish a lexical ordering between two strings, but that ordering can change among implementations. If a portable result is important, you must write your own comparison function. See also **strcoll** and **strxfrm**, below.

strcoll   **strcoll** — Use this function to determine the locale-specific lexical ordering of two null-terminated strings. You *must* know the current status of locale category **LC_COLLATE** to use this function wisely. (You must at least assume that someone else has set this category wisely.) Under some circumstances, you may want to use **strxfrm**, described below, instead.

strcpy   **strcpy** — If you can be certain that the destination **s1** and source **s2** do not overlap, **strcpy(s1, s2)** will perform the copy safely and rapidly. If the two might overlap, use **memmove(s1, s2, strlen(s2) + 1)** instead. *Do not* assume that either function accesses storage in any particular order.

strcspn   **strcspn** — You can think of **strcspn** as a companion to **strchr** that matches any of a set of characters instead of just one. That makes it similar to **strpbrk** as well. Note, however, that **strcspn** returns an *index* into the string instead of a pointer to an element. If it finds no match, it returns the index of the terminating null instead of a null pointer. Thus, you may find that the call **strcspn(s, "a")**, for example, is more convenient than either **strchr(s, 'a')** or **strpbrk(s, "a")**.

strerror **strerror** — Use **strerror(errcode)** to determine the null-terminated message string that corresponds to the error code **errcode**. (Chapter 3: **<errno.h>** describes the macro **errno** and the standard error codes.) **errcode** should be **errno** or one of the macros defined in **<errno.h>** whose name begins with **E**. Be sure to copy or write out the message before you call **strerror** again. A later call can alter the message. If you simply want to write to the standard error stream a message containing **strerror(errno)**, see **perror**, declared in **<stdio.h>**.

strlen   strlen — Use this function wherever possible to determine the length of a null-terminated string. It may well be implemented with inline code.

strncat   strncat — The strn in strncat(s1, s2, n2) refers to the string s2 the the function concatenates onto the end of the null-terminated string s1. The function copies at most n2 characters *plus* a terminating null if it doesn't copy a terminating null. Thus, strlen(s1) increases by at most n2 as a result of the call to strncat. That makes strncat a safer function than strcat, at the risk of truncating s2 to length n2.

strncmp   strncmp — This function offers the quickest way to determine whether two character sequences of the same known length match character for character up to and including any null character in both. You can also use it to establish a lexical ordering between two such character sequences, but that ordering can change among implementations. If a portable result is important, you must write your own comparison function.

strncpy   strncpy — If you can be certain that the destination s1 and source s2 do not overlap, strncpy(s1, s2, n2) will perform the copy safely. Note, however, that the function stores exactly n2 characters starting at s1. It may drop trailing characters, including the terminating null. It stores additional null characters as needed to make up a short count. If the two areas might overlap, use memmove(s1, s2, n2) instead. (You must then store the appropriate number of null characters at the end, if that is important to you.) *Do not* assume that either function accesses storage in any particular order.

strpbrk   strpbrk — You can think of strpbrk as a companion to strchr that matches any of a set of characters instead of just one. That makes it similar to strcspn as well. Note, however, that strcspn returns an *index* into the string instead of a pointer to an element. If it finds no match, it returns the index of the terminating null instead of a null pointer. Thus, you may find that the call strcspn(s, "abc"), for example, is more convenient than strpbrk(s, "abc").

strrchr   strrchr — Use this function to locate the last occurrence (the one having the highest subscript) of a character in a null-terminated string. The function type casts the second (search character) argument to *char*. That ensures that an argument expression of any character type behaves sensibly and predictably. A search failure returns a null pointer, however. Be sure to test the return value before you try to use it to access storage. Note that the call strrchr(s, '\0') returns a pointer to the terminating null. See also strchr, strcspn, and strpbrk, described above.

strspn   strspn — You can think of strspn as the complement to strcspn. It searches for a character that matches *none* of the elements in a set of characters instead of *any* one of them. strcspn also returns an index into the string or, if it finds no match, the index of the terminating null. Thus, the call strspn(s, "abc"), for example, finds the longest possible *span* of characters from the set "abc".

strstr   **strstr** — You write `strstr(s1, s2)` to locate the first occurrence of the substring `s2` in the string `s1`. A successful search returns a pointer to the *start* of the substring within `s1`. Note that a search failure returns a null pointer.

strtok   **strtok** — This is an intricate function designed to help you parse a null-terminated string into tokens. You specify the set of *separator* characters. Sequences of one or more separators occur between tokens. Such sequences can also occur before the first token and after the last. **strtok** maintains an internal memory of where it left off parsing a string. Hence, you can process only one string at a time using **strtok**. Here, for example, is a code sequence that calls the function **word** for each "word" in the string **line**. The code sequence defines a word as the longest possible sequence of characters not containing "white-space" — define here as a space, horizontal tab, or newline:

```
char *s;

for (s = line; (s = strtok(s, " \t\n")) != NULL; s = NULL)
    word(s);
```

The first call to **strtok** has a first argument that is not a null pointer. That starts the scan at the beginning of **line**. Subsequent calls replace this argument with **NULL** to continue the scan. If the return value on any call is not a null pointer, it points to a null-terminated string containing no separators. Note that **strtok** stores null characters in the string starting at **line**. Be sure that this storage is writable and need not be preserved for future processing.

You can specify a different set of separators on each call to **strtok** that processes a given string, by the way.

strxfrm   **strxfrm** — Use `strxfrm(s1, s2, n)` to map the null-terminated string `s2` to a (non-overlapping) version at `s1`. Strings you map this way can later be compared by calling **strcmp**. The comparison determines the locale-specific lexical ordering of the two strings that you mapped *from*. You *must* know the current status of locale category **LC_COLLATE** to use this function wisely. (You must at least assume that someone else has set this category wisely.) Under most circumstances, you may want to use **strcoll**, described above, instead. Use **strxfrm** if you plan to make repeated comparisons or if the locale may change before you can make the comparison. Use **malloc**, declared in `<stdlib.h>`, to allocate storage for `s1`, as in:

```
size_t n = strxfrm(NULL, s2, 0);
char *s1 = malloc(n + 1);

if (s1)
    strxfrm(s1, s2, n);
```

The first call to **strxfrm** determines the amount of storage required. The second performs the conversion (again) and stores the translated string in the allocated array.

Implementing <string.h>

The functions declared in <string.h> work largely independent of each other. The only exception is the pair strcoll and strxfrm. They perform the same essential operation two different ways. I discuss them last. The remaining functions each perform a fairly simple operation. Here, the challenge is to write them to be clear, robust, and efficient.

header   Figure 14.1 shows the file string.h. As usual, it inherits from the internal
<string.h> header <yvals.h> definitions that are repeated in several standard headers. I discuss the implemention of both the macro NULL and the type definition size_t in Chapter 11: <stddef.h>.

Figure 14.1:
string.h

```
/* string.h standard header */
#ifndef _STRING
#define _STRING
#ifndef _YVALS
#include <yvals.h>
#endif
        /* macros */
#define NULL    _NULL
        /* type definitions */
#ifndef _SIZET
#define _SIZET
typedef _Sizet size_t;
#endif
        /* declarations */
void *memchr(const void *, int, size_t);
int memcmp(const void *, const void *, size_t);
void *memcpy(void *, const void *, size_t);
void *memmove(void *, const void *, size_t);
void *memset(void *, int, size_t);
char *strcat(char *, const char *);
char *strchr(const char *, int);
int strcmp(const char *, const char *);
int strcoll(const char *, const char *);
char *strcpy(char *, const char *);
size_t strcspn(const char *, const char *);
char *strerror(int);
size_t strlen(const char *);
char *strncat(char *, const char *, size_t);
int strncmp(const char *, const char *, size_t);
char *strncpy(char *, const char *, size_t);
char *strpbrk(const char *, const char *);
char *strrchr(const char *, int);
size_t strspn(const char *, const char *);
char *strstr(const char *, const char *);
char *strtok(char *, const char *);
size_t strxfrm(char *, const char *, size_t);
char *_Strerror(int, char *);
        /* macro overrides */
#define strerror(errcode)  _Strerror(errcode, _NULL)
#endif
```

Only the function **strerror** has a masking macro. It shares the internal function **_strerror** with the function **perror**, declared in `<stdio.h>`. I discuss why on page 292.

Several other functions declared in `<string.h>` are serious candidates for implementing as builtin functions that generate inline code. A common practice is to give these builtin versions secret names. You then provide masking macros to gain access to the builtin functions. (See footnote 96 of the C Standard on page 6.) Thus, a production version of `<string.h>` could well include several additional masking macros.

function
memchr
Let's begin with the **mem** functions. Figure 14.2 shows the file **memchr.c**. The major concern of function **memchr** is to get various types right. You must assign both the pointer and the character arguments to dynamic data objects with different types. That lets you compare the array elements as type *unsigned char* correctly and efficiently. I wrote the **(void *)** type cast in the *return* expression for clarity, not out of necessity.

function
memcmp
Figure 14.3 shows the file **memcmp.c**. **memcmp**, too, is careful to perform *unsigned char* comparisons to meet the requirements of the C Standard.

function
memcpy
Figure 14.4 shows the file **memcpy.c**. I chose *char* as the working type within **memcpy** in the off chance that some computer architectures may favor it over *unsigned char*. (That's one of the justifications for having a "plain"

Figure 14.2:
memchr.c

```
/* memchr function */
#include <string.h>

void *(memchr)(const void *s, int c, size_t n)
    {                           /* find first occurrence of c in s[n] */
    const unsigned char uc = c;
    const unsigned char *su;

    for (su = s; 0 < n; ++su, --n)
        if (*su == uc)
            return ((void *)su);
    return (NULL);
    }
```

Figure 14.3:
memcmp.c

```
/* memcmp function */
#include <string.h>

int (memcmp)(const void *s1, const void *s2,
    size_t n)
    {                           /* compare unsigned char s1[n], s2[n] */
    const unsigned char *su1, *su2;

    for (su1 = s1, su2 = s2; 0 < n; ++su1, ++su2, --n)
        if (*su1 != *su2)
            return ((*su1 < *su2) ? -1 : +1);
    return (0);
    }
```

Figure 14.4:
memcpy.c

```
/* memcpy function */
#include <string.h>

void *(memcpy)(void *s1, const void *s2, size_t n)
    {                           /* copy char s2[n] to s1[n] in any order */
    char *su1;
    const char *su2;

    for (su1 = s1, su2 = s2; 0 < n; ++su1, ++su2, --n)
        *su1 = *su2;
    return (s1);
    }                                                                       □
```

Figure 14.5:
memmove.c

```
/* memmove function */
#include <string.h>

void *(memmove)(void *s1, const void *s2, size_t n)
    {                           /* copy char s2[n] to s1[n] safely */
    char *sc1;
    const char *sc2;

    sc1 = s1;
    sc2 = s2;
    if (sc2 < sc1 && sc1 < sc2 + n)
        for (sc1 += n, sc2 += n; 0 < n; --n)
            *--sc1 = *--sc2;                        /*copy backwards */
    else
        for (; 0 < n; --n)
            *sc1++ = *sc2++;                        /* copy forwards */
    return (s1);
    }                                                                       □
```

Figure 14.6:
memset.c

```
/* memset function */
#include <string.h>

void *(memset)(void *s, int c, size_t n)
    {                           /* store c throughout unsigned char s[n] */
    const unsigned char uc = c;
    unsigned char *su;

    for (su = s; 0 < n; ++su, --n)
        *su = uc;
    return (s);
    }                                                                       □
```

character type.) memcpy can assume that its source and destination areas do not overlap. Hence, it performs the simplest copy that it can.

function
memmove

Figure 14.5 shows the file memmove.c. The function memmove must work properly even when its operands overlap. Hence, it first checks for an overlap that would prevent the correct operation of an ascending copy. In that case, it copies elements in descending order.

Figure 14.7:
strncat.c

```
/* strncat function */
#include <string.h>

char *(strncat)(char *s1, const char *s2, size_t n)
    {                           /* copy char s2[max n] to end of s1[] */
    char *s;

    for (s = s1; *s != '\0'; ++s)
        ;                                       /* find end of s1[] */
    for (; 0 < n && *s2 != '\0'; --n)
        *s++ = *s2++;           /* copy at most n chars from s2[] */
    *s = '\0';
    return (s1);
    }
```

Figure 14.8:
strncmp.c

```
/* strncmp function */
#include <string.h>

int (strncmp)(const char *s1, const char *s2, size_t n)
    {                       /* compare unsigned char s1[max n], s2[max n] */
    for (; 0 < n; ++s1, ++s2, --n)
        if (*s1 != *s2)
            return ((*(unsigned char *)s1
                < *(unsigned char *)s2) ? -1 : +1);
        else if (*s1 == '\0')
            return (0);
    return (0);
    }
```

function
memset
Figure 14.6 shows the file `memset.c`. I chose *unsigned char* as the working type within `memset` in the off chance that some implementation might generate an overflow storing certain *int* values in the other character types.

function
strncat
Now consider the three `strn` functions. Figure 14.7 shows the file `strncat.c`. The function `strncat` first locates the end of the destination string. Then it concatenates at most n additional from the source string. Note that the function *always* supplies a terminating null character.

function
strncmp
Figure 14.8 shows the file `strncmp.c`. The function `strncmp` is similar to `memcmp`, except that it also stops on a terminating null character. And unlike `memcmp`, `strncmp` can use its pointer arguments directly. It type casts them to *pointer to unsigned char* only to compute a nonzero return value.

function
strncpy
Figure 14.9 shows the file `strncpy.c`. The function `strncpy` is likewise similar to `memcpy`, except that it stops on a terminating null. `strncpy` also has the unfortunate requirement that it must supply null padding characters for a string whose length is less than n.

strcat
strcmp
strcpy
Three of the `str` functions are direct analogs of the `strn` functions. Figure 14.10 through Figure 14.12 show the files `strcat.c`, `strcmp.c`, and `strcpy.c`. The functions `strcat`, `strcmp`, and `strcpy` differ only in not worrying about a limiting string length n. Of course, `strcpy` has no padding to contend with.

Figure 14.9:
`strncpy.c`

```
/* strncpy function */
#include <string.h>

char *(strncpy)(char *s1, const char *s2, size_t n)
    {                                     /* copy char s2[max n] to s1[n] */
    char *s;

    for (s = s1; 0 < n && *s2 != '\0'; --n)
        *s++ = *s2++;                /* copy at most n chars from s2[] */
    for (; 0 < n; --n)
        *s++ = '\0';
    return (s1);
    }
```

Figure 14.10:
`strcat.c`

```
/* strcat function */
#include <string.h>

char *(strcat)(char *s1, const char *s2)
    {                                     /* copy char s2[] to end of s1[] */
    char *s;

    for (s = s1; *s != '\0'; ++s)
        ;                                             /* find end of s1[] */
    for (; (*s = *s2) != '\0'; ++s, ++s2)
        ;                                             /* copy s2[] to end */
    return (s1);
    }
```

Figure 14.11:
`strcmp.c`

```
/* strcmp function */
#include <string.h>

int (strcmp)(const char *s1,
    const char *s2)
    {                               /* compare unsigned char s1[], s2[] */
    for (; *s1 == *s2; ++s1, ++s2)
        if (*s1 == '\0')
            return (0);
    return ((*(unsigned char *)s1
        < *(unsigned char *)s2) ? -1 : +1);
    }
```

Figure 14.12:
`strcpy.c`

```
/* strcpy function */
#include <string.h>

char *(strcpy)(char *s1, const char *s2)
    {                                         /* copy char s2[] to s1[] */
    char *s = s1;

    for (s = s1; (*s++ = *s2++) != '\0'; )
        ;
    return (s1);
    }
```

Figure 14.13:
strlen.c

```
/* strlen function */
#include <string.h>

size_t (strlen)(const char *s)
    {                                           /* find length of s[] */
    const char *sc;

    for (sc = s; *sc != '\0'; ++sc)
        ;
    return (sc - s);
    }
```

Figure 14.14:
strchr.c

```
/* strchr function */
#include <string.h>

char *(strchr)(const char *s, int c)
    {                       /* find first occurrence of c in char s[] */
    const char ch = c;

    for (; *s != ch; ++s)
        if (*s == '\0')
            return (NULL);
    return ((char *)s);
    }
```

Figure 14.15:
strcspn.c

```
/* strcspn function */
#include <string.h>

size_t (strcspn)(const char *s1, const char *s2)
    {           /* find index of first s1[i] that matches any s2[] */
    const char *sc1, *sc2;

    for (sc1 = s1; *sc1 != '\0'; ++sc1)
        for (sc2 = s2; *sc2 != '\0'; ++sc2)
            if (*sc1 == *sc2)
                return (sc1 - s1);
    return (sc1 - s1);                      /* terminating nulls match */
    }
```

function
strlen   Figure 14.13 shows the file `strlen.c`. The function `strlen` is probably the most heavily used of the functions declared in `<string.h>`. It is the leading contender for implementation as a builtin function. If that form exists, look for places where `strlen` masquerades as inline code. The functions `strcat` and `strncat` are two obvious examples.

function
strchr   Seven functions scan strings in various ways. Figure 14.14 shows the file `strchr.c`. The function `strchr` is the simplest of these functions. It is the obvious analog of `memchr`.

strcspn   Figure 14.15 through Figure 14.17 show the files `strcspn.c`, `strpbrk.c`,
strpbrk   and `strspn.c`. Both `strcspn` and `strpbrk` perform the same function. Only
strspn   the return values differ. The function `strspn` is the complement of `strcspn`.

Figure 14.16:
strpbrk.c

```c
/* strpbrk function */
#include <string.h>

char *(strpbrk)(const char *s1, const char *s2)
    {          /* find index of first s1[i] that matches any s2[] */
    const char *sc1, *sc2;

    for (sc1 = s1; *sc1 != '\0'; ++sc1)
        for (sc2 = s2; *sc2 != '\0'; ++sc2)
            if (*sc1 == *sc2)
                return ((char *)sc1);
    return (NULL);                          /* terminating nulls match */
    }
```

Figure 14.17:
strspn.c

```c
/* strspn function */
#include <string.h>

size_t (strspn)(const char *s1, const char *s2)
    {          /* find index of first s1[i] that matches no s2[] */
    const char *sc1, *sc2;

    for (sc1 = s1; *sc1 != '\0'; ++sc1)
        for (sc2 = s2; ; ++sc2)
            if (*sc2 == '\0')
                return (sc1 - s1);
            else if (*sc1 == *sc2)
                break;
    return (sc1 - s1);                      /* null doesn't match */
    }
```

Figure 14.18:
strrchr.c

```c
/* strrchr function */
#include <string.h>

char *(strrchr)(const char *s, int c)
    {                        /* find last occurrence of c in char s[] */
    const char ch = c;
    const char *sc;

    for (sc = NULL; ; ++s)
        {                                   /* check another char */
        if (*s == ch)
            sc = s;
        if (*s == '\0')
            return ((char *)sc);
        }
    }
```

function
strrchr

Figure 14.18 shows the file strrchr.c. The function strrchr is a useful complement to strchr. It memorizes the pointer to the rightmost occurrence (if any) in sc. The type cast in the *return* statement is necessary, in this case, because sc points to a constant type.

Figure 14.19:
strstr.c

```
/* strstr function */
#include <string.h>

char *(strstr)(const char *s1, const char *s2)
    {                            /* find first occurrence of s2[] in s1[] */
    if (*s2 == '\0')
        return ((char *)s1);
    for (; (s1 = strchr(s1, *s2)) != NULL; ++s1)
        {                                      /* match rest of prefix */
        const char *sc1, *sc2;

        for (sc1 = s1, sc2 = s2; ; )
            if (*++sc2 == '\0')
                return ((char *)s1);
            else if (*++sc1 != *sc2)
                break;
        }
    return (NULL);
    }
```
□

Figure 14.20:
strtok.c

```
/* strtok function */
#include <string.h>

char *(strtok)(char *s1, const char *s2)
    {                            /* find next token in s1[] delimited by s2[] */
    char *sbegin, *send;
    static char *ssave = "";                         /* for safety */

    sbegin = (s1) ? s1 : ssave;
    sbegin += strspn(sbegin, s2);
    if (*sbegin == '\0')
        {                                      /* end of scan */
        ssave = "";                            /* for safety */
        return (NULL);
        }
    send = strpbrk(sbegin, s2);
    if (*send != '\0')
        *send++ = '\0';
    ssave = send;
    return (sbegin);
    }
```
□

function
strstr   Figure 14.19 shows the file `strstr.c`. The function `strstr` calls `strchr` to find the first character of the string `s2` within the string `s1`. Only then does it tool up to check whether the rest of `s2` matches a substring in `s1`. The function treats an empty string `s2` as a special case. It matches the implicit empty string at the start of `s1`.

function
strtok   Figure 14.20 shows the file `strtok.c`. The function `strtok` is the last and the messiest of the seven string scanning functions. It doesn't look bad because it is written here in terms of `strspn` and `strpbrk`. It must contend, however, with writable static storage and multiple calls to process the same

string. It is probably at least as hard to use correctly as to write correctly. When **strtok** is not actively scanning an argument string, it points at an empty string. That prevents at least some improper calls from causing the function to make invalid storage accesses. (The function is still at risk if storage is freed for a string that it is scanning.)

strerror
_Strerror

Figure 14.21 shows the file **strerror.c**. It defines both **strerror** and the internal function **_Strerror**. (See page 292 for why **perror**, declared in **<stdio.h>** calls **_Strerror**.) **_Strerror** constructs a text representation of certain error codes in a buffer. It uses its own static buffer only when called by **strerror**. I supply here specific messages only for the minimum set of error codes defined in this implementation of **<errno.h>**. You may want to add more. Any unknown error codes print as three-digit decimal numbers.

Figure 14.21:
strerror.c

```
/* strerror function */
#include <errno.h>
#include <string.h>

char *_Strerror(int errcode, char *buf)
    {                   /* copy error message into buffer as needed */
    static char sbuf[] = {"error #xxx"};

    if (buf == NULL)
        buf = sbuf;
    switch (errcode)
        {                           /* switch on known error codes */
    case 0:
        return ("no error");
    case EDOM:
        return ("domain error");
    case ERANGE:
        return ("range error");
    case EFPOS:
        return ("file positioning error");
    default:
        if (errcode < 0 || _NERR <= errcode)
            return ("unknown error");
        else
            {                       /* generate numeric error code */
            strcpy(buf, "error #xxx");
            buf[9] = errcode % 10 + '0';
            buf[8] = (errcode /= 10) % 10 + '0';
            buf[7] = (errcode / 10) % 10 + '0';
            return (buf);
            }
        }
    }

char *(strerror)(int errcode)
    {               /* find error message corresponding to errcode */
    return (_Strerror(errcode, NULL));
    }
```

collation
functions

The last two functions declared in `<string.h>` help you perform locale-specific string collation. Both `strcoll` and `strxfrm` determine collation sequence by mapping strings to a form that collates properly when compared using `strcmp`. The locale category `LC_COLLATE` determines this mapping. (See Chapter 6: `<locale.h>`.) It does so by specifing the state table used by the internal function `_Strxfrm`. Thus, `strcoll` and `strxfrm` call `_Strxfrm` to map strings appropriately.

header
"xstrxfrm.h"

Figure 14.22 shows the file `xstrxfrm.h`. All the collation functions include the internal header `"xstrxfrm.h"`. It includes in turn the standard header `<string.h>` and the internal header `"xstate.h"`. (See the file `xstate.h` on page 100.) Beyond that, `"xstrxfrm.h"` defines the type `_Cosave` and declares the function `_Strxfrm`. A data object of type `_Cosave` stores state information between calls to `_Strxfrm`.

function
strxfrm

Figure 14.23 shows the file `strxfrm.c`. The function `strxfrm` best illustrates how the collation functions work together. It stores the mapped string in the buffer pointed to by `s1`, of length `n`. Once the buffer is full, the function translates the remainder of the source string to determine the full length of the mapped string. `strxfrm` stores any such excess characters in its own dynamic temporary buffer `buf`.

function
_Strxfrm

Figure 14.24 shows the file `xstrxfrm.c`. It defines the function `_Strxfrm` that performs the actual mapping. It does so as a finite-state machine executing the state table stored at `_Wcstate`, defined in the file `xstate.c`. (See page 107.)

`_Strxfrm` must be particularly cautious because `_Wcstate` can be flawed. It can change with locale category `LC_COLLATE` in ways that the Standard C library cannot control.

Note the various ways that the function can elect to take an error return:

- if a transfer occurs to an undefined state
- if no state table exists for a given state
- if the function makes so many state transitions since generating an output character that it must be looping
- if the state table entry specifically signals an error

Figure 14.22:
xstrxfrm.h

```
/* xstrxfrm.h internal header */
#include <string.h>
#include "xstate.h"
        /* type definitions */
typedef struct {
    unsigned char _State;
    unsigned short _Wchar;
    } _Cosave;
        /* declarations */
size_t _Strxfrm(char *, const unsigned char **, size_t,
    _Cosave *);                                          □
```

Figure 14.23:
strxfrm.c

```
/* strxfrm function */
#include "xstrxfrm.h"

size_t (strxfrm)(char *s1, const char *s2, size_t n)
    {          /* transform s2[] to s1[] by locale-dependent rule */
    size_t nx = 0;
    const unsigned char *s = (const unsigned char *)s2;
    _Cosave state = {0};

    while (nx < n)
        {                                     /* translate and deliver */
        size_t i = _Strxfrm(s1, &s, nx - n, &state);

        s1 += i, nx += i;
        if (0 < i && s1[-1] == '\0')
            return (nx - 1);
        else if (*s == '\0')
            s = (const unsigned char *)s2;              /* rescan */
        }
    for (; ; )
        {                                     /* translate and count */
        char buf[32];
        size_t i = _Strxfrm(buf, &s, sizeof (buf), &state);

        nx += i;
        if (0 < i && buf[i - 1] == '\0')
            return (nx - 1);
        else if (*s == '\0')
            s = (const unsigned char *)s2;              /* rescan */
        }
    }                                                                   □
```

The rest of _Strxfrm is simple by comparison. The function retains the wide-character accumulator (ps->_Wchar) as part of the state memory. That simplifies generating a sequence of mapped characters with a common component while in a given shift state. _Strxfrm returns after it fills the output buffer (with size characters) or whenever it encounters the terminating null character in the source string.

That can happen more than once. Note the careful way that strxfrm distinguishes the three reasons why _Strxfrm returns:

- If the last character delivered is a null character, the translation is complete. _Strxfrm delivers a null character if an error occurs. It also jiggers the stored state information to fail immediately should it be inadvertently called again for the same string.

- Otherwise, if the next source character is a null character, _Strxfrm wants to rescan the source string. _Strxfrm will not point past a null character in the source string.

- Otherwise, _Strxfrm wants to continue where it left off.

```
/* _Strxfrm function */
#include <limits.h>
#include "xstrxfrm.h"

size_t _Strxfrm(char *sout, const unsigned char **psin,
    size_t size, _Cosave *ps)
    {                          /* translate string to collatable form */
    char state = ps->_State;
    int leave = 0;
    int limit = 0;
    int nout = 0;
    const unsigned char *sin = *psin;
    unsigned short wc = ps->_Wchar;

    for (; ; )
        {                          /* perform a state transformation */
        unsigned short code;
        const unsigned short *stab;

        if (_NSTATE <= state
            || (stab = _Costate._Tab[state]) == NULL
            || (_NSTATE*UCHAR_MAX) <= ++limit
            || (code = stab[*sin]) == 0)
            break;
        state = (code & ST_STATE) >> ST_STOFF;
        if (code & ST_FOLD)
            wc = wc & ~UCHAR_MAX | code & ST_CH;
        if (code & ST_ROTATE)
            wc = wc >> CHAR_BIT & UCHAR_MAX | wc << CHAR_BIT;
        if (code & ST_OUTPUT && ((sout[nout++]
            = code & ST_CH ? code : wc) == '\0'
            || size <= nout))
            leave = 1;
        if (code & ST_INPUT)
            if (*sin != '\0')
                ++sin, limit = 0;
            else
                leave = 1;
        if (leave)
            {                          /* return for now */
            *psin = sin;
            ps->_State = state;
            ps->_Wchar = wc;
            return (nout);
            }
        }
    sout[nout++] = '\0';                          /* error return */
    *psin = sin;
    ps->_State = _NSTATE;
    return (nout);
    }
```
□

Figure 14.25:
strcoll.c

```
/* strcoll function */
#include "xstrxfrm.h"

        /* type definitions */
typedef struct {
    char buf[32];
    const unsigned char *s1, *s2, *sout;
    _Cosave state;
    } Sctl;

static size_t getxfrm(Sctl *p)
    {                                       /* get transformed chars */
    size_t i;

    do {                                /* loop until chars delivered */
        p->sout = (const unsigned char *)p->buf;
        i = _Strxfrm(p->buf, &p->s1, sizeof (p->buf), &p->state);
        if (0 < i && p->buf[i - 1] == '\0')
            return (i - 1);
        else if (*p->s1 == '\0')
            p->s1 = p->s2;                               /* rescan */
        } while (i == 0);
    return (i);
    }

int (strcoll)(const char *s1, const char *s2)
    {           /* compare s1[], s2[] using locale-dependent rule */
    size_t n1, n2;
    Sctl st1, st2;
    static const _Cosave initial = {0};

    st1.s1 = (const unsigned char *)s1;
    st1.s2 = (const unsigned char *)s1;
    st1.state = initial;
    st2.s1 = (const unsigned char *)s2;
    st2.s2 = (const unsigned char *)s2;
    st2.state = initial;
    for (n1 = n2 = 0; ; )
        {                               /* compare transformed chars */
        int ans;
        size_t n;

        if (n1 == 0)
            n1 = getxfrm(&st1);
        if (n2 == 0)
            n2 = getxfrm(&st2);
        n = n1 < n2 ? n1 : n2;
        if (n == 0)
            return (n1 == n2 ? 0 : 0 < n2 ? -1 : +1);
        else if ((ans = memcmp(st1.sout, st2.sout, n)) != 0)
            return (ans);
        st1.sout += n, n1 -= n;
        st2.sout += n, n2 -= n;
        }
    }
```

function
strcoll
Figure 14.25 shows the file `strcoll.c`. The function `strcoll` is somewhat more complex than `strxfrm`. It must translate *two* source strings a piece at a time so that it can compare their mapped forms. The type `Sctl` describes a data object that holds the information needed to process each source string. The internal function `getxfrm` calls `_Strxfrm` to update an `Sctl` data object.

The comparison loop within `strcoll` thus calls `getxfrm` for each source string that has no mapped characters in its `Sctl` buffer. That ensures that each source string is represented by at least one mapped character, if any such characters remain to be generated. `strcoll` compares all the mapped characters that it can. It returns zero only if both mapped strings compare equal character by character and have the same length.

Testing `<string.h>`

Figure 14.26 shows the file `tstring.c`. The test program performs several cursory tests of each of the functions declared in `<string.h>`. The header defines no unique macros or types, so there are no interesting sizes to display. If all goes well, the program simply displays:

```
SUCCESS testing <string.h>
```

References

R.E. Griswold, J.F. Poage, and I.P. Polonsky, *The SNOBOL4 Programming Language*, (Englewood Cliffs, N.J.: Prentice-Hall, Inc. 1971). The programming language SNOBOL pushes to the extreme both pattern matching and substitution within text strings. You may be surprised at what powerful programs you can base largely on string manipulations.

Exercises

Exercise 14.1 The following locale file defines a simple "dictionary" collation sequence that ignores punctuation and distinctions between uppercase and lowercase letters:

```
LOCALE DICT
NOTE dictionary collation sequence
collate[0, 0      ] '.'           $O $I $1
collate[0, 1:$#    ]                 $I $0
collate[0, 'a':'z'] $@           $O $I $0
collate[0, 'A':'Z'] $@+'a'-'A'   $O $I $0
collate[1, 0:$#    ] $@           $O $I $1
LOCALE end
```

Describe the mapping that it performs. Why does it rescan? Draw a state-transition diagram for this mapping.

Figure 14.26:
tstring.c
Part 1

```c
/* test string functions */
#include <assert.h>
#include <errno.h>
#include <stdio.h>
#include <string.h>

int main()
    {                       /* test basic workings of string functions */
    char s[20];
    size_t n;
    static const char abcde[] = "abcde";
    static const char abcdx[] = "abcdx";

    assert(memchr(abcde, 'c', 5) == &abcde[2]);
    assert(memchr(abcde, 'e', 4) == NULL);
    assert(memcmp(abcde, abcdx, 5) != 0);
    assert(memcmp(abcde, abcdx, 4) == 0);
        /* the following tests are interrelated */
    assert(memcpy(s, abcde, 6) == s && s[2] == 'c');
    assert(memmove(s, s + 1, 3) == s);
    assert(memcmp(memmove(s, s + 1, 3), "aabce", 6));
    assert(memcmp((char *)memmove(s + 2, s, 3) - 2,
        "bcece", 6));
    assert(memset(s, '*', 10) == s && s[9] == '*');
    assert(memset(s + 2, '%', 0) == s + 2 && s[2] == '*');
    assert(strcat(memcpy(s, abcde, 6), "fg") == s);
    assert(s[6] == 'g');
    assert(strchr(abcde, 'x') == NULL);
    assert(strchr(abcde, 'c') == &abcde[2]);
    assert(strchr(abcde, '\0') == &abcde[5]);
    assert(strcmp(abcde, abcdx) != 0);
    assert(strcmp(abcde, "abcde") == 0);
    assert(strcoll(abcde, "abcde") == 0);
    assert(strcpy(s, abcde) == s && strcmp(s, abcde) == 0);
    assert(strcspn(abcde, "xdy") == 3);
    assert(strcspn(abcde, "xzy") == 5);
    assert(strerror(EDOM) != 0);
    assert(strlen(abcde) == 5);
    assert(strlen("") == 0);
    assert(strncat(strcpy(s, abcde), "fg", 1) == s
        && strcmp(s, "abcdef") == 0);
    assert(strncmp(abcde, "abcde", 30) == 0);
    assert(strncmp(abcde, abcdx, 30) != 0);
    assert(strncmp(abcde, abcdx, 4) == 0);
    assert(strncpy(s, abcde, 7) == s
        && memcmp(s, "abcde\0", 7) == 0);
    assert(strncpy(s, "xyz", 2) == s
        && strcmp(s, "xycde") == 0);
    assert(strpbrk(abcde, "xdy") == &abcde[3]);
    assert(strpbrk(abcde, "xzy") == NULL);
    assert(strrchr(abcde, 'x') == NULL);
    assert(strrchr(abcde, 'c') == &abcde[2]);
    assert(strcmp(strrchr("ababa", 'b'), "ba") == 0);
    assert(strspn(abcde, "abce") == 3);
    assert(strspn(abcde, abcde) == 5);
```

**Continuing
tstring.c
Part 2**

```
        assert (strstr (abcde, "xyz") == NULL) ;
        assert (strstr (abcde, "cd") == &abcde [2]) ;
        assert (strtok (strcpy (s, abcde), "ac") == &s[1]) ;
        assert (strtok (NULL, "ace") == &s[3]) ;
        assert (strtok (NULL, "ace") == NULL
            && memcmp (s, "ab\0d\0\0", 6) == 0) ;
        n = strxfrm (NULL, abcde, 0) ;
        if (n < sizeof (s) - 1)
            assert (strxfrm (s, abcde, n + 1) == n
                && strlen (s) == n) ;
        puts ("SUCCESS testing <string.h>") ;
        return (0) ;
        }
```

□

Exercise 14.2 Modify the locale file in the previous exercise to order names that begin with **Mac** interchangeably with names that begin with **Mc**. Order **Mac** before **Mc** only if the names otherwise compare equal.

Exercise 14.3 Describe a precise specification for:

- how names sort in your telephone book
- how words sort in the dictionary you use
- how text lines sort in the computer sort utility you use

Can you define a locale that matches the behavior of each of these collation rules? How many states does it take to specify each?

Exercise 14.4 A simple calculator program recognizes the following tokens:

- numbers palatable to the function **strtod**, declared in **<stdlib.h>** (See the syntax diagram on page 351
- operators in the set [+ - * / = c]
- comments inside double quotes (")

These tokens are separated by spaces, horizontal tabs, and newlines. Such characters can, however, occur inside comments.

Write a function that reads characters from the standard input stream and parses them into tokens. Use the function **strtok**, declared in **<string.h>**. Rewrite the function to avoid using **strtok**. Which of the two versions do you prefer? Why?

Exercise 14.5 Identify the "missing" functions not declared in **<string.h>** (such as **strnlen** and **memrchr**). Write them. Can you add them to the Standard C library and still conform to the C Standard? Can you add their declarations to **<string.h>** and still conform?

Exercise 14.6 Measure a large corpus of code to determine the five functions declared in **<string.h>** that consume the most time. How much could you speed up a typical program if these functions were instantaneous? How much could you speed up a typical program if each of these functions ran five times faster? What are the comparable figures for the program you measured that would benefit most?

Exercise 14.7 [**Harder**] Write assembly language versions of the functions you identified in the previous exercise. Can you achieve a significant speedup just by altering the C code? How much faster is each function compared to the C version presented here?

Exercise 14.8 [**Very hard**] Modify a C compiler to generate inline code for the functions you identified in the previous two exercises. How much faster is each function compared to the versions discussed in the previous exercise?

Chapter 15: <time.h>

Background

Time and date calculations achieved a new level of sophistication under the UNIX operating system. Several of the developers of that system were amateur astronomers. They were sensitive to the need for representing times over a span of decades, not just years. They automatically reckoned time as Greenwich Mean Time (once GMT, now UTC), not just by the clock on the wall. They were, in short, more finicky than most about measuring and representing time on a computer.

That same attention to detail has spilled over into the Standard C library. Its scope is basically whatever was available in C under UNIX that didn't depend on the peculiarities of UNIX. As a consequence, you can do a lot with times and dates in Standard C. The functions declared in `<time.h>` provide the relevant services.

It stretches the truth a bit to say that these functions don't depend on the peculiarities of UNIX. Not all operating systems distinguish between local time and UTC. Even fewer allow different users to display times relative to different time zones. Some of the smallest systems can't even give you the time of day. Yet all implementations of C must take a stab at telling time wisely if they want to claim conformance to the C Standard.

weasel words The C Standard contains enough weasel words to let nearly everybody off the hook. A system need only provide its "best approximation" to the current time and date, or to processor time consumed, to conform to the C Standard. A vendor could argue that 1 January 1980 is always the best available approximation to any time and date. A customer can rightly quarrel about the low quality of such an approximation, but not whether it satisfies the C Standard.

What this means in practice is that a program should never take times too seriously. It can enquire about the current time (by calling `time`) and display what it gets in a variety of attractive formats. But it can't know for sure that the time and date are meaningful. If you have an application that depends critically upon accurate time stamps, check each implementation of Standard C closely.

What the C Standard Says

<time.h>

7.12 Date and time `<time.h>`

7.12.1 Components of time

The header `<time.h>` defines two macros, and declares four types and several functions for manipulating time. Many functions deal with a *calendar time* that represents the current date (according to the Gregorian calendar) and time. Some functions deal with *local time,* which is the calendar time expressed for some specific time zone, and with *Daylight Saving Time,* which is a temporary change in the algorithm for determining local time. The local time zone and Daylight Saving Time are implementation-defined.

NULL

The macros defined are **NULL** (described in 7.1.6); and

CLOCKS_PER_SEC

```
CLOCKS_PER_SEC
```

which is the number per second of the value returned by the **clock** function.

size_t

The types declared are **size_t** (described in 7.1.6);

clock_t

```
clock_t
```

and

time_t

```
time_t
```

which are arithmetic types capable of representing times; and

struct tm

```
struct tm
```

which holds the components of a calendar time, called the *broken-down time*. The structure shall contain at least the following members, in any order. The semantics of the members and their normal ranges are expressed in the comments.[137]

```
int tm_sec;   /* seconds after the minute — [0, 61] */
int tm_min;   /* minutes after the hour — [0, 59] */
int tm_hour;  /* hours since midnight — [0, 23] */
int tm_mday;  /* day of the month — [1, 31] */
int tm_mon;   /* months since January — [0, 11] */
int tm_year;  /* years since 1900 */
int tm_wday;  /* days since Sunday — [0, 6] */
int tm_yday;  /* days since January 1 — [0, 365] */
int tm_isdst; /* Daylight Saving Time flag */
```

The value of **tm_isdst** is positive if Daylight Saving Time is in effect, zero if Daylight Saving Time is not in effect, and negative if the information is not available.

7.12.2 Time manipulation functions

clock

7.12.2.1 The `clock` function

Synopsis

```
#include <time.h>
clock_t clock(void);
```

Description

The **clock** function determines the processor time used.

Returns

The **clock** function returns the implementation's best approximation to the processor time used by the program since the beginning of an implementation-defined era related only to the program invocation. To determine the time in seconds, the value returned by the **clock** function should be divided by the value of the macro **CLOCKS_PER_SEC**. If the processor time used is not available or its value cannot be represented, the function returns the value **(clock_t)-1**.[138]

difftime

7.12.2.2 The `difftime` function

Synopsis

```
#include <time.h>
double difftime(time_t time1, time_t time0);
```

Description

The **difftime** function computes the difference between two calendar times: **time1 - time0**.

mktime

Returns

The **difftime** function returns the difference expressed in seconds as a **double**.

7.12.2.3 The mktime function

Synopsis

```
#include <time.h>
time_t mktime(struct tm *timeptr);
```

Description

The **mktime** function converts the broken-down time, expressed as local time, in the structure pointed to by **timeptr** into a calendar time value with the same encoding as that of the values returned by the **time** function. The original values of the **tm_wday** and **tm_yday** components of the structure are ignored, and the original values of the other components are not restricted to the ranges indicated above.[139] On successful completion, the values of the **tm_wday** and **tm_yday** components of the structure are set appropriately, and the other components are set to represent the specified calendar time, but with their values forced to the ranges indicated above; the final value of **tm_mday** is not set until **tm_mon** and **tm_year** are determined.

Returns

The **mktime** function returns the specified calendar time encoded as a value of type **time_t**. If the calendar time cannot be represented, the function returns the value **(time_t)-1**.

Example

What day of the week is July 4, 2001?

```
#include <stdio.h>
#include <time.h>
static const char *const wday[] = {
        "Sunday", "Monday", "Tuesday", "Wednesday",
        "Thursday", "Friday", "Saturday", "-unknown-"
};
struct tm time_str;
/*...*/

time_str.tm_year    = 2001 - 1900;
time_str.tm_mon     = 7 - 1;
time_str.tm_mday    = 4;
time_str.tm_hour    = 0;
time_str.tm_min     = 0;
time_str.tm_sec     = 1;
time_str.tm_isdst   = -1;
if (mktime(&time_str) == -1)
        time_str.tm_wday = 7;
printf("%s\n", wday[time_str.tm_wday]);
```

time

7.12.2.4 The time function

Synopsis

```
#include <time.h>
time_t time(time_t *timer);
```

Description

The **time** function determines the current calendar time. The encoding of the value is unspecified.

Returns

The **time** function returns the implementation's best approximation to the current calendar time. The value **(time_t)-1** is returned if the calendar time is not available. If **timer** is not a null pointer, the return value is also assigned to the object it points to.

7.12.3 Time conversion functions

Except for the **strftime** function, these functions return values in one of two static objects: a broken-down time structure and an array of **char**. Execution of any of the functions may overwrite the information returned in either of these objects by any of the other functions. The implementation shall behave as if no other library functions call these functions.

7.12.3.1 The `asctime` function

Synopsis

```
#include <time.h>
char *asctime(const struct tm *timeptr);
```

Description

The **asctime** function converts the broken-down time in the structure pointed to by **timeptr** into a string in the form

```
Sun Sep 16 01:03:52 1973\n\0
```

using the equivalent of the following algorithm.

```
char *asctime(const struct tm *timeptr)
{
    static const char wday_name[7][3] = {
        "Sun", "Mon", "Tue", "Wed", "Thu", "Fri", "Sat"
    };
    static const char mon_name[12][3] = {
        "Jan", "Feb", "Mar", "Apr", "May", "Jun",
        "Jul", "Aug", "Sep", "Oct", "Nov", "Dec"
    };
    static char result[26];

    sprintf(result, "%.3s %.3s%3d %.2d:%.2d:%.2d %d\n",
        wday_name[timeptr->tm_wday],
        mon_name[timeptr->tm_mon],
        timeptr->tm_mday, timeptr->tm_hour,
        timeptr->tm_min, timeptr->tm_sec,
        1900 + timeptr->tm_year);
    return result;
}
```

Returns

The **asctime** function returns a pointer to the string.

7.12.3.2 The `ctime` function

Synopsis

```
#include <time.h>
char *ctime(const time_t *timer);
```

Description

The **ctime** function converts the calendar time pointed to by **timer** to local time in the form of a string. It is equivalent to

```
asctime(localtime(timer))
```

Returns

The **ctime** function returns the pointer returned by the **asctime** function with that broken-down time as argument.

Forward references: the **localtime** function (7.12.3.4).

7.12.3.3 The `gmtime` function

Synopsis

```
#include <time.h>
struct tm *gmtime(const time_t *timer);
```

Description

The **gmtime** function converts the calendar time pointed to by **timer** into a broken-down time, expressed as Coordinated Universal Time (UTC).

Returns

The **gmtime** function returns a pointer to that object, or a null pointer if UTC is not available.

7.12.3.4 The `localtime` function

Synopsis

```
#include <time.h>
struct tm *localtime(const time_t *timer);
```

Description

The **localtime** function converts the calendar time pointed to by **timer** into a broken-down time, expressed as local time.

Returns

The **localtime** function returns a pointer to that object.

7.12.3.5 The `strftime` function

Synopsis

```
#include <time.h>
size_t strftime(char *s, size_t maxsize,
        const char *format, const struct tm *timeptr);
```

Description

The **strftime** function places characters into the array pointed to by **s** as controlled by the string pointed to by **format**. The format shall be a multibyte character sequence, beginning and ending in its initial shift state. The **format** string consists of zero or more conversion specifiers and ordinary multibyte characters. A conversion specifier consists of a **%** character followed by a character that determines the behavior of the conversion specifier. All ordinary multibyte characters (including the terminating null character) are copied unchanged into the array. If copying takes place between objects that overlap, the behavior is undefined. No more than **maxsize** characters are placed into the array. Each conversion specifier is replaced by appropriate characters as described in the following list. The appropriate characters are determined by the **LC_TIME** category of the current locale and by the values contained in the structure pointed to by **timeptr**.

"**%a**" is replaced by the locale's abbreviated weekday name.

"**%A**" is replaced by the locale's full weekday name.

"**%b**" is replaced by the locale's abbreviated month name.

"**%B**" is replaced by the locale's full month name.

"**%c**" is replaced by the locale's appropriate date and time representation.

"**%d**" is replaced by the day of the month as a decimal number (**01-31**).

"**%H**" is replaced by the hour (24-hour clock) as a decimal number (**00-23**).

"**%I**" is replaced by the hour (12-hour clock) as a decimal number (**01-12**).

"**%j**" is replaced by the day of the year as a decimal number (**001-366**).

"**%m**" is replaced by the month as a decimal number (**01-12**).

"**%M**" is replaced by the minute as a decimal number (**00-59**).

"**%p**" is replaced by the locale's equivalent of the AM/PM designations associated with a 12-hour clock.

"**%S**" is replaced by the second as a decimal number (**00-61**).

"**%U**" is replaced by the week number of the year (the first Sunday as the first day of week 1) as a decimal number (**00-53**).

"**%w**" is replaced by the weekday as a decimal number (**0-6**), where Sunday is **0**.

"**%W**" is replaced by the week number of the year (the first Monday as the first day of week 1) as a decimal number (**00-53**).

"**%x**" is replaced by the locale's appropriate date representation.

"**%X**" is replaced by the locale's appropriate time representation.

"**%y**" is replaced by the year without century as a decimal number (**00-99**).

"**%Y**" is replaced by the year with century as a decimal number.

"**%Z**" is replaced by the time zone name or abbreviation, or by no characters if no time zone is determinable.

"**%%**" is replaced by **%**.

If a conversion specifier is not one of the above, the behavior is undefined.

Returns

If the total number of resulting characters including the terminating null character is not more than **maxsize**, the **strftime** function returns the number of characters placed into the array pointed to by **s** not including the terminating null character. Otherwise, zero is returned and the contents of the array are indeterminate.

Footnotes

137. The range [0, 61] for **tm_sec** allows for as many as two leap seconds.

138. In order to measure the time spent in a program, the **clock** function should be called at the start of the program and its return value subtracted from the value returned by subsequent calls.

139. Thus, a positive or zero value for **tm_isdst** causes the **mktime** function to presume initially that Daylight Saving Time, respectively, is or is not in effect for the specified time. A negative value causes it to attempt to determine whether Daylight Saving Time is in effect for the specified time.

Using <time.h>

The functions declared in **<time.h>** determine elapsed processor time and calendar time. They also convert among different data representations. You can represent a time as:

- type **clock_t** for elapsed processor time, as returned by the primitive function **clock**
- type **time_t** for calendar time, as returned by the primitive function **time** or the function **mktime**
- type *double* for calendar time in seconds, as returned by the function **difftime**
- type **struct tm** for calendar time broken down into separate components, as returned by the functions **gmtime** and **localtime**
- a text string for calendar time, as returned by the functions **asctime**, **ctime**, and **strftime**

You have a rich assortment of choices. The hard part is often identifying just which data represension, and which functions, you want to use for a particular application.

function strftime
The one complicated function declared in **<time.h>** (from the outside, at least) is **strftime**. You use it to generate a text representation of a time and date from a **struct tm** under control of a format string. In this sense, it is modeled after the print functions declared in **<stdio.h>**. It differs in two important ways:

- **strftime** does *not* accept a variable argument list. It obtains all time and date information from one argument.
- The behavior of **strftime** can vary considerably among locales. The locale category **LC_TIME** can, for example, specify that the text form of all dates follow the conventions of the French culture.

For example, the code fragment:

```
char buf[100];

strftime(buf, sizeof buf, "%A, %x", localtime(&t0));
```

might store in **buf** any of:

```
Sunday, 02 Dec 1979
dimanche, le 2 décembre 1979
Weekday 0, 02/12/79
```

If your goal is to display times and dates in accordance with local custom, then **strftime** gives you just the flexibility you need. You can even write multibyte-character sequences between the conversion specifiers. That lets you convert dates to Kanji and other large character sets.

conversion specifiers Here are the conversion specifiers defined for **strftime**. I follow each with an example of the text it produces. The examples, from Plauger and Brodie, all assume the "c" locale and the date and time Sunday, 02 December 1979 at 06:55:15 AM EST:

- **%a** — the abbreviated weekday name (**Sun**)
- **%A** — the full weekday name (**Sunday**)
- **%b** — the abbreviated month name (**Dec**)
- **%B** — the full month name (**December**)
- **%c** — the date and time (**Dec 02 06:55:15 1979**)
- **%d** — the day of the month (**02**)
- **%H** — the hour of the 24-hour day (**06**)
- **%I** — the hour of the 12-hour day (**06**)
- **%j** — the day of the year, from 001 (**335**)
- **%m** — the month of the year, from 01 (**12**)
- **%M** — the minutes after the hour (**55**)
- **%p** — the AM/PM indicator (**AM**)
- **%S** — the seconds after the minute (**15**)
- **%U** — the Sunday week of the year, from 00 (**48**)
- **%w** — the day of the week, from 0 for Sunday (**0**)
- **%W** — the Monday week of the year, from 00 (**47**)
- **%x** — the date (**Dec 02 1979**)
- **%X** — the time (**06:55:15**)
- **%y** — the year of the century, from 00 (**79**)
- **%Y** — the year (**1979**)
- **%Z** — the time zone name, if any (**EST**)
- **%%** — the per cent character (**%**)

I conclude with the usual description of the individual types and macros defined in **<time.h>**. It is followed by brief notes on how to use the functions declared in **<time.h>**.

shared   Note that the functions share two static data objects. All functions that
data return a value of type *pointer to char* return a pointer to one of these data
objects objects. All pointers that return a value of type *pointer to* **struct tm** return
a pointer to the other. Thus, a call to one of the functions declared in
<time.h> can alter the value stored on behalf of an earlier call to another
(or the same) function. Be careful to copy the value stored in one of these
shared data objects if you need the value beyond a conflicting function call.

NULL   NULL — See page 220.

CLOCKS_PER_SEC   CLOCKS_PER_SEC — The expression **clock()** / **CLOCKS_PER_SEC** measures
elapsed processor time in seconds. The macro can have any arithmetic type,
either integer or floating point. Type cast it to *double* to ensure that you can
represent fractions of a second as well as a wide range of values.

clock_t   clock_t — This is the arithmetic type returned by **clock**, described
below. It represents elapsed processor time. It can have any integer or
floating-point type, which need *not* be the same type as the macro
CLOCKS_PER_SECOND, above.

size_t   size_t — See page 219.

time_t   time_t — This is the arithmetic type returned by **time**, described below.
Several other functions declared in **<time.h>** also manipulate values of this
type. It represents calendar times that span years, presumably to the nearest
second (although not necessarily). Don't attempt to perform arithmetic on
a value of this type.

tm   tm — A structure of type **struct tm** represents a "broken-down time."
Several functions declared in **<time.h>** manipulate values of this type. You
can access certain members of **struct tm**. Its definition looks something
like:

```
struct tm {
    int tm_sec;        seconds after the minute (from 0)
    int tm_min;        minutes after the hour (from 0)
    int tm_hour;       hour of the day (from 0)
    int tm_mday;       day of the month (from 1)
    int tm_mon;        month of the year (from 0)
    int tm_year;       years since 1900 (from 0)
    int tm_wday;       days since Sunday (from 0)
    int tm_yday;       day of the year (from 0)
    int tm_isdst;      DST flag
```

The members may occur in a different order, and other members may also
be present. The DST flag is greater than zero if Daylight Savings Time (DST)
is in effect, zero if it is not in effect, and less than zero if its state is unknown.
The unknown state encourages the functions that read this structure to
determine for themselves whether DST is in effect.

asctime   asctime — (The **asc** comes from **ASCII**, which is now a misnomer.) Use
this function to generate the text form of the date represented by the
argument (which points to a broken-down time). The function returns a
pointer to a null-terminated string that looks like "**Sun Dec 02 06:55:15
1979\n**". This is equivalent to calling **strftime** with the format string "**%a**

%c" *in the* "C" *locale.* Call `asctime` if you want the English-language form regardless of the current locale. Call `strftime` if you want a form that changes with locale. See the warning about shared data objects, above.

clock   `clock` — This function measures elapsed processor time instead of calendar time. It returns –1 if that is not possible. Otherwise, each call should return a value equal to or greater than an earlier call during the same program execution. It is the best measure you can get of the time your program actually consumes. See the macro `CLOCKS_PER_SEC`, above.

ctime   `ctime` — `ctime(pt)` is equivalent to the expression `asctime(localtime(pt))`. You use it to convert a calendar time directly to a text form that is independent of the current locale. See the warning about shared data objects, above.

difftime   `difftime` — The only safe way compute the difference between two times `t1` and `t0` is by calling `difftime(t1, t0)`. The result, measured in seconds, is positive if `t1` is a later time than `t0`.

gmtime   `gmtime` — (The `gm` comes from `GMT`, which is now a slight misnomer.) Use this function to convert a calendar time to a broken-down UTC time. The member `tm_isdst` should be zero. If you want local time instead, use `localtime`, below. See the warning about shared data objects, above.

localtime   `localtime` — Use this function to convert a calendar time to a broken-down local time. The member `tm_isdst` should reflect whatever the system knows about Daylight Savings Time for that particular time and date. If you want UTC time instead, use `gmtime`, above. See the warning about shared data objects, above.

mktime   `mktime` — This function first puts its argument, a broken-down time, in canonical form. That lets you add seconds, for example, to the member `tm_sec` of a broken-down time. The function increases `tm_min` for every 60 seconds it subtracts from `tm_sec` until `tm_sec` is in the interval [0, 59]. The function then corrects `tm_min` in a similar way, then each coarser division of time through `tm_year`. It determines `tm_wday` and `tm_yday` from the other fields. Clearly, you can also alter a broken-down time by minutes, hours, days, months, or years just as easily.

`mktime` then converts the broken-down time to an equivalent calendar time. It assumes the broken-down time represents a local time. If the member `tm_isdst` is less than zero, the function endeavors to determine whether Daylight Savings Time was in effect for that particular time and date. Otherwise, it honors the original state of the flag. Thus, the only reliable way to modify a calendar time is to convert it to a broken-down time by calling `localtime`, modify the appropriate members, then convert the result back to a calendar time by calling `mktime`.

strftime   `strftime` — This function generates a null-terminated text string containing the time and date information that you specify. You write a format string argument to specify a mixture of literal text and converted time and date information. You specify a broken-down time to supply the encoded time and date information. The category **LC_TIME** in the current locale determines the behavior of each conversion. I describe how you write format strings starting on page 421. See the warning about shared data objects, above.

time   **time** — This function determines the current calendar time. It returns –1 if that is not possible. Otherwise, each call should return a value at the same time or later than an earlier call during the same program execution. It is the best estimate you can get of the current time and date.

Figure 15.1:
time.h

```
/* time.h standard header */
#ifndef _TIME
#define _TIME
#ifndef _YVALS
#include <yvals.h>
#endif
          /* macros */
#define NULL      _NULL
#define CLOCKS_PER_SEC  _CPS
          /* type definitions */
#ifndef _SIZET
#define _SIZET
typedef _Sizet size_t;
#endif
typedef unsigned int clock_t;
typedef unsigned long time_t;
struct tm {
    int tm_sec;
    int tm_min;
    int tm_hour;
    int tm_mday;
    int tm_mon;
    int tm_year;
    int tm_wday;
    int tm_yday;
    int tm_isdst;
    };
          /* declarations */
char *asctime(const struct tm *);
clock_t clock(void);
char *ctime(const time_t *);
double difftime(time_t, time_t);
struct tm *gmtime(const time_t *);
struct tm *localtime(const time_t *);
time_t mktime(struct tm *);
size_t strftime(char *, size_t, const char *,
    const struct tm *);
time_t time(time_t *);
#endif
```

Implementing `<time.h>`

The functions declared in `<time.h>` are quite diverse. Many wrestle with the bizarre irregularities involved in measuring and expressing times and dates. Be prepared for an assortment of coding techniques.

header Figure 15.1 shows the file `time.h`. As usual, it inherits from the internal
`<time.h>` header `<yvals.h>` definitions that are repeated in several standard headers. I discuss the implementation of both the macro **NULL** and the type definition `size_t` in Chapter 15: `<stddef.h>`.

`<yvals.h>` also defines two macros that describe properties of the primitive functions `clock` and `time`:

_CPS ▪ The macro `_CPS` specifies the value of the macro **CLOCKS_PER_SECOND**.

_TBIAS ▪ The macro `_TBIAS` gives the difference, in seconds, between values returned by `time` and the time measured from 1 January 1900. (This macro name does not appear in `<time.h>`.)

The values of these macros depend strongly on how you implement `clock` and `time`. This implementation represents elapsed processor time as an *unsigned int* (type `clock_t`). It represents calendar time as an *unsigned long* (type `time_t`) that counts UTC seconds since the start of 1 January 1900. That represents dates from 1900 until at least 2036. You have to adjust whatever the system supplies to match these conventions.

The macro `_TBIAS` is a kludge. Normally, you want to set it to zero. The version of `time` you supply should deliver calendar times with the appropriate starting point. UNIX, however, measures time in seconds since 1 January 1970. Many implementations of C offer a function `time` that matches this convention. If you find it convenient to use such a time function directly, then `<yvals.h>` should contain the definition:

```
#define _TBIAS ((70 * 365LU + 17) * 86400
```

That counts the 70 years, including 17 leap days, that elapsed between the two starting points. In several places, the functions declared in `<time.h>` adjust a value of type `time_t` by adding or subtracting `_TBIAS`.

function Figure 15.2 shows the file `time.c`. It defines the function `time` for a UNIX
time system. As usual, I assume the existence of a C-callable function with a reserved name that peforms the UNIX system service. For this version of `time`, the header `<yvals.h>` can define the macro `_TBIAS` to be zero.

function UNIX also provides an exact replacement for the function `clock`. So do
clock many implementations of C modeled after UNIX. Thus, you may not have to do any additional work. Just define the macro `_CPS` appropriately. For a PC-compatible computer, for example, the value is approximately 18.2.

Figure 15.3 shows the file `clock.c`. It defines a version of `clock` you can use if the operating system doesn't provide a separate measure of elapsed processor time. The function simply returns a truncated version of the calendar time. In this case, the header `<yvals.h>` defines the macro `_CPS` to be 1.

Figure 15.2:
time.c

```
/* time function -- UNIX version */
#include <time.h>


        /* UNIX system call */
time_t _Time(time_t *);

time_t (time)(time_t *tod)
    {                                               /* return calendar time */
    time_t t = _Time(NULL) + (70*365LU+17)*86400;

    if (tod)
        *tod = t;
    return (t);
    }                                                                         □
```

Figure 15.3:
clock.c

```
/* clock function -- simple version */
#include <time.h>

clock_t (clock)(void)
    {                                               /* return CPU time */
    return ((clock_t)time(NULL));
    }                                                                         □
```

Figure 15.4:
difftime.c

```
/* difftime function */
#include <time.h>

double (difftime)(time_t t1, time_t t0)
    {                                       /* compute difference in times */
    t0 -= _TBIAS, t1 -= _TBIAS;
    return (t0 <= t1 ? (double)(t1 - t0) : -(double)(t1 - t0));
    }                                                                         □
```

function
difftime

Figure 15.4 shows the file `difftime.c`. It is careful to correct the biases of both times before comparing them. It is also careful to develop a signed difference between two unsigned integer quantities. Note how the function negates the difference `t1 - t0` only after converting it to *double*.

header
"xtime.h"

The remaining functions all include the internal header `"xtime.h"`. Figure 15.5 shows the file `xtime.h`. It includes the standard header `<time.h>` and the internal header `"xtinfo.h"`. (See the file `xtinfo.h"` on page 100.) That internal header defines the type `_Tinfo`. It also declares the data object `_Times`, defined in the file `asctime.c`. (See page 437.) `_Times` specifies locale-specific information on the category `LC_TIME`.

The header `"xtime.h"` defines the macro `WDAY` that specifies the weekday for 1 January 1900 (Monday). It defines the type `Dstrule` that specifies the components of an encoded rule for determining Daylight Savings Time. (See the file `xgetdst.c` beginning on page 432.) And it declares the various internal functions that implement this version of `<time.h>`

Figure 15.5:
xtime.h

```
/* xtime.h internal header */
#include <time.h>
#include "xtinfo.h"
        /* macros */
#define WDAY    1                       /* to get day of week right */
        /* type definitions */
typedef struct {
    unsigned char wday, hour, day, mon, year;
    } Dstrule;
        /* internal declarations */
int _Daysto(int, int);
const char *_Gentime(const struct tm *, _Tinfo *,
    const char *, int *, char *);
Dstrule *_Getdst(const char *);
const char *_Gettime(const char *, int, int *);
int _Isdst(const struct tm *);
const char *_Getzone(void);
size_t _Strftime(char *, size_t, const char *,
    const struct tm *, _Tinfo *);
struct tm *_Ttotm(struct tm *, time_t, int);
time_t _Tzoff(void);                                            □
```

Figure 15.6:
gmtime.c

```
/* gmtime function */
#include "xtime.h"

struct tm *(gmtime)(const time_t *tod)
    {                            /* convert to Greenwich Mean Time (UTC) */
    return (_Ttotm(NULL, *tod, 0));
    }                                                           □
```

function
gmtime
Figure 15.6 shows the file gmtime.c. The function gmtime is the simpler of the two functions that convert a calendar time in seconds (type time_t) to a broken-down time (type struct tm). It simply calls the internal function _Ttotm. The first argument is a null pointer to tell _Ttotm to store the broken-down time in the communal static data object. The third argument is zero to insist that Daylight Savings Time is not in effect.

function
_Ttotm
Figure 15.7 shows the file xttotm.c. It defines the function _Ttotm that tackles the nasty business of converting seconds to years, months, days, and so forth. The file also defines the function _Daysto that _Ttotm and other functions use for calendar calculations.

function
_Daysto
_Daysto counts the extra days beyond 365 per year. To do so, it must determine how may leap days have occurred between the year you specify and 1900. The function also counts the extra days from the start of the year to the month you specify. To do so, it must sometimes determine whether the current year is a leap year. The function recognizes that 1900 was *not* a leap year. It doesn't bother to correct for the non-leap years 1800 and earlier, or for 2100 and later. (Other problems arise within just a few decades of those extremes anyway.)

```c
/* _Ttotm and _Daysto functions */
#include "xtime.h"

        /* macros */
#define MONTAB(year)    \
    ((year) & 03 || (year) == 0 ? mos : lmos)

        /* static data */
static const short lmos[] = {0, 31, 60, 91, 121, 152,
    182, 213, 244, 274, 305, 335};
static const short mos[] = {0, 31, 59, 90, 120, 151,
    181, 212, 243, 273, 304, 334};

int _Daysto(int year, int mon)
    {                       /* compute extra days to start of month */
    int days;

    if (0 < year)              /* correct for leap year: 1801-2099 */
        days = (year - 1) / 4;
    else if (year <= -4)
        days = 1 + (4 - year) / 4;
    else
        days = 0;
    return (days + MONTAB(year)[mon]);
    }

struct tm *_Ttotm(struct tm *t, time_t secsarg, int isdst)
    {                       /* convert scalar time to time structure */
    int year;
    long days;
    time_t secs;
    static struct tm ts;

    secsarg += _TBIAS;
    if (t == NULL)
        t = &ts;
    t->tm_isdst = isdst;
    for (secs = secsarg; ; secs = secsarg + 3600)
        {                               /* loop to correct for DST */
        days = secs / 86400;
        t->tm_wday = (days + WDAY) % 7;
            {                                       /* determine year */
        long i;

        for (year = days / 365;
            days < (i = _Daysto(year, 0) + 365L * year); )
            --year;                     /* correct guess and recheck */
        days -= i;
        t->tm_year = year;
        t->tm_yday = days;
            }
```

```
        {                                          /* determine month */
        int mon;
        const short *pm = MONTAB(year);

        for (mon = 12; days < pm[--mon]; )
            ;
        t->tm_mon = mon;
        t->tm_mday = days - pm[mon] + 1;
        }
    secs %= 86400;
    t->tm_hour = secs / 3600;
    secs %= 3600;
    t->tm_min = secs / 60;
    t->tm_sec = secs % 60;
    if (0 <= t->tm_isdst || (t->tm_isdst = _Isdst(t)) <= 0)
        return (t);                       /* loop only if <0 => 1 */
    }
}                                                                     □
```

_Daysto handles years before 1900 only because the function mktime can develop intermediate dates in that range and still yield a representable time_t value. (You can start with the year 2000, back up 2,000 months, and advance 2 billion seconds, for example.) The logic is carefully crafted to avoid integer overflow regardless of argument values. Also, the function counts *excess* days rather than total days so that it can cover a broader range of years without fear of having its result overflow.

_Ttotm uses _Daysto to determine the year corresponding to its time argument secsarg. Since the inverse of _Daysto is a nuisance to write, _Ttotm guesses and iterates. At worst, it should have to back up one year to correct its guess. Both functions use the macro MONTAB, defined at the top of the file, to determine how many days precede the start of a given month. The macro also assumes that every fourth year is a leap year, except 1900.

The isdst (third) argument to _Ttotm follows the convention for the isdst member of struct tm:

- If isdst is greater than zero, Daylight Savings Time is definitely in effect. _Ttotm assumes that its caller has made any necessary adjustment to the time argument secsarg.

- If isdst is zero, Daylight Savings Time is definitely *not* in effect. _Ttotm assumes that no adjustment is necessary to the time argument secsarg.

- If isdst is less than zero, the caller doesn't know whether Daylight Savings Time is in effect. _Ttotm should endeavor to find out. If the function determines that Daylight Savings Time is in effect, it advances the time by one hour (3,600 seconds) and recomputes the broken-down time.

Thus, _Ttotm will loop at most once. It calls the function _Isdst only if it needs to determine whether to loop. Even then, it loops only if _Isdst concludes that Daylight Savings Time is in effect.

function
_Isdst
Figure 15.8 shows the file `xisdst.c`. The function `_Isdst` determines the status of Daylight Savings Time (DST). `_Times._Isdst` points at a string that spells out the rules. (See the file `asctime.c` in Figure 15.16 for the definition of `_Times`. See page 111 for a description of the rule string.)

`_Isdst` works with the rules in encoded form. Those rules are not current the first time you call the function or if a change of locale alters the last encoded version of the string `_Times._Isdst`. If that string is empty, `_Isdst` looks for rules appended to the time-zone information `_Times._Tzone`. It calls `_Getzone` as necessary to obtain the time-zone information. It calls `_Gettime` to locate the start of any rules for DST. The function `_Getdst` then encodes the current array of rules, if that is possible.

Given an encoded array of rules, `_Isdst` scans the array for rules that cover the relevant year. It adjusts the day specified by the rule for any weekday constraint, then compares the rule time against the time that it is testing. Note that the first rule for a given starting year begins *not* in DST. Successive rules for the same year go in and out of DST.

function
_Getdst
Figure 15.9 shows the file `xgetdst.c`. It defines the function `_Getdst` that parses the string pointed to by `_Times._Isdst` to construct the array of rules. The first character of a (non-empty) string serves as a field delimiter, just as with other strings that provide locale-specific time information. The function first counts these delimiters so that it can allocate the array. It then passes over the string once more to parse and check the individual fields.

`_Getdst` calls the internal function `getint` to convert the integer subfields in a rule. No overflow checks occur because none of the fields can be large enough to cause overflow. The logic here and in `_Getdst` proper is tedious but straightforward.

function
localtime
Figure 15.10 shows the file `localtim.c`. The function `localtime` calls `_Ttotm` much like `gmtime`. Here, however, `localtime` assumes that it must convert a UTC time to a local time. To do so, the function must determine the time difference, in seconds, between UTC and the local time zone.

function
_Tzoff
The file `localtim.c` also defines the function `_Tzoff` that endeavors to determine this time difference (`tzoff`, in minutes). The time difference is not current the first time you call the function or if a change of locale alters the last encoded version of the string `_Times._Tzone`. If that string is empty, `_Tzoff` calls the function `_Getzone` to determine the time difference from environment variables, if that is possible.

However obtained, the string `_Times._Tzone` takes the form `:EST:EDT:+0300`. (See page 111.) `_Tzoff` calls the function `_Gettime` to determine the starting position (`p`) and length (`n`) of the third field (#2, counting from zero). The function `strtol`, declared in `<stdlib.h>` must parse this field completely in converting it to an encoded integer. Moreover, the magnitude must not be completely insane. (The maximum magnitude is greater than 12*60 because funny time zones exist on either side of the International Date Line.)

Figure 15.8:
xisdst.c

```c
/* _Isdst function */
#include <stdlib.h>
#include "xtime.h"

int _Isdst(const struct tm *t)
    {               /* test whether Daylight Savings Time in effect */
    Dstrule *pr;
    static const char *olddst = NULL;
    static Dstrule *rules = NULL;

    if (olddst != _Times._Isdst)
        {                               /* find current dst_rules */
        if (_Times._Isdst[0] == '\0')
            {                           /* look beyond time_zone info */
            int n;

            if (_Times._Tzone[0] == '\0')
                _Times._Tzone = _Getzone();
            _Times._Isdst = _Gettime(_Times._Tzone, 3, &n);
            if (_Times._Isdst[0] != '\0')
                --_Times._Isdst;            /* point to delimiter */
            }
        if ((pr = _Getdst(_Times._Isdst)) == NULL)
            return (-1);
        free(rules);
        rules = pr;
        olddst = _Times._Isdst;
        }
    {                                   /* check time against rules */
    int ans = 0;
    const int d0 = _Daysto(t->tm_year, 0);
    const int hour = t->tm_hour + 24 * t->tm_yday;
    const int wd0 = (365L * t->tm_year + d0 + WDAY) % 7 + 14;

    for (pr = rules; pr->wday != (unsigned char)-1; ++pr)
        if (pr->year <= t->tm_year)
            {                           /* found early enough year */
            int rday = _Daysto(t->tm_year, pr->mon) - d0
                + pr->day;

            if (0 < pr->wday)
                {                       /* shift to specific weekday */
                int wd = (rday + wd0 - pr->wday) % 7;

                rday += wd == 0 ? 0 : 7 - wd;
                if (pr->wday <= 7)
                    rday -= 7;                  /* strictly before */
                }
            if (hour < rday * 24 + pr->hour)
                return (ans);
            ans = pr->year == (pr + 1)->year ? !ans : 0;
            }
    return (ans);
    }
    }
```

```c
/* _Getdst function */
#include <ctype.h>
#include <stdlib.h>
#include <string.h>
#include "xtime.h"

static int getint(const char *s, int n)
    {                                            /* accumulate digits */
    int value;

    for (value = 0; 0 <= --n && isdigit(*s); ++s)
        value = value * 10 + *s - '0';
    return (0 <= n ? -1 : value);
    }

Dstrule *_Getdst(const char *s)
    {                                            /* parse DST rules */
    const char delim = *s++;
    Dstrule *pr, *rules;

    if (delim == '\0')
        return (NULL);
     {                                           /* buy space for rules */
    const char *s1, *s2;
    int i;

    for (s1 = s, i = 2; (s2 = strchr(s1, delim)) != NULL; ++i)
        s1 = s2 + 1;
    if ((rules = malloc(sizeof (Dstrule) * i)) == NULL)
        return (NULL);
     }
     {                                           /* parse rules */
    int year = 0;

    for (pr = rules; ; ++pr, ++s)
        {                                        /* parse next rule */
        if (*s == '(')
            {                                    /* got a year qualifier */
            year = getint(s + 1, 4) - 1900;
            if (year < 0 || s[5] != ')')
                break;                           /* invalid year */
            s += 6;
            }
        pr->year = year;
        pr->mon = getint(s, 2) - 1, s += 2;
        pr->day = getint(s, 2) - 1, s += 2;
        if (isdigit(*s))
            pr->hour = getint(s, 2), s += 2;
        else
            pr->hour = 0;
        if (12 <= pr->mon || 99 < pr->day || 99 < pr->hour)
            break;                    /* invalid month, day, or hour */
        if (*s != '+' && *s != '-')
            pr->wday = 0;
```

```
            else if (s[1] < '0' || '6' < s[1])
                break;                          /* invalid week day */
            else
                {                               /* compute week day field */
                pr->wday = s[1] == '0' ? 7 : s[1] - '0';
                if (*s == '+')                  /* '-': strictly before */
                    pr->wday += 7;              /* '+': on or after */
                s += 2;
                }
            if (*s == '\0')
                {                               /* done, terminate list */
                (pr + 1)->wday = (unsigned char)-1;
                (pr + 1)->year = year;
                return (rules);
                }
            else if (*s != delim)
                break;
            }
        free(rules);
        return (NULL);
        }
    }
```

Figure 15.10:
localtim.c

```
/* localtime function */
#include <stdlib.h>
#include "xtime.h"

time_t _Tzoff(void)
    {                               /* determine local time offset */
    static const char *oldzone = NULL;
    static long tzoff = 0;
    static const long maxtz = 60*13;

    if (oldzone != _Times._Tzone)
        {                           /* determine time zone offset */
        const char *p, *pe;
        int n;

        if (_Times._Tzone[0] == '\0')
            _Times._Tzone = _Getzone();
        p = _Gettime(_Times._Tzone, 2, &n);
        tzoff = strtol(p, (char **)&pe, 10);
        if (pe - p != n
            || tzoff <= -maxtz || maxtz <= tzoff)
            tzoff = 0;
        oldzone = _Times._Tzone;
        }
    return (tzoff * 60);
    }

struct tm *(localtime)(const time_t *tod)
    {                               /* convert to local time structure */
    return (_Ttotm(NULL, *tod + _Tzoff(), -1));
    }
```

Figure 15.11:
xgettime.c

```
/* _Gettime function */
#include <string.h>
#include "xtime.h"

const char *_Gettime(const char *s, int n, int *len)
    {                                   /*  get time info from environment */
    const char delim = *s ? *s++ : '\0';
    const char *s1;

    for (; ; --n, s = s1 + 1)
        {                                       /* find end of current field */
        if ((s1 = strchr(s, delim)) == NULL)
            s1 = s + strlen(s);
        if (n <= 0)
            {                                       /* found proper field */
            *len = s1 - s;
            return (s);
            }
        else if (*s1 == '\0')
            {                                       /* not enough fields */
            *len = 1;
            return (s1);
            }
        }
    }
```

**function
_Gettime**

Figure 15.11 shows the file **xgettime.c**. It defines the function **_Gettime** that locates a field in a string that specifies locale-specific time information. See the description of **_Getdst**, above, for how **_Gettime** interprets field delimiters. If **_Gettime** cannot find the requested field, it returns a pointer to an empty string.

**function
_Getzone**

Figure 15.12 shows the file **xgetzone.c**. The function **_Getzone** calls **getenv**, declared in **<stdlib.h>**, to determine the value of the environment variable **"TIMEZONE"**. That value should have the same format as the locale-specific time string **_Times._Tzone**, described above (possibly with rules for determining Daylight Savings Time bolted on).

**"TIMEZONE"
"TZ"**

If no value exists for **"TIMEZONE"**, the function **_Getzone** then looks for the environment variable **"TZ"**. That value should match the UNIX format **EST05EDT**. The internal function **reformat** uses the value of **"TZ"** to develop the preferred form in its static buffer.

If **_Getzone** finds neither of these environment variables, it assumes that the local time zone is UTC. In any event, it stores its decision in the static internal buffer **tzone**. Subsequent calls to the function return this remembered value. Thus, the environment variables are queried at most once, the first time that **_Getzone** is called.

**function
mktime**

Figure 15.13 shows the file **mktime.c**. The function **mktime** computes an integer **time_t** from a broken-down time struct **tm**. It takes extreme pains to avoid overflow in doing so. (The function is obliged to return the value −1 if the time cannot be properly represented.)

Figure 15.12:
xgetzone.c

```c
/* _Getzone function */
#include <ctype.h>
#include <stdlib.h>
#include <string.h>
#include "xtime.h"

        /* static data */
static const char *defzone = ":UTC:UTC:0";
static char *tzone = NULL;

static char *reformat(const char *s)
    {                                           /* reformat TZ */
    int i, val;
    static char tzbuf[] = ":EST:EDT:+0300";

    for (i = 4; 1 <= --i; )
        if (isalpha(*s))
            tzbuf[i] = *s++;
        else
            return (NULL);
    tzbuf[9] = *s == '-' || *s == '+' ? *s++ : '+';
    if (!isdigit(*s))
        return (NULL);
    val = *s++ - '0';
    if (isdigit(*s))
        val = 10 * val + *s++ - '0';
    for (val *= 60, i = 14; 10 <= --i; val /= 10)
        tzbuf[i] = val % 10;
    for (i = 8; 5 <= --i; )
        if (isalpha(*s))
                tzbuf[i] = *s++;
        else
            return (NULL);
    return (*s == '\0' ? tzbuf : NULL);
    }

const char *_Getzone(void)
    {                                   /* get time zone information */
    const char *s;

    if (tzone)
        ;
    else if ((s = getenv("TIMEZONE")) != NULL)
        {                                       /* copy desired format */
        if ((tzone = malloc(strlen(s) + 1)) != NULL)
            strcpy(tzone, s);
        }
    else if ((s = getenv("TZ")) != NULL)
        tzone = reformat(s);
    if (tzone == NULL)
        tzone = (char *)defzone;
    return (tzone);
    }
```

□

Figure 15.13:
mktime.c

```c
/* mktime function */
#include <limits.h>
#include "xtime.h"

time_t (mktime)(struct tm *t)
    {              /* convert local time structure to scalar time */
    double dsecs;
    int mon, year, ymon;
    time_t secs;

    ymon = t->tm_mon / 12;
    mon = t->tm_mon - ymon * 12;
    if (mon < 0)
        mon += 12, --ymon;
    if (ymon < 0 && t->tm_year < INT_MIN - ymon
        || 0 < ymon && INT_MAX - ymon < t->tm_year)
        return ((time_t)(-1));
    year = t->tm_year + ymon;
    dsecs = 86400.0 * (_Daysto(year, mon) - 1)
        + 31536000.0 * year + 86400.0 * t->tm_mday;
    dsecs += 3600.0 * t->tm_hour + 60.0 * t->tm_min
        + (double)t->tm_sec;
    if (dsecs < 0.0 || (double)(time_t)(-1) <= dsecs)
        return ((time_t)(-1));
    secs = (time_t)dsecs - _TBIAS;
    _Ttotm(t, secs, t->tm_isdst);
    if (0 < t->tm_isdst)
        secs -= 3600;
    return (secs - _Tzoff());
    }                                                                    □
```

Figure 15.14:
ctime.c

```c
/* ctime function */
#include <time.h>

char *(ctime)(const time_t *tod)
    {                     /* convert calendar time to local text */
    return (asctime(localtime(tod)));
    }                                                                    □
```

Figure 15.15:
strftime.c

```c
/* strftime function */
#include "xtime.h"

size_t (strftime)(char *s, size_t n, const char *fmt,
    const struct tm *t)
    {                                       /* format time to string */
    return (_Strftime(s, n, fmt, t, &_Times));
    }                                                                    □
```

Figure 15.16:
asctime.c

```
/* asctime function */
#include "xtime.h"

        /* static data */
static const char ampm[] = {":AM:PM"};
static const char days[] = {
    ":Sun:Sunday:Mon:Monday:Tue:Tuesday:Wed:Wednesday"
    ":Thu:Thursday:Fri:Friday:Sat:Saturday"};
static const char fmts[] = {
    "|%b %d %H:%M:%S %Y|%b %d %Y|%H:%M:%S"};
static const char isdst[] = {""};
static const char mons[] = {
    ":Jan:January:Feb:February:Mar:March"
    ":Apr:April:May:May:Jun:June"
    ":Jul:July:Aug:August:Sep:September"
    ":Oct:October:Nov:November:Dec:December"};
static const char zone[] = {""};              /* adapt by default */
static _Tinfo ctinfo = {ampm, days, fmts, isdst, mons, zone};
_Tinfo _Times = {ampm, days, fmts, isdst, mons, zone};

char *(asctime)(const struct tm *t)
    {              /* format time as "Day Mon dd hh:mm:ss yyyy\n" */
    static char tbuf[] = "Day Mon dd hh:mm:ss yyyy\n";

    _Strftime(tbuf, sizeof (tbuf), "%a %c\n", t, &ctinfo);
    return (tbuf);
    }
```

The first part of mktime determines a year and month. If they can be represented as type *int,* the function calls _Daysto to correct for leap days since 1900. mktime then accumulates the time in seconds as type *double,* to minimize further fretting about integer overflow. If the final value is representable as type time_t, the function converts it to that type. mktime calls _Ttotm to put the broken-down time in canonical form. Finally, the function corrects the time in seconds for Daylight Savings Time and converts it from local time to UTC. (The resultant code reads *much* easier than it wrote.)

time formatting functions   The remaining functions declared in `<time.h>` convert encoded times to text strings in various ways. All depend, in the end, on the internal function _Strftime to do the actual conversion. What varies is the choice of locale. The function asctime (and, by extension, the function ctime) convert times by a fixed format, following the conventions of the "C" locale regardless of the current state of the locale category LC_TIME. The function strftime, on the other hand, lets you specify a format that directs the conversion of a broken-down time. It follows the conventions of the current locale. Thus, one of the arguments to _Strftime specifies the locale-specific time information (of type _Tinfo) to use.

function asctime   Figure 15.16 shows the file asctime.c. It defines the function asctime that formats a broken-down time the same way irrespective of the current locale. The file also defines the data object **_Times** that specifies the locale-specific time information. And it defines the internal data object **ctinfo**, which replicates the time information for the "c" locale.

function
ctime
Figure 15.14 shows the file **ctime.c**. The function **ctime** simply calls **localtime**, then **asctime**, to convert its **time_t** argument. Thus, it always follows the conventions of the "c" locale.

function
strftime
Figure 15.15 shows the file **strftime.c**. The function **strftime** calls **_Strftime**, using the locale-specific time information stored in **_Times**. Thus, its behavior changes with locale.

function
_Strftime
Figure 15.17 shows the file **xstrftim.c**. It defines the internal function **_Strftime** that does all the work of formatting time information. **_Strftime** uses the macro **PUT**, defined at the top of the file **xstrftim.c**, to deliver characters. The macro encapsulates the logic needed to copy generated characters, count them, and limit the number delivered.

The internal function **_Mbtowc**, declared in **<stdlib.h>**, parses the format as a multibyte string using state memory of type **_Mbstate** that you provide on each call. The issues are the same as for **_Printf**, described on page 303.

function
_Gentime
Figure 15.18 shows the file **xgentime.c**. It defines the function **_Gentime** that performs the actual conversions for **_Strftime**. The function **_Gentime** consists primarily of a large *switch* statement that processes each conversion separately.

Each conversion determines a pointer **p** to a sequence of characters that gives the result of the conversion. It also stores a signed integer count at ***pn**. A positive count instructs **_Strftime** to generate the designated sequence of characters.

One source of generated characters is the function **_Gettime**, which selects a field from one of the strings in the locale-specific time information. Another is the internal function **getval**, also defined in the file **xgentime.c**, which generates decimal integers. **getval** stores characters in the accumulator provided by **_Strftime**.

_Gentime returns a negative count to instruct **_Strftime** to "push down" a format string for a locale-specific conversion. Three conversions change with locale — **%c**, **%x**, and **%X**. (The conversion **%x**, for example, becomes the format string "**%b %d %Y**" in the "c" locale.) You express these conversions as format strings that invoke the other conversions. (Page 111 describes how to write a locale file that alters these format strings.) Note that the function **_Strftime** supports only one level of format stacking.

The other internal function in the file **xgentime.c** is **wkyr**. It counts weeks from the start of the year for a given day of the year. The week can begin on Sunday (**wstart** is 0) or Monday (**wstart** is 1). The peculiar logic avoids negative arguments for the modulus and divide operators.

Figure 15.17:
xstrftim.c

```c
/* _Strftime function */
#include <stdlib.h>
#include <string.h>
#include "xtime.h"

        /* macros */
#define PUT(s, na)  (void)(nput = (na), \
    0 < nput && (nchar += nput) <= bufsize ? \
        (memcpy(buf, s, nput), buf += nput) : 0)

size_t _Strftime(char *buf, size_t bufsize, const char *fmt,
    const struct tm *t, _Tinfo *tin)
    {                                   /* format time information */
    const char *fmtsav, *s;
    size_t len, lensav, nput;
    size_t nchar = 0;

    for (s = fmt, len = strlen(fmt), fmtsav = NULL; ; fmt = s)
        {                               /* parse format string */
        int n;
        wchar_t wc;
        _Mbsave state = {0};

        while (0 < (n = _Mbtowc(&wc, s, len, &state)))
            {                           /* scan for '%' or '\0' */
            s += n, len -= n;
            if (wc == '%')
                break;
            }
        if (fmt < s)                    /* copy any literal text */
            PUT(fmt, s - fmt - (0 < n ? 1 : 0));
        if (0 < n)
            {                           /* do the conversion */
            char ac[20];
            int m;
            const char *p = _Gentime(t, tin, s++, &m, ac);

            --len;
            if (0 <= m)
                PUT(p, m);
            else if (fmtsav == NULL)
                fmtsav = s, s = p, lensav = len, len = -m;
            }
        if (0 == len && fmtsav == NULL || n < 0)
            {               /* format end or bad multibyte char */
            PUT("", 1);                 /* null termination */
            return (nchar <= bufsize ? nchar - 1 : 0);
            }
        else if (0 == len)
            s = fmtsav, fmtsav = NULL, len = lensav;
        }
    }
```

□

```
/* _Gentime function */
#include "xtime.h"

        /* macros */
#define SUNDAY  0                              /* codes for tm_wday */
#define MONDAY  1

static char *getval(char *s, int val, int n)
    {                                    /* convert a decimal value */
    if (val < 0)
        val = 0;
    for (s += n, *s = '\0'; 0 <= --n; val /= 10)
        *--s = val % 10 + '0';
    return (s);
    }

static int wkyr(int wstart, int wday, int yday)
    {                                         /* find week of year */
    wday = (wday + 7 - wstart) % 7;
    return (yday - wday + 12) / 7 - 1;
    }

const char *_Gentime(const struct tm *t, _Tinfo *tin,
    const char *s, int *pn, char *ac)
    {                                        /* format a time field */
    const char *p;

    switch (*s++)
        {                        /* switch on conversion specifier */
    case 'a':                              /* put short weekday name */
        p = _Gettime(tin->_Days, t->tm_wday << 1, pn);
        break;
    case 'A':                               /* put full weekday name */
        p = _Gettime(tin->_Days, (t->tm_wday << 1) + 1, pn);
        break;
    case 'b':                                /* put short month name */
        p = _Gettime(tin->_Months, t->tm_mon << 1, pn);
        break;
    case 'B':                                 /* put full month name */
        p = _Gettime(tin->_Months, (t->tm_mon << 1) + 1, pn);
        break;
    case 'c':                                   /* put date and time */
        p = _Gettime(tin->_Formats, 0, pn), *pn = -*pn;
        break;
    case 'd':                            /* put day of month, from 1 */
        p = getval(ac, t->tm_mday, *pn = 2);
        break;
    case 'H':                             /* put hour of 24-hour day */
        p = getval(ac, t->tm_hour, *pn = 2);
        break;
    case 'I':                             /* put hour of 12-hour day */
        p = getval(ac, t->tm_hour % 12, *pn = 2);
        break;
    case 'j':                             /* put day of year, from 1 */
        p = getval(ac, t->tm_yday + 1, *pn = 3);
```

```
                break;
        case 'm':                            /* put month of year, from 1 */
                p = getval(ac, t->tm_mon + 1, *pn = 2);
                break;
        case 'M':                            /* put minutes after the hour */
                p = getval(ac, t->tm_min, *pn = 2);
                break;
        case 'p':                                           /* put AM/PM */
                p = _Gettime(tin->_Ampm, 12 <= t->tm_hour, pn);
                break;
        case 'S':                        /* put seconds after the minute */
                p = getval(ac, t->tm_sec, *pn = 2);
                break;
        case 'U':                        /* put Sunday week of the year */
                p = getval(ac,
                    wkyr(SUNDAY, t->tm_wday, t->tm_yday), *pn = 2);
                break;
        case 'w':                        /* put day of week, from Sunday */
                p = getval(ac, t->tm_wday, *pn = 1);
                break;
        case 'W':                        /* put Monday week of the year */
                p = getval(ac,
                    wkyr(MONDAY, t->tm_wday, t->tm_yday), *pn = 2);
                break;
        case 'x':                                           /* put date */
                p = _Gettime(tin->_Formats, 1, pn), *pn = -*pn;
                break;
        case 'X':                                           /* put time */
                p = _Gettime(tin->_Formats, 2, pn), *pn = -*pn;
                break;
        case 'y':                            /* put year of the century */
                p = getval(ac, t->tm_year % 100, *pn = 2);
                break;
        case 'Y':                                           /* put year */
                p = getval(ac, t->tm_year + 1900, *pn = 4);
                break;
        case 'Z':                            /* put time zone name */
                if (tin->_Tzone[0] == '\0')
                    tin->_Tzone = _Getzone();            /* adapt zone */
                p = _Gettime(tin->_Tzone, 0 < t->tm_isdst, pn);
                break;
        case '%':                                           /* put "%" */
                p = "%", *pn = 1;
                break;
        default:                            /* unknown field, print it */
                p = s - 1, *pn = 2;
                }
        return (p);
        }
```
□

Figure 15.19:
ttime.c

```
/* test time functions */
#include <assert.h>
#include <stdio.h>
#include <time.h>

int main()
    {                       /* test basic workings of time functions */
    char buf[32];
    clock_t tc = clock();
    struct tm ts1, ts2;
    time_t tt1, tt2;
    static char *dstr = "Sun Dec 02 06:55:15 1979\n";
    static char *ptr = NULL;

    tt1 = time(&tt2);
    assert(tt1 == tt2);
    ts1.tm_sec = 15;
    ts1.tm_min = 55;
    ts1.tm_hour = 6;
    ts1.tm_mday = 2;
    ts1.tm_mon = 11;
    ts1.tm_year = 79;
    ts1.tm_isdst = -1;
    tt1 = mktime(&ts1);
    assert(ts1.tm_wday == 0);
    assert(ts1.tm_yday == 335);
    ++ts1.tm_sec;
    tt2 = mktime(&ts1);
    assert(difftime(tt1, tt2) < 0.0);
    assert(strcmp(asctime(localtime(&tt1)), dstr) == 0);
    assert(strftime(buf, sizeof (buf), "%S",
        gmtime(&tt2)) == 2);
    assert(strcmp(buf, "16") == 0);
    assert(tc <= clock());
    fputs("Current date -- ", stdout);
    time(&tt1);
    fputs(ctime(&tt1), stdout);
    puts("SUCCESS testing <time.h>");
    return (0);
    }                                                                    □
```

Testing `<time.h>`

Figure 15.19 shows the file `ttime.c`. The test program performs basic tests on all the functions declared in `<time.h>`. As a quality check, it also displays what the function `time` returns as the date and time when you run the program. If all goes well, the program displays something like:

```
Current date -- Sun Dec 02 06:55:15 1979
SUCCESS testing <time.h>
```

References

W.M. O'Neil, *Time and the Calendars*, (Sydney, N.S.W.: Sydney University Press, 1975). Calendars are notoriously idiosyncratic. This book tells you more than you probably want to know about the history of measuring calendar time. It also explains why days and dates are named and determined the way they are today.

Exercises

Exercise 15.1 Write a locale file that expresses the time conventions for the French language. You need to alter:

```
am_pm        days
dst_rules    months
time_zone    time_formats
```

Test your new locale. (Hint: You may want to commandeer test programs in this and earlier chapters as a starting point.)

Exercise 15.2 Determine the rule where you live for beginning and ending Daylight Savings Time. (If Daylight Savings Time is not observed where you live, then pick a place that does so where you might *like* to live.) Write a locale file that observes this rule. How has the rule changed over the last twenty years? Can you express all these changes succinctly in a locale-file specification for `dst_rules`?

Exercise 15.3 Many astronomers believe that the universe "began" approximately 15 billion years ago with a big bang. How many seconds have elapsed since the big bang? How many bits does it take to represent the seconds that have elapsed since the big bang?

Exercise 15.4 Leap years generally occur every multiple of four years. They generally do *not* occur every multiple of one hundred years. They *do* occur every multiple of four hundred years. Alter the function `_Daysto`, defined in the file `xttotm.c`, to determine leap years properly before 1801 and after 2099. Over what period does it make sense to have this function work properly?

Exercise 15.5 Write the function `long delta_days(int year, int mon, int delta_mon)` that counts the days in a span of months. The initial day is the first day of the month `mon` in the year `year`. The span of months is the signed value `delta_mon`. Why do you need to specify the initial year?

Exercise 15.6 Implement the primitive functions `clock` and `time` for your system. What can you say about the accuracy (and meaning) of the values returned by these functions?

Exercise 15.7 In recent years, astronomers have taken to adding "leap seconds" to certain years, just before midnight on New Year's Eve. (This corrects for the slowing rotation of the Earth.) Find a list of years that have added leap seconds. Correct for leap seconds at the appropriate place within the time functions.

Exercise 15.8 [**Harder**] Assemble a table of all the time zones in the world. Devise a mnemonic naming scheme for all the zones. Add a function that lets you specify your working time zone by this mnemonic name. What do you do about Daylight Savings Time?

Exercise 15.9 [**Very hard**] Devise a more orderly way to measure time. Get somebody with some authority to agree to adopt it.

Appendix A: Interfaces

This appendix summarizes what you have to do to interface this implementation of the Standard C library to a given execution envtronment. It is aimed primarily at those who intend to do something with the implementation that I have presented so far. Others may find parts that are of interest, if only to understand the issues involved. If your concern ends with the C Standard or with the advice to users, however, you can safely skip what follows.

Even among potential implementors, goals can vary widely. Some may wish only to mine the code presented here for a few useful gems. If so, your challenge is to find a consistent subset that meets your needs, then integrate it into an existing C implementation. Others may wish to displace completely an existing C library. If so, you have more work to do. I can only sketch those extra steps here.

assumptions I introduced the header **<yvals.h>** to summarize as many parameters as possible. Where that failed, I introduced the header **"yfuns.h"** to tailor the names of low-level primitives. I don't pretend that changing these headers alone will adapt this library to all sensible environments. The code is riddled with assumptions. Where those assumptions fail to hold, you have to alter the code to adapt it. Here are the assumptions you must verify:

- all files — Review the assumptions starting on page 9. Many parts of the library also assume that you can define writable static data objects within the library. See the discussion on page 36.

<ctype.h> ■ **<ctype.h>** — The files **xctype.c, xtolower.c,** and **xtoupper.c** assume that the execution character set is ASCII. Change the tables they contain for a different character set. These files also assume that a *char* occupies eight bits. If a *char* is larger, you may have to reconsider the approach based on tables.

<errno.h> ■ **<errno.h>** — The files **errno.c** and **errno.h** assume that you can maintain **errno** as a writable static data object. You may have to call a function on each access to **errno** to capture a deferred error report.

<float.h> ■ **<float.h>** — The files **float.h** and **xfloat.c** assume that the format for floating-point values is IEEE 754 or a closely related form. If the format(s) differ sufficiently, you may have to reconsider the approach based on the parameters in **<yvals.h>**.

<limits.h> ■ **<limits.h>** — The file **limits.h** assumes that a *char* occupies eight bits and an *int* occupies either two or four bytes, (See page 77.)

<locale.h> ■ **<locale>** — This code assumes knowledge of the inner workings of several parts of the library. Look for problems here if you change *any* code in: **<ctype.h>** (translation tables), **<limits.h>** (**MB_LEN_MAX**), **<stdlib.h>** (multibyte functions), **<string.h>** (collation functions), or **<time.h>** (locale-specific time information).

<math.h> ■ **<math.h>** — This code is at least as dependent on floating-point format as **<float.h>**, above. (See the discussion beginning on page 127.) Be prepared to make major changes if *double* retains more than 56 bits of precision or has a decimal base.

<stdarg.h> ■ **<stdarg.h>** — The file **stdarg.h** assumes that arguments passed to a function are stored in ascending storage locations following a predictable pattern. (See page 211.) You have to reconsider this approach if any of the assumptions fail to hold.

<stddef.h> ■ **<stddef.h>** — The macro **offsetof** in file **stddef.h** assumes that you can perform several tricks involving pointers and integers. (See page 222.) If any of those tricks fail, you must find an alternate set of tricks that does work. (Such a set must exist.)

primitives   Nineteen functions depend heavily on the execution environment. You can think of them as the basic primitives that interface this implementation to the execution environment. I made little or no attempt to provide parametric versions of these functions. Expect to make significant changes here. In many cases, you will find that existing functions in a C implementation can serve. Unless your goal is to displace completely an existing library, you can commandeer such functions rather than write your own. Here is a summary of the primitives:

<setjmp.h> ■ **<setjmp.h>** — The functions **setjmp** and **longjmp** must be written in assembly language specially for each implementation. You can probably adapt the file **setjmp.h** merely by altering the macro **_NSETJMP**, defined in the file **yvals.h**. Don't even think about using the example files **longjmp.c** and **setjmp.c**, however.

<signal.h> ■ **<signal.h>** — The files **raise.c** and **signal.c** must be modified to control hardware signals. Some systems provide a direct replacement for the function **signal**.

<stdio.h> ■ **<stdio.h>** — Nine functions and macros isolate most of the system dependencies from the rest of the code. The functions are in the files **remove.c**, **rename.c**, **tmpnam.c**, **xfgpos.c**, **xfopen.c**, and **xfspos.c**. The macros are **_Fclose**, **_Fread**, and **_Fwrite**, defined in the file **yfuns.h**. Some systems provide direct replacements for a few of these functions. Check carefully, however, that these candidates have the required behavior as well as the expected names.

<stdlib.h> ■ **<stdlib.h>** — Four functions and macros isolate most of the system dependencies from the rest of the code. The functions are in the files **getenv.c**, **system.c**, and **xgetmem.c**. The macro is **_Exit**, defined in the

Figure A.1:
yfuns.h

```
/* yfuns.h functions header -- UNIX version */
#ifndef _YFUNS
#define _YFUNS
            /* macros */
#define _Environ      (*_Envp)
#define _Fclose(str)      _Close((str)->_Handle)
#define _Fread(str, buf, cnt)  _Read((str)->_Handle, buf, cnt)
#define _Fwrite(str, buf, cnt) _Write((str)->_Handle, buf, cnt)
            /* interface declarations */
extern const char **_Envp;
int _Close(int);
void _Exit(int);
int _Read(int, unsigned char *, int);
int _Write(int, const unsigned char *, int);
#endif                                                                □
```

file **yfuns.h**. You can often use the file **getenv.c** presented here, given a suitable definition or declaration for the data object **_Envp** in the file **yfuns.h**.

<time.h> ▪ **<time.h>** — Two functions isolate most of the system dependencies from the rest of the code. The functions are in the files **clock.c** and **time.c**. You can write **clock.c** in terms of **time.c**, as I did here. That can be handy if the execution environment doesn't provide a separate measure of elapsed processor time.

header   Figure A.1 shows the file **yfuns.h**. It is a version of the header **"yfuns.h"**
"yfuns.h" that can work with many UNIX systems. It follows the same naming convention I have used for earlier UNIX examples. Here is the complete list of the names with external linkage that this implementation needs to have defined under UNIX. I follow each with its conventional UNIX library name:

_Environ	environ	_Lseek	lseek
_Clock	clock	_Open	open
_Close	close	_Read	read
_Execl	execl	_Sbrk	sbrk
_Exit	exit	_Signal	signal
_Fork	fork	_Time	time
_Getpid	getpid	_Unlink	unlink
_Kill	kill	_Write	write
_Link	link		

I list **_Environ** first because it names a data object. (Like the macro **errno**, defined in **<errno.h>**, it can be a function call that returns a pointer, if necessary.) All the rest name functions that provide UNIX system services. You may well have to write, or alter, assembly language files to supply these services.

You can cheat and replace the reserved names with the conventional names. That can be a quick way to get started using this implementation. But that shortcut also causes a few name collisions. And it violates the rules in the C Standard about the use of name spaces, of course.

Given the necessary primitives, you adapt the remainder of the code by altering the internal header `<yvals.h>`. It defines the following macros:

_ADNBND ■ _ADNBND — used by `stdarg.h` to back up an argument pointer (value typically 0, 1, 3, or 7)

_AUPBND ■ _AUPBND — used by `stdarg.h` to advance an argument pointer (value typically 0, 1, 3, or 7)

_C2 ■ _C2 — used by `limits.h` to distinguish two's-complement representation (value 1) from one's-complement or signed-magnitude (value 0)

_CPS ■ _CPS — used by `time.h` to determine the value of the macro CLOCKS_PER_SEC

_CSIGN ■ _CSIGN — used by `limits.h` to distinguish whether *char* can represent negative quantities (value nonzero) or only positive quantities (zero)

_D0 ■ _D0 — used by numerous files to determine the byte order of floating-point values in storage (value 0 or 3)

_DBIAS ■ _DBIAS — used by several files to determine the difference between a *double* characteristic and its signed exponent

_DLONG ■ _DLONG — used by several files to determine whether *long double* is IEEE 754 10-byte format (value nonzero) or the same as *double* (zero)

_DOFF ■ _DOFF — used by several files to determine the bit offset of a *double* characteristic in the most-significant word

_EDOM ■ _EDOM — used by `errno.h` to determine the value of the macro EDOM

_EFPOS ■ _EFPOS — used by `errno.h` to determine the value of the macro EFPOS

_ERANGE ■ _ERANGE — used by `errno.h` to determine the value of the macro ERANGE

_ERRMAX ■ _ERRMAX — used by `errno.h` to determine the range of error codes

_FBIAS ■ _FBIAS — used by `xfloat.c` to determine the difference between a *float* characteristic and its signed exponent

_FNAMAX ■ _FNAMAX — used by `stdio.h` to determine the value of the macro FILE-NAME_MAX

_FOFF ■ _FOFF — used by `xfloat.c` to determine the bit offset of a *float* characteristic in the more-significant word

_FOPMAX ■ _FOPMAX — used by `stdio.h` to determine the value of the macro FOPEN_MAX

_FRND ■ _FRND — used by `float.h` to determine the value of the macro FLT_ROUNDS

_ILONG ■ _ILONG — used by `limits.h` to distinguish whether *long* occupies 32 bits (value nonzero) or 16 bits (zero)

_LBIAS ■ _LBIAS — used by several files to determine the difference between a *long double* characteristic and its signed exponent

_LOFF ■ _LOFF — used by several files to determine the bit offset of a *long double* characteristic in the most-significant word

_MBMAX ■ _MBMAX — used by `limits.h` to determine the value of the macro MB_LEN_MAX

_MEMBND ■ _MEMBND — used by several files to enforce the worst-case storage boundary (value typically 0, 1, 3, or 7)

_NSETJMP ▪ _NSETJMP — used by setjmp.h to determine the size of the array of *int* jmp_buf

_NULL ▪ _NULL — used by several files to determine the value of the macro **NULL** (value 0, 0L, or (**void *)**0)

_SIGABRT ▪ _SIGABRT — used by signal.h to determine the value of the macro SIGABRT

_SIGMAX ▪ _SIGMAX — used by signal.h to determine the range of signal codes

_TBIAS ▪ _TBIAS — used by several functions to correct the starting point for calendar times represented as type time_t

_TNAMAX ▪ _TNAMAX — used by stdio.h to determine the value of the macro L_tmpnam

I give several examples of consistent sets of these parameters.

DEC VAX ULTRIX Figure A.2 shows the file yvals.h. It is a version of the header <yvals.h> that work with the VAX ULTRIX system. Most of the parameters are common to many versions of UNIX. The floating-point parameters describe the proprietary format supported by the VAX and the older PDP-11 computer architectures. That format does not truly support codes for Inf and NaN, but this library defines them anyway. So long as you perform no arithmetic operations on these special codes, they can survive to convey useful information.

GNU C under Sun UNIX You can easily modify this version of yvals.h to work with the GNU C compiler under Sun UNIX (using Motorola MC680X0 microprocessors). First, change the floating-point parameters to describe IEEE 754 formats:

```
#define _D0      0
#define _DBIAS   0x3fe
#define _DLONG   0
#define _DOFF    4
#define _FBIAS   0x7e
#define _FOFF    7
#define _FRND    1
#define _LBIAS   0x3fe
#define _LOFF    4
```

Then change the storage-alignment parameters:

```
#define _AUPBND  3U
#define _ADNBND  0U
#define _MEMBND  3U
```

You must also provide a set of renamed UNIX system services, of course.

complete libraries If your goal is to displace completely an existing library for a given compiler, you have two additional concerns:

▪ You must supply a *C startup header* that gets control initially from the operating system. That requires an intimate knowledge of how the operating system runs programs. The C startup header ensures that the call stack is properly set up, that static storage is properly initialized, and that the three standard streams are open. It calls **main**, then **exit** with the status returned from **main**. Operating systems vary considerably in how much of this work they do for you.

Figure A.2:
yvals.h

```
/* yvals.h values header -- VAX ULTRIX version */
#define _YVALS
         /* errno properties */
#define _EDOM    33
#define _ERANGE 34
#define _EFPOS  35
#define _ERRMAX 36
         /* float properties */
#define _D0      0
#define _DBIAS  0x80
#define _DLONG   0
#define _DOFF    7
#define _FBIAS  0x80
#define _FOFF    7
#define _FRND    1
#define _LBIAS  0x80
#define _LOFF    7
         /* integer properties */
#define _C2      1
#define _CSIGN   1
#define _ILONG   1
#define _MBMAX   8
typedef unsigned short _Wchart;
         /* pointer properties */
#define _NULL    (void *)0
typedef int _Ptrdifft;
typedef unsigned int _Sizet;
         /* setjmp properties */
#define _NSETJMP     80
         /* signal properties */
#define _SIGABRT     6
#define _SIGMAX      32
         /* stdio properties */
#define _FNAMAX 64
#define _FOPMAX 16
#define _TNAMAX 16
         /* stdlib properties */
#define _EXFAIL 1
         /* storage alignment properties */
#define _AUPBND 3U
#define _ADNBND 3U
#define _MEMBND 7U
         /* time properties */
#define _CPS     1
#define _TBIAS   0
```

- You must supply any *C runtime* functions that the generated code may call. That requires an intimate knowledge of how the compiler generates code. A *switch* statement, for example, often calls a runtime function rather than perform all the compares and branches with inline code. Compilers vary considerably in how much they depend on C runtime functions.

You will find little advantage to displacing completely the ULTRIX or GNU C libraries unless you have to contend with licensing issues.

Borland I also exercised the code in this book with the Borland Turbo C++ **Turbo** compiler. (I used the ANSI C compiler that comes with the package.) You **C++** have a broad range of choices in how much of the Borland library you choose to displace. You can even license the Borland library source code on reasonable terms to further broaden your choices. Here is a reasonable version of **yvals.h** for use with this compiler:

```
/* yvals.h values header -- Turbo C++ version */
#define _YVALS
        /* errno properties */
#define _EDOM   33
#define _ERANGE 34
#define _EFPOS  35
#define _ERRMAX 36
        /* float properties */
#define _D0     3
#define _DBIAS  0x3fe
#define _DLONG  1
#define _DOFF   4
#define _FBIAS  0x7e
#define _FOFF   7
#define _FRND   1
#define _LBIAS  0x3ffe
#define _LOFF   15
        /* integer properties */
#define _C2     1
#define _CSIGN  1
#define _ILONG  0
#define _MBMAX  8
typedef unsigned short _Wchart;
        /* pointer properties */
#define _NULL   (void *)0
typedef int _Ptrdifft;
typedef unsigned int _Sizet;
        /* setjmp properties */
#define _NSETJMP    10
        /* signal properties */
#define _SIGABRT    22
#define _SIGMAX     32
        /* stdio properties */
#define _FNAMAX 64
#define _FOPMAX 16
#define _TNAMAX 16
        /* stdlib properties */
#define _EXFAIL 1
        /* storage alignment properties */
#define _AUPBND 1U
#define _ADNBND 1U
#define _MEMBND 1U
        /* time properties */
#define _CPS    1
#define _TBIAS  ((70 * 365LU + 17) * 86400)
```

The C startup header that Borland supplies defines **abort** and **errno**. If you want to displace these, you must obtain the source code and modify it. Otherwise, your biggest worry is the way MS-DOS represents text files. You must discard (certain) carriage returns in **_Fread** and insert carriage returns before (certain) newlines in **_Fwrite**. You must also correct for these alterations in **_Fgpos** and **_Fspos**. For the remaining primitives, you will typically find more than adequate versions in the Borland library.

other systems   Other operating systems are much less inspired by UNIX. That makes them harder to pave over the way the C Standard requires. Usually, the worst offender is the input/output model. Files structured into records and blocks require delicate handling if streams are to behave robustly. It is particularly difficult to handle file-positioning requests properly in a file that has record or block structure.

IBM System/370   System/370 is an extreme example. It offers several operating systems, all steeped in conventions that long predate UNIX. Even the simplest of these operating systems requires a nontrivial interface to support Standard C properly. The biggest of them can easily call for system-specific code comparable in size and complexity to all the code in this book combined. Here is a case where you definitely want to build on the work of others.

freestanding programs   If your goal is to use this library to generate freestanding programs, you have a slightly different set of concerns. You have no operating system to lean on, or a vestigial one at best. An existing C cross compiler for the same computer architecture may supply you with C startup code and a C runtime tailored for a freestanding environment. A compiler designed to produce only hosted programs will leave you with work to do in both areas.

Many of the primitives you must supply can often be stubs in a freestanding environment. Consider an execution environment, for example, that supports only serial input and output of characters through a single port. The functions **_Fread** and **_Fwrite** need only deal with this port. The functions **_Fgpos**, **_Fopen**, etc. can all fail for any arguments. If your needs are modest, you can cut many corners here.

improvements   You may also wish to make an assortment of improvements. You can add error codes (to **errno.h** and **strerror.c**), for example. You can add signal codes (to **signal.h** and **raise.c**). You can implement a broad assortment of locales, and even build the more popular ones directly into the library. You can write enhanced versions of functions such as **div** and **strlen**, to name just two candidates. The list is endless, so I'll stop it here. But you don't have to. Good luck.

Appendix B: Names

This appendix lists the names of entities defined in this implementation of the library that have external linkage or are defined in one of the standard headers. They are the names that your program sees, for good or for ill. A function name that appears twice has a macro definition that masks its declaration in the standard header that declares it.

	Name	Header	File	Page
	BUFSIZ	<stdio.h>	stdio.h	276
	CHAR_BIT	<limits.h>	limits.h	76
	CHAR_MAX	<limits.h>	limits.h	76
	CHAR_MIN	<limits.h>	limits.h	76
	CLOCKS_PER_SEC	<time.h>	time.h	424
D	DBL_DIG	<float.h>	float.h	66
	DBL_EPSILON	<float.h>	float.h	66
	DBL_MANT_DIG	<float.h>	float.h	66
	DBL_MAX	<float.h>	float.h	66
	DBL_MAX_10_EXP	<float.h>	float.h	66
	DBL_MAX_EXP	<float.h>	float.h	66
	DBL_MIN	<float.h>	float.h	66
	DBL_MIN_10_EXP	<float.h>	float.h	66
	DBL_MIN_EXP	<float.h>	float.h	66
	EDOM	<errno.h>	errno.h	53
	EFPOS	<errno.h>	errno.h	53
	EOF	<stdio.h>	stdio.h	276
	ERANGE	<errno.h>	errno.h	53
	EXIT_FAILURE	<stdlib.h>	stdlib.h	354
	EXIT_SUCCESS	<stdlib.h>	stdlib.h	354
F	FILE	<stdio.h>	stdio.h	276
	FILENAME_MAX	<stdio.h>	stdio.h	276
	FLT_DIG	<float.h>	float.h	66
	FLT_EPSILON	<float.h>	float.h	66
	FLT_MANT_DIG	<float.h>	float.h	66
	FLT_MAX	<float.h>	float.h	66
	FLT_MAX_10_EXP	<float.h>	float.h	66
	FLT_MAX_EXP	<float.h>	float.h	66
	FLT_MIN	<float.h>	float.h	66
	FLT_MIN_10_EXP	<float.h>	float.h	66

Name	Header	File	Page
FLT_MIN_EXP	`<float.h>`	`float.h`	66
FLT_RADIX	`<float.h>`	`float.h`	66
FLT_ROUNDS	`<float.h>`	`float.h`	66
FOPEN_MAX	`<stdio.h>`	`stdio.h`	276
HUGE_VAL	`<math.h>`	`math.h`	138
INT_MAX	`<limits.h>`	`limits.h`	76
INT_MIN	`<limits.h>`	`limits.h`	76
LC_ALL	`<locale.h>`	`locale.h`	96
LC_COLLATE	`<locale.h>`	`locale.h`	96
LC_CTYPE	`<locale.h>`	`locale.h`	96
LC_MONETARY	`<locale.h>`	`locale.h`	96
LC_NUMERIC	`<locale.h>`	`locale.h`	96
LC_TIME	`<locale.h>`	`locale.h`	96
LDBL_DIG	`<float.h>`	`float.h`	66
LDBL_EPSILON	`<float.h>`	`float.h`	66
LDBL_MANT_DIG	`<float.h>`	`float.h`	66
LDBL_MAX	`<float.h>`	`float.h`	66
LDBL_MAX_10_EXP	`<float.h>`	`float.h`	66
LDBL_MAX_EXP	`<float.h>`	`float.h`	66
LDBL_MIN	`<float.h>`	`float.h`	66
LDBL_MIN_10_EXP	`<float.h>`	`float.h`	66
LDBL_MIN_EXP	`<float.h>`	`float.h`	66
LONG_MAX	`<limits.h>`	`limits.h`	76
LONG_MIN	`<limits.h>`	`limits.h`	76
L_tmpnam	`<stdio.h>`	`stdio.h`	276
M MB_CUR_MAX	`<stdlib.h>`	`stdlib.h`	354
MB_LEN_MAX	`<limits.h>`	`limits.h`	76
NULL	`<locale.h>`	`locale.h`	96
" "	`<stddef.h>`	`stddef.h`	223
" "	`<stdio.h>`	`stdio.h`	276
" "	`<stdlib.h>`	`stdlib.h`	354
" "	`<string.h>`	`string.h`	398
" "	`<time.h>`	`time.h`	424
RAND_MAX	`<stdlib.h>`	`stdlib.h`	354
SCHAR_MAX	`<limits.h>`	`limits.h`	76
SCHAR_MIN	`<limits.h>`	`limits.h`	76
SEEK_CUR	`<stdio.h>`	`stdio.h`	276
SEEK_END	`<stdio.h>`	`stdio.h`	276
SEEK_SET	`<stdio.h>`	`stdio.h`	276
SHRT_MAX	`<limits.h>`	`limits.h`	76
SHRT_MIN	`<limits.h>`	`limits.h`	76
SIGABRT	`<signal.h>`	`signal.h`	200
SIGFPE	`<signal.h>`	`signal.h`	200
SIGILL	`<signal.h>`	`signal.h`	200
SIGINT	`<signal.h>`	`signal.h`	200
SIGSEGV	`<signal.h>`	`signal.h`	200
SIGTERM	`<signal.h>`	`signal.h`	200
SIG_DFL	`<signal.h>`	`signal.h`	200

Name	Header	File	Page
SIG_ERR	\<signal.h>	signal.h	200
SIG_IGN	\<signal.h>	signal.h	200
TMP_MAX	\<stdio.h>	stdio.h	276
UCHAR_MAX	\<limits.h>	limits.h	76
UINT_MAX	\<limits.h>	limits.h	76
ULONG_MAX	\<limits.h>	limits.h	76
USHRT_MAX	\<limits.h>	limits.h	76
a abort	\<stdlib.h>	abort.c	379
abs	\<stdlib.h>	abs.c	355
acos	\<math.h>	acos.c	155
" "	\<math.h>	math.h	138
asctime	\<time.h>	asctime.c	437
asin	\<math.h>	asin.c	155
" "	\<math.h>	math.h	138
assert	\<assert.h>	assert.h	20
atan	\<math.h>	atan.c	156
atan2	\<math.h>	atan2.c	157
atexit	\<stdlib.h>	atexit.c	379
atof	\<stdlib.h>	atof.c	362
" "	\<stdlib.h>	stdlib.h	354
atoi	\<stdlib.h>	atoi.c	361
" "	\<stdlib.h>	stdlib.h	354
atol	\<stdlib.h>	atol.c	361
" "	\<stdlib.h>	stdlib.h	354
bsearch	\<stdlib.h>	bsearch.c	356
c calloc	\<stdlib.h>	calloc.c	375
ceil	\<math.h>	ceil.c	141
clearerr	\<stdio.h>	clearerr.c	287
clock	\<time.h>	clock.c	426
clock_t	\<time.h>	time.h	424
cos	\<math.h>	cos.c	152
" "	\<math.h>	math.h	138
cosh	\<math.h>	cosh.c	162
ctime	\<time.h>	ctime.c	436
difftime	\<time.h>	difftime.c	426
div	\<stdlib.h>	div.c	355
div_t	\<stdlib.h>	stdlib.h	354
errno	\<errno.h>	errno.c	54
exit	\<stdlib.h>	exit.c	379
exp	\<math.h>	exp.c	162
fabs	\<math.h>	fabs.c	140
fclose	\<stdio.h>	fclose.c	280
feof	\<stdio.h>	feof.c	288
ferror	\<stdio.h>	ferror.c	288
fflush	\<stdio.h>	fflush.c	298
fgetc	\<stdio.h>	fgetc.c	290
fgetpos	\<stdio.h>	fgetpos.c	289
" "	\<stdio.h>	stdio.h	276

g

S

_A

_D

Name	Header	File	Page
_LOCALE	`<locale.h>`	`locale.h`	96
_LOFF	`<yvals.h>`	`yvals.h`	450
_Ldbl	`<float.h>`	`xfloat.c`	68
_Ldtob	`"xstdio.h"`	`xldtob.c`	312
_Ldunscale	`"xmath.h"`	`xldunsca.c`	172
_Litob	`"xstdio.h"`	`xlitob.c`	310
_Loctab	`"xlocale.h"`	`xloctab.c`	117
_Locterm	`"xlocale.h"`	`xlocterm.c`	122
_Locvar	`"xlocale.h"`	`xlocterm.c`	122
_Log	`<math.h>`	`xlog.c`	166
_MATH	`<math.h>`	`math.h`	138
_MBMAX	`<yvals.h>`	`yvals.h`	450
_MEMBND	`<yvals.h>`	`yvals.h`	450
_Makeloc	`"xlocale.h"`	`xmakeloc.c`	120
_Mbcurmax	`<stdlib.h>`	`xstate.c`	107
_Mbsave	`<stdlib.h>`	`stdlib.h`	354
_Mbstate	`"xstate.h"`	`xstate.c`	107
_Mbtowc	`<stdlib.h>`	`xmbtowc.c`	367
_Mbxlen	`<stdlib.h>`	`mblen.c`	366
_Mbxtowc	`<stdlib.h>`	`mbtowc.c`	366
_NATS	`<stdlib.h>`	`stdlib.h`	354
_NCAT	`<locale.h>`	`locale.h`	96
_NERR	`<errno.h>`	`errno.h`	53
_NSETJMP	`<yvals.h>`	`yvals.h`	450
_NSIG	`<signal.h>`	`signal.h`	200
_NULL	`<yvals.h>`	`yvals.h`	450
_Nan	`"xmath.h"`	`xvalues.c`	139
_PU	`<ctype.h>`	`ctype.h`	37
_Poly	`"xmath.h"`	`xpoly.c`	151
_Printf	`"xstdio.h"`	`xprintf.c`	304
_Ptrdifft	`<yvals.h>`	`yvals.h`	450
_Putfld	`"xstdio.h"`	`xputfld.c`	308
_Randseed	`<stdlib.h>`	`rand.c`	359
_Readloc	`"xlocale.h"`	`xreadloc.c`	115
_Rteps	`"xmath.h"`	`xvalues.c`	139
_SETJMP	`<setjmp.h>`	`setjmp.h`	187
_SIGABRT	`<yvals.h>`	`yvals.h`	450
_SIGMAX	`<yvals.h>`	`yvals.h`	450
_SIGNAL	`<signal.h>`	`signal.h`	200
_SIZET	`<stddef.h>`	`stddef.h`	223
_SIZET	`<stdio.h>`	`stdio.h`	276
_SIZET	`<stdlib.h>`	`stdlib.h`	354
_SIZET	`<string.h>`	`string.h`	398
_SIZET	`<time.h>`	`time.h`	424
_SP	`<ctype.h>`	`ctype.h`	37
_STDARG	`<stdarg.h>`	`stdarg.h`	211
_STDDEF	`<stddef.h>`	`stddef.h`	223
_STDIO	`<stdio.h>`	`stdio.h`	276

_M

_S

Appendix C: Terms

This appendix lists terms that have special meaning within this book. Check here if you suspect that a term means more (or less) than you might ordinarily think.

A **access** — to obtain the value stored in a data object or to store a new value in the data object

address constant expression — an expression that you can use to initialize a static data object of some pointer type

allocated storage — data objects whose storage is obtained during program execution

alphabetic character — a lowercase or uppercase letter

alphanumeric character — an alphabetic character or a digit

ANSI — American National Standards Institute, the organization authorized to formulate computer-related standards in the U.S.

argument — an expression that provides the initial value for one of the parameters in a function call

argument-level declaration — a declaration for one of the arguments in a function definition or a function prototype

arithmetic type — an integer or floating-point type

array type — a data-object type consisting of a prespecified repetition of a data-object element

ASCII — American Standard Code for Information Interchange, the U.S. version of the standard character set ISO 646

assembly language — a programming language tailored to a specific computer architecture

assertion — a predicate that must be true for a program to be correct

assign — to store a value in a data object

assigning operator — an operator that stores a value in a data object, such as =, +=, or ++

assignment-compatible types — two data-object types that are valid on either side of an assigning operator

asynchronous signal — an important event not correlated with the execution of the program, such as someone striking an attention key

atomic — an indivisible operation that synchronizes two threads of control

B   **base** — the value used to weigh the digits in a positional number representation, such as base 8 (octal) or base 10 (decimal)

basic C character set — the minimum set of character codes needed to represent a C source file

beginning-of-file — the file position just before the first byte in a file

benign redefinition — a macro definition that defines an existing macro to have the same sequence of tokens spelled the same way and with white-space between the same pairs of tokens

bias — the value added to an exponent to produce the characteristic in a floating-point representation

binary — as opposed to text, containing arbitrary patterns of bits

binary stream — a stream that can contain arbitrary binary data

block — a group of statements in a C function enclosed in braces

block-level declaration — a declaration within a block

buffer — an array data object used as a convenient work area or for temporary storage, often between a program and a file

C   **C Standard** — a description of the C programming language adopted by ANSI and ISO to minimize variations in C implementations and programs

call tree — a hierarchical diagram showing how a group of functions call each other within a program

calling environment — the information in a stack frame that must be preserved on behalf of the calling function

category — part of a locale that deals with a specific group of services, such as character classification or time and date formatting

character — a data-object type in C that occupies one byte of storage and that can represent all the codes in the basic C character set

character class — a set of related character codes, such as digits, uppercase letters, or punctuation

character constant — a token in a C program, such as `'a'`, whose integer value is the code for a character in the execution character set

characteristic — the part of a floating-point representation that holds a biased exponent

close — to terminate a connection between a stream and a file

code — colloquial term for programming language text or the executable binary produced from that text

collate — to determine the ordering of two strings by some rule

compiler — a translator that produces an executable file

computer architecture — a class of computers that can all execute a common executable-file format

constant type — the type of a data object that you cannot store into (it is read-only) once it is initialized because it has the `const` type qualifier

control character — a character that performs a spacing or other control function instead of displaying as a graphic on a display device

conversion specification — a sequence of characters within a print or scan format that begins with a per cent and specifies the next conversion or transmission to perform

conversion specifier — the last character in a conversion specification, which determines the type of conversion or transmission to perform

converting type — altering the representation of a value of one type (as necessary) to make it a valid representation of a value of another type

cross compiler — a translator executing on one computer architecture that produces an executable file for use on a different computer architecture

currency symbol — the sequence of characters used to display to identify a monetary amount, such as $

D **data object** — a group of contiguous bytes in memory that can store a value of a given type

data object type — a type that describes a data object, as opposed to a function type

Daylight Savings Time — a period in the calendar year during which the local time zone is moved East one hour relative to UTC

decimal — the positional representation for numbers with base ten

decimal point — the character that separates the integer part from the fraction part in a decimal number

declaration — a sequence of tokens in a C program that gives meaning to a name, allocates storage for a data object, defines the initial content of a data object or the behavior of a function, and/or specifies a type

default — the choice made when a choice is required and none is specified

definition — a declaration that allocates storage for a data object, a declaration that specifies the behavior of a function, a declaration that gives a name to a type, or the *define* directive for a macro

device handler — that portion of an operating system that controls the operation of a specific I/O device

diagnostic — a message emitted by a C translator reporting an invalid program

digit — one of ten characters used to represent numbers, such as 3

domain error — calling a math function with an argument value (or values) for which the function is not defined

dot — the character . , often used as a decimal point

dynamic storage — data objects whose storage is allocated on entry to a block (or function) and freed when the activation of that block terminates, such as function parameters, `auto` declarations, and `register` declarations

E   **EBCDIC** — Extended Binary-Coded Decimal Interchange Code, a character encoding used extensively by IBM, particularly on the System/370

element — one of the repeated components of an array data object

end-of-file — the file position just after the last byte in a file

end-of-file indicator — a member of a `FILE` data object that records whether end-of-file was encountered during an earlier read

environment — those services provided by an operating system outside a C program but visible to it, such as files and environment variables

environment variable — a name that can be associated with a string by the environment

error indicator — a member of a `FILE` data object that records whether an error occured during an earlier operation

exception — a condition that arises during program execution that requires special handling, such as floating-point underflow

executable file — a file that the operating system can execute without further translation or interpretation

execution character set — the set of characters that a program uses when it executes

exponent — the component of a floating-point value that specifies to what power the base is raised before it is multiplied by the fraction

expression — a contiguous sequence of tokens in a C program that specifies how to compute a value and generate side effects

F   **field** — a contiguous group of characters that matches a pattern specified by a scan format conversion specification

file — a contiguous sequence of bytes that has a namename;file, maintained by the environment

file descriptor — a non-negative integer that designates a file while it is opened by a C program

file-level — that portion of a C source file outside any declaration

file-position indicator — an encoded value associated with an open file that specifies the next byte within the file to be read or written

file-positioning error — a request to alter the file-position indicator that cannot be honored

file-positioning functionsfunction;file-positioning — those functions that read or alter the file-position indicator

file name — the name used to designate a file by several functions in the Standard C library

finite-state machine — a computation whose actions are determined by a state value and a set of predicates, such as whether an input value matches certain specified values

floating-point type — any of the types *float*, *double*, or *long double*

format — a null-terminated string that determines the actions of a print, scan, or time function

formatted input — reading text and converting it to encoded values under control of a format, as with a scan function

formatted output — converting encoded values and writing them as text under control of a format, as with a print function

fraction — the component of a floating-point value that specifies a value in the range [1/base, 1) to a fixed precision

free — to release storage allocated for a data object during earlier program execution

function — a contiguous group of executable statements that accepts argument values corresponding to its parameters when called from within an expression and (possibly) returns a value for use in that expression

function prototype — a function declaration that includes enforcable declarations for the parameters to the function

G   **GMT** — Greenwich Mean Time, the older name for UTC

GNU C — a portable C compiler developed by an organization based in Massachusetts that makes its software widely avaialble

graphic — the visible representation of a printing character

H   **handle** — an alternate term for a file descriptor

header file — a text file that is made part of a translation unit by being named in an **#include** directive in a C source file

heap — that portion of memory that an executable program uses to store allocated data objects

hexadecimal — the positional representation for numbers with base 16

hole — a contiguous group of bits or bytes within a data object or argument list that does not participate in determining its value

I   **identifier** — a name

IEEE — Institute of Electrical and Electronic Engineers, one of the ANSI-authorized bodies that develops computer-related standards

implementation — a working version of a specification, such as a programming language

include file — a text file made part of a translation unit by being named in an **#include** directive in a C source file or another include file

infinity — a floating-point code that represents a value too large for finite representation

integer — a whole number, possibly negative or zero

integer constant expression — an expression that the translator can reduce to a known integer value at translation time

integer type — a data object type that can represent some contiguous range of integers including zero

Intel 80X86 — a popular family of microprocessors used in the IBM PC and compatibles

Intel 80X87 — a math coprocessor family that supports IEEE 754 floating-point arithmetic for the Intel 80X86 family

interface — a collection of functions and conventions that makes a service, such as input/output, available to a C program

international currency symbol — a three-letter code followed by either a space or a dot that specifies one of the world's currencies, as defined by ISO 4217:1987

interpreter — a translator that maintains control during program execution

invalid — not conforming to the C Standard

I/O — input and output

ISO — International Standards Organization, the organization charged with developing international conputer-related standards

K **knock out** — to prevent the linker from incorporating a library object module by providing a definition for a name with external linkage

L **letter** — one of the 52 characters, `a-z` and `A-Z`, in the English alphabet, plus possibly additional characters in other than the `"C"` locale

librarian — a program that maintains libraries of object modules

library — a collection of object modules that a linker can selectively incorporate into an executable program to provide definitions for names with external linkage

linker — a program that combines object modules to form an executable file

locale — a collection of infomation that modifies the behavior of the Standard C library to suit the conventions of a given culture or profession

locale-specific — subject to variation among locales

lowercase letter — one of the 26 characters, `a-z`, in the English alphabet, plus possibly additional characters in other than the `"C"` locale

lvalue — an expression that designates a data object

M **machine** — colloquial term for a distinct computer architecture

macro — a name defined by the `#define` directive that specifies replacement text for subsequent invocations of the macro in the translation unit

macro definition — the replacement text associated with a macro name

macro guard — a macro name used to ensure that a text sequence is incorporated in a translation unit at most once

macro, masking — a macro defintion that masks a declaration of the same name earlier in the translation unit

member — a data-object declaration that specifies one of the components of a structure or union declaration

mode — a qualifier that specifies two or more alternate behaviors, such as text versus binary mode for an open file

modifiable lvalue — an expression that designates a data object that you can store a new value into (having neither a constant nor an array type)

monetary — concerning currency, such as a monetary value

Motorola MC680X0 — a popular family of microprocessors used in the Apple Macintosh and some Sun workstations

Motorola MC68881 — a math coprocessor family that supports IEEE 754 floating-point arithmetic for the Motorola MC680X0 family

MS-DOS — a popular operating system by Microsoft Corporation for PC-compatible computers

multibyte character — a character from a large character set that is encoded as sequences of one or more conventional (one-byte) characters

multithread — supporting more than one program execution in a given time interval, possibly allowing interactions between the separate program executions

N **name** — a token from a large set used to designate a distinct entity — such as a function, macro, or member — in a translation unit

name space — a set of names distinguishable by context within a C program

native — the locale named by the empty string ""

not-a-number — a floating-point code that designates no numeric value, such as an undefined result

null character — the character with code value zero

null pointer — the value of a pointer type that compares equal to zero, and hence designates no function or data object

null-pointer constant — an integer constant expression, such as 0, that can serve in some context as a null pointer

O **object module** — the translated form of a translation unit, suitable for linking as part of an executable program

octal — the positional representation for numbers with base eight

offset — the relative address of a member or element within a containing data object, often expressed in bytes

one's-complement arithmetic — a positional binary encoding where the negative of a number is its bitwise complement

open — to form an association between a file and a stream

operand — a subexpression in a C expression acted on by an operator

operating system — a program that runs other programs, usually masking many variations among computers that share a common architecture

operator — a token in a C expression that yields a value of a given type, and possibly produces side effects, given one to three subexpressions as operands

overflow — computation of a value too small to be represented as the required integer or floating-point type

P   **parameter** — a data-object delcared in a function that stores the value of its corresponding argument on a function call

parse — to determine the syntactic structure of a sequence of tokens

PC — an IBM computer architecture developed in the early 1980s that has become the most widely used for personal computers

PDP-11 — a DEC computer architecture very popular throughout the 1970s, on which C and UNIX were first developed

period — alternate name for the dot character

PIP — Peripheral Interchange Program, used in older operating systems to convert among file and device formats

pointer type — a data-object type that represents addresses of a function or data-object type

portability — cheaper to move to another environment than to rewrite for that environment

POSIX — the IEEE 1003 Standard operating-system interface based on the system services provided by UNIX to application programs

precision — the number of distinct values that can be represented, often expressed in bits or decimal digits (which indicates the *logarithm* of the number of distinct values)

predicate — an expression that yields a binary result, usually nonzero for true and zero for false

preprocessor — that portion of a C translator that processes text-oriented directives and macro invocations

primitive — an interface function that performs an essential service, often one that cannot be performed another way

print function — one of the functions that convert encoded values to text under control of a format string

printable — giving a meaningful result, such as displaying a graphic or controlling the print position, when written to a display device

program — a collection of functions and data objects that a computer can execute to carry out the semantic intent of a corresponding set of C source files

program startup — the period in the execution of a program just before `main` is called

program termination — the period in the execution of a program just after `main` returns or `exit` is called

push back — to return a character to an input stream so that it is the next character read

punctuation — printable characters other than letters and digits, used to separate and delimit character sequences

R **range error** — calling a math function with an argument value (or values) for which the result is too large or too small to represent as a finite value

read function — one of the functions that obtain input from a stream

read-only — containing a stored value that cannot be altered

recursion — calling a function while an invocation of that function is active

representation — the number of bits used to represent a data-object type, along with the meanings ascribed to various bit patterns

reserved name — a name available for use only for a restricted purpose

round — to obtain a representation with reduced precision by some rule, such as round to nearest

rvalue — an expression that designates a value of some type (without necessarily designating a data object)

S **scan function** — one of the functions that convert text to encoded values under control of a format string

scan set — a conversion specifier for a scan function that specifies a set of matching characters

seek — to alter the file-position indicator for a stream to designate a given character position within a file

semantics — the meaning ascribed to valid sequences of tokens in a language

sequence point — a place in a program where the values stored in data objects are in a known state

side effect — a change in the value stored in a data object or in the state of a file when an expression executes

signal — an event that occurs during program execution that demands immediate attention

signal handler — a function that executes when a signal occurs

signed integer — an integer type that can represent negative as well as positive values

signed-magnitude arithmetic — a positional binary encoding where the negative of a number has its sign bit complemented

significance loss — a reduction in meaningful precision of a floating-point addition or subtraction caused by cancellation of high-order bits

source file — a text file that a C translator can translate to an object module

space — a character that occupies one print position but displays no graphic

stack — a list with a last in/first out protocol

stack frame — the data allocated on the call stack when a function is called

Standard C — that dialect of the C programming language defined by the ANSI/ISO C Standard

Standard C library — the set of functions, data objects, and headers defined by the C Standard, usable by any hosted C program

standard header — one of fifteen headers defined by the C Standard

state table — an array that defines the actions of a finite-state machine

statement — an executable component of a function that specifies an action, such as evaluating an expression or altering flow of control

static storage — data objects whose lifetime extends from program startup to program termination, initialized prior to program startup

store — to replace the value stored in a data object with a new value

stream — a data object that maintains the state of a sequence of reads, writes, and file-positioning requests for an open file

string — a sequence of characters stored in an array whose last (highest subscripted) stored value is a null character

string literal — a token in a C source file delimited by double quotes, such as `"abc"`, that designates a read-only *array of char* initialized to the specified character sequence with a null character added at the end

structure type — a data-object type consisting of a sequence of data-object members of different types

stub — a degenerate form of a function used as a place-holder for testing or before the function is implemented properly

Sun UNIX — a version of the UNIX operating system provided for the Sun workstation

synchronous signal — an important event arising out of the execution of the program, such as a zero divide

synonym — an alternate way of designating a type that is otherwise equivalent to the original type

syntax — the grammatical constraints imposed on valid sequences of tokens in a language

System/370 — an IBM computer architecture developed in the early 1960s that remains widely used, particularly for large to very large applications

system call — alternate term for a system service

system service — a request to an operating system to perform a service, such as writing to a device or obtaining the current time

T   **text** — a sequence of characters nominally suitable for writing to a display device (to be read by people)

text stream — a stream that contains text

thousands separator — the character used to separate groups of digits to the left of the decimal point (not necessarily groups of three)

thread of control — the execution of a program by a single agent

time zone — a region on Earth where local time is offset from UTC by a specified interval

token — a sequence of characters treated as a single element in a higher-level grammar

translation table — an array that specifies a mapping from one encoding to another

translation unit — a C source file plus all the files included by `#include` directives, excluding any source lines skipped by conditional directives

translator — a program that converts a translation unit to executable form

truncate — to round toward zero

Turbo C++ — an implementation by Borland International of ANSI C (and the newer language C++) for PC-compatible computers

two's-complement arithmetic — a positional binary encoding where the negative of a number is its bitwise complement plus one

type — the attribute of a value that determines its representation and what operations can be performed on it, or the attribute of a function that determines what arguments it expects and what it returns

type definition — a declaration that gives a name to a type

U **underflow** — computation of a value too small to be represented as the required floating-point type

union type — a data-object type consisting of an alternation of data-object members, only one of which can be represented at a time

UNIX — a machine-independent operating system developed in the early 1970s at AT&T Bell Laboratories, the first host for the C language

unsafe macromacro;unsafe — a macro that evaluates one or more of its arguments other than exactly once, hence a macro that does surprising things with arguments that have side effects

unsigned integer — an integer type that can represent values between zero and some positive upper limit

ULTRIX — the version of UNIX packaged and supported by DEC for the VAX computer architecture

uppercase letter — one of the 26 characters, `A-Z`, in the English alphabet, plus possibly additional characters in other than the `"C"` locale

UTC — Universal Time Coordinated, the modern term form GMT

V **variable** — older term for a data object

variable argument list — a list of arguments to a function that accepts additional arguments beyond its last declared parameter

VAX — a DEC computer architecture developed as a successor to the DEC PDP-11, on which C and UNIX are still widely used

void type — a type that has no representation and no values

volatile type — a qualified type for data objects that may be accessed by more than one thread of control

W   **WG14** — the ISO-authorized committee responsible for C standardization

white-space — a sequence of one or more space characters, possibly mixed with other characters such as horizontal tab

wide character — a code value of type `wchar_t` used to represent a very large character set

width — part of a conversion specification in a format that partially controls the number of characters to be transmitted

writable — can have its value altered, opposite of read-only

write function — one of the functions that deliver output to a stream

X   **X3J11** — the ANSI-authorized committee that developed the original C Standard

Z   **zero fixup** — replacing a floating-point underflow with an exact zero

Index